D0869082

The
INTERNATIONAL CRITICAL
COMMENTARY
on the Holy Scriptures of the Old and New Testaments

GENERAL EDITORS

G. I. DAVIES, F.B.A.
Professor of Old Testament Studies in the University of Cambridge
Fellow of Fitzwilliam College

AND

C. M. TUCKETT
Professor of New Testament Studies in the University of Oxford
Fellow of Pembroke College

CONSULTING EDITORS

J. A. EMERTON, F.B.A.
Emeritus Regius Professor of Hebrew in the University of Cambridge
Fellow of St John's College, Cambridge
Honorary Canon of St George's Cathedral, Jerusalem

AND

C. E. B. CRANFIELD, F.B.A.
Emeritus Professor of Theology in the University of Durham

FORMERLY UNDER THE EDITORSHIP OF

GENERAL EDITOR OF THE NEW SERIES

G. N. STANTON

FOUNDING EDITORS

S. R. DRIVER
A. PLUMMER
C. A. BRIGGS

THE EPISTLE TO
THE ROMANS

VOLUME I

A CRITICAL AND EXEGETICAL COMMENTARY

ON

THE EPISTLE TO THE ROMANS

BY

C. E. B. CRANFIELD

Emeritus Professor of Theology in the University of Durham

IN TWO VOLUMES

VOLUME I

Introduction and commentary on Romans I-VIII

t & t clark

T&T CLARK LTD
A Continuum imprint

The Tower Building
11 York Road
London SE1 7NX

80 Maiden Lane
Suite 704
New York, NY 10038

www.continuumbooks.com

Copyright © T&T Clark Ltd, 1975

All rights reserved. No part of this publication may be reproduced,
stored in a retrieval system, or transmitted, in any form or by any means,
electronic, mechanical, photocopying, recording or otherwise,
without the prior permission of T&T Clark Ltd.

First published 1975
Reprinted 1977 (with corrections)
Reprinted 1980 (with corrections)
Reprinted 1982
Reprinted 1985 (with corrections)
Reprinted 1987
Reprinted 1990 (with corrections)
Reprinted 1994
Reprinted 1998
Reprinted 2001 (with corrections)
Reprinted 2003
Reprinted 2004
Reprinted 2006
Reprinted 2007
Reprinted 2008
Reprinted 2010 (with corrections)

ISBN-10: 0 567 05040 8 (Hardback)
ISBN-10: 0 567 08405 1 (Paperback)
ISBN-13: 978 0 567 05040 3 (Hardback)
ISBN-13: 978 0 567 08405 7 (Paperback)

British Library Cataloguing-in-Publication Data
A catalogue record for this book is available from the British Library

Printed and bound in Great Britain by
the MPG Books Group, Bodmin and King's Lynn

PREFACE

A word of explanation is perhaps required with regard to the character of the translation of Romans included in this commentary. Commentators' translations are commonly intended to bring out as clearly and forcefully as possible the commentator's own conclusions concerning his author's meaning. When this is so, the translation, though it may be placed before the exegetical notes on each section, is really a summing up of the conclusions reached in those notes. My translation is designed rather to be a help to the reader at the earliest stage of his exegetical work. I have therefore refrained as far as I could from presupposing in it my own conclusions on controversial points, and have tried simply to represent as nearly as possible in English the Greek which has to be interpreted. One further point about the translation may be mentioned here: I have used the second person singular wherever it is used in the original, I have done this for the sake of exactness—though in this matter rather more than scholarly preciseness would seem sometimes to be at stake (as, for example, in 8.2).

My grateful thanks are due to the Rev. Professor T. F. Torrance and the Rev. Professor J. K. S. Reid; to the Rev. Principal M. Black; to the Rev. Dr. M. E. Glasswell, the Rev. Dr. E. W. Fasholé-Luke and the S.P.C.K.; to Dr. R. Banks and the Paternoster Press; and to Professor E. E. Ellis, Professor E. Grässer and Messrs. Vandenhoeck and Ruprecht, for allowing me to incorporate material contributed to the *Scottish Journal of Theology* (including *SJT* Occasional Paper 12), to *New Testament Studies,* and to the volumes in honour of the Rev. Canon H. A. E. Sawyerr, the Rev. Dr. L. Morris, and Professor W. G. Kümmel, respectively.

My other debts are far too numerous for it to be feasible for me to try to list them here. But I want particularly to acknowledge my indebtedness to those who taught me and, among them, especially to Alan D. Whitehorn, the outstanding excellence of whose teaching of the classical VIth, of which I was once a member, I have come to appreciate more and more with the passage of the years, and to whom I owe both personally and academically more than I can say; to my colleagues in the Theology Department of Durham University for much forbearance; to all those who as students have in the course of the last sixteen years faithfully attended my lectures on Romans and whose inspiration and encouragement have meant much to me; to the staff of Durham University Library for their helpfulness; to the craftsmen of Messrs. Morrison and Gibb Ltd., for their skill and carefulness; to my father, who in his 98th year still takes an interest in the progress of this work; to my daughters who, besides giving me some practical help, have been remarkably patient with an often much too preoccupied father; and, above all, to my wife, who has been my long-suffering and sympathetic helper and faithful and discerning critic. My deep indebtedness to the long succession of earlier commentators on the epistle I gladly acknowledge. (The commentaries of Ernst Käsemann and Matthew Black were, unfortunately, too late to be taken into account in volume one.) I dare to hope that this commentary will prove to be not altogether unworthy to be associated with such a company. Of the fact that—like all its predecessors known to me, without exception—it fails to come anywhere near to doing justice to the Epistle to the Romans, I am well aware.

Durham, *December, 1973.*   C. E. B. C.

NOTE ON THE SECOND IMPRESSION

I have taken this opportunity to correct a number of misprints, to make a few very slight alterations and additions, and also to refer (on p. 44) to three additional commentaries. I am very grateful to those who have drawn my attention to misprints—especially to the Rev. N. T. Wright, of Merton College, Oxford, who very kindly took the trouble to send me a list of those he had noticed.

C. E. B. C.

NOTE ON THE THIRD AND FIFTH IMPRESSIONS

Further corrections have been made in both the third and fifth impressions. In the latter account has been taken of the publication in 1979 of the twenty-sixth edition of the Nestle-Aland Greek New Testament.

C. E. B. C.

PREFACE TO THE TENTH IMPRESSION

In the successive impressions of this volume a number of errors
(as well as belatedly spotted misprints) have been corrected; an
attempt has been made to clarify obscurities; and some references
to later literature have been added, where this could be done without disturbing the pagination. As a result this tenth impression
differs considerably from the volume as originally published. I
think the changes made over the years add up to a significant
improvement.

In the last two decades a vast amount has been published on
Romans or having a bearing on it. While I have welcomed the
fresh light which has been shed and am grateful for having been
forced to return to the text again and again, and seriously to
ponder new questions, my understanding of the Epistle has not
been significantly changed and my enthusiasm for it remains
undiminished.

Durham, *September,* 2001.   C. E. B. C.

NOTE ON THE SIXTEENTH IMPRESSION

In this impression, in addition to corrections made on p.137, line
11, and on p.177, lines 21 and 26, I have done some rewriting of
pp. 151-53.

May I respectfully remind any reader who is finding the exegesis
of Romans 2 specially hard going (as I well remember that I did
myself when writing this commentary) that this same epistle also
includes 11.32 ('For God has imprisoned all in disobedience in
order that he may have mercy on all') and urge him or her to read
and to reflect on Karl Barth's sermon on that text preached to the
inmates of Basel Prison and published in his *Den Gefangenen
Befreiung,* Zollikon, 1959, pp. 92-102 (English translation,
Deliverance to the Captives, London 1961, pp. 85-92)?

Durham, *December,* 2009.   C. E. B. C.

CONTENTS OF VOLUME I

LISTS OF ABBREVIATIONS

Commentaries on Romans are cited by the author's name alone. Details are given below. Details of most other books and articles are given at the first citation. But certain general works, the references to which are widely distributed, are cited by abbreviated titles. These are listed below. Abbreviations of the titles of periodicals are listed separately.

COMMENTARIES ON ROMANS

(For the abbreviations CR, Cramer, *PG*, *PL*, and Staab, see the list of abbreviated titles of general works below.)

Abelard, Peter, *Commentarii super S. Pauli epistolam ad Romanos*, in *PL* 178, cols. 783–978.

Acacius, fragments in Staab.

Alford, H., *Greek Testament*, Cambridge, 1886 ([1]1849–61), 2, pp. 311–472.

Althaus, P., *Der Brief an die Römer* (NT Deutsch), Göttingen, [6]1949 ([1]1935).

Ambrosiaster, in *Commentaria in XIII epistolas beati Pauli*, in *PL* 17, cols. 45–184. Also a critical edition by H. J. Vogels in Corpus Scriptorum Ecclesiasticorum Latinorum 81 (1966–69).

Apollinarius, fragments in Staab.

Aquinas, Thomas, in *Super epistolas S. Pauli lectura*, ed. R. Cai, Turin, [8]1953, 1, pp. 5–230.

Asmussen, H., *Der Römerbrief*, Stuttgart, 1952.

Augustine, *Expositio quarumdam propositionum ex epistola ad Romanos*, in *PL* 35, cols. 2063–88; *Epistolae ad Romanos inchoata expositio*, in *PL* 35, cols. 2087–2106.

Barclay, W., *The Letter to the Romans* (Daily Study Bible), Edinburgh, [2]1957 ([1]1955).

Bardenhewer, O., *Der Römerbrief des heiligen Paulus* (Kurzgefasste Erklärung), Freiburg i.B., 1926.

Barmby, J., *Romans: Exposition* (Pulpit Commentary), London, 1890.

Barrett, C. K., *A Commentary on the Epistle to the Romans* (Black's NT Commentaries), London, 1957.

Barth, K., *The Epistle to the Romans* (Eng. tr. of *Der Römerbrief*, [6]1929 ([1]1919)), Oxford, 1933—cited as 'Barth, 1933'.

Barth, K., *A Shorter Commentary on Romans* (Eng. tr. of *Kurze Erklärung des Römerbriefes*, 1956), London, 1959—cited as 'Barth, *Shorter*'. The original German is occasionally cited as 'Barth, *KE*'.

Beck, J. T., *Erklärung des Briefes an die Römer*, 2 vols., Gütersloh, 1884.

Beet, J. A., *A Commentary on St. Paul's Epistle to the Romans*, London, [10]1902 ([1]1877).

Bengel, J. A., in *Gnomon Novi Testamenti*, London reprint of 3rd edition, 1862 ([1]1742), pp. 489–569.

Best, E., *The Letter of Paul to the Romans* (Cambridge Bible Commentary), Cambridge, 1967.

Beza (de Bèze), T., in *Annotationes maiores in Novum Dn. Nostri Iesu Christi Testamentum*, n.p., 1594 ([1]1556), part 2, pp. 3–152.

Bisping, A., *Erklärung des Briefes an die Römer* (Exegetisches Handbuch), Münster, 1870.

Black, M., *Romans* (New Century Bible), London, 1973.

Boylan, P., *St. Paul's Epistle to the Romans*, Dublin, 1934.

Bruce, F. F., *The Epistle to the Romans*, London, 1963.

Brunner, E., *The Letter to the Romans* (Eng. tr. of *Der Römerbrief*, 1956 ([1]1938)), London, 1959.

Calvin, J., in *The Epistles of Paul the Apostle to the Romans and to the Thessalonians*, tr. by R. Mackenzie, Edinburgh, 1961. Critical ed. by T. H. L. Parker and D. C. Parker in *Ioannis Calvini Opera Omnia*, Series II, Vol. XIII, Geneva, 1999.

Chrysostom, John, ʽΕρμηνεία εἰς τὴν πρὸς ʽΡωμαίους ἐπιστολήν, in *PG* 60, cols. 391–682.

Cornely, R., *Commentarius in S. Pauli Apostoli epistolas* 1, Paris, 1896.

Cranfield, C. E. B., *A Commentary on Romans 12–13*, Edinburgh, 1965.

Cyril of Alexandria, ʽΕρμηνεία εἰς τὴν πρὸς ʽΡωμαίους ἐπιστολήν, in *PG* 74, cols. 773–856.

Delitzsch, F., *Paulus des Apostels Brief an die Römer in das Hebräische übersetzt und aus Talmud und Midrasch erläutert*, Leipzig, 1870.

Denney, J., in *The Expositor's Greek Testament* 2, London, [3]1904 ([1]1900), pp. 555–725.

Didymus the Blind, fragments in Staab.

Diodore of Tarsus, fragments in Staab.

Dodd, C. H., *The Epistle of Paul to the Romans* (Fontana Books), London, 1959. This is a re-issue, with some revision, of the commentary published in 1932 in The Moffatt NT Commentary series.

Ephraem Syrus, in *Commentarii in epistolas d. Pauli*, tr. from the Armenian into Latin by the Mechitarist fathers, Venice, 1893.

Erasmus, D., in *In Novum Testamentum Annotationes*, Basel, 1527 ([1]1516), pp. 318–92.

Euthymius Zigabenus, in *Commentarius in XIV epistolas S. Pauli et VII catholicas*, ed. N. Calogeras, Athens, 1887, 1, pp. 5–185.

Fritzsche, C. F. A., *Pauli ad Romanos epistola*, 3 vols., Halle, 1836–43.

Fuchs, E., *Die Freiheit des Glaubens: Römer 5–8 ausgelegt*, Munich, 1949.

Gaugler, E., *Der Römerbrief* (Prophezei), 2 vols., Zurich, 1, 1958 ([1]1945); 2, 1952.

Gennadius, fragments in Cramer.

Gifford, E. H., *The Epistle of St. Paul to the Romans* (reprinted from The Speaker's Commentary), London, 1886.

Godet, F., *Commentary on St. Paul's Epistle to the Romans* (Eng. tr. of *Commentaire sur l'épître aux Romains*, 1879), 2 vols., Edinburgh, 1880–81.

Gore, C., *The Epistle to the Romans*, London, 1907.

Gutjahr, F. S., in *Die Briefe des hl. Apostels Paulus* 3, Graz, 1923.

Hammond, H., in *A Paraphrase and Annotations upon all the books of the New Testament, briefly explaining all the difficult places thereof*, London, [5]1681 ([1]1653), pp. 437–509.

Hodge, C., *A Commentary on the Epistle to the Romans* (revised ed. of commentary published in 1835), Philadelphia, 1864 (reprinted Grand Rapids, 1950).

Huby, J., *Saint Paul: Épître aux Romains* (Verbum Salutis), new ed. by S. Lyonnet, Paris, 1957 ([1]1940).

Hunter, A. M., *The Epistle to the Romans* (Torch Bible Commentaries), London, 1954.

John of Damascus, in Ἐκ τῆς καθόλου ἑρμηνείας Ἰωάννου τοῦ Χρυσοστόμου ἐκλογαὶ ἐκλεγεῖσαι, in *PG* 95, cols. 441–570.

Jowett, B., in *The Epistles of St. Paul to the Thessalonians, Galatians, and Romans*, London, 1855.

Jülicher, A., in *Die Schriften des Neuen Testaments* 2, Göttingen, [3]1917 ([1]1907).

Käsemann, E., *An die Römer* (Handbuch zum NT), Tübingen, 1973.

Kelly, W., *Notes on the Epistle to the Romans*, London, 1873.

Kirk, K. E., *The Epistle to the Romans* (Clarendon Bible), Oxford, 1937.

Knox, J., in *The Interpreter's Bible* 9, New York, 1954, pp. 355ff.

Kühl, E., *Der Brief des Paulus an die Römer*, Leipzig, 1913.

Kuss, O., *Der Römerbrief*, Regensburg, 1, 1957; 2, 1959.

Kutter, H., *Gerechtigkeit* (On Romans 1–8), Berlin, 1905.

Lagrange, M.-J., *Saint Paul: Épître aux Romains* (Études Bibliques), Paris, 1950 (^{1}1916).

Lapide, C. à (van den Steen), in *Commentaria in omnes d. Pauli Epistolas*, Antwerp, 1614.

Leenhardt, F.-J., *The Epistle to the Romans* (Eng. tr. of *L'Épître de Saint Paul aux Romains* (Commentaire du Nouveau Testament), 1957), London, 1961.

Liddon, H. P., *Explanatory Analysis of St. Paul's Epistle to the Romans*, London, 1893.

Lietzmann, H., *An die Römer* (Handbuch zum NT), Tübingen, 1933 (^{1}1906).

Lightfoot, J. B., in *Notes on Epistles of St. Paul*, London, 1895, pp. 237–305. (The notes stop at the end of chapter 7.)

Lipsius, R. A., in H. J. Holtzmann's *Handkommentar zum Neuen Testament*, 2, Tübingen, ^{2}1892.

Loane, M. L., *The Hope of Glory: an exposition of the eighth chapter in the Epistle to the Romans*, London, 1968.

Lombard, Peter, in *Collectanea in omnes divi Pauli epistolas*, in *PL* 191, cols. 1301–1534.

Luther, M., *Lectures on Romans*, tr. and ed. by W. Pauck, London, 1961. (Original German in Weimar edition of Luther's works, volume 56.)

Manson, T. W., in *Peake's Commentary on the Bible*, ed. M. Black and H. H. Rowley, London, 1962, pp. 940–53.

Martyr (Vermigli), Peter, *In epistolam S. Pauli Apostoli ad Romanos . . . commentarii doctissimi*, Basel, 1568 (^{1}1558).

Melanchthon, P., *Dispositio orationis in Epistolam Pauli ad Romanos*, 1529, in CR 15, cols. 441–92; *Commentarii in Epistolam Pauli ad Romanos*, 1540 (^{1}1532), in CR 15, cols. 493–796; *Epistolae Pauli scriptae ad Romanos Enarratio*, 1556, in CR 15, cols. 797–1052.

Melville, A., *Commentarius in divinam Pauli Epistolam ad Romanos*, Edinburgh, 1850 (from a transcript finished in 1601 at St. Andrews).

Meyer, H. A. W., *The Epistle to the Romans* (Eng. tr. of *Der Brief an die Römer* (Kritisch-exegetischer Kommentar über das NT), ^{5}1872 (^{1}1836)), Edinburgh, 1, 1881; 2, 1884.

Michel, O., *Der Brief an die Römer* (Kritisch-exegetischer Kommentar über das NT), Göttingen, ^{4}1966 (^{1}1955).

Moule, H. C. G., *The Epistle of Paul the Apostle to the Romans* Cambridge Bible for Schools and Colleges), Cambridge, 1879;

The Epistle of St. Paul to the Romans (The Expositor's Bible), London, 1894—cited as 'Moule'.

Murray, J., *The Epistle to the Romans* (New International Commentary on the NT), Grand Rapids, 1, ³1967 (¹1960); 2, 1965.

Nygren, A., *Commentary on Romans* (Eng. tr. of *Pauli Brev till Romarna*, 1944), London, 1952.

Oecumenius, Παύλου ἐπιστολὴ πρὸς 'Ρωμαίους, in *PG* 118, cols. 323–636.

Olshausen, H., *Der Brief des Apostels Paulus an die Römer*, Königsberg, ²1840 (¹1835).

Oltramare, H., *Commentaire sur l'épître aux Romains*, 2 volumes, Geneva, 1881–82.

Origen, *Commentaria in epistolam b. Pauli ad Romanos* (Latin tr. by Rufinus), in *PG* 14, cols. 837–1292; Greek fragments in A. Ramsbotham, 'The Commentary of Origen on the Epistle to the Romans', in *JTS* 13 (1911–12), pp. 209–224, 357–68, and 14 (1912–13), pp. 10–22; and in J. Scherer, *Le Commentaire d'Origène sur Rom 3.5–5.7*, Cairo, 1957 (cited as 'Scherer').

Pallis, A., *To the Romans: a commentary*, Liverpool, 1920.

Pareus (Waengler), D., *Commentarius in Epistolam ad Romanos*, Frankfurt, 1608.

Parry, R. St. J., *The Epistle of Paul the Apostle to the Romans* (Cambridge Greek Testament), Cambridge, 1912.

Pelagius, *Expositio in Romanos*, in A. Souter, *Pelagius's Expositions of Thirteen Epistles of St. Paul* 2 (Texts and Studies 9.2), Cambridge, 1926, pp. 6–126.

Photius, fragments in *PG* 101, cols. 1233–54.

Poole, M. in *Synopsis Criticorum aliorumque S. Scripturae Interpretum* 4, part 2, London, 1676, cols. 1–330.

Pseudo-Primasius, in *PL* 68, cols. 415–506.

Sanday, W., and Headlam, A. C., *A Critical and Exegetical Commentary on the Epistle to the Romans* (International Critical Commentary), Edinburgh, ⁵1902 (many times reprinted: ¹1895).

Schlatter, A., *Gottes Gerechtigkeit: ein Kommentar zum Römerbrief*, Stuttgart, ³1959 (¹1935).

Schmidt, H. W., *Der Brief des Paulus an die Römer* (Theologischer Handkommentar zum NT), Berlin, 1962.

Sedulius Scotus, in *PL* 103, cols, 9–128.

Severian of Gabala, fragments in Staab and Cramer.

Sickenberger, J., in *Die beiden Briefe des heiligen Paulus an die Korinther und sein Brief an die Römer* (Die Heilige Schrift des Neuen Testamentes), Bonn, ⁴1932.

Stuart, M., *A Commentary on the Epistle to the Romans*, Andover, N.H., 1832.

Szlichting, J., in *Commentaria posthuma in plerosque Novi Testamenti libros*, Amsterdam, 1665?-68, pp. 155-325.

Taylor, V., *The Epistle to the Romans* (Epworth Preacher's Commentaries), London, 1956.

Theodore of Mopsuestia, fragments in *PG* 66, cols. 787-876.

Theodoret, Ἑρμηνεία τῆς πρὸς Ῥωμαίους ἐπιστολῆς in *PG* 82, cols. 43-226.

Theophylact, Τῆς τοῦ ἁγίου Παύλου πρὸς Ῥωμαίους ἐπιστολῆς ἐξήγησις, in *PG* 124, cols. 335-560.

Tholuck, F. A. G., *Commentar zum Brief an die Römer*, Halle, [5]1856 ([1]1824).

Thomas Aquinas, see Aquinas, Thomas.

Vaughan, C. J., *St. Paul's Epistle to the Romans*, London, [5]1880 ([1]1857).

Weiss, B., *Der Brief an die Römer* (Kritisch-Exegetischer Kommentar über das NT), Göttingen, [4]1899 ([1]1881).

Wetstein, see Wettstein.

Wette, W. M. L. de, in *Kurzgefasstes exegetisches Handbuch zum Neuen Testament*, 3 vols., Leipzig, 1836-48.

Wettstein (Latinized as Wetstenius), J. J., Ἡ Καινὴ Διαθήκη: *Novum Testamentum Graecum editionis receptae cum lectionibus variantibus codicum MSS., editionum aliarum, versionum et patrum nec non commentario pleniore ex scriptoribus veteribus Hebraeis, Graecis et Latinis historiam et vim verborum illustrante* 2, Amsterdam, 1752, pp. 16-100.

Zahn, T., *Der Brief des Paulus an die Römer*, Leipzig, [3]1925 ([1]1910).

GENERAL WORKS

ADPB: *The Authorised Daily Prayer Book of the United Hebrew Congregations of the British Empire with a new translation by the late Rev. S. Singer*, London, [23]1954.

Antwort: E. Wolf, C. von Kirschbaum and R. Frey (ed.), *Antwort: Karl Barth zum siebzigsten Geburtstag*, Zollikon-Zurich, 1956.

Apostolic History: W. Ward Gasque and R. P. Martin (ed.), *Apostolic History and the Gospel: biblical and historical essays presented to F. F. Bruce on his 60th birthday*, Exeter, 1970.

Barrett, *From First Adam to Last*: C. K. Barrett, *From First Adam to Last: a study in Pauline theology*, London, 1962.

Barth, *CD*: K. Barth, *Church Dogmatics*, Edinburgh, 1936–69, being the English translation of the following.

Barth, *KD*: K. Barth, *Kirchliche Dogmatik*, Zollikon-Zurich, 1932–67.

Barth, M., et al., *Foi et Salut*: M. Barth, et al., *Foi et Salut selon S. Paul: colloque œcuménique à l'Abbaye de S. Paul hors les murs*, Rome, 1970.

Bauer: W. Bauer, *Griechisch-deutsches Wörterbuch zu den Schriften des Neuen Testaments und der übrigen urchristlichen Literatur*, Berlin, 1971 (corrected reprint of the revised and considerably expanded 5th edition of 1958). An English translation and adaptation of the 4th ed. of 1952 by W. F. Arndt and F. W. Gingrich under the title *A Greek-English Lexicon of the New Testament and other early Christian literature*, Cambridge, 1957, is available [1979: revised ed. advertised].

BDB: F. Brown, S. R. Driver and C. A. Briggs, *A Hebrew and English Lexicon of the Old Testament*, Oxford, corrected reprint, 1952 ([1]1907).

BDF: F. Blass and A. Debrunner, *A Greek Grammar of the New Testament and other early Christian literature*, Eng. tr. and revision of the 9th–10th German ed. incorporating supplementary notes of A. Debrunner, by R. W. Funk, Cambridge, 1961.

BFBS: 'H Καινὴ Διαθήκη, British and Foreign Bible Society, London, [2]1958.

BGU: *Ägyptische Urkunden aus den Museen zu Berlin: Griechische Urkunden*, 8 volumes, Berlin, 1895–1933.

BHH: B. Reicke and L. Rost (ed.), *Biblisch-historisches Handwörterbuch*, 3 volumes, Göttingen, 1962–66.

Bornkamm, *Early Christian Experience*: G. Bornkamm, *Early Christian Experience*, Eng. tr. of select articles from the following, London, 1969.

Bornkamm, *Gesammelte Aufsätze*: G. Bornkamm, *Gesammelte Aufsätze*, 4 volumes, Munich, 1959–71. (Volume 1 = *Das Ende des Gesetzes: Paulusstudien*; 2 = *Studien zu Antike und Christentum*; 3 and 4 = *Geschichte und Glauben*.)

Bornkamm, *Paul*: G. Bornkamm, *Paul* (Eng. tr. of *Paulus*, 1969), London, 1971.

Bousset, *Kyrios Christos*: W. Bousset, *Kyrios Christos: Geschichte des Christusglaubens von den Anfängen des Christentums bis Irenaeus*, Göttingen, [2]1921.

Bouttier, *Christianity*: M. Bouttier, *Christianity according to Paul* (Eng. tr. of *La condition chrétienne selon Saint Paul*, 1964), London, 1966.

Bruce, *Exegesis*: F. F. Bruce, *Biblical Exegesis in the Qumran Texts*, London, 1960.

Bultmann, 'Glossen': R. Bultmann, 'Glossen im Römerbrief', in *TLZ* 72 (1947), cols. 197–202.

Bultmann, *Stil*: R. Bultmann, *Der Stil der paulinischen Predigt und die kynisch-stoische Diatribe*, Göttingen, 1910.

Bultmann, *Theology*: R. Bultmann, *Theology of the New Testament* (Eng. tr. of *Theologie des Neuen Testaments*, [1]1948–53), 2 volumes, London, 1952–55.

Burton, *MT*: E. D. Burton, *Syntax of the Moods and Tenses in New Testament Greek*, Edinburgh, [3]1898 (reprinted).

Cambier, *L'Évangile de Dieu*: J. Cambier, *L'Évangile de Dieu selon l'Épître aux Romains* 1, Bruges, 1967. (Two further volumes planned.)

Cerfaux, *Le Chrétien*: L. Cerfaux, *Le Chrétien dans la théologie paulinienne*, Paris, 1962.

Cerfaux, *Le Christ*: L. Cerfaux, *Le Christ dans la théologie de Saint Paul*, Paris, 1951.

Chevallier, *Esprit*: M.-A. Chevallier, *Esprit de Dieu, Paroles d'Hommes: le rôle de l'esprit dans les ministères de la parole selon l'apôtre Paul*, Neuchâtel, 1966.

CIG: Corpus Inscriptionum Graecarum, Berlin, 1828–77.

CIL: Corpus Inscriptionum Latinarum, Berlin, 1863–1909.

CR: Corpus Reformatorum, Brunswick, 1834ff.

Cramer: J. A. Cramer, *Catenae Graecorum Patrum in Novum Testamentum* 4, Oxford, 1844 (reprinted Hildesheim, 1967).

Cullmann, *Christology*: O. Cullmann, *The Christology of the New Testament* (Eng. tr. of *Die Christologie des Neuen Testaments*, 1957), London, 1959.

Daube, *NTRJ*: D. Daube, *The New Testament and Rabbinic Judaism*, London, 1956.

Davies, *PRJ*: W. D. Davies, *Paul and Rabbinic Judaism: some Rabbinic elements in Pauline theology*, London, [2]1955 ([1]1948).

Deissmann, *Light*: G. A. Deissmann, *Light from the Ancient East* (Eng. tr. of *Licht vom Osten*, [4]1923 ([1]1908)), London, [2]1927.

Dittenberger, *Or.*: W. Dittenberger, *Orientis Graeci inscriptiones selectae*, 2 volumes, Leipzig, 1903–05.

Dittenberger, *Syll.*: W. Dittenberger *Sylloge inscriptionum Graecarum*, 4 volumes, Leipzig, [3]1915–24.

Dodd, *Bible and the Greeks*: C. H. Dodd, *The Bible and the Greeks*, London, 1935.

Foakes-Jackson and Lake, *Beginnings*: F. J. Foakes-Jackson

and K. Lake (ed.), *The Beginnings of Christianity*, Part I, 5 volumes, London, 1920–33.

Gerhardsson, *Memory and Manuscript*: B. Gerhardsson, *Memory and Manuscript: oral tradition and written transmission in Rabbinic Judaism and early Christianity*, Uppsala, 1961.

Guthrie, *Introduction*: D. Guthrie, *New Testament Introduction: the Pauline Epistles*, London, 1961.

Haenchen, *Apostelgeschichte*: E. Haenchen, *Die Apostelgeschichte* (Kritisch-exegetischer Kommentar über das NT), Göttingen, ³1959.

Hill, *GWHM*: D. Hill, *Greek Words and Hebrew Meanings: studies in the semantics of soteriological terms*, Cambridge, 1967.

HR: E. Hatch and H. A. Redpath, *A Concordance to the Septuagint and the other Greek versions of the Old Testament*, 2 volumes (the second including the supplement), Graz, 1954 (reprint of original edition, Oxford, 1897–1906).

IDB: G. A. Buttrick (ed.), *The Interpreter's Dictionary of the Bible*, 4 volumes, New York, 1962.

Jastrow, *Dictionary*: M. Jastrow, *A Dictionary of the Targumim, the Talmud Babli and Yerushalmi, and the Midrashic Literature*, 2 volumes, New York, 1950 (¹1903).

JB: The Jerusalem Bible, 1966.

Jeremias, *Jerusalem*: J. Jeremias, *Jerusalem in the Time of Jesus: an investigation into economic and social conditions during the New Testament period* (Eng. tr. of *Jerusalem zur Zeit Jesu*, ³1962), London, 1969.

Käsemann, *Perspektiven*: E. Käsemann, *Paulinische Perspektiven*, Tübingen, 1969.

Käsemann, *Questions*: E. Käsemann, *New Testament Questions of Today* (Eng. tr. of selections from the second volume of the following), London, 1969.

Käsemann, *Versuche*: E. Käsemann, *Exegetische Versuche und Besinnungen* 1 and 2 (in one volume), Göttingen, ²1965.

Kennedy, *Mystery Religions*: H. A. A. Kennedy, *St. Paul and the Mystery Religions*, London, 1913.

Kennedy, *Theology*: H. A. A. Kennedy, *The Theology of the Epistles*, London, 1919.

Kühner-Gerth: R. Kühner, *Ausführliche Grammatik der griechischen Sprache* II (Satzlehre), revised by B. Gerth, 2 volumes, Hanover, 1898–1904; reprinted 1955.

Kümmel, *Introduction*: W. G. Kümmel, *Introduction to the New Testament* (Eng. tr. of *Einleitung in das Neue Testament*, ³1965 (=14th ed. of Feine-Behm)), London, 1966.

Kuhn, *Konkordanz*: K. G. Kuhn, et al., *Konkordanz zu den Qumrantexten*, Göttingen, 1960.

LSJ: H. G. Liddell and R. Scott, *A Greek-English Lexicon*, revised and augmented by H. S. Jones and R. McKenzie, Oxford, 1940, reprinted 1953.

LSJ Suppl.: *A Supplement* to the above, ed. by E. A. Barber, assisted by P. Maas, M. Scheller and M. L. West, Oxford, 1968.

Manson, T. W., *Studies*: T. W. Manson, *Studies in the Gospels and Epistles*, ed. M. Black, Manchester, 1962.

Manson, W., 'Notes': W. Manson, 'Notes on the argument of Romans (chapters 1–8)', in A. J. B. Higgins (ed.), *New Testament Essays: Studies in Memory of T. W. Manson*, Manchester, 1959, pp. 150–64.

Merk: *Novum Testamentum Graece et Latine*, ed. A. Merk, Rome, [8]1957.

Metzger, *Text*: B. M. Metzger, *The Text of the New Testament: its transmission, corruption, and restoration*, Oxford, [2]1968.

MG: W. F. Moulton and A. S. Geden, *A Concordance to the Greek Testament according to the texts of Westcott and Hort, Tischendorf and the English Revisers*, Edinburgh, [3]1926.

MHT: J. H. Moulton, continued by W. F. Howard and N. Turner, *A Grammar of New Testament Greek*, 3 volumes, Edinburgh, 1906–63.

Michaelis, *Einleitung*: W. Michaelis, *Einleitung in das Neue Testament*, Bern, [2]1954.

MM: J. H. Moulton and G. Milligan, *The Vocabulary of the Greek Testament illustrated from the Papyri and other non-literary Sources*, London, 1930.

Moffatt: J. Moffatt, *A New Translation of the Bible*, London, 1926.

Moule, *Idiom-Book*: C. F. D. Moule, *An Idiom-Book of New Testament Greek*, Cambridge, [2]1959.

Munck, *Paul*: J. Munck, *Paul and the Salvation of Mankind* (Eng. tr. of *Paulus und die Heilsgeschichte*, 1954), London, 1959.

Murphy-O'Connor, *PQ*: J. Murphy-O'Connor (ed.), *Paul and Qumran: studies in New Testament exegesis*, London, 1968.

NEB: The New English Bible, 1970. Where it is necessary to distinguish between this and the first edition of the NEB NT of 1961, the former is cited as NEB[2] and the latter as NEB[1].

Neotestamentica et Patristica: W. C. van Unnik (ed.), *Neotestamentica et Patristica: eine Freundesgabe, Herrn Prof. Dr.*

Oscar Cullmann zu seinem 60. Geburtstag überreicht, Leiden, 1962.

Nestle: *Novum Testamentum Graece*, ed. Eberhard Nestle, [25]1963 (revised by Erwin Nestle and K. Aland), reprinted London, 1971.

OCD: N. G. L. Hammond and H. H. Scullard (ed.), *The Oxford Classical Dictionary*, Oxford, [2]1970, reprinted (with corrections) 1972.

PG: J.-P. Migne (ed.), *Patrologia Graeca*, Paris, 1857–66.

PL: J.-P. Migne (ed.), *Patrologia Latina*, Paris, 1844–64.

Prat, *Theology*: F. Prat, *Theology of St. Paul* (Eng. tr. of *La théologie de saint Paul*), 2 volumes, London, 1926–27.

Reitzenstein, *Mysterienreligionen*: R. Reitzenstein, *Die hellenistischen Mysterienreligionen*, Leipzig, [3]1927.

Reitzenstein, *Poimandres*: R. Reitzenstein, *Poimandres*, Leipzig, 1904.

RGG: *Die Religion in Geschichte und Gegenwart*, Tübingen, [2]1927–32; [3]1957–65.

Robert-Feuillet, *Introduction*: A. Robert and A. Feuillet (ed.), *Introduction à la Bible*, 2 volumes, Tournai, 1959. (An Eng. tr. of volume 2, *Introduction to the New Testament*, New York, 1965, is available.)

Robertson, *Grammar*: A. T. Robertson, *A Grammar of the Greek New Testament in the light of historical research*, London, 1914.

Roller, *Formular*: O. Roller, *Das Formular der paulinischen Briefe: ein Beitrag zur Lehre vom antiken Briefe*, Stuttgart, 1933.

RSV: The Revised Standard Version, 1952.

RV: The Revised Version, 1885 (OT and NT together; NT alone 1881; Apocrypha 1894).

SB: H. L. Strack and P. Billerbeck, *Kommentar zum Neuen Testament aus Talmud und Midrasch* 1–4, Munich, 1922–28; 5–6 (by J. Jeremias and K. Adolph), Munich, 1956–61.

Schelkle: K. H. Schelkle, *Paulus, Lehrer der Väter: die altkirchliche Auslegung von Römer 1–11*, Düsseldorf, [2]1956.

Schoeps, *Paul*: H. J. Schoeps, *Paul: the theology of the apostle in the light of Jewish religious history* (Eng. tr. of *Paulus: die Theologie des Apostels im Lichte der jüdischen Religionsgeschichte*, 1959), London, 1961.

Scott, *Christianity*: C. A. A. Scott, *Christianity according to St. Paul*, Cambridge, 1932 (reprint with a few corrections of 1st ed. of 1927).

Segond: La Sainte Bible, translated by L. Segond, 1880, subsequently revised.

Service in Christ: J. I. McCord and T. H. L. Parker (ed.), *Service in Christ: essays presented to Karl Barth on his 80th birthday*, London, 1966.

Souter: *Novum Testamentum Graece*, ed. A. Souter, Oxford, ²1947.

Staab: K. Staab, *Pauluskommentare aus der griechischen Kirche*, Münster, 1933.

Stauffer, *Theologie:* E. Stauffer, *Die Theologie des Neuen Testaments*, Stuttgart, ⁴1948. An Eng. tr., London, 1955, is available.

Strack, *Introduction:* H. L. Strack, *The Introduction to the Talmud and Midrash* (Eng. tr. of the author's revised copy of the 5th ed. (1921) of his *Einleitung in Talmud und Midrasch*), Philadelphia, 1931 (reprinted 1945).

Studia Paulina: J. N. Sevenster and W. C. van Unnik (ed.), *Studia Paulina in honorem Johannis de Zwaan septuagenarii*, Haarlem, 1953.

Taylor, *Names:* V. Taylor, *The Names of Jesus*, London, 1954

Taylor, *Person of Christ:* V. Taylor, *The Person of Christ in New Testament Teaching*, London, 1958.

Turner, *Insights:* N. Turner, *Grammatical Insights into the New Testament*, Edinburgh, 1965.

TWB: A. Richardson (ed.), *A Theological Word Book of the Bible*, London, 1950.

TWNT: G. Kittel (ed.), continued by G. Friedrich (ed.), *Theologisches Wörterbuch zum Neuen Testament*, Stuttgart, 1933ff. An Eng. tr. by G. W. Bromiley (*Theological Dictionary of the New Testament*, Grand Rapids, 1964ff) is also available.

UBS: *The Greek New Testament*, ed. K. Aland, M. Black, B. M. Metzger and A. Wikgren, published by the United Bible Societies, New York, London, Edinburgh, Amsterdam and Stuttgart, 1967.

VB: J.-J. von Allmen (ed.), *Vocabulary of the Bible* (Eng. tr. of *Vocabulaire Biblique*, 1954), London, 1958.

Vermes: G. Vermes, *The Dead Sea Scrolls in English*, Harmondsworth, 1962.

Weymouth: R. F. Weymouth, *The New Testament in Modern Speech*, London, 1929.

WH: *The New Testament in the Original Greek*, ed. B. F. Westcott and F. J. A. Hort, 2 volumes, Cambridge, 1881.

Whiteley, *Theology:* D. E. H. Whiteley, *The Theology of St. Paul*, Oxford, 1964.

Wikenhauser, *Introduction:* A. Wikenhauser, *New Testament*

Introduction (Eng. tr. of *Einleitung in das Neue Testament*, [2]1956), New York and Edinburgh, 1958.
Wiles, *Divine Apostle*: M. F. Wiles, *The Divine Apostle: the interpretation of St Paul's epistles in the early Church*, Cambridge, 1967.
Zuntz: G. Zuntz, *The Text of the Epistles: a disquisition upon the Corpus Paulinum*, London, 1953.

PERIODICALS

ABR: Australian Biblical Review, Melbourne.
Biblica: Biblica, Rome.
BJRL: Bulletin of the John Rylands Library, Manchester.
BT: Biblical Theology, Belfast.
BZ: Biblische Zeitschrift, Paderborn.
CBQ: Catholic Biblical Quarterly, Washington.
CJT: Canadian Journal of Theology, Toronto.
CV: Communio Viatorum, Prague.
EB: Estudios Bíblicos, Madrid.
EQ: Evangelical Quarterly, London.
ET: Expository Times, Edinburgh.
EvTh: Evangelische Theologie, Munich.
Expositor: The Expositor, London, 1880–1925.
Glotta: Glotta: Zeitschrift für griechische und lateinische Sprache, Göttingen.
HTR: Harvard Theological Review, Cambridge, Mass.
IKZ: Internationale kirchliche Zeitschrift, Bern.
Interpretation: Interpretation, Richmond, Virginia.
ITQ: Irish Theological Quarterly, Dublin; Maynooth.
JAOS: Journal of the American Oriental Society, Baltimore.
JBL: Journal of Biblical Literature, New Haven; Boston, Mass.; Philadelphia; Missoula.
JQR: Jewish Quarterly Review; London; Philadelphia.
JTS: Journal of Theological Studies, Oxford.
LV: Lumière et Vie, Lyons.
Mnemosyne: Mnemosyne: bibliotheca classica Batava, Leiden.
MTZ: Münchener theologische Zeitschrift, Munich.
NKZ: Neue kirchliche Zeitschrift, Erlangen, 1890–1939 (1934–39 under the name *Luthertum*).
NT: Novum Testamentum, Leiden.
NTS: New Testament Studies, Cambridge.
PTR: Princeton Theological Review, Philadelphia: Princeton, 1903–29.

RB: Revue biblique, Paris; Jerusalem.
RBén: Revue Bénédictine, Maredsous.
RechSR: Recherches de science religieuse, Paris.
RHPR: Revue d'histoire et de philosophie religieuses, Strasbourg.
RMP: Rheinisches Museum für Philogie, Bonn; Frankfurt a. M.
RQ: Revue de Qumran, Paris.
RSPT: Revue des sciences philosophiques et théologiques, Paris.
RTR: Reformed Theological Review, Hawthorn, Victoria.
SAB: Sitzungsberichte der preussischen (since 1948 *deutschen*) *Akademie der Wissenschaften zu Berlin*, Berlin.
SAH: Sitzungsberichte der Heidelberger Akademie der Wissenschaften, philosophische-historische Klasse, Heidelberg.
SBU: Symbolae Biblicae Upsalienses, Uppsala.
SEA: Svensk Exegetisk Årsbok, Uppsala.
SJT: Scottish Journal of Theology, Edinburgh; Cambridge;
ST: Studia Theologica, Lund.   [Edinburgh.
TB: Theologische Blätter, Leipzig, 1922–42.
Theology: Theology, London.
TLZ: Theologische Literaturzeitung, Leipzig.
TR: Theologische Rundschau, Tübingen.
TS: Theologische Studiën, Utrecht.
TSK: Theologische Studien und Kritiken, Hamburg; Gotha, 1828–1942.
TT: Theologisch Tijdschrift, Amsterdam; Leiden, 1867–1919.
TTod: Theology Today, Princeton, N.J.
TZ: Theologische Zeitschrift, Basel.
VD: Verbum Domini, Rome.
ZKT: Zeitschrift für katholische Theologie, Innsbruck.
ZNW: Zeitschrift für die neutestamentliche Wissenschaft, Giessen; Berlin.
ZST: Zeitschrift für systematische Theologie, Gütersloh, 1923–55.
ZTK: Zeitschrift für Theologie und Kirche, Tübingen.

OTHER ABBREVIATIONS

The abbreviations OT and NT are used throughout for the Old Testament and the New Testament, respectively. The abbreviations of the names of the books of the OT and NT and of the Apocrypha, which are printed without full point, will be readily understood. References to the Pseudepigrapha of the OT are according to the nomenclature employed in R. H. Charles, *The Apocrypha and Pseudepigrapha of the Old Testament in English*, Oxford, 1913. The Qumran texts are cited by the commonly used abbreviations (see, for example, Kuhn, *Konkordanz*, pp. v–vii). Tractates of the Mishnah, Talmud and Tosephta are cited by the abbreviations listed in H. Danby, *The Mishnah, translated from the Hebrew with introduction and brief explanatory notes*, Oxford, 1933, p. 806. The titles of other Rabbinic writings are either given in full or will be easily recognizable in the abbreviations used. Ancient Greek and Latin authors are designated by the names by which they are generally known (in unabbreviated form), and their works, where different works have to be distinguished, are indicated by abbreviated titles, in most cases those to be found in LSJ, pp. xvi–xli (see also Suppl., pp. vii–x), and in C. T. Lewis and C. Short, *A Latin Dictionary*, Oxford, 1966 ([1]1879), pp. vii–xi. A convenient list of the separate works of Philo (they are not listed in LSJ, p. xxxii) will be found at the end of the general introduction in each of the volumes of the Loeb edition of Philo.

The commentary is based on the Nestle text, which is presented in the lemmata even when in the following notes a variation from it is preferred; and the Nestle sigla have been used. For the MT the Württemberg Bible Society's *Biblia Hebraica*, Stuttgart, [6]1950, has been relied on, and for the LXX their *Septuaginta*, ed. A. Rahlfs, [7]1962. Hebrew is nearly always transliterated, the system followed being that set out in H. H. Rowley (ed.), *The Old Testament and Modern Study*, Oxford, 1951, p. xiii.

In 1979 the 26th edition of the Nestle-Aland *Novum Testamentum Graece* was published. A perusal of it will show that in Romans there are some thirty-three differences (marked by a dagger in the apparatus of Nestle[26]) between the text of Nestle[26] and that of Nestle[25]. To all of these reference is made within square brackets in the course of the commentary.

Readers working with Nestle[26] should note that, whereas it uses a Gothic H to denote the Hebrew (Masoretic) text of the OT and a Gothic M to denote the *Mehrheitstext* or Majority text, this commentary still adheres to the earlier Nestle use of Gothic H to denote the so-called Hesychian or Egyptian type of text and of Gothic K to denote the so-called Koine or Byzantine text-recension. To change from the apparatus of Nestle[25] to the apparatus of Nestle[26] as the basis of our presentation of text-critical evidence in this commentary is at this stage impracticable.

INTRODUCTION

Judging the proper function of the introduction to a commentary to be to furnish the reader with such information as will enable him to approach the detailed exegesis efficiently but with a still open mind rather than to present him with the commentator's ready-made answers to all important questions (in our view, an illegitimate procedure, because it can result in a pre-conditioning of the reader's mind to see the document through the commentator's eyes), we have decided to place both our general discussion of the theology of Romans and also our discussion of the difficult question of Paul's purpose or purposes in writing it[1] not in the introduction but in volume two at the end of the exegetical notes. The appropriate time for the commentator to set his own conclusions on these subjects before his reader is surely when the reader has completed his detailed exegetical work, and not before: in this way he will not be in so much danger of conditioning the reader's thinking, but will be submitting his conclusions to the reader's responsible judgment.

A chapter on the text of Romans is not included, since, while particular points of textual criticism will be fully discussed in the course of the commentary, on the more general textual questions the reader may now conveniently consult several excellent books on the text of the NT.[2]

I. AUTHENTICITY AND INTEGRITY

The denial of Paul's authorship of Romans by such critics as E. Evanson,[3] B. Bauer,[4] A. D. Loman[5] and R. Steck[6] is now

[1] What is said on this latter subject in chapter IV of this introduction will be limited to the indication of various questions needing to be kept in mind.

[2] Among these Metzger, *Text*, may be specially recommended. Attention may also be drawn to the series, Arbeiten zur neutestamentlichen Textforschung, published under the auspices of the Institut für neutestamentliche Textforschung of the University of Münster, and to the bulletins of the Stiftung zur Förderung der neutestamentlichen Textforschung (Münster i.W.).

[3] *The Dissonance of the Four generally received Evangelists, and the evidence of their respective authenticity examined*, Ipswich, 1792, pp. 257–61.

[4] *Kritik der paulinischen Briefe*, Berlin, 1852.

[5] 'Quaestiones Paulinae', in *TT* 16 (1882), pp. 141ff; 20 (1886), pp. 42ff; 387ff.

[6] *Der Galaterbrief nach seiner Echtheit untersucht, nebst kritischen Bemerkungen zu den paulinischen Hauptbriefen*, Berlin, 1888.

rightly relegated to a place among the curiosities of NT scholarship. Today no responsible criticism disputes its Pauline origin.[1] The evidence of its use in the Apostolic Fathers is clear,[2] and before the end of the second century it is listed and cited as Paul's. Every extant early list of NT books includes it among his letters. The external evidence of authenticity could indeed hardly be stronger; and it is altogether borne out by the internal evidence, linguistic, stylistic, literary, historical and theological. Since Paul's authorship is not now questioned, it is unnecessary to set out the evidence here.

But there is one question relating to the authorship of the epistle as a whole, which ought to be considered before we turn to the subject of integrity: it is the question of the precise part played by Tertius in the production of the epistle. That 16.22 (ἀσπάζομαι ὑμᾶς ἐγὼ Τέρτιος ὁ γράψας τὴν ἐπιστολὴν ἐν κυρίῳ) was not composed by Paul is clear. Recent commentators have for the most part been content to say simply that Paul was in the habit of dictating his letters. But it is necessary to ask whether Tertius means by ὁ γράψας τὴν ἐπιστολήν (i) that he wrote the letter in long-hand to Paul's dictation, or (ii) that he took it down in shorthand as Paul dictated it and then subsequently wrote it out in long-hand, or (iii) that, acting as a much more independent secretary, he himself composed the letter in accordance with Paul's instructions.[3] O. Roller, in an important book which has not received as much attention as might have been expected,[4] gave his support to (iii).[5] He maintained that the normal practice was either to write one's own personal letters in one's own hand (especially if they were short) or else—and this was more often done—to entrust the writing to a secretary, who would himself compose the letter on the basis of the instructions given him;[6] that the dictation

[1] C. H. Dodd, p. 9, goes so far as to say: 'The authenticity of the Epistle to the Romans is a closed question'.

[2] See especially 1 Clement 32.2 (cf. Rom 9.4f); 35.5 (cf. Rom 1.29–32); 50.6f (cf. Rom 4.7–9); Ignatius, Eph. 19.3 (cf. Rom 6.4); Magn. 6.2 (cf. Rom 6.17); 9.1 (cf. Rom 6.6); Trall. 9.2 (cf. Rom 8.11); Smyrn. 1.1 (cf. Rom 1.3f); Polycarp 3.3 (cf. Rom 13.8–10); 4.1 (cf. Rom 6.13 and 13.12); 6.2 (cf. Rom 14.10 and 12); 10.1 (cf. Rom 12.10).

[3] Acceptance of this third view would not, of course, necessarily involve assuming that Tertius received his instructions for the whole letter at once. We might think of him as submitting his draft of a part of the epistle for Paul's correction before receiving instructions for the next part.

[4] Das Formular der paulinischen Briefe: ein Beitrag zur Lehre vom antiken Briefe, Stuttgart, 1933.

[5] op. cit., p. 22f.

[6] op. cit., p. 14f; also pp. 295–300.

of letters (in the sense of the dictation of the full text of the letter as the scribe wrote) was exceptional,[1] since the extreme laboriousness and slowness of writing on papyrus with such pens and ink as were available[2] made such dictation excessively tedious and time-consuming; that shorthand was not used as early as Paul's time for taking down letters from dictation.[3] With regard to Romans, in particular, he further argued that the fact that Tertius composed 16.22 independently itself gives rise to doubts as to whether Paul dictated 16.21 and 23— and, in fact, the rest of the letter;[4] and that the chiastic arrangement of 1.8–15 and 15.28–33 (prayer—proposed visit in the one and proposed visit—prayer in the other) suggests composition by a secretary familiar with the stylistic convention that the beginning and conclusion of the 'context' of a letter should correspond, since this phenomenon occurs in no other Pauline letter.[5] He also suggested that some of the anacolutha and other unevennesses to be found in the Pauline epistles may be the result of Paul's own additions to, and corrections of, the drafts submitted for his approval.[6]

But Roller's arguments and the mass of fascinating illustrative material he brought together fall a long way short of proving that alternatives (i) and (ii) must be ruled out.[7] The former of these (that is, that Tertius wrote the letter in longhand to Paul's dictation) is by no means as unlikely as Roller thought. The last sentences of Cicero's letter of 12 July 45 B.C. to his friend Atticus,[8] in which he speaks of a letter he had written to the exceedingly fastidious Varro, show that Cicero judged it wiser, where it was specially important that the expression of his thoughts should be absolutely right, to dictate 'syllabatim' to Spintharus than to entrust the drafting to his highly competent and beloved secretary Tiro, though he apparently found this very tiresome. In view of the special importance and special difficulty of its subject matter and also

[1] op. cit., p. 16f; also pp. 300–4.
[2] op. cit., pp. 5–14; also pp. 257–95.
[3] op. cit., p. 17f; also pp. 305–34.
[4] op. cit., p. 22.
[5] op. cit., p. 470 (note 305).
[6] op. cit., p. 21f.
[7] Cf., e.g., E. Percy, *Die Probleme der Kolosser- und Epheser-briefe*, Lund, 1946, p. 10, n. 1; S. Lyonnet, 'De arte litteras exarandi apud antiquos', in *VD* 34 (1956), pp. 3ff.
[8] *Att.* 13.25.3: 'Sed, quaeso, epistula mea ad Varronem valdene tibi placuit? Male mi sit, si umquam quicquam tam enitar. Ergo ne Tironi quidem dictavi, qui totas περιοχὰς persequi solet, sed Spintharo syllabatim.' (On the manner of Cicero's 'dictation' to Tiro see Roller, op. cit., p. 307f.)

in view of its occasion, it hardly seems particularly unlikely
that Paul would dictate his letter to the Roman church—in
spite of its very much greater length—in the way in which
Cicero dictated his letter to Varro. After all, though he may
not have thought that he was producing a κτῆμα ἐς αἰεί, he
must surely have hoped that his letter would on more than one
occasion be read and listened to with a good deal of attention
by the Christians of Rome, and that they would ponder it and
discuss it among themselves. Moreover, with regard to the
slowness of such dictation, it is surely likely that even Paul
would be unable to formulate such a letter at any great speed.
Roller sometimes seems oblivious of the inherent probability
that the actual composition of Romans must have been a very
much more laborious process than that of composing an
ordinary personal or business letter. May not Paul have
needed quite as much time to compose it as did Tertius to
write it?

But alternative (ii), the view favoured by Sanday and
Headlam,[1] has also to be considered. Roller maintains that
there is no certain evidence of the existence of Greek tachygraphy earlier than the middle of the second century A.D.[2]
(The evidence for Latin tachygraphy is earlier.) But the fact
that Cicero used a Greek expression to denote shorthand-
writing in a letter to Atticus[3] strongly suggests that he derived
the art from Greeks. Whatever we make of the tradition that
Xenophon (5th–4th centuries B.C.) invented shorthand,[4] it
would seem that the possibility that Tertius made use of some
form of more or less rudimentary shorthand—we might
perhaps think of him taking down a few sentences at a time
in this way and then writing them out in long-hand while Paul
thought out his next few sentences—cannot be ruled out.

In view of what has been said above and also in view of the
inherent improbability that someone capable of the highly
original, closely-articulated and also extremely difficult thought
which has gone into the Epistle to the Romans would ever
have voluntarily entrusted the expression of it to another
person,[5] we conclude that Tertius either wrote the epistle in

---

[1] p. lx.
[2] p. 306f.
[3] *Att.* 13.32.3 (dated 29 May 45 B.C.). His words are: 'Et, quod ad te de
decem legatis scripsi, parum intellexisti, credo quia διὰ σημείων
scripseram.' (Cf. F. G. Kenyon, in *OCD*, p. 1033 (s.v. Tachygraphy).)
[4] Diogenes Laertius, *Vita Xen.* 2.48, speaks of him as πρῶτος
ὑποσημειωσάμενος τὰ λεγόμενα.
[5] The situation with regard to 2 Timothy, which (along with 1 Timothy
and Titus) Roller regards as authentic (cf. pp. 20f, 92–152), is of course

long-hand directly from Paul's dictation or else took it down first in shorthand, and that we may be confident that we have in the text which Tertius wrote the thought of Paul for all intents and purposes expressed as Paul himself expressed it.

We turn now to the question of integrity. The nineteenth century saw a number of theories of extensive interpolation put forward mainly by Dutch critics. First came the work of C. H. Weisse, *Beiträge zur Kritik der paulinischen Briefe an die Galater, Römer, Philipper und Kolosser*.[1] His example was followed—as Sanday and Headlam put it, 'with greater indiscreetness'[2]—by A. Pierson and S. A. Naber,[3] J. H. A. Michelsen,[4] D. Voelter[5] and W. C. van Manen.[6] The thoroughly arbitrary and subjective nature of these theories is now generally recognized. Also arbitrary and subjective are R. M. Hawkins, 'Romans: A Reinterpretation',[7] which also posits extensive interpolation, and the recent article in which J. Kallas attempts to prove that Rom 13.1–7 is un-Pauline.[8]

R. Bultmann's claim to detect a number of brief glosses (2.16; 6.17b; 7.25b–8.1; 10.17)[9] deserves to be taken more seriously; but in every case the passage in question can be explained satisfactorily without having recourse to this hypothesis (see the notes on these verses).

The most difficult and controversial problem which concerns the integrity of the epistle is the complex problem posed by the tangle of evidence bearing on the relation of chapters 15

altogether different. For one thing, the character of the contents is vastly different from that of Romans, and, for another, the circumstances indicated by 2.9 make it necessary to conclude that it was drafted by someone other than Paul.

[1] Leipzig, 1867.

[2] p. lxxxvi.

[3] *Verisimilia. Laceram conditionem Novi Testamenti exemplis illustrarunt* . . ., Amsterdam, 1886. A sample of this work is given by Sanday and Headlam, p. lxxxvif.

[4] 'Kritisch onderzoek naar den oudsten tekst van "Paulus' brief aan de Romeinen" ', in *TT* 20 (1886), pp. 372ff; 473ff; 21 (1887), pp. 163ff.

[5] 'Ein Votum zur Frage nach der Echtheit, Integrität und Composition der vier paulinischen Hauptbriefe', in *TT* 23 (1889), pp. 265ff; *Die Composition der paulinischen Hauptbriefe I: Der Römer- und Galaterbrief*, Tübingen, 1890.

[6] 'Marcions brief van Paulus aan de Galatiërs', in *TT* 21 (1887), pp. 382ff; 451ff; *Paulus II. De Brief aan de Romeinen*, Leiden, 1891.

[7] In *JBL* 60 (1941), pp. 129ff.

[8] 'Romans xiii.1–7: An Interpolation', in *NTS* 11 (1964–65), pp. 365ff.

[9] 'Glossen im Römerbrief', in *TL* 72 (1947), cols. 197–202.

and 16 to the rest of Romans.[1] The evidence which has to be explained may be set out as follows:

(i) The doxology, which is 16.25–27, is variously placed in the textual tradition—

- (a) at the end of chapter 16 by $\mathfrak{P}^{61}$ ℵ B C D 81 *al* it (UBS cites seven MSS.) vg sy^p sa bo aeth Cl Or Ambst.
- (b) at the end of chapter 14 by ℵ it (one MS.) sy^h *codd. apud* Or.
- (c) both at the end of chapter 14 and at the end of chapter 16 by AP 5 33 *pc.*
- (d) at the end of chapter 15 by $\mathfrak{P}^{46}$.
- (e) omitted altogether by G (but a space is left at the end of chapter 14) Mcion.

(ii) The 'grace' occurs twice in the ℵ text (both in 16.20 and in 16.24), but is omitted in 16.20 by D G it (UBS cites five MSS.) and as 16.24 by $\mathfrak{P}^{46}$ $\mathfrak{P}^{61vid}$ ℵ A B C 5 81 *al* it (one MS. according to UBS) vg^{codd} sa bo Or. Broadly speaking, the authorities which include the grace as 16.24 are those which have the doxology at the end of chapter 14 or else omit it altogether. A few authorities place 16.24 after 16.27.

(iii) G and *g* (with some support from Or) omit ἐν ῾Ρώμῃ in 1.7 (G also has ἐν ἀγάπῃ here instead of ἀγαπητοῖς) and τοῖς ἐν ῾Ρώμῃ in 1.15, that is, the only explicit references to Rome in the epistle.[2]

(iv) In the Vulgate codex Amiatinus, while the full sixteen chapters of Romans are included in the text, the last two of the fifty-one *breves* or section-summaries (taken over from a pre-Vulgate Latin version) correspond to 14.1–23 and 16.25–27, 15.1–16.24 being unrepresented.

(v) In the Vulgate MSS. 1648, 1792 and 2089 the text of Romans comprises only 1.1–14.23 followed immediately by 16.24–27.

(vi) Origen (col. 1290) says: 'Caput hoc [i.e. 16.25–27] Marcion, a quo scripturae evangelicae et apostolicae interpolatae sunt, de hac epistola penitus abstulit; et non solum hoc, sed et ab eo loco, ubi scriptum est: "omne autem, quod

---

[1] In his commentary as originally published Dodd was able to see here two quite separate questions, that of 'the two recensions' and that of the destination of chapter sixteen; but the discovery of $\mathfrak{P}^{46}$ has radically altered the situation. It is now, of course, no longer possible to say, as Dodd did then (p. xvii), that 'There is no textual evidence whatever for any separation between xv. and xvi.'; and the two questions cannot any more be properly treated as two quite separate questions.

[2] With reference to (iii) see further Michel, p. 43; Bruce, p. 25f; Zuntz, pp. 76, 228n, and 276; T. W. Manson, *Studies*, p. 227f.

non est ex fide, peccatum est" [i.e. 14.23], usque ad finem cuncta dissecuit.'[1]

(vii) Though there are things in chapters 15 and 16 which could well have been used against Marcion, Tertullian in his *Adversus Marcionem* never quotes from these chapters, and in one place (5.14) he refers to Rom 14.10 as 'in clausula' (which in the context can hardly mean anything other than 'in the concluding section (of the epistle)').[2] Tertullian, in fact, does not quote from Romans 15 or 16 in any of his works.

(viii) There are no quotations from these two chapters in Irenaeus or Cyprian; but Clement of Alexandria made use of them.

(ix) 16.25–27 makes (*pace, inter al.*, Nygren, p. 457, J. Cambier, in Robert-Feuillet *Introduction* 2, p. 450; Guthrie, *Introduction*, pp. 34–36; Bruce, p. 282) a rather un-Pauline impression.

(x) Chapter 16 consists to a large extent of greetings to individuals.

Three basic explanations of this evidence (there are, of course, a good many variations of them) have to be considered.

According to the first, Paul originally wrote 1.1–14.23 (without the references to Rome in 1.7 and 15) as a general letter for circulation among churches not of his foundation and which he had not visited, and then subsequently adapted it for sending to the church in Rome by the addition of the material which now follows 14.23 as well as by the insertion of the references to Rome in chapter one. But this explanation is most unlikely. For one thing, 1.8–13 contains statements (particularly vv. 8 and 13) so specific as to be hardly tolerable in a letter not intended for a particular church or at least a particular group of churches. A second, and even weightier, objection is that 14.23 is a most unsuitable ending for the letter even with the addition of the doxology of 16.25–27.[3] Dodd was surely justified in claiming that 14.23 'does not bring the argument of chap. xiv. to a conclusion worthy of the level on which it has been conducted' and that 'The plan of the epistle, which is more shapely than is usual in Paul's work, demands some such conclusion to its great argument as is found in xv. 7–13'.[4] That Paul was originally content to

---

[1] That 'dissecuit' is to be understood here as meaning 'cut off' rather than 'cut up' is to some extent confirmed by (vii) and (viii), and also by (i) (b), (iv) and (v).

[2] Tertullian's words are: 'Bene autem quod et in clausula tribunal Christi comminatur, utique judicis et ultoris, utique Creatoris; . . .'

[3] *Pace* F. C. Burkitt, *Christian Beginnings*, London, 1924, p. 127.

[4] p. 11.

conclude his letter at 14.23, and only later, in adapting it for Rome, felt the argument to be incomplete and so inserted 15.1–13 before adding the material with a specific relevance to the Roman church, is extremely improbable. The shortest form of the epistle, the existence of which is attested by (i) (b) and (c) and (iv) and (v) above, is rather to be explained as having originated with Marcion[1]—a supposition which is common to both the following explanations of the evidence. That, with the views which he had, he should have objected to 15.1–13 with its heavy concentration of OT quotations and such statements as 15.4 and 8, is easily understandable.[2] There is no difficulty in supposing that Marcion's text was then 'reproduced in greater or lesser degree in many orthodox lines of transmission, especially in western and, more particularly, Latin copies'.[3] The doxology, whatever its origin, was probably added in the first place to this text of Romans which ended with 14.23, because it was felt to need some sort of conclusion to round it off.[4] The variant readings of G in 1.7 and 15, which are the strongest point in favour of the first explanation of the evidence set out above, are difficult to account for. T. W. Manson's suggestion that Marcion excised the references to Rome, moved by resentment against the Roman church,[5]

---

[1] For the view that Marcion did not himself shorten the text but found it already mutilated see A. von Harnack, *Marcion*, Leipzig, 1921, p. 145*f: cf. Kümmel, *Introduction*, p. 224.

[2] T. W. Manson, *Studies*, p. 235, suggests that his anger against the Roman church for rebuffing him would account for the omission of 15.14–33.

[3] Bruce, p. 29.

[4] Though there are still some scholars who defend its originality at the end of chapter 16 (e.g. Nygren, Bruce), it seems much more probable that it was first attached to Romans for the purpose we have indicated, and then later attached at the end of chapter 16 and also after 15.33, having commended itself as a good conclusion, than that, being original at the end of chapter 16, it was taken from there to round off the shorter forms of the epistle. Whether it was specially composed for this purpose is disputed. Some (e.g. R. Schumacher, *Die beiden letzten Kapitel des Römerbriefes*, Münster i.W., 1929; Michaelis, *Einleitung*, p. 163f; Wiken-hauser, *Introduction*, p. 410f) maintain that it may be a fragment of another Pauline epistle; but the preservation of so small a fragment does not seem very likely. More probably it was composed, to round off Marcion's shortened text, either among Marcion's followers (in view of (vi) it is not to be ascribed to Marcion himself), or in the orthodox Church where this text-form was in use. If its origin is Marcionite, then it must have undergone orthodox expansion (cf. Harnack, in *SAB* 1919, pp. 531ff): the reference to the prophetic scriptures, in particular, can hardly be Marcionite. But an orthodox origin seems perfectly possible (cf. Eph 3.20f; 1 Tim 1.17; Jude 24f).

[5] *Studies*, p. 229f. But it is to be noted that there is no evidence that Marcion attempted to alter the title of the epistle.

is possibly the right solution; but perhaps rather more likely is the suggestion that the variants reflect an omission of the localizing references in liturgical use.[1]

The distinguishing characteristic of the second type of explanation is the contention that chapter 16 (or, according to some, 16.3–23) is not part of Paul's original letter to the Roman church. Though the suggestion has been made that it is a second letter to Rome, written from Puteoli (cf. Acts 28.13),[2] it is generally agreed by the upholders of this type of explanation that it was addressed to another church, Ephesus usually being suggested.[3] According to what is now the most popular form of this explanation, Paul wrote 1.1–15.33 and sent it to Rome, and then sent a copy of it supplemented by chapter 16 to the church in Ephesus. In support of this view, it is argued (i) that Paul is not likely to have sent so many greetings to individuals in a letter to the Roman church which he had not yet visited;

(ii) that Paul had had a longer ministry in Ephesus than anywhere else, and so would have many friends there;

(iii) that, in particular, Epaenetus, the ἀπαρχὴ τῆς ᾿Ασίας εἰς Χριστόν (16.5), and Prisca and Aquila (16.3: cf. Acts 18.2, 18f, 26; 1 Cor 16.19) would more probably be in Ephesus than in Rome;

(iv) that neither the authoritative and rather sharp tone (contrast 1.8–13; 15.14–33), nor the substance, of 16.17–20 accords with the supposition that chapter 16 was addressed to Rome, but both are understandable on the assumption that it was intended for the Ephesian church;

(v) that 15.33 appears to be the conclusion of a letter;

and, since the discovery of 𝔓⁴⁶, (vi) that—and this is the strongest argument in favour of the second explanation—𝔓⁴⁶ provides objective evidence of the existence of a text-form which ended with 15.33.

But these arguments are not as strong as on first sight they appear to be. With regard to (i), (ii) and (iii), a number of

---

[1] Cf., e.g., Lietzmann, p. 27. Manson objects that this hypothesis 'does not explain why the generalizing process was applied only to Romans, and possibly Ephesians, while all the other Pauline letters are left in their scandalous particularity' (p. 229); but it may be said in reply to this, that the other letters are by reason of their contents essentially and obviously particular, in a way in which the Epistle to the Romans is not.

[2] Cf. M. Albertz, *Die Botschaft des Neuen Testamentes* I/2, Zurich, 1952, p. 205.

[3] The suggestion that Romans 16 is a fragment of a Pauline letter to the church in Ephesus was made as early as 1829 by D. Schulz, in *TSK* 2 (1829), pp. 609ff.

points may be made: that Paul seems to have refrained from sending greetings to individuals in churches which he knew personally (there are none in 1 and 2 Corinthians, Galatians, Philippians and 1 and 2 Thessalonians), probably because he felt that where all were his friends it was invidious to single out particular individuals, but to have included them in writing to churches which he had not yet visited (there are such greetings in Colossians), probably because this seemed to be a good way of establishing contact, which is something he was certainly desirous of doing in writing to the Roman church; that, in view of Rome's position as the capital of the empire, the centre to which all roads led, it is not at all surprising that many of Paul's friends should find their way to Rome; that a number of Roman Jews, whom Paul might have got to know in other places during the period of their enforced absence from Rome after the expulsion of Jews from the capital by Claudius in A.D. 49, would probably by the time of Paul's writing of Romans have returned to Rome—among them Aquila and Prisca; that the description of Epaenetus as ἀπαρχὴ τῆς Ἀσίας εἰς Χριστόν would seem on the whole rather more natural in a letter addressed to a church outside, than in one to a church inside, the province of Asia. With regard to (iv), it is to be noted that Paul has already, as a matter of fact, used considerable frankness in the course of 12.1–15.13, and also that the warning may be read as a warning of a danger which has not yet materialized, and as such could be addressed to Rome as well as to Ephesus. (v) is not at all a strong argument; for it is improbable that 15.33 was intended as an epistolary concluding greeting, since, in contrast to all the concluding greetings in the Pauline corpus, it does not contain a reference to grace (cf. Roller, *Formular*, pp. 114–16, and Table 4 at the end of the book). We should rather compare 15.13; Phil 4.9; 1 Th 3.11–13. With regard to (vi), it must be said that, on the assumption that the original letter included chapter 16, there is no great difficulty in understanding how a text-form ending at 15.33 could come into existence. If any copy of Romans was sent by Paul to another church because of the general interest and importance of its contents, it would not be at all surprising if the last chapter were omitted as not being of general interest; and at a later date someone making a copy of Romans for the use of his own church might easily have omitted it for the same reason.

And not only can the different arguments put forward in support of this second explanation be quite easily countered; there are also some very serious difficulties which are inherent

in it in its various forms. Is it conceivable—for one thing—
that, if Paul were writing to the church in Ephesus, where he
had ministered so long, a covering letter to go with the copy of
his Roman letter he was sending them, he would have had
nothing more to say to them in it than we have in Romans 16?
To say, as Manson does,[1] that 'Any further information that
was asked for at Ephesus could doubtless be supplied verbally
by the bearer of the letter', does not meet the real difficulty;
for it would not be merely information that they would have
reason to look for, but some pastoral message specially
appropriate to them (vv. 17–20 can hardly be regarded as
enough), and its absence is made all the more inexplicable by
the fact that Paul had time to include so many greetings to
individuals. Moreover, our answer to (i) and (ii) above has
suggested not only that the presence of the greetings to
individuals is no objection to the view that chapter 16 was
addressed to Rome but also that it is a very serious difficulty
in the way of explaining that chapter as addressed to Ephesus.
And, if chapter 16 is really a covering letter to the Ephesian
church, how are we to explain the loss both of the epistolary
closing greeting (if we are right in thinking that 15.33 is not
likely to have been intended as this) of the Roman letter and
also of the 'prescript' of the letter to Ephesus? The suggestion
that chapter 16 is simply a Pauline fragment which has been
attached to the letter to the Romans has its own difficulties.
If the earlier, and presumably more substantial, part of a letter
was lost, would the latter part have been preserved, when it
consisted mostly of greetings? And, if it came to be attached
to the end of Romans, would there not have been left a trace
of the Pauline 'grace' at the end of chapter 15?

We conclude that the third explanation, according to which
Paul wrote 1.1–16.23 to the church in Rome, should be
accepted, as being capable of accounting for all the evidence
most convincingly.[2]

---

[1] p. 238f.

[2] On the relation of chapters 15 and 16 to the rest of the epistle see
further: D. de Bruyne, 'Les deux derniers chapitres de la lettre aux
Romains', in *RBén* 25 (1908), pp. 423ff; and 'La finale marcionite de la
lettre aux Romains retrouvée', in *RBén* 28 (1911), pp. 133ff; P. Corssen,
'Zur Überlieferungsgeschichte des Römerbriefes', in *ZNW* 10 (1909),
pp. 1ff, 97ff; A. von Harnack, in *SAB* 1919, pp. 527ff; Zahn, pp. 621ff;
Lagrange, pp. 380ff; Schumacher, op. cit.; J. Dupont, 'Pour l'histoire
de la doxologie finale de l'Épître aux Romains', in *RBén* 58 (1948),
pp. 3ff; T. W. Manson, *Studies*, pp. 225–41 ('St Paul's Letter to the
Romans—and Others', previously published in *BJRL* 31 (1948), pp.
224ff); B. N. Kaye, ' "To the Romans and others" revisited', in *NT* 18
(1976), pp. 37–77; H. Gamble, *The Textual History of the Letter to the
Romans* (Studies and Documents 42), Grand Rapids, 1977.

II. DATE AND PLACE OF WRITING

The epistle was written at a time when Paul was on his way to, or about to set out for, Jerusalem (15.25), and, since it was also (according to 15.19 and 23) a time when he felt that his pioneer missionary work in the eastern provinces of the empire had been completed, the journey in question cannot be an earlier one than that recorded in Acts 20 and 21. That it is this journey is confirmed by the agreement of 15.25–28 with Acts 24.17. For a long time Paul has wanted to visit Rome (1.10–13), but has so far been prevented from doing so (1.13; 15.22). Now he hopes that at last he will be able to visit Rome on his way to Spain (15.23f, 28); but first he has to go to Jerusalem with the proceeds of the collection which the churches of Macedonia and Achaia have made for the relief of the poor among the saints at Jerusalem (15.25–27). It is virtually certain that it was during Paul's three months in Greece (i.e. in the province of Achaia), to which Acts 20.2–3 refers, that Romans was written. No other period within the limits set by the indications of Romans 1 and 15 is likely to have been as suitable as this for the writing of something as substantial and as carefully thought out and composed as the Epistle to the Romans. It is highly probable, in view of Paul's intimate relationship with the Corinthian church, that he spent these three months in Corinth, the capital of the province; and there are a number of details in the epistle which may be taken as pointers to Corinth as its place of origin—the commendation in 16.1–2 of Phoebe, διάκονος of the church in Cenchreae, Corinth's eastern port, who, we may assume, was to carry the letter to Rome; the greeting in 16.23 from Gaius, in whose house Paul is staying, who may well be the same Gaius as is mentioned in 1 Cor 1.14 as one whom Paul had baptized in Corinth, and from Erastus ὁ οἰκονόμος τῆς πόλεως (cf. Acts 19.22; also 2 Tim 4.20, where it is said that Erastus stayed in Corinth).[1]

To place Romans in the framework of Paul's ministry is thus quite easy. What is very much more difficult is to convert this relative dating into a precise absolute dating. That it was written during the period of winter and early spring in one of the years between late A.D. 54 and early A.D. 59 is certain, but within those limits the opinions of scholars vary.

A dated inscription found at Delphi and first published

---

[1] These three details were already noted by Origen (col. 835) as pointers to Corinth as the place of composition. But see on 16.23.

early this century, which shows that Gallio was proconsul of Achaia in A.D. 52,[1] provides a starting-point from which we have to work forward. The proconsular governors of senatorial provinces normally held office for one year only. According to Dio Cassius,[2] Claudius had ordained that governors should set off for their provinces by the middle of April: the time of arrival in the province would naturally vary according to the distance from Rome. The most likely inference to be drawn from the Delphi inscription is that Gallio was proconsul of Achaia from mid-51 to mid-52; but, since Achaia was not very far from Rome, it is just conceivable that Gallio arrived in his province in the middle of 52 and immediately sent a report to Claudius and that Claudius then had time to reply and afterwards to be acclaimed Imperator for the twenty-seventh time before 1 August, and, since there is also a remote possibility that Gallio served for two years, we cannot rule out with absolute certainty the possibility of his governorship's having run from 52 to 53, or from 50 to 52, or from 51 to 53, or from 52 to 54. It is very probable that Paul's appearance before him (Acts 18.12ff) should be dated early in his governorship, since the Jews would be likely to hope to win a new governor to their side. So we may say that, in view of the Delphi inscription, it is highly likely that Paul's appearance before Gallio was in A.D. 51; but that any date between mid-50 and mid-54 is theoretically possible on the basis of the Delphi inscription. Taking the summer of A.D. 51 as the most probable date of the appearance before Gallio, we may try to work forward from there. According to Acts 18.18, Paul remained ἡμέρας ἱκανάς in Corinth after being dismissed by Gallio. He then sailed for Syria (v. 18) either in the autumn of 51 or in the spring of 52, spending a while in Ephesus on the way (vv. 19–21). Arriving at Caesarea, he went up and greeted the

---

[1] See Foakes-Jackson and Lake, *Beginnings* 5, pp. 460–4; Barrett, *The New Testament Background: Selected Documents*, London, 1956, p. 48f; E. Haenchen, *Apostelgeschichte*, ³1959, pp. 58–60; *BHH* 1, col. 512f (illustration); *IDB* 1, p. 604. The inscription is fragmentary, but enough of it remains to show that it reproduces a rescript of Claudius in response to a report from the proconsul Gallio. The reference to Claudius's having been acclaimed Imperator for the twenty-sixth time indicates a date probably later than 25 January A.D. 52 (we know from two inscriptions (CIL 3.i. 476 and 1977) that his twenty-second, twenty-third and twenty-fourth acclamations were in the eleventh year of his reign: if his twenty-sixth was also before 25 January 52, he would have been acclaimed five times in the one year—which is scarcely likely) and certainly earlier than 1 August 52, since by then he had been acclaimed for the twenty-seventh time.

[2] 60.17.3.

church (that is, probably, the church in Jerusalem), and then went down to Antioch (v. 22) and spent some time (χρόνον τινά) there (v. 23). It is just possible that all this was done before the summer of 52; and, if it was, he may have completed the journeying referred to in 18.23 and 19.1 during that summer. But it is perhaps rather more likely that it was not till the autumn of 53 that he reached Ephesus again (19.1). His stay in Ephesus was something between two and three years (cf. 19.8, 10; 20.31). So his return to Corinth by way of Macedonia (20.1–2) could conceivably have been late in 54, but was more probably late in 55 or even late in 56. Thus, working from the most probable date of Paul's appearance before Gallio, we arrive at the winter and early spring of 55–56 as the most likely time for the writing of Romans, with the winter and early spring of 56–57 and the same period in 54–55 as less probable alternatives (the former of these being in our view more probable than the latter).

But it is also necessary to try to establish the date when M. Antonius Felix was replaced as governor of Judaea by Porcius Festus, and to work back from it. It seems clear that Felix had become governor in 52, when Ventidius Cumanus was disgraced;[1] but the date of his recall by Nero is disputed. According to Josephus,[2] the Jews of Caesarea prosecuted him before the Emperor after his recall, and he would have been convicted of maladministration, had he not been the brother of Pallas, 'whom Nero at that time held in special esteem'. On the strength of this statement, it is often argued that Felix must have been recalled very early in Nero's reign, since—so it is alleged—Pallas would not have been able to exert such influence after his dismissal. Now the deposition of Pallas seems to have taken place towards the end of 55 (or possibly towards the end of 54).[3] But, if the period of two full years to

[1] Cf. Tacitus, *Ann.* 12.54; Josephus, *BJ* 2.247; *Ant.* 20.137. The account given by Tacitus would seem to be muddled. He represents Felix as already in 52 'iam pridem Iudaeae impositus', and as having ruled Samaria while Cumanus ruled Galilee.

[2] *Ant.* 20.182.

[3] Tacitus relates it (*Ann.* 13.14) immediately before his account of the murder of Britannicus who at the time of his death had almost reached his fourteenth birthday (*Ann.* 13.15: 'propinquo die quo quartum decimum aetatis annum Britannicus explebat'), the time when he would have assumed the *toga virilis*. According to Suetonius, *Claudius* 27, Britannicus was born 'on the twentieth day of his (i.e. Claudius's) reign and in his second consulship' ('vicesimo imperii die inque secundo consulatu'). The twentieth day of his reign was 13 February 41, but his second consulship did not begin until 42. If then the first part of the specification was intended as an actual date, i.e.

which Acts 24.27 refers is the time that Paul had already been a
prisoner (which is surely the natural meaning of the Greek),[1]
then to date the recall and prosecution of Felix before his
brother's dismissal would probably involve assigning Paul's
three months in Greece during which Romans was written to
the beginning of 53 (or possibly 52). And this would be quite
impossibly close to the date of his appearance before Gallio.
Moreover, the assumption that Felix was recalled so early falls
foul of Josephus's narrative in which a long list of events which
occurred in Palestine during Felix's governorship is placed
after the reference to Nero's accession. The assumption that
Pallas could only have had influence before his dismissal is
anyway unwarranted. For one thing, he was already an object
of Nero's dislike before he was dismissed; and, for another, his
dismissal was not a thoroughgoing disgrace—he was, in fact,
allowed to keep the huge fortune he had amassed and was able
to stipulate that there should be no retrospective inquiry into
any of his actions and that his accounts with the state should
be taken as balanced (Tacitus, *Ann*. 13.14). Once the notion
that Felix must have been recalled and prosecuted before the
dismissal of Pallas from office is out of the way, it is natural to
assign the change of governors to a considerably later date. The
impression given by Josephus is that, in comparison with that
of Felix, the governorship of Festus was short. If we date the
arrival of Festus in his province in the summer of 58 or 59,[2]
we shall not be far out. On this reckoning Paul's three months

---

13 February 41 (which would mean that the fourteenth birthday would
fall on 13 February 55), the second part is incompatible with it, and
Suetonius must have made a mistake. But it is quite probable that he
intended to indicate by the first part of his specification only the day
of the year (i.e. 13 February), and by the second part the year (i.e. 42)
of Britannicus's birth; and in this case the fourteenth birthday would be
13 February 56 (cf. Haenchen, *Apostelgeschichte*, p. 63, n. 3).

[1] *Pace* K. Lake, in Foakes-Jackson and Lake, *Beginnings* 5, pp. 465f,
471n., and others, who argue that the reference is to the time that
Felix had been governor.

[2] There is possibly some support for 59 in Eusebius's *Chronica*, as
Caird argues (*IDB* 1, p. 604f). In *Chron*. 2 (Migne *PG* 19, cols. 541 and
542) he dates the succession of Festus in the 55th year of Christ, the
10th of the reign of Agrippa II, and the 14th of the reign of Claudius.
But there must be a mistake here, since Eusebius knows well that it
was Nero who sent Festus (cf. *H.E.* 2.22.1). If Eusebius found just one
date in his source, the 10th year of Agrippa, he may perhaps have
mistakenly assumed that the reign of Agrippa II must be reckoned from
the death of Agrippa I: the 10th year of Agrippa would then coincide
with the 14th of Claudius. But the reign of Agrippa II was reckoned
as beginning from 1 Nisan 50, so that his 10th year would begin from
1 Nisan 59.

in Greece of Acts 20.3 would fall in the winter and early spring of 55–56 or 56–57.

We conclude that—within the period extending from late 54 to early 59 within which its composition must certainly fall— the Epistle to the Romans was most probably written either during the period comprising the last days of 55 and the early weeks of 56 or during that of the last days of 56 and the early weeks of 57.

III. THE CHURCH IN ROME

The Epistle to the Romans is our earliest witness to the existence of a church in Rome. But, since Paul can assure the Roman Christians that he has been desirous of visiting them ἀπὸ ἱκανῶν ἐτῶν (15.23: cf. the πολλάκις of 1.13), it is clear that there must have been Christians in Rome for at the very least three or four years before the time when Romans was written. It is probable that the statement of Suetonius, who was Hadrian's private secretary, that Claudius 'Iudaeos impulsore Chresto assidue tumultuantes Roma expulit' (*Claudius* 25) is evidence of the presence of Christianity in the capital by A.D. 49;[1] for it is more likely that the words 'impulsore Chresto' reflect in a confused way the fact that the riots originated in the Christian preaching of Christ (cf. its effects as recorded in Acts 13.50; 14.19; 17.5; 19.23ff)[2] than that they refer to the part played either by general messianic expectancy or by a Jewish agitator named Chrestus.[3] It is not necessary to assume that these riots must be connected with the first introduction of the gospel into Rome. It is intrinsically more likely, in view of the fact that there was at this time a freedom of circulation and movement such as the world had never seen before and, in particular, a constant movement to and

[1] The only ancient writer to give a precise date for this expulsion of the Jews by Claudius is Augustine's friend, Orosius, whose *Historia adversus paganos* was written early in the fifth century. He assigns it to the ninth year of Claudius (7.6: Migne, *PL* 31, col. 1075). His dating is generally accepted. It suits admirably the relation of Acts 18.2 (where this same expulsion is mentioned) to the account of Paul's appearance before Gallio (Acts 18.12ff), the date of which has been referred to above.

[2] For the confusion between 'Christus' and 'Chrestus' cf. Tertullian, *Apol.* 3; also Justin *1 Apol.* 4.

[3] For the view that the 'Chrestus' of Suetonius was 'some religious star whose appearance at Rome caused an upheaval among the Jews, but whose fame was sufficiently ephemeral for his precise identity to have been lost', see E. A. Judge and G. S. R. Thomas, 'The Origin of the Church at Rome', in *RTR* 25 (1966), pp. 84–87.

from Rome of officials, troops, merchants and many others, that Christianity was brought to Rome at a very early date (even if not quite so early as 'the autumn after the Crucifixion', mentioned in this connexion by Foakes-Jackson[1]).

It seems that the establishment of the gospel in Rome came about through the presence of Christians in the discharge of their ordinary secular duties or business rather than through any specially undertaken evangelistic enterprise. It is significant that neither in the Epistle to the Romans nor in the Acts of the Apostles (nor, for that matter, in any other NT document) is there any allusion to an initial evangelization in Rome by any particular missionary or missionaries. Ambrosiaster's statement that 'they had accepted faith in Christ without seeing any notable miracles or any of the apostles'[2] would seem to be applicable not just to the Gentile members of the Roman church (to whom he was referring) but to all, whether Gentile or Jewish, whose conversion had actually taken place in Rome. It is true that later tradition named Peter as the founder and first bishop of the Roman church (with an episcopate lasting twenty-five years).[3] But, since in its earliest form the tradition associated Paul with Peter, claiming both of them as co-founders,[4] and since there can be no question of Paul's having been a founder of the Roman church in the ordinary sense of the word, it is likely that all that was meant originally was that both Peter and Paul had been in Rome, had played a significant part in the early history of the Roman church, and had finally sealed their apostolic ministries by martyrdom in Rome or its immediate neighbourhood—and so were in a special sense the Roman church's apostles, whose mortal remains were in its possession. Since the Epistle to the Romans contains no reference at all to Peter, it is virtually certain that he was not in Rome at the time that Paul was writing, and highly probable that up to that time he had never been there.[5]

With regard to the composition of the Roman church at the time of Paul's writing, the question naturally arises whether it was predominantly Jewish-Christian or predominantly Gentile-

---

[1] *Peter, Prince of Apostles: A study in the history and tradition of Christianity*, London, 1927, p. 195.

[2] '. . . nulla insignia virtutum videntes, nec aliquem apostolorum, susceperant fidem Christi . . .' (col. 46).

[3] So, for example, the *Catalogus Liberianus* (A.D. 354).

[4] Cf. Irenaeus, *Adv. Haer.* 3.1.2; 3.3.1.

[5] *Pace* H. Lietzmann, 'Zwei Notizen zur Paulus', in *SAB* 1930. On the whole question of a residence of Peter in Rome see O. Cullmann, *Peter, Disciple, Apostle and Martyr*, Eng. tr., London, [2]1962.

Christian. Some[1] have argued that Jewish Christians formed
the majority. More common is the view that Paul was
addressing a mainly Gentile community.[2]

That the church in Rome included some Jews may be taken
as certain.[3] It is proved by the presence in the epistle of 15.7–12
and—if chapter 16 was addressed to Rome, as we are confident
that it was—by the fact that, among the people greeted, at the
very least Aquila (cf. Acts 18.2) and Andronicus, Junia(s) and
Herodion, whom Paul describes as his συγγενεῖς, were Jewish.
It is extremely probable that the Jewish element was
substantial. Claudius's edict of expulsion will have lapsed at
the time of his death, if not before: it may anyway have been
rather less indiscriminate than the references to it in Suetonius
and in Acts 18.2 suggest.[4] Those who had been expelled
will probably have lost no time in returning, once return
became possible. It is certain that early in Nero's reign the
Jewish community in Rome was once again strong and
flourishing.[5] As Dio Cassius observed,[6] the Jewish community
again and again showed an extraordinary resilience in the face
of setbacks and attempts at repression, and increased steadily.
In these circumstances it would be strange if there were not a
considerable number of Jews in the Roman church when Paul
wrote. But the evidence adduced as proving that the church
was predominantly Jewish falls a long way short of being
conclusive. Thus neither the constant engagement with the OT
to be seen throughout the epistle nor the use of the words

[1] e.g. F. C. Baur, *Paul the Apostle of Jesus Christ*, E. tr., 1 (²1876), pp. 331ff;
T. Zahn, *Introduction to the New Testament*, E. tr., Edinburgh, 1909, 1, p. 422;
W. Manson, *The Epistle to the Hebrews*, 1951, pp. 172ff; N. Krieger, 'Zum
Römerbrief', in *NT* 3 (1959), pp. 146ff; T. Fahy, 'St. Paul's Romans were
Jewish Converts', in *ITQ* 26 (1959–60), pp. 182–91.
[2] e.g. Sanday and Headlam, p. xxxiiif; Denney, pp. 561–67; Lagrange,
pp. xxi–xxiv; Barrett, p. 22; Kümmel, *Introduction*, pp. 218–20.
[3] *Pace* Munck, *Paul*, pp. 196, 200ff.
[4] Cf. Dio Cassius 60.6.6: τούς τε Ἰουδαίους πλεονάσαντας αὖθις ὥστε
χαλεπῶς ἂν ἄνευ ταραχῆς ὑπὸ τοῦ ὄχλου σφῶν τῆς πόλεως εἰρχθῆναι, οὐκ ἐξήλασε
μέν, τῷ δὲ δὴ πατρίῳ βίῳ χρωμένους ἐκέλευσε μὴ συναθροίζεσθαι, τές τε
ἑταιρείας ἐπαναχθείσας ὑπὸ τοῦ Γαΐου διέλυσε.
[5] It was not long before Nero became entangled with Otho's wife,
Poppaea Sabina, whom he subsequently married. She was attracted by
Judaism, and used her influence in the Jews' favour. On the whole
subject of the Jews in Rome reference may be made to J. Juster, *Les
Juifs dans l'empire romain*, Paris, 1914; G. La Piana, 'Foreign Groups
in Rome during the first centuries of the Empire', in *HTR* 20 (1927),
pp. 183ff; J. B. Frey, 'Les communautés juives à Rome aux premiers
temps de l'église', in *RechSR* (1930), pp. 275ff.
[6] 37.17.1: ἔστι καὶ παρὰ τοῖς Ῥωμαίοις τὸ γένος τοῦτο, κολουσθὲν μὲν πολλάκις,
αὐξηθὲν δὲ ἐπὶ πλεῖστον, ὥστε καὶ ἐς παρρησίαν τῆς νομίσεως ἐκνικῆσαι.

γινώσκουσιν γὰρ νόμον λαλῶ in 7.1 proves that Paul was writing to a predominantly Jewish-Christian church; for the OT was the Bible of the Gentile, as well as of the Jewish, Christian, and it is significant that Paul also assumes familiarity with, and reverence for, the OT in his letters to the Galatians and the Corinthians. The assumption that chapters 9–11 would only be of interest to Christians of Jewish race is quite unjustified, since the question of Israel was the question of God's faithfulness to His promises, and as such was the concern of the Gentile Christian just as much as it was the concern of the Jewish. W. Manson's contention that 'it is difficult to think of the question' of the Jew's advantage, taken up in 3.1ff, 'as having relevance to any body of hearers except a Jewish-Christian one'[1] is unconvincing; for, once again, it is the faithfulness of God which is in question. The reason why the Jew is addressed in the second person singular in 2.1ff, whereas in 1.18–32 the third person plural was used, may well be simply that, since his main concern in 1.18–3.20 is to show that there is no question of any man's being justified on the basis of his works, Paul directs his most vigorous efforts to demonstrating that the obvious possible exception, namely, the Jew, is in fact no exception. The ἡμῶν of 4.1 (Τί οὖν ἐροῦμεν εὑρηκέναι ᾿Αβραὰμ τὸν προπάτορα ἡμῶν κατὰ σάρκα;) is, of course, consonant with the Roman church's being predominantly Jewish-Christian; but the use of ἡμῶν would not be unnatural, if Paul knew that Jewish Christians were in a minority in the church he was addressing, or even if he knew it to be wholly Gentile (he could still associate himself with his fellow Jews, even if he knew that none of them was among the people he was addressing). And, if W. Manson was justified in claiming that in 3.21–26 Paul's interpretation of the Atonement 'is more closely related . . . to the central ritual idea of the Jewish sacrificial cultus than anywhere else in his Epistles',[2] and also that Romans contains no 'reference to gnosticising or pagan Hellenistic errors such as are charged by St. Paul upon other Churches',[3] neither feature necessarily proves the predominantly Jewish composition of the church in Rome: the former may simply reflect the fact that Romans is much more systematic than Paul's other extant letters, while the latter might perhaps be adequately explained by reference to Paul's specially 'delicate approach to this Church'—to use Manson's own phrase.[4] Ambrosiaster's

[1] op. cit., p. 174.
[2] op. cit., p. 175.
[3] op. cit., p. 173.
[4] ibid.

prologue to his commentary on Romans is sometimes cited as support for the view that the Roman church was at this time distinctly Jewish in character and outlook; but it is highly doubtful whether his statements[1] reflect anything more than either his own inferences from the epistle or the influence of Marcion's preconceptions.[2]

That the Roman church also included some Gentiles is, of course, absolutely clear from 11.13-32 and 15.7-12. If it continued to exist without any break when the Jews were expelled, that will presumably have been because by then some Gentiles had already been brought into its fellowship. That by the time when Paul was writing the Gentile element was considerable may be taken as quite certain. But the arguments put forward to prove that the Roman church was at this time predominantly Gentile fall—no less than those adduced to prove it was predominantly Jewish—far short of conclusiveness. The strongest concern 1.6 and 13 and 15.15f. But the words ἐν οἷς ἐστε καὶ ὑμεῖς κλητοὶ Ἰησοῦ Χριστοῦ may be understood as simply stating the fact that the Roman church is situated in the midst of the Gentile world (the implication being that it is therefore, though not founded by Paul, within the sphere of his apostolic commission), and, similarly, καθὼς καὶ ἐν τοῖς λοιποῖς ἔθνεσιν may be explained as a slightly inexact way of saying 'even as (I have already done) in the rest of the Gentile world'. In 15.15f Paul may be mentioning his apostleship of the Gentiles as the basis of his right to address the Roman church τολμηροτέρως and to put them in remembrance (they are, by virtue of their geographical situation, included in the sphere of his authority), without implying anything particular about the proportion of Gentiles to Jews in their community. The argument from the fact that, whereas the Jews are spoken of in the third person throughout 9.1–11.12,

---

[1] e.g. that the Christian Jews resident in Rome 'tradiderunt Romanis ut Christum profitentes, Legem servarent' (col. 45); that the Romans had received the faith of Christ 'ritu licet Judaico, in verbis potius quam in sensu; non enim expositum illis fuerat mysterium crucis Christi' (col. 46). It should, of course, be noted that the church could still have been racially mainly Jewish without being Judaistic in outlook and practice (Jewish Christians could of course differ widely), while, on the other hand, even if Gentiles were in the majority, it might still have had a Judaistic outlook.

[2] Cf. the Marcionite prologue to Romans: 'Romani sunt in partibus Italiae. Hi praeventi sunt a falsis apostolis et sub nomine domini nostri Jesu Christi in legem et prophetas erant inducti. Hos revocat apostolus ad veram et evangelicam fidem scribens eis a Corintho' (or 'ab Athenis').

the Gentiles are addressed in the second person in 11.13ff,[1] is surely quite illogical, since the Jews with whom Paul is mainly concerned in 9.1–11.12 are not Jewish Christians but the unbelieving Jews who could scarcely be addressed directly in a letter to a Christian community. What is said in 11.13ff is naturally understood as addressed to that element in the Roman church which could be tempted by the situation referred to in 9.1ff to adopt an altogether unchristian attitude of self-complacency and contemptuousness with regard to the Jews. There is no indication as to whether that element is a majority of the church or not.

The truth would seem to be that it is impossible to decide with anything like absolute certainty whether at the time Paul wrote to them the majority of the Roman Christians were Gentiles or Jews, and that we ought therefore to leave this question open. What is quite certain is that both the Jewish-Christian, and the Gentile-Christian, elements were considerable: it was clearly not a matter of an overwhelming majority and a tiny minority.

There are of course other questions which may be asked with regard to the composition of the Roman church besides the one we have been considering. It would, for example, be interesting to know what strata of society were represented in its membership. It is clear that some of the names of people greeted in chapter 16 are names of slaves or freedmen or freedwomen; but it should be remembered that slaves were quite often refined and well educated. That in Rome as elsewhere it was a matter of 'not many wise after the flesh, not many mighty, not many noble, are called' is likely; but it is also likely that some of the Christians in Rome were people of considerable means, and not impossible that one or two were possessed of considerable social status. There would seem to be a distinct possibility that Pomponia Graecina, the wife of Aulus Plautius, who had commanded the expedition to Britain in A.D. 43, a lady whom Tacitus describes as 'insignis femina', had come under the influence of Christianity: she was

---

[1] See, for example, Sanday and Headlam, p. 324, where they say with regard to 11.13: 'This verse and the references to the Gentiles that follow seem to show conclusively that St. Paul expected the majority of his readers to be Gentiles', and go on to quote with approval F. J. A. Hort's observation (*Prolegomena to St. Paul's Epistles to the Romans and the Ephesians*, London, 1895, p. 22): 'In all the long previous discussion bearing on the Jews, occupying nearly two and a half chapters, the Jews are invariably spoken of in the third person. In the half chapter that follows the Gentiles are constantly spoken of in the second person.' Cf. Kümmel, *Introduction*, p. 219.

accused of 'alien superstition' ('superstitionis externae rea'),
but left to her husband's jurisdiction, and was tried and
acquitted by a family council presided over by him just about
the time that the Epistle to the Romans was written.[1]

What organization the Roman church had we do not know.
From the arrangement of the greetings in chapter 16 (note
especially καὶ τὴν κατ' οἶκον αὐτῶν ἐκκλησίαν in v. 5, καὶ τοὺς σὺν
αὐτοῖς ἀδελφούς in v. 14, and καὶ τοὺς σὺν αὐτοῖς πάντας ἁγίους in
v. 15) it would appear that there were a number of different
groups. Did these groups meet on their own for worship? Did
they ever all meet together as a single 'church of God which is'
in Rome? In view of the evidence of chapter 16, of the fact that
the word ἐκκλησία is never used in Romans with reference to the
Christian community in Rome as a whole,[2] and of the size of
the area covered by the city of Rome, we ought to reckon with
the possibility that there may have been little, if any, central
organization and even that Phoebe may have had to make
contact with a number of separate churches rather than just
to deliver Paul's letter to the leadership of one single Roman
church. But the word 'possibility' is used here advisedly. The
statements of Bengel, '. . . neque adhuc in formam *ecclesiae*
redacti erant'[3] and 'Nondum Romae erat forma ecclesiae.
Accommodatum est igitur monitum *singulis* potius quam
universis'[4] express a certainty not warranted by the evidence.

Other matters which might have been discussed here will be
more conveniently referred to in connexion with the occasion
and purpose of the epistle.

IV. OCCASION AND PURPOSE

The occasion of the epistle is clear enough. What was said with
regard to the date and place of writing has already indicated
it. Paul has completed that pioneer missionary work in the east
which was to be done by him, and now he proposes, after he has
taken the proceeds of the collection made by the churches of
Macedonia and Achaia to Jerusalem, to go to Spain, there to

---

[1] Tacitus, *Ann.* 13.32.

[2] The word occurs in Romans only in 16.1, 4, 5, 16 and 23. It is
noticeable that in 1.7 it is not used (contrast 1 Cor 1.2; 2 Cor 1.1;
Gal 1.2; 1 Th 1.1; 2 Th 1.1; Philem 2), but instead πᾶσιν τοῖς οὖσιν ἐν 'Ρώμῃ
ἀγαπητοῖς θεοῦ, κλητοῖς ἁγίοις, though it is possible that the reason for
this was simply that, having anticipated the address by a statement in
the second person plural, Paul felt it more natural to keep to the plural
than to introduce a collective noun.

[3] p. 492 (on 1.7).

[4] p. 567f (on 16.17). A similar view is maintained by E. A. Judge and
G. S. R. Thomas, 'The Origin of the Church at Rome', in *RTR* 25 (1966),
pp. 81–93.

continue his missionary labours. He hopes to visit Rome on his way westward and to spend a short time with the church there, and then, refreshed by their fellowship, to journey on to his new mission field with their blessing, their interest, their support. So much is clear enough from 1.8–16a and 15.14–33. That at this point he should decide to write a letter to the church in Rome was perfectly natural.

What is less easy to understand is why he included 1.16b–15.13—and this precisely—in the letter. Or, to put the problem differently, what was it that determined the contents, the form, the emphases, of this main body of the epistle? Was it simply the inner logic of the gospel as Paul understood it? Or did either Paul's circumstances or those of the Roman church or both play a part, or a decisive part, or even the decisive part, in determining them? Did Paul feel perhaps that the mention of the gospel in 1.16a called for an exposition of it at considerable length, or that to present a balanced, objective, carefully reasoned account of the gospel was the appropriate way to introduce himself to a church to which he was as yet not known personally, since as an apostle he had no raison d'être apart from the gospel, or that for some other reason such a statement was required, and then simply allow himself to be led by the logic inherent in the gospel? Or did he perhaps feel compelled by misunderstanding or misrepresentation in one quarter or another to defend his doctrine, his missionary work, himself? (One might think, for instance, of the reference in 3.8 to people who misrepresented his teaching as being antinomianism, or of the possibility that behind the vehemence of 9.1–3 lies the knowledge of accusations of disloyalty to his own nation.) If the epistle was in some measure intended as an apologia, did the nature of the charges which were being warded off in any way shape or colour the theological exposition? How much did Paul know about the church (or churches) in Rome? Did any knowledge of any tendencies, tensions, divisions, or false teachings, within it, or of any danger threatening it from without, influence either his theological presentation or his ethical exhortation? Did Paul desire to combat some tendency to a false spirituality, to an individualistic piety, to anti-nomianism, to legalism, or to anti-semitism? Does 16.17–20 perhaps hold the clue to his purpose? Or should we perhaps see it in chapters 9 to 11? If so, where exactly is the emphasis laid? Is it on the fact of God's continuing faithfulness to Israel? Or on the fact that God's saving purpose includes Jew and Gentile alike (cf. the οὐ γάρ ἐστιν διαστολή of 3.22)? Or on the duty of Gentile Christians to have a brotherly regard for the still unbelieving Jews? Or on the fact that for all alike God's mercy is sheer mercy—so that glorying is utterly excluded? Or on the continuity of the people of God? Or is the clue to be found in 14.1–15.13? Or in the whole of 14.1–16.27? Is 14.1–15.13 perhaps to be understood not as a theoretical and abstract treatment of a practical problem but as referring to the circumstances which Paul knew to obtain in Rome, and was it his purpose to help to bring about the union of the divided Christians of Rome in a true fellowship of faith and mutual love?

The student of Romans will be well advised to bear all these, and a good many other similar questions in mind as he studies the epistle (remembering, of course, that the various possibilities indicated are by no means all mutually exclusive). But for the commentator to present him at this point with a carefully marshalled series of arguments in favour of a particular view of the purpose of the epistle would, in our view, be to render him a serious disservice. It is better to approach the detailed work of exegesis with as open a mind as possible on this matter. We shall hope to return to the subject at the end of the commentary.

V. LANGUAGE AND STYLE

It is not our intention to attempt to gather together here the things which will have to be said in various places throughout the commentary on matters which come under these heads, but only to make a few observations which may be useful to the reader in approaching the study of the epistle.

We take language first, and begin with vocabulary. The vocabulary of Romans shows no signs either of atticizing or of the opposite contemporary affectation of decorating one's prose with poetic expressions. But it is ample enough, and the reader has no sense of the writer's having been cramped or constrained in his choice of words. And this impression is borne out by a comparison of the ratio of vocabulary to word-total of Romans with that of other NT documents.[1] The range

---

[1] According to R. Morgenthaler, *Statistik des neutestamentlichen Wortschatzes*, Zurich, 1958, p. 164, the ratio of vocabulary to word-total of Romans is 1068:7094, whereas that of the Fourth Gospel is 1011:15420, that of Mark 1345:11229, that of Luke 2055:19404, that of Acts 2038:18374. On the other hand, Hebrews (1038:4942) and 1 Peter (545:1669) have, not surprisingly, a higher ratio than Romans, though proper allowance has, of course, to be made in interpreting these statistics for the fact that, the shorter the document is, the greater the ratio of vocabulary to word-total naturally tends to be (in a single sentence it may well be $x:x$).

of the vocabulary is in itself evidence of a degree of culture
and refinement. It includes, for example, such a good literary
word as ἀντιστρατεύεσθαι, which occurs nowhere else in the whole
Greek Bible, and various rather unusual words which are
specially appropriate in a particular context (e.g. ἀποκαραδοκία:
the substantive, as a matter of fact, is only attested in
Christian writings, but the cognate verb was used by Polybius).
It includes also words from the vocabulary of Greek moral
philosophy which had become part of the common language
of the more educated and thoughtful people of the Hellenistic
world (e.g. καθῆκον). In a considerable element of the
vocabulary of Romans, as of other NT documents, the
influence of the LXX is to be seen. There are the words which,
as used in Romans, are quite unintelligible unless seen in the
light of the LXX (e.g. δικαιοῦν, δικαίωσις (and, in some of their
occurrences, δίκαιος and δικαιοσύνη), κοινός, προσωπολημψία), and
also a much larger number of words, which, though up to a
point intelligible on the basis of ordinary secular Greek usage,
are certainly not given the full significance which they have in
Romans (or, in some cases, in some of their occurrences in
Romans), unless they are understood in the light of their use
(or the use of words connected with them) in the OT (e.g.
ἀλήθεια, διαθήκη, δόξα, δοῦλος (as used in 1.1), ἐκλογή, ἐπαγγελία,
καλεῖν, κύριος, νόμος, προγινώσκειν—to mention just a few).
Many of the words with strong LXX associations were
necessarily characteristic terms of Greek-speaking Christianity
from the very beginning, and, as used in Romans, have not
only their OT background but also their background in the
common usage of the Greek-speaking church. A tendency
toward the development of a technical terminology may be
observed, but it is important to realize that the technical
terminology has not yet hardened.

As far as the choice and management of grammatical con-
structions are concerned, the language of Romans is perfectly
competent. Occasionally the influence of a Semitic language
may be felt, but, whatever be the correct answer to the question
whether Paul was brought up in Tarsus or in Jerusalem,[1] there
is nothing in Romans to suggest that the author was thinking
in Aramaic. The evidence suggests rather that, when writing
or speaking Greek, Paul also thought perfectly naturally in
Greek.

As far as style is concerned, the epistle shows considerable

[1] See, for instance, W. C. van Unnik, *Tarsus or Jerusalem: the City of Paul's Youth*, Eng. tr., London, 1962.

variety. The style varies with the subject matter. Quite often it approximates closely to the style of the Hellenistic diatribe. Sometimes it is the style of liturgical utterance or of the solemn confession of faith. Sometimes there are resemblances to Jewish Wisdom, sometimes to the manner of Jewish biblical exegesis such as we find in some of the Qumran texts, sometimes to the rules of the Rabbis. There is nothing to suggest familiarity with classical Greek literature (the quotation from Menander in 1 Cor 15.33 does not prove that Paul had read Menander, for the verse may well have been a popular quotation); and there is little, if any, evidence of the concern for literary grace for its own sake which is characteristic of classical Greek prose. John Chrysostom recognized that it was no use looking for the smoothness of Isocrates, the majesty of Demosthenes, the dignity of Thucydides, or the sublimity of Plato in Paul's letters, and admitted Paul's poverty τῇ λέξει and the simplicity and artlessness (ἁπλῆν . . . καὶ ἀφελῆ) of his composition;[1] and Gregory of Nyssa speaks of Paul as adorning his sentences μόνῃ τῇ ἀληθείᾳ.[2] For the most part the real grandeur of Romans as a piece of literature derives from its content and from the sincerity, directness, and personal involvement of the author. At the same time, it would be quite incorrect to assume that the epistle is totally devoid of literary elegance; for it affords clear evidence that Paul knew the various figures of speech of the rhetoricians and that it came naturally to him to make use of them from time to time. As examples may be cited the instances of assonance in 1.29 (φθόνου φόνου) and 31 (ἀσυνέτους ἀσυνθέτους); of climax in 5.3–5; 8.29f; 10.14f; of paronomasia in 12.3; 14.23; of parallelism in 2.6–10, 21–23; 8.33–35; 12.6ff; 13.7.[3] But these things are used by Paul unselfconsciously, not as ends in themselves but as natural means to the forceful and compelling expression of what he has to say. It is the content that is all-important. And it is to this concentration on the content of what has to be expressed and subordination of outward form to it that at any rate some of his anacolutha should be attributed. For example, that in 5.12ff is surely not a case of a period's failing to be 'wirklich glücklich':[4] the truth is rather that at this particular point the broken construction suits the exigencies of the subject matter (cf. the notes in loc.). It should certainly not be

---

[1] PG 48, col. 669.
[2] PG 45, col. 253.
[3] Some of these examples were pointed out by Augustine, De doct. Christ. 4.7ff.
[4] Michel, p. 23.

cited as evidence of inability to manage a longish period competently. A notable example of genuine eloquence is to be seen in 8.31–39.[1]

It will perhaps not be out of place to mention here something which, while it is very obvious, is sometimes overlooked by students of the epistle—the importance of watching carefully the connectives linking the sentences. Whereas in English it is not at all unusual for sentences to be set down one after the other without connexion, in ancient Greek it was normal to link each sentence with the preceding one by means of a connective of one sort or another. The Greek custom has two great advantages: it helps the writer to think clearly and logically and it enables the reader to know what was the connexion of thought in the writer's mind between his sentences. In those parts of the NT where much of the material consists of independent units of oral tradition which have been brought together the connectives are naturally not very helpful; and in passages of ethical exhortation they tend to be omitted (e.g. in 12.9–21). But, where there is continuous argument, they are a most important clue to the author's meaning, of which full use should be made. In the exegesis of Romans one is well advised to watch the connectives with the utmost attentiveness, wherever they are present—and in the first eight chapters they nearly always are. Paul uses them competently enough.

VI. STRUCTURE

It is generally agreed that 1.1–17 includes not only the epistolary opening formula and a paragraph concerned with Paul's relations with the Roman church but also a statement (whether it consists of vv. 16–17 or of vv. 16b–17 or simply of v. 17 is disputed) of the theological theme to be worked out in the main body of the epistle; that 9.1–11.36 and 12.1–15.13 are two main divisions; and that from 15.14 onward is a continuation of what was begun in 1.8ff. It is also very widely agreed that 1.18–8.39 contains two main divisions of the epistle; but there is disagreement as to where within 1.18–8.39 the break between the two divisions comes.

For discussion of this last question and of other matters relating to the structure of the epistle and for justification of

---

[1] For an interesting discussion of Paul's style see E. Norden, *Die antike Kunstprosa vom sechsten Jahrhundert vor Christus bis in die Zeit der Renaissance*, Stuttgart, ⁶1958 (¹1898), pp. 492–510. Reference may also be made to Lagrange, pp. xlv–liii.

the following analysis the reader may be referred—in order to avoid unnecessary repetition—to the various introductions to main divisions, sections and sub-sections to be found in the commentary, which are intended to clarify the movement of Paul's argument.

ANALYSIS OF THE EPISTLE

(iii) The indwelling of the Spirit—the gift of hope (8.17–30)

(iv) Conclusion both to section V. 4 and also at the same time to the whole of the foregoing argument of the epistle (8.31–39)

VI. THE UNBELIEF OF MEN AND THE FAITHFULNESS OF GOD (9.1–11.36)

1. The subject of this main division of the epistle is introduced (9.1–5)

2. The unbelief and disobedience of men are shown to be embraced within the work of the divine mercy (9.6–29)

3. Israel is without excuse, but in the light of scripture we may hope that the fact that Gentiles believe will provoke Israel to jealousy: the OT quotation in the last verse strikes a hopeful note in that, while it indicates the dreadfulness of Israel's sin by showing the goodness of Him against whom they have sinned, it focuses attention not on Israel's sin but on God's goodness toward Israel (9.30–10.21)

4. God has not cast off His people (11.1–32)

5. Conclusion to this main division (11.33–36)

VII. THE OBEDIENCE TO WHICH THOSE WHO ARE RIGHTEOUS BY FAITH ARE CALLED (12.1–15.13)

1. The theme of this main division of the epistle is set forth (12.1–2)

2. The believer as a member of the congregation in his relations with his fellow members (12.3–8)

3. A series of loosely connected items of exhortation (12.9–21)

4. The believer's obligation to the state (13.1–7)

5. The debt of love (13.8–10)

6. The eschatological motivation of Christian obedience (13.11–14)

7. The 'strong' and the 'weak' (14.1–15.13)

VIII. CONCLUSION TO THE EPISTLE (15.14–16.27)[1]

[1] An extremely ingenious analysis was proposed by Bengel (p. 494f), according to which the three themes, (i) 'de fide et justitia', (ii) 'de salute sive vita', and (iii) 'de Omni credente, Judaeo et Graeco', which he saw in 1.16–17, are not only treated in 1.18–4.25, 5.1–8.39, and 9.1–11.36, respectively, but also recur in the same order in the paraclesis of 12.1–15.13 (in 12.3–13.10 he sees paraclesis 'de fide, et (quia per fidem lex statuitur (3.31)) de amore, quem fides parit, deque justitia erga homines', and notes that faith is expressly mentioned in 12.3 and 6,

VII. HISTORY OF EXEGESIS

There can be few documents, if any, which have had more study concentrated on them than the Epistle to the Romans. We know of very many more commentaries on it (and there is, of course, a vast amount of valuable exegesis of this epistle outside the commentaries) than can be mentioned in this chapter, and we do not doubt that the number of extant commentaries which are quite unknown to us may well exceed the full number of those of which we know. All we can hope to do here is just to give some idea of the richness of this exegetical tradition.[1]

That this tradition is so rich, that the Epistle to the Romans has drawn to itself so many commentaries, is certainly not

and love in 12.9 and 13.8, and that justice is defined in 13.7a; in 13.11–14 paraclesis 'de salute', salvation being explicitly mentioned in 13.11; and finally paraclesis 'de conjunctione Judaeorum et gentium' in 14.1–15.13); but, as far as 12.1–15.13 is concerned, this is surely far too subtle.

On the structure of the epistle reference may be made, further, to: K. Prümm, 'Zur Struktur des Römerbriefes', in *ZKT* 72 (1950), pp. 333–49; A. Feuillet, 'Le plan salvifique de Dieu d'après l'épître aux Romains', in *RB* 57 (1950), pp. 336–87, 489–529, and 'La citation d'Habacuc 2.4 et les huit premiers chapitres de l'épître aux Romains', in *NTS* 6 (1959–60), pp. 52–80; N. A. Dahl, 'Two Notes on Romans 5', in *ST* 5 (1951–52), pp. 37–48; S. Lyonnet, 'Note sur le plan de l'épître aux Romains', in *RechSR* 39 (1951–52), pp. 301–16; J. Dupont, 'Le problème de la structure littéraire de l'épître aux Romains', in *RB* 62 (1955), pp. 365–97.

[1] I have been very much aware of this tradition throughout my study of the epistle, and I hope that my interest in the history of interpretation will be to some extent reflected in the following commentary; but reference may be made here to the existence of several studies in the history of interpretation by scholars who, confining their attention to very brief passages, have been able to go into the history in much greater detail than would be at all feasible in a commentary on a whole biblical book and to produce something like the core resulting from a geologist's boring. Mention may be made of F. Keienburg, *Die Geschichte der Auslegung von Römer 13.1–7*, Gelsenkirchen, 1956; W. Affeldt, *Die weltliche Gewalt in der Paulus-Exegese: Röm 13.1–7 in den Römerbriefkommentaren der lateinischen Kirche bis zum Ende des 13. Jahrhunderts*, Göttingen, 1969; and of the following doctoral theses: H. Gieraths, *Knechtschaft und Freiheit der Schöpfung: eine historisch-exegetische Untersuchung zu Röm 8.19–22*, Catholic Theological Faculty, Bonn University, 1950; W. C. Brownson, *Protestant Exegesis of Romans 8.26f: a history and evaluation*, Princeton Theological Seminary, 1963; C. M. Kempton Hewitt, *Life in the Spirit: a study in the history of interpretation of Romans 8.12–17*, Durham University, 1969; and also of the series of studies being published in Tübingen under the general title of 'Beiträge zur Geschichte der neutestamentlichen Exegese' under the editorship of Oscar Cullmann and others. I am specially indebted to Dr Hewitt who worked with me here in Durham.

surprising in view of the important part which this document
has played in the history of the Church and of Christian life
and thought. As the most systematic and complete exposition
of the gospel that the NT contains, it has naturally seemed to
have a very special place in the Bible. That Martin Luther
called it 'das rechte Heubtstück des newen Testaments, und
das allerlauterste Evangelium'[1] and went on to recommend
that every Christian should learn it by heart, and that John
Calvin observed that 'if we understand this Epistle, we have a
passage opened to us to the understanding of the whole of
scripture',[2] is well known; but the recognition of the special
importance of Romans is no peculiarity of Protestantism.

The student of the epistle who consults but a single commentary is perforce involved to some extent in a conversation
not only with St Paul but also with this long exegetical
tradition; for every reputable commentary carries a great deal
of this tradition—even if the commentator is himself largely
ignorant of the more distant sources of the things which he
says. But to gain something more than an altogether superficial knowledge of the course of the tradition is to learn a
deep respect and affection for, and gratitude to, those who have
laboured in the field before one, irrespective of the barriers
between different confessions, theological and critical view-
points, nations and epochs; to learn to admire the engagement
with Paul's thought of some of the greatest minds from the
third to the twentieth century, but also to be humbled by the
discovery that even the weakest and least perceptive have
from time to time something worth while to contribute;
to learn that it is naïve to imagine that old commentaries are
simply superseded by new ones,[3] since, even the good commentator, while he will have some new insights of his own and
will be able to correct some errors and make good some
deficiencies of the past, will also have his own particular blind
spots and will see less clearly, or even miss altogether, some

[1] *Luthers Werke: Die Deutsche Bibel* 7, p. 3 (Weimar ed.).
[2] Calvin, p. 2.
[3] The observation of T. W. Manson in the new Peake's Commentary,
p. 953, at the end of his select bibliography ('Careful study of Barrett,
Dodd, and Sanday and Headlam will provide the English reader with
practically all the information he needs in order to reach his own
understanding of the Apostle's meaning'), was surely ill-advised—and
not at all in character. But he probably did not mean to give the
impression which his words are liable to give. The present writer
certainly does not wish any one to imagine that the previous I.C.C.
commentary on Romans may safely be forgotten when this commentary
has appeared.

things which some one before him has seen clearly;[1] and, above all, to learn that all commentators (including those who in the next few pages will be most highly praised and also—and this is perhaps the most difficult lesson for any commentator to grasp—oneself) have feet of clay, and that therefore both slavish deference to any of them and also presumptuous self-confidence must alike be eschewed.

The earliest extant commentary on Romans[2] is that of Origen (c. 185–c. 254).[3] It has survived in the abridged Latin translation by Tyrannius Rufinus (c. 345–c. 410). There are also a number of quite short fragments of the original Greek which have been preserved in the *Philocalia* and in catenae. A much longer fragment, or rather a series of excerpts from the commentary on Rom 3.5–5.7 and covering twenty-eight pages of papyrus codex, turned up among the papyri discovered at Tura in 1941. It is long enough to provide a valuable means of testing the reliability of the Latin version of Rufinus; and it has on the whole vindicated it[4]—a very important result of the discovery, in view of the suspicion with which the Latin version has so long been regarded. The commentary is full of interest. It comes from the time of Origen's settlement in Caesarea. Origen brought to his study of the text of Romans a tremendously powerful intellect, immense learning (his knowledge of the whole Bible is extremely impressive, and he was, of course, also deeply learned in pagan literature and thought), a scholarly patience and attentiveness to detail, and

[1] Very salutary are the following words of Wiles (*Divine Apostle*, p. 132): 'We have come to the end of our study and the question that immediately arises in our minds is the question "How far then did the early commentators give a true interpretation of Paul's meaning?" Yet the very form in which the question arises is not without danger. It implies the assumption that we have a true interpretation of Paul's meaning—or at least a truer one than that of those whom we have studied—in the light of which theirs may be tested and judged. It may be so; but we as much as they are children of our own times and there may well be aspects of Pauline thought to which we are blinded by the particular presuppositions and patterns of theological thinking in our own day. If therefore we seek to pass judgement on other interpreters it can only be in the recognition that we also stand in need of judgement, even and perhaps especially when we are least conscious of that need.'

[2] Clement of Alexandria (c. 150–c. 215) apparently commented very briefly on all the Pauline epistles in his lost work, *The Hypotyposes* (cf. Eusebius, *H.E.* 6.14.1).

[3] For bibliographical details of this and the other commentaries mentioned in this chapter reference should be made to the list of abbreviated titles (pp. xiii–xviii).

[4] Cf. H. Chadwick, 'Rufinus and the Tura Papyrus of Origen's Commentary on Romans', in *JTS* n.s. 10 (1959), pp. 10–42; Wiles, *Divine Apostle* p. 6.

a deep sincerity. Again and again he shows his perceptiveness by his recognition of the questions which need to be asked. But, while there is a great deal in the commentary which is valuable and suggestive, there is certainly also a good deal which is merely fanciful, and, even in Rufinus's abridgement, it is excessively discursive and verbose.

Of the fourth century commentaries of Acacius of Caesarea (died 366), the 'semi-Arian', of Diodore of Tarsus (died c. 390), the teacher of Chrysostom and Theodore, of Apollinarius (c. 310–c. 390) and of the blind Alexandrian theologian, Didymus (c. 313–398), only fragments have survived.[1] But from the end of the century we have the splendid contribution of John Chrysostom (c. 347–407). Pioneer and accomplished master of the practice of 'preaching through' biblical books, he has left us expositions of all Paul's epistles, that of Galatians being in the form of a commentary, the others being sequences of sermons. His custom was to give in the earlier part of a sermon a careful exegesis of the passage with which he was concerned, discussing matters of grammar, exact meanings of words, and different possible interpretations of clauses and sentences, and then to follow up his exegesis with a forceful and pointed application of the passage, or of some part or aspect of it, to himself and his Antiochene congregation (of leaving the biblical message in the air, lost in safe generalities, the fault of so many preachers, he certainly cannot fairly be accused). As an Antiochene theologian he eschewed allegorizing, and his sermons are free from the sort of fancies to which Origen was prone. With his moral earnestness and deep compassion for the poor and the weak, Chrysostom is specially strong in exposition of the explicitly ethical sections and specially alert to the ethical implications of what is not primarily ethical. He is less strong in plumbing the depths of the great theological questions which engage Paul's mind or in following Paul in his theological mountaineering; and it must be admitted that he can at times be distinctly pedestrian. But, when full account is taken of their obvious weak points, his Homilies on Romans, characterized as they are by accomplished scholarship, linguistic and literary sensitivity, and spiritual insight, as well as by a shrewd and sympathetic knowledge of human nature, must be recognized as a distinguished and permanently valuable contribution to the exegesis of the epistle—a contribution which no commentator on Romans worth his salt is ever likely to ignore.

[1] They are included in Staab.

The other great Antiochene commentator was Theodore (c. 350–428), bishop of Mopsuestia in Cilicia, who seems to have written on practically every book of the Bible. Unfortunately, the bulk of his works have perished; but among what has survived we have quite a number of fragments of the original Greek of his commentary on Romans (also fragments of the commentaries on 1 and 2 Corinthians together with a fifth century Latin translation of those on the rest of the Pauline epistles). They are extraordinarily interesting on account of the independence and originality of the thought, the careful attention to detail (e.g. the punctuation of 6.21, the significance of λογιζόμεθα in 3.28, the force of ἵνα in 7.4), the attempts to clarify important theological terms (e.g. the treatment of σάρξ with reference to 7.5), and the concern to elucidate the continuity of the argument. His eschatological emphasis enables him to bring out something of Paul's thought that is generally missed by Patristic commentators (so, for example, it is interesting to set his comments on 13.11 and 12 beside those of other Patristic writers: in connexion with v. 12 he speaks explicitly of the παρουσία of Christ).

Of the commentary by Cyril of Alexandria (died 444) we have a fairly substantial collection of excerpts (they take up about forty columns of Migne). His comments, though devoid of literary gracefulness, are often discerning and repay study. Of particular interest is his contribution to the exegesis of 5.12. Fragments have also survived of the commentaries of Severian of Gabala (fl. c. 400), the rival and opponent of Chrysostom, and of Gennadius (died 471), the opponent of Cyril's Christological teaching and later Patriarch of Constantinople.

Five other Greek commentaries must be mentioned: those of Theodoret (c. 393–c. 458), John of Damascus (c. 675–c. 749), Oecumenius of Tricca (10th century), Theophylact (11th and early 12th century) and Euthymius Zigabenus (early 12th century). They are all heavily indebted to John Chrysostom, but Theodoret, Theophylact and Euthymius, at any rate, contribute something worth while of their own.

From the Syriac-speaking church the commentaries on the Pauline epistles by Ephraem Syrus (c. 306–73) have survived only in an Armenian translation.[1]

The earliest Latin commentary on Romans which has come down to us is that of the author who is commonly referred to as Ambrosiaster because his works were long preserved among

---

[1] They are available in a Latin translation, *Ephraemi Syri commentarii in epistolas divi Pauli nunc primum ex armenico in latinum sermonem a patribus Mekitharistis translati*, Venice, 1893.

those of Ambrose.[1] From him we have commentaries on all thirteen Pauline epistles. They were written during the pontificate of Damasus, probably between 374 and 379. Interesting on account of the form of Old Latin text on which they are based they certainly are; but any one who supposed them to be of interest only as a quarry for textual critics would be very far indeed from the mark. The Romans commentary is remarkable for its maturity of scholarship, suggestiveness, and admirable succinctness. Though we must reject many of his interpretations (as, for example, his anticipation of Barth's and T. W. Manson's interpretation of ἐκ πίστεως εἰς πίστιν in 1.17), his comments rarely fail to be thought-provoking.

There is much in the later writings of Augustine of Hippo (354–430), which is of immense importance in the history of the exegesis of Romans;[2] but in the way of actual commentary on the epistle he has left us only two slight pieces, an exposition of a selection of eighty-four statements contained in it (all the chapters of Romans are represented), which takes just twenty-four columns of Migne, and the beginning (covering only 1.1–7) of what would have been a very substantial commentary, had it ever been completed. Both were written c. 394, when his conversion (incidentally, it was his reading of a couple of verses of Romans, 13.13f, which was the final pressure that precipitated this conversion)[3] lay less than a decade behind him and he had not yet come to the insights characteristic of his theological maturity.

One needs neither a special sympathy with Pelagianism nor the sort of nationalistic fervour which led Milton to make excessive claims for Wyclif,[4] to recognize in Pelagius (died

[1] Augustine cited the commentary on Romans as by St Hilary; but in all the MSS. but one and by most mediaeval writers the commentaries are attributed to Ambrose. It was Erasmus who in modern times first rejected Ambrosian authorship, and invented the name 'Ambrosiaster'. A suggestion which has met with a good deal of favour is that the author was Isaac, a convert from Judaism, who opposed Damasus; but it is far from being established.

[2] Worthy of special mention is his discussion of Rom 7.7–25 and 9.10–29 in book I of his De diversis quaestionibus ad Simplicianum Libri II of A.D. 396/7 (for its importance for Augustine see his references in Retract. 2.1 [27]; De praedest. sanct. 4.8; De dono persever. 20.52; 21.55). I am indebted to my colleague, Mr Gerald Bonner, for drawing my attention to some passages of Augustine, which I should otherwise have missed.

[3] Confessions 8.12.

[4] Cf. Areopagitica, Everyman's Library edition, p. 31f: 'Yet that which is above all this, the favour and the love of Heaven, we have great argument to think in a peculiar manner propitious and propending towards us. Why else was this Nation chosen before any other, that out

after 418), the first known British commentator on Romans, a considerable biblical scholar. His commentary shows a deep and extensive knowledge of scripture, familiarity with earlier and contemporary biblical scholarship (from his thirteen Pauline commentaries it seems that he knew and made use of Rufinus's translation of Origen, the commentaries of Ambrosiaster and Chrysostom, the two works of Augustine just mentioned, some of Jerome's works, and probably also the writings of Theodore of Mopsuestia), a by no means insignificant spiritual insight, great moral earnestness and a pleasing and succinct style. His commentary belongs to the latter half of the first decade of the fifth century. It was subsequently worked over by Cassiodorus (c. 485–c. 580), and was variously ascribed to Jerome, Primasius and Augustine. Mention may also be made of the commentary ascribed to Primasius of Hadrumetum but probably originating in the school of Cassiodorus[1] and of the commentary of the Irishman Sedulius Scotus.[2]

From the Middle Ages a number of western commentaries on Romans have come down to us (we have already listed some mediaeval Greek commentaries). Mention may be made of those of Haimo of Auxerre (9th century)[3] and Bruno (c. 1032–1101), the founder of the Carthusians, those in the *Glossa ordinaria*, traditionally associated with Walafrid Strabo (9th century), and the *Glossa interlinearis* of Anselm of Laon (died 1117) and his assistants, those of Peter Abelard (1079–1142), Hervé of Bourgdieu (died about 1150) and Peter Lombard (c. 1100–1160), and that in the *Postilla Litteralis* of Nicholas of Lyra (c. 1270–1340). But altogether outstanding among mediaeval commentaries is that of Thomas Aquinas (c. 1225–1274). One does not have to read very far in it to realize that one is observing an immensely powerful intellect at work. His commentary is admirably succinct and beautifully clear (with a very liberal use of 'primo', 'secundo' and 'tertio'). It is notable for its close attentiveness to, and extraordinarily precise logical analysis of, the Pauline text. The author's

---

of her, as out of Sion, should be proclaimed and sounded forth the first tidings and trumpet of Reformation to all Europe? And had it not been the obstinate perverseness of our prelates against the divine and admirable spirit of Wickliff, to suppress him as a schismatic and innovator, perhaps neither the Bohemian Huss and Jerome [of Prague], no nor the name of Luther or of Calvin, had been ever known: the glory of reforming all our neighbours had been completely ours.'

[1] In *PL* 68, cols. 415–506.
[2] In *PL* 103, cols. 9–128.
[3] Not Haimo of Halberstadt, to whom it is often ascribed.

knowledge of the Bible and indebtedness to earlier exegesis is evident, but there is no ostentatious flaunting of erudition. The humility characteristic of the true scholar shows itself both in his sense of the importance of allowing the text to bear its own natural meaning and resisting the temptation to force interpretations upon it with masterful violence (reflected in his use of such language as 'recte ac faciliter potest intelligi',[1] 'Potest tamen, licet extorte, exponi etiam ...',[2] '... nisi forte quis extorte velit exponere ...')[3] and also in the fairness and fullness with which he expounds alternative interpretations which he himself does not accept. A good example of the latter feature is to be seen in the discussion of 7.14ff,[4] where, noting that v. 14b can be explained either as spoken by Paul 'in persona hominis in peccato existentis' or as spoken by him 'in persona sua, id est, hominis sub gratia constituti', he goes on to show at length 'qualiter haec verba et sequentia diversimode possunt utroque modo exponi', at the same time indicating clearly his own judgment (which is surely right!) that the explanation which understands Paul to be speaking of the man who is under grace is to be preferred ('quamvis secunda expositio melior sit').

With the Renaissance and Reformation there began a tremendous proliferation of commentaries on Romans. So from this point on we shall not attempt even just to list all the more important ones, but propose to say something about the contributions of Luther and Calvin, and then (apart from a reference to one specially attractive work of the eighteenth century) to refer the reader to Sanday and Headlam, pp. civ–cix, for a brief account of a selection of mainly Protestant work from the end of the sixteenth century to the time of their own commentary, and to Cornely, p. 25f, for an account of Catholic commentaries of the sixteenth to nineteenth centuries,[5] and to use the remaining space at our disposal to give some indication of contributions which have appeared since the publication of the commentaries of Sanday and Headlam and of Cornely.

Luther's commentary, consisting of a marginal gloss, an interlinear gloss, and scholia or continuous expositions, is in fact the notes on the basis of which he delivered his famous

---

[1] p. 103 (570).
[2] p. 103 (571).
[3] p. 104 (576).
[4] pp. 101ff (§§ 558ff).
[5] Reference may also be made to the very long, though by no means complete, list of commentaries in Meyer I, pp. xviii–xxix.

course of lectures on the epistle at 6.0 a.m. on Mondays and Fridays from Easter 1515 to the early autumn of 1516, and it is important in reading it to realize that it was written not for publication but for his own use in the lecture-room (comparison with students' notes which have survived would seem to indicate that, while he dictated philological notes more or less verbatim, he considerably abbreviated the scholia). Luther's own manuscript was sold by his grandsons to the Margrave of Brandenburg and subsequently 'lost' in the Royal Library of Berlin: it did not come to light, as far as Luther scholarship was concerned, until the beginning of the twentieth century. In the preparation of his lectures Luther relied largely on the traditional exegesis but also on the most recent work, in particular, the commentaries on Romans in Lorenzo Valla's *Adnotationes in latinam Novi Testamenti interpretationem*, edited by Erasmus and published in Paris in 1505, and in the *Epistolae Pauli Apostoli* of the French Humanist, Jacques Lefèvre d'Étaples, published in 1512, and, from Romans 9 onward, Erasmus's edition of the Greek New Testament and his *Annotationes in Novum Testamentum*, which were published early in 1516. The great importance of Luther's lectures lies in the clarity with which, helped in part by the stimulus he derived from the writings of Augustine, Bernard of Clairvaux, and Johann Tauler, and from the encouragement and advice of Johann von Staupitz, he saw aspects of Paul's thought which by the end of the Middle Ages had come to be but dimly perceived or altogether lost sight of, and so found his way to a truer understanding of the nature of sin, of justification, of grace, of faith, of divine election and of the love to God and to men required of Christians. (Unfortunately, the English translation, published in 1961, by giving for the most part only the scholia (which, as we have seen, Luther himself greatly abbreviated in lecturing) and omitting the glosses (which were clearly an important part of the lectures), is liable to give—in spite of the translator's clear statement of what he has done—a distorted impression of the whole and to encourage the not infrequently expressed notion that Luther was less concerned than he should have been with detailed exegesis.) In addition to his lectures of 1515–16, Luther also contributed to the exposition of Romans the very interesting and illuminating preface to the epistle (first printed in the German New Testament of 1522 and printed in a slightly different form in the 1546 German Bible), which is associated with John Wesley's experience in Aldersgate Street, London, in May 1738.

Calvin's commentary on Romans was first published in 1540.

It was the first of his biblical commentaries, but he had behind him the experience of his commentary on Seneca's *De clementia* (published in 1532) and of two editions of his *Institutio* (1536 and 1539). The dedicatory preface addressed to Simon Grynée, professor of Greek in Basel, shows that he had been deeply pondering the problems which face a commentator. T. H. L. Parker, in his invaluable *Calvin's New Testament Commentaries*, London, 1971, has well brought out the significance of what is said about the commentaries of Melanchthon and Bucer in this preface to Grynée.[1] Calvin is indicating his conscious rejection for his own biblical commentaries of the method, derived from Cicero who in turn had derived it from Aristotle, of establishing the meaning of a document by searching out its τόποι or *loci*, i.e. its definitive concepts,[2] which Melanchthon had adopted in his *Commentarii in epistolam Pauli ad Romanos* of 1532 with the result that, while he dwelt at length on what he regarded as the principal points, 'he neglected many points which require attention',[3] and also of the combination of it with straightforward commentary which had made Bucer's *Romans*[4] of 1536 so intolerably verbose. He will leave the discussion of *loci* to his *Institutio*, and in his commentaries keep strictly to the text and to the task of elucidating what is actually said in it.[5] In his commentary on this epistle we have a magnificent example of that 'perspicua brevitas', which he and Grynée had in their conversations in Basel agreed was the chief virtue of a commentator.[6] Making full use of the best scholarly help available (e.g. that of Budé, Erasmus, Bucer) and taking pains to make sure that the Greek text which he translates into Latin is as reliable as possible,[7] he takes care not to allow his commentary to come between the text and the reader, seeking to unfold the mind of Paul as expressed in the written words as faithfully, simply and succinctly as he can. And, in drawing out the relevance of the text to his sixteenth century readers, he never forgets that the document he is expounding must be understood as a first-century document. 'For Calvin,' as Parker puts it, 'the historical document is of

---

[1] See especially pp. 26–54.
[2] It had been expounded by R. Agricola in his *De inventione dialectica* first published in 1479.
[3] Calvin, p. 3: cf. also the previous page.
[4] For the proper title, itself unconscionably verbose, reference may be made to Parker, op. cit. p. 172.
[5] Cf. Parker, op. cit., p. 53f.
[6] Calvin, p. 1.
[7] On Calvin's Greek text and the evidence of his use of the edition of Simon de Colines (Colinaeus) of 1534 see Parker, op. cit., pp. 93–123.

prime importance; it cannot be dispensed with; it cannot be left aside in favour of the substance that is extracted from it: in brief, it must never cease to be a historical document'.[1] If we had to choose just one word to characterize Calvin's commentary on Romans, it would be the word 'humble'; for it seems to us to display to an outstanding degree that humility before the text which is shared to some degree by every commentator on a historical document who is of any worth, the humility which seeks, not to master and manipulate, but to understand and to elucidate. The humility of Calvin's commentary is, of course, also at the same time the humility of the believer before what he sincerely believes to be the Word of God,[2] 'that most sacred of all things on earth', which one must strive with all one's might to avoid handling 'with unclean or even ill-prepared hands'.[3] This humility lies behind his quest for 'perspicua brevitas', his patient detailed exegesis, his refusal to shirk difficulties and his respect for the natural meaning of the text; it prevents him from imagining that his own exegesis can claim finality and makes him ready to leave some questions undecided; it emboldens him to dare to stand alone among commentators, where respect for the text seems to him to require it, and at the same time makes him set before himself a high standard of scholarly courtesy.[4] That he is not always humble, that he falls short of the standards which he himself did so much to clarify for succeeding commentators, of course, goes without saying.

The commentary from the eighteenth century to which we referred above as being 'specially attractive', and which we cannot forbear to mention, is that in J. A. Bengel's *Gnomon Novi Testamenti* (first published in 1742), which is remarkable for its fine scholarly judgment (Bengel was, of course, an accomplished scholar, who is of great importance in the history of New Testament textual criticism), and theological perceptiveness, and as—in its original Latin—an outstanding masterpiece of compression.

---

[1] Parker, op. cit., p. 91.

[2] On Calvin's understanding of the Bible as the Word of God see especially W. Niesel, *The Theology of Calvin*, Eng. tr., London, 1956, pp. 22–39; J. K. S. Reid, *The Authority of Scripture: a study of the Reformation and Post-Reformation understanding of the Bible*, London, 1957, pp. 29–55; Parker, op. cit., pp. 56–68.

[3] Calvin, p. 4.

[4] We have in mind the words of the preface to Grynée (p. 4): 'When, therefore, we depart from the views of our predecessors, we are not to be stimulated by any passion for innovation, impelled by any desire to slander others, aroused by any hatred, or prompted by any ambition.'

At the close of the nineteenth century two outstanding full-scale commentaries were published, one in Scotland and one in France. The former, by two Anglican scholars, Sanday and Headlam, has been for over three-quarters of a century—deservedly—the main large commentary for English-speaking students. Its merits are too well known to need recital here; but any one who has worked with it for many years is likely to have become more and more grateful for its thoroughness and exactness, its massive learning and sound judgment—though even of this most distinguished work one has occasionally to observe that 'bonus dormitat Homerus' (as, for example, when one reads on p. ciii that 'Exegesis was not Luther's strong point' or on p. 331—after ten and a half chapters of Romans and in spite of Deut 7.7f—of 'those national qualities which Israel inherits, and which caused it to be selected as the Chosen People'). The latter, by the Catholic, Cornely, is not as well known among Protestant students as it deserves to be. This is no doubt due in part to the deterrent effect of the prospect of above eight hundred pages of Latin (though Cornely's Latin is, as a matter of fact, exceptionally lucid) and in part to the excellence of Lagrange's commentary (later published) which has made it seem adequate by itself to represent Catholic scholarship. But, while Protestants would find a good many things in it to disagree with and the more thin-skinned of them might be inclined to regard some features as offensive, there is no doubt that it has much of real value to offer. It was not for nothing that Lagrange referred to its 'tact exégétique, très modéré et très sûr'.[1]

The years from the opening of the twentieth century up to the outbreak of the First World War saw the appearance in quick succession of the noteworthy commentaries of Denney, Lietzmann (a mine of historical and philological information), Jülicher, Gore, Zahn, Parry and Kühl. The magnificent commentary of Lagrange, distinguished by formidable learning and sound scholarly judgment, was published during the war.

The publication of Barth's first commentary on Romans, which Karl Adam likened to the falling of 'a bomb on the playground of the theologians',[2] came just after the war—though, as far as the English-speaking world was concerned, its action was somewhat delayed, since the translation by Hoskyns (made from the sixth German edition which was very different from that of 1919) did not appear till 1933. Of its

[1] p. x.
[2] Quoted in J. McConnachie, *The Significance of Karl Barth*, London, 1931, p. 43.

importance as a turning-point in the history of theology there
can be no doubt, and Barrett was certainly right to say that
'to read it must be reckoned an essential part of a theological education';[1] but, while it rendered the Church, and can
still render it, a much-needed service, it has very serious
deficiencies as an exposition of Romans, and to take it for
one's main aid in studying the epistle would be to demonstrate
one's failure to learn from Barth's maturer thinking and one's
lack of an essential element in theological seriousness, a sense
of humour. Barth himself has given a necessary warning in a
valuable autobiographical passage in the *Church Dogmatics*, in
the course of which he quotes with reference to his Romans
commentary the words of Demetrius in *A Midsummer Night's
Dream*: 'Well roared, Lion'.[2] To the same period as the
successive editions of Barth's *Römerbrief* belong the commentaries of Pallis, Gutjahr and Bardenhewer.

To the 1930's belong Dodd's commentary with its psychological approach (it has the brilliance which is characteristic of
Dodd's works, but is marred by an over-hasty readiness to
conclude that Paul has been caught napping),[3] the Irish
Catholic commentary of Boylan, Schlatter's refreshingly independent and very impressive *Gottes Gerechtigkeit*, the useful
commentaries of Althaus and Kirk, and the brief exposition by
Brunner.

From the period of the Second World War three valuable
commentaries must be mentioned. The first to appear was that
by the French Catholic scholar, Huby, which, while it is
greatly indebted to Lagrange, is by no means the work of a
mere *pedisequus*, but makes its own distinctive contribution
(it was reissued with valuable additional notes by Lyonnet in
1957). It was followed by the original Swedish version of
Nygren's commentary, which was later to appear in German
and English translations. Nygren's exposition of chapters one
to eight, with its stress on the thought of the two aeons, is
interesting and refreshing; but his treatment of the second
half of the epistle and particularly of the last five chapters
seems almost perfunctory[4]—a disappointment after his most
emphatic insistence in his introduction on the essential unity

---

[1] 'New Testament Commentaries: III. Epistles and Revelation', in
ET 65 (1953–4), p. 177.
[2] 5.1.272. The quotation is in *CD* II/1, p. 635 (= *KD*, II/1, p. 715).
[3] See, for instance, his comment on 3.1, his final paragraph on 3.1–8,
his comment on 7.4 and his final paragraph on 7.1–6.
[4] As against 253 pages in the German version for the introduction and
the commentary on Rom 1–8, there are 38 on chapters 9–11, and only
32 on chapters 12–16.

of the epistle.[1] The third commentary to be mentioned here is Gaugler's, the first volume of which was published in 1945, the second following a few years later. It is one of the very best of modern expositions of the epistle. Though designed to be intelligible to the Greekless layman and therefore necessarily lacking the sort of detailed technical discussion which is appropriate to a full-scale critical commentary, it bears on every page the impress of a mind distinguished by great learning, profound theological insight and shining sincerity. Its attractiveness for the layman stems from its marvellous lucidity and its general liveliness of style, never from superficiality. Gaugler was himself a Swiss Old Catholic, but his commentary reflects his familiarity with, and sympathetic understanding of, the different theological traditions.

The years 1954–1956 saw the publication of Knox's commentary, an important contribution from America, of the brief, popular expositions of Hunter, Barclay and Taylor, of the fine full-scale commentary by Michel, a worthy fellow to the commentaries of Sanday and Headlam and of Lagrange, an example of German *Gründlichkeit* at its very best, coupled with sound scholarly sense (of Michel one can say, what can be truly said of but few commentators, that even the careful and sharp-sighted reader will seldom catch him out quite unaware of a question which needs to be asked),[2] and of Barth's *Kurze Erklärung des Römerbriefs*.[3] The last mentioned, while it is only brief and does not give much help in matters of detail, is, in our judgment, extraordinarily perceptive and suggestive. The exposition of Romans 8 may be mentioned as specially illuminating.[4] In 1957 Britain, Switzerland and Germany each made a significant contribution. Barrett's commentary, hampered though it is to some extent by the requirements of the series of which it is a part, is always interesting and well written and worthy of close attention. That of Leenhardt, with its valuable stress on the importance for Paul of the people of God, is very stimulating, though one might perhaps express disappointment that, with the dedication it bears, it should fail (just like so many other recent commentaries) to recognize

---

[1] p. 17.

[2] Michel's commentary has since been considerably expanded and improved.

[3] The English translation published in 1959 is, unfortunately, unreliable: in one place (p. 138) the translator [or rather, as I now (1978) learn, a member of his publisher's staff] has even allowed himself, having failed to understand the point which was being made, to change Barth's biblical reference—disastrously.

[4] Attention may be drawn at this point to the considerable sections of very valuable Romans exegesis in the *Church Dogmatics*.

at all clearly Paul's positive attitude to the OT law. Kuss, whose 1957 contribution was but the beginning of what looks like being one of the longest and fullest of all commentaries on Romans, is splendid in his thoroughness, and deserves our prayers that he may have long life and health to complete the work.

Since the beginning of 1960 we have had Murray's two-volume commentary, which is admirable in its learning and carefulness, and often sound in its judgments, but somehow leaves the impression, at least in the mind of one student, that the author did not offer very serious resistance to the temptation, which is of course common to us all, to conduct inquiries with one's mind already made up that the answer to emerge shall be the one which suits one's own preconceptions. To this period belong also Bruce's commentary, which though short is valuable (it is very much fuller on some points than on others), the yet shorter but still useful commentaries of T. W. Manson and Best, and a *Vorarbeit* of the present work, *A Commentary on Romans 12–13*. And, finally, our rule of keeping in this chapter to actual commentaries may perhaps be so far relaxed as to allow mention of J. Cambier's important *L'Évangile de Dieu selon l'Épître aux Romains*, of which the first volume (*L'Évangile de la Justice et de la Grâce*) was published in 1967 (it contains a great deal of exegesis), the various contributions bearing on Romans in Käsemann's *Exegetische Versuche und Besinnungen* and *Paulinische Perspektiven*, and Minear's *The Obedience of Faith*.

Mention may also be made now of Käsemann's impressive commentary and the much smaller, but valuable, commentary by Black which have just appeared (1973).

Since the first impression was printed, two further commentaries in English have come to hand: R. Bowen, *A Guide to Romans* (Theological Education Fund Study Guide 2), London, 1975; and J. C. O'Neill, *Paul's Letter to the Romans*, Harmondsworth, 1975. The former is a useful help to study, compressing much into a short space and in straightforward language. The latter, while containing valuable insights, much interesting information and evidence of the author's very considerable erudition, is, in our judgment, so extremely subjective and arbitrary in its rejection of the Pauline authorship of a large proportion of the epistle, that, while its challenge will no doubt have to be answered by someone, it is much to be hoped that not all who are writing on Romans will feel obliged to accept the author's suggestion (p. 11) that they must 'put aside all their previous comments' and 'suspend' their own work until they have dealt with his claims. One older commentary (not mentioned in the above section on the history of exegesis), to the merit of which my attention has been drawn by Mr. Gervase Duffield, namely, that by Peter Martyr, I hope to be able to consult in working over the material to be published in volume 2.

I

SUPERSCRIPTION, ADDRESS AND SALUTATION
(1.1–7)

The widely held assumption that the formula to be found at the beginning of a Pauline letter is to be explained as a modification and expansion of the ordinary Greek epistolary 'prescript' or opening protocol was challenged by E. Lohmeyer,[1] on the ground that, whereas the Greek prescript consists of a single sentence in the form ὁ δεῖνα τῷ δεῖνι χαίρειν (sc. λέγει),[2] in the Pauline formula the salutation proper invariably stands as an independent sentence. Since both the two-sentence form and the use of first and second person pronouns in the salutation, which it makes possible, are also features of the ancient western Asiatic epistolary style,[3] he argued that it was on the western Asiatic rather than on the Greek convention that the Pauline formula was based. But, while it is possible that the western Asiatic convention had some influence in the formation of the Pauline formula, the following considerations suggest that it is more likely that its basis was the ordinary Greek prescript:

(i) In closing his letters Paul followed the Greek custom by writing a 'subscription' in his own hand (see on 16.20b);

(ii) The first part of the Pauline formula follows the form of the Greek prescript exactly (the sender's name in the nomina-

---

[1] 'Probleme paulinischer Theologie: I. Briefliche Grussüberschriften', in ZNW 26 (1927), pp. 158ff.

[2] The ordinary Latin form was similar; e.g., 'Quintus Marco fratri salutem dicit'. The last two words were usually abbreviated as 'S.D.', or it might be 'S.D.M.' or 'S.D.P.', the 'M' standing for 'multam', the 'P' for 'plurimam'.

[3] Lohmeyer refers to 2 Macc 1.1ff (a letter from Jews to Jews); to R. H. Pfeiffer, 'Assyrian epistolary formulae', in JAOS 43, part 1 (1923), pp. 26–40 (for Babylonian-Assyrian letters), from which he cites as a typical official formula, 'To the King, my lord, thy servant so and so. Greetings to the King, my lord! May Nabu and Marduk bless the King, my lord!'; J. A. Knudtzon, Die Briefe von Tel-el-Amarna (Vorderasiatische Bibliothek 72), nos. 68, 69, 71, 74, and others; Pap. Sachau, 4.1,2; 6,2; 10.2,3; 11.2f,12–14, 43; Dan 6.25; 1 Pet 1.2; 2 Pet 1.2; 2 Baruch 78.2; SB 3, p. 1 (on Rom 1.1 A.a). But see Roller, Formular, pp. 213–38; also G. Friedrich, 'Lohmeyers These über das paulinische Briefpräskript kritisch beleuchtet', in TLZ 81 (1956), cols. 343–6.

tive followed by the recipient's in the dative): the Asiatic form
was different—the recipient was often mentioned before the
sender, and sometimes the sender's name was omitted;
(iii) The fact that Paul used his Roman name and not his
Jewish name, 'Saul', suggests that he would be likely, at any
rate when writing as ἐθνῶν ἀπόστολος (11.13) to Gentiles or to a
church including a large number of Gentiles, to follow (or
adapt) Greek rather than Jewish convention in a matter of
external form of this sort. While it is no doubt possible that the
two-sentence structure of the Pauline formula derives from
the west-Asiatic custom, it is rather more likely that it is
simply the natural result of the decision to put a specifically
Christian and theological content into the salutation, which
could hardly be conveniently done within the tight one-
sentence construction. And, when once the salutation became
an independent sentence, the use of first and second person
pronouns was natural.[1]

If it was, then, the normal Greek prescript which was the
basis of the Pauline, Paul certainly modified and expanded it
in a most remarkable manner. Roller was surely right in
thinking that the prescript must have struck the recipients of
one of Paul's letters as extremely strange, when they read or
heard it for the first time.[2] While in ancient Greek private
letters to comparative strangers the ὁ δεῖνα τῷ δεῖνι χαίρειν form
was followed exactly and without any expansion, in intimate

---

[1] Friedrich has claimed (op. cit., col. 346) that the lack of definite
articles in the Pauline salutation and also the use of the words χάρις and
εἰρήνη are best explained as deriving from the west-Asiatic epistolary
formula: indeed he goes so far as to say, 'Sie [i.e. the Pauline salutation]
stammt aus dem orientalischen Briefformular'. But the absence of
articles is not surprising: εἰρήνη ὑμῖν is a natural enough greeting, and
there is therefore no difficulty over the omission of the article with the
first two nouns; and this omission would tend to carry with it the
omission before θεοῦ, and so before πατρός and κυρίου. And, while it is
interesting that neo-Assyrian and neo-Babylonian epistolary formulae
could combine the wish that the person addressed might have peace or
salvation with the wish that Asshur or Nabu and Marduk might be
gracious to him, the words χάρις and εἰρήνη are such central words of
the gospel that we scarcely need to look so far afield for an explanation
of Paul's use of them in his salutation.

[2] *Formular*, p. 88. The astonishment will not have ceased with the
prescript. The length of the letter—not to mention the contents!—must
also have amazed the recipients. The great majority of ancient Greek
and Latin letters are very short. Private letters seldom extended beyond
one side of a papyrus sheet (that is, between about 150 and 250 words,
if the hand was not a professional scribe's). The longest of Cicero's
letters is 4530 words, whereas Romans contains over 7000 (according
to Roller, 7101). Even Philemon is a good deal longer than the average
Greek or Latin letter.

letters a certain degree of variation (e.g. the introduction of terms of endearment and the use of direct address in the second person) was not unusual, and in official letters the superscription and the address were often expanded by the introduction of titles. Paul's use of the first and second persons in the superscription and address as well as in the salutation (in Romans both first and second persons appear in the superscription and salutation, but neither of them in the address) is a point of contact with the intimate letter prescript; but the resemblance of the Pauline prescript to that of Greek and Latin official letters is more striking, and probably conveyed to the recipients a suggestion of a solemn and authoritative mandate.[1] So, in addition to the astonishment which the Pauline prescript's extraordinary length and theological weight will have caused, there must also have been surprise at its combination of features associated with the most intimate kind of letter with features reminiscent of a Roman imperial mandate. The most important thing about Paul's adaptation and expansion of the prescript is, of course, his making it the vehicle of a specifically Christian and theological content.

In the Romans prescript, which is longer than that of any other Pauline epistle (taking thirteen lines of Nestle text: the next longest are the prescripts of Galatians with ten lines and I Corinthians with seven and a half), each of the three parts has been given a substantial theological content. Much the most extensive expansion is in the superscription which runs to six verses. The reason for this is of course Paul's special need to introduce himself, since the church to which he is writing is one to which he is not personally known, since he hopes soon to visit it, and since it is the church in Rome. (It is to be noted that in the whole Pauline corpus the only letters in which no one is associated with Paul in the superscription are Romans, Ephesians, I and 2 Timothy and Titus.) But in introducing himself he naturally refers to his mission, and this leads to a highly significant definition of the gospel which it is his mission to proclaim. This definition, which takes vv. 2–4, is presupposed in vv. 9, 15 and 16, when the gospel is referred to. What follows in vv. 5 and 6 has an obvious and very important bearing on Paul's relations with the Roman church and his proposed visit. Thus we see particularly clearly in Romans Paul's radical transformation of the Greek epistolary prescript. In his hands it has ceased to be a mere

---

[1] Cf. Roller, *Formular*, p. 88.

protocol, standing outside the 'context' or body of the letter, and has become an integral part of it.[1]

[1]Paul, slave of Christ Jesus, apostle by *God's* calling, set apart for *the work of proclaiming* God's message of good news, [2]which he promised beforehand through his prophets in the holy scriptures, [3]concerning his Son, who was born of David's seed according to the flesh, [4]who was appointed Son of God in power according to the Spirit of holiness from the resurrection of the dead, even Jesus Christ our Lord, [5]through whom we received grace and apostleship in order to bring about, for his name's sake, obedience of faith among all the Gentiles, [6]among whom you also are, you who are called of Jesus Christ, [7]to all in Rome beloved of God, saints by *God's* calling: grace to you and peace from God our Father and the Lord Jesus Christ.

1. Παῦλος. In view of the prominence in Scripture of Jacob-Israel and Simon-Peter, it is hardly surprising that the Apostle of the Gentiles has often been thought of as another example of significant re-naming. But the suggestion that Saul's name was changed to Paul at the time of his conversion is altogether unlikely, there being absolutely no support for it in the NT.[2] Scarcely more probable is Chrysostom's idea that God changed Saul's name on his 'ordination';[3] for—apart from the analogy of Simon Peter (Mk 3.16)—the only shred of evidence in its favour is the fact that the name Paul is first introduced in Acts at 13.9—soon after what is related in 13.2–3. More persistently maintained has been the view that Saul took the name of his distinguished convert, Sergius Paulus, the governor of Cyprus.[4] But, while it is true that the name is first introduced in the course of the section in which the governor's conversion is related, it is introduced three verses before the statement that the governor ἐπίστευσεν (Acts 13.12); moreover, it is introduced without any hint that it was a new name

---

[1] On the ancient Greek epistolary prescript in general and the Pauline prescript in particular see especially Roller, *Formular*; also G. Funaioli, *Studi in Letteratura Antica* 1, Bologna, 1948, pp. 157–74; M. van den Hout, 'Studies in early Greek Letter-writing', in *Mnemosyne* 4th ser., 2, pp. 19–41, 138–51; H. Koskenniemi, *Studien zur Idee und Phraseologie des griechischen Briefes bis 400 n. Chr.*, Helsinki, 1956.

[2] That the author of Acts had no such idea is clear from the fact that, while Saul's conversion is related in chapter 9, the name Paul is not introduced until 13.9.

[3] *PG* 60, col. 209 (on Acts 13.9). His words are: Ἐνταῦθα τὸ ὄνομα αὐτοῦ ἀμείβεται μετὰ τῆς χειροτονίας, ὅπερ καὶ ἐπὶ τοῦ Πέτρου γεγένηται. Cf. col. 395 (on Rom 1.1): Τίνος ἕνεκεν μετέθηκε τὸ ὄνομα αὐτοῦ ὁ Θεός, καὶ Σαῦλον ὄντα Παῦλον ἐκάλεσεν; Ἵνα μηδὲ ταύτῃ τῶν ἀποστόλων ἔλαττον ἔχῃ, ἀλλ' ὅπερ ἔσχεν ἐξαίρετον ὁ κορυφαῖος τῶν μαθητῶν, τοῦτο καὶ αὐτὸς κτήσηται, καὶ πλείονος οἰκειώσεως ὑπόθεσιν λάβῃ.

[4] By, e.g., Jerome, *De vir. ill.* 5 (*PL* 23, col. 646); Augustine, *Conf.* 8.4 (contrast *De Spir. et litt.* 7.12; *Serm.* 279.5; 315.7); Bengel, p. 437; Meyer, on Acts 13.9.

($\acute{o}$ καί in 13.9 certainly does not suggest this), and, further, it is intrinsically improbable that the apostle would have assumed his convert's name, whether on account of his worldly distinction or in gratitude for his assistance (particularly inappropriate is the appeal to the analogy of such Roman names as Africanus or Germanicus—Paul is hardly likely to have thought of his convert as a conquest to be boasted of). Had Paul not been a Roman citizen, it would have been natural to suppose that 'Paul' was simply a Gentile name possessed by him from childhood alongside his Jewish name 'Saul';[1] for the use of a Gentile name in addition to a Jewish, particularly one more or less like-sounding, was by NT times a well-established custom among Hellenistic Jews.[2] But, since Paul was a Roman citizen, the matter is rather more complicated. It is very probable that he possessed the three names characteristic of a Roman citizen, a *praenomen* or personal name, a *nomen* or clan name and a *cognomen* or family name.[3] It is probable that one of the two names given in Acts 13.9 was one of Paul's official *tria nomina*, and the other a *signum* or *supernomen*, an unofficial, informal name, additional to the three official names, such as was common at this time in the east.[4] 'Saul' in a Latinized form could have been the apostle's *cognomen*, and 'Paulus' his *signum*. But it is much more likely that it was the other way round, that 'Paulus' was his *cognomen*[5] and 'Saul' in

---

[1] So, e.g., Origen, cols. 836–38; Aquinas, p. 5f (he mentions the views of Chrysostom and Jerome, but prefers the explanation that 'Paulus fuit a principio binomius'); Calvin, p. 13.

[2] Cf., e.g., Acts 1.23; 12.25; 13.1; Col 4.11. See also SB 2, pp. 711–13.

[3] Cf. Juvenal, *Sat.* 5.127: '. . . tamquam habeas tria nomina' (i.e., as if you were a Roman citizen); Plutarch, *Mar.* 1. The *Lex Julia municipalis* (drafted by Julius Caesar) had laid down that Roman citizens living in the *municipia, coloniae* and *praefecturae* of Italy were to be registered by the three names.

[4] Cf. G. A. Harrer, 'Saul who also is called Paul', in *HTR* 33 (1940), pp. 19–33; also M. Lambertz, 'Zur Doppelnamigkeit in Ägypten', in *Jahresbericht über das K.K. Elisabeth-Gymnasium in Wien* 26 (1911) and 'Zur Ausbreitung des Supernomen oder Signum im römischen Reiche', in *Glotta* 4 (1913), pp. 78–143; 5 (1914), pp. 99–170; H. Wuilleumier, 'Étude historique sur l'emploi et la signification des Signa', in *Mémoires à l'Académie des Inscriptions et Belles-Lettres* 13 (1933), pp. 559–696. ὁ καί (Latin: 'qui et') was a regular formula in connexion with *signa*, and, as Lambertz has shown (*Glotta* 4, pp. 133 and 140: see also 130f), the *signum* could either follow or precede the other name, being separated from it by the ὁ καί.

[5] A slave who became a citizen by being granted his freedom regularly assumed the *praenomen* and *nomen* of his master, but retained his own slave-name as a *cognomen*: similarly, a free-born provincial who obtained Roman citizenship took the *praenomen* and *nomen* of the citizen who proposed him or of the emperor who granted the citizenship, but

its Semitic form his *signum*. That in his work as a missionary among the Gentiles he should have preferred to use one of his Roman names is readily understandable. The complete disappearance of two of Paul's names may seem surprising; but Paul, while ready to insist on his Roman citizenship when to do so might be to the advantage of his mission, is not likely to have emphasized it in his dealings with his fellow Christians, most of whom were of inferior worldly status, and he may well have chosen to use only one of his names in view of the fact that most of his fellow Christians only possessed one name. If only one of the *tria nomina* was to be used, it would naturally be the *cognomen*, since that was the most distinctive.[1]

Paul styles himself 'δοῦλος of Christ Jesus'. The background of this self-designation is to be found in the OT. For the Greek in the classical tradition it was well-nigh impossible to use a word of the δοῦλος group without some feeling of abhorrence. That the subjects of an oriental monarch could willingly describe themselves as his δοῦλοι was to him revolting, and to use such language with reference to men's relations to the gods never came naturally to him (it is characteristic of him that, except in the worship of the chthonian deities (when the gesture was not expressive of humility but of the will to get close to them physically), he did not kneel in worship). But in the OT the language of slavery is frequently used both with reference to the relation of the subject, and especially of the courtier, to a human ruler and of men to God. In the LXX δουλεύειν is in fact the commonest expression for the service of God in the sense of total allegiance and not just isolated acts of worship. The expression '*eḇeḏ YHWH*, δοῦλος κυρίου, or an equivalent, is a title of honour accorded to Moses, Joshua, David and the prophets (e.g. Josh 14.7; 24.29; Judg 2.8; 2 Kgs 17.23; Ps 89.3). For Paul every Christian is a δοῦλος Χριστοῦ (1 Cor 7.22f; Eph 6.6: cf. also Rom 12.11; 14.18; 16.18; 1 Cor 3.23; 6.19f; Col 3.24). The term expresses the total belongingness, total allegiance, correlative to the absolute ownership and

retained his native name as his *cognomen*. But with the next generation (and Paul was a citizen of at least the second generation according to Acts 22.28) the native *cognomen* was often exchanged for a regular Roman or Italian family name. 'Paullus' (less correctly 'Paulus') was a well-known family name found in several different *gentes* or clans. (One or two examples of 'Paullus' serving as a *praenomen* are known; but they are so rare that we scarcely need to reckon seriously with the possibility of its being the apostle's *praenomen*.)

[1] It was, of course, common practice among the Romans to use less than the full complement of names in referring to someone: one might, for example, use the *praenomen* and *nomen* or the *praenomen* and *cognomen* or the *cognomen* alone

authority denoted by κύριος used of Christ.¹ But when δοῦλος Χριστοῦ Ἰησοῦ (or Ἰησοῦ Χριστοῦ) is used, as here, as a self-designation (cf. Gal 1.10; Phil 1.1: cf. also Jas 1.1; 2 Pet 1.1), it probably carries, in addition to the personal confession of commitment, a reference to the writer's special office, in the fulfilment of which he is in a special sense Christ's slave.

Χριστοῦ Ἰησοῦ. The words should probably here be read in this order with 𝔓¹⁰ B *pc c e* vg^codd Ir Ambst Aug. The fact that Paul did quite often put 'Christ' before 'Jesus' is a strong indication that (despite opinions to the contrary²) he did not habitually think of 'Christ' as just a proper name.³ It is quite probable that he adopted this order here with the intention of giving special emphasis right at the beginning of the epistle to the fact that the One, whose slave he was, was the fulfilment of God's promises and of Israel's age-old hope.

κλητὸς ἀπόστολος. The verbal adjective κλητός occurs in Romans also in vv. 6 and 7, and in 8.28, the noun κλῆσις in 11.29, and the verb καλεῖν in 4.17; 8.30 (twice); 9.7, 12, 24, 25, 26. The verb καλεῖν, which corresponds to the Hebrew *ḳārā'* (e.g. Isa 42.6; 48.15; 49.1; 51.2), is used to denote God's gracious call to life and salvation, which is always at the same time a call to faith, obedience, service. For Paul all Christians are κλητοί (cf. vv. 6 and 7; 8.28; 1 Cor 1.2, 24); but this is not to say that κλητὸς ἀπόστολος means therefore simply 'Christian apostle'.⁴ The word κλητός here expresses the thought of divine calling in opposition to human self-appointment —it is not on the basis of presumptuous human ambition but on the basis of God's call that Paul is an apostle.⁵ Compare Gal 1.1 (though there it is authorization by men rather than self-appointment that is contrasted with divine calling).⁶

The word ἀπόστολος (which appears in association with Paul's name in the superscriptions of all the Pauline epistles except Philippians, 1 and 2 Thessalonians and Philemon) occurs in Romans only here and in 11.13 and 16.7: in addition, ἀποστολή occurs in 1.5 and ἀποστέλλειν in 10.15. The use of ἀπόστολος in the NT is less close to its use in classical Greek than it is to the Jewish use of its Hebrew and Aramaic

---

¹ On Paul's use of the language of slavery in connexion with the Christian life see also the notes on 6.15–23.
² e.g. Lietzmann, p. 23; Taylor, *Names*, p. 21f.
³ Cf. Cullmann, *Christology*, p. 134. Bornkamm, *Early Christian Experience*, p. 76, rightly claims that 'Christ' is for Paul usually a title.
⁴ *Pace* K. L. Schmidt, in *TWNT* 3, p. 495.
⁵ Cf. Calvin, p. 14.
⁶ On κλητός, καλεῖν, etc. see further K. L. Schmidt, in *TWNT* 3, pp. 488ff.

linguistic equivalents, *šālîaḥ* and *šᵉlîḥā'* respectively, which denote an authorized agent or representative. It is sometimes used in a quite general way of an emissary (e.g. Jn 13.16; 2 Cor 8.23; Phil 2.25); but it is also used as a technical term to denote (i) the Twelve, and (ii) a larger number including Barnabas and Paul (Acts 14.14) and Andronicus and Junia(s) (Rom 16.7). Paul, while we have no reason to doubt his sincerity in acknowledging himself to be the least of the apostles and unworthy to be an apostle at all inasmuch as he had persecuted God's Church (1 Cor 15.9) and may be sure that he also freely admitted that he was not a first-hand source of historical tradition concerning the life and teaching of Jesus as were the Twelve (he certainly did not fulfil the conditions indicated in Acts 1.21f) but was himself dependent on the witness of those who were apostles before him (Gal 1.17) for his knowledge both of the details of Jesus's ministry and of the substance of His teaching, nevertheless asserted vehemently the equality of the authority of his apostleship with theirs. This claim he seems to have based on the facts that he too had seen the risen Lord (1 Cor 9.1), had received his commission directly from Christ Himself (Gal 1.1: cf. Acts 26.15–18), and had had his commission divinely confirmed by the signs of an apostle accompanying his labours (2 Cor 12.12). The use of the word 'apostle' here indicates that Paul claims the attention of the Roman church to what follows not on the ground of his own personal worth and wisdom but by virtue of the commission he has received from Christ. The word points away from the apostle's person to Him whose apostle he is. It is thus both a very humble word and also at the same time expressive of the most august authority.[1]

---

[1] On ἀπόστολος see further: K. H. Rengstorf, in *TWNT* 1, pp. 406–48; id., *Apostolat und Predigtamt* (1934), Stuttgart, ²1954; J.-L. Leuba, *Recherches exégétiques relatives à l'apostolat dans le Nouveau Testament*, Neuchâtel thesis, 1936; G. Sass, *Apostelamt und Kirche: eine theologisch-exegetische Untersuchung des paulinischen Apostelbegriffs*, Munich, 1939; R. N. Flew, *Jesus and His Church*, London, 1938; M. Barth, *Der Augenzeuge: eine Untersuchung über die Wahrnehmung des Menschensohnes durch die Apostel*, Zurich, 1946; K. E. Kirk (ed.), *The Apostolic Ministry*, London, 1946; R. Liechtenhan, *Die urchristliche Mission*, Zurich, 1946; E. Schweizer. *Das Leben des Herrn in der Gemeinde und ihren Diensten*, Zurich, 1946; A. Fridrichsen, *The Apostle and his Message*, Uppsala, 1947; H. von Campenhausen, 'Der urchristliche Apostelbegriff', in *ST* 1 (1948), pp. 96–130; T. W. Manson, *The Church's Ministry*, London, 1948; H. Mosbech, 'Apostolos in the NT', in *ST* 2 (1949), pp. 166–200; J. Munck, 'Paul, the Apostles, and the Twelve', in *ST* 3 (1950), pp. 96–110; A. Ehrhardt, *The Apostolic Succession*, London, 1953; E. Lohse,

ἀφωρισμένος εἰς εὐαγγέλιον θεοῦ is better construed as a third phrase in apposition to Παῦλος (alongside δοῦλος Χριστοῦ Ἰησοῦ and κλητὸς ἀπόστολος) than as in apposition to κλητὸς ἀπόστολος.[1] A comma should therefore be placed after ἀπόστολος.[2] Nevertheless the phrase does of course throw light on the meaning of κλητὸς ἀπόστολος, since it is parallel to it, just as δοῦλος Χριστοῦ Ἰησοῦ also does. The apostle's function is indeed to serve the gospel by an authoritative and normative proclamation of it (cf. v. 5, where the meaning of ἀποστολή is elucidated by what follows). ἀφωρισμένος refers not to the separation of Paul from the religious community of Judaism,[3] nor yet to the separation described in Acts 13.2,[4] but to God's consecration of him for his future task (cf. Gal 1.15: also Isa 49.1; Jer 1.5). In the LXX ἀφορίζειν is used of setting apart to God the firstborn of man and beast (Exod 13.12), of offering the firstfruits (Num 15.20), of consecrating the Levites to the divine service on behalf of Israel (Num 8.11), and also of God's separating Israel from the other nations to be His special possession (Lev 20.26). It is often used in association with ἅγιος or ἁγιάζειν (so, e.g., in Lev 20.26), and once it actually represents a derivative of the Hebrew verb ḳādaš (Ezek 45.4), which in the Pi'el and Hiph'il means to set apart, consecrate. It is the Hiph'il of ḳādaš (represented by ἁγιάζειν in the LXX), which is used in Jer 1.5, a passage which Paul probably had in mind when composing Gal 1.15 and quite possibly here also, and mûḳdāš is the equivalent (so far as the sense is concerned) of ἀφωρισμένος here.[5] The suggestion that, in using the Greek word ἀφωρισμένος, Paul may have had in mind the name 'Pharisee' (it is of course a widely-favoured explanation of the name that it was derived from pāraš and meant 'separated one')[6] and wanted to make the point that he was now, as a

'Ursprung und Prägung des christlichen Apostolates', in *TZ* 9 (1953), pp. 259–75; D. W. B. Robinson, 'Apostleship and Apostolic Succession', in *RTR* 13 (1954), pp. 33–42; E. M. Kredel, 'Der Apostelbegriff in der neueren Exegese', in *ZKT* 78 (1956), pp. 169–93, 257–305; W. Schmithals, *The Office of Apostle in the Early Church*, Eng. tr., London, 1971; C. K. Barrett, *The Signs of an Apostle*, London, 1969; R. Schnackenburg, 'Apostles before and during Paul's time', in *Apostolic History*, pp. 287–303.

[1] Cf. Michel, p. 35. To take the phrase as in apposition to κλητὸς ἀπόστολος, which is itself in apposition to Παῦλος, would be very clumsy, while the explanation of ἀφωρισμένος, κ.τ.λ. as co-ordinate with κλητός is, in the absence of καί, impossible.

[2] As in AV, RV, etc.   [3] So Augustine, col. 2089.

[4] Sanday and Headlam, p. 5, mention this as part of what is meant.

[5] Cf. SB 3, p. 4.

[6] Cf., e.g., M. Black, in *IDB* 3, p. 776; Jeremias, *Jerusalem*, p. 246 (further bibliographical information, ibid., n. 1).

Christian, a true 'Pharisee' or 'separated one',[1] while perhaps just possible, is surely not very likely; for this thought is not really in accord with the way in which ἀφωρισμένος is actually used here—for one thing, the separation to which the name 'Pharisee' referred (if indeed it was derived from *pāraš*) was most probably separation *from* uncleanness, while that denoted by ἀφωρισμένος here is separation (or consecration) *to* a holy task; and for another thing, 'Pharisee' was a name applied to *all* the members of a particular religious community or party, while the last four words of this verse (like the two preceding phrases) are descriptive of Paul not simply as a Christian, but as one having a *special* ministry within the Christian community.

Paul knows himself as one who has been separated, consecrated, by God εἰς εὐαγγέλιον θεοῦ —for (that is, for the task of proclaiming) God's message of good news.[2] For the right understanding of εὐαγγέλιον here and elsewhere in the NT

[1] Accepted by, e.g., Nygren, p. 45f; Michel, p. 36; Barrett, p. 17 (more tentatively). Nygren not only accepts this suggestion without question but goes farther and, interpreting Paul's former separatedness as a matter of separation *for the law*, sees here in the very first verse of the epistle a reference to the 'basic juxtaposition of law and gospel which, from one point of view, is the theme of Romans'. But this is surely *ei*segesis rather than exegesis! The appeal to ἐγὼ Φαρισαῖός εἰμι (present tense) in Acts 23.6 (e.g. Michel, p. 36) as supporting the contention that Paul thought of himself as being, as a Christian, a 'Pharisee' or 'separated one' in a new and special sense can hardly be sustained; for (quite apart from the question whether so much historical weight ought to be put on the use of a particular tense in Acts) Φαρισαῖος can hardly bear a different sense when used of Paul in this verse from that which it bears in the same verse when used of his family (υἱὸς Φαρισαίων), and the natural explanation of the present tense is surely that the author of Acts (rightly, in our opinion) depicts Paul as still feeling, as a Christian, a certain degree of attachment to Pharisaism which made it natural for him to take sides with the Pharisees against the Sadducees.

[2] G. Friedrich (*TWNT* 2, p. 727) seems to suggest that in the Pauline epistles εὐαγγέλιον sometimes denotes the act of proclaiming (e.g. in 1 Cor 9.14 (second occurrence); 2 Cor 2.12; 8.18; Phil 4.3) and sometimes, as when it is the object of a verb of speaking or hearing, the content of the proclamation (e.g. 1 Cor 15.1; Gal 1.12; 2.2), as though these were two distinct alternative significations. In Rom 1.1–2 he understands εὐαγγέλιον in the sense of the proclamation of the gospel but the following relative pronoun in the sense of the content of the gospel. But to understand a noun to have one sense when it appears as the antecedent of the relative and then to take the relative pronoun to denote a different sense of that noun is surely extremely awkward. Is it not a preferable explanation of the data to say that in Paul εὐαγγέλιον always denotes the message of good news, but that sometimes the context (as ἀφωρισμένος εἰς here) may indicate that it is used in a slightly pregnant way, the thought of the message's proclamation (which is always present in the word) coming specially to the fore?

the use of the root *bśr* in the OT is of fundamental importance. The noun *bᵉśôrāh/bᵉśōrāh* occurs only six times (twice meaning 'reward for bringing good news'); but the verb in the Pi'el occurs often (it is nearly always represented in the LXX by the middle of εὐαγγελίζειν) and means 'to announce good news' (e.g. 1 Kgs 1.42; Jer 20.15), especially of victory (e.g. 1 Sam 31.9). Of special importance are the occurrences in Ps 40.9 [MT: 10; LXX: 39.10]; 96 [LXX: 95].2; Isa 40.9; 41.27; 52.7; 60.6; 61.1; Nah 1.15 [MT, LXX: 2.1]: they have to do with the in-breaking of God's reign, the advent of His salvation, vengeance, vindication. But there is also a pagan background to the NT use of εὐαγγέλιον. For the inhabitants of the Roman Empire it had special associations with the Emperor-cult, since the announcements of such events as the birth of an heir to the Emperor, his coming-of-age, and his accession, were referred to as εὐαγγέλια. There is thus in the Christian use of the word an implicit contrast between that εὐαγγέλιον which may truly be termed εὐαγγέλιον θεοῦ (for this phrase compare 15.16; Mk 1.14; 2 Cor 11.7; 1 Th 2.2, 8, 9; 1 Pet 4.17: the omission of the articles here has the effect of giving it additional emphasis and solemnity) and these other εὐαγγέλια which represent the pretentious claims of self-important men. The message of good news Paul has to proclaim is God's authoritative Word. Its source[1] is none other than God Himself. A further definition of it follows in vv. 2–4.[2]

2. ὃ προεπηγγείλατο διὰ τῶν προφητῶν αὐτοῦ ἐν γραφαῖς ἁγίαις. Having already defined εὐαγγέλιον by the genitive θεοῦ, Paul proceeds to define it further by means of a relative clause as the fulfilment of God's promises[3] through His prophets[4] in the OT.[5]

---

[1] The genitive θεοῦ indicates origin. We may render it by 'from God' or simply by 'God's' or 'of God'. Barrett's 'God is now setting forth' (p. 15) is an unwarranted limitation of the sense. God is the author of the message not only in that it is He who is now setting it forth, speaking through those who proclaim it, but also in that He has purposed it from all eternity, promised it in the OT scriptures (cf. v. 2), and brought it into being by the gospel events to which Paul refers with a perfect tense in, for example, 3.21.

[2] On εὐαγγέλιον see further G. Friedrich, in *TWNT* 2, pp. 705–35.

[3] The two-preposition compound προεπαγγέλλεσθαι occurs in the NT only here and in 2 Cor 9.5. Its only known pre-Pauline occurrence is in an inscription of 84 B.C. (*Inschriften von Priene*, ed. F. Hiller von Gärtringen, 1906, 113.71). The force of the προ- is to emphasize the thought of priority already present in ἐπαγγέλλεσθαι. The one-preposition compound ἐπαγγέλλεσθαι (see on 4.21) occurs fifteen times in the NT—always, apart from two occurrences in the Pastorals, in the sense 'promise', while the noun ἐπαγγελία (see on 4.13) occurs much more frequently, especially in the Pauline epistles and particularly in Romans and Galatians. But, deeply rooted in the OT though the thought of God's promising is, it is

He thus underlines its trustworthiness.[1] The verse is formally a statement about the gospel, with which we may compare such things as the latter part of 3.21 and the repeated κατὰ τὰς γραφάς of 1 Cor 15.3f: it is also, indirectly, a statement about the OT, a claim that it is to be understood as pointing forward to the gospel. Thus Paul introduces at the very beginning of the epistle the subject of the right interpretation of the OT with which he will be concerned throughout its course. Karl Barth has rightly underlined the fact of this epistle's insistent concentration upon this theme.[2] It was the life's theme of the Jewish scribe who had become a Christian apostle and 'the theme around which the controversies moved which he aroused in the Church and had to overcome, and consequently it was undoubtedly', as Barth has pointed out, 'the most

not expressed there in the terminology of ἐπαγγέλλεσθαι (the earliest occurrences of ἐπαγγέλλεσθαι and ἐπαγγελία with reference to God's promises would seem to be Ps. Sol. 7.9 (10); 12.7 (6); 17.6 (5)). See further J. Schniewind and G. Friedrich, in *TWNT* 2, pp. 573–83.

[4] By 'prophets' here we should probably understand not just those whom we normally think of as OT prophets nor yet all whose combined legacy makes up the second division of the Hebrew Scriptures, but the inspired men of the OT generally, including such as Moses (cf. Acts 3.22) and David (cf. Acts 2.30f) For 'his (i.e. God's) prophets' cf. Lk 1.70; Acts 3.21 (cf. also 'thy prophets' in Rom 11.3).

[5] As in the case of εὐαγγέλιον θεοῦ in v. 1, the absence of the article gives additional solemnity: it does not make the expression indefinite—it is clear that the OT is meant. Compare διὰ ... γραφῶν προφητικῶν in 16.26 and ἱερὰ γράμματα (according to the reading preferred by Nestle) in 2 Tim 3.15. (See also BDF, § 255, on the omission of the article in prepositional phrases.) The characteristic NT designation of the OT is the simple αἱ γραφαί. This is the only place in the NT where ἅγιος is used in connexion with γραφαί. There is also Rom 7.12, where the law is said to be ἅγιος, and once the adjective ἱερός is used in this connexion (2 Tim 3.15). This use of ἅγιος or ἱερός reflects Jewish usage, both Rabbinic and Hellenistic (the Rabbinic expression is kiṯᵉḇē hakkōḏeš, while αἱ ἱεραὶ γραφαί occurs frequently in Philo). ἐν γραφαῖς ἁγίαις, as well as διὰ τῶν προφητῶν αὐτοῦ, qualifies προεπηγγείλατο (it was through His prophets and it was in the Scriptures that God promised the gospel)— Barrett's translation 'which in the past he promised through his prophets, whose word still stands in Holy Writ' (p. 15), which has the effect of making the relation of ἐν γραφαῖς ἁγίαις to προεπηγγείλατο indirect instead of direct, is hardly justifiable.

[1] Its correspondence to the promises attests its truth (cf. Bengel, p. 490: 'Veritas promissionis et veritas impletionis se invicem confirmat'). And the fact that it has been promised by God from of old proves that it is no mere novelty (cf. Chrysostom, col. 396: 'Ἐπειδὴ δὲ καινοτομίαν ἐνεκάλουν τῷ πράγματι, δείκνυσιν αὐτὸ πρεσβύτερον Ἑλλήνων ὂν καὶ ἐν τοῖς προφήταις προδιαγραφόμενον: also Calvin, p. 15). In illustration of the ancient suspicion of what is merely of recent origin Michel cites Josephus, *Contra Ap.* 1.2ff.

[2] *Shorter*, pp. 10–13. (*KE*, pp. 10–14.)

suitable theme if he wanted to introduce himself, or rather not himself but his cause, to people who so far only knew him from hearsay'.[1] It is a truly penetrating insight to which Martin Luther gives expression in his preface to Romans when he says that it seems as if in this epistle St Paul wanted to set forth in a brief summary the whole Christian and evangelical doctrine and show the way to the understanding of the whole of the OT, and that there is no doubt that he who has this epistle in his heart is possessed of the light and power of the OT.[2]

3–4. It is very much better to place a comma at the end of v. 2 and take vv. 3–4 as an attribute of εὐαγγέλιον[3] than to understand them as a continuation of the relative clause;[4] for this punctuation yields a better balanced sentence and avoids an unbroken string of three relative clauses, the second depending on the first and the third on the second, which connecting vv. 3–4 with v. 2 involves. Having already defined εὐαγγέλιον first by θεοῦ and then by a relative clause (v. 2), Paul now defines it yet further by indicating its content: the message of good news concerns God's Son, Jesus Christ our Lord.

That in these two verses Paul is making use of the language of an already existing confessional formula,[5] though it is hardly as certain as it is sometimes assumed to be, seems highly probable. For him at this particular point, when he is introducing himself to the Roman church, to underline his fundamental agreement with his fellow Christians in this way would make good sense. The facts that there is no other direct reference to Christ's Davidic descent in the Pauline corpus except in 2 Tim 2.8 and that ὁρίζειν is nowhere else used by Paul may be seen as supporting this view. Whether there was any tension between the theology of this formula—if this view is correct—and Paul's own thought is not clear. It may be that κατὰ σάρκα and κατὰ πνεῦμα ἁγιωσύνης are Pauline additions (though it is to be noted that πνεῦμα ἁγιωσύνης is not an expression which

[1] *Shorter*, p. 11.
[2] *Die deutsche Bibel* (Weimar ed.) 7, p. 27: 'Darumb es auch scheinet, als habe S. Paulus in dieser Epistel wollen ein mal in die kürtze verfassen, die gantze Christliche und Evangelische lere, und einen Eingang bereiten in das gantze alte Testament. Denn on zweivel, wer diese Epistel wol im hertzen hat, der hat des alten Testaments liecht und krafft bey sich.'
[3] With Souter, UBS: cf. RV, RSV, NEB, JB.
[4] With WH, Nestle, Merk, BFBS.
[5] Cf., e.g., Cullmann, *The Earliest Christian Confessions*, Eng. tr., London, 1949, pp. 55ff; Bultmann, *Theology* 1, p. 49. This view is, however, rejected by A. Fridrichsen, *The Apostle and his Message*, Uppsala, 1947.

he uses elsewhere). We do not have to assume that the original intention of the formula must have been adoptionist. Our present concern is anyway with Paul's meaning, and for this the words περὶ τοῦ υἱοῦ αὐτοῦ are decisive. This language is thoroughly characteristic of Paul (cf. v. 9 of this chapter; 5.10; 8.3, 29, 32; 1 Cor 1.9; 15.28; 2 Cor 1.19; Gal 1.16; 2.20; 4.4, 6; Eph 4.13; Col 1.13; 1 Th 1.10; and also passages such as 2 Cor 1.3 which describe God as the Father of Jesus Christ). It is clear that, as used by Paul with reference to Christ, the designation 'Son of God' expresses nothing less than a relationship to God which is 'personal, ethical and inherent',[1] involving a real community of nature between Christ and God.[2] The position of the words τοῦ υἱοῦ αὐτοῦ—being placed, so to speak, outside the bracket, they are naturally taken to control both participial clauses alike—would seem to imply that the One who was born of the seed of David was already Son of God before, and independently of, the action denoted by the second participle.

τοῦ γενομένου ἐκ σπέρματος Δαυίδ. Though it seems that some Jews of the NT period did not regard descent from David as an absolutely essential qualification of the Messiah (Rabbi Akiba may be cited as an example; for he hailed Simeon 'Bar-Cochba' as Messiah—a man who, as far as we know, never claimed Davidic descent), it is clear that the expectation that the Messiah would belong to the family of David was strongly established (compare, in addition to the evidence of the NT itself, Ps. Sol. 17.23(21); 4QpIsaᵃ; 4QPB; 4QFl).[3] Its OT basis is to be seen in such passages as 2 Sam 7.16; Ps 89.3f, 19ff; Isa 11.1, 10; Jer 23.5f; 30.9; 33.14–18; Ezek 34.23f; 37.24f. These words assert the Davidic descent of Jesus, in agreement with the testimony of other parts of the NT (cf. Mt 1.1, 2–16, 20; Lk 1.27, 32, 69; 2.4; 3.23–31; Acts 2.30; 2 Tim 2.8; Rev 5.5; 22.16: that the author believed Jesus to have been of David's house is probably to be inferred from Jn 7.42). On the historical credibility of this claim reference may be made to Jeremias, *Jerusalem*, pp. 275–302 (cf. E. Stauffer, *Jesus and His Story*, Eng. tr., London, 1960, p. 22f; Cullmann, *Christology*, pp. 127–30). The claim not only has an apologetic significance (drawing attention to Jesus' possession of an important messianic qualification and underlining the correspondence

[1] Scott, *Christianity*, p. 255.
[2] Cf., e.g., Taylor, *Person of Christ*, pp. 43ff; Cullmann, *Christology*, pp. 292–4.
[3] For English translations of the last three see Vermes, pp. 226f, 224 and 244, respectively.

between promise and fulfilment (cf. v. 2)), but also endorses
the reality of those promises on which Israel's messianic hopes
were founded and implicitly acknowledges the true and
inalienable dignity of the succession of the kings of David's
line (the fact that they dimly and unworthily, but nonetheless
really, foreshadowed Him who was to come, in whom God's
promise to David would be finally and completely honoured).

But in both Matthew and Luke, while Jesus' Davidic
descent is asserted emphatically, it is also at the same time
indicated that Joseph, through whom the descent is traced
(Mt 1.16, 20; Lk 1.27; 2.4; 3.23), was not the natural father of
Jesus (Mt 1.18–25; Lk 1.34f); the implication of the narratives
is that Jesus' Davidic descent rests on Joseph's having
accepted Him as his son and thereby legitimized Him.[1] It is
possible that Paul's use here and also in Gal 4.4 and Phil 2.7
of γίνεσθαι rather than γεννᾶσθαι (which he does sometimes use
but never in connexion with the birth of Jesus)[2] may reflect
knowledge on his part of the tradition of Jesus' birth without
natural human fatherhood;[3] though γίνεσθαι is certainly
sometimes used with reference to birth (cf. Bauer, s.v. I.1.a),
it is not the ordinary word to denote it.[4]

κατὰ σάρκα. Paul's uses of the noun σάρξ present a bewilder-
ing variety of nuances, and we shall often have to try to
discover the precise sense which it bears in a particular
passage. The phrase κατὰ σάρκα itself can have more than one
sense. Thus its significance here is quite different from that

[1] It is significant that in Mt 1.21 Joseph is commanded to name the
Child (we assume that καλέσεις is to be read there), and in v. 25 is
presumably the subject of ἐκάλεσεν. To give the name was to accept the
child as one's son. Joseph's acceptance of Jesus as his son would have
conferred on Him all the legal rights of legitimate sonship (cf. SB 1,
p. 35, where B.B. 8.6 is cited in support; Stauffer, op. cit., p. 25. We
may understand the use of οἱ γονεῖς αὐτοῦ in Lk 2.41 and 43 in this light.
[2] A few minuscule MSS. do in fact have γεννωμένου here, and it has
the support of syh: the equivalent 'natus' was a variant known to
Augustine. The Vulgate has 'qui factus est ei' (there is no known Greek
support for the 'ei').
[3] Cf., e.g., H. E. W. Turner, 'Expository Problems: The Virgin Birth',
in ET 68 (1956–7), p. 12.
[4] On the subject of the Virgin Birth reference may be made to G. H.
Box, The Virgin Birth of Jesus, London, 1916; V. Taylor, The Historical
Evidence for the Virgin Birth, Oxford, 1920; J. G. Machen, The Virgin
Birth of Christ, London, 1930; M. Dibelius, Jungfrauensohn und Krippen-
kind, Heidelberg, 1932; K. L. Schmidt, 'Die jungfräuliche Geburt Jesu
Christi', in TB 14 (1935), cols. 289–97; Barth, CD I/2, pp. 172–202 (=
KD I/2, pp. 187–221); D. A. Edwards, The Virgin Birth in History and
Faith, London, 1943; T. D. Boslooper, The Virgin Birth, London, 1962;
R. E. Brown, The Virginal Conception and Bodily Resurrection of
Jesus, Paramus, N. J., 1973; J. McHugh, The Mother of Jesus in the
New Testament, London, 1975; C. Cranfield, in SJT 41 (1988), pp. 177–89.

which it has in, for example, 8.4, 5, 12. The closest parallel
to the present instance is in 9.5. Both there and here it is best
understood as meaning 'as a man', 'so far as His human
nature is concerned'. By using it Paul implies that the fact
of Christ's human nature, in respect of which what has just
been said is true, is not the whole truth about Him. 'Son of
David' is a valid description of Him so far as it is applicable,
but the reach of its applicability is not coextensive with the
fullness of His person (cf. Mk 12.35–37). But this is not to say
that κατὰ σάρκα defines Christ's kinship with David as something
belonging only to His earthly, historical life.[1] So to interpret
it is to impose upon it—quite unjustifiably[2]—a meaning
inconsistent with the truth (fundamental for Paul as for the
other NT writers) of the resurrection of Jesus. For belief in the
resurrection of Jesus necessarily involves believing that, as the
risen and exalted Lord, He still possesses the same human
nature—albeit glorified—as He assumed in the Incarnation.[3]
We take it then that κατὰ σάρκα here indicates that the words
τοῦ γενομένου ἐκ σπέρματος Δαυίδ are used of the Son of God in
respect of His human nature, not that the kinship with David
which they express is to be thought of as limited to the days
of His earthly life. (The view that κατὰ σάρκα must refer not to
Christ's manhood but to the period of His earthly life, His state
of humiliation, springs from the assumption that κατὰ σάρκα
and κατὰ πνεῦμα ἁγιωσύνης and the two participial clauses as
wholes must be closely parallel, with which is often combined
the desire to avoid an interpretation which might seem to

---

[1] As seems to be implied by some exegetes, e.g., W. Manson, 'Notes',
p. 153 ('. . . the earthly life (κατὰ σάρκα) in which Jesus appeared as
Davidic Messiah'); Michel, p. 39 ('. . . "Fleisch" . . . bezeichnet hier . . .
die leibliche und räumliche Gebundenheit an die Erde im Unterschied
von der Welt des Geistes (und der Geister) und des Himmlischen');
E. Schweizer, in TWNT 7, p. 125f ('Wie R 1,3f . . . zeigt, übernimmt
Paulus schon einen Sprachgebrauch, der . . . die irdische Sphäre als die
der σάρξ der himmlischen als der der πνεύματα oder des πνεῦμα gegen-
überstellt').

[2] The fact that σάρξ is occasionally used with the intention of indicating earthly life as such (Heb 5.7; Gal 2.20; Phil 1.22 (cf. 24)) is, in view of
the variety of nuance which σάρξ is generally recognized as having in the
NT, certainly no justification for imposing this meaning here.

[3] It is precisely this, that He is now at God's right hand not only as
God but also as Man, that is the new thing about the exaltation of
Christ over against the glory possessed by the Son of God from eternity
(2 Cor 8.9—πλούσιος ὤν). But, in insisting that Christ's relation to David
is not something concluded with His earthly life, we are not forgetting
that real otherness of the resurrection life to which Mk 12.25 bears
witness, nor that justice has also to be done to Paul's οὐκ ἔνι Ἰουδαῖος οὐδὲ
Ἕλλην (Gal 3.28).

imply that Christ only became the Son of God at the Resurrection.)

τοῦ ὁρισθέντος[1] υἱοῦ θεοῦ ἐν δυνάμει κατὰ πνεῦμα ἁγιωσύνης ἐξ ἀναστάσεως νεκρῶν. The first of the two participial clauses has just characterized the Son of God, whom the message of good news concerns, by reference to the event of His human birth, singling out for special mention the relationship to David into which it brought Him. And now the second characterizes Him by reference to another event, namely, His resurrection, though in this case the event itself as such is specified not by the participle but by a dependent phrase. (It is noteworthy that a similar combination of references to Christ's Davidic descent and to His resurrection is to be found in 2 Tim 2.8.) The clause contains an unusually large number of problems: (i) Does ὁρίζειν here mean 'appoint', 'constitute' or 'declare', 'show to be'? (ii) Does ἐν δυνάμει qualify ὁρισθέντος or υἱοῦ θεοῦ? (iii) What is the significance of κατὰ πνεῦμα ἁγιωσύνης? (iv) What sense does ἐξ have? (v) How is νεκρῶν to be explained?

With regard to (i), there is little doubt that we should decide for the meaning 'appoint', 'constitute', 'install'. The verb means properly 'delimit', hence, by natural extension, 'define' (in the sense of setting forth the essential nature of something), since this is an intellectual delimiting. It came to be used very frequently with the meaning, 'fix', 'determine', 'appoint'; and this is the sense it has in all its other occurrences in the NT.[2] No clear example, either earlier than, or contemporary with, the NT, of its use in the sense 'declare' or 'show to be' has been adduced. This being so, it is probably right to conclude that the support for this interpretation afforded by various Greek

[1] The tendency observable in the Latin tradition to use 'praedestinatus' here is no proof of the existence of an early variant προορισθέντος. There is no trace of such a reading in any extant Greek biblical MS. Eusebius refers to Marcellus's reading προορισθέντος as a corrupting of the text (*PG* 24, col. 737: ὁ δέ, οὐκ οἶδα ποίᾳ διανοίᾳ, κἀνταῦθα διαστρέφει τὴν ἀποστολικὴν λέξιν· ἀντὶ τοῦ ὁρισθέντος ποιήσας προορισθέντος), and the presence of προορισθέντος in Epiphanius's quotation of this passage (*PG* 41, col. 969) is probably either a slip of memory or due to Latin influence. 'Praedestinatus' is found in the Latin translation of Irenaeus, in some Old Latin MSS. and in the Vulgate. Origen, col. 849, refers to its prevalence in Latin MSS., but affirms that 'destinatus' is more accurate. Jerome, who was well aware of the difference in meaning between ὁρίζειν and προορίζειν, no doubt allowed the translation 'qui praedestinatus est' to stand here in the Vulgate on the strength of the conviction which he expressed in his comment on Eph 1.5 (*PL* 26, col. 448) that 'Differentiam . . . Graeci sermonis προορίσας et ὁρισθέντος Latinus sermo non explicat'. That ὁρισθέντος is the true reading there can be no doubt.

[2] Lk 22.22; Acts 2.23; 10.42; 11.29; 17.26, 31; Heb 4.7.

Fathers[1] is due to a doctrinal consideration rather than to their superior knowledge of Greek usage.

With regard to (ii), while it is perhaps not possible to decide with absolute certainty, the following points may be made in favour of understanding ἐν δυνάμει as qualifying υἱοῦ θεοῦ: first, that ἐν δυνάμει is used elsewhere in the NT (Mk 9.1; 1 Cor 15.43; 1 Th 1.5) in the sense 'invested with power'; and, secondly, that the sense which results from taking ἐν δυνάμει with υἱοῦ θεοῦ accords well, while the sense which is yielded by taking it with ὁρισθέντος, suggestive as it is of adoptionism (on the assumption that ὁρισθέντος means 'who was appointed'), seems to accord ill, not only with Paul's teaching in other places but also with the presence of τοῦ υἱοῦ αὐτοῦ at the beginning of v. 3.

The meaning of the first six words of this clause then is probably 'who was appointed Son-of-God-in-power' (that is, in contrast with His being Son of God in apparent weakness and poverty in the period of His earthly existence). Consideration of (iii) we postpone for the moment. With regard to (iv), ἐξ is by some understood to mean 'since', 'from the time of', by others 'on the ground of'. Of these interpretations the former is to be preferred. Christ's resurrection was scarcely the ground of His exaltation; but it was the event which was the beginning of His exalted life.[2] As to (v), the genitive plural νεκρῶν is variously explained as meaning 'from the dead', the preposition being omitted so as to avoid repeating ἐκ,[3] or as being due to the fact that ἀνάστασις νεκρῶν was a stereotyped expression, almost a compound word, or as used because Christ was not raised for Himself alone but as the firstfruits of the dead,[4] or as being merely a generalizing or allusive plural.[5] The last of these explanations should possibly be preferred as being the simplest.

We have now to consider (iii), which is the most difficult of these problems. Every word of the phrase is itself problematic

---

[1] e.g. Chrysostom, col. 397 (Τί οὖν ἐστιν, Ὁρισθέντος; Δειχθέντος, ἀποφανθέντος, κριθέντος, ὁμολογηθέντος παρὰ τῆς ἁπάντων γνώμης καὶ ψήφου. . . .)

[2] Cf. Huby, p. 44f ('le point de départ et le premier acte de cette exaltation définitive').

[3] Cf. Lietzmann, p. 25. He thinks that ἐξ ἀναστάσεως νεκρῶν was used instead of ἐκ τῆς ἀναστάσεως αὐτοῦ (τῆς) ἐκ νεκρῶν for the sake of euphony and brevity.

[4] Cf. Bengel, p. 491 ('. . . innuitur, cum resurrectione Christi penitus conjunctam esse resurrectionem omnium'): Nygren, pp. 49–51. Augustine, col. 2063 ('mortuorum vero resurrectionem memorat, quia in ipso omnes crucifixi sumus, et resurreximus'), seems to be thinking more along the lines of Col 3.1.

[5] See BDF, § 141 init.; also Turner, Insights, pp. 27, 69.

(which of its possible senses does κατά have? who or what is meant by πνεῦμα? is ἁγιωσύνης simply equivalent to ἅγιον, or does it mean 'of holiness' or 'of sanctification'?); and widely differing explanations of the phrase as a whole have been suggested. A good many exegetes[1] have argued that the Holy Spirit cannot be intended by πνεῦμα, because—so it is alleged— the parallelism between κατὰ σάρκα and κατὰ πνεῦμα ἁγιωσύνης necessitates taking πνεῦμα to refer to something inherent in Christ, and not to another Person of the Trinity. On the assumption that the Holy Spirit is not meant, the choice seems to be between taking the phrase to refer to the human spirit of Christ 'distinguished . . . from that of ordinary humanity by an exceptional and transcendent Holiness'[2] and understanding it as referring to His divinity. In support of the latter inter- pretation Lagrange argues that, if σάρξ in v. 3 indicates Christ's humanity, πνεῦμα must necessarily indicate His divinity. He understands Paul's meaning to be that at His resurrection Christ was definitively established in that role which was fully consonant with the divine nature which had all along been His, namely, the role of Son of God invested with might. Such OT passages as Gen 6.3; Ps 56.4 [LXX: 55.5]; Job 10.4; Isa 31.3, he suggests, help to explain how Paul could refer to Christ's divine nature in terms of 'spirit'.[3] But to many commentators both ancient and modern the identi- fication of πνεῦμα ἁγιωσύνης with the Holy Spirit has seemed natural. On this assumption, several possible interpretations present themselves. One is, taking κατά to mean 'in the sphere of', to understand the phrase as characterizing Christ's appointment as Son of God in power as an eschatological event, the beginning of God's new creation.[4] Or, taking κατά in its sense of 'according to', it is possible to explain the phrase as indicating that it was by the power of the Holy Spirit that the establishment of Christ as mighty Son of God (or possibly

[1] e.g. Sanday and Headlam, p. 9; Lagrange, p. 7; Huby, p. 45.

[2] Sanday and Headlam, p. 9. They compare Heb 2.17; 4.15. In their paraphrase on p. 2 the phrase is represented by 'in virtue of the Holiness inherent in His spirit'.

[3] p. 8. He says: '. . . κατὰ πνεῦμα indique nécessairement l'autre être propre du Christ, celui qu'il avait tout d'abord et qui l'autorise à être constitué Fils de Dieu aux yeux de tous. . . . Il est . . . établi Fils de Dieu investi de puissance, comme il convenait à sa nature propre. Cette nature ne peut être que la divinité. . . . Conformément à la nature spirituelle très sainte qui était en lui. . . .' Cf., e.g., Bengel, p. 491; Cornely, pp. 40–42; Huby, p. 45f. (The objection of Sanday and Headlam, p. 9, that this interpretation comes close to the teaching of Apollinarius would seem to rest on a misconception of the meaning of σάρξ in v. 3.)

[4] Cf. Michel, p. 38f; also Barrett, p. 18.

His resurrection) was accomplished. But we are inclined to think that the most probable explanation is that which (taking κατά as meaning 'according to') understands the phrase to refer to the Holy Spirit, who, as given by the exalted Christ, is the manifestation of His power and majesty, and so the guarantee of His having been appointed Son of God in might.[1] It may be that πνεῦμα ἁγιωσύνης simply reflects the Hebrew expression rûaḥ haqqōdeš:[2] this could be, whether the phrase is Paul's own or part of a pre-Pauline formula taken over by him. Or it may be that ἁγιωσύνη has the meaning 'sanctification' (cf. 2 Cor 7.1; 1 Th 3.13), and that Paul had specially in mind the sanctifying work of the Spirit (cf. chapter 8).[3] Even if πνεῦμα ἁγιωσύνης was used only as a stronger form of πνεῦμα ἅγιον, the thought of sanctification would not be far from Paul's mind in mentioning the Holy Spirit.[4]

[1] Cf., e.g., Chrysostom, col. 397 (. . . ἀπὸ τοῦ Πνεύματος οὖπερ ἐδίδου τοῖς πιστεύουσιν εἰς αὐτόν, καὶ δι' οὗ πάντας ἁγίους ἐποίει· διό φησι, Κατὰ Πνεῦμα ἁγιωσύνης · Θεοῦ γὰρ ἦν μόνου τὰ τοιαῦτα δῶρα χαρίζεσθαι); Augustine, col. 2063 ('. . . id est, quia Spiritus donum acceperunt post ejus resurrectionem . . .'); Aquinas, quoted below in n. 3; Leenhardt, p. 37; Bruce, p. 73.

[2] Found in Rabbinic literature. Cf. Ps 51.11 [MT: 13]; Isa 63.10f; 1QS 4.21; 8.16; 9.3; 1QH 7.6f; 9.32: also Test. Levi 18.7.

[3] Cf. Aquinas, p. 12f: 'Dicit ergo quod Christus sit Filius Dei in virtute, apparet secundum Spiritum sanctificationis, id est secundum quod dat Spiritum sanctificantem, quae quidem sanctificatio incoepit ex resurrectione mortuorum Iesu Christi Domini nostri, id est ex mortuis secundum illud Io. vii, 30: Nondum erat Spiritus datus quia nondum Iesus fuerat glorificatus: quod non sic intelligendum quod nullus, ante Christi resurrectionem, Spiritum sanctificantem acceperit, sed quia ex illo tempore, quo Christus resurrexit, incoepit copiosius et communius Spiritus sanctificationis dari.'

[4] To the possible objections to the interpretation preferred above to the effect that, had Paul intended a reference to the Holy Spirit, he would have used πνεῦμα ἅγιον, and that this interpretation fails to give to κατὰ πνεῦμα ἁγιωσύνης a sense properly parallel to that of κατὰ σάρκα, it may be replied that, if ἁγιωσύνης was not part of an underlying pre-Pauline formula, Paul may well have used it in order to bring out specially the thought of sanctification as the Holy Spirit's work, and the incommensurability of τοῦ γενομένου ἐκ σπέρματος Δαυίδ and τοῦ ὁρισθέντος υἱοῦ θεοῦ ἐν δυνάμει made a really strict parallelism impossible anyway.

On the problems of the two principal clauses of vv. 3 and 4 reference may be made to (in addition to the literature already cited): M. E. Boismard, 'Constitué Fils de Dieu', in RB 60 (1953), pp. 5–17; E. Schweizer, 'Röm 1.3f und der Gegensatz von Fleisch und Geist vor und bei Paulus', in EvTh 15 (1955), pp. 563–71; A. J. B. Higgins, 'The OT and some aspects of NT Christology', in CJT 6 (1960), pp. 200–10; L. C. Allen, 'The OT Background of (προ)ὁρίζειν in the NT', in NTS 17 (1970–71), pp. 104–8; E. Linnemann, 'Tradition und Interpretation in Röm 1.3f', in EvTh 31 (1971), pp. 264–75; J. D. G. Dunn, 'Jesus—Flesh and Spirit: an exposition of Rom 1.3–4', in JTS, n.s., 24 (1973), pp. 40–68.

Ἰησοῦ Χριστοῦ τοῦ κυρίου ἡμῶν stands in apposition to τοῦ υἱοῦ αὐτοῦ in v. 3.[1] Paul concludes his definition of the message of good news which he has been appointed to proclaim by adding the full title of Him who is its content. This title 'designates the glorified Christ, the incarnate Son of God, placed close to the Father and at the right hand of His majesty, to whom His believers render adoring worship'.[2] For a full discussion of κύριος as used of Christ see on 10.9. When, as here, a personal pronoun in the genitive is combined with it, the sense of personal commitment and allegiance is brought out.[3]

5. δι' οὗ. It was through the mediation of the risen and glorified Jesus Christ, the Lord, as Paul had special reason to acknowledge (cf. 1 Cor 9.1; 15.8; Gal 1.1, 12, 16; Acts 9.3ff; 22.6ff; 26.12ff), that the gift was received.

ἐλάβομεν. The most probable explanation of the use of the plural here is not that Paul had in mind the fact that all Christians had received grace,[4] nor yet that he was associating the other apostles with himself as recipients of grace and apostleship,[5] but that it is a writer's plural,[6] employed here perhaps as suiting the formal statement of authority (vv. 8ff, where the singular is used, are more personal).

χάριν καὶ ἀποστολήν may be understood either as denoting two distinct things, grace (i.e., God's undeserved favour which is the very basis of the Christian life) and apostleship (i.e., the office of apostle)[7] or as an example of hendiadys, denoting the grace, or undeserved favour, of apostleship, the office of

[1] The 'Iesu Christi Domini nostri' of the Vulgate is no doubt due to a mistaken connexion with 'resurrectione mortuorum': the ablative is required by the sense in agreement with 'de Filio suo'.

[2] Huby, p. 46 (my translation).

[3] Cf. W. Foerster, in *TWNT* 3, p. 1091f. The sense which the personal pronoun carries in this connexion was given classical expression in the first question and answer of the Heidelberg Catechism: 'Was ist dein einziger Trost im Leben und im Sterben? Dass ich mit Leib und Seele im Leben und im Sterben nicht mein, sondern meines treuen Heilandes Jesu Christi Eigentum bin, . . .'

[4] So, e.g., Augustine, col. 2092; Barrett, p. 21.

[5] So, e.g., Sanday and Headlam, p. 10; Schlatter, p. 22.

[6] Cf., e.g., Lagrange, p. 10; Leenhardt, p. 38f. For other examples in Paul's epistles see 3.8–9; 1 Cor 9.11ff; 2 Cor 1.12ff; (1 Th 2.18?) 1 Th 3.1f (cf. v. 5). The alternation between singular and plural in several of these passages is to be noted. On the writer's plural see further: K. Dick, *Der schriftstellerische Plural bei Paulus*, Halle, 1900; Roller, *Formular*, pp. 169ff (critical of Dick); BDF, § 280 (though ἐλάβομεν here is given a different explanation); Moule, *Idiom-Book*, p. 118f. Also Cranfield, 'Changes of Person and Number in Paul's Epistles', in M. D. Hooker and S. G. Wilson (ed.), *Paul and Paulinism*, London, 1982, pp. 283ff.

[7] So, e.g., Augustine, col. 2092; Pelagius, p. 9; Sanday and Headlam, p. 11; Lagrange, p. 10; Barrett, p. 21; JB.

apostle as a gracious gift undeserved by any human worth.[1] Of these the latter is surely to be preferred, since a statement that Paul has received grace through Christ is scarcely necessary here. What is apposite is simply a statement of his authority in respect of the Gentile world. That he should indicate, however, that he had not received this authority because of any merit of his own would be thoroughly appropriate.[2] With this verse Paul returns, after his definition of the gospel, to the subject of his apostleship introduced in v. 1. On χάρις see on v. 7. For its use in connexion with Paul's apostleship compare, for example, 12.3; 15.15; 1 Cor 3.10; Gal 2.9.

εἰς: 'for the purpose of bringing about'.

ὑπακοὴν πίστεως has been variously understood as meaning: (i) 'obedience to the faith' (i.e., to faith in the sense of *fides quae creditur*, the body of doctrine accepted); (ii) 'obedience to faith' (i.e., to the authority of faith); (iii) 'obedience to God's faithfulness attested in the gospel'; (iv) 'the obedience which faith works'; (v) 'the obedience required by faith'; (vi) 'believing obedience'; (vii) 'the obedience which consists in faith'.

The first three of these interpretations assume that the genitive is objective, the fourth and fifth that it is subjective, the sixth that it is adjectival, the last that it is a genitive of apposition or definition (cf. σημεῖον . . . περιτομῆς in 4.11). Of these the one which seems to us to suit best the structure of Paul's thought in Romans is (vii). The equivalence for Paul of faith in God and obedience to Him may be illustrated again and again from this epistle.[3] Paul's preaching is aimed at obtaining from his hearers true obedience to God, the essence of which is a responding to His message of good news with faith. It is also

---

[1] So, e.g., Chrysostom, col. 398 (τουτέστιν, Οὐχ ἡμεῖς αὐτὸ κατωρθώσαμεν τὸ γενέσθαι ἀπόστολοι · οὐδὲ γὰρ καμόντες πολλὰ καὶ πονέσαντες, τὴν ἀξίαν ταύτην ἐλάχομεν · ἀλλὰ χάριν ἐλάβομεν, καὶ τῆς ἄνωθεν δωρεᾶς τὸ κατόρθωμα γέγονεν) ; Calvin, p. 17; Barth, *Shorter*, p. 16; Bruce, p. 74.

[2] On hendiadys in the NT see BDF, § 442 (16). Two obvious examples are ἐπὶ τῇ συνέσει καὶ ταῖς ἀποκρίσεσιν αὐτοῦ in Lk 2.47 and περὶ ἐλπίδος καὶ ἀναστάσεως νεκρῶν in Acts 23.6. In classical literature such examples as Virgil's 'molemque et montes' and 'ferro et compagibus' (Aen. 1.61 and 293) are familiar.

[3] For example, compare 1.8 (ἡ πίστις ὑμῶν καταγγέλλεται ἐν ὅλῳ τῷ κόσμῳ) with 16.19 (ἡ γὰρ ὑμῶν ὑπακοὴ εἰς πάντας ἀφίκετο); 10.16a (ἀλλ' οὐ πάντες ὑπήκουσαν τῷ εὐαγγελίῳ); with 10.16b ('Ησαΐας γὰρ λέγει · κύριε, τίς ἐπίστευσεν τῇ ἀκοῇ ἡμῶν;); 11.23 (ἐὰν μὴ ἐπιμένωσιν τῇ ἀπιστίᾳ) with 11.30 (τῇ τούτων ἀπειθείᾳ) and 11.31 (οὕτως καὶ οὗτοι νῦν ἠπείθησαν); and 15.18 (οὐ γὰρ τολμήσω τι λαλεῖν ὧν οὐ κατειργάσατο Χριστὸς δι' ἐμοῦ εἰς ὑπακοὴν ἐθνῶν) with the verse we are considering.

true to say that to make the decision of faith is an act of obedience toward God and also that true faith by its very nature includes in itself the sincere desire and will to obey God in all things.[1] On πίστις see further on vv. 8, 16 and 17.

ἐν πᾶσιν τοῖς ἔθνεσιν: 'among all the Gentiles'. It has sometimes been maintained that ἔθνη should here be taken in its proper inclusive sense as meaning 'nations';[2] but, if that were its meaning, the ἐν οἷς in v. 6 would seem to be pointless, and it is surely natural to understand it here in the light of Paul's special commission to the Gentiles (cf., e.g., 11.13f; Gal 2.8f).

ὑπὲρ τοῦ ὀνόματος αὐτοῦ is better understood as meaning 'for the sake of His name' in the sense of 'for the glory of His name'[3] (i.e., in order that He Himself may be known and glorified) than as meaning 'in His name',[4] or 'on His behalf'.[5] It is a reminder that the true end of the preaching of the gospel and of the winning of men to faith is not just the good of those to whom the preaching is directed, but also—and above all—the glorification of Christ, of God.[6]

6. ἐν οἷς ἐστε καὶ ὑμεῖς κλητοὶ Ἰησοῦ Χριστοῦ is, of course, grammatically a relative clause dependent on ἔθνεσιν, but, as far as the thought is concerned, it is really parenthetic; for a statement about the people addressed is unexpected before the datives of v. 7 and, placed where it is, disturbs the flow of the prescript. If κλητοὶ Ἰησοῦ Χριστοῦ is taken closely with the preceding words, the point intended must presumably be that the Roman Christians too (who are in some sense ἐν τοῖς ἔθνεσιν) are κλητοὶ Ἰησοῦ Χριστοῦ as well as Paul (described as κλητὸς ἀπόστολος in v. 1).[7] But there seems to be no reason for inserting this just here: the natural place for it would surely be after πᾶσιν τοῖς οὖσιν ἐν ʽΡώμῃ. We should probably therefore put a comma after ὑμεῖς, and understand the words to mean: 'among whom are you also, you who are called . . .' In this case, what is emphasized is that the Roman Christians

---

[1] Cf., inter al., Althaus, p. 7; Schlatter, p. 22 (specially interesting and illuminating is his statement to the effect that it is only when God's message is replaced by a doctrine offering instruction about God that a gap between faith and obedience appears); Barth, CD II/1, pp. 26 and 37 (= KD II/1, pp. 27 and 39f).

[2] e.g. by Gifford: see also Michel, p. 42.

[3] So, e.g., Bauer, s.v. ὄνομα I.4.c.θ. Cf. Ps 106.8; Ezek 20.9, 14.

[4] So, e.g., Pelagius (p. 9), who compares Jn 20.21b and Mt 10.40a.

[5] So, e.g., Barrett, p. 21.

[6] Cf. especially 15.7 and see on that verse and also on 1.21 (οὐχ ὡς θεὸν ἐδόξασαν).

[7] This 'as well as Paul' would seem to be the significance of the καί before ὑμεῖς.

also are ἐν τοῖς ἔθνεσιν, and a plausible motive for inserting the words just here is not far to seek, namely, Paul's desire to indicate that the Roman church, though not founded by him, is nevertheless within the sphere of his apostolic commission, and that he therefore has a right to address it in the way he is doing. The words ἐν οἷς ἐστε καὶ ὑμεῖς are very often taken to be a clear indication that the Roman church was at this time predominantly Gentile;[1] but they could quite as well simply refer to its geographical situation in the midst of the Gentile world.[2] It would be reasonable for Paul to regard even a predominantly Jewish church, if situated at the heart of the Roman Empire, as within his sphere of responsibility. This verse certainly does not by itself settle the question of the racial composition of the Roman church. On this question see pp. 17–21. The members of the church are 'called of Jesus Christ', i.e., called by Him (to insist, as some do,[3] that Ἰησοῦ Χριστοῦ must be taken as a possessive genitive is surely, especially in view of the proximity of the grammatically closely parallel ἀγαπητοῖς θεοῦ in v. 7, doctrinaire). On κλητός see further both on v. 1 and on v. 7.

7. πᾶσιν τοῖς οὖσιν ἐν Ῥώμῃ ἀγαπητοῖς θεοῦ, κλητοῖς ἁγίοις. Those to whom the letter is addressed are at last named. It is to all the Christians in Rome, not just to the leaders or to the people greeted by name in chapter 16. The word πᾶσιν is emphatic, and the emphasis is reiterated by the πάντων in v. 8 (cf. 15.33). The words ἀγαπητοῖς θεοῦ, κλητοῖς ἁγίοις, which are substantially equivalent to 'Christians', must be connected closely with οὖσιν ἐν Ῥώμῃ (on the variant reading which omits ἐν Ῥώμῃ see pp. 6–11); for Paul is, of course, not addressing all the inhabitants of Rome, but all in Rome who are Christians. The adjective ἀγαπητός[4] is most frequently used

---

[1] So, e.g., Sanday and Headlam, p. 12; Barrett, p. 22.

[2] Had the thought been of the church's being made up mostly of Gentiles, ἐξ ὧν (cf., e.g., οἱ ἐξ Ἰσραήλ in 9.6) would probably have been more natural than ἐν οἷς (cf. Schlatter, p. 23). For the geographical sense cf. Acts 21.21: τοὺς κατὰ τὰ ἔθνη πάντας Ἰουδαίους.

[3] e.g. Sanday and Headlam, p. 12; Lagrange, p. 11; Barrett, p. 22; and cf. NEB. It should not be assumed that the fact that elsewhere in the Pauline epistles it is (where the subject of the action is explicit) God the Father rather than Christ who is said to call, must mean that Paul avoided on principle speaking of Christ as calling. It is significant that he can, for example, refer both to God's love (e.g. 8.39) and to Christ's love (e.g. 8.35), both to God's grace (e.g. 5.15) and to Christ's grace (ibid.), and can name together the Father and Christ as the source of grace and peace (as he does in v. 7).

[4] The variant reading ἐν ἀγάπῃ (G d* vgam Ambst Pelag) for ἀγαπητοῖς is not likely to be original. It can scarcely have originated in unconscious assimilation to Jude 21. Most probably it is to be connected with the

in the NT with reference to the love of Christians for their
fellow Christians (so in 12.19; 16.5, 8, 9, 12), but it is probably
true to say that where it is so used the thought of the love of
God for sinful men, which is the basis of the love of Christians
for each other, is not far away. In 11.28 it is used with
reference to God's love for unbelieving Israel. The perfect
passive participle ἠγαπημένος is several times used of God's
love much as ἀγαπητός is used here (so 9.25; Col 3.12; 1 Th 1.4;
2 Th 2.13). The thought of God's love as the basis of the
existence of Christians is of course quite often expressed by
means of ἀγάπη and ἀγαπᾶν (e.g., 5.8; 8.39). It is significant
that Paul mentions not their love for God but that which is
fundamental—God's love for them, God's choice of them.[1]

The word κλητός, already used in vv. 1 and 6,[2] also emphasizes the divine action. They are κλητοὶ ἅγιοι, i.e., ἅγιοι by
virtue of having been called.[3] The NT idea of God's calling has
a significant background in the OT (see, for example, Isa 49.1;
50.2; 65.12; 66.4; Jer 7.13: compare also Prov 1.24, where the
reference is to Wisdom's calling) and also in later Judaism
(particularly interesting are: 1QM 3.2 ('On the trumpets
calling the congregation they shall write, *The Called of God*');
4.9–11 ('When they set out for battle they shall write, on the
first standard *Congregation of God*, . . . on the seventh standard
The Called of God, . . .'); CD 2.11 ('And in all of them He raised
for Himself men called by name, that a remnant might be
left to the Land, . . .'); 4.3f ('The *sons of Zadok* are the elect
of Israel, the men called by name who shall stand at the end of
days)).[4] As used by Paul, καλεῖν denotes God's effectual
calling: the κλητοί are those who have been called effectually,
who have been summoned by God and have also responded to
His summons.

variant which omits the reference to Rome (it is interesting that G
attests both variants): πᾶσιν τοῖς οὖσιν ἐν ἀγάπῃ θεοῦ would appear to be
a generalizing substitute for πᾶσιν τοῖς οὖσιν ἐν ῾Ρώμῃ ἀγαπητοῖς θεοῦ, and
the Latin readings which combine 'in caritate (or 'dilectione') Dei' with
'Romae' the result of the re-introduction of the reference to Rome into
the corrupted text. See pp. 6–11.

[1] Cf. Augustine, col. 2093, who adds the comment: 'Prior enim dilexit
nos ante omnia merita, ut et nos eum dilecti diligeremus'.

[2] On Paul's repetition of κλητός in this paragraph Chrysostom
comments (col. 399): Τοῦτο δὲ οὐ περιττολογῶν ποιεῖ, ἀλλὰ βουλόμενος αὐτοὺς
τῆς εὐεργεσίας ἀναμνῆσαι.

[3] Cf. Augustine, col. 2093: '*Vocatis* autem *sanctis*, non ita intelligendum
est, tamquam ideo vocati sunt, quia sancti erant; sed ideo sancti effecti,
quia vocati sunt'; and Pelagius, p. 10: 'Sanctis vocatione Dei, non
merito sancti[tatis]'.

[4] Translations from Vermes, pp. 127, 129, 98 and 100 respectively.
The Hebrew phrases are ḳerû'ê 'ēl and ḳerî'ê (haš)šēm.

The term ἅγιος also has a significant history. The root meaning of *ḳāḏôš* seems to be 'marked off', 'separate','withdrawn from ordinary use'. Whereas in the paganism surrounding Israel it was applied predominantly to objects, places and human persons, and only rarely to the actual deity, in the OT it is chiefly of God Himself that it is used, and the holiness of places, objects and human persons is hardly ever conceived in a merely impersonal, mechanical sense, but is thought of as derived from the personal will of God and therefore always involving an encounter with the personal demands of the living God who claims the absolute allegiance of His people. It is this difference, and not simply its ethical content, as is sometimes alleged, which distinguishes the OT conception of holiness from the pagan. The 'holiness' of God denotes the absolute authority with which He confronts men. But this authority was the authority of Him who had revealed Himself as merciful and righteous; and under the influence of the prophets the ethical element in 'the holy' was strongly emphasized. The term 'holy', applied to Israel, expressed the fact that they were God's special people. Their holiness derived from God's gracious choice, and it involved the obligation on their part to seek to be and do what was in accordance with the revealed character of their God by obedience to His law (see especially the 'Holiness Code' of Lev 17–26). Paul's use of ἅγιος rests squarely upon this OT foundation. Those who have been called by the holy God are holy in virtue of His calling and are thereby claimed for holiness of life (see on εἰς ἁγιασμόν in 6.19, 22).[1]

The view that Paul's combination of κλητός and ἅγιος (cf. 1 Cor 1.2) may have been suggested by the expression κλητὴ ἁγία which occurs in the LXX (Exod 12.16; ten times in Lev 23; Num 28.25)[2] does not seem particularly likely; for the combination was natural enough to have suggested itself to him independently.[3] The fact that Paul does not here make use of the word ἐκκλησία has been noted; but it is probably

[1] See further: O. Procksch and K. G. Kuhn, in *TWNT* I, pp. 87ff; W. Eichrodt, *Theology of the Old Testament* I, Eng. tr., London, 1961, pp. 270–82; also bibliography in Bauer, s.v. ἅγιος.

[2] See Sanday and Headlam, p. 12f; Huby, p. 50 (where it is put forward more cautiously). The expression κλητὴ ἁγία represents *miḳrā' ḳōḏeš* (RV: 'an holy convocation') which the translators seem not to have understood.

[3] Since the word κλητός was already in Paul's mind and he apparently wanted to emphasize it as linking himself and those to whom he was writing (vv. 1 and 6), while ἅγιοι was a thoroughly obvious word for him to use in addressing the members of a church (cf. 1 Cor 1.2; 2 Cor 1.1; Eph 1.1; Phil 1.1; Col 1.2).

unwise to make much of it[1]. It occurs in Romans only in chapter 16 (five times). It is in 1 and 2 Corinthians that it occurs most frequently in the Pauline corpus, the occurrences being specially widely dispersed in 1 Corinthians. It is perhaps possible that, having anticipated the address by a statement in the second person plural in v. 6, Paul felt it more natural to keep to the plural and not introduce a collective noun.

χάρις ὑμῖν καὶ εἰρήνη ἀπὸ θεοῦ πατρὸς ἡμῶν καὶ κυρίου Ἰησοῦ Χριστοῦ. Exactly the same formula is used in 1 Cor 1.3; 2 Cor 1.2; Gal 1.3; Eph 1.2; Phil 1.2; Philem 3 (also, without ἡμῶν in 2 Th 1.2, and without ὑμῖν and with the addition of τοῦ σωτῆρος ἡμῶν in Tit 1.4)[2]. Instead of the ordinary Greek greeting χαίρειν (sc. λέγει), which is found in the NT in Acts 15.23; 23.26; Jas. 1.1, Paul uses the direct form of a wish, χάρις ὑμῖν (sc. ἔστω) καὶ εἰρήνη,[3] which has the effect of leaving the nominative Παῦλος, κ.τ.λ. and the dative πᾶσιν τοῖς οὖσιν, κ.τ.λ. hanging. By using χάρις at this point Paul makes the third part of the epistolary prescript into the vehicle of a profound theological and evangelical meaning; for χάρις, which in the LXX (in the books of the Jewish canon) almost always represents ḥēn, in the NT characteristically denotes—this is the meaning which it has here—God's undeserved love revealed in Christ and so may be said to sum up the whole gospel in a single word. It occurs twenty-four times in Romans (besides v. 5 and the present verse, in 3.24; 4.4, 16; 5.2, 15 (twice), 17, 20, 21; 6.1, 14, 15, 17; 7.25; 11.5, 6 (three times); 12.3, 6; 15.15; 16.20);[4] and its various nuances and emphases will call for comment later on.[5]

[1] See p. 22.

[2] The shorter formulae in Col 1.2 and 1 Th 1.1 are, as one would expect, assimilated in many MSS. to the fuller form which we have here.

[3] While it is perhaps probable that the salutation of the Pauline prescript was based on the Semitic greeting šālôm (which allowed the possibility of expansion by the association of other substantives with it) rather than on the (practically invariable) χαίρειν of the Greek letter-formula (cf. Roller, *Formular*, p. 61; W. Foerster, in *TWNT* 2, p. 142, n. 78), the possibility that Paul in using the word χάρις here (even if not aware of the linguistic connexion between this word and the χαίρειν which would be expected in a Greek letter at this point) was at least conscious of the similarity of sound between the two words, and expected his readers also to be conscious of it, can certainly not be ruled out. We may also recognize the possibility that the Pauline salutation had first been developed for liturgical use (whether by others or by Paul himself), and that its employment as an epistolary greeting was secondary (cf. E. Lohmeyer, in *ZNW* 26 (1927), p. 161f).

[4] Also in 16.24, which is not likely to be part of the original text of Romans.

[5] On χάρις reference should be made to H. Conzelmann and W. Zimmerli, in *TWNT* 9, pp. 363-93, and to the many works listed by them on p. 363, to which should certainly be added Barth, *CD* (see the

With regard to εἰρήνη, 'peace' was of course the common greeting of the Semitic world (cf., e.g., Gen 43.23; Judg 19.20; 1 Sam 25.6), and was used in epistolary salutations (cf., e.g., LXX Dan 4.37c; Theod. Dan 6.26; Tanchuma, *wayyišlaḥ* 39a: other examples are given in SB 3, p. 25). Sometimes in the opening greeting of a letter another noun was associated with it: so the Pauline combination is not without antecedents. In 2 Macc 1.1 χαίρειν and εἰρήνην ἀγαθήν are combined in an epistolary salutation, and in 2 Bar. 78.2 we find 'mercy and peace'. It has sometimes been suggested that Paul's χάρις καὶ εἰρήνη may owe something to Num 6.24ff; but it is to be noted that there, though the RV 'be gracious' represents the Hebrew verb that is cognate with *ḥen* (the word rendered in the LXX by χάρις), the LXX has ἐλεῆσαι. In any case χάρις and εἰρήνη together well express the sum of evangelical blessings. εἰρήνη occurs in Romans also in 2.10; 3.17; 5.1; 8.6; 14.17, 19; 15.13, 33; 16.20, and it is clear that it has differing shades of meaning in different passages. It is likely that the thought which here is uppermost is that of peace with God (cf. 5.1–11, which includes, as well as εἰρήνην ἔχομεν πρὸς τὸν θεόν in v. 1, the occurrences of καταλλάσσεσθαι and καταλλαγή in vv. 10 and 11),[1] though Paul may also have had in mind the blessings which result from reconciliation with God.[2] On εἰρήνη see further G. von Rad and W. Foerster, in *TWNT* 2, pp. 398ff, and see also the notes on the other occurrences of the word in Romans cited above. The words which follow (ἀπὸ θεοῦ, κ.τ.λ.) indicate the source from which Paul looks for grace and peace for the Roman Christians. No distinction between God as the source and Christ as the means or agent is expressed in this verse, though there are features of the preceding verses (e.g. the δι' οὗ of v. 5) which might perhaps be said to suggest it (cf. 1 Cor 8.6). The striking juxtaposition of God and Christ while clearly not, by itself a proof that Paul believed Christ to be divine in the fullest sense, is a strong pointer in that direction; and it has of course to be seen alongside many other pointers in the same direction to be found in Romans—we have already met more than one in these first seven verses—and also in the other Pauline epistles. The words πατρὸς ἡμῶν anticipate the teaching of 8.14–17 (see notes there). On the title κύριος (here without the genitive pronoun) see on v. 4 and on 10.9.

indices of the various volumes s.v. 'grace' or *KD* Registerband s.v. 'Gnade').

[1] Cf. Augustine, col. 2093: 'Pax vero ipsa qua reconciliamur Deo'.

[2] On χάρις ὑμῖν καὶ εἰρήνη as a whole Michel's comment is very apt: 'Im Gruss wird der Inhalt der Botschaft als Segenswunsch der Gemeinde zugesprochen' (p. 44).

II

PAUL AND THE ROMAN CHURCH
(1.8–16a)

The first sentence (after the protocol) of an ancient Greek letter was very often of a pious nature, informing the recipient of the writer's prayer to the gods on his behalf. The prayer was sometimes a thanksgiving, but more often a petition: it was usually concerned with the recipient's health. Thus, formally, the beginning of Romans follows contemporary convention. But the character and content of Paul's thanksgiving are very far from being conventional. The subject of it is not the health or outward prosperity of those to whom he is writing, but the fact that their faith is everywhere reported. He goes on to assure them in an extremely solemn and emphatic manner of his unceasing prayer for them, in which is included the prayer that God may permit him to visit them. He explains that he desires to see them in order that he may be able to impart to them a spiritual blessing for their strengthening; but, recognizing as a true apostle of Christ that what he has just said, while true, only tells part of the relevant truth, he brings out in v. 12—to regard this as a mere *captatio benevolentiae* is quite uncalled for!—the reciprocal nature of the benefit to be expected. Verse 13 is intended, it seems, to guard against the possibility that some in the Roman church may think that his not having already come to them reflects a lack of will on his part. Verses 14–16a are a solemnly expressed declaration of the obligation which Paul recognizes as laid upon him as apostle of the Gentiles and of his eagerness to preach the gospel, in accordance with it, to the Christians in Rome in particular, in confirmation of the reality of which eagerness he adds the challenging personal confession, 'For I am not ashamed of the gospel'.

⁸First, I thank my God through Jesus Christ for you all, that *the news of* your faith is being published abroad in all the world. ⁹For God, whom I serve in my spirit in *the proclamation of* the gospel of his Son, is my witness, how unceasingly I make mention of you ¹⁰always in my prayers, asking if by any means now at last I may succeed in coming to you, if it be God's will. ¹¹For I long to see you, in order that I may impart to you some spiritual gift, so that you

may be strengthened, ¹²or rather in your midst to be comforted together with you, each through the other's faith, both yours and mine. ¹³But I do not want you to be ignorant, brethren, of the fact that I have often purposed to come to you—but up till the present I have been prevented—in order that I might obtain some fruit among you also even as *I have done* in the rest of the Gentile world. ¹⁴I am a debtor both to the Greeks and to the barbarians, both to the wise and to the foolish: ¹⁵so my eager desire is to preach the gospel to you also who are in Rome. ¹⁶ᵃFor I am not ashamed of the gospel.

8. Πρῶτον μέν is used here, as in 3.2 and 1 Cor 11.18, without any further item following. For this see Bauer, s.v. πρῶτος 2.b; BDF, § 447(4). Possibly it was intended in some such sense as 'From the very outset' or 'Above all';¹ but quite probably Paul meant to make a further point in continuation, and then omitted to do so.

εὐχαριστῶ. Compare 1 Cor 1.4; Phil 1.3; Col 1.3; 1 Th 1.2; 2 Th 1.3; Philem 4: in Galatians the thanksgiving is significantly omitted, while in 2 Corinthians and Ephesians it is in the form of a 'blessing' or *bᵉrākāh*. A prayer to the gods for the correspondent's health is found at the beginning of many papyrus letters:² thanksgivings occur much less frequently.

τῷ θεῷ μου strikes a personal note which is reminiscent of some passages in the Psalms (e.g. Ps 3.7; 5.2; 7.1, 3; 13.3; 22.1, 2, 10). Paul only rarely calls God 'my God' in this way—in Phil 1.3 and Philem 4, which are similar contexts to this,³ and otherwise only in 2 Cor 12.21 and Phil 4.19.

διὰ Ἰησοῦ Χριστοῦ. Cf. 7.25; Col 3.17 (also Eph 5.20: εὐχαριστοῦντες . . . ἐν ὀνόματι τοῦ κυρίου ἡμῶν Ἰησοῦ Χριστοῦ τῷ θεῷ). Christ is Mediator not only of God's approach to men (as, e.g., in v. 5), but also, as the risen and exalted Lord, of their responding approach to God in worship. Origen comments: 'Agere autem Deo gratias, hoc est sacrificium laudis offerre; et ideo addit *per Jesum Christum*, velut per Pontificem magnum'.⁴

περί⁵ πάντων ὑμῶν: not just for some of them, but for them all (cf. πᾶσιν in v. 7).⁶

¹ Examples of πρὸ μὲν πάντων and other similar expressions used in this way without any answering δέ are common in the openings of papyrus letters (cf., e.g., P. Tebt. 412 and 418; BGU 2.423 and 632).
² Cf., e.g., Πρὸ μὲν πάντων εὔχομαί σε ὑγιαίνειν in BGU 2.423 and also 632.
³ Also, according to some MSS., in 1 Cor 1.4.
⁴ Col. 854.
⁵ On the use of περί see BDF, § 229 (1). There is a variant ὑπέρ here as in a number of other places where περί is similarly used (e.g. Col 1.3).
⁶ Origen's comment (col. 854) is interesting: '. . . observans invenies quod ubi dicit *pro omnibus* se gratias agere, culpas aliquas graves aut

ἡ πίστις ὑμῶν: that is, the fact of your faith, the fact that you believe. Nothing is said here about their faith's being specially great, deep or strong, or in any other way superior to that of other Christians, though commentators of very different backgrounds have agreed in discovering some such suggestion in the text.[1] There is no justification for reading it into the statement that their faith καταγγέλλεται ἐν ὅλῳ τῷ κόσμῳ which means simply that the fact that they believe, the fact that also in the imperial capital there is a church of Jesus Christ, is being published abroad far and wide.[2] This fact in itself is enough to call forth his thanksgiving. And the implication of his thanking God for it is that he recognizes it to be God's work, God's gift.[3]

9. μάρτυς γάρ μού ἐστιν ὁ θεός. Compare 2 Cor 1.23; 11.31; Gal 1.20; Phil 1.8; 1 Th 2.5, 10; and also Rom 9.1; 2 Cor 2.17; 12.19. Here, as seems also to be the case in the other instances of oaths in Paul's letters, the statement made is one the truth of which the readers cannot prove for themselves, since it concerns his inward life.[4] The question as to how Paul's oaths stand in relation to Mt 5.33–37 and Jas 5.12 has, naturally, often been asked. The traditional answer that the very fact that Paul does swear is itself one indication that Mt 5.33ff and Jas 5.12 are not to be understood as forbidding all oaths without exception seems to us to be along the right lines.[5] The fact that he appeals to God as witness here is evidence of the

---

probra in eos non exaggerat; ubi autem notat aliquos vel arguit, non addit ad gratiarum actionem, quod *pro omnibus* gratias agat, sicut et ad Corinthios vel ad Colossenses. Ad Galatas vero omnino nec ponit gratiarum actionem . . .'

[1] e.g. Cornely, p. 55f; Barrett, p. 24 (' "Your faith" does not mean "the Christian faith *which* you, in common with all other Christians, hold", for this would be pointless in a thanksgiving; but "the faith *as* you hold it", that is, the understanding, constancy, and charity with which you hold it'—surely a strange piece of argumentation); Bruce, p. 75 ('News that he has received about the high and renowned quality of their faith calls forth deep thanksgiving from Paul, . . .').

[2] ἐν ὅλῳ τῷ κόσμῳ is no doubt to be recognized as an instance of hyperbole (cf. 1 Th 1.8).

[3] Cf. Calvin, p. 20: 'If thanksgiving is the acknowledgment of a benefit, whoever thanks God for faith acknowledges that it is His gift'.

[4] So in 2 Cor 1.23 it is Paul's inner motive (φειδόμενος ὑμῶν) which is in question. Note that in 1 Th 2.5 a distinction is drawn between what the Thessalonians themselves know and what is beyond the scope of their verification, while in 1 Th 2.10 we may suppose Paul's intention to be to appeal to his readers' own knowledge as witness so far as it reaches, and to call God as witness to the truth where it is beyond their ken.

[5] Cf., e.g., Augustine, *De mend.* 15; Aquinas, p. 16f; Calvin, p. 21f; also Calvin, *Inst.* 2.8.26–27; and Article 39 of the Church of England.

great importance he attaches to their knowing that he prays for them continually.

ᾧ λατρεύω ἐν τῷ πνεύματί μου ἐν τῷ εὐαγγελίῳ τοῦ υἱοῦ αὐτοῦ. The relative clause is by no means a mere embellishment, but is of real significance in connexion with Paul's oath; for it points to the fact that his praying for them is an integral part of his service of God and therefore something about which it is specially fitting for him to appeal to God to bear witness. The latter part of the clause indicates the sphere in which he is active in the service of God:[1] his sphere of service is the great work of publishing the message of good news concerning God's Son (the genitive τοῦ υἱοῦ is objective: cf. περὶ τοῦ υἱοῦ αὐτοῦ in v. 3). In 15.16 he speaks of his service in cultic terms, and the verb used in the present verse (λατρεύειν) is one which in the LXX, wherever it is used in the books of the Hebrew canon in connexion with God, denotes cultic service (though this includes cultic service understood more profoundly in the light of the prophets' teaching). So it would seem that Kuss is justified in saying that by his use of λατρεύειν Paul designates his service 'as worship, as the fulfilment of his glorification of God' ('als Gottesdienst, als den Vollzug seiner "Gottes-verehrung" ').[2] But to speak of 'priestly service', as some commentators do, is to go too far; for cultic service was not limited to the functions of priests, and it is possible that in 15.16 Paul had in mind the service of the Levite rather than that of the priest.[3] The word 'serve' would seem an adequate translation of λατρεύειν. The phrase ἐν τῷ πνεύματί μου is difficult, and has been very variously interpreted:

(i) as referring to the Spirit of God dwelling in him (e.g. W. G. Kümmel, *Römer 7 und die Bekehrung des Paulus*, Leipzig, 1929, p. 33);

(ii) as indicating a spiritual (Christian) service contrasted with a carnal (pagan or Jewish) service (e.g. Chrysostom, col. 403);

(iii) as meaning 'wholeheartedly' (e.g. Pelagius, p. 10: 'in toto corde et prompta deuotione');

(iv) as meaning 'sincerely' (e.g. Calvin, p. 22: 'from the heart ... with sincere devotion of heart . . .' in contrast with a mere external appearance);

(v) as indicating 'the organ of service', that by using which he accomplishes his service (e.g., Sanday and Headlam, p. 20);

(vi) as indicating that his whole person is engaged (e.g.

---

[1] It seems better to understand it thus than as indicating that by which he serves (or in which his service consists).

[2] p. 17.

[3] See on 15.16, and also on λατρείαν in 12.1.

Michel, p. 46f: 'dieser . . . Dienst beansprucht den Geist, damit den ganzen Menschen, sein Denken, Wollen und Handeln');

(vii) as meaning 'in my spirit', with reference to his praying as being the inward side of his apostolic service contrasted with the outward side consisting of his preaching, etc. (e.g. Althaus, p. 10: ' "Dienst am Evangelium" tut er nicht nur durch die nach aussen tretenden Akte der Verkündigung und Seelsorge, sondern auch "in seinem Geiste", innerlich durch das Reden des Herzens mit Gott und die Fürbitte für die Gemeinden').

Of these the last seems best to suit the context, and it does no violence to the Greek. It should therefore be accepted as the most probable interpretation. We understand the clause then as referring to one part of Paul's service of God in the promulgation of the gospel, namely, that part which he fulfils inwardly and secretly, his constant prayer for the churches.

ὡς[1] ἀδιαλείπτως μνείαν ὑμῶν ποιοῦμαι. The expression μνείαν ποιεῖσθαι with a genitive, meaning 'to mention', which occurs also in classical Greek (e.g. Plato, *Phdr.* 254a), is used in the NT only, as here, of mentioning someone in one's prayers (Eph 1.16; 1 Th 1.2; Philem 4).[2]

10. It is difficult to decide whether to connect πάντοτε ἐπὶ τῶν προσευχῶν μου with the preceding, or with the following, words. The awkwardness of having two adverbs so nearly synonymous as ἀδιαλείπτως and πάντοτε in the same clause tells quite strongly in favour of placing the comma at the end of v. 9; but perhaps the considerations which favour putting it after προσευχῶν μου are rather stronger. There is, first, the point that, if the comma is placed at the end of v. 9, there is then nothing in the last clause of that verse to indicate that μνείαν ποιοῦμαι refers to mentioning in prayer. And, secondly, while it is perfectly understandable that Paul should say that he always mentions the Roman Christians when he prays, it seems questionable whether he would be so likely to say that whenever he prays he always asks that he may be allowed to visit them (did this particular desire really occupy quite so prominent a place in his thoughts?). And, with regard to the argument on the other side, it may be said that the two adverbs are not exactly synonymous, since ἀδιαλείπτως brings

---

[1] Lietzmann's view (p. 28) that ὡς here is used for ὅτι does not commend itself: it is rather to be taken in its sense 'how' and connected closely with the following adverb.

[2] Examples of its use in connexion with pagan prayer are to be found in P. Lond. 42.6 (2nd cent. B.C.); Epigr. Gr. 983.2ff (1st cent. B.C.); BGU 632.5 (2nd cent. A.D.).

out specifically the idea of uninterruptedness. But absolute certainty about this question seems impossible.

After δεόμενος one might have expected ὅπως (as in Acts 8.24) or ἵνα (as in Lk 22.32). By the use of εἴ πως the special degree of submissiveness to the divine will which characterized the prayer is indicated.[1] Compare the use of εἰ ἄρα in Acts 8.22.

ἤδη ποτέ: 'now at last'. The ποτέ expresses the feeling that there has been enough time of waiting.[2] Compare Phil 4.10; also Arrian, *Epict.* 3.24.9 (οὐκ ἀπογαλακτίσομεν ἤδη ποθ' ἑαυτούς...;).[3]

εὐοδωθήσομαι. Lagrange's contention (p. 14) that the passive carries an implicit reference to the divine action should not, in view of the verb's usage,[4] be pressed. The thought of an actual journey is not present in the verb which is used here metaphorically.

ἐν τῷ θελήματι τοῦ θεοῦ. Compare 15.32; Acts 18.21; 1 Cor 4.19; 16.7; Heb 6.3; Jas 4.15. That Jews of Paul's day were well aware of the truth that 'man proposes, God disposes' goes without saying; but the common use of such formulae as 'God willing', 'if God wills', seems to have been less characteristic of Judaism than of the ancient pagan world.[5]

ἐλθεῖν πρὸς ὑμᾶς. An explanation of Paul's desire to visit the Roman church follows in vv. 11–15. In 15.24 a further consideration is referred to. That it is important is not to be doubted; but to brush aside the reasons indicated in chapter 1 as merely 'reasons of a sort' and to insist that 'the basic reason' is his need to use Rome as a base for his Spanish mission, as Barrett does,[6] is surely arbitrary.

11. ἐπιποθῶ: 'I long' (cf. 2 Cor 5.2; 9.14; Phil 1.8; 2.26; 1 Th 3.6; 2 Tim 1.4).

ἵνα τι μεταδῶ χάρισμα ὑμῖν πνευματικόν. He longs to see them in order that he may impart to them, share among them (for the use of μεταδιδόναι compare 12.8 (and see note there); Lk 3.11; Eph 4.28; 1 Th 2.8), a spiritual gift. The noun χάρισμα

---

[1] Cf. Lagrange, p. 14. εἴ πως occurs also in 11.14 and Phil 3.11, but in neither of these verses is it preceded by a verb of requesting.

[2] The objection of Sanday and Headlam, p. 20, to the AV and RV rendering 'now at length' that it does not translate the ποτέ is hardly fair. See LSJ, s.v. πότε III.1.b. and 2.

[3] Cited by Lietzmann, p. 28.

[4] See Bauer, s.v. εὐοδόω.

[5] Though this does not mean that there is anything positively un-Jewish in Paul's use of this formula here. See J. H. Ropes, *A Critical and Exegetical Commentary on the Epistle of St. James*, Edinburgh, 1916, p. 279f; M. Dibelius, *Der Brief des Jakobus*, Göttingen, ⁸1957, p. 215, and Ergänzungsheft, p. 21; G. Schrenk, in *TWNT* 3, p. 46; SB, 3, p. 758.

[6] p. 25.

is used in Romans in several different ways: (i) to denote
generally God's gracious gift in Jesus Christ (5.15, 16: it is
probably to be understood similarly in 6.23); (ii) in the plural
to denote the gracious gifts bestowed by God on Israel (11.29);
(iii) in 12.6, to denote a special gift or endowment bestowed on
a member of the Church by God in order that it may be used
by that member in His service and in the service of men.
Examples—not an exhaustive list—of χαρίσματα in this last
sense are mentioned in 12.6–8 and in 1 Cor 12, and Paul's most
extensive teaching on the subject is in 1 Cor 12–14. He connects these gifts closely with the Spirit—so much so, that he
sometimes uses the neuter plural of the adjective πνευματικός
by itself to denote them (e.g. in 1 Cor 14.1). It is the Holy
Spirit who mediates them to the members of the Church. The
present occurrence of χάρισμα is often understood as an
example of this third usage; but it is probably better to take
the word here in a more general sense as denoting a blessing
or benefit to be bestowed on the Christians in Rome by God
through Paul's presence.[1] There is an intentional indefiniteness
(τι . . . χάρισμα), due to the fact that he has not yet learned
by personal encounter what blessing they particularly stand
in need of.

According to Michel,[2] Paul is here seeking to legitimize
himself in the eyes of the πνευματικοί in the Roman church as
being himself also a πνευματικός, though without admitting
the validity of their claims. But, while it is to be admitted that
there are places in this epistle which reflect concern about the
dangers of a false spirituality rooted in alien Hellenistic ideas
similar to that with which Paul had to contend in Corinth, it
may be doubted whether he had these πνευματικοί in mind
when he used the adjective πνευματικός here. He may well
have introduced the word in qualification of χάρισμα, because
he believed that the blessing which he hoped God would
bestow on the Roman Christians through his coming to them
would be mediated by the Holy Spirit, or—perhaps more
probably—simply to indicate in a more general way the sort
of blessing he had in mind.[3]

εἰς τὸ στηριχθῆναι ὑμᾶς. Paul's hope is that by the imparting
of the gift they may be strengthened, that is, strengthened as
Christians, strengthened in faith and obedience. For the use of
στηρίζειν compare 16.25; also Lk 22.32; Acts 18.23; 1 Th 3.2, 13;

[1] Cf. Chevallier, Esprit, 143–5.
[2] p. 48.
[3] Cf. the use of πνευματικός in 15.27.

2 Th 2.17; 3.3; 1 Pet 5.10.[1] On the articular infinitive in the accusative used with εἰς see BDF, § 402 (2); Burton, *MT*, §§ 409–13; Moule, *Idiom-Book*, pp. 140 and 141.

12. τοῦτο δέ ἐστιν occurs in the NT only here. It differs from the common τοῦτ᾽ ἔστιν (meaning 'that is to say'), in that it does not simply repeat in different language what has just been said, but actually amends the effect of what has been said by expressing a complementary truth.[2] τοῦτο does not refer merely to στηριχθῆναι (as though εἰς τὸ στηριχθῆναι ὑμᾶς were being corrected to εἰς τὸ συμπαρακληθῆναι, κ.τ.λ.), but to everything following ἐπιποθῶ γάρ.[3] Paul's desire to see them in order to be the means of their receiving a blessing will only be rightly understood, if it is seen as part of his desire for a mutual παράκλησις between him and them. To regard v. 12 as evidence of embarrassment on Paul's part at the anomalousness of his plans to visit a church not founded by himself (cf. 15.20), as does Barrett,[4] and to see in it a calculated *captatio bene-volentiae*, as does Kuss,[5] are alike uncalled for. There seems to be no cogent reason for refusing to accept the verse at its face-value as the sincere expression of a real humility (cf. the last clause of 15.24 and the note on it). An apt comment is Calvin's: 'Note how modestly he expresses what he feels by not refusing to seek strengthening from inexperienced beginners. He means what he says, too, for there is none so void of gifts in the Church of Christ who cannot in some measure contribute to our spiritual progress. Ill will and pride, however, prevent our deriving such benefit from one another.'[6]

---

[1] Cf. in the LXX, e.g., Exod 17.12; Judg 19.5, 8; Ps 50.14 [RV: 51.12]; 1 Macc 14.14; and also the use of *sāmak* in the Qumran texts, e.g. 1QS 4.5; 8.3; 1QH 1.35; 2.9; 7.6. See further G. Harder, in *TWNT* 7, pp. 653ff. We may also compare the use of βεβαιοῦν in 1 Cor 1.8; 2 Cor 1.21; Col 2.7.

[2] Cf. Leenhardt, p. 44, n. *.

[3] *Pace* Kuss, p. 18.

[4] p. 25.

[5] p. 18: cf. p. 20 ('sie [i.e. 'die freundliche Konzession V.11' (*sic:* ?12)] hatte freilich sowieso mehr rhetorischen—wenn man will: konvention-ellen oder taktischen—Sinn gehabt'). A not so very dissimilar line is taken by Chrysostom, col. 404f. He sees here the prudent teacher (Ὄρα σοφίαν διδασκάλου), and, though he salutes Paul's humility (βαβαί, πόση ἡ ταπεινοφροσύνη) and speaks eloquently of it, he goes on to say: Τοῦτο δὲ ἔλεγεν, οὐχ ὡς αὐτὸς χρῄζων τῆς παρ᾽ ἐκείνων συμμαχίας, ἄπαγε · πῶς γὰρ ὁ τῆς Ἐκκλησίας στῦλος, ὁ σιδήρου καὶ πέτρας στερρότερος, . . .; ἀλλ᾽ ἵνα μὴ καταφορικὸν ποιήσῃ τὸν λόγον. . . .

[6] p. 24. Cf. Barth, *Shorter*, p. 18 ('He takes it seriously that Jesus Christ is over him and the rest of the Church, and that he, Paul himself is not over and above the Church but lives in the Church, receiving as well as giving').

συμπαρακληθῆναι might perhaps be translated 'to be comforted and encouraged together with you'. It seems more probable (*pace* Calvin)[1] that παρακαλεῖν here has its sense of 'comfort', 'encourage', than that it means 'exhort', in view of the rest of the verse. See further on παρακαλῶ in 12.1, ὁ παρακαλῶν, ἐν τῇ παρακλήσει in 12.8, and the use of παράκλησις in 15.4 and 5. (The double compound συμπαρακαλεῖν is found in classical Greek (Plato, Xenophon, Polybius), meaning 'exhort together', 'invite at the same time'.)

ἐν ὑμῖν is more probably local ('among you') than instrumental ('through you').[2]

διὰ τῆς ἐν ἀλλήλοις πίστεως ὑμῶν τε καὶ ἐμοῦ: 'through the faith which is in each other (i.e., 'each through the other's faith'), both yours and mine'—through the meeting between their faith and his. Such an encounter must mean a mutual comforting, encouraging, strengthening. For the meaning of πίστις see on vv. 5 and 8.

13. For **οὐ θέλω δὲ ὑμᾶς ἀγνοεῖν** compare 11.25; I Cor 10.1; 12.1; 2 Cor 1.8; I Th 4.13.[3] This formula is used by Paul to introduce a piece of information which is in one way or another of special importance, and each time it is accompanied by the vocative ἀδελφοί (see below). Apparently he regards it as important to emphasize that his long-standing desire to see them has been so seriously felt that it has on a number of occasions led him to make definite plans to visit them. Does he wish to counter a possible reproach of neglectfulness?[4] (So far from having a feeling of embarrassment about visiting this particular church which he has not founded, he seems to regard it as his clear duty to visit it.)

ἀδελφοί. Compare 7.1, 4; 8.12; 10.1; 11.25; 12.1; 15.14, 30; 16.17. In all of these passages there seems to be an appreciable heightening of the sense of intimacy between Paul and those to whom he is writing. Thus in 11.25 he is sharing a μυστήριον with them, while here and in 10.1 and 15.30 he is speaking about himself, in a personal way, more or less confidingly—

---

[1] p. 24.

[2] The variant ὑμῖν is doubtless an attempt to provide a dative to be governed by the συμ- of the verb, the variant ὑμᾶς an attempt to improve the grammar on the (we think, mistaken) assumption that συμπαρακληθῆναι was meant to be parallel to εἰς τὸ στηριχθῆναι ὑμᾶς, as is also Michelsen's conjectural emendation, ἐμέ.

[3] The positive formula γινώσκειν σε θέλω occurs quite often in Hellenistic letters (some examples cited by Michel, p. 49, n. 1).

[4] Cf. Chrysostom, col. 406: Κατόρθωσας τοίνυν ὅπερ ἐσπούδαζεν ὁ Παῦλος (τί δὲ τοῦτο ἦν; Τὸ δεῖξαι, ὅτι οὐ καταφρονῶν αὐτῶν οὐκ ἤρχετο, ἀλλὰ καὶ σφόδρα ἐπιθυμῶν ἐκωλύετο), καὶ τὸ ἔγκλημα ἀποδυσάμενος τῆς ῥαθυμίας, καὶ πείσας ὅτι αὐτῶν οὐχ ἧττον ἐκεῖνος ἰδεῖν αὐτοὺς ἐπεθύμει.

about his past intentions, his innermost feelings, his appre-
hensions concerning the future. In 15.14 he speaks of his
confidence in the Christian maturity of his readers. In 12.1 and
in 16.17 (cf. also 8.12) he is probably particularly conscious of
the relationship between himself and those he is addressing,
as he takes up the pastoral task of exhortation. (See also on
τῇ φιλαδελφίᾳ in 12.10a.)

ὅτι πολλάκις προεθέμην ἐλθεῖν πρὸς ὑμᾶς. The verb προτίθεσθαι
is stronger than βούλεσθαι or θέλειν. So προεθέμην here says more
than ἠθελήσαμεν in 1 Th 2.18: the implication of this clause is
that on a number of occasions Paul's wish to see them has
actually been transformed into a more or less definite plan to
visit them. For the use of the aorist tense see BDF, § 332(2).

καὶ ἐκωλύθην ἄχρι τοῦ δεῦρο is parenthetic, the following
final clause being dependent not on ἐκωλύθην but on προεθέμην
ἐλθεῖν. The καί is adversative—'and yet', 'but'.[1] In the similar
statement in 1 Th 2.18 Paul refers to Satan as having hindered
him; but here, with reference to hindrances of a different sort,
he uses the simple passive—perhaps with the thought of God's
action in mind. He refers again in 15.22 to his having been
prevented from visiting them, and the διό at the beginning of
that verse is perhaps to be taken as indicating that it was
because of the activity of evangelization reflected in the
preceding verses that he had been unable to visit them.
Calvin's explanation of ἐκωλύθην is as likely as any that have
been suggested: 'We may take this to mean that the Lord
employed him in more urgent business, which he could not
have neglected without damage to the Church'.[2]

ἵνα τινὰ καρπὸν σχῶ καὶ ἐν ὑμῖν καθὼς καὶ ἐν τοῖς λοιποῖς ἔθνεσιν
indicates the purpose for which he had planned to come to
Rome. καρπός is no doubt used here as in Phil 1.22 to denote
the return to be hoped for from apostolic labours, whether
new converts gained or the strengthening of the faith and
obedience of those already believing.[3] The τινά may possibly
express a certain reserve and circumspection felt to be appropriate in speaking of fruit to be obtained by him in a church
he has not founded,[4] or it may simply reflect his knowledge
that it is not he but God who gives the increase (cf. 1 Cor 3.6).
In view of the extent of Paul's labours as ἐθνῶν ἀπόστολος

---

[1] See Bauer, s.v. καί I.2.g; Moule, *Idiom-Book*, p. 178; BDF, § 442 (1).
[2] p. 25.
[3] Cf. the thought of Mt 9.37f; Lk 10.2; Jn 4.36; 15.16. The suggestion
that the reference is to a contribution to his collection for Jerusalem
(see K. F. Nickle, *The Collection: a Study in Paul's Strategy*, London,
1966, p. 70) is scarcely probable.
[4] Cf. Leenhardt, p. 45.

(11.13), the amount of the Gentile world he had already traversed, he could scarcely exclude much longer from his operations Rome, the very centre of the Gentile world. On the possible bearing of these words on the question of the composition of the Roman church, see p. 20.

14. Ἕλλησίν τε καὶ βαρβάροις, σοφοῖς τε καὶ ἀνοήτοις ὀφειλέτης εἰμί. The asyndeton adds to the solemnity of the statement. The interpretation of the two pairs of contrasted terms is not as free of difficulties as many commentators seem to have taken for granted. At least the following possibilities need to be considered: (i) Each pair of contrasted terms denotes the whole of mankind, and the two groupings are identical; (ii) Each pair denotes the whole of mankind, but the two pairs represent different groupings; (iii) The first pair denotes the whole of Gentile humanity, but the second the whole of mankind; (iv) Both pairs denote the whole of Gentile humanity, and both groupings are identical; (v) Both pairs denote the whole of Gentile humanity, but they represent different groupings of the same totality. Of these, (iii), which seems to be the view of Huby,[1] is surely the least probable; for it is natural to assume that both pairs refer to the same totality. In favour of (i) and (ii), it may be said that in vv. 16 and 17 as well as in the argument which follows Paul has the whole of mankind in sight, and also that it is clear that he regarded himself as, at any rate to some extent, ὀφειλέτης to his own countrymen (cf. 9.1–5; 11, 13f). That, from a Greek point of view, the Jews formed no 'third race', but could be accommodated either among the Greeks or among the barbarians, is also true. Nevertheless, the fact that he has just referred to his mission to the Gentiles makes it natural enough to refer here simply to the sum of Gentile mankind. The change of perspective which this interpretation implies between v. 14 and v. 16 does not seem to be a serious objection, since there is anyway (on any interpretation of v. 14) a significant change in the connotation of Ἕλλην between v. 14 and v. 16. We incline then to the view that either (iv) or (v) is to be accepted. Between these it is very difficult to decide. Both of them are possible. (iv) has had its supporters from early times down to the present.[2] But there are several considerations which suggest that (v) is more likely to be right. For one thing, the division into Greeks and barbarians was so well established as to make an explanation of it in different terms superfluous. Moreover, σοφοῖς τε καὶ ἀνοήτοις

---

[1] p. 56f ('*La Gentilité* (ἔθνη) . . . le genre humain . . .').
[2] e.g. Pelagius, p. 11 ('Sapientes Graecos [apud quos omnis philosophia est], barbaros insipientes appellat'); Calvin, p. 25; Kuss, p. 19.

would not be particularly illuminating as an explanation of
Ἕλλησίν τε καὶ βαρβάροις, since it would only be appropriate
if understood on a conventional level. While it is true that Paul
quite often uses σοφός and σοφία in a more or less ironical way,
there is nothing in this context to suggest that he is doing so
here; but, if σοφός and ἀνόητος are intended at all seriously,
they can hardly be used as synonyms for 'Greek' and 'bar-
barian'. The Greeks themselves knew that there were wise
barbarians and foolish Greeks. How much more would Paul
realize it! And, if, when he used the word βάρβαρος here, he
really had in mind some of the Spaniards whom he hoped to
evangelize (15.24),[1] is he likely to have described the βάρβαροι
so sweepingly as ἀνόητοι?

We take it then that by Ἕλληνες are meant all those Gentiles
who are possessed of Graeco-Roman culture, and by βάρβαροι
all the rest of the Gentiles;[2] and that σοφοῖς τε καὶ ἀνοήτοις
represents a different grouping of the Gentiles, which divides
them into those who are intelligent and educated, on the one
hand, and, on the other hand, those who lack intelligence and
education. Here both pairs of terms appear to be used in a
thoroughly objective, factual manner, without overtones of
irony, complacency, prejudice or contemptuousness. While in
the first grouping the thought is probably of communities, in
the second it is rather of individuals.

To all the Gentiles, to those of them who are 'barbarians' no
less than to those who are 'Greeks', and to the ἀνόητοι as much

---

[1] Cf. H. Windisch, in *TWNT* I, p. 549f. In Paul's day many Spaniards
were, of course, thoroughly romanized (the inhabitants of the region of
the Baetis, i.e. the Guadalquivir, were, according to Strabo (64/63 B.C.–
A.D. 21 at least), already at an earlier date so romanized that they had
forgotten their own language); but some parts of the country, and
particularly the north-west, were much less civilized. See on 15.24.

[2] On the words Ἕλλην and βάρβαρος see H. Windisch's articles in
TWNT I, pp. 544ff; 2, pp. 501ff. Whereas Paul elsewhere uses Ἕλλην
in contrast to 'Jew' (so with the significance of 'Gentile', 'pagan'), he
here uses it according to normal Greek usage as the opposite to βάρβαρος.
The idea that someone who is not Greek by race could be in a real sense
a Ἕλλην is to be found already in Plato, *Mx.* 245d. By NT times it was
normal, when thinking of the contrast Ἕλλην/βάρβαρος to include under
the former term all who shared Hellenic civilization and culture. So
Romans were in this sense 'Greeks', though not of course all inhabitants
of Rome, since by this time many lived there who would certainly have
been regarded as βάρβαροι. The word βάρβαρος is in origin onomatopoeic,
being an attempt to reproduce the impression which those talking
languages other than Greek made on Greek ears (cf. the way the word
is used with reference to the twittering of birds in Aristophanes, *Av.*
199). As used here by Paul, it no doubt covers all non-Hellenized
communities (Jews excepted) whether within the Roman Empire or
outside it.

as to the σοφοί,[1] Paul knows himself to be a debtor, that is, having an obligation to them in the sense that God has laid upon him a duty toward them. His debt to them is constituted by the fact that God has appointed him ἐθνῶν ἀπόστολος.[2] For the use of ὀφειλέτης here compare 8.12 and Gal 5.3: the use in 15.27 is different, for there the thought of obligation to someone because of a benefit received from that person is present. Compare also the occurrences of the verb in 13.8 and 15.1, and the notes thereon. Paul's desire to come to Rome, then, is not just a matter of his own personal inclination: it is a matter of his duty before God as apostle of the Gentiles.

15. οὕτως here indicates that the fact about to be stated is a consequence of the fact which has just been stated. Paul's eagerness spoken of here is something which arises from the general obligation of which he is conscious. This use of οὕτως is related to, but is not quite the same thing as, the inferential use found in 6.11.

τὸ κατ' ἐμὲ πρόθυμον has been variously explained: (i) Some take τὸ κατ' ἐμέ as the subject of which πρόθυμον is the predicate, a neuter periphrasis for the first person singular personal pronoun with some such sense as 'I, so far as it rests with me'; (ii) Others take τὸ κατ' ἐμέ as adverbial ('so far as it rests with me'), the subject being ἐγώ to be understood; (iii) Others take all four words together as the subject and (ἐστιν) . . . εὐαγγελίσασθαι as the predicate ('my eager desire is . . .'). Of these (i) is not very likely to be right.[3] The difficulty in the way of (ii) is the neuter πρόθυμον, though this could perhaps be explained as a slip or possibly as a case of attraction.[4] (iii) should probably be preferred.[5]

---

[1] Michel notes with justice (p. 50) that Paul thereby distinguishes himself from the Greek philosophers, who deliberately sought the educated and refined, and were inclined to despise the ignorant and stupid. Cf. 1 Cor 1.26–29.

[2] It is not probable (*pace* Barclay, p. 8) that Paul was also thinking of himself as having been put under an obligation to them by benefits conferred by them. Indebted to individual Gentiles he doubtless was, but there could be no question of his being a debtor to them all in this sense as he was in the sense indicated above. (That Paul's duty is grounded in a benefit received is of course true, but this benefit is God's gift in Christ, not anything conferred by the Gentiles.)

[3] *Pace* Sanday and Headlam, p. 21f.

[4] Cf. Moule, *Idiom-Book*, p. 58. There is early Latin support for interpreting the sentence in this way—d, the Latin translation of Origen, and Ambrosiaster.

[5] Cf. Bauer, s.v. πρόθυμος and s.v. κατά II.7b; BDF, § 224 (1); Michel, p. 51. For κατά with the accusative as a circumlocution for a possessive genitive or possessive adjective compare, e.g., Acts 17.28; 18.15; Eph 1.15: for τὸ πρόθυμον used for ἡ προθυμία compare 3 Macc 5.26; also, e.g., Thucydides, 3.82.8; Plato, *Lg.* 9.859b.

καὶ ὑμῖν: 'to you also', that is, to those in Rome in addition to all those to whom he had already preached the gospel (cf. καθὼς καὶ ἐν τοῖς λοιποῖς ἔθνεσιν in v. 13).[1]

τοῖς ἐν Ῥώμῃ. On the omission of these words in G see pp. 6–11, and compare the same manuscript's omission of ἐν Ῥώμῃ in v. 7.

εὐαγγελίσασθαι. Kuss sees a contradiction between this and what he calls Paul's 'friendly concession' in v. 12.[2] But Paul's preaching the gospel to them (εὐαγγελίζεσθαι is here used of preaching to those who are already believers)[3] is in no way incompatible with his receiving comfort and encouragement from them: it does not at all imply that in relation to them he must be someone who only gives and does not also receive. There is therefore no good reason to conclude, as Kuss does,[4] that he must already have forgotten what he said only three verses earlier and that that must therefore have been mere rhetoric, or merely conventional or tactical.

16a. οὐ γὰρ ἐπαισχύνομαι τὸ εὐαγγέλιον explains how it is that Paul eagerly desires to preach the gospel in Rome also, even in Rome, the imperial capital, the 'princeps urbium', and at the same time forms the transition to the statement in vv. 16b–17 of the theme of the epistle as a whole. The negative formulation is not to be explained as a mere example of litotes (such as is found frequently in Acts),[5] but rather as reflecting Paul's sober recognition of the fact that the gospel is something of which, by the very nature of the case, Christians will in this world constantly be tempted to be ashamed. We may compare Mk 8.38 = Lk 9.26 (it is possible that Paul is consciously echoing this dominical saying, a tradition of which may well have been known to him, but that he is can hardly be proved); also 2 Tim 1.8. Paul knows full well the inevitability of the temptation to be ashamed of the gospel in view of the continuing hostility of the world to God, on the one hand, and, on the other, the nature of the gospel itself, its unimpressiveness over against the impressiveness of the world, the fact that God (because He desires to leave men room to make a free personal decision of faith rather than to compel them) has intervened in history for the salvation of men not in obvious might and majesty but in a veiled way which was bound to look to the

---

[1] The addition of ἐν before ὑμῖν (D* pc g vgam) is perhaps to be explained as assimilation to the ἐν ὑμῖν in v. 13.

[2] p. 19f. His reference to v. 11 is presumably a mistake: v. 12 must surely be meant.

[3] Cf. G. Friedrich, in TWNT 2, p. 717, lines 13ff.

[4] p. 20.

[5] e.g. 12.18; 14.28; 17.4, 12; 19.11, 23f; 20.12; 21.39; 27.20; 28.2.

world like abject weakness and foolishness.[1] Since the presence
of this temptation is a constant feature not just of the life
of all Christian preachers but of all Christian life, it is surely
unnecessary to search for special reasons (as, for example, that
Paul has been accused of not having the courage to face the
imperial capital[2]) to account for his saying what he does.

III

THE THEME OF THE EPISTLE IS STATED
(1.16b–17)

These one and a half verses are at the same time both an
integral part of Paul's expression of his readiness to preach the
gospel in Rome and also the statement of the theological theme
which is going to be worked out in the main body of the
epistle. While it is no doubt formally tidier to treat them as
part of the division which began with 1.8, the logical structure
of the epistle stands out more boldly when they are presented
as a separate main division.

> **16b**For it is God's saving power for every one who believes, both for
> the Jew first and for the Greek. **17**For in it God's righteousness is
> being revealed from faith to faith, even as it is written: 'But he who is
> righteous by faith shall live'.

16b. δύναμις γὰρ θεοῦ ἐστιν εἰς σωτηρίαν.[3] The reason why Paul
is not overcome by the temptation to be ashamed of the gospel,
but, on the contrary, exults in it and lives to proclaim it, is
that he knows that this apparently weak and foolish message
is really, in spite of all appearances, power, and not just one
power over against others, but the supreme power, the
almighty power of God Himself directed toward the salvation
of men, God's almighty saving power. Paul's thought of the
message as being effective power (cf. 1 Cor 1.18) is to be

---

[1] The words τοῦ Χριστοῦ read after εὐαγγελίου by ℵ al are no doubt an
example of the clarifying addition such as is often to be found in the
NT textual tradition.

[2] So M. Barth, in M. Barth, et al., *Foi et Salut*, p. 45f.

[3] The omission of εἰς σωτηρίαν by G is no doubt accidental, due perhaps
to unconscious assimilation to other passages (such as 1 Cor 1.18) where
δύναμις θεοῦ stands without qualification.

understood in the light of such OT passages concerning the divine word as Gen 1.3, 6, etc.; Ps 147.15; Isa 40.8b; 55.10f; Jer 23.29 (cf. also Wisd 18.14–16).[1]

Both δύναμις and σωτηρία, together with their cognates, figure prominently in Hellenistic religion, and the actual phrase δύναμις . . . θεοῦ εἰς σωτηρίαν is closely paralleled in P. Oxy. 11.1381. 215–218 (. . . εἰς πάντα γὰρ τόπον διεπεφοίτηκεν ἡ τοῦ θεοῦ δύναμις σωτήριος—the god is Asklepios). The existence of Hellenistic parallels to Paul's language here is hardly surprising, since saving power is naturally what most religions are concerned with. The suggestion that δύναμις . . . εἰς σωτηρίαν here is to be understood on the analogy of the ideas of the magical papyri as denoting a healing formula or healing power or an initiation which empowers for the journey to heaven and the vision of God and brings about deification[2] is altogether unlikely. The suggestion that in the statement that the gospel is God's saving power there is an implicit opposing of the gospel to the law[3] should also be rejected: it is surely not called for by anything in the context, but arises from false preconceptions about Paul's attitude to the law.[4]

In Paul's letters σώζειν and σωτηρία are used only in connexion with men's relations with God, ῥύεσθαι being employed where deliverance from ordinary temporal dangers is concerned. They have primarily an eschatological reference. This is explicit in 1 Cor 5.5 (ἐν τῇ ἡμέρᾳ τοῦ κυρίου), but is clear also in Rom 5.9f; 13.11; 1 Cor 3.15; Phil 1.28; 2.12;

---

[1] Bultmann's suggestion (see *JBL* 83 (1961), p. 14, n. 5) that δύναμις . . . εἰς σωτηρίαν is to be understood as meaning 'die Möglichkeit zum Heil' is surely to be rejected.

[2] Cf. A. Dieterich, *Eine Mithrasliturgie*, 3rd ed. 1923, p. 46f; J. Weiss, *Der erste Korintherbrief*, Göttingen, 1910, p. 26.

[3] According to Nygren, p. 67, the thought of the powerlessness of the law (he compares τὸ ἀδύνατον τοῦ νόμου in 8.3) is present in the background here. W. Grundmann refers to the Jewish identification of God's power with the law (cf., e.g., *Mekilta* Exod 15.13: ' "Thou hast guided them in thy strength" (Exod 15.13): by virtue of the law, which they will receive in the future. "Thy strength": that is nothing other than the law, as it is written: "The LORD will give strength unto his people" (Ps 29.11)'), and understands Paul's point to be that it is not the law but the gospel which is really God's power (*TWNT* 2, pp. 298, 309, 310). But to see here in 1.16 polemic against the law or even against Jewish misunderstanding of the law is surely, in view of the fact that the law is not mentioned until 2.12, eisegesis rather than exegesis.

[4] That Paul, while strongly opposed to legalism, saw a close positive relation between the law and Christ/the gospel/the righteousness of God, will become clear in the course of our study of Romans (cf., e.g., the notes on 3.21, 31; chapter 7 passim; 8.4; 9.31f; 10.4ff; and the essay on 'The Theology of Romans' in volume 2).

1 Th 5.8f; 2 Th 2.13. What may be called the negative content of salvation is indicated in 5.9: it is salvation from the final eschatological manifestation of the wrath of God. But there is also a positive content. It is the restoration of the δόξα which sinful men lack (compare the contrast between justification/ reconciliation and salvation in 5.9f with the contrast between justification and glorification in 8.30; compare also the description in Phil 3.20f of the work of Christ as σωτήρ as the transformation of τὸ σῶμα τῆς ταπεινώσεως ἡμῶν so that it becomes σύμμορφον τῷ σώματι τῆς δόξης αὐτοῦ), the earnestly awaited final manifestation of the believer's adoption, which is also the ἀπολύτρωσις τοῦ σώματος ἡμῶν (8.23). While salvation is characteristically spoken of with future tenses, Paul can use a past tense in connexion with it (thus in 8.24 we have the statement ἐσώθημεν which, however, is qualified by τῇ ... ἐλπίδι: compare ἐδόξασεν in 8.30),[1] since the decisive act of God, by which the believer's final salvation has been secured, has already been accomplished, and also a present tense, as in 1 Cor 1.18; 2 Cor 2.15, to describe the believer's present waiting and hoping and struggling which have salvation for their goal.[2]

What Paul is saying here, then, is that the gospel is God's effective power active in the world of men to bring about deliverance from His wrath in the final judgment and re-instatement in that glory of God which was lost through sin—that is, an eschatological salvation which reflects its splendour back into the present of those who are to share it. (The significance of εἰς σωτηρίαν will be further clarified by consideration of Paul's understanding of ζήσεται in v. 17.) The gospel is this by virtue of its content, its subject, Jesus Christ. It is He Himself who is its effectiveness. His work was God's decisive act for men's salvation, and in the gospel, in the message of which He is the content, He presents Himself to men as it were clothed in the efficacy of His saving work.

παντὶ τῷ πιστεύοντι. The appropriate response to the message, the response it calls for, is faith—faith in the message, and so faith in Jesus Christ who is its content and in God who has acted in Him and whose power the message is. For all who do respond with faith the gospel is effective unto salvation. But here we have to beware of the possibility of very serious misunderstanding. Nygren has rightly warned against thinking of faith as being 'prior to the gospel and independent of it. It

[1] Cf. also Eph 2.5, 8; 2 Tim 1.9; Tit 3.5.
[2] On σῴζειν and σωτηρία see further W. Foerster and G. Fohrer, in *TWNT* 7, pp. 966ff (especially 992–996).

arises only through one's meeting with the gospel'.[1] It is not a
qualification which some men already possess in themselves so
that the gospel, when it comes to them, finds them eligible to
receive its benefits. Faith, in the sense in which the term is
used here, can exist only as response to the gospel (or its OT
foreshadowing). And it is also wrongly conceived, if it is
thought of as being, as a man's response to the gospel, a
contribution from his side which, by fulfilling a condition
imposed by God, enables the gospel to be unto salvation for
him. In that case, faith would itself be in the last resort a
human meritorious work, a man's establishment of his own
claim on God by virtue of something in himself. But it is of the
very essence of faith, as Paul understands it, that it is opposed
to all human deserving, all human establishing of claims on
God (cf., e.g., 3.20–22, 28; 4.2–5; 9.32; Gal 2.16; 3.2, 5). For
Paul man's salvation is altogether—not almost altogether—
God's work; and the faith spoken of here is the openness to the
gospel which God Himself creates, the human response of
surrender to the judgment and unmerited mercy of God which
God Himself brings about—God who not only directs the
message to the hearer but also Himself lays open the hearer's
heart to the message. And yet this faith, as God's work in a
man, is in a real sense more truly and fully the man's own
personal decision than anything which he himself does of
himself; for it is the expression of the freedom which God has
restored to him—the freedom to obey God. But it is not till
chapter eight that this secret of faith is revealed.[2] The παντί
emphasizes the fact that the gospel is God's power effective
unto salvation for all those who thus accept it, without
exception and without distinction. It strikes a note which
sounds again and again through the epistle: compare, for
example, 1.5; 3.9, 12, 19, 20, 22, 23; 4.16; 5.12, 18; 8.32; 10.4,
11, 12, 13; 11.32; 15.11.

Ἰουδαίῳ τε πρῶτον καὶ Ἕλληνι. That πρῶτον should be read is
hardly to be doubted. It is surely much more probable that its
absence in some witnesses (B G sa Marcion Ephraem) is the
result of deliberate omission on the part of Marcion than that
its presence in the great majority of witnesses is due to

---

[1] p. 78.
[2] On the uses of πιστεύειν with accusative, dative, εἰς, ἐπί, ὅτι, see
Bauer, s.v.; and for bibliography on 'faith' see ibid., s.v. πίστις , to which
bibliography Barth, CD IV/1, pp. 608–42 and 740–79 (=KD IV/1, pp.
679–718 and 826–72) should be added (see also indices of the various
volumes of CD s.v. 'faith' or Registerband s.v. 'Glaube'). See also the
essay on 'The Theology of Romans' at the end of volume 2 of this
commentary.

assimilation to 2.9 and 10. The presence of πρῶτον in 2.9 and 10 is itself a very strong reason for thinking it likely that Paul would also have inserted it here, and the probability is confirmed by much else in the epistle. The phrase as a whole underlines and explicates the preceding παντί. The word τε (though its presence is simply ignored by RV, RSV, NEB and JB) is suggestive of the fundamental equality of Jew and Gentile[1] in the face of the gospel (the gospel is the power of God unto salvation for believing Jew and believing Gentile alike), while the word πρῶτον indicates that within the framework of this basic equality there is a certain undeniable priority of the Jew.[2] In view of chapters nine to eleven it is hardly admissible to explain this πρῶτον as referring merely to the historical fact that the gospel was preached to the Jews before it was preached to the Gentiles, or, while allowing a reference to the special position of the Jews in the *Heilsgeschichte*, to cite Gal 3.28 and Eph 2.14f as proof that this πρῶτον is, in Paul's view, something now abolished, as Nygren does.[3] Rather must we see it in the light of Paul's confident statement in 11.29 that ἀμεταμέλητα . . . τὰ χαρίσματα καὶ ἡ κλῆσις τοῦ θεοῦ. The paradoxical insistence both on the fact that there is no διαστολή (3.22; 10.12) and also at the same time on the continuing validity of the 'Ιουδαίῳ . . . πρῶτον (in spite of the actual order of salvation disclosed in 11.25f) belongs to the substance of the epistle. On this see further on chapters nine to eleven.

17. δικαιοσύνη γὰρ θεοῦ ἐν αὐτῷ ἀποκαλύπτεται ἐκ πίστεως εἰς πίστιν is introduced in explanation and confirmation (γάρ) of v. 16b: the gospel is God's δύναμις εἰς σωτηρίαν παντὶ τῷ πιστεύοντι because in it δικαιοσύνη θεοῦ is being revealed ἐκ πίστεως εἰς πίστιν. The pronoun αὐτῷ refers back to τὸ εὐαγγέλιον in v. 16a, which was the unexpressed subject of v. 16b; and the present tense (contrast the tense of πεφανέρωται in 3.21) is used, because here the thought is of the revelation in the on-going preaching

---

[1] *Ἕλλην* has here, being used in antithesis to 'Jew', the sense 'non-Jewish', 'Gentile' (contrast v. 14, where it was opposed to βάρβαρος). See Bauer, s.v. 2; *TWNT* 2, pp. 501ff. Paul uses the plural with this sense in 3.9: so his use of the word is not to be explained simply as due to the impossibility of using ἔθνος as the singular of ἔθνη meaning 'Gentiles'.

[2] The suggestion that πρῶτον is to be taken not just with 'Ιουδαίῳ but with 'Ιουδαίῳ τε ... καὶ Ἕλληνι (Paul being understood either as contrasting Jew and Greek with the βάρβαροι and ἀνόητοι mentioned in v. 14 (so Zahn) or else as meaning that the Jews, as striving after righteousness, and the Greeks, as possessed of wisdom, are specially in danger and therefore to be called first to faith (so Kühl)) is quite unlikely.

[3] p. 73.

of the message. The choice of the verb ἀποκαλύπτειν[1] underlines the fact that, though the gospel is proclaimed by human lips, the revelation of δικαιοσύνη θεοῦ in the proclamation is God's doing (cf. the statement in v. 16b that the gospel is God's power).

In coming to a conclusion with regard to the meaning of δικαιοσύνη θεοῦ in this verse we have tried to take full account of the most recent, as well as of earlier, discussion. But the bulk of it is so immense and the positions maintained by different scholars depend to such an extent on detailed arguments, that it is impossible to give, within reasonable limits, an account of the debate which is fair to those who have contributed to it.[2] We shall therefore give a relatively full bibliography on the subject and, for the rest, concentrate on the presentation of what we are convinced is the right interpretation, with some reference to other views but without attempting to outline the actual course of the debate. We also hope to return to the subject in the essay on the theology of Romans at the end of the commentary.

We begin with the bibliography. The following must be mentioned (in addition, of course, to the contributions of the various commentaries): Luther, WA 54, p. 185f; O. Zänker, 'Δικαιοσύνη Θεοῦ bei Paulus', in ZST 9 (1931–2), pp. 398–420; G. Quell and G. Schrenk, in TWNT 2, pp. 176ff (includes bibliography up to 1933 on p. 194); R. Gyllenberg, 'Die paulinische Rechtfertigungslehre und das Alte Testament', in Studia Theologica I, Riga, 1935, pp. 35–52; H.-D. Wendland, Die Mitte der paulinischen Botschaft: Die Rechtfertigungslehre des Paulus im Zusammenhange seiner Theologie, Göttingen, 1935; Dodd, Bible and the Greeks, pp. 42ff; S. Lyonnet, 'De "Justitia Dei" in Epistola ad Romanos', in VD 25 (1947), pp. 23ff, 118ff, 129ff, 193ff, 257ff; Bultmann, Theology I, pp. 270–85; A. Oepke, 'Δικαιοσύνη Θεοῦ bei Paulus in neuer Beleuchtung', in TLZ 78 (1953), 257–64; Barth, C.D IV/1, pp. 514–642 (=KD IV/1, pp. 573–718); S. Schulz, 'Zur Rechtfertigung aus Gnaden in Qumran und bei Paulus', in

---

[1] It is used in the NT 26 times (Mt 10.26; 11.25, 27 = Lk 12.2; 10.21, 22, respectively; Mt 16.17; Lk 2.35; 17.30; Jn 12.38; Rom 1.17, 18; 8.18; 1 Cor 2.10; 3.13; 14.30; Gal 1.16; 3.23; Eph 3.5; Phil 3.15; 2 Th 2.3, 6, 8; 1 Pet 1.5, 12; 5.1), while ἀποκάλυψις is used 18 times (Lk 2.32; Rom 2.5; 8.19; 16.25; 1 Cor 1.7; 14.6, 26; 2 Cor 12.1, 7; Gal 1.12; 2.2; Eph 1.17; 3.3; 2 Th 1.7; 1 Pet 1.7, 13; 4.13; Rev 1.1). It would seem that in every NT occurrence of these words (including 2 Th 2.3, 6 and 8) the reference is to a divine revealing. See further A. Oepke, in TWNT 3, pp. 565ff.

[2] Even those who have devoted whole monographs to the subject of the righteousness of God in Paul's thought have been conscious of the difficulty to which we refer (cf., e.g., Ziesler, op. cit. infra, pp. 1 and 15).

ZTK 56 (1959), pp. 155–85; W. Grundmann, 'Der Lehrer der Gerechtigkeit von Qumran und die Frage nach der Glaubensgerechtigkeit in der Theologie des Apostels Paulus', in *RQ* 2 (1959–60), pp. 237–59 (Eng. tr. of a revised form of this in Murphy-O'Connor, *PQ*, pp. 85ff); E. Käsemann, 'Gottesgerechtigkeit bei Paulus', in *ZTK* 58 (1961), pp. 367–78 (Eng. tr. of this in Käsemann, *Questions*, pp. 168ff); R. Bultmann, 'Δικαιοσύνη Θεοῦ', in *JBL* 83 (1964), pp. 12–16; P. Stuhlmacher, *Gerechtigkeit Gottes bei Paulus*, Göttingen, 1965; Cambier, *L'Évangile de Dieu* 1, especially pp. 37–40; Hill, *GWHM*, pp. 82–162; K. Kertelge, *'Rechtfertigung' bei Paulus*, Münster, 1967; M. Barth, 'Rechtfertigung: Versuch einer Auslegung paulinischer Texte im Rahmen des Alten und Neuen Testamentes', in M. Barth, et al., *Foi et Salut*, pp. 137–209; J. A. Ziesler, *The Meaning of Righteousness in Paul: a linguistic and theological enquiry*, Cambridge, 1972.

The ranges of meaning which the words δίκη, δίκαιος, δικαιοσύνη and δικαιοῦν have in ordinary Greek may be indicated as follows:

The original meaning of δίκη, the basic word of the group, was probably 'custom', 'that which is customary'. In Hesiod's *Works and Days*, 256f, Δίκη is the virgin daughter of Zeus, described as honoured and revered by the gods who dwell on Olympus. For Solon, the great Athenian legislator of the early sixth century B.C., δίκη was the divine law both of the universe and of civic life, the true norm of human conduct, 'justice', 'right'. Later the juristic reference which was implicit in the word came to predominate (cf. LSJ, s.v. III and IV), and it is used with such senses as 'judgment', 'lawsuit', 'trial', 'penalty', 'satisfaction'.

The adjective δίκαιος describes the man whose conduct conforms to δίκη. It means 'observant of custom' or 'of duty', 'just', 'righteous'. According to Aristotle's *Nicomachean Ethics* 1129ᵃ34, τὸ δίκαιον is 'that which is lawful and fair' (τὸ νόμιμον καὶ τὸ ἴσον). While δίκαιος is often used in non-moral senses (it can mean, for example, 'precise', 'exact', 'fit for use', 'genuine'), it is characteristically an ethical term. It can refer to the fulfilment of obligations to gods as well as to men, but more usually refers to relations between men.

The noun δικαιοσύνη denotes the quality of being δίκαιος. It is used both to denote a particular virtue, the civic virtue of the honest, law-abiding citizen who faithfully discharges his obligations (along with wisdom, temperance and courage, it was one of the four cardinal virtues), and also as a comprehensive term for all the virtues taken together as a single whole. Occasionally it is used specifically of the justice which is the concern of a judge.

The verb δικαιοῦν is used, with an impersonal object, in such senses as 'deem right', 'claim as a right', 'allow', and, with a personal object, with the meaning 'treat justly', especially in the sense of passing sentence on, condemning and punishing.[1]

But the ranges of meaning of these words were significantly altered through their being regularly used in the LXX to represent the Hebrew words of the ṣdḳ group. The basic idea of the noun ṣeḍeḳ seems to have been that of conformity to a norm. Where ṣeḍeḳ is used in connexion with the conduct of persons, it refers to the fulfilment of the obligations arising from a particular situation, the demands of a particular relationship. As far as Israel was concerned the supremely important relationship was the covenant between God and His people; and ṣeḍeḳ in the OT is to be understood in the context of the Covenant. The adjective ṣaddîḳ is used to describe those whose conduct and character, whether specifically in relation to the administration of justice or quite generally, are characterized by ṣeḍeḳ. But there are passages in which ṣaddîḳ, used of Israel or of the individual Israelite, refers to status rather than to ethical condition (see, for example, Ps 32.11 in the light of vv. 1, 2 and 5; Isa 60.21). The cognate verb used in the Qal, can mean (i) 'be just', 'be righteous' (e.g. Job 35.7; Ps 19.9 [MT: 10]; 51.4 [MT: 6]); (ii) 'be in the right' in the sense of having a just cause (e.g. Gen 38.26); (iii) 'be justified', 'be declared righteous' (e.g. Ps 143.2; Isa 43.26). In the Hiph'il (and occasionally in the Pi'el), it means 'justify', 'declare righteous', 'acquit' (e.g. Exod 23.7; Deut 25.1; Prov 17.15): there is also one place (Dan 12.3), where the Hiph'il seems to mean 'make righteous', 'turn to righteousness'. The noun ṣeḍāḳāh can denote (i) righteousness in government and in administering justice (whether in acquitting or punishing); (ii) righteousness in the sense of that which is ethically right; (iii) being in the right in the sense of having a just cause; (iv) the action of acquitting, of conferring a status of righteousness on, vindicating; (v) the righteous status bestowed, vindication; (vi) in the plural, righteous acts (whether of God or of men).

---

[1] The usage which comes nearest to the Pauline is that found in Polybius 3.31.9 (to defend or secure someone's right): cf. the use of the passive in Aristotle, *E.N.* 1136a 18ff. The use of the passive in *Corp. Herm.* 13.9 apparently to denote a moral transformation may perhaps reflect knowledge of Paul's language as understood by some Greek interpreters: it is without any parallel in classical Greek.

That Paul's use of the words δίκαιος, δικαιοσύνη and δικαιοῦν (and also of δικαίωμα and δικαίωσις) reflects his familiarity with, and is to a very considerable extent moulded by, the LXX use of them to render words of the ṣdḳ group is clear, and is generally agreed. It is most obvious in the case of the verb δικαιοῦν; for none of the occurrences of δικαιοῦν in the Pauline epistles (in Romans alone it occurs fifteen times) can be at all tolerably explained on the basis of the word's use in secular Greek. But, in spite of the general agreement on the importance of the LXX here, there is far from being general agreement as to the precise significance which these words have in Paul.

We must notice first the centuries-old dispute as to whether δικαιοῦν and (when they are used in connexion with justification) its cognates refer simply to status or to status and also ethical character—or, to put it otherwise, as to whether justification is simply the bestowal of a righteous status, God's acquittal of the sinner, or both that and also a making righteous in an ethical sense, moral regeneration. Roman Catholic scholars have generally maintained that justification includes moral renewal, though they have stated and defended this position in various ways: Protestants have generally taken the opposite view. While it should be freely admitted that the Protestant position has sometimes been stated misleadingly or seriously distorted so that Catholics have had good reason to be suspicious and alarmed (a good many Protestants have put far too little emphasis on sanctification, and some have even seemed inclined to frown on the appearance of moral earnestness as though it must necessarily be evidence of a weakening loyalty to the doctrine of *sola fide*), there seems to us to be no doubt that δικαιοῦν, as used by Paul, means simply 'acquit', 'confer a righteous status on', and does not in itself contain any reference to moral transformation. This conclusion is surely forced upon us by the linguistic evidence. It would also seem to be borne out by the structure of Paul's argument in Romans. But, while sanctification is distinct from justification, the two things are not to be separated; for, as Calvin insisted,[1] to 'imagine that Christ bestows free justification upon us without imparting newness of life' is shamefully to 'rend Christ asunder'. Justification is indeed basic for Paul, but it is not the whole of what God does for us in Christ, and 'we cannot receive righteousness in Christ without at the same time laying hold on sanctification'.[2]

The other main disagreement concerns the question whether

[1] p. 121.
[2] Calvin, p. 8.

in the phrase δικαιοσύνη θεοῦ in 1.17; 3.21, 22 (cf. 10.3) θεοῦ is
to be understood as a subjective genitive or as a genitive of
origin,[1] or—to put it differently—whether δικαιοσύνη refers to
an activity of God[2] or to a status of man resulting from God's
action, righteousness as a gift from God. In support of the
view that θεοῦ is a subjective genitive and δικαιοσύνη refers
to God's activity, a number of arguments have been advanced:

(i) That in 3.5 (θεοῦ δικαιοσύνην) θεοῦ must be a subjective
genitive (cf. also 3.25, 26).

(ii) That, in view of the parallelism of structure between
v. 17a and v. 18, the fact that θεοῦ in v. 18 is a subjective
genitive suggests that θεοῦ in v. 17a is likely also to be one,
and the fact that ὀργή refers to an activity of God suggests that
δικαιοσύνη is likely also to do so.

(iii) That, in view of the connexion between v. 17 and v. 16b,
the phrase δύναμις θεοῦ in v. 16b tells in favour of taking θεοῦ
in v. 17 as a subjective genitive and understanding δικαιοσύνη
to refer to God's activity, God's saving power in action.

(iv) That in the OT ṣeḏāḵāh, when the reference is to God's
ṣeḏāḵāh, refers to an activity of God, the activity of His
saving power. (It has sometimes been suggested that Paul was
echoing Ps 98.2, in which three of the key ideas of Rom
1.16b–17 occur—in the LXX version [97.2], τὸ σωτήριον αὐτοῦ,
ἀπεκάλυψεν, τὴν δικαιοσύνην αὐτοῦ.)

(v) That the expression 'the righteousness of God'[3] was a
technical term of late-Jewish apocalyptic for God's saving
justice, which embraces His sovereign and triumphant faithfulness to His covenant and to His creation, His forgiving mercy,
His laying claim to obedience (among other passages, 1QS
10.25f; 11.12; 1QM 4.6; Test. Dan 6.10; Enoch 71.14; 99.10;
101.3 are appealed to). It is claimed that Paul took over,
radicalized and universalized this Jewish apocalyptic technical
term.[4] So, according to Käsemann, 'δικαιοσύνη θεοῦ is for Paul
God's sovereignty over the world revealing itself eschatologically in Jesus'.[5]

These arguments appear quite impressive at first sight
(and since the contributions of Käsemann and Stuhlmacher it
has been fashionable to maintain the view that θεοῦ is a

---

[1] That in 3.5 θεοῦ is a subjective genitive is hardly to be doubted.

[2] That it refers to righteousness as an attribute of God is not likely,
though this has sometimes been maintained.

[3] Käsemann, *Questions*, p. 172, and Stuhlmacher, op. cit., pp. 142ff,
trace it back to Deut 33.21, the only place in the OT where the actual
expression ṣiḏqaṯ YHWH occurs.

[4] Cf. Käsemann, *Questions*, pp. 172, 178.

[5] *Questions*, p. 180.

subjective genitive and δικαιοσύνη refers to God's activity); but they are not really very cogent. With regard to (i), Bultmann has rightly refused to allow that for Paul to use the same expression in different senses in different contexts would have to be labelled 'Inkonsequenz'.[1] To assume that 'eine einheitliche Interpretation' must necessarily be preferable to an interpretation which allows δικαιοσύνη θεοῦ to have more than one sense in Paul[2] is merely arbitrary. With regard to (ii) and (iii), it may be said that, while they have a certain plausibility, they are in no way conclusive. And as to (iv) and (v), it must be said that, while it is of course true that the righteousness language of the OT and of late Judaism is the background against which Paul's expression δικαιοσύνη θεοῦ must be understood, there is no reason to assume that he must have used the language he took over just precisely as it had been used. We must allow for the possibility of his having used what he took over with freedom and originality.[3] These arguments from the OT and late Judaism cannot therefore be decisive.

We must now consider what can be said in favour of the other view, namely, that θεοῦ is a genitive of origin and that δικαιοσύνη refers to man's righteous status which is the result of God's action of justifying.[4]

(i) There are several occurrences of δικαιοσύνη in the Pauline letters which seem to afford strong support for it. In Rom 10.3 it is surely natural (*pace* Stuhlmacher, op. cit., pp. 91ff) to understand τὴν τοῦ θεοῦ δικαιοσύνην to mean the status of righteousness which is given by God, since it is opposed to τὴν ἰδίαν [δικαιοσύνην], that is, a status of righteousness achieved by their own efforts, and the following τῇ δικαιοσύνῃ τοῦ θεοῦ is best taken in the same sense. This interpretation of Rom 10.3 is strongly confirmed by Phil 3.9, where ἐμὴν δικαιοσύνην τὴν ἐκ νόμου is contrasted with τὴν διὰ πίστεως Χριστοῦ, τὴν ἐκ θεοῦ δικαιοσύνην ἐπὶ τῇ πίστει, in which the ἐκ is specially significant. In 1 Cor 1.30 (. . . Χριστῷ Ἰησοῦ, ὃς ἐγενήθη σοφία ἡμῖν ἀπὸ θεοῦ, δικαιοσύνη τε καὶ ἁγιασμὸς καὶ ἀπολύτρωσις . . .) not only σοφία but also the other three abstract nouns are qualified by ἀπὸ θεοῦ: so we have the thought of Christ as being our righteousness from God, that is, surely, the one in whom we have a righteous status. In 2 Cor 5.21 (. . . ἵνα ἡμεῖς γενώμεθα δικαιοσύνη θεοῦ ἐν αὐτῷ) δικαιοσύνη

[1] *JBL* 83, p. 12. [2] Stuhlmacher, op. cit., p. 14: cf. pp. 23, 27f, 36, 40ff.
[3] It should be noted that ṣidḳaṭ 'ēl in the Qumran texts has been interpreted differently from the way in which Stuhlmacher understands it by other scholars, as he himself indicates (cf. pp. 148ff).
[4] Augustine's 'justitia Dei, non qua Deus justus est, sed qua induit hominem, cum justificat impium' in *De Spir. et litt.* 9.15 (on Rom 3.21: cf. 11.18 on 1.17) may be noted here.

θεοῦ is best explained as an instance of the use of the abstract for the concrete, δικαιοσύνη being equivalent to δικαιωθέντες (cf. Bauer, s.v. δικαιοσύνη, 3). In other words, θεοῦ here is a genitive of origin and δικαιοσύνη denotes the righteous status bestowed on men. In Rom 5.17 we have the phrase τὴν περισσείαν... τῆς δωρεᾶς τῆς δικαιοσύνης, in which τῆς δικαιοσύνης can scarcely be anything other than an objective genitive, so an explicit reference to righteousness as God's gift.

(ii) In the verse we are here specially concerned with the words ἐκ πίστεως εἰς πίστιν strongly support the view that δικαιοσύνη θεοῦ must refer to the status of righteousness conferred on man by God's action. It is extremely difficult to see how ἐκ πίστεως εἰς πίστιν can at all convincingly be shown to be a natural expression for Paul to have used, if he meant by δικαιοσύνη θεοῦ God's activity.

(iii) The Habakkuk quotation (1.17b) seems also to tell in favour of this view; for it focuses attention on the justified man, not on God's act of justifying him.

(iv) Most important of all, in our judgment, is the fact that to take δικαιοσύνη θεοῦ in 1.17 to refer to the righteous status bestowed by God agrees better with the structure of the argument of the epistle, in which 1.18–4.25 expounds the words ὁ δίκαιος ἐκ πίστεως and 5.1–8.39 the promise that the man who is righteous by faith ζήσεται. The focusing of attention on the status of righteousness is to be observed in 2.13 (... δίκαιοι παρὰ [τῷ] θεῷ, ... δικαιωθήσονται); 3.20 (διότι ἐξ ἔργων νόμου οὐ δικαιωθήσεται πᾶσα σὰρξ ἐνώπιον αὐτοῦ), 24 (δικαιούμενοι δωρεάν ...), 28 (λογιζόμεθα γὰρ δικαιοῦσθαι πίστει ἄνθρωπον χωρὶς ἔργων νόμου); 4.2 (εἰ γὰρ Ἀβραὰμ ἐξ ἔργων ἐδικαιώθη ...), 13 (διὰ δικαιοσύνης πίστεως); 5.1 (Δικαιωθέντες οὖν ἐκ πίστεως ...), 9 (δικαιωθέντες), 19 (... οὕτως ... δίκαιοι κατασταθήσονται οἱ πολλοί); and most probably also in διὰ δικαιοσύνης in 5.21 and διὰ δικαιοσύνην in 8.10. It is this fourth argument which ought surely to be regarded as decisive.

The last word in this debate has clearly not yet been spoken. It would therefore be irresponsible to claim that the question has been conclusively decided either way. But, in view of what has been said above and especially of point (iv) in favour of the latter position, we regard the interpretation which takes θεοῦ as a genitive of origin and δικαιοσύνη as referring to the righteous status which is given by God as being much the more probable.[1] The theological objections which Käsemann

---

[1] Some commentators have felt that the arguments on both sides are so strong that the best solution is to conclude that Paul is here using δικαιοσύνη θεοῦ in a double sense, meaning at the same time God's

has raised to it, namely, that it involves an isolating of the
gift from the Giver and an anthropocentric rather than
theocentric understanding of the gospel, and that it is
individualistic,[1] are important and require to be taken very
seriously; but, while these objections may well lie against the
theology of Bultmann, whose contributions on the subject
Käsemann had specially in mind, it is, in our view, perfectly
possible to hold that Paul meant by δικαιοσύνη θεοῦ in some of
the places where he uses the expression the status of righteousness which may be had as a gift from God, without in any way
compromising the theocentricity of Paul's theology or making
his gospel merely individualistic. Paul's focusing attention on
the man who is righteous by faith is bound up with the use
which he makes of Hab 2.4; but everything he says about the
justified man is said within the context of the gospel, which
for Paul is certainly not a gospel of man's self-understanding,
but the gospel of God (cf. 1.1).

The words ἐκ πίστεως εἰς πίστιν have been understood in
many different ways: e.g. as meaning 'from the faith of the
OT to the faith of the NT' or 'from the faith of the law to the
faith of the gospel',[2] 'from the faith of the preachers to the
faith of the hearers',[3] 'from faith in one article to faith in
another',[4] 'from present faith to future',[5] 'from the faith of
words (whereby we now believe what we do not see) to the
faith of the things, that is, realities (whereby we shall hereafter
possess what we now believe in)',[6] 'from God's faithfulness to
man's faith',[7] or as indicating a growth in faith (for the form
of expression compare πορεύσονται ἐκ δυνάμεως εἰς δύναμιν in
LXX Ps 83.8 and perhaps μεταμορφούμεθα ἀπὸ δόξης εἰς δόξαν
in 2 Cor 3.18 and for the idea of a growth in faith 2 Cor 10.15;
2 Th 1.3).[8] Against all of these interpretations there is the
serious objection that they involve taking ἐκ πίστεως in a
different sense from that which it has in the Habakkuk

righteous activity and its result in man's situation. But it is surely more
likely that Paul meant to focus attention either on the one or on the
other, though it is of course true—and this needs to be emphasized—
that a direct reference to either carries with it an indirect reference to
the other.

[1] Cf. *Questions*, pp. 168 (n. *), 173 (n. 4), 175f, 180f.
[2] e.g. Tertullian, *Adv. Marc.* 5.13; Origen, col. 861 (cf. 858).
[3] Augustine, *De Spir. et litt.*, 11.18.
[4] An interpretation mentioned by Aquinas, p. 20 (103).
[5] Another interpretation mentioned by Aquinas.
[6] Augustine, *Quaest. Evang.* 2.39.
[7] Ambrosiaster, col. 56 ('ex fide Dei promittentis in fidem hominis
credentis'); Barth, 1933, p. 41; *Shorter*, p. 22f; Manson, p. 942.
[8] e.g. Sanday and Headlam, p. 28; Lagrange, p. 20.

quotation as used by Paul. Other suggestions are: that the ἐκ πίστεως means 'by faith 'and the εἰς πίστιν is to be explained as an instance of the abstract used for the concrete, being equivalent to εἰς τοὺς πιστεύοντας (cf. 3.22);[1] that the whole phrase indicates that the δικαιοσύνη θεοῦ has faith both as its ground and as its goal;[2] that the phrase is simply a rhetorical formulation to express ἐκ πίστεως specially emphatically;[3] that it makes no sense, and that πίστιν should be emended to Ἰησοῦν Χριστόν.[4] Of these the suggestion that it is an emphatic equivalent of ἐκ πίστεως, the εἰς πίστιν having much the same effect as the 'sola' of 'sola fide', would seem to be much the most probable.

The structure of the sentence suggests that ἐκ πίστεως εἰς πίστιν was intended to be connected with ἀποκαλύπτεται; but it is probable that in Paul's thought it was linked rather with δικαιοσύνη θεοῦ. Confirmation of this view is provided both by the Habakkuk quotation, in which Paul almost certainly meant ἐκ πίστεως to be connected with δίκαιος, and also by 3.21f, where the thought of this verse is taken up and the repetition of the δικαιοσύνη θεοῦ of 3.21 in v. 22 makes it quite clear that διὰ πίστεως [Ἰησοῦ] Χριστοῦ is to be connected with it rather than with the verb πεφανέρωται.[5] The sense of the whole sentence may then be set out as follows: For in it (i.e. in the gospel as it is being preached) a righteous status which is God's gift is being revealed (and so offered to men)—a righteous status which is altogether by faith.

καθὼς γέγραπται· ὁ δὲ δίκαιος ἐκ πίστεως ζήσεται. In confirmation of v. 17a Paul cites Hab 2.4b. The sense of the Hebrew wᵉṣaddîḳ be'ᵉmûnāṭô yihyeh is that the righteous shall be preserved alive because of his faithfulness, that is, his steadfast loyalty. The original reference was probably not to the individual righteous man but to the Jewish people contrasted with their heathen oppressors in their puffed up pride, and the life referred to was probably political survival; but the tendency to understand the words with reference to the individual will have made itself felt quite early. The LXX has ὁ δὲ δίκαιος ἐκ πίστεώς μου ζήσεται, in which ἐκ πίστεώς μου could mean either 'because of my [sc. God's] faithfulness' or 'because of his faith in me'.[6] Paul in quoting retains neither the third person pronoun of

[1] e.g. Cornely, p. 71; Hill, GWHM, p. 157.
[2] e.g. Lightfoot, p. 250.
[3] e.g. Lietzmann, p. 31.
[4] Pallis, p. 40.
[5] Cf. Nygren, p. 79.
[6] In the Codex Alexandrinus μου is placed before, instead of after, ἐκ πίστεως, and so connected with ὁ δίκαιος. Compare Heb 10.38.

the MT nor the first person pronoun of the LXX. The sentence
is also quoted in Gal 3.11 and Heb 10.38. That it came to be of
special importance for some Jews is indicated by *bMakk.* 23ᵇ,
which tells us that Rabbi Simlai (about A.D. 250) had asserted
that the 613 commandments received by Moses had been summed up by David in eleven commandments (Ps 15), by Isaiah in
six (Isa 33.15f), by Micah in three (Mic 6.8), by Isaiah again in
two (Isa 56.1), and finally by Amos in one (Amos 5.4), but that
Rabbi Nachman ben Isaac (about A.D. 350) had substituted
Hab 2.4b for Amos 5.4 as the summary in one commandment.[1]
The interpretation given in 1QpH 8.1–3 is interesting: 'Interpreted, this concerns all those who observe the Law in the
House of Judah, whom God will deliver from the House of
Judgement because of their suffering[2] and because of their
faith in the Teacher of Righteousness.' Paul in taking up the
prophet's statement understands it in the light of the gospel.
So, as used now by him, πίστις has here the same sense as it
has in v. 17a; and ζήσεται refers not to political survival but to
the life with God, which alone is true life, the life which the
believer is to begin to enjoy here and now, but which he will
enjoy in its fullness in the eschatological future. To understand
the significance of ζήσεται for Paul, one must refer to 2.7;
4.17; 5.17, 18, 21; 6.4, 10, 11, 13, 22, 23; 7.10; 8.2, 6, 10, 13;
10.5; 12.1.

It remains to ask whether ἐκ πίστεως is to be connected with
the verb, as it is in the LXX and as the equivalent expressions
are in the MT and the Targum, or, as was suggested by
Beza[3] and has since been maintained by many interpreters,[4]
with ὁ δίκαιος. In favour of the former alternative there are two
very obvious and considerable arguments: first, that Paul
must have known that in the original *be'emûnātô* was connected with *yihyeh* and in the LXX ἐκ πίστεώς μου with
ζήσεται; and, secondly, that, had he meant ἐκ πίστεως to be

---

[1] Cf. SB 3, pp. 542–4. There is dispute as to whether in this use of
Hab 2.4 *'emûnāh* was understood as being the true fulfilment of the
whole Torah or merely adherence to monotheism as the minimal
requirement of a Jew.
[2] Or perhaps *'āmāl* should here rather be rendered by 'toil'? Is the
reference to the toil of obedience to the law? (Cf. Bruce, *Exegesis*, p. 82.)
[3] p. 15.
[4] e.g. Bengel, who says on the ἐκ πίστεως in v. 17a: 'Construe, *justitia
ex fide*, ut mox, *justus ex fide*' (p. 495), and then comments on these
words, 'Omnia confirmat illud, *Justus ex fide, vivet*' (p. 496); Lietzmann,
p. 31; Lagrange, p. 20; Bultmann, *Theology* 1, p. 319; Nygren, who
argues the case very fully, pp. 85ff; Gaugler 1, p. 37f; Barrett, p. 31;
Kuss, p. 24.

connected with ὁ δίκαιος, he ought to have written ὁ δὲ ἐκ
πίστεως δίκαιος ζήσεται. It is also sometimes claimed that
ζήσεται alone without the support of ἐκ πίστεως is weak. But
the first of these arguments is by no means conclusive, since
Paul could quote the OT with considerable freedom; in reply
to the second, it is surely enough to point out that Paul is
quoting, not formulating something quite independently; and
the third rests on a misunderstanding, a failure to recognize
the significance of ζῆν, ζωή, ζωοποιεῖν, in Romans, to which
attention was drawn above. On the other side, the following
arguments may be adduced in support of connecting ἐκ πίστεως
with ὁ δίκαιος: (i) The immediate context requires it; for the
context contains no direct reference to living by faith, but
does contain a direct reference to righteousness by faith, if, as
urged above, ἐκ πίστεως εἰς πίστιν was in Paul's mind linked
with δικαιοσύνη. (ii) The structure of the epistle requires it;
for 1.18–4.25 expounds the meaning of ὁ δίκαιος ἐκ πίστεως,
while 5.1–8.39 expounds the meaning of the promise that the
man who is righteous by faith ζήσεται. (In this connexion it
is interesting to note that in 1.18–4.25 πίστις occurs nineteen
times and πιστεύειν eight times, whereas in 5.1–8.39 they
occur only twice[1] and once respectively; and that, whereas in
1.18–4.25 ζωή occurs only once and ζῆν not at all, each of them
occurs twelve times in 5.1–8.39.) (iii) The connexion between
righteousness and faith is made explicitly in 5.1 in the words
which summarize the argument of the preceding division
(Δικαιωθέντες οὖν ἐκ πίστεως) and also in 4.11 (σφραγῖδα τῆς
δικαιοσύνης τῆς πίστεως), 13 (διὰ δικαιοσύνης πίστεως); 9.30
(δικαιοσύνην δὲ τὴν ἐκ πίστεως) and 10.6 (ἡ δὲ ἐκ πίστεως
δικαιοσύνη οὕτως λέγει). We conclude (pace Leenhardt[2] and
Michel[3]) that ἐκ πίστεως is almost certainly to be connected with
ὁ δίκαιος rather than with ζήσεται.

---

[1] And one of these occurrences (that in 5.1) is in a summary of the
foregoing argument, i.e. of what lies outside chapters 5 to 8.

[2] p. 58 (Fr.: p. 35).

[3] p. 55.

IV

THE REVELATION OF THE RIGHTEOUSNESS WHICH IS FROM GOD BY FAITH ALONE—'HE WHO IS RIGHTEOUS BY FAITH' EXPOUNDED (1.18–4.25)

This is the first of the four great blocks of material which compose the main body of the epistle (the others being 5.1–8.39, 9.1–11.36, and 12.1–15.13), Paul's first and fundamental contribution to the elucidation of the statement in 1.17 that God's righteousness is being revealed in the gospel, from faith to faith, and also to the exposition of the Habakkuk quotation in the same verse, 'He who is righteous by faith shall live'.

The heart of this main division is the section comprised by 3.21–26, the function of which is to establish the truth of the 'is being revealed' of 1.17, to establish that God's righteousness is actually being revealed now, whenever and wherever the gospel is being preached. This it does by describing the revelation which has already taken place in the past, the revelation of God's righteousness in the gospel events themselves. Without that prior revelation there could be no authentic revelation of God's righteousness in the Church's preaching; but, since God's righteousness has indeed been manifested in the gospel events, the fact of its being revealed in the preaching of the gospel is established, and so also the fact of the existence of the man 'who is righteous by faith'.

This central section is preceded by one (1.18–3.20), the purpose of which is to support the 'from faith to faith' of 1.17 and the qualification of 'he who is righteous' in the same verse by the words 'by faith', to make it clear that there can be no question of any other righteousness of men before God than that which is 'from faith to faith'. It is followed by two sections, the former (3.27–31) drawing out something implicit in it, namely, that glorying, that is, the assertion of a claim on God on the ground of one's works, is altogether ruled out, and the latter (4.1–25) confirming the former by showing that, according to Scripture, not even Abraham had a right to glory.

IV. I. IN THE LIGHT OF THE GOSPEL THERE IS NO QUESTION
OF MEN'S BEING RIGHTEOUS BEFORE GOD OTHERWISE
THAN BY FAITH (1.18–3.20)

The above title is an attempt to bring out as clearly as possible
the relation of this section to the statement of the theological
theme of the epistle in 1.17. This whole section supports the
words 'from faith to faith' and 'by faith' in that verse.

The question is often asked—not unnaturally—whether the
extremely dark picture of human life which is presented here
is not grossly unfair. Certainly, if we read this section as an
historian's assessment of the moral condition of his contemporaries made on the same sort of basis as is normally
used when one is attempting a relative evaluation, and so go
on to compare it with other people's moral assessments of
other epochs, the result will be thoroughly unfair to Paul's
contemporaries. But the truth is that Paul is not attempting
to give an assessment of this sort at all. What he says must be
understood as said on the basis of 1.16b–17 and 3.21–26. In
other words, it is not Paul's judgment of his contemporaries
that we have here, but the gospel's judgment of men, that is,
of all men, the judgment the gospel itself pronounces, which
Paul has heard and to which he has himself submitted.[1] The
section depicts man as he appears in the light of the cross of
Christ. It is not a description of specially bad men only, but the
innermost truth of all of us, as we are in ourselves.

The burden of the section is summed up in the statements,
'There is no one who is righteous, not even one' (3.10) and 'all
have sinned and lack the glory of God' (3.23).

(i) *Man under the judgment of the gospel*
(1.18–32)

[18]For God's wrath is being revealed from heaven against every kind
of ungodliness and unrighteousness of men who try to suppress the
truth by their unrighteousness; [19]for what is knowable of God is

---

[1] This is not to deny that Paul has borrowed many thoughts and
expressions of late Judaism (parallels may be cited in, for example,
the Wisdom of Solomon, the Testaments of the Twelve Patriarchs, the
Sibylline Oracles, the Qumran texts, the Letter of Aristeas and the
Rabbinic literature). He has indeed borrowed much; but he has transformed what he has borrowed by putting it to serve a radically different
purpose—instead of a polemic of one group of human beings against
another, the testimony to a universal accusation against all men without
exception which can be recognized and submitted to only in the light
of the gospel.

manifest in their midst, for God has made it manifest to them. ²⁰For his invisible attributes are clearly seen since the creation of the world, being perceived by means of the things he has made, even both his eternal power and divinity, so that they are without excuse, ²¹because, though they have known God, they have not glorified him as God or given him thanks, but have become futile in their reasonings, and their uncomprehending heart has been darkened. ²²Pretending to be wise, they have shown themselves fools, ²³and exchanged the glory of the immortal God for the likeness of the form of mortal man and of birds and fourfooted animals and reptiles. ²⁴Wherefore God delivered them up, in *their abandonment to* the lusts of their own hearts, to uncleanness, so that among them their bodies are dishonoured.

²⁵They have actually exchanged the truth of God for the lie, and worshipped and served the creature instead of the Creator, who is blessed for ever: Amen. ²⁶Wherefore God has delivered them up to passions which bring dishonour: for both their females have exchanged natural intercourse for that which is contrary to nature, ²⁷and likewise also the males, having abandoned natural intercourse with the female, have burned in their lust for one another, males with males perpetrating shamelessness and receiving in their own persons the due wages of their deludedness.

²⁸And, as they have not seen fit to take God into account, God has delivered them up to a reprobate mind, to do the things which are morally wrong, ²⁹filled with all manner of unrighteousness, wickedness, ruthlessness, depravity, full of envy, murder, rivalry, treachery, malice, whisperers, ³⁰slanderers, haters of God, insolent, arrogant, boastful, inventive of *novel* forms of evil, disobedient to parents, ³¹without understanding, without loyalty, without natural affection, without pity. ³²They know God's righteous decree that those who practise such things deserve death; yet they not only do them, but actually applaud others who practise them.

That in this sub-section Paul has in mind primarily the Gentiles is no doubt true. But it may be doubted whether we shall do justice to his intention, if we assume—as many interpreters seem inclined to do—that these verses refer exclusively to them. In v. 18 he uses the general term 'men', and nowhere in the sub-section does he use either 'Gentiles' or 'Greek'. In describing men's idolatry in v. 23 he echoes the language of Ps 106.20 and Jer 2.11, the former of which refers to Israel's worship of the golden calf and the latter to Israel's forsaking the Lord for other gods at a much later date. And the main point of 2.1–3.20 is precisely that the Jew, who thinks himself entitled to sit in judgment on the Gentiles, himself does the very same things that he condemns in them (cf. especially 2.3). The implication would seem to be that Paul himself reckoned that, by describing—as he certainly was doing in 1.18–32—the obvious sinfulness of the heathen, he was, as a matter of fact, describing the basic sinfulness of fallen man as such, the inner reality of the life of Israel no less than of that of the Gentiles. And the correctness of this view is confirmed by the fact that the 'Wherefore' at the beginning of 2.1, which has proved so baffling to commentators, becomes, on this assumption, perfectly intelligible: if 1.18–32 does indeed declare the truth about *all* men, then it really does follow from it that the man who sets himself up as a judge of his fellows is without excuse. So we understand these verses as the revelation of the gospel's judgment of all men, which lays bare not only the idolatry of ancient and modern paganism but also the idolatry ensconced in Israel, in the Church, and in the life of each believer.

The carefully balanced structure of the central part (vv. 22–28) of this sub-section looks as if it may have been specially designed to suggest a correspondence between sin and punishment such as is noted in, for example, 2 Macc 5.9f; 9.1–10.28; 13.3–8; Wisd 11.6f, 15f; 12.23; 18.4f; Philo, *In Flacc.* 20. It does not seem far-fetched to see intentional correspondences between ἤλλαξαν τὴν δόξαν . . . θεοῦ in v. 23 and τοῦ ἀτιμάζεσθαι, κ.τ.λ. in v. 24, between μετήλλαξαν τὴν ἀλήθειαν, κ.τ.λ. in v. 25 and μετήλλαξαν τὴν φυσικήν, κ.τ.λ. in v. 26, and between οὐκ ἐδοκίμασαν τὸν θεὸν ἔχειν ἐν ἐπιγνώσει in the earlier, and εἰς ἀδόκιμον νοῦν in the later, part of v. 28 (in this last case οὐκ ἐδοκίμασαν/ ἀδόκιμον is simply a word-play, but it draws attention to a substantial correspondence between the refusal to take God into account and the mind's becoming ἀδόκιμος).[1]

18. Ἀποκαλύπτεται γὰρ ὀργὴ θεοῦ. We must first try to decide what is the connexion of thought between this verse and what precedes it. Some interpreters are reluctant to allow γάρ to have its ordinary sense of 'for' here. Thus Lagrange, though he does translate it by 'for' (*car*), speaks of its indicating 'a mild opposition' (*une légère opposition*),[2] while Moffatt boldly renders it by 'but', and Dodd in his commentary (based on the Moffatt translation) has the sentence: 'The adversative conjunction *but* in 1.18 shows that the revelation of God's *anger* is contrasted, and not identified, with the revelation of His righteousness'.[3] Now it is of course true that in certain special circumstances γάρ can acquire some adversative force;[4] but, in the absence of such special circumstances, there would seem to be no justification (apart from a theological presupposition that it is appropriate to contrast δικαιοσύνη θεοῦ and ὀργὴ θεοῦ)

---

[1] Cf. especially the articles by Klostermann and Jeremias cited in the note on v. 22.

[2] p. 21.

[3] p. 45. Cf. Huby, p. 79; Stuhlmacher, op. cit., pp. 78, 80f; and JB, standard ed., p. 269, note n.

[4] e.g. in dialogue, if a 'No' is omitted and γάρ introduces a reason for this unexpressed 'No'. See LSJ, s.v.

for giving to γάρ here any other than its normal meaning. But even those who accept that γάρ means 'for' offer a variety of interpretations. Thus Barth in his shorter commentary understands γάρ as indicating a connexion with v. 16a (v. 18 giving a further reason why Paul has no need to be ashamed of the gospel);[1] Sanday and Headlam, who do not discuss γάρ specifically, see the section which begins with this verse as being explanatory of v. 17 (or of vv. 16 and 17) in that it shows the need for the revelation of the δικαιοσύνη θεοῦ, the need for God's saving action (they say: 'St. Paul has just stated what the Gospel is; he now goes on to show the necessity for such a Gospel. The world is lost without it');[2] and Barrett, who also sees γάρ as indicating the connexion with v. 17, thinks that the implication is that the manifestation of divine wrath described in vv. 18ff is thought of by Paul as demonstrating or supporting the truth of the statement that the righteousness of God is being revealed (he explains that, since for Paul both the revelation of the righteousness of God and the revelation of the wrath of God are properly eschatological events though being anticipated in history, it 'follows logically (assuming Paul's premises) that if the revelation of wrath can be demonstrated (as Paul believes), the revelation of righteousness is demonstrated too': thus, according to Barrett, Paul is appealing to the 'observable situation' depicted in the latter part of the chapter as proof that the righteousness of God is being revealed).[3]

The last of these explanations must surely be rejected; for the argument it attributes to Paul is one which could have been thought to have cogency only on the assumption that this 'observable situation' was something new—an assumption Paul is hardly likely to have entertained. He must surely have known that such corruption of life and consequent disasters had marked every period of previous history, and that an observable situation which was not radically different from that obtaining five hundred or a thousand years before could not demonstrate the fact of the revelation of the righteousness of God in the recent events of Christ's ministry and in the

[1] p. 25f. He writes: 'I am not ashamed of the Gospel over against the powers of the metropolis of Rome; because at all events the Gospel as God's almighty work of salvation pronounces God's condemnation of man; because it is more than obvious that I need not be ashamed of the Gospel but that over against the Gospel the Gentile world as concentrated in Rome ought to be ashamed of itself'.
[2] p. 40.
[3] p. 34.

subsequent proclamation of them as good news from God.[1]
Barth's explanation should also be rejected; for, important
though Paul's statement (v. 16a) that he is not ashamed of the
gospel undoubtedly is, it is made simply as support for his
statement of his readiness to preach in Rome (v. 15), whereas
vv. 16b–17, which it serves to introduce, are clearly the
statement of the theme of the epistle as a whole. It is surely
more probable that the section beginning with v. 18 is intended
as support for something in the actual statement of Paul's
theme than that it is merely intended to support the relatively
incidental statement of v. 16a. The explanation offered by
Sanday and Headlam (and others) is preferable to the two
explanations we have just rejected. But it surely requires
some refinement. It may be suggested that γάρ is to be explained
as indicating the relation of the whole section 1.18–3.20 to 1.17
as support not for its claim that the righteousness from God is
being revealed but for its claim that this righteousness is ἐκ
πίστεως εἰς πίστιν. When it is recognized that the purpose of
1.18–3.20 is to support the claim that the righteousness from
God, now being revealed in the message of good news, is ἐκ
πίστεως εἰς πίστιν, the structure of the argument of the epistle
is considerably clarified. We take it then that the point of the
γάρ is that the revelation of the wrath of God against men's
sin makes it abundantly clear that there can be no question of
men's having a status of righteousness before God in any other
way than ἐκ πίστεως εἰς πίστιν.

The second question about these words which needs to be
answered is: What is meant by ὀργὴ θεοῦ? Dodd has argued
that by this phrase Paul did not mean to indicate a personal
reaction on God's part but 'some process or effect in the realm
of objective facts',[2] 'an inevitable process of cause and effect
in a moral universe'.[3] But, when he says, 'we cannot think
with full consistency of God in terms of the highest human
ideals of personality and yet attribute to Him the irrational
passion of anger',[4] he is begging the question by assuming that

---

[1] It is to be noted that to regard the wickedness and consequent disasters
of the present, though not substantially different in kind from those of past
ages, as a sign of the imminence of God's decisive redemptive action, as an
apocalyptist might, is one thing: to appeal to them as demonstrating that this
action has occurred in particular events of the recent past and is occurring in
their proclamation in the present as good news from God is another thing
altogether.

[2] p. 49.

[3] p. 50.

[4] p. 50.

anger is always an irrational passion. Certainly it sometimes is; but there is also an anger which is thoroughly rational. That Paul would attribute to God a capricious, irrational rage is more than improbable. But a consideration of what Dodd calls 'the highest human ideals of personality' might well lead us to question whether God could be the good and loving God, if He did not react to our evil with wrath. For indignation against wickedness is surely an essential element of human goodness in a world in which moral evil is always present. A man who knows, for example, about the injustice and cruelty of *apartheid* and is not angry at such wickedness cannot be a thoroughly good man; for his lack of wrath means a failure to care for his fellow man, a failure to love.

We shall not understand what Paul means by the wrath of God, until we recognize, first, that, in seeking the measure of help which human analogies can afford, we must look not to the lower, irrational kind of human anger, but to the higher kind, the indignation against injustice, cruelty and corruption, which is an essential element of goodness and love in a world in which moral evil is present; and, secondly, that even the very highest and purest human wrath can at the best afford but a distorted and twisted reflection of the wrath of God, since the wrath of men (our Lord alone excepted) is always more or less compromised by the presence of sin in the one who is wroth, whereas the wrath of God is the wrath of Him who is perfectly loving, perfectly good. The third thing to be said here—and it is the really decisive thing—will become clear from what is said now in answer to the third question about the opening words of this verse, namely, What is meant by Ἀποκαλύπτεται?

With regard to this question, it must be said at once that it is very easy to get from reading vv. 18ff the impression that Paul is thinking here of the revelation of God's wrath as taking place in the frustrations, futilities and disasters which result from human ἀσέβεια and ἀδικία. But Paul himself has given a pretty clear indication in the parallelism in language and structure between vv. 17 and 18 that this is not his meaning. In v. 17 he has stated that δικαιοσύνη θεοῦ is being revealed in the gospel, that is, in the on-going proclamation of the gospel. And this statement presupposes a prior revelation of δικαιοσύνη θεοῦ in the gospel events themselves, a revelation indicated by the perfect πεφανέρωται in 3.21. In view of the parallelism between vv. 17 and 18, the most natural way of taking v. 18 is to understand Paul to mean that ὀργὴ θεοῦ also is being revealed *in the gospel*, that is, in the on-going proclamation of

the gospel, and to recognize that behind, and basic to, this
revelation of the wrath of God in the preaching, is the prior
revelation of the wrath of God in the gospel events. This
interpretation of v. 18, which is suggested by the parallelism
we have noted, is confirmed by the fact that the sense thus
obtained is thoroughly Pauline and by the further fact that
according to it the early chapters of Romans have a much
more closely-knit character than other interpretations
imply.[1]

The two revelations referred to in these two verses are then
really two aspects of the same process. The preaching of Christ
crucified, risen, ascended and coming again, is at the same time
both the offer to men of a status of righteousness before God
and the revelation of God's wrath against their sin. In the
gospel the divine mercy and the divine judgment are inseparable from each other: the forgiveness offered to us is
forgiveness without condoning. And this is so because in the
gospel events themselves there was wrought for men no cheap
or superficial forgiveness, but God's costly forgiveness.

Now the third and most important thing about the wrath
of God (omitted above) has become clear. It is that we do not
see the full meaning of the wrath of God in the disasters
befalling sinful men in the course of history: the reality of the
wrath of God is only truly known when it is seen in its revelation in Gethsemane and on Golgotha.[2]

ἀπ' οὐρανοῦ might seem at first sight to correspond to ἐν αὐτῷ
in the parallel sentence, v. 17a, since both phrases are adverbial
with a local significance; and one might be inclined to assume
that a contrast is intended between the revelation of the
righteousness of God in the preaching of the gospel and the
revelation of God's wrath 'from heaven' (in the sense of its

---

[1] In this paragraph we are deeply indebted to Barth, *Shorter*, p. 24f.
[2] See also on 3.24–26. The word ὀργή occurs elsewhere in Romans
eleven times (2.5 (twice), 8; 3.5; 4.15; 5.9; 9.22 (twice); 12.19; 13.4, 5),
the reference always being to the divine wrath. Reference should be
made to G. Stählin *et al.*, in *TWNT* 5, pp. 382–448: to the bibliography
on p. 382 should be added: E. R. Bevan, *Symbolism and Belief*, London,
1938, pp. 206–51; R. V. G. Tasker, *The Biblical Doctrine of the Wrath
of God*, London, 1951; A. T. Hanson, *The Wrath of the Lamb*, London,
1957; Barth, *KD* II/1, pp. 442ff (*CD* II/1, pp. 393ff); *KD* IV/1, pp. 434ff
(*CD* IV/1, pp. 392ff), and other references (see indices). Reference may
also be made to C. E. B. Cranfield, *The Gospel according to Saint Mark*,
Cambridge, ⁴1972, pp. 431, 433 and 458f, on Mk 14.34, 36, and 15.34,
respectively, and, with regard to the present verse, 'Romans 1.18', in
SJT 21 (1968), pp. 330–35; and G. Herold, *Zorn und Gerechtigkeit bei
Paulus: eine Untersuchung zu Röm 1.16–18*, Berne, 1973, which I have
not yet been able to see.

being revealed in fearful apocalyptic catastrophes such as are alluded to in Mk 13.24f or Rev 15.5–7). But, in view of what was said above on ἀποκαλύπτεται, it is unlikely that any such contrast is in Paul's mind. The truth seems rather to be that the two adverbial phrases are not meant to correspond to each other, and that, so far from intending to contrast the one thing's being revealed in the gospel with the other's being revealed 'from heaven', Paul would—had he been questioned —have replied that the wrath, as well as the righteousness, is being revealed in the gospel, and that the righteousness no less than the wrath is being revealed from heaven. The purpose of ἀπ' οὐρανοῦ would seem to be simply to emphasize the utter seriousness of the ὀργὴ θεοῦ as being really *God's* wrath: it amounts in fact to an underlining of θεοῦ.[1]

ἐπὶ πᾶσαν ἀσέβειαν καὶ ἀδικίαν ἀνθρώπων τῶν τὴν ἀλήθειαν ἐν ἀδικίᾳ κατεχόντων indicates the object against which God's wrath is directed. The wrath which is being revealed is no nightmare of an indiscriminate, uncontrolled, irrational fury, but the wrath of the holy and merciful God called forth by, and directed against, men's ἀσέβεια and ἀδικία. In this disclosure, which takes place again and again in the preaching of the gospel (as the prior, altogether decisive, disclosure in the gospel events themselves is proclaimed), not only is the reality of the divine wrath unveiled, but its object is also unmasked and raked with light. According to some interpreters, ἀσέβεια[2]

---

[1] The word 'heaven', though occurring in Romans only here and in 10.6, is used in the Bible very frequently to denote God's own place, i.e., that place, which, in contrast to earth, is altogether mysterious and beyond the reach of men's scrutiny. As God's 'dwelling place' (e.g. 1 Kgs 8.30: for the idea cf., out of a multitude of possible references, Eccles 5.2; Mt 5.16; 6.9; 7.21; 10.32; Mk 11.25, 26), heaven is the place toward which men direct their prayers (e.g. 2 Chr 30.27; 32.20), the place in which God hears them (e.g. 1 Kgs 8.30, 32; Neh 9.27) and from which He speaks to them (e.g. Exod 20.22; Deut 4.36) and sends them help (e.g. Ps 57.3). It is His 'throne' (e.g. Isa 66.1; Mt 5.34; 23.22) and also the sphere where His will is done (Mt 6.10). While He is 'Lord of heaven and earth' (e.g. Mt 11.25), heaven stands in a special relation to Him, and the phrase 'the God of heaven' can be used as a designation of the true God (e.g. Neh 1.4; Dan 2.19, 44; in the NT only in Rev. 11.13; 16.11). As is well known, the word 'heaven' came to be used as a way of referring to God without mentioning Him. When ὁ ἐν τοῖς οὐρανοῖς or ὁ οὐράνιος is used to qualify πατήρ as applied to God (e.g. Mt 5.16, 48; 6.1, 9, 14, 26, 32), it is a confession of that majesty, mystery and holiness which call for deepest reverence on the part of men, and, when it is πατὴρ ἡμῶν or πατὴρ ὑμῶν that is so qualified, a reminder of the unutterable grace which those expressions signify. See further H. Traub and G. von Rad, in *TWNT* 5, pp. 496–543; Barth, *CD* III/3, pp. 369–531, especially 418–76 (= *KD* III/3, pp. 426–623, especially 486–558).

[2] It occurs also in 11.26, and ἀσεβής in 4.5; 5.6.

and ἀδικία[1] here denote two distinct categories of sinfulness, namely, those covered by the first four of the Ten Commandments and by the last six, respectively.[2] But, in view of the fact that the single πᾶσαν embraces both ἀσέβειαν and ἀδικίαν, and the fact that in the participial clause ἀδικίᾳ by itself is apparently meant to represent the double expression,[3] it is more probable that they are here used as two names for the same thing combined in order to afford a more rounded description of it than either gives by itself (ἀσέβεια focusing attention on the fact that all sin is an attack on the majesty of God, ἀδικία on the fact that it is a violation of God's just order).[4] The words which follow are a penetrating description of the essential nature of sin. The verb κατέχειν is used in its sense of 'hold down', 'suppress';[5] and the present participle is to be understood as having a conative force.[6] Sin is always (cf. v. 25) an assault upon the truth (that is, the fundamental truth of God 'as Creator, Judge, and Redeemer',[7] which, because it is the truth, must be taken into account and come to terms with, if man is not to live in vain), the attempt to suppress it, bury it out of sight, obliterate it from the memory; but it is of the essence of sin that it can never be more than an *attempt* to suppress the truth, an attempt which is always bound in the end to prove futile.

[1] ἀδικία occurs also in v. 29, and in 2.8; 3.5; 6.13; 9.14; and ἄδικος in 3.5.

[2] Cf., e.g., Schlatter, p. 49; Michel, p. 62; Leenhardt, p. 61, n. † (Fr.: 36, n. 3).

[3] That, by using at this point ἀδικία by itself, Paul meant to indicate that impiety has its ultimate source in immorality (in the wider sense of the word), is quite unlikely: the sequel clearly suggests that, on the contrary, Paul understood moral corruption to be rooted in a false relationship to God.

[4] For the view that the two nouns together denote one and the same thing cf. Nygren, p. 100f; W. Foerster, in *TWNT* 7, p. 188f. In this connexion it is significant that in the LXX several Hebrew words are represented both by ἀσέβεια and by ἀδικία.

[5] Cf. Bauer, s.v. 1. β. The meanings 'possess' and 'hold fast' are unsuitable to the context. There is nothing in this section to support the idea that the reference is to men's combining orthodox belief and unrighteousness of life. Such a knowledge as is referred to in vv. 19-21 could scarcely be described as possessing the truth, and still less as holding it fast.

[6] For the conative present indicative (τῶν . . . κατεχόντων is of course equivalent to a relative clause with a verb in the present indicative) cf. BDF, § 319. The general failure of translators and commentators to notice the conative force of κατεχόντων has had the effect of turning Paul's words into a cheerless statement which ill accords with the tenor of his argument in which the inherent futility of sin is again and again being emphasized.

[7] Barrett, p. 34.

19. διότι. It is difficult to decide whether this verse should be understood as giving the reason for God's wrath (so vindicating God's fairness) or as justifying the language of the preceding participial clause by showing that men do indeed have sufficient knowledge[1] of the truth to warrant their being described as trying to suppress it. Though the former alternative is commonly accepted, it might perhaps be claimed for the latter alternative that it yields a rather better articulated sequence of thought; but, in any case, the general sense of the passage is not substantially affected by the decision we reach on this point.

τὸ γνωστὸν τοῦ θεοῦ. While elsewhere in the NT (in which, apart from its use here and twice in John, its occurrences are confined to Luke and Acts) γνωστός always means 'known', in classical Greek and also in the LXX it sometimes has the meaning 'knowable'; and there is little doubt that this is its sense here, since, if it meant 'known', the sentence could scarcely be regarded as anything but a tautologism.[2] The phrase as a whole must mean 'that which is knowable (to man) of God', i.e. 'God, in so far as He is knowable (to man)'. Paul's main purpose in putting as the subject of this sentence τὸ γνωστὸν τοῦ θεοῦ rather than ὁ θεός was probably to safeguard the truth of the mysteriousness and hiddenness of God. He may perhaps also have felt it more appropriate in view of the fact that the only revelation he was thinking of here was the revelation of the Creator in His creation. The phrase should not be taken to imply a belief that fallen man is capable in himself of a knowledge, in the sense of a subjective knowledge, of God. It should rather be interpreted as meaning either 'God, in so far as men ought to be able to know Him—though, being fallen, they cannot as a matter of fact do so' or—and this seems more likely—'God, in so far as He is objectively knowable, i.e. knowable in the sense of being experienceable' (cf. on γνόντες in v. 21).

φανερόν ἐστιν. A real revelation of τὸ γνωστὸν τοῦ θεοῦ has taken place. God (in so far as He is knowable) is truly manifest.

ἐν αὐτοῖς: 'in their midst' rather than 'within them'. For an

[1] With regard to the sense in which they may be said to know the truth, see below on the rest of this verse, on v. 20 and also on γνόντες in v. 21.

[2] γνωστός is taken to mean 'knowable' by Origen, col. 863; and he has been followed by very many, including Aquinas, the AV, and a great many moderns. The Vulgate on the other hand has 'quod notum est Dei', and this interpretation still has supporters. The phrase has also been taken to mean 'the fact that God is known' (cf. Prat, *Theology* 1, p. 195f).

assertion that God is manifest within them in the sense that the revelation has been inwardly apprehended by them would be incompatible with what is said in v. 21; and it is unlikely, in view of the reference in v. 20 to seeing (we take it that καθορᾶται does refer to physical sight: see below on v. 20f), that Paul meant to refer here exclusively to the existence and functioning of men's inward capacities (as, for example, of their consciences, as is often suggested) as manifestation of God. The meaning is rather that τὸ γνωστὸν τοῦ θεοῦ is manifest in their midst. In their midst and all around them and also in their own creaturely existence (including of course what is inward as well as what is external) God is objectively manifest: His whole creation declares Him.

ὁ θεὸς γὰρ αὐτοῖς ἐφανέρωσεν is added to make it clear that God's being manifest in His creation is the result of His own deliberate self-disclosure and not something in any way independent of His will.

20f. τὰ γὰρ ἀόρατα αὐτοῦ ἀπὸ κτίσεως κόσμου τοῖς ποιήμασιν νοούμενα καθορᾶται, ἥ τε ἀΐδιος αὐτοῦ δύναμις καὶ θειότης provides, as a matter of fact, an explanation of v. 19b; but it is probably more natural to understand γάρ as marking the relation of v. 20f as a whole to v. 18f than that of only the first part of v. 20 to v. 19b. τὰ . . . ἀόρατα αὐτοῦ . . . καθορᾶται is a notable oxymoron, no doubt intentional.[1] By τὰ . . . ἀόρατα αὐτοῦ are meant God's invisible attributes (see further on ἥ τε ἀΐδιος, κ.τ.λ.). For the invisibility of God compare Jn 1.18; Col 1.15; 1 Tim 1.17; Heb 11.27 (see also Gen 32.30; Exod 24.10f; 33.20–23; Judg 6.22f; 13.20ff; Isa 6.5). There is little doubt that ἀπὸ κτίσεως κόσμου should be taken to mean 'since the creation of the world', ἀπό being understood in a temporal sense (cf. Mt 24.21; 25.34; Mk 10.6; 13.19; Lk 11.50; 2 Pet 3.4; Rev 13.8; 17.8) and κτίσις in its sense of 'act of creating': this is much more natural than to take the phrase to mean 'from the created universe' (an idea which is anyway sufficiently expressed by τοῖς ποιήμασιν). The point made is that the self-revelation of God here referred to has been continuous ever since the creation. It is extremely difficult to arrive at a firm conclusion about the precise meaning of τοῖς ποιήμασιν νοούμενα καθορᾶται, and various explanations of these words are current. Thus some understand νοούμενα as virtually equivalent to an adverbial expression modifying καθορᾶται (indicating that the seeing referred to is a seeing with the mind's eye) and connect τοῖς ποιήμασιν with the combination νοούμενα καθορᾶται as a whole; while others regard τοῖς ποιήμασιν νοούμενα as an

---

[1] Cf. (Ps.-)Aristotle, Mu. 399b. 14ff: ἀόρατος τοῖς ἔργοις ὁρᾶται.

ordinary participial clause explanatory of καθορᾶται, some
of them taking both νοούμενα and καθορᾶται to refer to physical
sight, others taking them both to refer to mental perception.[1]
If the last explanation is accepted (it may certainly be argued
that usage favours this interpretation of νοούμενα), the mental
perception signified by νοούμενα and καθορᾶται must, in view of
the tenor of the context, be understood in a strictly limited
sense. But the fact that the oxymoron ἀόρατα . . . καθορᾶται is
clearly deliberate should probably encourage us to understand
καθορᾶται (and therefore also νοούμενα) as referring to physical
sight and the sentence as a whole as a paradoxical assertion
that God's invisible attributes are actually seen in, and through,
His creation.[2] ἥ τε ἀίδιος αὐτοῦ δύναμις καὶ θειότης is a clarification of τὰ ἀόρατα αὐτοῦ, to which it stands in apposition.
ἀιδιότης is an attribute of God in Wisd 2.23. The adjective
ἀίδιος occurs in the LXX only in Wisd 7.26 and as a variant in
4 Macc 10.15; in the NT only here and in Jude 6. It is found in
pagan Greek from early times (e.g. Homeric Hymns, Hesiod),
but is a favourite with Philo. The thought of God's eternity is
of course common enough in the Bible, but it is characteristically expressed by other words (αἰώνιος, ζῶν). God's δύναμις is
referred to again and again in Scripture, and power is so
characteristic of God that ἡ δύναμις can be used as a periphrasis for the divine Name (Mt 26.64 = Mk 14.62). The term
θειότης (divinitas, 'divinity') first appears in biblical Greek in
Wisd 18.9, and occurs in the NT only here. It is a Hellenistic
term (Plutarch, Lucian, Hermetic corpus, etc.) denoting the
divine nature and properties; and is to be distinguished from
θεότης (deitas, 'deity'), which denotes the divine personality
(in the NT only Col 2.9).[3] The phrase 'vis et natura deorum' in
Cicero, N.D. 1.18.44, is an interesting parallel to the combination of δύναμις and θειότης here.[4]

---

[1] To take καθορᾶται to refer to physical seeing and νοούμενα to refer to
mental perception is hardly possible, since it is natural to understand
the action denoted by the participle to be either prior to, or contemporaneous with, and not subsequent to, that denoted by the indicative.

[2] The κατα- of the verb is intensive—so 'are clearly seen' or perhaps
'cause themselves to be clearly seen' (if the passive is to be understood
in the sense described in BDF, § 314). On ἀόρατος and καθορᾶν see further
W. Michaelis, in TWNT 5, pp. 370f and 379–81, respectively; and on
νοεῖν J. Behm, in TWNT 4, pp. 947–50. It is surely more natural in this
context (pace Michel, p. 63) to take ποιήματα in its specific sense of
'things made' (cf., e.g., Eph 2.10) than in the general sense of 'works'
(including deeds).

[3] See further H. S. Nash, 'Θειότης-Θεότης (Rom 1.20; Col 2.9)', in
JBL 18 (1899), pp. 1–34.

[4] Cited Michel, p. 63, n. 3.

εἰς τὸ εἶναι αὐτοὺς ἀναπολογήτους is, in view of the following causal clause, better understood as consecutive ('so that they are without excuse') than as final.[1] It is the key to the proper understanding of what Paul is saying in vv. 19–21. The result of God's self-manifestation in His creation is not a natural knowledge of God on men's part independent of God's self-revelation in His Word, a valid though limited knowledge, but simply the excuselessness of men in their ignorance. A real self-disclosure of God has indeed taken place and is always occurring, and men ought to have recognized, but in fact have not recognized, Him. They have been constantly surrounded on all sides by, and have possessed within their own selves, the evidences of God's eternal power and divinity, but they have not allowed themselves to be led by them to a recognition of Him. Barrett is surely correct over against a great many interpretations of this passage when he declares: 'It is not Paul's intention' in these verses 'to establish a natural theology; nor does he create one unintentionally'.[2] For the thought of men's being without excuse compare Wisd 13.8.[3]

διότι introduces a statement (it includes vv. 22 and 23 as well as v. 21) in explanation of the last clause. It takes up the thought of the latter part of v. 18 and clarifies it. Verses 19 and 20 have already shown that the fact that God has manifested Himself to them renders them without excuse, and this thought is taken up by the words γνόντες τὸν θεόν; but, for the rest, vv. 21–23 focus attention on the conduct for which (having had God's self-manifestation) they are without excuse, that conduct already hinted at in the last words of v. 18.

γνόντες τὸν θεόν: that is, knowing[4] God in the sense that in their awareness of the created world it is of Him that all along, though unwittingly, they have been—objectively—aware.

---

[1] Cf., e.g., Chrysostom, col. 413; Burton, MT, § 411; Lagrange, p. 24f; Kuss, p. 37. The contrary view is taken by, e.g., Michel, p. 65; Barrett, p. 36.

[2] p. 35.

[3] On v. 19f see further A. Fridrichsen, 'Zur Auslegung von Röm 1.19f', in ZNW 17 (1916), pp. 159–68; Barth, Shorter, pp. 26–29; id., CD I/2, pp. 303ff; II/1, pp. 118ff; IV/1, p. 394; IV/3, pp. 187f and 200 (= KD I/2, pp. 331ff; II/1, pp. 131ff; IV/1, p. 436; IV/3, pp. 215 and 229); Bornkamm, Early Christian Experience, pp. 47ff; A. Feuillet, 'La connaissance naturelle de Dieu par les hommes d'après Rom 1.18–23', in LV 14 (1954), pp. 63–80; S. Lyonnet, 'De naturali Dei cognitione (Rom 1.18–23)', in Quaestiones in epistolam ad Romanos 1, Rome, 1955, pp. 68–108; also E. Brunner and K. Barth, Natural Theology, London, 1946.

[4] The aorist participle is used since their experience of God has necessarily always gone before their failure to recognize its true significance and act accordingly.

They have in fact experienced Him—His wisdom, power, generosity—in every moment of their existence, though they have not recognized Him. It has been by Him that their lives have been sustained, enriched, bounded. In this limited sense they have known Him all their lives.

οὐχ ὡς θεὸν ἐδόξασαν ἢ ηὐχαρίστησαν. Having experience of God's self-manifestation, they ought to have glorified Him as God and given Him thanks; but they did not do so. The verb δοξάζειν (it occurs five times in Romans) is used in 11.13 of Paul's glorifying his ministry to the Gentiles, in 8.30 (with God as subject and man as object) of God's giving men a share in His own glory (cf. 3.23; 5.2; 8.18, 21), and here and in 15.6 and 9 (with man as subject and God as object) of the response which men owe to God's glory of recognizing Him as God, as their Creator and the Lord of their life, in humble trust and obedience (cf. 4.20; 15.7). See further on 15.6, and also on δόξαν in 1.23; and, for a suggestive discussion of the meaning of man's glorification of God, Barth, *CD* II/1, pp. 667 ff. (=*KD*, II/1, pp. 753ff). The words ἢ ηὐχαρίστησαν single out for special mention one particular element in the glorification which they owed to God. They ought to have recognized their indebtedness to His goodness and generosity, to have recognized Him as the source of all the good things they enjoyed, and so to have been grateful to Him for His benefits.[1]

ἀλλὰ ἐματαιώθησαν ἐν τοῖς διαλογισμοῖς αὐτῶν. Instead of glorifying God and being grateful to Him, they became futile[2] in their reasonings. This is the only occurrence of the verb ματαιοῦν in the NT, but other words of the μάτην group occur between them thirteen times. In the LXX the word-group is prominent, and represents a number of different Hebrew roots. One particularly significant usage is in connexion with idolatry, idols being referred to as μάταια, that is, mere useless nothings. The verb occurs in association with μάταια used in this sense in the question asked by God in Jer 2.5: Τί εὕροσαν οἱ πατέρες ὑμῶν ἐν ἐμοὶ πλημμέλημα, ὅτι ἀπέστησαν μακρὰν ἀπ' ἐμοῦ καὶ ἐπορεύθησαν ὀπίσω τῶν ματαίων καὶ ἐματαιώθησαν; Paul no doubt means to indicate the futility which is the inevitable result of loss of touch with reality. It is to be seen, in particular,

---

[1] For Jewish condemnation of the pride of the Gentiles, which withholds from God His glory, and of their ingratitude, see the numerous passages quoted in SB 3, pp. 44–46.
[2] Some (e.g. Michel, p. 65) see in the passives ἐματαιώθησαν and ἐσκοτίσθη a reference to God's judicial action; but the way in which the reference to the divine action is introduced in v. 24 seems to us to tell against this suggestion.

in their thinking, in referring to which Paul uses a word which in the Bible often has a distinctly pejorative connotation (e.g. Mk 7.21; Lk 5.22; 6.8; 9.47;and Ps 94[LXX: 93].11, which is quoted in 1 Cor 3.20).[1] All their thinking suffers from the fatal flaw, the basic disconnexion from reality involved in their failure to recognize and to glorify the true God.

καὶ ἐσκοτίσθη ἡ ἀσύνετος αὐτῶν καρδία. Paul uses καρδία to denote a man's inward, hidden[2] self as a thinking,[3] willing[4] and feeling[5] subject. The fact that καρδία is qualified by ἀσύνετος ('uncomprehending', 'void of understanding') suggests that it is the intellectual element of their inner lives which here is particularly in mind. Their heart has become darkened[6] (on the passive see above on ἐματαιώθησαν) as a result of their failure to recognize the true God. It is important to understand the significance of this statement correctly. It implies no contempt for reason (those Christians who disparage the intellect and the processes of rational thought have no right at all to claim Paul as a supporter). But it is a sober acknowledgment of the fact that the καρδία as the inner self of man shares fully in the fallenness of the whole man, that the intellect is not a part of human nature somehow exempted from the general corruption, not something which can be appealed to as an impartial arbiter capable of standing outside the influence of the ego and returning a perfectly objective judgment.[7] See further on v. 28 (ἀδόκιμον νοῦν) and 12.2 (τῇ ἀνακαινώσει τοῦ νοός).

22. φάσκοντες εἶναι σοφοὶ ἐμωράνθησαν drives home the contrast between human pretension and actual fact. The asyndeton makes the statement specially striking. For all their

---

[1] Cf. Bengel, p. 497 ('διαλογισμοῖς, cogitationibus) variis, incertis, stultis'); E. Hatch, *Essays in Biblical Greek*, Oxford, 1889, p. 8; G. Schrenk, in *TWNT* 2, pp. 96–8.

[2] e.g. 2.29; 1 Cor 4.5; 14.25; 2 Cor 5.12; 1 Th 2.17.

[3] e.g. 10.6, 8, 9; 1 Cor 2.9; 2 Cor 3.15; 4.6; Eph 1.18.

[4] e.g. 2.5, 15; 1 Cor 7.37; 2 Cor 8.16; 9.7; 1 Th 3.13.

[5] e.g. 1.24; 9.2; 2 Cor 7.3; Phil 1.7; Col 4.8.

[6] For the imagery of the darkening of the heart (or mind) cf. Eph 4.18; also Test.Reuben 3.8; and the complementary idea of the illumination of the heart in 2 Cor 4.6.

[7] The Christian should of course be aware not just of such obvious facts as that judgment is often warped by self-interest and the processes of rational thought often exploited for base purposes, but also of the innumerable much more subtle ways in which the processes of thought are deflected, distorted and debilitated by the egotism of the thinker (e.g. the scholar's inability to criticize his own arguments and theories as rigorously as he does those of others). The darkening to which this sentence testifies means that, even at its best, the thinking of fallen men is never perfectly objective.

emphatic claims[1] to be wise, they have shown themselves fools.[2]
For the substance of the sentence compare 1 Cor 1.21 (the
theme of the contrast between wisdom and folly runs through
the whole of 1 Cor 1.18–25). The idea that Paul is here alluding
to the philosophers in particular is rightly rejected by Calvin;[3]
for, if he were, then v. 23 would be an inappropriate sequel,
since idolatry did not originate with them. The reference is
much more general and fundamental. Compare the descriptions
in Gen 3.6ff and 11.4ff of supposed wisdom which proves to be
folly.[4]

**23. καὶ ἥλλαξαν[5] τὴν δόξαν τοῦ ἀφθάρτου θεοῦ ἐν ὁμοιώματι εἰκόνος
φθαρτοῦ ἀνθρώπου καὶ πετεινῶν καὶ τετραπόδων καὶ ἑρπετῶν.** This
statement that men have exchanged the glory of the eternal
God for mere likenesses of the forms of mortal men, birds, beasts
and creeping things, echoes the language used of Israel in LXX
Ps 105[MT:106].20 (καὶ ἠλλάξαντο τὴν δόξαν αὐτῶν ἐν ὁμοιώματι
μόσχου ἔσθοντος χόρτον) with reference to the making of the
golden calf (Exod 32) and in Jer 2.11 (εἰ ἀλλάξονται ἔθνη θεοὺς
αὐτῶν; καὶ οὗτοι οὔκ εἰσιν θεοί. ὁ δὲ λαός μου ἠλλάξατο τὴν δόξαν
αὐτοῦ, ἐξ ἧς οὐκ ὠφεληθήσονται) with reference to their forsaking
the Lord for other gods at a much later time. Compare also for
the use of ὁμοίωμα and εἰκών and for the classification of the
idols Deut 4.16–18 (μὴ ἀνομήσητε καὶ ποιήσητε ὑμῖν ἑαυτοῖς
γλυπτὸν ὁμοίωμα, πᾶσαν εἰκόνα, ὁμοίωμα ἀρσενικοῦ ἢ θηλυκοῦ,
ὁμοίωμα παντὸς κτήνους τῶν ὄντων ἐπὶ τῆς γῆς, ὁμοίωμα παντὸς
ὀρνέου πτερωτοῦ, ὃ πέταται ὑπὸ τὸν οὐρανόν, ὁμοίωμα παντὸς
ἑρπετοῦ, ὃ ἕρπει ἐπὶ τῆς γῆς, ὁμοίωμα παντὸς ἰχθύος, ὅσα ἐστὶν ἐν
τοῖς ὕδασιν ὑποκάτω τῆς γῆς). Paul uses δόξα here differently
from the way in which it is used in the psalm-verse and in Jer
2.11 (in these two OT passages the reference is to Israel's glory,
whereas Paul here refers to God's glory), but the substantial
meaning is much the same, since what is meant by Israel's
glory is God Himself. In extra-biblical Greek the primary
meaning of δόξα is 'opinion', its secondary meaning 'the opinion
which others have of one', so 'repute', 'good repute', 'glory'.
But in the Bible the meaning 'opinion' has almost completely

---

[1] For the use of φάσκειν cf. Gen. 26.20; 2 Macc 14.32; Acts 24.9; 25.19.
[2] Cf. Jer 10.14; Ecclus 23.14.
[3] p. 33.
[4] On this and the following verses reference may be made to E.
Klostermann, 'Die adäquate Vergeltung in Röm 1.22–31', in *ZNW* 32
(1933), pp. 1–6; J. Jeremias, 'Zu Röm 1.22–32', in *ZNW* 45 (1954),
pp. 119–21.
[5] The variant ἠλλάξαντο may be explained as assimilation to LXX
Ps 105[MT: 106].20. It is also an easier reading, since Attic usage
preferred the middle of this verb when the sense intended was 'give in
exchange'.

disappeared, and δόξα has acquired a new meaning as a result of its being used to translate the Hebrew *kābôd*, namely, 'glory', 'splendour', 'majesty', with reference to external appearance. So it is used to denote the manifest majesty of God (e.g. LXX Ps 96[MT: 97].6; Exod 40.35; Isa 6.3; 40.5). In the NT it can further denote the divine quality of life. But in this verse it is best understood as referring to that self-manifestation of the true God spoken of in vv. 19 and 20. (On δόξα see further on 2.7; 3.7, 23; and G. von Rad and G. Kittel, in *TWNT* 2, pp. 235–58.) The use of ἐν with the dative to indicate the object acquired in the exchange reflects the *bᵉ* of the underlying Hebrew.[1] ὁμοίωμα has here the sense 'likeness', 'image', as in LXX Ps 105.20 and Deut 4.16–18,[2] while εἰκών here denotes the actual form of man, bird, etc., which the likeness reproduces (cf. G. Kittel, in *TWNT* 2, p. 393f).[3] With regard to the animal images reference may be made to (in addition to Deut 4.16ff) e.g. Wisd 11.15; 12.24; 13.10, 14; Ep. Arist. 138 (other references in SB 3, pp. 60–2) and also to J. Gray, in *IDB* 2, pp. 673–8 on 'Idol' and 'Idolatry'.

24. διό indicates that what is related in this verse was God's response to the perverseness of men just described in vv. 22–23.

παρέδωκεν αὐτοὺς ὁ θεός is repeated like a refrain in vv. 26 and 28. If the sentence of which these words are a part stood quite on its own, παρέδωκεν would be patient of a wide variety of interpretations; but, since this sentence has its context in Romans, that interpretation has the best claim to be accepted —all other things being equal—which agrees best with the thought of the rest of the epistle. Dodd has attempted to minimize any suggestion of a direct judicial act on God's part. 'All through this passage', he says, 'the disastrous progress of evil in society is presented as a natural process of cause and effect, and not as the direct act of God. . . . The act of God is no more than an abstention from interference with their free choice and its consequences.'[4] But the thrice-repeated παρέδωκεν αὐτοὺς ὁ θεός is surely so emphatic as to suggest that a deliberate, positive act of God is meant. Another view which is surely to be rejected is that which understands παρέδωκεν to

---

[1] See BDB, s.v.[מְסֻרָה]2. But the indication of the object acquired in exchange by ἐν and the dative occurs also in classical Greek (see Sophocles, *Ant.* 945).

[2] In Deut 4.12, 15, ὁμοίωμα is used in a different sense—to denote a visible form.

[3] On the words ὁμοίωμα and εἰκών see further J. Schneider, in *TWNT* 5, pp. 191–7, and G. von Rad, H. Kleinknecht and G. Kittel, in *TWNT* 2, pp. 378–96.

[4] p. 55.

imply that God actually impelled men to uncleanness, actually made them sin. Chrysostom rightly rejected this explanation;[1] for it is hardly reconcilable with the fundamental biblical doctrine of God's absolute goodness. We must rather think in terms of God's permitting (in the sense not of authorizing but of not preventing), of His withholding His help which alone could prevent.[2] A further question of the greatest importance still remains to be considered: Did Paul mean by παρέδωκεν an act which was absolute and final, or an act of definitely limited intent? The English expression 'give up' (used by the AV and RV here) is liable to suggest a finality which the verb παραδιδόναι certainly does not always imply. It is significant that the same verb is used in 8.32 of God's delivering up His Son to death for our sake:[3] while this fact in no way calls in question the seriousness of what is meant by παρέδωκεν here, it ought to put us on our guard against too readily assuming that Paul must mean that God gave these men up for ever. It seems more consistent with what is said elsewhere in the epistle (e.g. in chapter 11) to understand the meaning to be that God allowed them to go their own way, in order that they might at last learn from their consequent wretchedness to hate the futility of a life turned away from the truth of God.[4] We suggest then that Paul's meaning is neither that these men fell out of the hands of God, as Dodd seems to think,[5] nor that God washed His hands of them; but rather that this delivering them up was a deliberate act of judgment and mercy on the part of the God who smites in order to heal (Isa 19.22), and that throughout the time of their God-forsakenness God is still concerned with them and dealing with them.[6]

[1] By implication, when (col. 414) he uses the words οὐχὶ αὐτὸς ὠθῶν of the general to whom he likens God.

[2] Cf. Chrysostom's statement (col. 414): Τὸ δὲ Παρέδωκεν ἐνταῦθα Εἴασεν ἐστίν. In his illustration of the general he goes on to use the words γυμνῶν τῆς ἑαυτοῦ βοηθείας.

[3] On παραδιδόναι, which, besides this occurrence and its two other occurrences in the present chapter, occurs in Romans also in 4.25; 6.17 and 8.32; see on 4.25 and also F. Büchsel, in *TWNT* 2, pp. 171–4.

[4] Cf. Chrysostom, col. 415, where it is stated that God let them go, ἵνα κἂν οὕτω τῇ πείρᾳ μαθόντες, ὧν ἐπεθύμησαν, φύγωσι τὴν αἰσχύνην.

[5] He says (p. 55): 'Paul . . . sees that the really awful thing is to fall out of His hands, and to be left to oneself in a world where the choice of evil brings its own moral retribution'. But did God let men fall out of His hands? Dodd's dislike of the biblical doctrine of the wrath of God seems here to have betrayed him into the enunciation of a singularly cheerless and unevangelical doctrine.

[6] We might perhaps compare Calvin's comment on Hos 12.4 that God fights with us with His left hand, and defends us with His right hand. (*Commentaries on the Twelve Minor Prophets.* Eng. tr., Edinburgh, 1846, p. 425). See also Barth, *CD* II/2, pp. 486ff (= *KD* II/2, pp. 540ff).

ἐν ταῖς ἐπιθυμίαις τῶν καρδιῶν αὐτῶν is more probably to be understood as indicating men's actual condition, the character of their life (i.e. as having the meaning which it would clearly have, were the word πορευομένους inserted) than as instrumental.[1] For this expression compare Ecclus 5.2: μὴ ἐξακολούθει τῇ ψυχῇ σου καὶ τῇ ἰσχύι σου πορεύεσθαι ἐν ἐπιθυμίαις καρδίας σου. It describes the life of those who acknowledge no higher criterion than their own wayward desires.

εἰς ἀκαθαρσίαν indicates the state into which they have been given up, the prison to which they have been delivered. Compare the use of παραδιδόναι with εἰς θάνατον (e.g. Mt 10.21), εἰς φυλακήν (e.g. Acts 8.3), εἰς χεῖρας ἀνθρώπων (e.g. Mt 17.22), εἰς θλῖψιν (Mt 24.9). ἀκαθαρσία is used particularly of sexual immorality. It occurs in association with πορνεία in 2 Cor 12.21; Gal 5.19; Eph 5.3; Col 3.5. The connexion between immorality and idolatry is enunciated in Wisd 14.12: 'Ἀρχὴ γὰρ πορνείας ἐπίνοια εἰδώλων, εὕρεσις δὲ αὐτῶν φθορὰ ζωῆς. There is no need to limit the reference to sexual immorality here and in the following verses to the immorality practised in the name of religion in the various pagan cults, though Paul probably did have this in mind.

τοῦ ἀτιμάζεσθαι τὰ σώματα αὐτῶν ἐν αὐτοῖς may be explained variously, as final[2] or consecutive[3] or simply epexegetic.[4] The second of these explanations is perhaps to be preferred to the third: the first seems least likely. ἀτιμάζεσθαι is apparently taken as middle by Greek commentators, as also by the Vulgate, the AV, and some modern commentators; but evidence of the use of this verb in the middle elsewhere in ancient Greek has not been adduced. It is probably better to take it as passive.[5] The reading αὐτοῖς is to be preferred to ἑαυτοῖς on the ground of better attestation and also because the reflexive would be a natural improvement as soon as the tendency to understand the verb as middle made itself felt. (There is no justification here for reading αντοις as αὐτοῖς.) Various interpretations of ἐν αὐτοῖς have been offered, the main ones being: (i) 'among them';[6] (ii) 'among themselves' (cf. εἰς ἀλλήλους in v. 27);[7] (iii) 'through themselves' (i.e. in an

---

[1] It is taken as instrumental by, e.g., Barrett, pp. 32, 38. The Vulgate obliterates the distinction between ἐν and εἰς in this verse by rendering both by 'in' with the accusative.

[2] So, e.g., Zahn, p. 98; Lagrange, p. 28.

[3] So, e.g., BDF, § 400 (2); Bauer, s.v. ὁ II.4.b. γ.

[4] So, e.g., Barrett, p. 38.

[5] If the variant ἑαυτοῖς were preferred, this would weigh in favour of the middle.

[6] So, e.g., Sanday and Headlam, p. 46.

[7] So, e.g., RV; Bisping; Michel, p. 67, as one of two alternatives.

instrumental sense);[1] (iv) 'in their own persons' (i.e. being affected in their own persons).[2] Of these the first is perhaps the most natural. We may understand the sense to be that the result of their having been delivered up to uncleanness is that among them their bodies are dishonoured and abused. (On the suggestion that Paul intended to bring out a correspondence between their abuse of God's glory (v. 23: cf. v. 21) and their bodies' being dishonoured see the introduction to this subsection.)

25 can be understood as connected closely with v. 24,[3] and Οἵτινες (it would then be printed with a lower case) can be explained as introducing a relative clause indicating a cause of the action described in the preceding main sentence (cf. the Latin 'qui' or 'quippe qui' followed by a subjunctive). The meaning would then be 'seeing that they'. But the action described in v. 24 has already been assigned a cause by the use of διό looking back to vv. 22–23. Moreover, the διὰ τοῦτο of v. 26 connects v. 25 with v. 26. It seems better therefore to follow those who see a break between vv. 24 and 25 rather than between vv. 25 and 26.[4] We may then render Οἵτινες in some such way as 'They actually', and take vv. 25–27 as repeating, and at the same time in some respects spelling out more fully, what has already been indicated in vv. 22–24.

μετήλλαξαν τὴν ἀλήθειαν τοῦ θεοῦ ἐν τῷ ψεύδει repeats the general sense of v. 23, μετήλλαξαν corresponding to ἤλλαξαν, τὴν ἀλήθειαν τοῦ θεοῦ to τὴν δόξαν τοῦ θεοῦ, and ἐν τῷ ψεύδει to ἐν ὁμοιώματι, κ.τ.λ. We may compare τῶν τὴν ἀλήθειαν ἐν ἀδικίᾳ κατεχόντων in 1.18. For the use of ψεῦδος in connexion with idolatry compare the use of šeķer in, for example, Isa 44.20, where the LXX has ψεῦδος; Jer 10.14, where in the LXX the adjective ψευδής is used. In the present verse it is perhaps rather more satisfactory to understand by 'the truth of God' the reality consisting of God Himself and His self-revelation and by 'the lie' the whole futility of idolatry than to explain them as simply cases of the use of the abstract for concrete (so equivalent to

---

[1] So, e.g., Bauer, s.v. ἀτιμάζω; Barrett, p. 38.
[2] So, e.g., Gutjahr; Lagrange, p. 28; Lietzmann, p. 32; Michel, p. 67, as first of two alternatives; Kuss, p. 49.
[3] So, e.g., Sanday and Headlam, pp. 40, 46; Lagrange, p. 28; Michel, pp. 59, 67.
[4] So Nestle; Klostermann, 'Die adäquate Vergeltung in Röm 1.22–31', in *ZNW* 32 (1933), p. 2f; Huby, p. 93. This is not, of course, to deny the fact that the relative marks a connexion with v. 24, in that its antecedent is contained in it. ὅστις is used frequently by Paul (in Romans also 1.32; 2.15; 6.2; 9.4; 11.4; 16.4), and not always in precisely the same way.

τὸν ἀληθινὸν θεόν and τοῖς ψευδέσι θεοῖς, respectively).[1] Contrast the reference in 1 Th 1.9b to the opposite exchange which takes place when men respond to the gospel.

καὶ ἐσεβάσθησαν καὶ ἐλάτρευσαν. σεβάζεσθαι (it occurs in the NT only here: σέβεσθαι occurs ten times, mostly in Acts) means 'reverence', 'worship'; λατρεύειν means 'serve', and in the LXX, when used in connexion with God, always denotes specifically cultic service. To regard the two verbs as indicating internal and external worship respectively, as did Bengel,[2] is not justified, since σεβάζεσθαι can denote external acts of religious veneration as well as inward feelings of reverence and awe. What we have here is probably to be explained as an example of the combination of two expressions, in which the first indicates what is meant in a more general way and the second defines it more precisely.[3] In Deut 4.19 we have a somewhat similar combination: μὴ . . . προσκυνήσῃς αὐτοῖς καὶ λατρεύσῃς αὐτοῖς. . . .

τῇ κτίσει.[4] With idolatry goes the worship of created things themselves.[5] Compare the way in which Deut 4 passes from the subject of the making of images (vv. 16–18) to that of the worship of sun, moon and stars (v. 19).

παρὰ τὸν κτίσαντα. παρά with the accusative here has the sense 'rather than', 'in preference to', 'instead of'. Compare Lk 18.14 (λέγω ὑμῖν, κατέβη οὗτος δεδικαιωμένος εἰς τὸν οἶκον αὐτοῦ παρ' ἐκεῖνον), where the NEB renders παρ' ἐκεῖνον—probably correctly—'and not the other'. This use is an extension of the quite well-established use in the sense 'more than'.[6] For the general thought compare Wisd 13.1–9; Philo, Op. Mund. 2 (τινὲς γὰρ τὸν κόσμον μᾶλλον ἢ τὸν κοσμοποιὸν θαυμάσαντες).

ὅς ἐστιν εὐλογητὸς εἰς τοὺς αἰῶνας· ἀμήν. In Jewish manner Paul attaches to his reference to God a bᵉrākāh or benediction.

---

[1] Cf., e.g., Michel, p. 68: the opposite view is taken by Sanday and Headlam, p. 46; Kuss, p. 49, and by a good many others. For an interesting parallel to this sentence see Philo, Vit. Mos. 2.167 (ὅσον ψεῦδος ἀνθ' ὅσης ἀληθείας ὑπηλλάξαντο), with reference to the episode of Exod 32.

[2] p. 497: 'ἐσεβάσθησαν, coluerunt) interne.—ἐλάτρευσαν, serviverunt) externe.'

[3] Cf. W. Foerster, in TWNT 7, p. 173.

[4] The dative is required by λατρεύειν, though σεβάζεσθαι takes a direct object.

[5] It seems rather more likely that by τῇ κτίσει is meant 'the creature', 'the created thing' than 'the creation (as a whole)' (pace Bauer, s.v. 1.b.β).

[6] See Bauer, s.v. παρά III.3 (though one might question whether all the instances adduced for the meaning 'instead of' really bear that meaning); LSJ, s.v. C.III.2.

Compare the very common Rabbinic formula, *hakkādôš bārûk hû'*. See also on 9.5. Reference may also be made to SB 2, p. 310, and 3, p. 64. The addition of ἀμήν gives to the benediction a note of special solemnity and also of personal involvement.[1]

26. διὰ τοῦτο connects the following statement with v. 25 in the same way that διό connected v. 24 with vv. 22–23.

παρέδωκεν αὐτοὺς ὁ θεός. See above on v. 24.

εἰς πάθη ἀτιμίας answers to εἰς ἀκαθαρσίαν in v. 24. ἀτιμίας (a genitive of quality, the meaning of the phrase being 'passions which bring dishonour') takes up the τοῦ ἀτιμάζεσθαι, κ.τ.λ. of v. 24.

The γάρ indicates that vv. 26b–27 are explanation and substantiation of v. 26a.

θήλειαι. The use of the adjectives meaning 'female' and 'male' rather than the words γυνή and ἀνήρ is appropriate here, since it is the sexual differentiation as such on which attention is specially concentrated (cf. Gen 1.27; Mt 19.4 = Mk 10.6; Gal 3.28). As to why Paul chose to mention the women before the men, the suggestion of Kuss that it was in order to give more emphasis to the male perversion by referring to it in the latter part of the sentence and dealing with it more fully[2] seems more probable than either the suggestion that he was influenced by the narrative in Gen 3,[3] or the suggestion that it was because he felt the women's guilt the more shocking because of their greater endowment with modesty.[4]

μετήλλαξαν echoes v. 25: the thought would seem to be present that there is a correspondence between this exchange and that described in v. 25.

τὴν φυσικὴν χρῆσιν εἰς τὴν παρὰ φύσιν. Precisely what is meant only becomes clear in the light of v. 27, the ὁμοίως of which implies that these words must refer to unnatural sexual relations between women. The use of χρῆσις as a periphrasis for sexual intercourse was well-established (cf. Bauer, s.v. 3). By φυσικός (here used to describe that which is κατὰ φύσιν) and παρὰ φύσιν Paul clearly means 'in accordance with the intention of the Creator' and 'contrary to the intention of the Creator', respectively. For this appeal to 'nature' in the sense of the order manifest in the created world compare 1 Cor 11.14, where ἡ φύσις αὐτή might almost be translated 'the very way God

[1] Cf. 9.5; 11.36; 15.33; 16.24. See further H. Schlier, in *TWNT* I, pp. 339–42.
[2] p. 50.
[3] So Michel, p. 68.
[4] So, e.g., Cornely, p. 99; Murray I, p. 47.

has made us'. That Paul had some awareness of the great importance which φύσις had had in Greek thought for many centuries is not impossible; that he was aware of its use in contemporary popular philosophy is very likely. He was at any rate using a word which—significantly—is not to be found in the LXX except in Wisdom and 3 and 4 Maccabees. But, for all its far-reaching and varied Greek background,[1] the decisive factor in Paul's use of it is his biblical doctrine of creation. It denotes that order which is manifest in God's creation and which men have no excuse for failing to recognize and respect (cf. what was said above on vv. 19 and 20).

27. ὁμοίως τε καί: 'and likewise also'—so RV rightly. *Pace* BDF, § 444(1)n., there does not seem to be any sufficient reason for preferring the variant δέ to τε.[2] ὁμοίως is, of course, commonly followed by καί.

ἐξεκαύθησαν. Compare the use of πυροῦσθαι in 1 Cor 7.9 of natural sexual desire which is unfulfilled.

ἄρσενες ἐν ἄρσεσιν. To construe this closely with what follows results in a more pointed sentence than is obtained by placing a comma after ἄρσεσιν (as is done by WH).

ἀσχημοσύνην. This noun occurs elsewhere in the NT only in Rev 16.15; the adjective ἀσχήμων occurs in 1 Cor 12.23, and the verb ἀσχημονεῖν in 1 Cor 7.36 and 13.5. RV 'unseemliness' is rather too weak: 'shamelessness' would be nearer the mark. Compare Ecclus 26.8; 30.13; Arrian, *Epict.* 2.5.23; Philo, *Leg. All.* 2.66; 3.158; Josephus, *Ant.* 16.223; Or. Sib. 5.389.

κατεργαζόμενοι. κατεργάζεσθαι is specially frequent in Romans (also 2.9; 4.15; 5.3; 7.8, 13, 15, 17, 18, 20; 15.18) and 2 Corinthians. In so far as a distinction is maintained between κατεργάζεσθαι and ἐργάζεσθαι, the former is always the stronger word, carrying such meanings as 'carry out', 'accomplish', 'effect' (the compound expressing intensification), while the latter is weaker (e.g. 'do', 'practise'); but the compound came, through over-use, to be very often no more than a synonym of the simple verb. See Bauer's articles on the two verbs; also G. Bertram, in *TWNT* 2, pp. 631ff; 3, pp. 635–7.

τὴν ἀντιμισθίαν ἣν ἔδει τῆς πλάνης αὐτῶν. It has been recognized from early times that the reference is more probably to their sexual perversion itself as the punishment for their abandon-

---

[1] On this see H. Koester, in *TWNT* 9, pp. 246ff. A perusal of the index of H. Ritter and L. Preller, *Historia Philosophiae Graecae*, Gotha, [10]1934, s.v. φύσις, or even of the article on the word in LSJ, is enough to show how far-reaching this background is. It should be noted that παρὰ φύσιν is used in connexion with homosexual intercourse by both Philo (*Spec. Leg.* 3.39) and Josephus (*Contra Ap.* 2. 273).

[2] Cf. Kuss, p. 50.

ment of the true God than to a necessary or appropriate but unspecified punishment for their sexual perversion.[1] The noun ἀντιμισθία has so far only been found in Christian writings, but the adjective ἀντίμισθος occurs in Aeschylus, *Supp.* 270, and the noun ἀντιμίσθιον in Pseudo-Callisthenes, 3.26. It is difficult to decide precisely what is meant by ἦν ἔδει. Does it refer to a necessity grounded in God's decision (cf. παρέδωκεν in v. 26), or to the fact that such moral confusion is a natural consequence of turning from God (cf. Bengel's *'quam oportuit*, naturali sequela'—p. 498), or to the appropriateness of the punishment to the wrong committed, so to its deservedness? 'Error' (AV and RV) is an adequate rendering of πλάνη here only if it is understood in the strongest sense it can have, as denoting a thoroughly serious going astray from the truth in thought and/or in conduct. πλάνη occurs elsewhere in the NT in Mt 27.64; Eph 4.14; 1 Th 2.3; 2 Th 2.11; Jas 5.20; 2 Pet 2.18; 3.17; 1 Jn 4.6; Jude 11.

ἐν ἑαυτοῖς: 'in their own persons'. As in v. 24, there is a variation in the textual tradition between ἑαυτοῖς and αὐτοῖς: here the former should probably be preferred (even were αὐτοῖς read, the meaning would be the same).

ἀπολαμβάνοντες. The ἀπο- emphasizes the deservedness of the punishment (the ἀντι- of the variant would have the same force).

The fact that ancient Greek and Roman society not only regarded paederasty with indulgence but was inclined to glorify it as actually superior to heterosexual love is too well known to need to be dwelt on here. References in classical literature are frequent and widespread. Few indeed were the voices raised in protest from within Graeco-Roman society, but there were some. It is only fair to remember that Greece and Rome had no monopoly in homosexuality: it was common also in the Semitic world. To the Jews it was an abomination (see, e.g. Gen 19.1–28; Lev 18.22; 20.13; Deut 23,17f; 1 Kgs 14.24; 2 Kgs 23.7; Isa 1.9; 3.9; Lam 4.6; Wisd 14.26; Test. Levi 17.11; Or. Sib. 2.73; 3.596ff; Philo, *Spec. Leg.* 3.39, etc.), and Paul clearly shared his fellow-countrymen's abhorrence of it. In the NT compare 1 Cor 6.9; 1 Tim 1.10; 2 Pet 2.6ff; Jude 7; and also—for dominical words which must not be overlooked in this connexion—Mt 10.14f; 11.23f.

28. καθὼς οὐκ ἐδοκίμασαν τὸν θεὸν ἔχειν ἐν ἐπιγνώσει is parallel to v. 22f and v. 25. καθώς has here the sense 'since', 'because'.[2]

---

[1] By, e.g., Chrysostom, col. 418; Calvin, p. 36f; Beet, p. 61; Denney, p. 593; Lagrange, p. 30; Michel, p. 69; Murray 1, p. 48f; Kuss, p. 50.
[2] See Bauer, s.v. 3; BDF, § 453 (2). Cf. the use of 'as' in English to introduce a causal clause.

δοκιμάζειν (also 2.18; 12.2; 14.22) can mean 'test' or 'approve (as a result of testing)', so, with an infinitive, 'see fit', and, negatived (as here), 'not see fit', 'refuse'.[1] τὸν θεὸν ἔχειν ἐν ἐπιγνώσει is to know God in the sense of acknowledging Him, reckoning with Him, taking Him into account in the practical affairs of one's life. For the expression τινὰ ἔχειν ἐν see Bauer, s.v. ἔχω I.7.a, where such parallels as ἐν ὀργῇ ἔχειν τινά and ἐν ἡδονῇ ἔχειν τινά are quoted. The verb ἐπιγινώσκειν is generally used simply as a synonym for γινώσκειν, but there are occurrences where it is plausible to see a special intensive force in the ἐπι- (e.g. 1 Cor 13.12—though for a contrary opinion see R. Bultmann, in *TWNT* 1, p. 703, 38ff). The compound substantive ἐπίγνωσις (also 3.20; 10.2) is, in the NT and other early Christian literature, only used with reference to a religious or moral knowledge. A strong sense is required here by the context. It must denote a knowledge which goes beyond that indicated by γνόντες τὸν θεόν in v. 21, and which in fact includes the δοξάζειν and εὐχαριστεῖν to which that verse refers. What they have refused to do is seriously to take God into account.

παρέδωκεν αὐτοὺς ὁ θεός.[2] See above on vv. 24 and 26.

εἰς ἀδόκιμον νοῦν is parallel to εἰς ἀκαθαρσίαν in v. 24 and εἰς πάθη ἀτιμίας in v. 26. There is a word-play—οὐκ ἐδοκίμασαν/ ἀδόκιμον—which it is difficult to reproduce at all satisfactorily in English. Because they have rejected God as not worth reckoning with, God has delivered them into a condition in which their minds are fit only to be rejected as worthless, useless for their proper purpose, disreputable. The proper meaning of ἀδόκιμος (it occurs in the NT also in 1 Cor 9.27; 2 Cor 13.5, 6, 7; 2 Tim 3.8; Tit 1.16; Heb 6.8) is 'failing the test', 'disqualified', hence 'unsatisfactory', 'useless', 'disreputable', 'reprobate'. For the thought here compare v. 21 (ἐσκοτίσθη ἡ ἀσύνετος αὐτῶν καρδία), and see note there. Here it is particularly the mind in respect of its moral functions that Paul is concerned with, as the next words make clear. The ἀδόκιμος νοῦς is a mind so debilitated and corrupted as to be a quite untrustworthy guide in moral decisions.

ποιεῖν τὰ μὴ καθήκοντα is parallel to τοῦ ἀτιμάζεσθαι τὰ σώματα αὐτῶν ἐν αὐτοῖς in v. 24. The use of the participle of καθήκειν to denote either one's due or one's duty had long been common (cf., e.g., Herodotus 7.104; Xenophon, *Cyr.* 1.2.5; Menander,

---

[1] W. Grundmann, in *TWNT* 2, p. 262, ascribes to δοκιμάζειν with the infinitive a somewhat different sense, namely, 'für notwendig erachten'.

[2] The omission of ὁ θεός (ℵ* A *pc*) looks like an accidental omission—possibly due to τὸν θεόν earlier in the verse.

575¹); but the term τὸ καθῆκον is especially associated with the Stoics, for whom it was an ethical technical term (both Zeno of Citium (4th–3rd century B.C.), the founder of the Stoic philosophy, and Panaetius (2nd century B.C.) wrote treatises entitled περὶ τοῦ καθήκοντος), the Latin equivalent being 'officium'.² The negative τὰ μὴ καθήκοντα is used in 2 Macc 6.4 of things which ought not to be brought into the temple and in 3 Macc 4.16 of things which ought not to be uttered. As used in Rom 1, it denotes generally what is morally wrong.

29–31 comprise a list of vices³ arranged in three⁴ distinct groups: (i) four abstract nouns in the dative singular all qualified by πάσῃ and dependent on the participle πεπληρωμένους, which stands in apposition to αὐτούς in v. 28; (ii) five nouns in the genitive singular all depending on the adjective μεστούς, which is also in apposition to αὐτούς; (iii) a series of twelve items all of which are directly in apposition to αὐτούς, the first seven of them being positive and the last five negative. Within these groupings a tendency to a further grouping in pairs according to rhetorical rather than substantial considerations is noticeable (thus φθόνου and φόνου, ἀσυνέτους and ἀσυνθέτους feature assonance; ἐφευρετὰς κακῶν and γονεῦσιν ἀπειθεῖς are a pair of two-word phrases; and the last two items both have the privative α- besides having a certain relatedness of meaning).

ἀδικίᾳ. Compare v. 18.

πονηρίᾳ πλεονεξίᾳ κακίᾳ. The order in which these items are given varies in the textual tradition, and sometimes a fourth is

¹ In the Menander line the expression used is actually ποιεῖν τὸ καθῆκον.
² Cf. Diogenes Laertius 7.92, 107–9; Cicero, Att. 16.11.4; Arrian, Epict. 2.17.31.
³ Similar lists of vices (there are of course also lists of virtues) occur in 13.13; 1 Cor 5.10f; 6.9f; 2 Cor 12.20; Gal 5.19–21; Eph 4.31; 5.3–5; Col 3.5, 8; 1 Tim 1.9f; 2 Tim 3.2–5; Tit 3.3; 1 Pet 4.3. Cf. Wisd 14.25f; 3 Bar. 4.17; 8.5; 13.4; Test. Reub. 3.3–6; Test. Jud. 16.1; 2 Enoch 10.4f. Lists of virtues and vices were popular among the Stoics. See further: Lagrange, 'Le catalogue de vices dans l'épître aux Romains, 1.28–31', in RB, n.s.8 (1911), pp. 534–49; B. S. Easton, 'NT Ethical Lists', in JBL 51 (1932), pp. 1–12; A. Vögtle, Die Tugend- und Lasterkataloge im NT, Münster, 1936; S. Wibbing, Die Tugend- und Lasterkataloge im NT, Berlin, 1959; E. Kamlah, Die Form der katalogischen Paränese im NT, Tübingen, 1964; O. J. F. Seitz, in IDB 3, pp. 137–9.
⁴ Some, however, see the last twelve items as falling into two or even three distinct groups. Thus Jülicher, for example, sees a group of seven and a group of five items; Zahn, who sees the division at the same place, takes ψιθυριστάς and the following five words to be only three items, each consisting of a noun and qualifying adjective, so that he gets two groups, one of four items and one of five; while Kuss sees three groups, of six, two, and four items, respectively.

added, namely, πορνείᾳ. That πορνείᾳ should be read is unlikely: it may have been introduced by mistake in place of πονηρίᾳ (D G and a few other MSS. which have πορνείᾳ omit πονηρίᾳ), but its addition is anyway easily understandable, since there is no reference (unless perhaps in πλεονεξίᾳ) to sexual immorality in this list of vices. There have been many attempts to make out a definite distinction between πονηρία and κακία; but the results have been unconvincing.[1] πλεονεξία denotes the ruthless self-assertion of 'the man who will pursue his own interests with complete disregard for the rights of others and for all considerations of humanity'.[2] It is sometimes associated with sexual vices (e.g. 1 Cor 5.10f; Eph 4.9; 5.3, 5), and sex is indeed one of the spheres in which it is manifested; but πλεονεξία never denotes simply lust.

Between **φθόνου** and **φόνου**—in addition to the assonance—there is a certain inner connexion (cf. Gen 4.1ff; Mt 27.18 = Mk 15.10). We might perhaps go further, and suggest that all the evils denoted by the four genitives which follow φθόνου are very often to be explained as fruits of envy. The omission of **δόλου** by A is probably accidental.

κακοηθείας. It is a mistake to assume, as Sanday and Headlam,[3] Michel,[4] Barrett,[5] Barclay[6] do, that Paul is likely to have used this word in the special sense indicated by Aristotle, Rh. 1389[b]20 and 1416[b]10, of putting the worst construction on everything;[7] for this is clearly a special connotation. He is surely much more likely to have used it here in its ordinary general sense of 'malice', 'malignity', 'spite'. In Ammonius (1st–2nd century A.D.), περὶ ὁμοίων καὶ διαφόρων λέξεων (Valckenaer, p. 148), it is defined as κακία κεκρυμμένη. It occurs in LXX Esth 8.12(f) [=Add. Esth 16.6]; 3 Macc 3.22; 7.3; 4 Macc 1.4; 3.4 (bis). We may accept Grundmann's conclusion that here in Rom 1 it denotes conscious and intentional malice.[8]

ψιθυριστάς, καταλάλους. Both words denote people who go about

[1] See G. Harder, in *TWNT* 6, pp. 546–66 (especially 565).

[2] Dodd, p. 53. See further Bauer, s.v. πλεονεξία, and also πλεονεκτέω and πλεονέκτης; LSJ, under πλεονεκτέω and πλεονεξία. For Aristotle's understanding of πλεονεξία see the passages listed in the index of I. Bywater's Oxford edition of the *Ethica Nicomachea* under πλεονεκτεῖν, πλεονέκτης and πλεονεξία.

[3] p. 47.

[4] p. 70.

[5] p. 40.

[6] p. 29.

[7] 1389[b]20 has the sentence: ἔστι γὰρ κακοήθεια τὸ ἐπὶ τὸ χεῖρον ὑπολαμβάνειν πάντα.

[8] *TWNT* 3, p. 486.

to destroy other people's reputations by misrepresentation.[1] The difference between ψιθυριστής and κατάλαλος is that the former denoted specifically one who whispers his slanders in his listener's ear, whereas the latter means a slanderer quite generally, irrespective of whether he whispers his calumnies or proclaims them from the house-tops—though the fact that it is used immediately after ψιθυριστής makes it natural to understand it to refer here in particular to the more open sort of slanderer. The ψιθυριστής is, of course, the more vicious and dangerous kind, inasmuch as he is one against whom there is virtually no human defence.

θεοστυγεῖς. In classical Greek θεοστυγής seems always to have a passive sense, 'hated by the gods', and the Vulgate understands it here as 'hateful to God'; but an active sense fits the present context much better and should be accepted.[2] There is little really to be said in favour of insisting on a passive sense here,[3] and still less for taking θεοστυγεῖς as qualifying καταλάλους.[4] Hatred of God is, of course, common to all sinful men; but Paul perhaps applies the term particularly to those in whom it is specially strident.

ὑβριστάς. Cognate with ὕβρις (the word which denotes the insolent pride, familiar theme of classical Greek tragedy, which brings upon the man who indulges it νέμεσις, the retribution of the gods, but which was also used to denote any wanton act of violence against another man bespeaking contempt for his person), ὑβριστής means, according to LSJ, a 'violent, wanton, licentious, insolent man'. In the NT it occurs only here and in I Tim 1.13, though the verb ὑβρίζειν and the noun ὕβρις occur, respectively, five and three times. It is best understood here as signifying the man who, in his confidence in his own superior power, wealth, social status, physical strength, intellectual or other ability, treats his fellow men with insolent contemptuousness and thereby affronts the majesty of God.

ὑπερηφάνους,[5] ἀλαζόνας. For this association compare Wisd 5.8; Stobaeus, Flor. 85.16 (quoted by Field). ὑπερήφανος is adequately

[1] The cognate nouns ψιθυρισμός and καταλαλιά are coupled together in 2 Cor 12.20; I Clement 30.3; 35.5 (but this last passage is anyway echoing Rom 1.29-31).
[2] Cf. the Latin version used by Cyprian ('abhorrentes Deo'); Theodoret, col. 65; Euthymius, p. 21; Calvin, p. 38; Sanday and Headlam, p. 47; Bauer, s.v.
[3] Pace Lagrange, p. 33, et al.
[4] As is done by Barrett, p. 40, following Pallis.
[5] The word is associated with ὑβριστής in Aristotle, Rh. 1390ᵇ33. ὑπερηφανία is included in the list of evil things proceeding out of the heart of men, which is given in Mk 7.21f.

represented by 'arrogant'. ἀλαζών denotes the man who tries
to impress others by making big claims. It was used of the
braggart, the charlatan, the quack, the impostor. The word is
probably used here with the graver end of its range of meaning
in mind. We may think of the 'frantic boast and foolish word'
of the heathen heart, the sort of thing which is reflected in
Isa 10.7–11, in fact all the presumptuous claims and ostentatious behaviour of men by which they seek to impress one
another, and very often delude themselves.

ἐφευρετὰς κακῶν and γονεῦσιν ἀπειθεῖς are associated simply
because they are both two-word phrases. The former of them,
far from being 'a curious expression',[1] is an incisive characterization of men's capacity for committing 'The oldest sins
the newest kind of ways'—we may think especially of their
inventiveness in finding ever more hateful methods of hurting
and destroying their fellow men.

ἀσυνέτους and ἀσυνθέτους are linked by assonance rather than
meaning. For ἀσύνετος see v. 21. The background to its use
here is without doubt biblical. Compare Ps 92.6 [LXX: 91.7];
Wisd 1.5; 11.15; Ecclus 15.7; 21.18; 22.13, 15, in all of which
ἀσύνετος is used in the LXX; also the much larger number of
places where in the LXX ἄφρων occurs (e.g. Ps 53.1 [LXX:
52.2]; Prov 6.12; 10.1; Isa 59.7), and the presence of ἀφροσύνη
in Mk 7.22. In the OT foolishness, lack of understanding, can
have a distinctly moral and religious connotation. ἀσύνθετος
also has an OT background, which is overlooked by the
Vulgate rendering 'incompositos' (reflecting the the use of the
word by Plato and Aristotle in the sense 'uncompounded').
The word occurs four times in LXX Jeremiah (3.7, 8, 10, 11)
with the meaning 'treacherous' (it represents Hebrew bāḡaḏ,
bāḡôḏ). The cognate verb ἀσυνθετεῖν is also used in the LXX:
it means 'deal treacherously' (e.g. Ps 73 [LXX: 72] .15; 78
[LXX: 77] .57; 119 [LXX: 118] .158). And the abstract noun
ἀσυνθεσία occurs too, though only once in a canonical book.
The adjective (unless the variant ἀσυνετώτατος should be read)
already has its biblical sense of 'treacherous', 'faithless',
'inconstant', 'unreliable', in Demosthenes 19.136.

ἀστόργους:[2] 'without natural affection'. Among the various
words for 'love' in Greek στοργή was the one which particularly
denoted family affection. In this connexion Barclay aptly
refers to the prevalence in the Graeco-Roman world of Paul's
day of the practice of exposing unwanted babies and also of

---

[1] Barrett, p. 41.
[2] The addition of ἀσπόνδους (C 𝕶 pl lat) would seem to be assimilation
to 2 Tim 3.3.

actual infanticide.[1] Paul's contemporary, Seneca, takes for granted the drowning of weakly or deformed babies: 'Portentosos fetus exstinguimus, liberos quoque, si debiles monstrosique editi sunt, mergimus. Non ira, sed ratio est, a sanis inutilia secernere'.[2]

ἀνελεήμονας requires no explanation.

32. οἵτινες τὸ δικαίωμα τοῦ θεοῦ ἐπιγνόντες, ὅτι οἱ τὰ τοιαῦτα πράσσοντες ἄξιοι θανάτου εἰσίν, οὐ μόνον αὐτὰ ποιοῦσιν, ἀλλὰ καὶ συνευδοκοῦσιν τοῖς πράσσουσιν. This has perplexed readers from early times, and the difficulty experienced has caused a very considerable disturbance in the textual tradition. The main difficulty has been that the sentence, as it stands, seems to imply that to approve of the evil deeds of others is even worse than to do the same deeds oneself, and this implication has been felt—and is still felt by some commentators[3]—to be untrue. Hence the disturbance in the textual tradition of the last part of the verse. Here, while the text of the Vulgate as printed by Wordsworth and White has a form agreeing with the Greek ('non solum ea faciunt sed et consentiunt facientibus'), the Clementine Vulgate has an 'et' before 'non solum' and also adds 'qui' both before 'ea' and before 'consentiunt', thus giving a quite different sense, namely, that the statement that those who do such things are worthy of death applies not only to those who actually do them but also to those who applaud others who do them. This has, in addition to considerable Latin support, the support of the variant attested by B, ποιοῦντες and συνευδοκοῦντες instead of ποιοῦσιν and συνευδοκοῦσιν; and is already anticipated in the echo of this verse contained in 1 Clement 35.6 (ταῦτα γὰρ οἱ πράσσοντες στυγητοὶ τῷ θεῷ ὑπάρχουσιν· οὐ μόνον δὲ οἱ πράσσοντες αὐτά, ἀλλὰ καὶ οἱ συνευδοκοῦντες αὐτοῖς). But that this form of the text represents a corruption of what Paul wrote was recognized by Isidore of Pelusium, who explains it as due to the failure of some people to see how consenting could be worse than doing.[4]

---

[1] p. 32f. [2] De ira 1.15.

[3] e.g. Barrett, p. 41. WH obelized the whole text from ὅτι to τοῖς as probably corrupt, because they too could not see how to applaud a bad action could be worse than doing it.

[4] Epistolae 5.159 (PG 78, col. 1417). His words are worth quoting. Having stated his own view of the specially grave position of the man whose judgment is so corrupted that he actually approves of and praises those who do evil, he appeals to Paul in support thus: καὶ διὰ τοῦτο Παῦλος ἔφη · Οὐ μόνον αὐτὰ ποιοῦσιν, ἀλλὰ καὶ συνευδοκοῦσι τοῖς πράττουσιν. Τὸ γὰρ ἐπαινεῖν καὶ συνηγορεῖν τοῦ πράττειν χεῖρον εἰκότως ὡρίσατο, and then goes on to say: ὅπερ τινὲς μὴ συνέντες, ἑρμηνεῦσαι βουληθέντες, παραπεποιῆσθαι ἐνόμισαν, καὶ οὕτως αὐτὸ τάξαι οὐκ ὤκνησαν · "Οὐ μόνον οἱ ποιοῦντες αὐτὰ ἀλλὰ καὶ οἱ συνευδοκοῦντες τοῖς πράττουσιν", ἵνα μεῖζον ᾖ τὸ ποιεῖν, καὶ ἔλαττον τὸ συνευδοκεῖν. Cf. 5.74 (PG 78, col. 1369).

Another difficulty, which was probably a factor contributing to the corruption of the text of the earlier part of the verse, alongside the fact that the substitution of participles for indicatives in the latter part (in Latin the addition of the double 'qui') had left the sentence without a main verb, was that of understanding how the heathen could be said to know that such evil-doers are in God's sight deserving of death. So we get the insertion of 'non intellexerunt' after 'cognovissent' in the Latin (d e vg^{cl} Or Cypr Lcf Ambst) and of οὐκ ἐνόησαν (D*) or οὐκ ἔγνωσαν (G) or οὐ συνῆκαν (15) in the Greek.

It remains to consider the verse in the form which we may assume to be original. We may take δικαίωμα to mean God's just ordinance or decree, the substance of which is indicated by the following ὅτι- clause (whereas those who introduced 'non intellexerunt' and its various equivalents clearly understood the δικαίωμα of God to be something quite distinct from the content of the ὅτι- clause—probably God's righteous requirement, i.e., of a way of life consistent with the truth of God (cf. vv. 18 and 25)). ἐπιγνόντες[1] may be interpreted in a way similar to that in which we understood γνόντες in v. 21. Paul's thought would seem to be that in that knowledge of God which they have had objectively though not subjectively (see on v. 21) there was all along included an objective knowledge of His righteousness and of His uncompromising hostility to evil, and therefore of the ultimate penalty of their evil-doing. That the reference of θανάτου is to this ultimate penalty of sin in God's creation, and not to death as a penalty for particular wrong-doings according to an actual code of law, is surely clear; for—for one thing—many of the things listed in vv. 29–31 could not conceivably carry a death penalty in any code. With regard to the latter part of the verse, Barrett argues that the difficulty can be solved only by seeing what is said here in the light of chapter 2. Before proceeding to show that those who strongly disapprove of the sinful actions which have been listed are themselves under the same condemnation (the burden of 2.1ff), Paul slips in an indication that those who approve of others' wrong-doing are under condemnation as well as those who do these things—so Barrett attempts to get rid of the emphasis on ἀλλὰ καὶ συνευδοκοῦσιν τοῖς πράσσουσιν.[2] But it is doubtful whether the Greek can really bear this interpretation—if this was what Paul had in mind, he has

---

[1] The variant ἐπιγινώσκοντες, possibly due to the presence of the present participles, πράσσοντες and πράσσουσιν (and in B also ποιοῦντες and συνευδοκοῦντες), would not give a substantially different sense.

[2] p. 41.

expressed his meaning in a very surprising way. And, in any case, there is no need to explain away the natural meaning of the words; for it is surely true, as Apollinarius,[1] Chrysostom,[2] Isidore of Pelusium,[3] Calvin,[4] and a good many others have seen, that the man who applauds and encourages[5] others in doing what is wicked is, even if he never actually commits the same wicked deed himself, not only as guilty as those who do commit it, but very often more guilty than they. There are several factors involved. Apollinarius drew attention to one of them when he said: ὁ μὲν γὰρ ποιῶν, μεθύων τῷ πάθει, ἡττᾶται τῆς πράξεως· ὁ δὲ συνευδοκῶν, ἐκτὸς ὢν τοῦ πάθους, πονηρίᾳ χρώμενος, συντρέχει τῷ κακῷ.[6] To draw attention to the fact that the man who does the wrong will often be under great pressure, as for instance that of passion, whereas the man who looks on and applauds will not normally be under any similar pressure, is not at all to diminish the guilt of the doer, but it is to reveal the greater culpability of the applauder. His attitude will very often be the reflection of a settled choice. But there is also the fact that those who condone and applaud the vicious actions of others are actually making a deliberate contribution to the setting up of a public opinion favourable to vice, and so to the corruption of an indefinite number of other people. So, for example, to excuse or gloss over the use of torture by security forces or the cruel injustices of racial discrimination and oppression, while not being involved in them directly, is to help to cloak monstrous evil with an appearance of respectability and so to contribute most effectively to its firmer entrenchment.[7]

---

[1] As quoted in Cramer, p. 10.

[2] col. 423.

[3] *PG* 78, cols. 1369 and 1417, already cited above.

[4] p. 38f: 'It is the height of evil when the sinner is so completely void of shame that he is not only pleased with his own vices, . . . but also encourages them in others by his consent and approval. . . . Paul, it seems, meant to condemn here something more grievous and wicked than the mere perpetration of vice. I do not know what this may be, if we do not mean that which is the height of wickedness—when wretched men, casting away all shame, undertake the patronage of vice rather than the righteousness of God.'

[5] For συνευδοκεῖν cf. 1 Macc 1.57; 2 Macc 11.24, 35; Lk 11.48; Acts 8.1; 22.20; 1 Cor 7.12, 13; also the interesting parallels in Test. Asher 6.2 and Seneca, *Ep. mor.* 39.6 (cited by Michel, p. 71, n. 2).

[6] Cramer, p. 10.

[7] On the verbs πράσσειν and ποιεῖν see note on 7.15.

(ii) *Jewish man is no exception*
(2.1–3.20)

¹Wherefore thou hast no excuse, man, whoever thou art who judgest *another*; for wherein thou judgest the other thou condemnest thyself; for thou doest the same things, thou that settest thyself up as a judge. ²But we know that God's judgment is justly pronounced against those who practise such things. ³And dost thou reckon, thou man that judgest those that practise such things and yet doest them thyself, that thou shalt escape God's judgment? ⁴Or despisest thou the wealth of his kindness and forbearance and patience, refusing to see that God's kindness is meant to lead thee to repentance? ⁵But thou art storing up for thyself on account of thine obstinacy and unrepentant heart wrath in the day of wrath and of the revelation of the righteous judgment of God, ⁶who will recompense every man according to his works, ⁷to those who by steadfast perseverance in the good work seek glory and honour and immortality eternal life, ⁸but to those who are self-seeking and disobey the truth but obey unrighteousness there will be wrath and fury. ⁹There will be tribulation and distress as the lot of every individual man who works what is evil, both of the Jew first and also of the Greek, ¹⁰but glory and honour and peace for every one who works what is good, both for the Jew first and also for the Greek. ¹¹For there is no partiality with God.

¹²For, while all those who have sinned in ignorance of the law will also perish even though they did not have the law, all those who have sinned knowing the law will be judged on the basis of the law; ¹³for it is not the hearers of the law who are righteous with God, but the doers of the law will be pronounced righteous. ¹⁴For when Gentiles which do not possess the law by nature actually do the things which the law requires, they themselves, though not possessing the law, are a law for themselves. ¹⁵They actually give proof of the fact that the work which the law requires is written on their hearts, and their own conscience will testify to them and their thoughts among themselves will accuse or even excuse them ¹⁶on the day on which God judges the secrets of men through Christ Jesus according to the gospel which I preach.

¹⁷But, if thou hast the name of 'Jew' and reliest on the law and gloriest in God ¹⁸and knowest his will and canst discern the things which are essential, being instructed out of the law, ¹⁹and art confident that thou art a guide of the blind, a light of those in darkness, ²⁰an educator of the foolish, a teacher of the immature, having in the law the embodiment of knowledge and of truth, —²¹thou then, who teachest another, dost thou not teach thyself? thou, who preachest that one should not steal, dost thou steal? ²²thou, who sayest that one should not commit adultery, dost thou commit adultery? thou, who abhorrest idols, dost thou commit sacrilege? ²³While thou gloriest in the law, thou dishonourest God by transgressing the law. ²⁴For God's name is blasphemed among the Gentiles on your account, even as Scripture says.

²⁵For circumcision is indeed profitable, provided thou dost practise the law; but if thou art a transgressor of the law, thy circumcision has become uncircumcision. ²⁶If then an uncircumcised man observes the righteous requirements of the law, will not his uncircumcision be reckoned as circumcision? ²⁷And the man who is by virtue of his birth

an uncircumcised Gentile but who fulfils the law will judge thee, who for all thy possession of Scripture and circumcision art a transgressor of the law. ²⁸For it is not the outward *Jew* who is a Jew *in the fullest sense,* nor is it the outward *circumcision* in the flesh which is circumcision *in the fullest sense;* ²⁹but *it is* the inward Jew *who is a Jew in the fullest sense,* and *it is* the circumcision of the heart (wrought by the Spirit and not merely a matter of fulfilment of the letter of the law) *which is circumcision in the fullest sense.* This man's praise is not from men but from God.

¹What advantage then does the Jew have? Or what profit is there in circumcision? ²An altogether great advantage. First, that they were entrusted with the oracles of God. ³What then? If some have failed to respond with faith, shall their lack of faith render God's faithfulness ineffective? ⁴God forbid! We confess rather that God is true, and all men liars, even as Scripture says, '. . . in order that thou mayest be acknowledged as righteous in thy words and mayest overcome when thou contendest'.
⁵But if our unrighteousness actually shows up the righteousness of God, what are we then to say? Is God unrighteous in that he inflicts his wrath *on us?* (I am giving expression to thoughts which are very human.) ⁶God forbid! For in that case how shall God judge the world? ⁷But if the truth of God has been more abundantly manifested to his glory, by means of my lie, why am I still judged as a sinner? ⁸And do we then say (as certain people slanderously allege that we say), 'Let us do evil, that good may come of it'? Those who so slander us are deservedly condemned.
⁹What then? Do we *Jews* have an advantage? Not in every respect; for we have already laid the charge against both Jews and Greeks that they are all under sin, ¹⁰even as Scripture testifies:

'There is no one who is righteous, not even one,
¹¹   there is no one who has understanding,
      there is no one who seeks God.
¹²All have turned aside, together they have become useless;
      there is no one who shows kindness,
      no, not as much as one.

¹³An open grave is their throat,
    with their tongues they are wont to deceive,
    the poison of asps is under their lips.
¹⁴   Their mouth is full of cursing and bitterness.

¹⁵Swift are their feet to shed blood,
¹⁶   destruction and misery mark their ways,
¹⁷and the way of peace they have not known.
¹⁸   There is no fear of God before their eyes.'

¹⁹But we know that whatever the law says it speaks to those who possess the law, in order that every mouth may be stopped and the whole world stand guilty before God. ²⁰For no flesh shall be justified before him on the ground of having done what the law requires; for through the law *comes* the knowledge of sin.

That in 2.17ff Paul is apostrophizing the typical Jew is clear; but there is no explicit indication before v.17 that it is the Jews whom he has in mind. So the question arises: At what point does he turn his attention to them? Is it at v.17? Or has he the Jews already in mind from the beginning of the chapter?

Some interpreters maintain that in vv. 1ff Paul is thinking of the morally superior among the Gentiles,[1] others that the thought is quite general, embracing all, whether Jews or Gentiles, who are inclined to judge their fellows.[2] But there are weighty reasons for thinking that Paul had the Jews in mind right from 2.1. The following may be mentioned:

(i) The notable points of contact between 2.1ff and chapters eleven to fifteen of Wisdom (see the notes on the verses) strongly suggest that Paul was thinking of just such Jewish assumptions as are expressed in those chapters.

(ii) While Paul certainly believed that the heathen also were recipients of God's mercy, the emphatic nature of the language of v. 4 suggests the probability that he had in mind the special privileges of Israel and the extraordinary patience of God in the face of His chosen people's unfaithfulness and stubbornness.

(iii) The references to Jews and Greeks (that is, in the contexts, Gentiles) in 1.16; 2.9, 10; 3.9 suggest that in the construction of 1.18–3.20 Paul would be likely to keep to this twofold division of mankind: a brief reference in passing to the morally superior among the Gentiles might be understandable, but scarcely the lengthy treatment which 2.1ff would be.

(iv) The way in which the name 'Jew' is introduced in v.17 does not suggest that Paul is at this point turning his attention to a different group of people.

(v) An attitude of moral superiority toward the Gentiles was so characteristic of the Jews (as vv. 18ff themselves indicate), that, in the absence of any indication to the contrary, it is natural to assume that Paul is apostrophizing the typical Jew in 2.1ff.

(vi) A confident expectation of special indulgence (see v. 3) was equally characteristic of them.

(vii) If our understanding of the purpose of 2.12–16 is correct, then those verses are a further pointer in the same direction.

In view of these considerations we conclude that the

[1] e.g., Pelagius, who (p. 24), commenting on 2.21, says: 'similiter [ut] gentibus dixerat: "qui enim alium iudicas, te ipsum condemnas" ', and Leenhardt, p. 74 (Fr.: 44), who argues that, if vv. 1–11 were addressed to the Jews, they would interrupt the flow of the discourse from 1.18 to 2.16 (he understands 1.18–32 to refer to mankind in general, including the Jews, and 2.14–16 to refer to the natural man), and would also duplicate several things said in vv. 17ff; and that the vocabulary used in vv. 1–11 is different from that used where Paul is definitely addressing or speaking about the Jews (e.g. there is no mention of the law).

[2] e.g., Barrett, p. 43, on the ground that vv. 9ff and vv. 12–16 apply to both Jews and Gentiles.

probability that Paul is already thinking of the Jews in 2.1 is
very strong.

The sub-section falls into six paragraphs. In 2.1–11 Paul,
making use of apostrophe, declares those who condemn others
but themselves do the very same things, to be without excuse.
They must not think to escape the judgment of God, who, as
Scripture testifies, will render to each man according to his
deeds, judging all men, Jew and Gentile alike, without respect
of persons. The second paragraph (2.12–16) contains the first
direct and explicit reference in the epistle to the law, and
makes the point that knowledge of the law does not in itself
constitute any defence against the judgment of God. In the
third paragraph (2.17–24), now apostrophizing the typical Jew
by name, Paul draws attention to the disastrous contradictions
by which his life is characterized.

In the next paragraph (2.25–29) he refers to a ground of
Jewish confidence which has not been mentioned before,
namely, circumcision. Circumcision profits, if one obeys the
law, but, if one is a transgressor of the law, one's circumcision
has become uncircumcision; and, conversely, the uncircumcised
man's uncircumcision will be counted as circumcision, if he
does what the law requires. Neither this nor the distinction
which Paul goes on to draw between the outward Jew and the
inward Jew, and between outward circumcision and the
circumcision of the heart, should be understood without
reference to 3.1–4; 4.9–12; 9.1–11.36. The fact that Paul gives
the answer which he does in 3.2 to the questions in 3.1 and the
fact that in 3.4 he firmly rejects the suggestion that Israel's
lack of faith will make God's faithfulness ineffective should
discourage us from understanding v. 25b to mean that the
circumcision of the disobedient Jew is simply annulled
(though it is often so understood).[1] Paul has not said that the
transgressor's circumcision profits nothing; he has not taken
away the sacramental character of circumcision,[2] though he
has certainly indicated that it does not place a man out of
range of God's judgment.[3] The point of v. 25b would seem to
be that it is possible for a circumcised Jew to stand, by reason

[1] It is noticeable that even commentators, who show their awareness
of the connexion between these verses and 3.1ff in their comments on
3.1ff, often fail altogether to take 3.1ff into account in their comments
on 2.25–29.

[2] *Pace* Kuss, p. 89. In this connexion Calvin, p. 54f, is illuminating.

[3] God's faithfulness to His sacraments, which should not be denied,
does not mean that He will not judge severely those who have received
them, requiring much of all those to whom much has been given
(Lk 12.48). The relevance of what Paul says here about circumcision to

of his disobedience, in a negative relation to God's purpose in history. (On this and on the distinction between the outward and the inward Jew in v. 28f see further, in addition to the notes on the verses, what is said on chapters nine to eleven.)

The fifth paragraph is 3.1–8. Paul recognizes that what he has said in 2.25–29 is very liable to be misunderstood as implying that the Jews have after all no privilege and that there is no profit at all in circumcision. So in the first four verses of this paragraph he seeks to deal with this possible misunderstanding. But in the course of warding off this possible misunderstanding he lays himself open to another, and, recognizing that he has done so, he digresses from his argument for the last four verses of the paragraph, in order to guard against it. With the beginning of the sixth and last paragraph of the sub-section (3.9–20) Paul returns to his argument after the digression of vv. 5–8. While what was said in vv. 2–4 certainly does mean that the reality and greatness of the Jews' privilege are not to be denied, it would be wrong to infer that they are at an advantage in absolutely every respect. In one respect, in particular, they have no advantage: as far as having a claim on God in virtue of their merit is concerned, they are in exactly the same position as the Gentiles—having, equally with them, no claim at all. The fact that all men alike are under sin's power is then confirmed by the catena of OT quotations in vv. 10–18. So far from imagining themselves to be excepted from God's condemnation of human sinfulness, the Jews must accept it as certainly including themselves, since what is said in the Scriptures concerns first and foremost the people of the Scriptures. And, if the Jews are no exception, then it is clear that all mankind must stand guilty before God. There is no question of the Jews' being justified by God on the ground of obedience to the law: the effect of the law is to reveal men's sinfulness.

1. Διό (we have already had the word in 1.24) has given interpreters of Paul a good deal of trouble. The difficulty they have experienced in trying to explain 2.1 as following logically upon 1.32 has given rise to a remarkable variety of suggestions: for example, that διό has lost its logical force and is here used simply as a colourless transition particle;[1] that it

Christian baptism has often been noted. So, e.g., Chrysostom, col. 490 (Οὕτω καὶ Χριστιανοῦ οὐδὲν ἔσται κέρδος πίστιν μὲν ἔχοντος καὶ τὴν ἀπὸ τοῦ βαπτίσματος δωρεάν, πᾶσι δὲ τοῖς πάθεσι ὑποκειμένου· μείζων γὰρ οὕτως ἡ ὕβρις ἔσται καὶ πλείων ἡ αἰσχύνη); Calvin, p. 55; Gaugler 1, p. 70.

[1] So Lietzmann, pp. 37–39; E. Molland, in *Serta Rudbergiana*, Oslo, 1931, pp. 43–52; Michel, p. 73.

should be emended to δίς;[1] that it should be explained as
anticipating what follows;[2] that v. 1 is a gloss;[3] that διό
connects v. 1 with 1.32a, v. 32b being parenthetic;[4] that it
looks back to 1.18–32 as a whole.[5] The last of these is surely
the most natural solution; but its acceptance has been hindered,
particularly for those who feel sure that Paul has the Jews in
mind right from the beginning of chapter 2, by the common
assumption that in 1.18–32 he is concerned *exclusively* with the
Gentiles. And, on this assumption, it is indeed difficult to see
any sense in which 2.1 can be said to follow from 1.18–32.
How can it follow from the fact that the Gentiles fall under the
condemnation declared in 1.18–32 that the Jew is without
excuse if he judges? Nygren has suggested[6] that the clue to
the understanding of διό is the recognition that in addressing
himself to the Jews in 2.1ff Paul has in mind the attitude
which comes to expression in Wisd 11–15. In those chapters
it is accepted that Jews also are guilty of the sins for which the
Gentiles are condemned but it is assumed that they will be
differently judged (so 15.2: καὶ γὰρ ἐὰν ἁμάρτωμεν, σοί ἐσμεν,
εἰδότες σου τὸ κράτος, and 11.9f: ὅτε γὰρ ἐπειράσθησαν, καίπερ
ἐν ἐλέει παιδευόμενοι, ἔγνωσαν πῶς μετ᾽ ὀργῆς κρινόμενοι ἀσεβεῖς
ἐβασανίζοντο· τούτους μὲν γὰρ ὡς πατὴρ νουθετῶν ἐδοκίμασας,
ἐκείνους δὲ ὡς ἀπότομος βασιλεὺς καταδικάζων ἐξήτασας, and
12.22: Ἡμᾶς οὖν παιδεύων τοὺς ἐχθροὺς ἡμῶν ἐν μυριότητι
μαστιγοῖς). On the assumption that the person addressed
in 2.1 admits that he too commits the sins with which the
Gentiles have been charged, the διό is perfectly appropriate
(so Nygren suggests), since in this case 2.1a is indeed logically
consequential on 1.18–32. But, while the relevance of Wisd
11–15 to the interpretation of Rom 1–2 is not to be denied, it
is surely much simpler and more satisfactory to recognize that
in 1.18–32 (though no doubt Paul has especially in mind the
sins of the Gentile world) it is not exclusively the sin of the

---

[1] A. Fridrichsen, in *Symbolae Osloenses* 1 (1922), p. 40, and in *RHPR* 3
(1923), p. 440.
[2] Cf. Murray 1, p. 56, who mentions this as a possibility which cannot
be dismissed. But is there any other evidence of διό being used in this
way?
[3] So Bultmann, 'Glossen', col. 200. He argues that 2.2 connects well
with 1.32, and that 2.1 is to be regarded as a gloss intended to sum up
the sense of 2.2f or as the conclusion to be drawn from the implicit 'No'
answering the question in v. 3 (Bultmann has 'V.2', but must surely
mean v. 3).
[4] So Barrett, p. 43.
[5] So, e.g., Sanday and Headlam, p. 55; Meyer 1, p. 102.
[6] p. 116f.

Gentiles which is being declared, but the sin of all men. The διό then presents no difficulty.

ἀναπολόγητος εἶ, ὦ ἄνθρωπε πᾶς ὁ κρίνων. Since the gospel reveals the fact of the universal sinfulness of men, the man who sets himself up to judge[1] other men is without excuse (for ἀναπολόγητος cf. 1.20)—he has no ground at all on which to stand. That the truth thus stated applies to the heathen moralist, to the civil magistrate,[2] to the ministers of the Church,[3] is indeed true; but Paul himself, it is scarcely to be doubted, was thinking especially of the typical Jew. The direct address in the second person singular, which is characteristic of, but not of course peculiar to, the Hellenistic diatribe, is used for the sake of vividness in this and the following verses (cf. 2.17ff; 8.2; 9.19f; 11.17ff; 13.3f; 14.4, 10, 15, 20–22).[4]

ἐν ᾧ γὰρ[5] κρίνεις τὸν ἕτερον, σεαυτὸν κατακρίνεις. τὰ γὰρ αὐτὰ πράσσεις ὁ κρίνων is naturally taken to mean that the man who judges his fellow man is thereby condemning himself because he himself is guilty of the same sorts of wrong-doing as the man he judges. Barrett has objected to this interpretation on the ground of the real moral superiority of the Jews and also of Gentile moral philosophers (he does not accept that this is addressed exclusively to the Jews), and suggested that Paul's point is rather that the act of judging is itself an attempt to put oneself in the place of God, and so the same idolatry essentially as is manifested in the sins referred to in the latter part of chapter 1.[6] But this is surely a very forced interpretation of Paul's Greek. Barrett's objection is answered, if we recognize that τὰ . . . αὐτά need not imply that the judge sins in precisely the same ways. There are, for example, more ways than one of breaking the seventh commandment, as is made clear in Mt 5.27f. On the verb πράσσειν (used here and also in vv. 2 and 3) and the distinction between it and ποιεῖν (used in v. 3) see on 7.15 (cf. also 1.32).

2. οἴδαμεν δὲ[7] ὅτι τὸ κρίμα τοῦ θεοῦ ἐστιν κατὰ ἀλήθειαν

---

[1] For the various shades of meaning which κρίνειν can express (cf. the English 'judge') see Bauer, s.v.

[2] Cf. Chrysostom, col. 423; but a few lines later he makes it clear that he does not think that Paul is addressing only rulers.

[3] Cf. Origen, col. 873f.

[4] For a good example in the OT see Ps 34.13f [LXX: 33.14f].

[5] The addition of κρίματι (C* 69 al sy^h) is to be explained as assimilation to Mt 7.2.

[6] p. 43f.

[7] The variant γάρ is less well-attested than δέ, which should be read. The substitution of γάρ for δέ here is not difficult to understand, but it is . less appropriate.

ἐπὶ τοὺς τὰ τοιαῦτα πράσσοντας is not intended to be taken as the imagined reply of the representative Jew whom Paul is addressing, as Dodd for example understands it,[1] but is Paul's own statement of what he knows to be common ground between himself and the person addressed. There are similar occurrences of οἴδαμεν δέ in 3.19; 8.28; 1 Tim 1.8, and of οἴδαμεν γάρ in 7.14; 8.22; 2 Cor 5.1. In each case οἴδαμεν introduces a statement which the writer can assume will meet with general acceptance on the part of those to whom he is writing or whom he has in mind. The use of οἴδαμεν (without a conjunction) in 1 Cor 8.1 and 4 is somewhat different, but in these verses too it introduces a statement of common ground (Paul is admitting that these Corinthians do have knowledge, before proceeding to point out that knowledge breeds conceit, and admitting that idols have no real existence, before proceeding to remind them that, since not all men understand this, one ought to be careful not to exercise one's freedom in such a way as to injure a weak brother). κατὰ ἀλήθειαν here means, of course, not 'truly' but 'according to truth'. What is being said of the divine judgment[2] is not that it truly is (that there truly is such a thing), but that it is in accordance with the facts (i.e., is just). The same point is expressed negatively in v. 11.

3. λογίζῃ δὲ τοῦτο, ὦ ἄνθρωπε ὁ κρίνων τοὺς τὰ τοιαῦτα πράσσοντας[3] καὶ ποιῶν αὐτά, ὅτι σὺ ἐκφεύξῃ τὸ κρίμα τοῦ θεοῦ; is closely connected with vv. 1 and 2, the language of which it echoes. It, in fact, applies the generally acknowledged truth stated in v. 2 to the person addressed in v. 1. In view of that truth, does he really reckon[4] to be a special case,[5] to escape the judgment of God?[6] That there were Jews who did

---

[1] p. 58: cf. Barrett, p. 44.

[2] κρίμα here means 'judgment' in the sense of sentence of condemnation (see Bauer, s.v., 4.b).

[3] P has, instead of the first eleven words, νομίζεις οὖν ὁ ταῦτα πράσσων, but this reading is not likely to be original.

[4] This is the first of nineteen occurrences of λογίζεσθαι in Romans. In extra-biblical Greek it was used both as a technical term in commercial language for calculating cost, debts, etc., and also to denote objective, dispassionate thought (e.g. in Plato). In the LXX it mainly represents ḥāšaḇ, from which it derives a certain enrichment of signification, since it is used to denote a thinking in which feeling and will are involved, and sometimes with reference to God's purposing and also to men's disposition in relation to God. On its special uses in the Pauline epistles see further on v. 26; 3.28; 4.3; 6.11; 8.18; 9.8. See further H. W. Heidland, in TWNT 4, pp. 287–95.

[5] σύ is emphatic, bringing out the folly of such an assumption of partiality on the part of God.

[6] As in v. 2, κρίμα here denotes the sentence of condemnation.

reckon precisely this is clear from, for example, Wisd 15.2.

4. ἢ τοῦ πλούτου τῆς χρηστότητος αὐτοῦ καὶ τῆς ἀνοχῆς καὶ τῆς μακροθυμίας καταφρονεῖς, ἀγνοῶν ὅτι τὸ χρηστὸν τοῦ θεοῦ εἰς μετάνοιάν σε ἄγει;[1] is not an alternative interpretation of the Jew's attitude to that put forward in v. 3, but rather a different, and heightened, statement of it (cf. the use of a question introduced by ἤ in 1 Cor 9.6 to press home the point just made by a previous question: Lagrange cites also an example in Arrian, *Epict.* 1.6.32). The Jew's assumption that he is going to escape God's judgment actually amounts to contempt for God's kindness. For the use of πλοῦτος followed by the genitive to express abundance of something compare 9.23; 2 Cor 8.2; Eph 1.7, 18; 2.7; 3.16; Col 1.27; 2.2. Of the three abstract nouns in the genitive χρηστότης is specially emphasized, being picked up by τὸ χρηστόν in the participial clause. The piling up of synonymous or near-synonymous expressions is reminiscent of the language of prayer (cf., e.g., 1 Kgs 8.22ff; Neh 9.17; Dan 9.4ff; Wisd 15.1; Rev 4.11; 5.9, 12) and also of solemn exhortation (e.g. Deut 30). For God's χρηστότης compare, for example, 11.22, and also, e.g., Ps 25 [LXX: 24] .7, 8; 31.19 [LXX: 30.20]; 34.8 [LXX: 33.9]; 86 [LXX: 85] .5; 100 [LXX: 99] .5; 119 [LXX: 118] .68; 136 [LXX: 135] .1; 145 [LXX: 144] .9; Mt 11.30; Lk 6.35; Eph 2.7; Tit 3.4; 1 Pet 2.3. Both ἀνοχή (in the LXX only in 1 Macc 12.25 and there not in the same sense; in the NT only here and 3.26) and μακροθυμία (cf., e.g., Exod 34.6; Num 14.18; Neh 9.17; Ps 7.12[LXX only]; 86[LXX: 85].15; 103 [LXX: 102].8; 145[LXX: 144].8; Joel 2.13; Jon 4.2; Nah 1.3; Ecclus 5.4; 18.11) are used of God's forbearance, His holding back his wrath. It is significant that both χρηστός and μακρόθυμος are used of God in Wisd 15.1, and that the thought of patience (expressed by other words) occurs a number of times in Wisd 11–15.

The participle ἀγνοῶν and its dependent clause are clearly not intended as an extenuation of the guilt of the person addressed, but as a clarification of καταφρονεῖς. The attitude described amounts to contempt of God's goodness in that it is a wilful refusal to recognize (it is clear that ἀγνοεῖν denotes here a thoroughly blameworthy not-knowing) the fact that God's goodness both affords to those who are its objects the opportunity for, and also summons them to, repentance.[2]

---

[1] The variant ἐνάγει (33 (Hier)) for σε ἄγει is not significant: it could easily have arisen by a simple error in copying.

[2] μετάνοια occurs in the Pauline corpus only here and in 2 Cor 7.9, 10; 2 Tim 2.25, and μετανοεῖν only in 2 Cor 12.21 (there is also the occurrence

That τὸ χρηστὸν τοῦ θεοῦ εἰς μετάνοιαν . . . ἄγει (in the sense of being intended and designed to produce it) was a well-established truth in Judaism is clear from, for example, Wisd 11.23; 12.10, 19; but the tendency was to recognize this with regard to the heathen but to fail to see that it was applicable also —and indeed particularly—to the Jew.

5. κατά: here probably 'because of', 'on account of'.[1]

σκληρότητα. Compare 9.18; also Deut 9.27. Compare also the use of σκληροκαρδία in Mt 19.8 = Mk 10.5; Mk 16.14 (cf. Deut 10.16; Jer 4.4; Ezek 3.7) and of σκληροτράχηλος in Acts 7.51 (cf., e.g., Exod 33.3, 5; 34.9; Deut 9.6, 13). In the OT these words are particularly used with reference to Israel.

θησαυρίζεις σεαυτῷ ὀργὴν ἐν ἡμέρᾳ ὀργῆς καὶ ἀποκαλύψεως[2] δικαιοκρισίας[3] τοῦ θεοῦ. The use of θησαυρίζειν is ironical. Compare LXX Prov 1.18. The metaphor is elsewhere used of storing up something desirable, as in Mt 6.20. Because of his stubbornness and impenitence the person addressed is storing up for himself God's wrath to be experienced in the future. The words ἐν ἡμέρᾳ ὀργῆς καὶ ἀποκαλύψεως δικαιοκρισίας τοῦ θεοῦ are usually taken closely with ὀργήν, i.e., as indicating when the wrath is to be experienced (namely, in the final judgment). But Barth has suggested that these words should rather be taken with θησαυρίζεις, i.e. as characterizing the present time, in which the storing up is taking place, as the time of God's wrath and of the revelation of His righteous judgment.[4] We should then compare 1.18 in which the present tense (ἀποκαλύπτεται) is used of the wrath of God, and understand Paul's thought to be that even now, when God's wrath and His righteous judgment are actually being revealed as the gospel is preached, the person whom he is addressing cannot

of ἀμετανόητος in v. 5). The fact that these words are so seldom used by Paul certainly does not mean that repentance is not important for him. The explanation of it is rather that repentance is for him an integral element of πίστις. He may well also have felt that the word itself had been devalued by the tendency in Judaism to understand it legalistically. See further J. Behm and E. Würthwein, in *TWNT* 4, pp. 972–1004.

[1] Cf. Bauer, s.v. II.5.a.δ.

[2] There is considerable support for the addition before δικαιοκρισίας of καί, which has the effect of making ἀποκαλύψεως parallel with ὀργῆς and δικαιοκρισίας; but intrinsic probability is against it, and it is possible to account for it as due to a careless reader's puzzlement at the combination ἀποκαλύψεως δικαιοκρισίας. The variant ἀνταποδόσεως for ἀποκαλύψεως in A also looks like a not very perceptive attempted improvement.

[3] See BDF, § 119 (3); Bauer, s.v. *Pace* Sanday and Headlam who claim (p. 56) that this word denotes 'not so much the character of the judgement as the character of the judge', there is probably no difference of meaning between δικαιοκρισίας here and δικαίας κρίσεως in 2 Th 1.5.

[4] *Shorter*, p. 34 (*KE*, p. 39).

think of anything better to do than to go on storing up wrath for himself by his self-righteous, impenitent attitude. It is not at all easy to decide between these alternatives. Neither of them can fairly be charged with doing violence to the Greek; and neither can be disqualified on the ground of being inconsonant with Paul's thought in general. The argument from 1.18 is strong support for the latter interpretation. It is possibly strengthened by the fact that 2.5 is near enough to the beginning of 2.1–3.20 to be regarded as standing in a roughly corresponding position in that section to that in which 1.18 stands in the parallel section 1.18–32. And the fact that Paul did not place the words under consideration next to θησαυρίζεις cannot fairly be urged against this interpretation, since his intention to introduce the quotation in v. 6 adequately explains the word-order adopted (it was clearly desirable to place τοῦ θεοῦ as near as possible to ὅς). But, in view of the contents of vv. 6–10, the former interpretation ought probably to be preferred; for it does seem a good deal more natural to understand these verses as direct explication of ἀποκαλύψεως δικαιοκρισίας than as only indirect support for it, which is what they would be, if ἡμέρᾳ ὀργῆς καὶ ἀποκαλύψεως δικαιοκρισίας τοῦ θεοῦ referred not to the time of the final judgment but to the present time.

6. ὃς ἀποδώσει ἑκάστῳ κατὰ τὰ ἔργα αὐτοῦ echoes the language of Ps 62.12 [LXX: 61.13]; Prov 24.12. That God's judgment will be according to men's deeds is again and again affirmed in Scripture—in the NT no less strongly than in the OT. We may compare, in the OT, in addition to the passages just mentioned, e.g. Eccles 12.14; Isa 3.10f; Jer 17.10; Hos 12.2, and, in the NT, Mt 7.21; 16.27; 25.31–46; Jn 5.28f; 2 Cor 5.10; 11.15b; Gal 6.7–9; Eph 6.8; Col 3.24f; 2 Tim 4.14; 1 Pet 1.17; Rev 2.23; 20.12f; 22.12. The question of the compatibility of this affirmation with what Paul says elsewhere (e.g. in 3.20a, 21f, 28) in connexion with justification must be discussed in the light of vv. 6–11 as a whole, since the summary statement of this verse is spelled out in vv. 7–10 and confirmed by v. 11. But it can be said at this point that there is nothing in this verse to support the suggestion that Paul is here speaking only from an OT point of view; that the plain future indicative ἀποδώσει is no encouragement to take these verses as merely hypothetical; but also that the ἀπο- of ἀποδιδόναι, while it is true that it suggests that what is being rendered is in some sense due, need not imply the idea of equivalence; and that it must not be assumed that κατὰ τὰ ἔργα αὐτοῦ is simply a way of saying 'what his deeds deserve' or 'according to his deserts'.

7. τοῖς μὲν καθ' ὑπομονὴν ἔργου ἀγαθοῦ δόξαν καί τιμὴν καὶ
ἀφθαρσίαν ζητοῦσιν and the parallel formulation in v. 8 stand in
apposition to ἑκάστῳ in v. 6, and indicate two categories of men. Barrett's paraphrase of the words by
'To those who with patient endurance look beyond their
own well-doing to the glory, honour, and incorruption God
alone can give'[1] does intolerable violence to the Greek. The
words καθ' ὑπομονὴν ἔργου ἀγαθοῦ must surely mean
something like 'by steadfast perseverance in good works'
(or 'in the good work').[2] The expression ἔργον ἀγαθόν
has been variously interpreted. Some understand Paul to
mean such goodness of life as would be a real fulfilling of
God's law and would actually merit salvation but to be
speaking here from a pre-evangelical point of view (not
taking account of the revelation of the δικαιοσύνη θεοῦ
referred to in 1.17; 3.21ff) and also hypothetically (such
goodness of life not in fact being found among men), the
purpose of what is here said being merely to contribute to the
demolishing of the Jews' claims; others take him to be
referring to faith as being the good work required by God;
and others think the reference is to goodness of life, not
however as meriting God's favour but as the expression of
faith. It is to be noted that Paul speaks of those who seek
(ζητοῦσιν) glory, honour and incorruption, not of those
who deserve them. δόξα, τιμή and ἀφθαρσία here denote
eschatological gifts of God already firmly associated in Jewish
thought with the resurrection life of the blessed (cf. δόξα . . . καί
τιμὴ καὶ εἰρήνη in v. 10, and also εἰς ἔπαινον καὶ δόξαν καὶ τιμὴν
ἐν ἀποκαλύψει Ἰησοῦ Χριστοῦ in I Pet 1.7).

ζωὴν αἰώνιον is the direct object of ἀποδώσει. The
expression is a comprehensive term for final blessedness.[4]

8. τοῖς δὲ ἐξ ἐριθείας καὶ ἀπειθοῦσι τῇ ἀληθείᾳ πειθομένοις δὲ τῇ
ἀδικίᾳ corresponds to τοῖς μέν, κ. τ. λ. in the previous verse,
being also in apposition to ἑκάστῳ. It indicates the other
category of men, and contains a threefold characterization
of them. Of the three elements of this characterization the

[1] p. 42.
[2] Cf. BDF, § 163. ὑπομονή occurs also in 5.3, 4; 8.25; 15.4, 5, and
the cognate verb in 12.12.
[3] For τιμή cf. Jn 12.26b; also 1 Sam 2.30; Ps 91.11.
[4] Cf. 5.21; 6.22, 23; also Gal 6.8; 1 Tim 1.16; 6.12; Tit 1.2; 3.7; Mt 19.29;
25.46; Mk 10.17, 30; Lk 10.25; 18.18, 30; Jn 3.15, etc. The noun ζωή
occurs here for the first time in Romans: it occurs also four times in
chapter 5, three times in chapter 6, four times in chapter 8, and once
each in chapters 7 and 11, while the verb ζῆν, which we have already
had in 1.17, is used in all twenty-three times in Romans.

second (i.e. ἀπειθοῦσι τῇ ἀληθείᾳ) and third (i.e. πειθομένοις ... τῇ ἀδικίᾳ) are straightforward enough. The only commentary on them that is necessary is a comparison of the words τῶν τὴν ἀλήθειαν ἐν ἀδικίᾳ κατεχόντων in 1.18. But the first element is puzzling. The meaning which ἐριθεία has in the NT[1] is disputed. In the RV it is represented by 'faction': so here τοῖς ... ἐξ ἐριθείας[2] is rendered 'unto them that are factious'. Barrett rejects this translation on the ground that it 'assumes the derivation of ἐριθεία from ἔρις (strife)';[3] but, while the AV rendering 'unto them that are contentious' might perhaps be suspected of resting on a false connexion of ἐριθεία with ἔρις,[4] the Revisers cannot fairly be held guilty of such a mistake. They doubtless had in mind the sense which the word has in Aristotle, *Pol.* 1302[b]4 and 1303[a]14 (cf. the use of the verb ἐριθεύεσθαι in 1303[a]16), where it is used of canvassing for public office, intriguing.[5] Such intriguing involved the creation of a faction. So the RV rendering can be defended on the basis of the use of the word in Aristotle. If it is right, then Paul may perhaps be understood to refer here to the fact that those who disobey the truth of God and give themselves to unrighteousness constitute a faction in opposition to God.[6] However, it is possibly rather more likely that in the NT ἐριθεία has a more general sense which could be an extension of that which it has in Aristotle—namely, 'self-seeking' or 'selfishness'.[7] The first element in the threefold description contained in this verse could then be taken to refer to the basic egotism of sinful men which lies behind their disobedience to the truth and their obedience to unrighteousness. Barrett's suggestion (based on the view that, since ἐριθεία is derived from ἔριθος which means 'a hireling', it 'should therefore mean the activity, or characteristics, or mind, of a hireling') that it is 'very probable that Paul intends by means of this word to describe the motives ... of those who look on their works as achievements of their own, complete in themselves, by means

---

[1] It occurs in 2 Cor 12.20; Gal 5.20; Phil 1.17; 2.3; Jas 3.14, 16, as well as here. Outside the NT it occurs but rarely.

[2] For οἱ ἐκ ... cf., e.g., οἱ ἐκ νόμου in 4.14; οἱ ἐκ πίστεως in Gal 3.7; οἱ ἐκ περιτομῆς in Gal 2.12.

[3] p. 47.

[4] Elsewhere the AV renders ἐριθεία by 'strife'. Cf. the use of *contentio* and *rixa* in the Vulgate.

[5] It is not difficult to guess how words cognate with ἔριθος ('hired servant') came to be used of such intrigues; for they were not carried on without money changing hands.

[6] Cf., e.g., Sanday and Headlam, p. 57.

[7] Cf. Bauer, s.v.

of which they may acquire rights'[1] builds too much on ety-
mology to be convincing. Moreover, while the appropriateness
of ascribing the motives to which Barrett refers to Jewish
legalists is of course obvious, it is not quite so obvious that
Paul would be likely to ascribe them to pagan Gentiles—and
vv. 9 and 10 make it clear that what is said in vv. 6–8 is said
with reference to Jews and Gentiles alike.

ὀργὴ καὶ θυμός. Instead of using the accusative, as with
ζωὴν αἰώνιον in v. 7, Paul slips into a different construction
in the middle of his sentence. With these nominatives the verb
'to be' has to be understood. The two nouns are probably used
simply as synonyms,[2] the second having the effect of strengthening and emphasizing the first. The divine wrath is of course
meant.

9. θλῖψις καὶ στενοχωρία.[3] The arrangement is chiastic,
these words answering to ὀργὴ καὶ θυμός, the rest of v. 9 to the
earlier part of v. 8, and v. 10 to v. 7. θλῖψις can denote tribulation of various kinds. The reference here is to the effects of the
eschatological wrath of God. See further H. Schlier, in *TWNT*
3, pp. 139–48, especially 146f. στενοχωρία, which occurs in the
NT only in the Pauline letters (four times: in addition, the
cognate verb occurs three times), is generally taken, in view of
2 Cor 4.8, to be a stronger term than θλῖψις, with which it is
associated in 8.35 and 2 Cor 6.4, as well as here.[4] It may be
that in this verse its addition simply has the effect of emphasizing and heightening θλῖψις But the view, maintained by,
for example, Aquinas,[5] Calvin,[6] and Karl Barth,[7] that when
Paul uses the two words together he intends by θλῖψις outward
affliction and by στενοχωρία inward distress or anguish, though
it cannot be said to be firmly established, seems to possess
considerable plausibility. See further G. Bertram, in *TWNT* 7,
pp. 604–8, especially 607f. The θλῖψις and στενοχωρία referred to
here are, in any case, effects of the divine ὀργὴ καὶ θυμός
mentioned in v. 8.

ἐπὶ πᾶσαν ψυχὴν ἀνθρώπου means no more than 'as the

---

[1] p. 47f. Cf. Zahn, pp. 115–18; Barth, 1933, pp. 61–63.
[2] If any distinction were intended, ὀργή would probably be used of
the inner feeling of wrath and θυμός of its outward expression (cf. LSJ,
s.v. θυμός, II.4); but it is not at all likely that this distinction was
intended here.
[3] The alternative punctuation with commas after θυμός and στενοχωρία
yields a less satisfactory structure.
[4] The two words are associated together also in LXX Deut 28.53,
55, 57; Isa 8.22;˙30.6.
[5] p. 36 (200).
[6] p. 187.
[7] *CD* IV/3, p. 614f (= *KD* IV/3, p. 704).

lot of every individual man', the introduction of the word
ψυχή here being merely a reflection of the Hebrew use of
nepeš in the sense of 'person' (cf., e.g., LXX Num 19.20;
31.40; Deut 10.22). The suggestion that this expression was
used in order to indicate that it is the souls of men which will
suffer the punishment (so Lagrange[1]) should be rejected.

τοῦ κατεργαζομένου (see on 1.27) τὸ κακόν expresses simply
and directly what was expressed in v. 8 by a threefold
characterization.

Ἰουδαίῳ τε πρῶτον καὶ Ἕλληνι. For the emphasis, in this and
the next verse, both on the equal relevance to both Jew and
Gentile of what is being said, and also at the same time on
the special precedence of the Jew, see on 1.16, and also on 3.1f,
9, and on chapters 9 to 11. For the aspect of Jewish priority
indicated in this verse compare Amos 3.2; Lk 12.48.[2]

10. For δόξα and τιμή compare v. 7. For εἰρήνη see on 1.7.
Here it is more or less equivalent to σωτηρία.

παντὶ τῷ ἐργαζομένῳ. The simple dative is now used instead of
ἐπί and the accusative and the simple verb instead of the compound probably just for the sake of variety.[3]

11. οὐ γάρ ἐστιν προσωπολημψία παρὰ τῷ θεῷ is added in
confirmation of what has been said in vv. 6–10. Compare
Gal 2.6; Eph 6.9; Col 3.25: also Acts 10.34. In the Hebrew OT
there are several expressions for 'showing partiality', which
include the word for 'face': *nāśā' pānîm, hikkîr pānîm, hāḏar
pānîm*. Of these the first is the commonest. It can be used in a
good sense—'be gracious to', 'show consideration for' (e.g.
Deut 28.50; 2 Kgs 3.14; Job 42.8f; Lam 4.16); but it is often
used in a bad sense—'be unduly influenced by', 'show partiality toward' (e.g. Lev 19.15; Deut 10.17; Ps 82.2; Prov 18.5).
In the LXX it is sometimes represented by πρόσωπον λαμβάνειν,
and it is from this LXX expression that the NT words

[1] p. 46f.

[2] Dodd's comment (p. 59), 'In the thought of Paul it is little more
than a survival of his inherited and deeply ingrained feeling that
somehow his own people must receive special treatment', seems strangely
unperceptive. Dodd's over-confidence in the reliability of his guesses
about Paul's psychology has surely led him astray here.

[3] Though a distinction is sometimes seen between κατεργάζεσθαι in
v. 9 and ἐργάζεσθαι in v. 10 (so, e.g., Severian, in Cramer, p. 11: 'Ἐπὶ μὲν
τοῦ κακοῦ, τὴν κατάκρισιν ὥρισεν, οὐχ ἁπλῶς ἀλλ' ἐπὶ τῶν κατεργαζομένων · ἐπὶ
δὲ τοῦ ἀγαθοῦ τὴν δόξαν, οὐ μόνον ἐπὶ τῶν κατεργαζομένων, ἵνα δι' ἑκατέρων τοῦ
θεοῦ τὸ ἀγαθὸν δειχθῇ, καὶ ὅτι κατακρίνει οὐχ ἁπλῶς τοὺς ἐργαζομένους, ἀλλὰ
τοὺς κατεργαζομένους · καὶ ὅτι τιμᾷ τοὺς ἁπλῶς ἐργαζομένους τὸ ἀγαθόν. Cf. the
same author quoted by Cramer, p. 10: ἔστι γὰρ ἐργάζεσθαι παλαίοντα, μὴ
νικώμενον δέ. τὸ δὲ κατεργάζεσθαι, τῆς μετ' ἐπιμελείας ἐργασίας ἐστι τοῦ κακοῦ).
See on 1. 27.

προσωπολημ-πτεῖν, -ψία, -πτης and ἀπροσωπολήμπτως
derive. In the NT the sense conveyed is always bad.

We are now in a position to look at vv. 6–11 as a whole and to try to
decide how the passage may best be understood. It will be of the
greatest importance to keep firmly in mind the actual direction in
which Paul's argument is going. In 1.18-32 he has spoken of the
judgment which the gospel pronounces on humankind generally. In
chapter 2 he has set about showing that those who imagine that they are
exceptions to this general condemnation are in fact not exceptions at
all. Though he does not explicitly use the name 'Jew' until v.17, it
seems highly probable (as we have seen)[1] that Paul has the Jews in
mind right from the beginning of chapter 2 and that the whole of
chapter 2 is an apostrophizing of the typical Jew (note the use of the
second person singular from v.1 onwards). Paul recognizes in him a
combination of two highly dangerous ingredients. On the one hand,
there is a signally complacent self-righteousness of the sort classically
illustrated by the attitude of the Pharisee in Luke 18.9-14. On the other
hand, there is an unshakable confidence that God's covenant with
Israel must mean, in spite of the emphatic warning of Amos 3.2 ('You
only have I known of all the families of the earth: therefore I will visit
upon you all your iniquities'), that God will, while judging the Gentiles
with severity, treat the members of the people Israel with special
indulgence and leniency as suggested in Wisdom ('For when they were
tried, albeit but in mercy chastened, they learned how the ungodly were
tormented, being judged with wrath: for these as a father, admonishing
them, thou didst prove; but those, as a stern king, condemning them,
thou didst search out'[2] and 'While therefore thou dost chasten us, thou
scourgest our enemies ten thousand times more'[3]). It is the attitude
which results from the combination of these two ingredients which
Paul recognizes as constituting an extraordinarily effective obstacle in
the way of any true faith in God and also of any truly brotherly relations
with fellow human beings, and which he challenges in his
apostrophizing of the typical Jew: 'Wherefore thou hast no excuse,
man, whoever thou art who judgest *another;* for wherein thou judgest
the other, thou condemnest thyself; for thou doest the same things, thou
that settest thyself up as a judge' (2.1).

Paul's direct address to the typical Jew is leading up to the conclusion in
chapter 3 that, while human beings' lack of faith will not be able to
render God's faithfulness ineffectual,[4] and, while the fact that Israel has
been entrusted with the oracles of God remains an altogether great
advantage of the Jews,[5] both Jews and Gentiles equally are 'all under
sin' and, in the words of the OT catena in 3.10 ff, 'There is no one
who is

---

[1] Cf p,138f.
[2] Wisd 11.9-10.
[3] Wisd 12.22.
[4] 3.3.
[5] 3.2.

righteous, not even one',[6] and the only hope for human beings, whether Jews or Gentiles, is God's altogether undeserved gift of a status of righteousness before Himself through the redemptive work of Jesus Christ.[7]

If we keep firmly in mind the direction of Paul's argument, we shall, we think, be less likely to be attracted by the notion that we can actually discern the detailed shape of a doctrine of the final judgment in what he has written. Some commentators (including the present writer in earlier impressions of this commentary) have perhaps been rather too ready to try to systematize here. While Paul certainly believed that God is, and will be, the just Judge of all humankind, and indications of this may be seen throughout the epistle, it is surely a mistake to look for a systematic doctrine of God's final judgment either in chapter 2 or elsewhere in Romans. Paul surely did not intend to give to believers in Jesus Christ any encouragement to indulge in a Christian self-complacency answering to the Jewish self-complacency against which his apostrophizing of his contemporary typical Jew is such an eloquent warning – although Christians through the centuries may sometimes have managed to discover such encouragement in what he has written.

Clearly the point which Paul wanted to make after vv. 3–5, and to make emphatically, was that for the Jew to rely complacently on the fact of his knowledge of God and of God's will, as though a merely formal knowledge (that is, a knowledge which is not existential, which stops short of obedience) were enough, is folly, since God's judgment will take account of men's deeds. It is ἔργα which is the operative word in v. 6, and the importance of ἔργα is further underlined in v. 13 (cf. the emphatic ποιῶσιν in v. 14). So the accent in vv. 7–10 is on the negative side, on the warning these verses contain for the Jew in his complacency. This is confirmed by v. 11. Thus the intention of vv. 6–11 fits naturally into place (and the same may also be said of vv. 12–16 and of vv. 25–29) within the over-all function of 2.1–3.20 which is to show that the Jew is no exception to the verdict of the gospel that no man—apart of course from the one man, Jesus Christ— *deserves* God's favour.

---

[6] 3.10.
[7] 3.21-26.

It is absolutely vital to the true understanding of these verses to recognize that the statement of v. 6 is not made in a legalistic sense—it is not an assertion of requital according to *deserts*—and that it is not implied in vv. 7 and 10 that the people referred to *earn* eternal life. The ἔργον ἀγαθόν is not regarded as constituting a claim upon God, but as the expression of faith and repentance. The good work no more earns salvation than does the evil work. The difference between them is the difference between evidence of openness to God's judgment and mercy and evidence of the persistence of a proud and stubborn self-righteousness. The insistence on the necessity of ἔργα which we have here, which should be compared with what is to be seen in such passages as Mt 7.21 and 25.31ff,[1] has nothing to do with the idea that one can be justified ἐξ ἔργων, i.e. earn one's justification by one's works. There is then, we would suggest, nothing in these verses which is incompatible with Paul's doctrine of justification by faith.

12 begins a new paragraph within the sub-section. The connexion of thought with vv. 1–11 is very close. But now there is introduced for the first time in the epistle a direct and explicit reference to the law (an indirect reference may be recognized in vv. 1 and 3, for the reader is no doubt expected to realize that it is on the basis of his knowledge of the law that the Jew presumes to judge others). The main point made in this paragraph is that knowledge of the law does not in itself constitute any defence against the judgment of God.

The sentence Ὅσοι γὰρ ἀνόμως ἥμαρτον, ἀνόμως καὶ ἀπολοῦνται provides some illustration of the truth stated in v. 11; but it seems to be introduced more as a foil to the following sentence which is co-ordinate with it than for its own sake. The emphasis falls rather on καὶ ὅσοι ἐν νόμῳ ἥμαρτον, διὰ νόμου κριθήσονται. While those who have sinned[2] in ignorance of the law will perish (that is, will be condemned

---

[1] And also, if we understand the passage correctly, in Jas 2.14-26 (cf. C.E.B. Cranfield, 'The Message of James', in *SJT* 18 (1965), pp. 338–42).

[2] On the use of the aorist in this verse see Burton, *MT,* § 54. It may be described as a collective historical aorist (cf. 3.23), the aorist being used because the sins referred to are thought of as together constituting a past event. Since no interval is envisaged between the completion of the sum of sins and the time of speaking, a perfect is required in English. But it is possible—indeed, probable—that here the statements of past fact are made proleptically as from the viewpoint of the last judgment.

in the final judgment) even though they did not have the law,[1] those who have sinned knowing the law (ἐν νόμῳ indicates the circumstances under which they sinned, namely, the direct opposite to those denoted by ἀνόμως at the beginning of the verse) will be judged by God according to the standard provided by the law. That in each reference to law here it is the law of God, the OT law, which is intended is not to be doubted.[2]

13. οὐ γὰρ οἱ ἀκροαταὶ νόμου δίκαιοι παρὰ [τῷ] θεῷ, ἀλλ' οἱ ποιηταὶ νόμου δικαιωθήσονται supports v. 12b, and brings to clear expression the main point of this paragraph. With the contrast between hearers of the law and doers of it compare Jas 1.22f, 25. The fact that hearing is here opposed to doing indicates that the hearing referred to is not hearing in the fuller sense which the words šāmaʿ and ἀκούειν can have in the Bible (as, for example, in Gen 3.17; Exod 15.26; Deut 4.30; Josh 1.18; Isa 1.19; Jer 11.3; 12.17; Mic 5.15 [MT: 14]), but a 'hearing only' which falls short of heeding and obeying. Those who are merely hearers of the law in this narrow sense are certainly not possessed of any status of righteousness before God (that δίκαιοι here refers to status in relation to God rather than moral quality is clear—compare δικαιωθήσονται in the latter half of the verse). It is rather those who are doers of the law who will be justified at the last judgment (δικαιοῦν is here used with reference to the ultimate eschatological verdict).[3] That doing what the law commands is the decisive thing, and not just hearing it and knowing about it, was a truth familiar to the Rabbis;[4] but, though Paul takes

---

[1] With ἀνόμως in this verse cf. χωρὶς νόμου in 7.9 and also the use of ἄνομος in 1 Cor 9.21.

[2] *Pace* Sanday and Headlam (p. 58) *et al.*, who take νόμος when used without the article here and in vv. 13 and 14, and also e.g. in 3.20f; 4.15, to mean law in general. The view, already expressed by Origen (according to Rufinus, col. 944: the Greek text of the commentary on 3.21 omits this passage—see Scherer, p. 152f), that it was Paul's custom to place the article before νόμος when he was using it with reference to the OT law and that, when he omits the article, he is using the word in a general sense, cannot be sustained—not even to the limited extent approved by Sanday and Headlam. It is safe to assume that in Paul's epistles νόμος refers to the OT law unless the context clearly shows this to be impossible. On this matter and on the whole subject of Paul's understanding of the law reference may be made to the extended discussion at the end of this commentary.

[3] In connexion with δίκαιοι and δικαιωθήσονται see further on 1.17.

[4] Cf., e.g., the words ascribed to Rabban Simeon, the son of Rabban Gamaliel I (Paul's own teacher) in *Aboth* 1.17: 'not the expounding [of the Law] is the chief thing but the doing [of it]; and he that multiplies words occasions sin'. Further interesting material is given in SB 3, pp. 84ff.

up a Rabbinic doctrine, he is giving it fresh content. In its context in Romans this sentence can hardly be intended to imply that there are some who are doers of the law in the sense that they so fulfil it as to earn God's justification. Rather is Paul thinking of that beginning of grateful obedience to be found in those who believe in Christ, which though very weak and faltering and in no way deserving God's favour, is, as the expression of humble trust in God, well-pleasing in His sight.[1]

14-16.[2] The most natural explanation of the γάρ would seem to be that these verses are thought of as confirming v. 13b—v. 13b, which might at first sight appear to conflict with the καὶ ᵀΕλληνι of v. 10, does not in fact do so, since those Gentiles who do the things the law requires stand in a real positive relation to the law (vv. 14b and 15a) and so may be regarded as included in the reference of οἱ ποιηταὶ νόμου in v. 13b.

The words ἔθνη[3] . . . τὰ τοῦ νόμου ποιῶσιν pose again both the problems common to vv. 7, 10 and 13b and also the special problem posed by καὶ ᵀΕλληνι in v. 10; and are interpreted variously. The following possibilities have to be considered: (i) to understand them to mean that some pagan Gentiles do in fact, on the basis of a natural moral law, fulfil God's law's demands[4] and so merit His favour; (ii) to understand them as meant only hypothetically, their purpose being to underline the essential equality before God of Jews and

---

[1] Our understanding of this verse will naturally follow the way in which we understand vv. 6–11. See the notes on those verses and in particular the discussion which follows the note on v. 11.

[2] Among the literature bearing on the interpretation of this passage may be mentioned: Lietzmann, p. 40f; E. Norden, *Agnostos Theos*, Leipzig and Berlin, 1913; M. Pohlenz, 'Paulus und die Stoa', in *ZNW* 42 (1949), pp. 69ff; W. Mundle, 'Zur Auslegung von Röm 2.13ff', in *TB* 13 (1934), cols. 249ff; W. Kranz, 'Das Gesetz des Herzens', in *RMP* n.s. 94 (1951), pp. 222ff; F. Flückiger, 'Die Werke des Gesetzes bei den Heiden (nach Röm 2.14ff)', in *TZ* 8 (1952), pp. 17–42; Kuss, pp. 69–76; also 'Die Heiden und die Werke des Gesetzes (nach Röm 2.14–16)', in *MTZ* 5 (1954), pp. 77ff; J. B. Souček, 'Zur Exegese von Röm 2.14ff' in *Antwort*, pp. 99ff; B. Reicke, 'Natürliche Theologie nach Paulus', in SEA 22–23 (1957–58), pp. 154–67; G. Bornkamm, *Gesammelte Aufsätze* 2, pp. 93–118; A. Walker, 'Die Heiden und das Gericht', in *EvTh* 20 (1960), pp. 302ff; Barth, *CD* II/2, p. 604; IV/1, pp. 33f, 395; IV/2, p. 561; IV/4, p. 7f (=*KD* II/2, p. 672; IV/1, pp. 33f, 437; IV/2, p. 635; IV/4, p. 8f).

[3] The AV's 'the Gentiles' is incorrect. There is no article here in the Greek, and the meaning is 'Gentiles', the reference being to some, not to all, Gentiles. Cf. 9.30.

[4] Some, who follow this line of interpretation, take Paul to mean by τὰ τοῦ νόμου ποιεῖν a fulfilment of the whole law, others understand him to mean only a doing from time to time of things which are in accordance with the law.

Gentiles; (iii) to interpret them as referring to a secret, hidden faith, known only to God, mysteriously existing in some pagan hearts, or to the works by which it expresses itself; (iv) to take ἔθνη to refer to the Gentile Christians. Of this last interpretation also two forms may be distinguished: (a) that which understands τὰ τοῦ νόμου ποιῶσιν of the Gentile Christians' faith, and (b) that which takes it to refer to those works of obedience which, though but imperfect and far from deserving God's favour, are the expression of their hearts' faith. Of the interpretations we have listed (i) should be rejected as hardly compatible with 3.9, 20, 23, and (ii) on the ground that there is nothing here to suggest that Paul is speaking merely hypothetically. Interpretation (iv), which is found already in Ambrosiaster[1] and Augustine,[2] and is maintained by Barth in his shorter commentary,[3] seems to us most likely. Verses 26–29 would seem to tell in its favour. The Gentile Christians are referred to simply as τὰ ἔθνη in 11.13 and 15.9. And, as between (a) and (b), (b) should, in our view, be preferred.

Before trying to clarify the meaning of τὰ μὴ[4] νόμον ἔχοντα we must decide whether φύσει is to be connected with the words which follow it (i.e. τὰ τοῦ νόμου ποιῶσιν) or with these words. It has usually been connected with τὰ τοῦ νόμου ποιῶσιν,[5] and Paul's meaning has commonly been taken to be that it is as a result of their possession of natural law (Paul's use of φύσις being understood in the light of Stoic teaching)[6] that some Gentiles do the things required by God's law (whatever sense is given to this statement). But a comparison of the other occurrences of φύσις in the Pauline corpus[7] suggests rather the connexion of φύσει with the preceding words and the interpretation of ἔθνη τὰ μὴ νόμον ἔχοντα φύσει as meaning 'Gentiles which do not possess the law by nature,

[1] col. 68.
[2] Contra Jul. 4.3.25; De Spir. et litt. 26.43ff.
[3] p. 36. But see also J. B. Souček, op. cit. supra.
[4] It is wrong to read a special significance into the use of μή here, as Sanday and Headlam for example do; for in the NT it is the use of οὐ rather than the use of μή, to negate a participle, which requires special explanation. See BDF, §§ 426 and 430.
[5] In fact, this connexion has tended to be taken for granted to the exclusion of any reference to the other possibility. This is so even in the case of those who have understood ἔθνη to refer to Gentile Christians (see, e.g., Augustine, Contra Jul. 4.3.25, where φύσει is understood as referring to nature renewed by grace).
[6] See on 1.26.
[7] They are 1.26; 2.27; 11.21, 24 (three times); 1 Cor 11.14; Gal 2.15; 4.8; Eph 2.3. The word occurs elsewhere in the NT only in Jas 3.7 and 2 Pet 1.4. See the notes on 1.26; 11.21 and 24. The one Pauline occurrence which might seem to point in the opposite direction is 1 Cor 11.14.

i.e. by virtue of their birth' (cf. especially ἡ ἐκ φύσεως ἀκροβυστία in v. 27 of this chapter, ἡμεῖς φύσει Ἰουδαῖοι καὶ οὐκ ἐξ ἐθνῶν ἁμαρτωλοί in Gal 2.15, and also ἤμεθα τέκνα φύσει ὀργῆς ὡς καὶ οἱ λοιποί in Eph 2.3).[1] Moreover, if we are right in understanding ἔθνη to refer to the Gentile Christians, there is a further point in favour of taking φύσει with what precedes—it would not be strictly accurate to describe the Gentile Christians as μὴ νόμον ἔχοντα, since as Christians they would of course have some knowledge of the law, but to describe them as μὴ νόμον ἔχοντα φύσει would be thoroughly appropriate, since, while they possessed the law as Christians, they did not possess it by virtue of their birth (as did the Jews). While the question whether Paul meant φύσει to be taken with what precedes it or with what follows cannot be decided with complete certainty,[2] we regard the former alternative as much more probable. And, if φύσει is taken with what precedes, then it simply makes explicit the sense which τὰ μὴ νόμον ἔχοντα would have to have anyway (if by ἔθνη the Gentile Christians are meant), even if φύσει were connected with what follows.

νόμον μὴ ἔχοντες adds no new thought, but simply picks up τὰ μὴ νόμον ἔχοντα in the first half of the verse.

ἑαυτοῖς εἰσιν νόμος. ἑαυτῷ εἶναι νόμος is a stereotyped expression used by Greek writers with reference to the man of superior virtue who does not need the guidance or sanctions of external law.[3] As used here, it must clearly be interpreted in close relation to what is said in v. 15a. Those who understand ἔθνη . . . τὰ τοῦ νόμου ποιῶσιν according to the first or second interpretation listed above take these words as a statement of these particular Gentiles' knowledge of, and reverence for, that moral law which is innate in their human nature. But, on the assumption that the Gentiles referred to are Christians, the

---

[1] Cf. Bengel, p. 502. Barth's shorter commentary seems to afford evidence of a wavering between the two possibilities (on p. 41 of the German original we read: '. . . so dass sie nun . . . in ihrer menschlichen Natur, ohne das Gesetz zu haben, tun, was das Gesetz fordert . . .', but on p. 42: '. . . obwohl sie das Gesetz nicht haben, obwohl sie von Natur Heiden sind'). But see Souček, in *Antwort*, pp. 99ff.

[2] There are several reasons for this: (i) a reasonably satisfactory sense can be ascribed to the verse, whichever way we connect φύσει; (ii) the order of the words is not decisive (in this connexion we may note that, where Paul uses a participle with the definite article as here, he quite often places a word or words depending on the participle after it instead of before it—see, e.g., vv. 9, 10, 21, 22; 14.1, 18); and (iii) Paul's use of φύσις elsewhere is not absolutely decisive.

[3] Cf., e.g., Aristotle, *E.N.* 1128a 31–32 (in the course of his discussion of 'the mean' in the matter of humour, Aristotle speaks of the behaviour of the refined and well-bred man, and concludes: ὁ δὴ χαρίεις καὶ ἐλευθέριος οὕτως ἕξει, οἷον νόμος ὢν ἑαυτῷ).

158   COMMENTARY ON ROMANS

sense of these words will rather be that, although they have
not been brought up by virtue of their birth in the possession
of God's law (like Jews), they now know it and actually have
in their hearts the earnest desire to obey it (see further on
v. 15).

οἵτινες. See on 1.25: compare also 1.32; 6.2; 9.4; 11.4; 16.4,
6, 7, 12.

ἐνδείκνυνται: 'show', 'exhibit', 'give proof of'. ἐνδεικνύναι
(in the NT only in the middle) occurs also in 9.17, 22; 2 Cor
8.24; Eph 2.7; 1 Tim 1.16; 2 Tim 4.14; Tit 2.10; 3.2; Heb 6.10,
11, and the noun ἔνδειξις occurs in 3.25, 26; 2 Cor 8.24; Phil
1.28. The present tense should be understood to refer to the
present time, and not—in spite of v. 16—as a futuristic
present.[1]

τὸ ἔργον τοῦ νόμου: 'the work which the law requires'
(surely not 'the effect of the law', as Barrett, who sees this
'effect' or 'stamp' of the law as identical with their conscience,
suggests[2]). An exact equivalent of this is not found in Rabbinic literature,[3] but a closely similar expression occurs in 2
Bar. 57.2 (in the plural). Elsewhere Paul uses the plural
ἔργα νόμου (3.20, 28; Gal 2.16; 3.2, 5, 10) in a concrete sense
—meaning the works as actually performed;[4] but here 'the
work which the law requires' means not the required work as
accomplished, but the required work in the sense of the
prescription contained in the law. Michel finds the use of the
singular here surprising;[5] but compare τὸ δικαίωμα τοῦ νόμου
in 8.4. In both cases the singular may be explained as intended
to bring out the essential unity of the law's requirements, the
fact that the plurality of commandments is no confused and
confusing conglomeration but a recognizable and intelligible
whole. We might perhaps compare Jn 6.29, in which the
τὰ ἔργα τοῦ θεοῦ of the preceding question is replaced by
τὸ ἔργον τοῦ θεοῦ.

γραπτὸν ἐν ταῖς καρδίαις αὐτῶν. That we have here a deliberate reminiscence of Jer 31[LXX: 38].33 is emphatically denied
by many commentators, on the ground that the Jeremiah
passage refers to an eschatological work of God to be wrought
on Israel, while the present passage is (allegedly) concerned
with a non-eschatological fact of Gentile life.[6] The expression

[1] *Pace*, e.g., C. Maurer, in *TWNT* 7, p. 915.
[2] p. 52f.
[3] Cf. SB 3, pp. 160–62.
[4] For which the Rabbis used *miṣwōt* (see SB 3, p. 161).
[5] p. 83.
[6] So, e.g., Michel, pp. 80 and 83.

'written on the heart' is accordingly explained as a specially emphatic way of indicating the inescapability of the divine requirement. But, as soon as it is recognized that the Gentiles whom Paul has in mind are Gentile Christians, the objection to seeing here an intentional reference to Jer 31.33 disappears; for it is abundantly clear that Paul did think that God's eschatological promises were already beginning to be fulfilled through the gospel in the lives of believers, both Jews and Gentiles. And the verbal similarity between τὸ ἔργον τοῦ νόμου γραπτὸν ἐν ταῖς καρδίαις αὐτῶν and the LXX form of Jer 31.33 (δώσω νόμους μου εἰς τὴν διάνοιαν αὐτῶν καὶ ἐπὶ καρδίας αὐτῶν γράψω αὐτούς), which is part of a passage (Jer 31.31–34) to which Paul refers elsewhere (see 1 Cor 11.25; 2 Cor 3.2, 3, 6, 14; 6.16), is so close that it is difficult to avoid the conclusion that Paul has the Jeremiah verse in mind. We take it then that Paul is deliberately echoing Jer 31 [LXX: 38] .33, and that his thought is that in these Gentiles who are believers in Christ God's promise that He would establish His law by creating in His people a sincere and earnest desire to obey it is being fulfilled.

συμμαρτυρούσης αὐτῶν τῆς συνειδήσεως καὶ μεταξὺ ἀλλήλων τῶν λογισμῶν κατηγορούντων ἢ καὶ ἀπολογουμένων, ἐν ᾗ ἡμέρᾳ* κρίνει ὁ θεὸς τὰ κρυπτὰ τῶν ἀνθρώπων κατὰ τὸ εὐαγγέλιόν μου διὰ Χριστοῦ Ἰησοῦ. In these one and a half verses we are faced by an unusually large number of difficult problems.

It will be best to begin with the use of the word συνείδησις. C. A. Pierce rendered an important service to scholarship by his book, *Conscience in the New Testament*,[1] in particular by his demonstration of the fallacy of the commonly-held assumption of the Stoic origin of Paul's use of συνείδησις and by his careful survey and clarification of the uses of συνείδησις and related terms in classical and non-Christian Hellenistic Greek. He has shown that συνείδησις, the substantivally-used neuter participle συνειδός and (though much less frequently) σύνεσις can all be used as substantival equivalents of the verbal expression αὐτῷ συνειδέναι (though συνείδησις and σύνεσις are also used—and it is important to remember this—as equivalents of the simple συνειδέναι[2]), and that the use of this group of expressions 'is found again and again, throughout the range of Greek writing as a whole—not in literature only—from the sixth century B.C. to the seventh century A.D.'[3] It is popular, not philosophical, in origin. The basic idea conveyed is that of

---

* [N²⁶: ἡμέρᾳ ὅτε. But an original ᾗ ἡμέρᾳ better explains the other two readings?]
[1] London, 1955.   [2] σύνεσις is, in fact, so used in the great majority of its occurrences.   [3] op. cit., p. 16f.

knowledge shared with oneself—so, in particular, these expressions denote a painful knowledge shared with oneself of having done wrong or (less frequently) a knowledge—not painful—of one's innocence, or, in other words, what is signified by such English expressions as 'a bad conscience', 'a good conscience', 'a clear conscience'. Subsequent discussion has directed attention to various points in Pierce's treatment of the subject which seem open to dispute. Thus it has been argued that he has not paid sufficient attention to Hellenistic Judaism; that his explanation of some of the Pauline passages in which συνείδησις occurs is not convincing; and that there is more in συνείδησις as used by Paul than can be accommodated in the pattern of classical and Hellenistic usage. To some extent the difference of opinion between Pierce and some of his critics (and also some who have written on the subject independently of him), reflected in this last contention, turns on the question whether certain Pauline instances of συνείδησις should be excluded from consideration under the heading of Paul's idea of conscience, on the ground that they are instances of its use as a substantival equivalent not of αὐτῷ συνειδέναι but of the simple συνειδέναι, or should be regarded as marking a special Pauline development of the idea of conscience. But, as far as the present instance is concerned, there is little doubt, in view of the use of συμμαρτυρεῖν and of the genitive absolute which follows (μεταξὺ ἀλλήλων, κ.τ.λ.), that συνείδησις is here used in its common Greek sense of knowledge shared with oneself whether of one's having done wrong or of one's innocence. There is—so far as we can see—no justification in Paul's sentence for identifying the Gentiles' συνείδησις with τὸ ἔργον τοῦ νόμου γραπτὸν ἐν ταῖς καρδίαις αὐτῶν or (on the basis of such an identification) seeing here the idea of the conscience as an internal law or law-giver. On συνείδησις see further on 9.1 and 13.5, and also, in addition to Pierce's book, C. Maurer, in *TWNT* 7, pp. 897–918 (bibliography on p. 897f), and Margaret E. Thrall, 'The Pauline Use of Συνείδησις', in *NTS* 14 (1967–68), pp. 118–25.

We must next note the questions posed by συμμαρτυρούσης, though we shall not attempt to answer them independently of the consideration of several further problems which are presented by the rest of vv. 15b–16. The verb συμμαρτυρεῖν can mean either (i) 'bear witness along with' (in this case, it is implied that there is at least one other witness besides the subject of the verb, and an accompanying dative, if there is one, will indicate this other witness), or (ii) simply 'bear witness', 'testify', 'assure' (in this case, the συν- merely strengthens the idea conveyed by the simple verb, and the accompanying dative, if there is one, indicates the recipient of the testimony).[1] So the question arises: Is συμμαρτυρεῖν used here in sense (i) or in sense (ii)? And, if we decide that it is used in sense (i), we are faced with another question, namely, that of the identity of the other witness or witnesses. Other questions posed by συμμαρτυρούσης are: When is this bearing witness supposed to take place? and What are we to understand its content to be?

At this point we have to ask about the relation of καὶ μεταξὺ ἀλλήλων τῶν λογισμῶν κατηγορούντων ἢ καὶ ἀπολογουμένων to συμμαρτυρούσης αὐτῶν τῆς συνειδήσεως, and about the relation of v. 16 to what immediately precedes. With regard to the former question, the suggestion that the witness of conscience belongs to the present and the debate of the λογισμοί to the time of the last judgment is very much less likely than the view that these two genitive absolute formulations must be taken closely together, the second being understood as clarifying the first. On this view there can be no difference of time between them. To the latter question radically different answers have been given. Those who assume that the witness of the Gentiles' conscience is mentioned as being evidence that, in spite of their not having the law in the way the Jews have it, they nevertheless in a real sense know it, naturally find the connexion of v. 16 with v. 15 difficult, since (on the assumption that both parts of v. 15b belong closely together) it implies that the witness of the conscience is to take place at the time of the final judgment, whereas, on their understanding of the matter, it must needs be a phenomenon of the present. Various suggestions have been made with a view to removing the difficulty: e.g. that v. 16 should be connected with v. 13 (or with v. 12), and vv. 14–15 (or 13–15) explained as a parenthesis;[2] that v. 16 should be emended by the addition of καὶ δικαιωθήσονται before ἐν ᾗ ἡμέρᾳ;[3] that v. 16 should be omitted as a gloss reminiscent of 1 Cor 4.5;[4] that vv. 14–15 should be omitted as a gloss;[5] that ἐν ᾗ ἡμέρᾳ should be omitted;[6] that the day on which God judges should be understood as meaning not the final judgment day but any day;[7] that some such supplement as 'this will be made manifest'

[1] Cf. Bauer, s.v., and see also on 8.16 and 9.1.
[2] e.g. Sanday and Headlam, p. 62.
[3] e.g. Pohlenz.
[4] e.g. Bultmann, 'Glossen', col. 200f.
[5] e.g. J. Weiss, according to Bultmann, ibid.
[6] e.g. BDF, § 382 (3).
[7] e.g. J. C. von Hofmann, according to Bultmann, ibid.

should be supplied before ἐν ᾗ ἡμέρᾳ.[1] But the difficulty disappears, if we understand the witness of conscience referred to here—it is not implied that this is the only witness borne by it—to be the witness it will bear at the time of God's final judgment. We may then take v. 16 closely with v. 15b.

To return now to συμμαρτυρούσης, it may be suggested that this συμμαρτυρεῖν is to be thought of as taking place at the time of the last judgment and consisting in the attestation of the fact that they now in the present time show the work of the law written on their hearts. The words καὶ μεταξὺ ἀλλήλων τῶν λογισμῶν κατηγορούντων ἢ καὶ ἀπολογουμένων may be understood as explaining how this συμμαρτυρεῖν is accomplished. It is by means of this internal debate (ἀλλήλων must surely refer to the λογισμοί, not to the ἔθνη), in which, as a matter of fact, their thoughts will do more accusing than excusing (it was presumably because Paul recognized this that he put κατηγορούντων first and also inserted καὶ before ἀπολογουμένων), since these Gentile Christians will know that their lives fell very far short of the perfect fulfilment of the law's requirement (cf. 7.14ff)—at the same time, in the midst of their painful awareness of their sinfulness, their thoughts will also be able to remind them that they truly believed and had begun to have their lives turned in the direction of obedience. Through this mêlée of accusing and defending thoughts the reality of their commitment will be attested. With regard to the question whether συμμαρτυρεῖν is here used in sense (i) or sense (ii), it may be said that, if it is understood in sense (i), then the only feasible 'other witness' would be the Gentiles in question (αὐτοῖς to be supplied from αὐτῶν), not the law, as Barrett maintains[2] (it would surely anyway have to be the work of the law, not the law); but that, on the whole, it seems more likely that συμμαρτυρεῖν is used here in sense (ii), and means simply 'testify'. This testimony is conceivably thought of as being addressed to God the Judge; but it seems rather more probable that the thought is of each man's being assured by his own conscience.

If in v. 16 κρινει is accentuated κρίνει, as in Nestle, then it is to be explained as a present tense used to express the future (see BDF, § 323). But it may be that it should be accentuated κρινεῖ. In any case the reference to the final judgment is quite clear.

That the secrets of men's hearts are all known to God is axiomatic in Scripture (e.g. 1 Sam 16.7; 1 Chron 28.9; Ps 139.1f,

[1] e.g. Althaus, p. 20.
[2] p. 53.

23; Jer 17.10; Mt 6.4,6, 18; Heb 4.12f), and the conviction that
He will take them into account in His judgment can hardly be
separated from it. The insight expressed in v. 16 has of course
to be held together with the truth declared in v. 6. The
recognition that God will take into account the innermost
secrets of men's hearts, and that His judgment will therefore
be far different from the superficial judgment which human
judgment necessarily is, in no way calls in question the
seriousness of the biblical stress on the importance of concrete
deeds (cf. note on v. 6).[1] With τὰ κρυπτὰ τῶν ἀνθρώπων here
should be compared the striking contrasts in vv. 28–29
between the ἐν τῷ φανερῷ Jew and the ἐν τῷ κρυπτῷ Jew, and
between the ἐν τῷ φανερῷ circumcision and the circumcision of
the heart.

It is not immediately clear exactly what it is that is κατὰ
τὸ εὐαγγέλιόν μου (the phrase also occurs in 16.25 and 2 Tim 2.8:
cf. 2 Cor 4.3; 1 Th 1.5; 2 Th 2.14). Is it that God will judge
the world? Or that He will judge the world διὰ Χριστοῦ Ἰησοῦ?
Or that Gentiles will also (as is implied in view of the context)
be included in this judgment through Christ? Or that God will
judge τὰ κρυπτὰ τῶν ἀνθρώπων? Barrett rejects the first three of
these suggestions on the ground that none of these represents a
position peculiar to Paul, and prefers the last[2] (though it
seems doubtful whether the idea that God will judge the
secrets of men's hearts can plausibly be regarded as specially
Pauline). But the order of the words surely favours connecting
κατὰ τὸ εὐαγγέλιόν μου with διὰ Χριστοῦ Ἰησοῦ; and it is probable that by 'my gospel' Paul did not mean a peculiarly
Pauline form of the gospel but simply the gospel which he
preached together with other Christian preachers.[3]

17. Εἰ δέ. The reading ἴδε (ℵ 33 al) is no doubt secondary,
an attempt to remove the anacoluthon (reading Εἰ δέ, we have
a protasis to which there is no answering apodosis, the construction being broken off at the end of v. 20). The δέ sets
vv. 17ff in an adversative relation to vv. 12–16.

σύ. See on the use of the second person singular in v. 1.

Ἰουδαῖος ἐπονομάζῃ. Here for the first time in this chapter
there is an explicit reference to the fact that the person who
is being addressed is a Jew. Though ἐπονομάζεσθαι could of

---

[1] Barrett's 'not . . . but . . .' (p. 54: 'God's judgement does not rest
upon the observable behaviour . . . but upon the secret things of the
heart . . .') could be seriously misleading.

[2] p. 54.

[3] The suggestion, mentioned by Eusebius, H.E. 3.4.7, that by 'my
gospel' Paul meant the Gospel according to St Luke, though highly
fanciful, is not without interest.

course be used in the sense 'be surnamed' (it was, as a matter of fact, not uncommon for Diaspora Jews to use Ἰουδαῖος as a surname), it is here no doubt used in a general sense ('be named', so 'be known to be', 'claim to be'). It is possible that the thought of a contrast between having the name of Jew and being an ἐν τῷ κρυπτῷ Jew (v. 29) is present; but too much should not be made of this, since, while there is an element of irony in each of the following items by which the Jew is described in vv. 17–20, 'they are not merely ironical, but also a sincere acknowledgement of the position and the mission which the Jews have in fact been given in the Gentile metropolis and in the whole Gentile world'.[1] Throughout vv. 17–20 Paul appears to be deliberately taking up claims which were actually being made by his fellow Jews, echoing the very language in which they were being expressed (see SB 3, pp. 96–105).

ἐπαναπαύῃ νόμῳ. ἐπαναπαύεσθαι (middle) occurs in the NT only here and in Lk 10.6. The meaning it has here is 'rest upon', so 'rely on', 'rest one's hopes on'. It is used a number of times in the LXX (e.g. 2 Kgs 5.18; 7.2, 17; Ezek 29.7; Mic 3.11; 1 Macc 8.11[RV:12]). The Jew is absolutely right to be seriously concerned with God's law, to follow after it (cf. 9.31) with the utmost diligence, and to rely on it as God's true and righteous word. But the trouble is that he follows after it ἐξ ἔργων instead of ἐκ πίστεως (cf. 9.32), and relies on it in the sense of thinking to fulfil it in such a way as to put God in his debt or of imagining complacently that the mere fact of possessing it gives him security against God's judgment.

καυχᾶσαι ἐν θεῷ. Again, to boast or glory in God is a thoroughly good thing, if it is the sort of boasting in Him which truly gives Him the glory, a truly humble boasting in His goodness and mercy; but it is an altogether different matter, if it is the sort which is a self-centred boasting in Him as a basis for one's own self-importance. This is the first occurrence in Romans of a word of the word-group καυχᾶσθαι, καύχημα, καύχησις, which has considerable importance in Paul's epistles (in Romans see also v. 23; 3.27; 4.2; 5.2, 3, 11; 15.17; and the two occurrences of the compound κατακαυχᾶσθαι in 11.18). These words are used in the LXX pejoratively to denote boastful self-glorification on the level of human relations (its connotation in classical Greek) and also the pride and self-confidence in relation to God which are the mark·of the nābāl or 'fool'; they are also used favourably of boasting

---

[1] Barth, *Shorter*, p. 37.

in God and in His saving deeds, a boasting which is not self-centred but means a looking away from one's self to God. This latter kind of boasting, glorying, exultation, had its place in worship and would be consummated in the coming salvation-time. The use of this word-group in the NT is almost exclusively Pauline.[1] For Paul there is a right boasting in God (5.11: it is here also through Christ); in Christ (Phil 3.3); in the hope of the glory of God (5.2); in the cross of Christ (Gal 6.14); in tribulations (5.3)—not as something meritorious on the part of those who suffer them but as part of the discipline by which God teaches them to wait patiently for His deliverance; in weaknesses (2 Cor 12.5, 9: cf. 11.30)—because it is in the context of His servants' weakness that Christ's power is manifested; and in the faith of one's fellow Christians and the success of the apostolic mission seen as resulting from the work of Christ or of God (15.17f; 2 Cor 7.4, 14; 8.24; 9.2f). But all boasting which is essentially a boasting in man, in flesh, is illegitimate (1 Cor 1.29; 3.21; 4.7; 2 Cor 5.12b). Specially to be noted is the use of καύχησις in 3.27 of the act of asserting a claim on God on the ground of one's works, of claiming to have put God in one's debt, and of καύχημα in 4.2 to denote such a claim upon God. See further R. Bultmann, in *TWNT* 3, pp. 646–54.[2]

18 refers to a knowledge and discernment on the part of the Jew, which Paul certainly regarded as real and important though paradoxically compounded with a disastrous failure of comprehension (cf. notes on 10.2 and 19).

γινώσκεις τὸ θέλημα: sc. *τοῦ θεοῦ* (cf. the Rabbinic use of *rāṣ̌ôn* absolutely to denote the will of God[3]).

δοκιμάζεις. See on 1.28. The precise meaning of the word here will depend on the meaning given to the following expression.

τὰ διαφέροντα. The verb διαφέρειν (when used intransitively) can mean 'differ', and so 'stand out', 'excel', 'matter', 'be essential'. The whole expression δοκιμάζειν τὰ διαφέροντα (it occurs also in Phil 1.10) could therefore mean 'distinguish the things which differ', so perhaps 'know right from wrong' (as the NEB renders it),[4] or 'distinguish (or 'approve') the

---

[1] καυχᾶσθαι 35 times in the Pauline epistles, twice in James; καύχημα 10 times in Paul, once in Hebrews; καύχησις 10 times in Paul, once in James.

[2] Also E. A. Judge, 'Paul's boasting in relation to contemporary professional practice', in *ABR* 16 (1968), pp. 37–50.

[3] See G. Schrenk, in *TWNT* 3, p. 54, line 35, and p. 58, n. 19.

[4] Cf. Euthymius, quoted by Sanday and Headlam, p. 65: διακρίνεις τὰ διαφέροντα ἀλλήλων · οἷον καλὸν καὶ κακόν, ἀρετὴν καὶ κακίαν.

things which are excellent' (and ought therefore to be chosen);[1] but it is more probable that the meaning is 'distinguish the things which matter (or 'are essential')', the antithesis of διαφέροντα being ἀδιάφορα. It is possible that Mt 23.23 provides the right clue to Paul's meaning. The Jew, with his knowledge of such passages in the law as Deut 6.4f and Lev 19.18, is in a position to discern τὰ βαρύτερα τοῦ νόμου, and in fact does discern them, though often failing signally to act accordingly.

κατηχούμενος ἐκ τοῦ νόμου can be connected with δοκιμάζεις τὰ διαφέροντα alone (so NEB), but is more naturally connected with both the preceding statements. It is through the instruction which he has received from the law that the Jew knows the will of God and discerns the things which are essential. κατηχεῖν (see H. W. Beyer, in TWNT 3, pp. 638-40) can have either the more general sense of 'inform' (as in Acts 21.21, 24) or the more specific sense of 'instruct', as here (cf. Acts 18.25; 1 Cor 14.19; Gal 6.6). Paul here uses of the Jew's instruction by the law a term which elsewhere he uses of instruction in the gospel.

19f. πεποιθώς τε σεαυτὸν ... εἶναι. On the construction see Bauer, s.v. πείθω, 2.b. This reference to the Jew's confident conviction is certainly not to be understood as merely ironical; for not only was it his divine vocation to be all the things which Paul lists in these two verses, but it is also true that to some extent he was in fact all these things.[2] The real indebtedness of the Gentile to the Jew is not to be denied or glossed over. It is only when what the Jew is and does is seen *coram Deo* that its complete inadequacy comes to light.

ὁδηγὸν ... τυφλῶν. Compare, e.g., Isa 42.7; 1 Enoch 105.1; Or. Sib. 3.195 (οἱ πάντεσσι βροτοῖσι βίου καθοδηγοὶ ἔσονται); but also Isa 42.19f; Mt 7.3–5; 15.14; 23.16, 24.

φῶς τῶν ἐν σκότει. Compare, e.g., Isa 42.6 (εἰς φῶς ἐθνῶν), 7 (καθημένους ἐν σκότει); 49.6; Wisd 18.4; Test. Levi 18.9; 1QSb 4.27f.

παιδευτήν: 'an educator'.[3] Though in the NT παιδεία and παιδεύειν usually convey the idea of correction by chastise-

---

[1] Cf. Bengel's explanation of the expression in Phil 1.10: 'Non modo prae malis bona sed in bonis optima'.

[2] The suggestion that in this and the next verse Paul is quoting phrases from a Jewish writing intended for proselytes (Lietzmann, p. 43) is not unlikely but remains unproven.

[3] On the concept of παιδεία in ancient Greece and for information on the OT and Jewish background of the NT idea of παιδεία, see G. Bertram, in TWNT 5, pp. 596ff. Reference may also be made to W. Barclay *Educational Ideals in the Ancient World*, London, 1959.

ment,¹ and this idea is clearly present in παιδευτής in its only other occurrence in the NT (Heb 12.9), it is hardly likely that Paul had it in mind here. The thought is rather of the general influence of Jewish moral standards in the Gentile world and perhaps also, in particular, the practical moral guidance given by Jewish teachers of the law to those aspiring to become proselytes.

ἀφρόνων. In comparison with the Jews, many Gentiles could indeed be described as ἄφρονες, as far as moral standards were concerned.

διδάσκαλον. The word, when set side by side with παιδευτής, may perhaps be taken to indicate rather more theoretical instruction. Again, we may think both of the ordinary Jew in his contacts with Gentiles and also perhaps, in particular, of those actually engaged in instructing converts from paganism.

νηπίων. For the use of νήπιος with reference to those needing elementary instruction compare 1 Cor 3.1; Eph 4.14; Heb 5.13.

ἔχοντα τὴν μόρφωσιν τῆς γνώσεως καὶ τῆς ἀληθείας ἐν τῷ νόμῳ explains the confidence referred to in v. 19. It forms something of a climax, and after it the construction changes. Michel notes that both γνῶσις and ἀλήθεια are solemn words.² They denote the objects of men's longings and aspirations and are suggestive of the claims of philosophy and of the various religions, besides being important biblical words. The Jew's confidence that he can be the four things just mentioned rests on his conviction that in the law he possesses the embodiment of knowledge and truth, i.e. knowledge and truth in a form which can be grasped, expressed clearly and understandably.³ Paul shows later on how the Jews have disastrously misunderstood the law; but the claim that in possessing the law they possessed the embodiment of knowledge and truth is one which he nowhere contradicts.⁴

21 and 22 consist of four sentences which can be read either as statements or—more naturally—as accusatory rhetorical questions. They are all similar in structure, apart from the

---

¹ See especially Heb. 12.5–11.
² p. 88.
³ μόρφωσις can mean the act of forming or the result of such an act, that which is formed, the form, the outward form, manifestation. See J. Behm, in *TWNT* 4, p. 761f.
⁴ Cf. Barrett, p. 56: 'The Jew is persuaded that in the (book of the) law he has truth in visible form. Paul does not disagree with him; he himself says little less in vii.12, 14'. By contrast, the statement of Behm in *TWNT* 4, p. 762, lines 21–23 ('Dies Werturteil, das Paulus in offenbar ironischem Tone wiedergibt, deckt sich—trotz R 7.7ff; 2.13ff; 3.31; 9.4; 13.8—durchaus nicht mit seinem eigenen Urteil über die Bedeutung des Gesetzes') is surely to be rejected.

fact that only the first contains the negative particle οὐ, and so, if it is read as a question, anticipates an affirmative answer (though ironically), while the others, if read interrogatively, are open questions.

ὁ ... διδάσκων ἕτερον σεαυτὸν οὐ διδάσκεις; The phenomenon of the teacher who teaches others but not himself is mentioned in *Aboth R. Nathan* 29 (8ᵃ);[1] but what for the Rabbis is a possibility which, unfortunately, is sometimes actualized, is apparently regarded by Paul as characteristic of Jewish life.

ὁ κηρύσσων μὴ κλέπτειν κλέπτεις; ὁ λέγων μὴ μοιχεύειν μοιχεύεις; ὁ βδελυσσόμενος τὰ εἴδωλα ἱεροσυλεῖς; Numerous passages referring to individual teachers whose conduct was a contradiction of their teaching may be cited from Rabbinic writings in illustration of each of these questions;[2] but the fact that isolated instances of all these things were to be found among the Jews was, as far as Paul's argument was concerned, beside the point.[3] Even the extremely dark picture of the state of Jewish morals in the decades preceding the destruction of Jerusalem presented in the lamentation of Rabbi Johanan ben Zakkai (died *c.* A.D. 80) in *TSot.* 14.1ff, quoted in SB 3, p. 106,[4] scarcely implies, as Paul does, that all contemporary Jews are guilty of the evils which are described. It is anyway of course quite certain that there were many Jews in Paul's day who were not guilty of theft, adultery or temple-robbing (or sacrilege), in the ordinary sense of the words. Some commentators, therefore, feeling the need for an interpretation of κλέπτεις, μοιχεύεις, and ἱεροσυλεῖς, which makes them true of all Jews, have understood them to refer to what the Jews as a whole had done with regard to

---

[1] 'Thou hast many a man who teaches himself but does not teach others; many a man who teaches others but does not teach himself; many a man who teaches himself and others; and many a one who teaches neither himself nor others. . . . The man who teaches others but does not teach himself. How, for example? A man learns a piece of teaching twice or thrice, then teaches it to others, and then concerns himself with it no further, but forgets it; that is one who teaches others but does not teach himself' (SB 3, p. 107).

[2] e.g., in connexion with the first of these questions, *Deut R.* 2 (198ᵇ) (quoted in SB 3, p. 107): 'Rabbi Simlai (about A.D. 250) said: . . . There sits a learned one and publicly proclaims before the congregation: Thou shalt not lend on interest! and he himself lends on interest. He says: Thou shalt not steal! and he himself steals'. SB 3, pp. 109–11, provide a considerable amount of material illustrative of the fact that, in respect of the seventh commandment, the conduct even of respected Rabbis often belied the strictness of their teaching; and pp. 113–15 give instances of robbing by Jews both of heathen temples and of the temple in Jerusalem.

[3] Cf. Barrett, p. 56.

[4] Cf. also (from earlier times) Test. Levi 14.4–8; Ps. Sol. 8.8–13 (especially v. 13: οὐ παρέλιπον ἁμαρτίαν, ἣν οὐκ ἐποίησαν ὑπὲρ τὰ ἔθνη).

Jesus Christ and were doing with regard to His followers.[1]
Others have explained—and this seems more probable—that
Paul is thinking in terms of a radical understanding of the law
(cf. Mt 5.21-48). Where the full seriousness of the law's
requirements is understood, there it is recognized that all are
transgressors.[2]

It seems on the whole better to explain μοιχεύεις simply
along the lines suggested by Mt 5.27-32 than to see here also a
reference to adultery in the religious sense (Hos 1-3; Jer 3;
Ezek 16, etc.).[3]

With regard to ὁ βδελυσσόμενος[4] τὰ εἴδωλα, it is to be noted
that in Paul's time it could be confidently assumed that there
was no longer any idolatry in Israel.[5] This confidence is already
expressed at an earlier date in Jth 8.18. To the Jew who is
confident of his complete purity in respect of idolatry Paul
addresses the accusation ἱεροσυλεῖς. It is often argued that,
contrasted as it is with ὁ βδελυσσόμενος τὰ εἴδωλα, it must refer
to ἱεροσυλία committed against idol-temples.[6] If this argument
is accepted, we may understand Paul's point to be that the
Jew who is so confident in his purity from idolatry is as a
matter of fact not free from its taint. Paul would presumably
be referring to the sort of thing illustrated in SB 3, p. 113f—the
use by Jews of articles stolen (whether by themselves or others)
from idol-shrines and the casuistry of Rabbis who invented
various exceptions to the categorical prohibition of Deut 7.25f
—and probably also to still more subtle forms of complicity
in idolatry. But the view that what Paul is contrasting with
the Jew's abhorrence of idolatry out of loyalty to the one true
God is his actually committing ἱεροσυλία against the true God
does not seem impossible. If it is accepted, it is probably
better not to assume that Paul must have in mind the robbing
of the Jerusalem temple (the sort of thing referred to in, e.g.,
Test. Levi 14.5; Ps. Sol. 8.12(11); CD 6.15), but to understand
him to be using ἱεροσυλεῖν in the more general sense of 'commit

[1] e.g. Barth, *Shorter*, p. 37f (*KE*, p. 43). It is interesting that Pelagius,
p. 25, says on ὁ κηρύσσων, κ.τ.λ., 'Quidam dicunt: abscondendo ab
hominibus furaris Christum'.
[2] Cf. Barrett, p. 56.
[3] *Pace* Barrett, p. 57, with which may be compared Pelagius, p. 25:
'Non est una moechia: nam omne quod totum deo debet anima, si
alicui praeter deum reddideris, moecharis'.
[4] In the LXX βδελύσσεσθαι is frequently used to denote abhorrence of
idolatry and everything connected with it. It usually represents *ti'ēb* or
šiḳḳēṣ.
[5] Cf. SB 3, p. 111f.
[6] So, e.g., in SB 3, p. 113; G. Schrenk, in *TWNT* 3, p. 256; Kuss, p. 86.
It was already understood in this way by Chrysostom, col. 434.

sacrilege'. Again, we may take him to be thinking not only of behaviour which is obviously sacrilegious, but also of less obvious and more subtle forms of sacrilege.[1]

23. ὃς ἐν νόμῳ καυχᾶσαι, διὰ τῆς παραβάσεως τοῦ νόμου τὸν θεὸν ἀτιμάζεις is more naturally read as a statement than as a question, in view of the fact that the following verse is a confirmation of its truth (γάρ). The change of construction (the use of ὅς and the indicative after the series of four participles with the article) also suggests that this is not a further question. It sums up vv. 21 and 22.

With ἐν νόμῳ καυχᾶσαι compare ἐπαναπαύῃ νόμῳ in v. 17, and see on καυχᾶσαι in that verse. Just as there is a right, but also a wrong, boasting or exulting in God, so too with the law. Gratefully and humbly to exult in it as the gracious revelation of God's merciful will is right, but to boast in it in the sense of thinking to use it as a means to putting God in one's debt and of regarding one's knowledge of it as conferring on one the right to look down on one's fellow men is altogether wrong. That Paul is not using καυχᾶσθαι simply in a bad sense[2] here is clear from the fact that ἐν νόμῳ καυχᾶσαι is contrasted with διὰ τῆς παραβάσεως τοῦ νόμου τὸν θεὸν ἀτιμάζεις. The Jew ought to boast in the law, but the truth is that his actual boasting in the law is to a very large extent the wrong sort of boasting in the law.

διὰ τῆς παραβάσεως τοῦ νόμου τὸν θεὸν ἀτιμάζεις sums up the situation indicated by means of the examples κλέπτεις, μοιχεύεις, ἱεροσυλεῖς. The Jew's conduct, which gives the lie to his doctrine and profession, is transgression[3] of God's law, and as such it is a dishonouring of God.[4]

24. τὸ γὰρ ὄνομα τοῦ θεοῦ δι' ὑμᾶς βλασφημεῖται ἐν τοῖς ἔθνεσιν, καθὼς γέγραπται is an appeal to Scripture[5] in support (γάρ)

[1] See further G. Schrenk, in TWNT 3, pp. 254–6; also LSJ, s.vv. ἱεροσυλέω, etc.; and Bauer, s.vv. ἱεροσυλέω and ἱερόσυλος.

[2] Pace Bultmann, in TWNT 3, p. 649, line 10f.

[3] On παράβασις (used also in 4.15; 5.14) and παραβάτης (vv. 25 and 27) see J. Schneider, in TWNT 5, pp. 733–38. The idea contained in these words, as they are used in the NT, is that of the transgression of a known, concrete divine commandment.

[4] Paul's assumption that to transgress the law is to dishonour God agrees with the Rabbinic teaching, according to which to obey God's commandments is a sanctification of His name resulting in its glorification, and to disobey the commandments is a profaning of God's name resulting in its dishonouring. Cf. SB 1, pp. 411–18.

[5] The position of καθὼς γέγραπται after, rather than before, the quotation has been noted from early times (e.g., Pelagius, p. 25: 'Praeposterato ordine ante posuit testimonium quam diceret scriptum: ita enim dicentis sermo delapsus est, ut quod ex propria intentione

of what has just been said, the quotation being an adaptation of the LXX version of the last part of Isa 52.5 (δι' ὑμᾶς διὰ παντὸς τὸ ὄνομά μου βλασφημεῖται ἐν τοῖς ἔθνεσιν), which itself differs from the MT by the omission of *kolhayyôm* and the addition of δι' ὑμᾶς and ἐν τοῖς ἔθνεσιν. Isa 52.5 referred originally to the reviling of God's name by the oppressors of Israel on account of Israel's misfortunes. The LXX's variations from the MT made the way easier for Paul's application of the words to the reviling of God's name by the Gentiles on account of the Jews' disobedience to His law.[1] This verse of Isaiah is also echoed in 2 Pet 2.2. Compare Ezek 36.20ff for Paul's thought.[2] Israel, whose special vocation it was to sanctify God's name by its obedience and so promote the glory of God's name, is actually the cause of its being dishonoured.

25. περιτομὴ μὲν γὰρ ὠφελεῖ ἐὰν νόμον πράσσῃς. The γάρ indicates the connexion between vv. 25–29 and what precedes. One of the chief grounds of Jewish confidence has so far not been mentioned—circumcision. So, in order to complete this part of his argument and meet an obvious objection from the Jewish side, and in clarification and confirmation of what he has just been saying, Paul now turns to the subject of circumcision. The μέν, which looks forward to the following δέ, introduces the free admission that, in the case of the Jew who does what the law requires,[3] circumcision[4] is profitable.[5] Of this there can be no doubt; for it is an institution appointed by God, a token ('ôṯ, σημεῖον) of the covenant made by God with Israel and a pledge of the covenant blessings (cf. Gen 17; Rom 4.11).

dicebat, eodem sensu scriptum in propheta repperiret'; cf. Sanday and Headlam, p. 67). See, on Paul's use of Scripture, the concluding essay in volume 2.

[1] Though in the LXX δι' ὑμᾶς no doubt means 'because of your misfortunes'.

[2] Unlike Isa 52.5, Ezek 36.20ff is used a number of times in Rabbinic writings to support the charge which Paul here expresses by means of the Isaiah verse. (See SB 3, p. 118.)

[3] νόμον πράσσειν (cf. the Hebrew expression 'āśāh 'eṯ-hattôrāh used in *Siphre* Deut 32.30) occurs nowhere else in the NT; but compare οἱ ποιηταὶ νόμου in v. 13 and τὸν νόμον ποιεῖν in Gal 5.3. On πράσσειν see on 7.15. Here what is meant would seem (in view of vv. 26 and 27) to be not a perfect fulfilment of the radical demands of the law, but a real faith in God and the serious engagement with obedience which springs therefrom (cf. Murray 1, p. 85f).

[4] περιτομή can have three different meanings: (i) the act of circumcising; (ii) the state of having been circumcised; (iii) the community of the circumcised, i.e. the Jews. It is used here in sense (ii).

[5] ὠφελεῖν occurs in Romans only here. Cf. 1 Cor 13.3; 14.6; Gal 5.2; Heb 4.2; 13.9.

ἐὰν δὲ παραβάτης νόμου ᾖς, ἡ περιτομή σου ἀκροβυστία γέγονεν. With these words Paul challenges the Jew's complacent reliance upon circumcision as 'a certain passport to salvation'.[1] His words are generally taken to mean that, if a Jew is a transgressor of the law, his circumcision is annulled;[2] and, taken by itself, this sentence certainly can bear this meaning. But the sentence does not stand by itself. In 3.3 Paul is going to reject with emphasis the suggestion that the ἀπιστία of the Jews τὴν πίστιν τοῦ θεοῦ καταργήσει, and the burden of chapter 11 is going to be that God has not cast off His people. Moreover, it is noticeable—though not often noticed—that Paul does not say here (as, in view of the first part of the verse, we might expect him to do), ἡ περιτομή σου οὐδὲν ὠφελεῖ. That would indeed have been strange in view of 3.1 (... ἢ τίς ἡ ὠφέλεια τῆς περιτομῆς; πολὺ κατὰ πάντα τρόπον). It seems therefore better to understand v. 25b to mean, not that the Jew's circumcision has been annulled in God's sight,[3] but that he has become uncircumcised in heart (i.e. one whose heart is far from God and whose life is a contradiction of his membership of the Covenant people),[4] and now, though still a member of God's special people to whom God is still faithful, stands in his human existence in a negative, and no longer in a positive, relation to God's purpose in history, and is outside that Israel within Israel, to which Paul refers in 9.6ff. (See further on vv. 28 and 29 below.)

26. ἐὰν οὖν ἡ ἀκροβυστία τὰ δικαιώματα τοῦ νόμου φυλάσσῃ, οὐχ ἡ ἀκροβυστία αὐτοῦ εἰς περιτομὴν λογισθήσεται; ἀκροβυστία can denote: (i) the foreskin; (ii) the state of being uncircumcised; (iii) the community of the uncircumcised, i.e.

---

[1] The phrase is Barrett's (p. 58). The relevant Rabbinic material includes such statements as: 'Circumcised men do not descend into Gehenna' (*Exod R.* 19 (81ᶜ); 'Rabbi Levi (*c.* A.D. 300) said: At the last Abraham will sit at the entrance to Gehenna and will not let any circumcised man of Israel go down there' (*Gen R.* 48 (30ᵃ); 'Circumcision will deliver Israel from Gehenna' (Tanchuma B, ḥayyê Sarah 60ᵇ.8). Only in certain extreme cases is the saving power of circumcision believed to be ineffective. See SB 1, p. 119 (the last three quotations under 3); and 4, pp. 37ff, 1049ff, 1063ff.

[2] So, e.g., SB 3, p. 119; Michel, p. 90f; Barrett, p. 58; Kuss, p. 89.

[3] The contention of SB 3, p. 119, accepted by Michel (p. 90), that 'the corresponding λογισθήσεται' in v. 26 shows that γέγονεν must here be used in the sense of the Rabbinic na'ᵃśāh kᵉ and mean 'is reckoned as', 'counts as' (sc. in God's judgment), seems at first sight impressive; but it rests on an unwarranted assumption, namely, that vv. 25b and 26 must be strictly parallel in all respects.

[4] For the recognition already in the OT that the circumcised can be uncircumcised of heart see Jer 9.25f: cf. 4.4; Deut 10.16; 30.6; and also Jer 6.10 (uncircumcised ear).

the Gentile world, or the individual Gentile (the word ἀκρόβυστος is not used in the LXX or in the NT: its earliest attestation is in Ignatius and Aquila). In the first part of the verse it is used in sense (iii)—that here it denotes the individual is clear from the context and is probably confirmed by the use of αὐτοῦ in referring back—and in the second part of the verse in sense (ii). φυλάσσειν was already used in classical Greek of observing a law. For its use in connexion with the OT law compare Mt 19.20 = Mk 10.20 = Lk 18.21; Acts 7.53; 21.24; Gal 6.13. For τὰ δικαιώματα τοῦ νόμου ('the righteous requirements of the law') compare 8.4, where the singular is used. On the assumption that Paul is not putting forward merely for the sake of argument an hypothesis which he does not expect to be fulfilled,[1] we must understand τὰ δικαιώματα τοῦ νόμου φυλάσσῃ to mean, not a perfect fulfilment of the law's demands (for, according to Paul, only one man, the circumcised Jesus, ever accomplished this[2]), but a grateful and humble faith in God and the life turned in the direction of obedience which is its fruit. We take it he has in mind the Gentile Christians. The οὐχ indicates that an affirmative answer is presupposed. So the question is tantamount to a positive statement—one which general Rabbinic opinion would certainly have rejected categorically.[3] The meaning of εἰς περιτομὴν λογισθήσεται is that his uncircumcision will be reckoned[4] by God as circumcision—in other words, in God's sight he will count as a member of the people of Israel.

[1] Cf. what was said above on pp. 151–53.

[2] Cf. 3.20, 23; and see on 10.5.

[3] Cf. SB 3, pp. 119–21, where a wealth of Rabbinic material is quoted in support of their statement (on p. 120), 'Der Nichtisraelit, der die Tora beobachtete, trat nach allgemeiner Überzeugung durchaus nicht als gleichberechtigt dem Israeliten an die Seite; er blieb vielmehr, eben weil er ein Unbeschnittener war, für Gott ein Ferner u. Fremder, ja er zog sich sogar Strafe zu, weil er sich mit Dingen befasste, die ihm nicht befohlen waren'. The view expressed by Rabbi Meïr (c. A.D. 150), quoted in SB 3, p. 79 ('Whence do we know that a Gentile too, who, occupies himself with the Torah, is as the High Priest? The scripture teaches: "The man, who does them, shall live through them", Lev 18.5. It does not say "priest" or "Levite" or "Israelite", but "man". That shows that a Gentile too, who occupies himself with the Torah, is as the High Priest' (BK 38ᵃ; also in A. Zar. 3ᵃ, and in Sanh. 59ᵃ)) was not generally accepted.

[4] On λογίζεσθαι see on 2.3. Its use in the present verse is similar to that in 4.3, in which Gen 15.6 is quoted. The idea of 'reckoning something to someone as' is expressed by the Rabbis in a number of different ways (see SB 3, pp. 121–3). The reference of the future tense is perhaps better not limited to the final judgment, since 11.17ff clearly presupposes that God has already reckoned the Gentile believers true members of His special people.

Compare what is said in 11.17ff about the Gentile Christians' having been grafted into Israel.

27. κρινεῖ. Compare Mt 12.41f=Lk 11.31f. The meaning is not that the Gentile will assume the role of judge, but rather that he will be a witness for the prosecution in the sense that his obedience will be evidence of what the Jew ought to have been and could have been.[1]

ἡ ἐκ φύσεως ἀκροβυστία. ἀκροβυστία is again used in a concrete sense (sense (iii) in the note on v. 26). The whole phrase must surely mean 'the man who is by virtue of his birth an uncircumcised Gentile' (see on v. 14—φύσει).[2]

τὸν νόμον τελοῦσα. For τελεῖν used of fulfilling the law compare Jas 2.8: Paul nowhere else uses it in this connexion (the nearest approach to a parallel to this use of the verb in the Pauline epistles would seem to be Gal 5.16). τὸν νόμον τελεῖν must clearly have the same general sense as τὰ δικαιώματα τοῦ νόμου φυλάσσειν in v. 26, and it is probable that τελεῖν is here used simply as a synonym of φυλάσσειν.

διά is best explained as simply 'διά of attendant circumstances'.[3] The situation in which the Jew is a transgressor of the law is that of a man who possesses 'Scripture and circumcision'.

γράμματος καὶ περιτομῆς. The explanation of this as an instance of hendiadys ('literal circumcision')[4] can claim to have some support in the language of v. 29, and gives a satisfactory sense. But it seems rather more probable that the phrase is intended to indicate the Jew's possession of two different things, Scripture (the law would probably be specially in mind) and circumcision, the word γράμμα perhaps being used not just to emphasize the Scripture's concreteness as something written, visible, tangible, but because of Paul's awareness of the externality of the Jew's possession of Scripture (cf. the use of γράμμα in v. 29).

---

[1] Cf. Leenhardt, p. 88. This is more probable than the explanation given by Kuss, p. 90: 'vor Gottes Gericht besser gestellt ist als'.

[2] Hardly 'der leiblich Unbeschnittene' (Michel, p. 85, in his translation of the section) or 'der Heide in seiner natürlichen Unbeschnittenheit' (Michel, p. 92). The NEB rendering 'He may be uncircumcised in his natural state, . . .', can scarcely be intended in the sense it naturally bears, for in his natural state the Jew also is uncircumcised. The whole phrase is absent from G; but it is much more likely that it was omitted either accidentally or because it seemed difficult than that Pallis was right in regarding it as a secondary amplification.

[3] *Pace* G. Schrenk, in *TWNT* I, p. 765, who maintains that it has here also its instrumental force. The idea which Schrenk sees expressed here is surely foreign to this particular context.

[4] Cf. Calvin, p. 56. On hendiadys see BDF, § 442 (16).

28f. forms the climax of the sub-section. Its expression is strikingly concise and elliptic. We may set it out with the addition of supplements thus—

οὐ γὰρ ὁ ἐν τῷ φανερῷ (᾿Ιουδαῖος) ᾿Ιουδαῖός ἐστιν, οὐδὲ ἡ ἐν τῷ φανερῷ ἐν σαρκὶ (περιτομή) περιτομή (ἐστιν) · ἀλλ᾿ ὁ ἐν τῷ κρυπτῷ ᾿Ιουδαῖος (᾿Ιουδαῖός ἐστιν), καὶ περιτομὴ καρδίας ἐν πνεύματι οὐ γράμματι (περιτομή ἐστιν), οὗ ὁ ἔπαινος οὐκ ἐξ ἀνθρώπων (ἐστὶν) ἀλλ᾿ ἐκ τοῦ θεοῦ.[1] Paul has already referred in v. 16 to the fact that God judges the secrets (τὰ κρυπτά) of men (see note there). He now draws a distinction between the person who is to all outward appearance a Jew and the person who is inwardly a Jew, and claims that it is the latter, and not the former, who is a Jew—in the sense Paul here gives to the term (what precisely it is will have to be discussed below). In the light of vv. 25 and 26 it is implied both that not all outward Jews are Jews in the special sense, and also that not all Jews in the special sense are outward Jews. At the same time a similar distinction is drawn between outward circumcision ἐν σαρκί[2] and circumcision of the heart ἐν πνεύματι οὐ γράμματι. The idea of circumcision of the heart is one that goes back to Deuteronomy (cf. Lev 26.41; Deut 10.16; 30.6; Jer 4.4; 9.26). Paul further defines this circumcision as ἐν πνεύματι οὐ γράμματι. By this he most probably intends to indicate that the circumcision of the heart is not accomplished by the mere fulfilment of the letter of the law's requirement, but is a miracle, the work of God's Spirit.[3]

The concluding relative clause probably contains an intentional play on the connexion between Yᵉhûḏî ('Jew') and the Hebrew verb meaning 'praise' (the Hiph'il of yāḏāh) and its derivatives, a word-play going back to Gen 29.35; 49.8, and well known in Judaism. ἔπαινος is probably to be understood

---

[1] Various ways of supplementing Paul's words have been suggested (see, e.g., Sanday and Headlam, p. 68), according to how much of what is actually expressed is regarded as belonging to the subject, and how much to the predicate; but the above suggestion seems most natural.

[2] The Rabbis also spoke of circumcision as 'in the flesh' (cf., e.g., *Exod R.* 19 (81ᶜ): 'He said to them: If the seal of Abraham is not in your flesh, you may not eat (of the meal)'; Targum Ct 3.8: '... and every one of them had the seal of circumcision in his flesh, as it was sealed in the flesh of Abraham ...': see also *ADPB*, p. 305).

[3] That πνεῦμα here denotes the human spirit is unlikely, since the inwardness of this circumcision is already adequately expressed by καρδίας. Moreover, in 7.6 and 2 Cor 3.6 (two other Pauline passages in which πνεῦμα and γράμμα are contrasted) πνεῦμα refers to the Holy Spirit. The conviction that the circumcision of the heart has to be accomplished by God Himself is already to be seen in Deut 30.6 (cf. Jub. 1.23). In Od. Sol. 11.1–3 it is connected with the Holy Spirit.

here eschatologically (cf. v. 10—δόξα . . . καὶ τιμή). For the contrast between praise from God and praise from men compare Jn 5.41, 44; 12.43.

It is clear that in these verses Paul is in some sense denying the name of Jew to those who are only outwardly Jews and not also secretly and inwardly, and at the same time according it to those who are secret, inward Jews but not outward Jews at all. Is he then denying that those Jews who in some sense are not Jews have any part in the promises made to Israel? Is he implying that henceforth the elect people of God consists only of those whom he describes as inward Jews, i.e., of Jewish Christians together with Gentile Christians, or, in other words, that the Christian Church alone is the heir to all the promises? Taken by themselves, these verses would seem to be patient of such a construction. They have certainly often been understood in this sense, and Paul has appeared as the father of those 'who have denied to the Jewish people their election privileges and promises', simply 'transferring them to Christianity as the new Israel of God'.[1] But these verses do not stand by themselves, and, if they are to be interpreted in the light of 3.1–4 and also of 9.1–11.36, they can hardly bear this meaning. The true explanation of them is rather that in them Paul is using 'Jew' in a special limited sense to denote the man who in his concrete human existence stands by virtue of his faith in a positive relation to the on-going purpose of God in history, and that, while they certainly do imply that many who are outwardly Jews are outside what may be called 'the Israel within Israel', they should not be taken as implying that those who are Jews only outwardly are excluded from the promises. (See further on 3.1–4 and especially on 9.1–11.36.)

1. Τί οὖν τὸ περισσὸν τοῦ Ἰουδαίου, ἢ τίς ἡ ὠφέλεια τῆς περιτομῆς; is no frivolous objection. What has just been said in chapter 2, and particularly in vv. 25–29, might indeed seem to imply that there is no advantage of the Jew over the Gentile and no profit in circumcision. But, if this really were the implication of Paul's argument, then it would have called in question the truthfulness of the OT or the faithfulness of God; for, according to the testimony of the OT, God chose this nation out of all mankind to be His special people and gave them circumcision as a token of the covenant which He had made with them. If then there really is no advantage of the Jew and no profit in circumcision, this must

[1] Schoeps, *Paul*, p. 234.

mean either that the OT is a false witness or else that God has not been faithful to His word. The question raised is nothing less than the question of the credibility of God.

2. πολὺ κατὰ πάντα τρόπον.[1] According to Dodd, The logical answer on the basis of Paul's argument is, "None whatever!" ' and the answer which Paul has given is to be explained as the result of his deeply engrained Pharisaic and patriotic prejudice.[2] With regard to the latter part of this judgment, it must be said that to see nothing more than prejudice behind Paul's answer is strange unperceptiveness. For, as we have already seen in connexion with v. 1, to deny that the Jew has a real advantage and that circumcision does profit is to impugn either the faithfulness and consistency of God or the fundamental veracity of the OT. How could Paul then, as a serious theologian, have answered differently?

With reference to the former part of Dodd's judgment, we have to consider whether what Paul has said in chapter 2 (and particularly in w. 25-29) and his strong affirmation in this verse are really irreconcilable. It must first be submitted that πολὺ κατὰ πάντα τρόπον does not mean 'much of every sort', but 'an advantage altogether great and important'. Paul is not asserting here that the Jew far outstrips the Gentile in every sort of advantage one might think of, including every sort of petty advantage which a man might reckon as advantage; but that the Jew has an advantage, a priority, a privilege, a preeminence, which is altogether great and important. What this pre-eminence is becomes clear from the reference in the latter part of the verse to one aspect of it. It is the fact of God's special choice of Israel, the fact that it is through this nation that God's covenant with mankind has been made, the fact that it is in Jewish flesh that the redemption of the world was to be, and now has been, accomplished. Of the greatness of this pre-eminence there can be—within the framework of biblical faith—no doubt. But this tremendous pre-eminence never involved exemption from God's judgment—in fact, it

[1] Pelagius (p. 271) argued that these words should be understood as part of the objection attributed to the Jew: he, in fact, regarded the whole of vv. 1-4 as an objection, and v. 5 as the beginning of Paul's reply. He found it difficult to accept v. 2a as giving Paul's own view. But, though interesting in connexion with the history of exegesis, Pelagius's explanation of these verses is clearly unsatisfactory.

[2] p. 68. Dodd does not himself use the word 'prejudice' here, but I think it fairly represents his meaning. He says: 'His Pharisaism—or shall we say, his patriotism?—was too deeply engrained for him to put right out of his mind the idea that somehow the divine covenant with mankind had a "most favoured nation clause" '.

meant that the Jews were always in a particularly exposed position in relation to it (cf. Amos 3.2). Those who stood nearest to the working out of God's saving purpose could be blind and deaf and uncomprehending, and, where they were rebels against God's grace, that grace could enable others who stood far off to believe. Thus they fundamentally misunderstood their special position when they thought of it as a ground for self-complacency and all too human glorying. But to challenge the falsehood of Jewish complacency and draw attention to the fact that the Jews were for the most part excluding themselves from an active and voluntary participation in the working out of God's gracious purpose was by no means to deny the reality of their pre-eminence which rests not on the faithfulness of men but on the grace and faithfulness of God.

πρῶτον μὲν [γὰρ] ὅτι ἐπιστεύθησαν τὰ λόγια τοῦ θεοῦ. The reading πρῶτοι γάρ (instead of πρῶτον μὲν [γὰρ] ὅτι), which is found in Origen and Eusebius and in the MS. 1739, is no doubt to be rejected: it is easily explicable as a way of removing the awkwardness of a πρῶτον μέν which is not followed by any ἔπειτα δέ (a consciousness on the part of Gentile Christians of having also been entrusted with the λόγια τοῦ θεοῦ subsequently could perhaps have been a further motive for the change). Accepting πρῶτον μέν, we may assume that Paul intended to mention other aspects of the Jew's περισσόν, but then omitted to do so (cf. 1.8, where there is another πρῶτον μέν without a following ἔπειτα δέ). Paul does in fact give a list of Jewish privileges in 9.4f. Whether γάρ should be read or not is more difficult to decide. It could perhaps be an intrusion (possibly due to the influence of Origen's text): on the other hand, its very awkwardness should perhaps incline us to regard it as original. ὅτι is better understood as meaning 'that' than as meaning 'because' (cf. Michel, p. 95, n. 4). For the use of the passive of πιστεύειν with an accusative with the meaning 'to be entrusted with something' compare 1 Cor 9.17; Gal 2.7; 1 Th 2.4; 1 Tim 1.11. The association of ἐπιστεύθησαν, ἠπίστησαν, ἀπιστία, and πίστιν in this and the next verse is striking. τὰ λόγια[1] τοῦ θεοῦ has

---

[1] On λόγιον see G. Kittel, in *TWNT* 4, pp. 140–43 (on the question of the derivation of the word see p. 140, n. 1, contributed by A. Debrunner); J. W. Doeve, 'Some notes with reference to τὰ λόγια τοῦ Θεοῦ in Romans 3.2', in *Studia Paulina*, pp. 111–23. In classical Greek it was used especially to denote an oracle given by a god. In the LXX it is used of a particular word of God (Isa 28.13), of God's commandments (Deut 33.9), but more commonly of the word of God quite generally, so that there is little if any difference of meaning between λόγιον τοῦ θεοῦ and

been variously understood as referring to the law, to the promises made to Israel, to those utterances in the OT 'which stand out as most unmistakably Divine; the Law as given from Sinai and the promises relating to the Messiah',[1] to the OT as a whole, to God's self-revelation in the whole *Heilsgeschichte* both of the OT and of the NT.[2] It is perhaps best (*pace* Kuss, p. 100) to take it in the widest sense. The Jews have been given God's authentic self-revelation in trust to treasure it and to attest and declare it to all mankind.[3] The gospel events and all the *Heilsgeschichte* which preceded them and attested them beforehand took place not 'an irgendeiner beliebigen Stelle der Welt'[4] but in the midst of this people. They alone have been the recipients on behalf of mankind of God's message to mankind.[5]

3. Τί γάρ; εἰ ἠπίστησάν τινες, μὴ ἡ ἀπιστία αὐτῶν τὴν πίστιν τοῦ θεοῦ καταργήσει; Two interrelated questions have to be considered first: What punctuation is to be adopted within the verse? and How much, if any, of the verse is to be assigned to an imaginary objector? It is possible either to put a question mark after γάρ and then to put a comma after τινες, or to put no punctuation after γάρ but a question mark after τινες. With regard to the other question, the following possibilities present themselves: (i) (with either punctuation) to take the whole verse as an objection; (ii) (again with either punctuation) to take the whole verse as Paul's own; and (iii) (punctuation with nothing after γάρ and a question mark after τινες) to take τί γὰρ εἰ ἠπίστησάν τινες; as an objection, and the rest of the verse as Paul's reply. On the whole, it seems best to take the whole verse as Paul's own

λόγος τοῦ θεοῦ. In Ps 119 [LXX: 118] both words are used many times indiscriminately (in some verses the textual tradition wavers between the two terms).

[1] Sanday and Headlam, p. 70.
[2] Cf. G. Kittel, in *TWNT* 4, p. 141f; also Barth, *Shorter*, p. 39: 'The Jews are and remain the nation entrusted with the words, the revelations of God up to and including the person of Jesus Christ'.
[3] The use of ἐπιστεύθησαν is significant. Paul does not say that the Jews have been given the λόγια τοῦ θεοῦ but that they have been entrusted with them—i.e. they have been given them not to do what they like with them but to conduct themselves towards them according to the will of Him who has entrusted them to them, and to Him they will have to give account. Cf. Mt 25.14-30. Calvin's comment is apt: 'The Jews were, firstly, keepers of the oracles of God, and secondly stewards' (p. 59).
[4] G. Kittel, in *TWNT* 4, p. 142.
[5] Cf. Barth, *Shorter*, p. 39: 'The Gentiles, when they attain to faith, can in a way only be their [i.e., the Jews'] guests. It must remain at this: "Salvation comes from the Jews" (John 4.22)'.

thought; for, while it seems to carry on quite naturally the thought of v. 2, neither the verse as a whole nor the first part of it by itself seems particularly natural at this point as an objection. And, although either punctuation yields a good sense if the whole verse is regarded as Paul's own, it seems rather more natural to take τί γάρ as a separate question (cf. Phil 1.18).

We have next to decide how ἠπίστησαν and ἀπιστία are to be understood. The words ἀπιστεῖν and ἀπιστία can mean either 'be unfaithful' and 'unfaithfulness' respectively or 'be unbelieving' and 'unbelief'. One might perhaps be inclined to think that, coming just after ἐπιστεύθησαν and just before τὴν πίστιν τοῦ θεοῦ (which here must mean 'the faithfulness of God'), these words would more likely be intended in the former sense. But Sanday and Headlam were probably right to maintain[1] that they refer to unbelief, which is the idea they convey in almost all the other places in which they occur in the NT (ἀπιστεῖν occurs in all eight times in the NT, and ἀπιστία eleven times), and which ἀπιστία carries in the three other places in which it occurs in Romans (4.20; 11.20, 23). Their view is shared by many other commentators from early times on. We take it then that the thought conveyed by ἠπίστησαν in relation to the ἐπιστεύθησαν of the previous verse is not that these Jews have proved unfaithful to their trust but that they have failed to believe the λόγια τοῦ θεοῦ entrusted to them. But, with regard to the further question of translating these words, it is highly desirable, since the series of four cognate words here is clearly not accidental, to translate them in such a way as to bring out, if at all possible, the connexion between them. This might just be done, though not altogether satisfactorily, by using 'were entrusted', 'have refused to trust', 'lack of trust', 'trustworthiness', for the four words. Perhaps it is better to sacrifice the verbal connexion with ἐπιστεύθησαν, and translate the other words in some such way as 'have failed to respond with faith', 'lack of faith', and 'faithfulness'. In any case, it is important to recognize that we have here more than just a play on words: there is, in the Bible, a real inward connexion between faith-belief and faithfulness. The Jews' unbelief was also, as a matter of fact, unfaithfulness to the covenant; and Paul may well, while referring primarily to their unbelief, have had also in mind the thought of their unfaithfulness.[2]

[1] p. 71.
[2] Cf. Sanday and Headlam, p. 71 ('At the same time the one sense rather suggests than excludes the other').

τινες here is meiosis (intended presumably to 'lessen the hardness' of the censure):[1] compare 11.17 (Εἰ δέ τινες τῶν κλάδων ἐξεκλάσθησαν, . . .). The μή introducing the question indicates that a negative answer is anticipated. τὴν πίστιν τοῦ θεοῦ must here mean 'the faithfulness of God' (contrast, e.g., διὰ πίστεως Ἰησοῦ Χριστοῦ in 3.22, where the meaning is 'through faith in Jesus Christ'). The verb καταργεῖν is found in Euripides, Polybius, LXX (four times—all in 2 Esdras), a few times in papyri, and twenty-seven times in the NT (twenty-five times in the Pauline corpus, and once in Luke and once in Hebrews). Its basic meaning is 'to put out of action', 'to make ineffective' (the simple verb ἀργεῖν, from ἀργός, a contraction of ἀεργός, means 'to be idle'); but it can also carry the stronger sense of 'abolish' and in the passive can mean 'to be removed out of the sphere of effectiveness' of someone or something (so in 7.2 and 6; Gal 5.4). Here it clearly has its basic sense of 'make ineffective'. (See further on 3.31; 4.14; 6.6; 7.2, 6; and G. Delling, in *TWNT* 1, pp. 453–5.)

The sense of the verse as a whole is that it is unthinkable that God's faithfulness to His covenant with Israel should be rendered ineffective even by the Jews' unbelief.

4. μὴ γένοιτο is a formula of strong denial used frequently by Paul (in Romans also vv. 6 and 31; 6.2, 15; 7.7, 13; 9.14; 11.1, 11)—always after a question. It also occurs frequently in Epictetus. It is not really equivalent to the Hebrew *ḥālîlāh*;[2] for, though μὴ γένοιτο is indeed used in association with other words to represent *ḥālîlāh* in association with other words, *ḥālîlāh* is not used on its own.

γινέσθω δὲ ὁ θεὸς ἀληθής. The use of the imperative is a vigorous way of stating the true situation after the emphatic rejection of an altogether false suggestion. The Vulgate 'est' rightly recognizes that the imperative here is declaratory in meaning, though, as Lagrange notes,[3] Erasmus's 'Immo sit' brings out the precise nuance of the Greek better.[4] 'We confess rather that God is true' just about gives the sense. γίνεσθαι does not here convey any idea of becoming, but is used simply as equivalent to εἶναι (see Bauer, s.v. γίνομαι, II).[5] In ἀληθής the thought of God's faithfulness to His promises is

---

[1] Cf. Calvin, p. 59.   [2] *Pace* Michel, p.96, n. 2.
[3] p. 65.
[4] Cf. Cyril, col. 776: ἀντὶ τοῦ, νοείσθω τε καὶ λεγέσθω πρὸς ἡμῶν ἀληθής, καθοριζέσθω δὲ ὥσπερ ἀνθρώπου παντὸς τοῦ ψεύδους τὸ κατηγόρημα.
[5] This is surely a more natural explanation than that of Sanday and Headlam, p. 71 ('the transition which the verb denotes is often from a latent condition to an apparent condition, and so here, "prove to be", "be seen to be" ').

no doubt specially prominent, though it would be wrong to exclude reference to other aspects of His truth. Calvin well describes this statement of Paul's as 'the primary axiom of all Christian philosophy'.[1]

πᾶς δὲ ἄνθρωπος ψεύστης is reminiscent of the psalmist's cry of dismay in Ps 116.11 [LXX: 115.2], where the LXX has ἐγὼ εἶπα ἐν τῇ ἐκστάσει μου Πᾶς ἄνθρωπος ψεύστης. In contrast to the truthfulness of God stands the falsehood of men. Over against Him all men are liars. This—it is, of course, a continuation of the declaration introduced by γινέσθω—is best understood as a general characterization of men in contrast to God.[2]

καθάπερ γέγραπται refers forward to the quotation from Ps 51 which follows, not to the preceding reminiscence of Ps 116. καθάπερ occurs in the NT seventeen times (in Romans here and in 4.6; 9.13; 10.15; 11.8; 12.4, six times in 1 and 2 Corinthians, four times in 1 Thessalonians, and once in Hebrews). In each place where it occurs in Romans there is a variant reading, there being a natural tendency to substitute a more common for a rather rare word. It is a thoroughly Attic expression, and in the NT is a slightly literary touch.[3]

ὅπως ἂν δικαιωθῇς ἐν τοῖς λόγοις σου καὶ νικήσεις ἐν τῷ κρίνεσθαί σε is an exact quotation of the LXX version[4] of Ps 51.4b [LXX: 50.6b], except for the use of the future indicative νικήσεις where the LXX has νικήσῃς.[5] It is a final

---

[1] p. 60.

[2] Cf. Lagrange, p. 64. Others explain it in various ways: e.g. Sanday and Headlam (p. 72) take Paul to be referring particularly to the Jews' assertion that God's promises have not yet been fulfilled; Barrett (p. 63) understands the point to be that God's truth is to be believed, 'even though maintaining it (in the teeth of human unfaithfulness) leads to the conclusion that all men are liars'.

[3] Cf. Robertson, *Grammar*, p.967. [Nestle²⁶ reads καθώς.]

[4] The LXX translator took zākāh ('be pure') to mean 'conquer' (cf. the way the verse is understood in *Sanh.* 107ᵃ, quoted in SB 1, p. 135); this is a sense the word came to have in later usage (cf. Aramaic *rekā'*). Whether he intended κρίνεσθαι to be taken as passive or middle is not clear, nor which way Paul understood it. If it is passive, then the idea is of God's being judged by men—a bold image. But κρίνεσθαι (middle) means 'to contend in a law-suit' (e.g. Job 9.3; 13.19; Isa 50.8; Jer 2.9; 1 Cor 6.1, 6). In favour of taking κρίνεσθαι here as middle it may be said (i) that the meaning 'contend' accords better with νικήσῃς/νικήσεις; (ii) that 'contend' is not so different from 'judge', which is the sense of the Hebrew form, as is 'be judged'; and (iii) that the image of God and men contending against each other in a law-suit is a familiar one (cf., e.g., Mic 6.1ff).

[5] There is a variant reading νικήσῃς here in Rom 3.4, but it should no doubt be rejected as being easily explicable as assimilation to the LXX and also anyway an easier reading. On the use of the future indicative in a final clause see BDF, § 369 (3).

clause, which in the psalm should probably be understood as being dependent not on the preceding half-verse but on v. 3 [LXX: 5]: the psalmist (according to the title, David) recognizes and confesses his sin as committed against God Himself, in order that through his confession God might be acknowledged as just in His judgment.[1] The quotation serves here as support for the general idea expressed in the words γινέσθω ... ὁ θεὸς ἀληθής, πᾶς δὲ ἄνθρωπος ψεύστης, inasmuch as (understood in conjunction with the preceding half-verse of the psalm) it speaks of God's righteousness over against man's sinfulness. It is possible that Paul also had in mind, in connexion with what he had just said in v. 3, the fact that the case of David (to whom of course the psalm was attributed) was an outstanding example of God's faithfulness in the face of grievous sin (cf., e.g., Ps 89.35; Isa 55.3; Lk 1.32, 69; Rom 1.3).[2]

5. εἰ δὲ ἡ ἀδικία ἡμῶν θεοῦ δικαιοσύνην συνίστησιν, τί ἐροῦμεν; μὴ ἄδικος ὁ θεὸς ὁ ἐπιφέρων τὴν ὀργήν; At this point Paul's thought takes an unexpected turn. It seems likely that the experience he had already had of having his doctrine of grace misunderstood and misrepresented (cf. v. 8) had made him specially sensitive to the danger of being misinterpreted (by opponents and perhaps also by professed supporters) as an advocate of what was later to be called antinomianism.[3] At any rate, he saw that a false inference could be drawn from what he had just said (vv. 3 and 4), and so digressed from his argument for four verses (vv. 5–8) in order to guard against it. It is possible that he had in mind the half-verse of Ps 51 (σοὶ μόνῳ ἥμαρτον καὶ τὸ πονηρὸν ἐνώπιόν σου ἐποίησα) immediately preceding the one he had just quoted:[4] taken as a whole, the psalm-verse seems, if it is not recognized that the final clause is really dependent on the previous verse (ὅτι τὴν ἀνομίαν μου ἐγὼ γινώσκω, κ.τ.λ.), to be saying that the psalmist's sin was actually committed in order that God might be acknowledged to be just.[5] But it is rather more

[1] For the use of δικαιοῦν of acknowledging God to be in the right, acknowledging His justice, cf. Ps. Sol. 2.15 (16) ('Εγὼ δικαιώσω σε, ὁ θεός, ἐν εὐθύτητι καρδίας, ὅτι ἐν τοῖς κρίμασίν σου ἡ δικαιοσύνη σου, ὁ θεός); 3.5 (Προσέκοψεν ὁ δίκαιος καὶ ἐδικαίωσεν τὸν κύριον . . .); 4.8 (9); 8.7.

[2] Cf. Leenhardt, p. 92 (Fr.: 55).

[3] Cf. Kuss, p. 102f.

[4] Cf., e.g., Lagrange, p. 65; Barrett, p. 63f.

[5] The Rabbinic explanations of Ps 51.4 [MT: 6] in *Yalkut Reub.* on Gen 8.21 and *Sanh.* 107ᵃ, quoted in SB 3, p. 135, are startling: according to them, David's motive in sinning with Bath-sheba was to prevent God's word in Gen 8.21 ('the imagination of man's heart is evil from his youth') from being falsified.

probable that the starting-point of Paul's thought in vv. 5–8 is what he himself has said in vv. 3–4a, as illuminated by the quotation in v. 4b;[1] and that ἡ ἀδικία ἡμῶν and θεοῦ δικαιοσύνην refer to the Jews' unbelief (Paul associating himself with his countrymen, as in v. 9 (προεχόμεθα)) and to God's faithfulness to His covenant, respectively, or that Paul is already generalizing on the basis of what has been said in vv. 3 and 4, and means by ἡ ἀδικία ἡμῶν the sinfulness of men quite generally. The point of the first question of v. 5, then, is to draw attention to the difficulty which presents itself, if it is really true that the unbelief of the Jews actually serves to show up[2] the faithfulness of God (or the sinfulness of men generally to show up the righteousness of God). The second question indicates the nature of the difficulty, though it does not present it in the form of an objection (if it were intended as an objector's question, it would of course have been introduced by οὐκ—'Is not God unjust . . .?'),[3] but in the form of a rhetorical question anticipating a negative answer (μὴ ἄδικος ὁ θεός . . .;—'Is God unjust . . .?'). For the use of ἐπιφέρειν in ὁ ἐπιφέρων τὴν ὀργήν ('who inflicts His wrath') compare Ep. Arist. 253 (θάνατον) and Josephus, Ant. 2. 296 (πληγήν).

κατὰ ἄνθρωπον λέγω. The same expression is used in Gal 3.15, and similar ones occur in Rom 6.19 and 1 Cor 9.8; but it is to be noted that the precise sense conveyed varies.[4] Here these words are a parenthetic apology for having presented (even though in a clearly deprecatory way) a thought which is all too human in its weakness and folly,[5] an apology which has the effect of underlining Paul's repudiation of the thought, already indicated by the μή.

6. μὴ γένοιτο· ἐπεὶ πῶς κρινεῖ[6] ὁ θεὸς τὸν κόσμον; Paul rejects the notion that God is guilty of injustice on the ground that to ascribe injustice to God is essentially absurd, since it is tantamount to a denial of what must be held to be axiomatic, namely, that God is the eschatological Judge of the

[1] On this view, as on the one just mentioned, the ὅπως of the quotation is important. It is surprising that the NEB simply omits it altogether.

[2] For this use of συνιστάναι cf. 5.8; 2 Cor 6.4; 7.11; Gal 2.18.

[3] The possibility of explaining it as an example of a hesitant question introduced by μή (see BDF, § 427 (2)) hardly comes in question.

[4] Cf. SB 3, p. 136, where the further point is made that this variation shows that we have not here a stereotyped expression. But see Daube, NTRJ, pp. 394–6.

[5] It is an apology for the fact that the thought to which Paul has given expression is marked by the foolishness and weakness which are characteristic of human thinking, not for having spoken of God as if He were a man, as Sanday and Headlam suggest (p. 69: cf. p. 73).

[6] The accentuation κρινεῖ is surely to be preferred to κρίνει (present).

world (i.e. of all men). That God who shall judge the world is just is a fundamental certainty of all theological thinking (cf., e.g., Gen 18.25; Deut 32.4; Job 8.3; 34.10ff). God would in fact not be God at all, if He were unjust.

ἐπεί is here used elliptically, as in 11.6, 22; 1 Cor 14.16; 15.29; Heb 10.2, the sense being 'for otherwise', 'else'.[1] Paul's thought here, set out fully, is: 'for, if my rejection of the suggestion that God is unjust is not right, how can it be true that God shall judge the world?'[2]

7. εἰ δὲ ἡ ἀλήθεια τοῦ θεοῦ ἐν τῷ ἐμῷ ψεύσματι ἐπερίσσευσεν εἰς τὴν δόξαν αὐτοῦ, τί ἔτι κἀγὼ ὡς ἁμαρτωλὸς κρίνομαι; The thought, which was expressed in v. 5b in a form which indicated that it was being repudiated, is now brought forward again[3]—this time in the form of an objection (the use of the first person singular is simply rhetorical). If the truth of God (cf. τὴν πίστιν τοῦ θεοῦ in v. 3, ὁ θεὸς ἀληθής in v. 4, and θεοῦ δικαιοσύνην in v. 5) has really been more abundantly manifested, to His glory, by means of my lie (cf. ἡ ἀπιστία αὐτῶν in v. 3, πᾶς δὲ ἄνθρωπος ψεύστης in v. 4, and ἡ ἀδικία ἡμῶν in v. 5), why am I still judged as a sinner? How can it be fair for a man to be blamed for his falsehood, when it has actually redounded to God's glory?

8. καὶ μὴ καθὼς βλασφημούμεθα καὶ καθώς φασίν τινες ἡμᾶς λέγειν ὅτι ποιήσωμεν τὰ κακὰ ἵνα ἔλθῃ τὰ ἀγαθά; ὧν τὸ κρίμα ἔνδικόν ἐστιν poses a number of interrelated problems. It will be convenient to begin with the question of the punctuation to be adopted (apart from the matter of the parenthesis καθώς, κ.τ.λ., which we shall consider later). The following possibilities have been suggested: (i) a comma at the

---

[1] The usage is found in classical Greek (e.g. Plato, *Euthphr.* 9b; Xenophon, *Cyr.* 2.2.31) as well as in Hellenistic. See BDF, § 456 (3); Bauer, s.v. 2.

[2] The two other ways of understanding ἐπεί here ('if God is not to use his wrath' and 'if God does not punish Jews (as well as Gentiles)') mentioned by Barrett, p. 64, are clearly less probable.

[3] It is a moot question whether δέ or γάρ should be read. In favour of γάρ it may be said that it not only has very strong attestation (see the fuller apparatus to this verse in UBS) but would also seem to be the more difficult reading, since it must mark the connexion of this verse not with the sentence immediately preceding it but with v. 5b (indicating that v. 7 is explication of v. 5b), whereas δέ marks v. 7 as standing in an adversative relation to v. 6 (a reply to it). We are inclined to agree with UBS in accepting γάρ, though recognizing that a considerable doubt remains. That the notion presented in v. 5b should be reintroduced here in a different form is perhaps a little surprising, but certainly not so surprising as to warrant Cornely's conclusion (p. 164f) that it must be a Gentile objection which is being presented in v. 7 (ψεύσματι referring to the lie of idolatry).

end of v. 7, another comma after ἀγαθά, and a question mark
at the end of this verse; (ii) a comma at the end of v. 7,
a question mark after ἀγαθά, and a full stop at the end of
the verse; (iii) a question mark at the end of v. 7, a comma
after ἀγαθά, and a question mark at the end of the verse;
(iv) a question mark at the end of v. 7, a question mark after
ἀγαθά, and a full stop at the end of the verse. The effect of (i)
is to make vv. 7 and 8 one composite question. It is to be
rejected on the ground that, according to it, we should have
objections left without any sort of answer, and also on the
ground that, if it were accepted, we should have a very
awkward combination of the first person singular and the
first person plural in the same question. (ii) might perhaps be
acceptable, if ὧν τὸ κρίμα ἔνδικόν ἐστιν could be understood as a
short, sharp answer to the objections; but (*pace* Sanday and
Headlam,[1] Lagrange,[2] *et al.*, who maintain that ὧν refers to
those who put forward the sort of objection which has been
mentioned) ὧν can scarcely refer to any but the τινες,[3] in which
case ὧν τὸ κρίμα ἔνδικόν ἐστιν is not a reply to the objections
but only a condemnation of Paul's calumniators. Both (iii)
and (iv) separate v. 8 from v. 7, and make it possible to
interpret the verse as a whole as some sort of answer to v. 7.
(iv) should be preferred to (iii), as being a more natural
punctuation, provided it is not taken to imply any dissociation
of ὧν from τινες.

The construction of the verse is unusually clumsy and
tangled. Paul apparently wanted to refer to the fact that there
were some people who were falsely alleging that he himself
maintained the viewpoint which he was here describing, and
vehemently[4] to repudiate their allegation, and he has attempted to do this by means of a parenthesis. This parenthesis
begins with the first καθώς, but it is not clear whether it
includes ὅτι or not. The ὅτι (which in any case must be *recitativum*) can either be understood as inside the parenthesis,
having been inserted redundantly, though not altogether

[1] p. 74.
[2] p. 67.
[3] Cf., Michel, p. 97, n. 4, Barrett, p. 61.
[4] Paul's use of βλασφημεῖν, a particularly strong expression, is to be
noted. Michel, p. 97, rightly observes that this allegation touched Paul
at his most sensitive point, because it concerned the seriousness of his
witness. In view of Paul's language it is much more likely that he is
referring to accusations levelled against him by opponents of his doctrine
than that he has in mind the misapprehensions of converts, though
there is little doubt that the antinomian misunderstanding appeared
among Paul's converts very quickly (cf. chapter 6).

unnaturally, after λέγειν, or else construed with μή (outside the parenthesis).

Even when the parenthesis has been isolated, the construction of the rest of the sentence is still difficult, and it is variously explained. The following possibilities require to be noticed: (i) Those who punctuate with only a comma at the end of v. 7 generally understand the force of τί to carry over from v. 7 (so 'and why not');[1] (ii) Others, who understand the main part of v. 8, not as actually continuing the question in v. 7, but as a further objection set alongside it, explain μή as introducing a hesitant question, either taking it directly with ποιήσωμεν ('And should we perhaps . . . do evil . . .?') or with ellipse of λέγομεν (or λέγωμεν) and taking ὅτι as outside the parenthesis ('And do we perhaps say (or 'should we perhaps say') . . . Let us do evil . . .?'); (iii) We may understand μή as introducing a question expecting a negative answer, i.e., a rhetorical question which is in fact a reply to the objection in v. 7, either (a) taking μή directly with ποιήσωμεν ('And should we then . . . do evil . . .?') or (b) assuming an ellipse of λέγομεν and taking ὅτι as outside the parenthesis ('And do we then say . . . Let us do evil . . .?'). Of these possibilities, (i) and (ii) should, we believe, be rejected for the reasons already indicated above.[2] Between (iii) (a) and (b) there is not much to choose, but perhaps (iii) (b) should be preferred as being rather neater.

We take v. 8, then, to consist of a rhetorical question (expecting the answer 'No'), which serves as a rejoinder to the objection expressed in v. 7, incorporating a parenthesis which refers to the fact that some people actually allege that Paul himself teaches the attitude which he is here repudiating, and followed by a condemnation of the people to whom the parenthesis refers.[3]

9. Τί οὖν; προεχόμεθα; οὐ πάντως· προῃτιασάμεθα γὰρ 'Ιουδαίους τε καὶ Ἕλληνας πάντας ὑφ'ἁμαρτίαν εἶναι is another particularly difficult verse. In view of the interrelatedness of the problems, which concern text, punctuation and interpretation, it will be best to set out the whole range of the main problems before attempting to discuss any of them.

First, the main textual variations may be shown as follows: (i) Nearly all authorities attest either (a) προεχόμεθα (א B etc.),

---

[1] On this interpretation, μή is of course not the word which introduces a question anticipating a negative answer (according to this interpretation, an affirmative answer is in fact expected), but must be explained as due to the use of the subjunctive (see BDF, § 427 (4)).

[2] In connexion with the question of punctuation.

[3] The κρίμα referred to (κρίμα here means 'judgment' in the sense of 'sentence of condemnation') is presumably that pronounced by God.

or (b) προεχώμεθα (A L), or (c) προκατέχομεν περισσόν (D* G Ψ 104 Or⁽ᴸᵃᵗ⁾ Ambst and other Fathers).

(ii) The words οὐ πάντως are omitted by those authorities which have the reading (i) (c), and also by a few attesting προεχόμεθα.[1]

(iii) ἠτιασάμεθα is read instead of προῃτιασάμεθα by D* G pc, supported by lat.

(iv) γάρ is omitted by D* syᴾ.

(v) πρῶτον is added after τε by A.

Secondly, there are the following questions concerning punctuation, on the assumption that the text printed by Nestle is correct:

(i) Should a question mark or no punctuation be placed after οὖν?

(ii) Should no punctuation mark be placed after οὐ and a colon after πάντως, or a comma after οὐ and nothing after πάντως?

Thirdly, there are the problems of interpretation. These are centred on προεχόμεθα and οὐ πάντως. The basic sense of προέχειν is 'hold before'. In the middle it means 'hold before oneself', and so, metaphorically, 'put forward as a pretext or excuse'. In the active it is also used intransitively, meaning 'jut out', 'project', 'have the start' (e.g. in running), 'be superior to', 'surpass', 'excel' (either with a genitive or absolutely). Since προεχόμεθα may be either middle or passive, the following possibilities have to be considered:

(i) that it is middle with a proper middle force. One would then have expected a direct object to be expressed ('put . . . forward as an excuse'), but Paul—it has been argued—could conceivably have used it without a direct object with such a sense as 'excuse oneself', 'make excuses' or 'prevaricate'. The subject might be 'we Jews' or perhaps the same as that of προῃτιασάμεθα later in the verse, i.e. 'we' meaning Paul himself.

(ii) that it is middle with an active force. The meaning would then be: 'Have we (Jews) any advantage over them (sc. the Gentiles)?' No other examples of the middle of this verb used in this way have been adduced.

(iii) that it is passive, the meaning being: 'Are we (Jews) excelled by them?' or 'Are we worse off than they?'

πάντως (it occurs in the NT nine times in all, four times in Luke and Acts and five in Romans and 1 Corinthians), like the English 'altogether', modifies the negative adverb, if placed before it (thus πάντως οὐ properly means 'altogether not'), but is itself modified by the negative, if placed after it (thus

---

[1] UBS gives a fuller apparatus as far as (i) and (ii) are concerned than does Nestle.

οὐ πάντως properly means 'not altogether'). But there is some
evidence of οὐ πάντως being used where one would expect
πάντως οὐ (see, for example, Epictetus, *Ench*. 1.5; and (from a
much earlier date) Theognis (Elegiacus), 305); and the Vulgate
renders οὐ πάντως here by 'Nequaquam'.

We are now in a position to attempt to reach some conclusions. With regard to the textual variations (i) and (ii), there
seems to be little doubt that the words προεχόμεθα οὐ πάντως
should be read; for they are strongly attested, and their
difficulty also tells in their favour. The substitution of
προκατέχομεν περισσόν (without οὐ πάντως) for προεχόμεθα οὐ
πάντως would be readily understandable, the resulting question
τί οὖν προκατέχομεν περισσόν; being so much easier, while the
alteration in the opposite direction would be most unlikely.
And the reading προεχώμεθα looks like an attempted improvement by someone who understood the verb in its proper
middle sense and so felt a deliberative question was required.

The decision to read προεχόμεθα οὐ πάντως involves putting
a question mark after οὖν, since if τί were the object of
προεχόμεθα the answer would naturally be οὐδέν rather than
οὐ πάντως.

With regard to the interpretation of προεχόμεθα, explanation
(iii), though grammatically quite unobjectionable, must surely
be rejected (*pace* Lightfoot, Field, Sanday and Headlam, and
the RV) on the ground that the sense yielded is unsuitable to
the context. Even if the question 'Are we (Jews) inferior (to
the Gentiles)?' is conceivable as an immediate sequel to
2.17–29, it is surely altogether inappropriate after 3.1–8.[1]
Explanation (i) would connect v. 9 with the preceding verses,
but it seems very doubtful whether προέχεσθαι used by itself
could bear the sense 'have an excuse' (or 'excuse oneself') and
the possibility of taking τί as the object of προεχόμεθα seems to
be ruled out by οὐ πάντως, as we have seen. Explanation (ii),
while not without difficulty (if this was Paul's meaning, why
did he not use the active προέχομεν?), seems much the most
likely. It would not be the only case of the use of a middle
form, where an active is to be expected: Lagrange[2] refers to
ἡρμοσάμην in 2 Cor 11.2 (cf. Bauer, s.v. ἁρμόζω 3), and further
examples are given in BDF, § 316 (1). It has the support of the
Vulgate rendering 'praecellimus eos ?'. And the variant

---

[1] The explanation of προεχόμεθα (understood as passive) as meaning
'Are we (Jews) preferred (to the Gentiles) in God's sight?' put forward
by Olshausen, followed by Vaughan and Liddon, can hardly be said
to be more than a counsel of despair.

[2] p. 69.

προκατέχομεν περισσόν is also in its own way, as Lagrange observed, a witness to this interpretation.

Turning now to οὐ πάντως, we may begin by setting aside the suggested punctuation οὐ, πάντως προῃτιασάμεθα γάρ . . ., as improbable. The fact that it entails making γάρ the third word of a sentence in itself tells against it—though it is certainly true that occasionally γάρ is the third or even fourth word (so in 2 Cor 1.19) of a sentence. But in this case, where the natural tendency would be to connect πάντως with the negative, it is hard to believe that Paul, had he meant πάντως to be connected with what follows, would not have placed γάρ immediately after it. Many commentators, following the Vulgate's 'nequaquam', understand Paul to be using οὐ πάντως in the sense which properly belongs to πάντως οὐ—as a strong negative, 'Certainly not', 'By no means'.[1] After long hesitation, we have come to the conclusion that this view should be abandoned, and the interpretation 'Not altogether', 'Not in every respect', adopted.[2] The fact that in both the other places, in which Paul uses πάντως in conjunction with οὐ, the meaning is the natural one (in 1 Cor 16.12 we have πάντως οὐ, and the meaning is 'altogether not', while in 1 Cor 5.10 we have οὐ πάντως, and the meaning is 'not altogether') strongly suggests that here too his usage is likely to be correct. Furthermore, the meaning 'not altogether' is, as a matter of fact, better suited to the context. Paul has said in 3.2 that the Jew has an advantage which is great and important in every respect. He now indicates that, while the Jews have this altogether great advantage, they are not at an advantage in every respect. (These two statements are not contradictory.[3]) There is at least one respect in which they are at no advantage—the matter of sinfulness, of having no claim on God in virtue of their merit.[4]

[1] So, e.g., Cornely, Lipsius, Sanday and Headlam, Barrett, Murray: cf. RV, RSV, NEB, JB.

[2] Cf., e.g., Lietzmann, p. 47; Lagrange, p. 69; Michel, p. 98; Gaugler 1, p. 75f.

[3] If, however, οὐ πάντως is taken to mean here 'Certainly not!', there is at any rate something very much like a formal contradiction—though it might perhaps be maintained that in 3.1f the reference is to what the Jews have received, whereas the first person plural in this verse refers to their persons (cf. Aquinas, p. 49 (273): 'Sic igitur dicendum est quod supra ostendit praerogativam divinorum beneficiorum, unde non dixit quod Iudaeus esset excellentior, sed quod aliquid esset Iudaeo amplius *donatum*; hic autem excludit excellentiam personarum, quia illi qui divina beneficia acceperunt, non sunt illis debite usi').

[4] Calvin, p. 65, with some justification sees a significance in the fact that, when Paul was speaking of the pre-eminence of the Jews (v. 1f),

It is this which the following sentence makes clear. It supports and explains (γάρ) 'Not in every respect' by the reminder that Paul has already (προ-) charged both Jews and Gentiles alike with being—all of them—under sin. This he has indeed done in 1.18–2.29. Here the noun ἁμαρτία occurs for the first time in Romans (we have had the verb ἁμαρτάνειν in 2.12, ἁμαρτωλός in 3.7, and also such closely related words as ἀσέβεια (1.18) and ἀδικία (1.18, 29; 2.8; 3.5)). For the expression ὑφ' ἁμαρτίαν compare 7.14 (ἐγὼ δὲ σαρκινός εἰμι, πεπραμένος ὑπὸ τὴν ἁμαρτίαν); Gal 3.22 (ἀλλὰ συνέκλεισεν ἡ γραφὴ τὰ πάντα ὑπὸ ἁμαρτίαν . . .), and, for the general sense of ὑπό with the accusative here, also Gal 3.25 (. . . οὐκέτι ὑπὸ παιδαγωγόν ἐσμεν); 4.2 (. . . ὑπὸ ἐπιτρόπους ἐστὶν καὶ οἰκονόμους . . .); 4.3 (. . . ὑπὸ τὰ στοιχεῖα τοῦ κόσμου ἤμεθα δεδουλωμένοι). Paul thinks of sin as a power which has got control of man, and there is a marked tendency to personification in his references to it—encouraged, no doubt, by the memory of Gen 3. Very seldom does he use ἁμαρτία in the plural to denote actual sins committed (e.g. 1 Cor 15.3), whereas in other parts of the NT the plural use is predominant. Paul, when he uses ἁμαρτία, thinks rather of sin as a power controlling man than of the individual sins which man commits. Since it is in Rom 5–7 that he develops most fully his thought about sin (almost half the occurrences in the whole *corpus Paulinum* of words of the ἁμαρτάνειν group, and well over half the occurrences of the noun ἁμαρτία, are to be found in Rom 5–7), we may refer forward to the notes on those chapters for further discussion.

It remains to refer to textual variations (iii), (iv) and (v). The reading ἠτιασάμεθα may well be simply due to Latin influence, there not being an equivalent verb to προαιτιᾶσθαι. The support for the omission of γάρ is insufficient to warrant omitting it. The πρῶτον in A between τε and καί is no doubt to be explained as assimilation to 1.16; 2.9 and 10.

10–18 may be taken together. They are a catena of OT quotations in confirmation of the charge which Paul has levelled against both Jews and Gentiles that they are all under sin's power. The catena has been constructed with considerable care and artistry, so as to form a real new unity out of a multiplicity of excerpts. It is arranged in three strophes, the first (vv. 10–12) consisting of two sets of three lines, the second (vv. 13–14) and third (vv. 15–18) each consisting of two sets of two lines. The six times repeated οὐκ ἔστιν (it occurs

he referred to them in the third person, but here, where he is 'stripping them of every privilege, he numbers himself among them to avoid giving offence'.

five times in vv. 10–12—once more than in the original psalm-passage—and once in v. 18) and the πάντες of v. 12 express the theme of the cento, the universality of sin's hold on men, and drive home the πάντας of v. 9. It is possible that this particular cento was already in use in Christian worship and that Paul adopted it for his present purpose; but, in any case, it is thoroughly apposite here. Among the Rabbis the stringing together of quotations from different books of the OT was a familiar practice, but they did not normally run the quotations together but introduced each one with a formula of quotation.

Verses 10–12 are an abridgement and adaptation of the LXX version of the last part of v. 1 and of vv. 2 and 3 of Ps 14 [LXX: 13], which are repeated in a not quite identical form in Ps 53 [LXX: 52]. The LXX text is as follows: . . . οὐκ ἔστιν ποιῶν χρηστότητα, οὐκ ἔστιν ἕως ἑνός. κύριος ἐκ τοῦ οὐρανοῦ διέκυψεν ἐπὶ τοὺς υἱοὺς τῶν ἀνθώπων τοῦ ἰδεῖν εἰ ἔστιν συνίων ἢ ἐκζητῶν τὸν θεόν. πάντες ἐξέκλιναν, ἅμα ἠχρεώθησαν, οὐκ ἔστιν ποιῶν χρηστότητα, οὐκ ἔστιν ἕως ἑνός. Paul has freely adapted the first line (when it is repeated in v. 3 he reproduces it verbatim). It is possible that he had Eccles 7.20 in mind,[1] a verse which contained the word δίκαιος, which Paul has introduced here and which is, of course, along with its cognates, an essential element in the thought of the epistle (cf., 1.17, 18, 29; 2.8, 13; 3.5, 20, 21, etc.). That δίκαιος here is intended to convey the thought of righteous standing before God as well as that of moral righteousness (cf. the 'do justly' of Mic 6.8) is highly probable. Verse 11 is a free adaptation of Ps 14.2. συνίων (from συνίειν, a collateral form of συνιέναι) is used both in the psalm and by Paul with reference to religious and moral understanding. With ὁ[2] ἐκζητῶν τὸν θεόν we have an explicit reference to man's relation to God. References to 'seeking' God are of course to be found very frequently in the OT (compare, for example, Exod 33.7; 2 Chron 15.12, 13, 15; Ezra 8.22; Ps 9.10; 24.6; 27.8 (in Pss examples are specially numerous); Prov 28.5; Isa 9.13; 31.1; 51.1; 55.6; Jer 29.13; Zeph 1.6).[3]

---

[1] It is interesting that this verse of Ecclesiastes was the favourite verse of the Tannaite Rabbi Eliezer ben Hyrcanus (fl. end of 1st century A.D.), according to Sanh. 101a. His teaching of the general sinfulness of mankind comes close to Paul's teaching, whereas the usual doctrine of the Rabbis insisted on man's freedom to choose between the good and the bad impulses. (Cf. Schoeps, Paul, p. 185.)

[2] There is textual support for omitting the article before συνίων and ἐκζητῶν in this verse and also before ποιῶν in v. 12, but this is probably simply assimilation to the LXX text.

[3] In the LXX both ζητεῖν and ἐκζητεῖν are used to represent both bikkēš and dāraš in this connexion.

Verse 12 is, apart from the addition of the article before
ποιῶν, an exact quotation of the LXX version of Ps 14.3. The
word χρηστότης is used in this psalm both in v. 1 and in v. 3,
but the LXX translation of Ps 53 has in both places ἀγαθόν
(the MT has in both psalms the word *ṭôḇ*).

The first two lines of v. 13 are an exact quotation of the
latter half of LXX Ps 5.10 [RV: 9].[1] The psalmist is describing
the ruthless enemies against whom he prays for God's help.
By describing their throat as an open grave he perhaps
intended to indicate the deadly effects of their speech[2] or
perhaps the inner corruption which it expresses. Such is the
reality of their speech, although the flatteries[3] of their tongues
may give a different impression. The last line of v. 13 is an
exact quotation of the latter half of the LXX version of
Ps 140.3 [LXX: 139.4]. This psalm is another complaint and
prayer for help against cruel enemies, and this verse vividly
characterizes the malignancy of their slanders. Verse 14,
which completes the second strophe of the cento, is a quotation
(slightly adapted) of the first part of LXX Ps 9.28 [RV: 10.7].
Whether Pss 9 and 10, which are combined into one in some
Hebrew MSS., the LXX and the Vulgate, were originally the
lament of an individual concerning the wicked in Israel or a
communal lament over foreign oppressors is disputed. As used by
Paul, the words ὧν τὸ στόμα[4] ἀρᾶς καὶ πικρίας γέμει make a fitting
conclusion to the description of the sinfulness of men's speech.

Verses 15–17 are an abridgement of Isa 59.7–8a, verses which
describe the sins of the Jewish people, and which in the LXX
run as follows: οἱ δὲ πόδες αὐτῶν ἐπὶ πονηρίαν τρέχουσιν
ταχινοὶ ἐκχέαι αἷμα · καὶ οἱ διαλογισμοὶ αὐτῶν διαλογισμοὶ ἀφρόνων,
σύντριμμα καὶ ταλαιπωρία ἐν ταῖς ὁδοῖς αὐτῶν. καὶ ὁδὸν εἰρήνης
οὐκ οἴδασιν, . . . And, finally, v. 18, which is (except for the
alteration of αὐτοῦ to αὐτῶν) an exact quotation of LXX
Ps 35.2b [RV: 36.1b], concludes the third strophe and at the
same time forms a fitting climax to the whole cento. As far as

---

[1] The whole of vv. 13–18 was interpolated into the text of LXX Ps 13,
so as to follow straight on after the words quoted in v. 12. They thence
found their way into the Roman and Gallican Psalters (though in the
latter they were originally obelized). The interpolation was also included
in Coverdale's Bible and in the Great Bible, from which it was taken
over into the English Book of Common Prayer and was retained in
the 1662 revision.

[2] Cf. Jer 5.16, where the same image is used with reference to a
quiver.

[3] The Hebrew *yaḥălîqûn* conveys the idea of smooth talk, flattery.
On the form ἐδολιοῦσαν see BDF, § 84 (3).

[4] The addition of the redundant genitive pronoun αὐτῶν after στόμα
in B 33 represents assimilation to the LXX text.

the original Hebrew of Ps. 36.1 [MT: 2] is concerned, neither
the text nor the sense is certain. It is not clear whether 'my
heart' or 'his heart' should be read in the first half of the verse.
According to some scholars the verse represents sin itself as
speaking, and the second half of the verse is sin's claim that
God Himself has no regard for men's fear of Him; according
to others, the second half of the verse is a description of the
wicked. Clearly it was in this latter sense that Paul understood
it, as his use of the plural αὐτῶν indicates.

The choice and arrangement of the quotations in this cento
have been very variously explained, sometimes with much
subtlety and ingenuity. For the suggestion that the intention
was to show that sin has hold not only of every man without
exception but also of every part of the human personality
there is obviously something to be said.[1] But it is probably
wise not to look for a hard and fast pattern here. It must be
remembered that for the whole of what we have called the first
strophe Paul (or conceivably someone else before him) has kept
to Ps 14.1–3, apart from the possible trace of a reminiscence of
Eccles 7.20 in the first line: so what pattern there is within
the first strophe is anyway the psalmist's. It looks as if this
psalm-passage was chosen for the sake of its testimony to the
fact that all men without exception are sinners. It is expressed
in fairly general terms—for the most part, but not exclusively,[2]
with reference to men's relation to God. In the second strophe
three different sources have been resorted to: so here the
pattern which emerges may more fairly be attributed to the
selector. The strophe concentrates on men's speech, and the
amount devoted to this subject in relation to the length of the
whole cento is striking. Bengel observes aptly: 'Magna peccati
pars in verbis est'.[3] We may compare the stress laid on the
importance of right speaking in the Epistle of James (1.19, 26;
3.1–12). After this concentration on words the last strophe
directs attention to deeds—to the fratricidal character of
men's conduct.[4] The words σύντριμμα καὶ ταλαιπωρία ἐν ταῖς

[1] Cf. A. Feuillet, 'Le plan salvifique de Dieu d'après l'épître aux
Romains', in RB 57 (1950), p. 350. Reference may also be made to
Bengel, p. 506, where he comments: 'Genus, *non est justus*. sequuntur
partes: affectus et studia, v. 11.12.: sermo, v. 13.14.: actiones, v.
15.16.17.: gestus et nutus, v. 18.'

[2] *Pace* Leenhardt, p. 95f (Fr.: p. 55). ὁ ποιῶν χρηστότητα, in particular,
seems rather to refer to human relations.   [3] p. 506.

[4] What characterizes this strophe in contrast with the preceding one
is not the fact that it deals with 'the corruption of human relations'
(so Leenhardt, p. 96)—for these are of course also affected by the
corruption of speech—but rather the fact that it deals with deeds as
opposed to words.

ὁδοῖς αὐτῶν indicate the dire results of their activities with poetic evocativeness: wherever they go, they leave behind them a trail of destruction and misery. In this context it seems natural to understand καὶ ὁδὸν εἰρήνης οὐκ ἔγνωσαν to mean that they do not know how to go about to establish true peace among themselves, though some commentators take the reference of εἰρήνης to be rather to salvation (cf. Lk 1.79). Finally, οὐκ ἔστιν φόβος θεοῦ ἀπέναντι τῶν ὀφθαλμῶν αὐτῶν indicates the root of their evil deeds and also of their evil words—in fact, the very essence of their sinfulness. It is by his eyes that a man directs his steps. So to say that there is no fear of God[1] before his eyes is a figurative way of saying that the fear of God has no part in directing his life, that God is left out of his reckoning, that he is a practical, whether or not he is a theoretical, atheist.

19. οἴδαμεν δέ, See on 2.2.

ὅσα ὁ νόμος λέγει is naturally understood to include the quotations contained in the immediately preceding verses (vv. 10–18). Since these come from the Writings and the Prophets, and not from the Pentateuch, ὁ νόμος must be used here, as it is also in 1 Cor 14.21; Jn 10.34; 15.25, and as *tôrāh* is quite often used by the Rabbis,[2] to denote the OT as a whole.[3]

τοῖς ἐν τῷ νόμῳ λαλεῖ. For ἐν τῷ νόμῳ compare not ὑπὸ νόμον in 6.14 and 15, the sense of which is quite different, but ἐν νόμῳ in 2.12. οἱ ἐν τῷ νόμῳ are those who possess the law (cf. the negative expression τὰ μὴ νόμον ἔχοντα in 2.14), those who know it (cf. γινώσκουσιν . . . νόμον λαλῶ in 7.1). But there is no need to assume (as do many commentators) that νόμος must here have its ordinary narrower sense: here too, as in the earlier part of the sentence, it can quite well have its wider

---

[1] For the biblical teaching on the fear of God cf., e.g., Gen 22.12; 42.18; Deut 4.10; 5.29; 6.2, 13; Job 1.1; Ps 19.9; 22.23; 34.9, 11; 90.11; 111.10; 112.1; Prov 1.7; 3.7; 8.13; 9.10; 14.27; Eccles 12.13; Isa 8.12f; Jer 32.39; Mt 10.28=Lk 12.5; Acts 9.31; 10.35; 2 Cor 7.1; 1 Pet 1.17. 2.17. See also the notes on 8.15; 11.20; 13.7. See also H. Balz and G. Wanke, in *TWNT* 9, pp. 186–216.

[2] For examples see SB 2, p. 542; 3, p. 159.

[3] This has been recognized from early times. Cf., e.g., Chrysostom, col. 441: ὅτι τὴν Παλαιὰν [sc. Διαθήκην] πᾶσαν νόμον καλεῖν εἴωθεν ὁ Παῦλος. The facts that the Law is distinguished from the Prophets in v. 21 and that there is only one other place where Paul definitely uses νόμος in the wider sense are not serious objections to this interpretation here. The suggestion that ὁ νόμος means law generally, including the law of conscience, is altogether improbable. Hardly any more probable is the suggestion that ὅσα ὁ νόμος λέγει is not meant to include the preceding quotations but simply refers to the law's affirmations about the connexion between sin and punishment.

sense and denote the OT as a whole. Compare 3.2, where it
was said of the Jews that they were entrusted with τὰ λόγια
τοῦ θεοῦ. We take it then that in τοῖς ἐν τῷ νόμῳ Paul refers to
the Jews as those who possess the OT scriptures (or—less
probably—as those who possess the law in the narrower sense).
The difference between λαλεῖ here and λέγει in the earlier part
of the sentence is much the same as that between 'speaks' and
'says' in English: λέγειν is the natural word to use where the
thought is concentrated on the substance of what is said,
whereas λαλεῖν draws attention to the act of speaking. The
question which remains to be answered is: What does Paul
mean when he claims that all the things which Scripture says
are spoken to the Jews? Aquinas, noting that a good deal in
the OT concerns other nations, understands Paul to mean that
whatever the OT says *indeterminate*, i.e., without explicit
indication of its reference, concerns the Jews.[1] But perhaps we
should rather take Paul's meaning to be that everything which
the OT says (including the things which are said about
Gentiles) is indeed addressed in the first instance to the Jews
and is intended for their instruction, so that, so far from
imagining themselves excepted from its condemnations of
human sinfulness, they ought to accept them as applying first
and foremost to themselves.

ἵνα πᾶν στόμα φραγῇ καὶ ὑπόδικος γένηται πᾶς ὁ κόσμος τῷ θεῷ
should probably be understood as final (one purpose which
God has in directing His word to His own people is that
every human mouth . . .), though some[2] explain it as consecutive. The emphatic πᾶν and πᾶς (cf. the οὐ . . . πᾶσα of
the following verse) are no reason at all for thinking that by
τοῖς ἐν τῷ νόμῳ Paul did not mean the Jews.[3] Paul's thought
is that, with the proof that the Jews (the people who might
seem to have reason to regard themselves as an exception)
are in fact no exception, the proof that the entire human race
lies under God's judgment is finally completed. If the Jews are
shown by Scripture to be ὑφ' ἁμαρτίαν, there is no question of
any Gentile's not being ὑφ' ἁμαρτίαν. The words στόμα φραγῇ[4]
evoke the picture of the defendant in court, who, given the
opportunity to speak in his own defence, is speechless because

[1] p. 51 (293).
[2] e.g. Lagrange, p. 71.
[3] *Pace* Murray 1, p. 106.
[4] The expression στόμα φράσσειν occurs also in Heb 11.33. Cf. the use
of ἀποφράσσειν in 1 Macc 9.55, and of ἐμφράσσειν in the LXX version of
Job 5.16; Ps 63.11 [LXX: 62.12]; 107 [LXX: 106].42, and in Dan (Th)
6.23 Cf. also. the references in Judg 18.19; Job 21.5; 29.9; 40.4 to laying
the hand on the mouth.

of the weight of the evidence which has been brought against him and (as Calvin puts it)[1] 'without saying a word awaits his condemnation'. The word ὑπόδικος presents a certain amount of difficulty. It is used in extra-biblical Greek to describe someone who is guilty in the sense of having offended against the law and so made himself liable to prosecution and punishment. A dative associated with it may denote either the judicial authority in relation to which one is ὑπόδικος, or—and this is more common—the injured party with a right to satisfaction. The word occurs in the NT only here. In this case it is more likely that the thought expressed by the dative is that God is the judicial authority concerned than that He is the injured party. It is difficult to determine the exact force of ὑπόδικος τῷ θεῷ; but, in view of the way in which ὑπόδικος γένηται πᾶς ὁ κόσμος τῷ θεῷ is associated with πᾶν στόμα φραγῇ, it would seem that 'answerable to God' (suggested by Sanday and Headlam),[2] the NEB rendering 'exposed to the judgement of God', and Barrett's 'brought to trial before God',[3] on the one hand, say too little, while, on the other hand, Michel's assertion that ὑπόδικος is equivalent to κατάκριτος[4] says too much. The picture intended to be evoked by ὑπόδικος . . . τῷ θεῷ in this context is probably that of men standing at God's bar, their guilt proven beyond all possibility of doubt, awaiting God's sentence of condemnation.[5] ὁ κόσμος here as in v. 6 means 'the world of men', 'mankind'.

20. διότι (it also occurs in 1.19, 21; 8.7, 21) is better understood here as equivalent to ὅτι meaning 'for' than as equivalent to ὅτι meaning 'because'.[6] In the present verse it introduces a confirmation from Scripture of what has just been said in v. 19. Ps 143.2b is echoed, though it is to be noted that there is no γέγραπται here to indicate expressly that the OT is being quoted.[7]

ἐξ ἔργων νόμου is not part of the quotation but is Paul's own addition. It clarifies the psalmist's statement, the intention of which was not to deny altogether the possibility of justification, but only (as is suggested by v. 2a) to deny the possibility of a man's being justified on the basis of his deserts. We have already had the phrase τὸ ἔργον τοῦ νόμου in 2.15.

[1] p. 68.
[2] p. 80.
[3] p. 66.
[4] p. 101.
[5] On ὑπόδικος see further C. Maurer, in *TWNT* 8, pp. 556–8.
[6] *Pace* Lagrange, p. 71. On the distinction see BDF, § 456 (1).
[7] Cf. Gal 2.16, where also the same psalm-verse is echoed without any formula of quotation.

The plural ἔργα νόμου is also used in v. 28, and in Gal 2.16 (three times); 3.2, 5, 10: in all the Galatians occurrences, as here, the expression used is ἐξ ἔργων νόμου. According to Barrett, ἔργα νόμου 'are not good works simply, but works done in obedience to the law and *regarded as*, in themselves, a means of justification'.[1] But (whatever may be the truth with regard to Gal 3.2, 5, 10) there seems to be no compelling reason for assuming that ἔργα νόμου has here the pejorative sense of 'works . . . *regarded as*, in themselves, a means of justification'. The point Paul is making here is surely not that no flesh will be justified in God's sight on the ground of works regarded as in themselves a means of justification (i.e. works done in a legalistic spirit), but that no flesh will be justified in God's sight on the ground of works—that is, no man will earn justification by his obedience to God's requirements. The reason why this is so is that ἔργα νόμου in the sense of such a perfect obedience as would merit justification are not forthcoming.[2] That this is the thought is confirmed by the content of the latter part of the verse. See my *On Romans*, 1998, pp. 1–14.

οὐ δικαιωθήσεται πᾶσα σάρξ ἐνώπιον αὐτοῦ. The LXX version of Ps 143 [LXX: 142].2b runs as follows ὅτι οὐ δικαιωθήσεται ἐνώπιόν σου πᾶς ζῶν (MT: kî lōʼ yiṣdaḳ lᵉpānêḵā ḳol ḥāy). The sentence contains two Hebraisms, the use of οὐ . . . πᾶς in the sense of οὐδείς[3] and the use of σάρξ in the sense of ἄνθρωποι. The second is due to Paul who has substituted πᾶσα σάρξ for the πᾶς ζῶν of the LXX. The same variation is to be found in Gal 2.16 too. Very probably it is due to Paul's quoting from memory—or perhaps we should rather say 'echoing' the scriptural text. bāśār is of course frequently used in the OT to denote man in his frailty and mortality in contrast with God (e.g. Gen 6.3; 2 Chron 32.8; Job 10.4; Ps 78.39; Jer 17.5), and kol bāśār is often used with the meaning 'all mankind' (e.g. Gen 6.12, 13; Ps 145.21; Isa 40.5, 6).

διὰ γὰρ νόμου ἐπίγνωσις ἁμαρτίας[4] is added in support (γάρ)

---

[1] p. 70 (cf. Michel, p. 101: 'Die ἔργα νόμου sind hier die Werke, die der Mensch tut, um durch Erfüllung eines Gebotes vor Gott gerecht zu werden').

[2] And the ἔργα νόμου which *are* forthcoming where the promise of Jer 31.33 is being fulfilled (see on 2.15), that is, ἔργα νόμου in the sense of faith and the true, though imperfect, works of obedience in which it expresses itself—these, of course, while accepted by God, constitute no claim to justification.

[3] See BDF, § 302 (1).

[4] In this connexion it is interesting to compare the Hellenistic aphorism, ἀρχὴ σωτηρίας γνῶσις ἁμαρτήματος (cf. Seneca, *Ep. mor.* 28: 'Initium est salutis notitia peccati. Egregie mihi hoc dixisse videtur

of what has just been said. So far from its being true that there are men who so adequately fulfil the law's requirements as to earn justification for themselves, the truth is rather that the condition of all men is such that the primary effect of the law in relation to them is to show up their sin as sin and themselves as sinners.[1]

IV. 2. THE MANIFESTATION OF THE RIGHTEOUSNESS WHICH IS FROM GOD IN THE GOSPEL EVENTS (3.21–26)

This short section is, as has already been indicated, the centre and heart of the main division to which it belongs. We may go farther and say that it is the centre and heart of the whole of Rom 1.16b–15.13. It stands out by reason of the distinctiveness of its style: it reads like a solemn proclamation.[2] Notable, in particular, are the emphatic 'But now' followed by the perfect tense, the fewness of the verbs especially in the latter part of the section,[3] the impressive repetition of key-phrases,[4] the striking use of prepositional phrases placed one after the other without connexion.[5] It stands out much more of course by virtue of its content; for it proclaims the fact that the one decisive, once for all, redemptive act of God, the revelation both of the righteousness which is from God and also of the wrath of God against human sin, the once for all revelation which is the basis of the continuing revelation of the righteousness (1.17) and of the wrath (1.18) of God in the preaching of the gospel, has now taken place. It shows that the heart of the gospel preached by Paul is a series of events in the

Epicurus. Nam qui peccare se nescit, corrigi non vult; deprehendas te oportet antequam emendes'), though Pallis's suggestion (p. 65) that its influence is to be seen in Paul's statement is not particularly likely.

[1] Bultmann's confident assertion that 'this sentence (coming after vv. 10–19) does not, of course, mean that *through the Law* man is led to knowledge of what sin is, but does mean that by it he is *led into sinning*' (*Theology* 1, p. 264) is improbable; for there is no suggestion at all in this context of the thought of the law as ἀφορμή, which Paul introduces in 7.5, 7–11. It is a mistake to read into ἐπίγνωσις here a special meaning which is often thought to attach—but more probably does not—to the use of γινώσκειν and εἰδέναι in 7.7.

[2] Cf. Michel, p. 103, who speaks of its style as being 'proklamatorisch', and compares that of 1 Cor 11.24f.

[3] There are only five finite verbs in the six verses, and four of them are in the first three, προέθετο standing alone in vv. 24–26.

[4] δικαιοσύνη θεοῦ in vv. 21 and 22, and εἰς (πρὸς τὴν) ἔνδειξιν τῆς δικαιοσύνης αὐτοῦ in vv. 25 and 26.

[5] In v. 25f we have διὰ . . . ἐν . . . εἰς . . . διὰ . . . ἐν . . . πρὸς . . . ἐν . . εἰς . . .

past (not just the crucifixion of Christ—for the Cross by itself would have been no saving act of God—but the crucifixion together with the resurrection and exaltation of the Crucified), a series of events which is *the* Event of history, an act which as the decisive act of God is altogether effective and irreversible. It attests the fact that what we have to do with in the gift of righteousness, with which Romans is concerned, is nothing less than God's costly forgiveness, which, whereas forgiveness on cheaper terms would have meant God's abandonment of His faithful love for man and the annihilation of man's real dignity as His morally accountable creature, is altogether worthy of the righteous, loving, faithful God, who does not insult or mock His creature man by pretending that his sin does not matter, but rather Himself bears the full cost of forgiving it right-eously—lovingly.[1]

---

[1] On the grounds that ἱλαστήριον occurs only here in Paul's letters, that elsewhere, apart from places where traditional material is being used (Rom 5.9; 1 Cor 10.16; 11.25, 27), Paul refers not to Christ's blood but to His cross, and that the idea of the divine righteousness as requiring the expiation of former sins is nowhere else found in Paul's writings, Bultmann has argued (*Theology* 1, p. 46) that 3.24f should be recognized as a pre-Pauline formula which Paul has taken over, adding δωρεὰν τῇ αὐτοῦ χάριτι and διὰ πίστεως. Käsemann has attempted in his short study, 'Zum Verständnis von Römer 3.24–26' (*Versuche* 1, pp. 96–100) to improve on Bultmann's arguments. He draws attention to the absence of anything in v. 24 to correspond to the πάντες of v. 23; the terminology of v. 24f (in addition to the particulars cited by Bultmann, he mentions πάρεσις, προγεγονότα ἁμαρτήματα, προτίθεσθαι used —so he maintains—in the sense 'set forth publicly', and ἀπολύτρωσις used of the already accomplished redemption as, at the least, not characteristic of Paul); the overladen style with its genitival construc-tions and prepositional connexions; and the substantial divergence which he sees between the formally parallel clauses εἰς ἔνδειξιν . . . τοῦ θεοῦ and πρὸς τὴν ἔνδειξιν . . . τῷ καιρῷ (he understands δικαιοσύνη in v. 25 to denote a divine attribute but in v. 26 God's eschatological saving action). According to Käsemann, Paul has made use of a Jewish-Christian formula which he valued because it spoke of the salvation-event (*Heilsereignis*) in terms of justification brought about through Christ's death, but has corrected it not only by inserting δωρεὰν τῇ αὐτοῦ χάριτι and διὰ πίστεως, but also by adding a corrective parallel to v. 25b in the words πρὸς τὴν ἔνδειξιν τῆς δικαιοσύνης αὐτοῦ ἐν τῷ νῦν καιρῷ, and then binding together these two clauses (vv. 25b and 26a) with their parallel structures but basically different view-points by means of v. 26b. But to accept Käsemann's account of these verses requires a very great deal of credulity. In the construction of a paragraph as vital and central to his whole argument as this paragraph is, Paul is scarcely likely to have gone to work in the way Käsemann would have us envisage. It is very much more probable that these verses are Paul's own independent and careful composition reflecting his own preaching and thinking (cf. Cambier, *L'Évangile de Dieu*, p. 78f), and that the overladen style is the result, not of the incorporation of a *Vorlage* and the need to provide

²¹But now God's righteousness, attested by the law and the prophets, has been manifested apart from the law, ²²namely, that righteousness of God which is through faith in Jesus Christ for all who believe. For there is no distinction; ²³for all have sinned and lack the glory of God, ²⁴being justified freely by his grace through the redemption *accomplished* in Christ Jesus; ²⁵whom God purposed to be by the shedding of his blood a propitiatory sacrifice, *the benefit to be appropriated* by faith, in order to prove his righteousness (*this was necessary* on account of the overlooking of past sins ²⁶in God's forbearance), in order, *I say,* to prove his righteousness in the present time, so that he might be righteous even in justifying the man who believes in Jesus.

21. Nυνὶ δέ. In view of the presence of πεφανέρωται the contention of some commentators that νυνί has a purely logical force here must surely be rejected, and its temporal significance firmly maintained. It emphasizes the fact that the contrast marked by δέ, so far from being merely a contrast between two ideas, that of justification ἐξ ἔργων νόμου and that of justification χωρὶς νόμου, is a contrast between the impossibility of justification by works, on the one hand, and, on the other hand, the *fact* that in the recent past a decisive event has taken place, by which a justification which is God's free gift πεφανέρωται, and now is πεφανερωμένη. It is not unfair to claim that this νυνί points to the decisiveness for faith of the gospel events in their objectiveness as events which took place at a particular time in the past and are quite independent of, and distinct from, the response of men to them.[1]

χωρὶς νόμου is an adverbial phrase modifying πεφανέρωται. In 7.8 and 9 it is used to indicate the law's absence; but it can scarcely have that meaning here, since it is clear that Paul did not think that the law was absent at the time of the manifestation referred to—on the contrary, passages like Gal 3.13 and 4.4 suggest that he thought that it was deeply involved in the gospel events. The words are most naturally understood in relation to ἐξ ἔργων νόμου and διὰ νόμου in v. 20—as indicating that the δικαιοσύνη θεοῦ of which vv. 21 and 22 speak is manifest as something which has not been earned by men's fulfilment of the law. In other words, χωρὶς νόμου here is equivalent in significance to χωρὶς ἔργων νόμου in v. 28 and χωρὶς ἔργων in 4.6. To appeal to these words as evidence that Paul regarded the law as superseded and set aside by the gospel as something now out of date and irrelevant is surely perverse.

it with correctives, but of the intrinsic difficulty of interpreting the Cross at all adequately and perhaps also, in part, of the natural tendency to fall into a more or less liturgical style when speaking of so solemn a matter.

[1] Cf. O. Cullmann, *Salvation in History*, Eng. tr., London, 1967, p. 322.

δικαιοσύνη θεοῦ is no doubt to be understood both here and in v. 22 in the same sense as it has in 1.17, that is, as meaning a status of righteousness before God which is God's gift.

πεφανέρωται. In 1.17 the present indicative passive of ἀποκαλύπτειν was used, because the reference was to the revelation taking place in the on-going preaching of the gospel: here the use of a past tense indicates that the thought is of the revelation in the gospel events themselves, the perfect being preferred to the aorist because that which was made manifest in those events has ever since remained manifest. The verb φανεροῦν (in Romans also in 1.19 and 16.26) is more or less synonymous with ἀποκαλύπτειν.[1] The contrast between two periods of time which is implied is the contrast between the period before, and the period after, the decisive manifestation of δικαιοσύνη θεοῦ: it is important in interpreting this verse to beware of the danger (to which some commentators have succumbed) of sliding over inadvertently from this contrast to some other contrast quite foreign to Paul's meaning.

μαρτυρουμένη ὑπὸ τοῦ νόμου καὶ τῶν προφητῶν is formally a statement about δικαιοσύνη θεοῦ, but in fact it is both this and also at the same time a statement about the OT;[2] for it affirms not only that the righteousness which is God's gift has the attestation of the OT or—to put it otherwise —that the gospel is continuous with the OT, but also that the OT is properly understood as witness to this righteousness —in other words, to the gospel, to Jesus Christ. The thought expressed here is to be found again and again in Romans (cf., e.g., 1.2; the whole of chapter 4; 9.25–33; 10.6–13, which is especially interesting in this connexion; 10.16–21; 11.1–10, 26–29; 15.8–12), though Paul nowhere else uses μαρτυρεῖν to express it.[3] That this attestation of the gospel by the OT is of

---

[1] It is probably a post-classical word (for the occurrence in Herodotus 6.122 is textually doubtful), though the adjective φανερός is of course classical. In the NT it is used more frequently than ἀποκαλύπτειν (49 occurrences as against 26), though the noun φανέρωσις occurs only twice as against 19 occurrences of ἀποκάλυψις. It is used both with reference to Christ's manifestation in His historical life and also with reference to His final coming. See further R. Bultmann and D. Lührmann, in *TWNT* 9, pp. 4–7.

[2] For the use of this twofold designation for the OT as a whole cf., e.g., Mt 5.17; 7.12; 22.40; Acts 24.14; 28.23; and see further SB 1, p. 240; 3, p. 164f.

[3] Paul in fact does not use μαρτυρεῖν often (it occurs only eight times in the whole Pauline corpus). By contrast it occurs thirty-three times in Jn. It is used in connexion with the witness of the OT to Christ in Jn 5.39 (cf. also its frequent use in connexion with John the Baptist,

fundamental importance for Paul is indicated by the solemn
way in which he insists on it here in what is one of the great
hinge-sentences on which the argument of the epistle turns.
(See, further, the essay on the theology of Romans in volume
2.)

22. δικαιοσύνη δὲ θεοῦ διὰ πίστεως ['Ιησοῦ] Χριστοῦ, εἰς
πάντας τοὺς πιστεύοντας. The δέ introduces a closer definition,
as in 9.30; 1 Cor 2.6; Gal 2.2; Phil 2.8: the δικαιοσύνη θεοῦ
of which Paul is speaking is through faith in Christ, and
further, it is for all who believe. The subject is repeated for
the sake of clarity (cf. the repetition of the object in 9.30 and
1 Cor 2.6). διὰ πίστεως ['Ιησοῦ] Χριστοῦ defines the righteousness in question as that which is received by means of faith in
Christ (cf. Phil 3.9: . . . μὴ ἔχων ἐμὴν δικαιοσύνην τὴν ἐκ νόμου,
ἀλλὰ τὴν διὰ πίστεως Χριστοῦ . . .). For πίστις see on 1.5, 16, 17.
The genitive Χριστοῦ[1] expresses the object of faith (cf. v. 26;
and also Mk 11.22; Acts 3.16; Gal 2.16 (twice), 20; 3.22; Eph
3.12; Phil 3.9; Col 2.12).[2] Here for the first time in the epistle
Christ is explicitly referred to as the object of faith. εἰς πάντας
τοὺς πιστεύοντας makes the point that the δικαιοσύνη θεοῦ is
for *all* who believe: compare παντὶ τῷ πιστεύοντι,'Ιουδαίῳ τε . . .
καὶ"Ελληνι in 1.16.[3] The originality of the words καὶ ἐπὶ πάντας
attested by western and Byzantine authorities after εἰς πάντας
is maintained by Nygren on the ground of its correspondence
to the ἐπὶ πᾶσαν ἀσέβειαν καὶ ἀδικίαν ἀνθρώπων of 1.18;[4] but his
argument is hardly convincing, and it seems more likely that
the longer reading is simply a conflation of an original εἰς πάντας
with a variant ἐπὶ πάντας which is represented by the 'super
omnes' of some Vulgate MSS.

οὐ γάρ ἐστιν διαστολή (cf 10.12a: οὐ γάρ ἐστιν διαστολὴ
'Ιουδαίου τε καὶ "Ελληνος) supports πάντας; but in its turn it is
explained and qualified by the two following verses, in the
light of which Michel's comment to the effect that the abolition
of distinction to which Paul refers includes the abolition

in whose witness that of the OT may in a sense be said to be summed
up—a theological truth to which the Crucifixion of the Isenheim altar-
piece of Grünewald has given eloquent expression).
[1] 'Ιησοῦ is omitted by B and by Marcion. It is possible—it is scarcely
justified to put it more strongly—it is not original here. [N[26] omits [ ].]
[2] The suggestion that it should be understood as subjective (J. Haussleiter,
'Der Glaube Jesu Christi und der christliche Glaube: ein Beitrag zur
Erklärung des Römerbriefes', in *NKZ* 2 (1891), pp. 109–45 and 205–30) is, in
spite of recent support, unconvincing. See my *On Romans*, 1998, pp. 81–97.
[3] That this language is misunderstood if it is taken to imply that faith is a
prior condition we have already seen (see notes on 1.16b).
[4] pp. 150–52.

of the privilege of Israel¹ may be seen to say too much. **23** and **24** indicate the scope of v. 22b. It is not to be understood as a denial of the truth affirmed in v. 2 (cf. 9.4f; 11.17f, 28f; and also the πρῶτον in 1.16), but only as a denial that there is any distinction in respect of the δικαιοσύνη θεοῦ. All alike may receive this righteousness by faith and none has any claim to it on the ground of merit; for all alike—Jews as well as Gentiles—have sinned, and receive righteousness as a free gift altogether undeserved.

πάντες continues the emphasis on universality which has already been noted (vv. 9, 10, 11, 12, 19, 20, 22), and this verse (23) as a whole sums up the conclusion to the argument of 1.18–3.20.²

ἥμαρτον: 'have sinned'. For the use of the aorist here see on 2.12.

ὑστεροῦνται τῆς δόξης τοῦ θεοῦ. Taken by itself, ἡ δόξα τοῦ θεοῦ could, of course, mean 'the approbation of God', as it does in Jn 12.43 (cf. 5.44), and it is so understood here by some.³ But it is more probable that the reference is to that share in the divine glory, which, according to Jewish thought,⁴ man possessed before he fell away from his true relationship to God and which will be restored in the eschatological future (cf. 5.2; 8.18, 21, 30). As a result of sin all men lack⁵ this illumination by the divine glory. Here both the tense of the verb and the fact that its subject is πάντες should be noted. They clearly imply that not only all other men but also all believers still lack this 'glory of God'. Attempts to soften this or to explain it away have the disastrous effect of

¹ p. 105. His words are: 'Der Allgemeinheit der Knechtschaft (Röm 3.9) tritt die Allgemeinheit des Glaubens gegenüber; aber in diesem Fall bedeutet Allgemeinheit Aufhebung der Unterschiede, auch Aufhebung des Vorrechts Israels'. Contrast the carefully qualified statement of Sanday and Headlam, p. 84: 'The Jew has (in this respect) no real advantage over the Gentile; both alike need a righteousness which is not their own; and to both it is offered on the same terms'.

² For the summing up of the preceding section at the beginning of a new section cf. 5.1 and 8.1.

³ e.g. Calvin, p. 74; Denney, p. 610.

⁴ Cf. *Gen R.* 12.5 (on 2.4); 3 Bar. 4.16 ('. . . . as Adam . . . was divested of the glory of God . . .'); Apoc. Mos. 21.6 ('And to me he saith, "O wicked woman! what have I done to thee that thou hast deprived me of the glory of God?" ').

⁵ ὑστερεῖν means 'be behind', 'come too late', so 'fail to obtain', 'lack', also 'be inferior to' and 'fail' or 'be wanting'. The passive (so e.g. Bauer s.v., but LSJ regards these occurrences as middle, except for those which are aorist, and similarly Sanday and Headlam, p. 84) is also used with the meanings 'suffer want' and 'lack'. The other Pauline occurrences are 1 Cor 1.7; 8.8; 12.24; 2 Cor 11.5, 9; 12.11; Phil 4.12.

obscuring the transcendent majesty of the glory which is yet
to be ours. This is not to deny that there is a relative glory
which already illumines the lives of believers—Paul can speak
elsewhere of their being transformed 'from glory to glory'
(2 Cor 3.18); but the decisiveness of the distinction between
these two glories should not be blurred.[1]

There has been a good deal of discussion of the relation of
v. 24 to its context. The difficulty of the explanation which
lies nearest to hand, namely, that δικαιούμενοι is dependent on
the πάντες of v. 23, is that, on this view, what seems to be a
substantial contribution to the thought of the paragraph as
a whole (if ὅν in v. 25 is understood as introducing an ordinary
relative clause, it actually includes the whole of vv. 24–26) is
formally part of the explanation of οὐ γάρ ἐστιν διαστολή, which
itself supports the πάντας of v. 22a. The various possibilities,
as Sanday and Headlam see them,[2] may be set out as follows:
(i) to understand v. 24 to 'mark a detail in, or assign a proof of,
the condition described by ὑστεροῦνται'; (ii) to understand
ὑστεροῦνται . . . δικαιούμενοι as equivalent to ὑστεροῦνται . . . καὶ
δικαιοῦνται or to ὑστερούμενοι δικαιοῦνται; (iii) to take δικαιούμενοι
as the beginning of a new and independent sentence; (iv) to
regard vv. 22b–23 as practically a parenthesis and to understand δικαιούμενοι to refer to πάντας τοὺς πιστεύοντας in v. 22a,
though put in the nominative under the influence of the πάντες
in v. 23. Sanday and Headlam and also a good many others
favour (iv), and it certainly has attractions. But the analysis
of possibilities reproduced above is perhaps rather too mechanical. It may be suggested that the best solution is to take
v. 24 as dependent on the πάντες of v. 23 (cf. (i) above), and to
understand it to be adding (and this is rather different from
(i)) an indication, in further explanation of οὐ γάρ ἐστιν
διαστολή, of what is, in view of what has already been said in
vv. 21–22a, the other side of the picture presented in v. 23;
but at the same time to recognize that in filling out the
explanation of v. 22b Paul has, as a matter of fact, also made a
substantial addition to the treatment of the main theme of
the paragraph.

The verb δικαιοῦν (it has already been used in 2.13; 3.4 and
20) is here used for the first time in Romans 'directly and
positively in reference to what is the leading theme of this
epistle'.[3] For its meaning see on δικαιοσύνη θεοῦ in 1.17.

δωρεάν (the accusative of δωρεά used as an adverb)

[1] See also on 5.2; 8.18, 21, 30.
[2] p. 85.
[3] Murray I, p. 114.

corresponds to the Hebrew *ḥinnām*. Found as early as the fifth century B.C., it occurs in the NT nine times (in addition to the present instance, Mt 10.8 (twice); Jn 15.25; 2 Cor 11.7; Gal 2.21; 2 Th 3.8; Rev 21.6; 22.17). It describes here the manner of their justification as that of a free gift, gratis.

τῇ αὐτοῦ χάριτι points to the origin of their justification in the undeserved love of God. Thus δωρεάν and τῇ αὐτοῦ χάριτι support and confirm each other. On χάρις see on 1.7.

The interpretation of διὰ τῆς ἀπολυτρώσεως is controversial. While some insist that the thought of a λύτρον, a ransom paid, is present in the word ἀπολύτρωσις here,[1] others maintain that it means simply 'deliverance', 'emancipation', without any reference to the payment of a ransom.[2] But in this matter an absolutely confident assertion of either view can hardly be justified; for, on the one hand, the possibility that Paul used ἀπολύτρωσις here without any thought of a ransom paid cannot be ruled out in the face of the evidence of the LXX's use of λυτροῦσθαι and other derivatives of λύτρον;[3] and, on the other hand, in view of the fact that 'in the use of the word λύτρον and its derivatives in profane Greek literature

---

[1] e.g. Sanday and Headlam, p. 86; Lagrange, p. 74; B. B. Warfield, 'The New Testament Terminology of Redemption', in *PTR* 15 (1917), pp. 201–49; L. Morris, *The Apostolic Preaching of the Cross*, London, 1955; Murray I, p. 115f. Barrett, p. 76, inclines to the view that the word 'has not completely lost its original sense of "ransoming", emancipation by the payment of a price'. (That the ransom—if the idea of ransom is present—is not thought of as paid to the devil of course goes without saying.)

[2] e.g. F. Büchsel, in *TWNT* 4, p. 357f; Cambier, *L'Évangile de Dieu* I, pp. 84ff; Hill, *GWHM*, pp. 49ff (though pp. 75–76 seem to show a certain amount of hesitation).

[3] In most of its occurrences in the LXX λυτροῦσθαι represents either *g'l* or *pdh*, the former of which denotes primarily the exercise of the next of kin's rights, whether in avenging blood or, more often, in the redemption of alienated property or of kinsmen who have been enslaved, while the latter is used of the redemption of the firstborn and of a man's payment of a ransom to redeem his own life that is forfeit. Both these Hebrew verbs came to be used—and so λυτροῦσθαι also is used— metaphorically of deliverance from various distresses and dangers, as, e.g., from a wild beast, from death, and, above all, of God's deliverance of Israel from Egyptian bondage and from Babylonian exile. In these instances—and there are many of them—there is no question of the payment of a ransom (the suggestion, made by B. F. Westcott in his *Commentary on the Epistle to the Hebrews*, London, ³1903, p. 296, that the idea of the ransom paid is preserved in these instances in the thought of the effort expended, or of the love or self-sacrifice involved, in the action, is hardly to be accepted). That Paul should use ἀπολύτρωσις in a sense in which several λύτρον-words are used in the LXX would be natural enough, and natural too for him to see a parallel between the act of liberation accomplished by God in Christ and the act of liberation by which God had set His people free from slavery in Egypt.

there is a marked consistency in the retention and expression
of the ransom idea',[1] the presence of the ransom idea also in a
considerable number of the occurrences of these words in the
LXX, the fact that the use of ἀπολύτρωσις in connexion with
the manumission of slaves (in which a payment was involved)
must have been familiar to many of Paul's readers,[2] the
rareness of this particular word in the LXX (it occurs only
once—in Dan 4.34), the references in 1 Cor 6.20 and 7.23 to
Christians as having been bought with a price (cf. Gal 3.13;
4.5),[3] and the presence in the NT of Mk 10.45 = Mt 20.28;
Acts 20.28; 1 Tim 2.6; 1 Pet 1.18f; 2 Pet 2.1; Rev 5.9, the
possibility that Paul did have in mind the thought of a ransom
paid, when he used ἀπολύτρωσις here, cannot be excluded
either.[4] We must therefore leave this question open. (As a
translation of ἀπολύτρωσις here the traditional word 'redemption' seems most appropriate: it is preferable to such words as
'deliverance' and 'ransoming' which would have the effect of
foreclosing the issue one way or the other, since, when used in
a theological context, it can, but does not necessarily, suggest
the thought of a payment's being made.) What can be said
with confidence about διὰ τῆς ἀπολυτρώσεως is that it indicates
that the believer's righteous status has been brought about by
God by means of a definite and decisive[5] action on His own

[1] Hill, GWHM, p. 52.

[2] This is clearly not a case where we are forced (as we are with
δικαιοῦν) to understand Paul's use of a word according to its use in the
LXX because only by so doing can we give it any satisfactory sense.

[3] Cambier's attempt to dispose of this evidence (op. cit., p. 87) is
hardly convincing.

[4] The other nine occurrences of ἀπολύτρωσις in the NT (8.23; Lk 21.28;
1 Cor 1.30; Eph 1.7, 14; 4.30; Col. 1.14; Heb 9.15; 11.35) are naturally
often appealed to by those who would settle this issue; but they cannot
decide it.

[5] That Paul intended to indicate something decisive is of course
clear, irrespective of the amount of weight we give to Chrysostom's
distinction between ἀπολύτρωσις and λύτρωσις (he comments (col. 444)
with reference to the use of the former word here: Καὶ οὐχ ἁπλῶς
εἶπε "λυτρώσεως" ἀλλ', "ἀπολυτρώσεως", ὡς μηκέτι ἡμᾶς ἐπανελθεῖν πάλιν ἐπὶ
τὴν αὐτὴν δουλείαν). Hill's observation (p. 71) about the meaning of this
comment of Chrysostom's would appear to be a guess on the basis of
an isolated quotation. But Chrysostom refers a number of times to
Paul's use of ἀπο-compounds. In his comment on ἀποστυγοῦντες in 12.9
he mentions ἀπολύτρωσις along with other examples: Σφόδρα μισοῦντες.
Τὸ γὰρ "ἀπὸ" τοῦτο πολλαχοῦ ἐπιτάσεώς ἐστι παρ' αὐτῷ · ὡς ὅταν λέγῃ
"ἀποκαραδοκίαν", καὶ "ἀπεκδεχόμενοι", καὶ "ἀπολύτρωσιν". See also on 8.19,
23; 10.20. Büchsel's statement (TWNT 4, p. 354) to the effect that the
use of ἀπολύτρωσις in preference to λύτρωσις in the NT is to be explained
as due simply to the liking of Hellenistic Greek for compounds should,
in our judgment, be regarded with some reserve, at any rate as far as
Paul is concerned.

part. Something more of the nature and significance of that action is disclosed in the following four words and also in verses 25 and 26; but it is already clear from the fact that διὰ τῆς ἀπολυτρώσεως is linked with δικαιούμενοι that the slavery from which this action of God has redeemed must be the slavery of sin in the sense of subjection to sin's effects, that is, to God's condemnation, God's wrath, the condition of having an unrighteous status before Him.

τῆς ἐν Χριστῷ Ἰησοῦ is naturally explained as intended to indicate that it was in and through[1] Christ Jesus, that is, in and through His Person and Work, that God accomplished His redeeming action. The thought is of the accomplishment of the redeeming action in the past, not of the availability of redemption in the present through union with Christ. Paul perhaps used ἐν Χριστῷ Ἰησοῦ (which, along with ἐν Χριστῷ, he seems to have used normally with reference to the glorified Christ) rather than ἐν Ἰησοῦ Χριστῷ or ἐν Ἰησοῦ, because the action in question included not only the passion and death of Jesus Christ but also their sealing by His resurrection and ascension. We may compare the use of ἐν Χριστῷ Ἰησοῦ in 8.2 (see notes on that verse).

The whole of 25 and 26 is a single relative clause depending on Χριστῷ Ἰησοῦ in v. 24. It consists of a main element followed by three formulations equivalent to final clauses which together serve to clarify the key-word ἱλαστήριον.

ὃν προέθετο ὁ θεός. The verb προτιθέναι occurs only three times in the NT (in 1.13, here, and in Eph 1.9). The main meanings which it can have, when used in the middle (as it is in all its NT occurrences), are: (i) 'propose to oneself', 'purpose'; (ii) 'set forth publicly', 'display'.[2] Both these possibilities with regard to προέθετο have found support from early times. Sanday and Headlam argued that (ii) should be preferred on the ground that the immediate context is 'full of terms denoting publicity (πεφανέρωται, εἰς ἔνδειξιν, πρὸς τὴν ἔνδειξιν)', and compared Gal 3.1 (. . . οἷς κατ᾽ ὀφθαλμοὺς Ἰησοῦς Χριστὸς προεγράφη ἐσταυρωμένος);[3] and this view is widely favoured.[4] It is sometimes even taken for granted without

___

[1] ἐν may be explained as instrumental (cf. the ἐν in v. 25).

[2] Bauer gives only these two meanings for the middle as used in early Christian literature, though he mentions as of interest in connexion with this verse the fact that there is some evidence that at least the active could have the sense 'offer (sc. a sacrifice)': LSJ indicates a rather greater variety of meanings for the middle in the much wider range of Greek with which it is concerned.

[3] p. 87.

[4] e.g. Nygren, p. 158f; Michel, p. 107; Barrett, p. 77 (though with some tentative inclination to take the meaning to be 'set forth as a

discussion. But there are strong reasons for preferring (i). In both its other NT occurrences—and one of them is in this epistle (1.13)—προτίθεσθαι definitely means 'purpose'; and 'purpose' is also the meaning of the cognate noun πρόθεσις in eight of its twelve occurrences in the NT (in the others it is used with reference to the shewbread).[1] In 8.28 and 9.11 πρόθεσις is used of God's gracious purpose of election. Support for the meaning 'purpose' for προέθετο here is to be found in the comments of Origen,[2] Ambrosiaster,[3] and Chrysostom.[4] It is true that the double accusative is difficult on this view; but a parallel construction with προορίζειν, a verb of similar meaning, is to be seen in 8.29, and it is significant that this difficulty did not weigh with Origen and Chrysostom. The meaning 'purpose' has been accepted in modern times by, *inter al.*, J. B. Lightfoot, p. 271; Lagrange, p. 75; Cambier, *L'Évangile de Dieu*, p. 91; NEB ('designed'); JB ('appointed').[5] There is, in our view, little doubt that 'purposed' should be preferred to 'set forth publicly'. In addition to what has already been said in its favour, it may further be suggested that it makes rather better theological sense in the context; for, true though it is that the idea of publicity is present in the context, v. 26b indicates Paul's concern with something even more important than men's being made aware of God's righteousness, namely, God's being righteous. A reference to God's eternal purpose strikes us as even more apposite at this point than a reference to the fact that the Cross was something accomplished in the sight of men. Chrysostom's comment (Δηλῶν δὲ πάλιν οὐ νεώτερον τοῦτο ὂν οὐδὲ καινόν, φησί,

sacrifice'); Kuss, p. 155; Bruce, p. 107. This interpretation is to be found already in Pelagius, who comments: '*Quem proposuit deus*. In promptu ante oculos omnium posuit, ut qui redemi uult accedat' (p. 33).

[1] On πρόθεσις see notes on 8.28.

[2] Scherer, p. 156 (. . . πάλαι προέθετο ὁ θεὸς ἐσόμενον ἱλαστήριον . . .); cf. Rufinus's Latin, col. 949 ('*proposuit* enim intelligitur quasi prius posuit, hoc est priusquam esset. Quod enim est ponitur, quod nondum proponitur').

[3] col. 80 ('*Quem proposuit Deus propitiatorem fidei*. Hoc dicit quia in Christo proposuit Deus, id est, disposuit propitium se futurum humano generi, si credant').

[4] col. 444, which will be quoted in the text below.

[5] Schoeps, *Paul*, p. 146, is inclined to accept the suggestion made by Gottlieb Klein, *Studien über Paulus*, Stockholm, 1918, p. 96, on the basis of this understanding of προέθετο, that it was intended as an echo of *yir'eh* in Gen 22.8 ('Abraham said, God will provide himself the lamb for a burnt offering, my son': God has provided Christ as ἱλαστήριον). But, while the Jewish theology of the Binding of Isaac may perhaps have had some influence on Paul, this particular suggestion in support of this possibility does not seem very likely.

Προέθετο. Καὶ εἰπών, Προέθετο ὁ Θεός, καὶ δείξας τοῦ Πατρὸς
τὸ κατόρθωμα, τὸ αὐτὸ δείκνυσι καὶ τοῦ Υἱοῦ ὄν· ὁ μὲν γὰρ
Πατὴρ προέθετο, ὁ δὲ Χριστὸς ἐν τῷ αὐτοῦ αἵματι τὸ πᾶν
κατώρθωσεν) is suggestive. We take it that by ὃν προέθετο ὁ
θεός Paul means to emphasize that it is God who is the origin
of the redemption which was accomplished in Christ Jesus
(cf. 2 Cor 5.19 (. . . θεὸς ἦν ἐν Χριστῷ κόσμον καταλλάσσων
ἑαυτῷ . . .) and also that this redemption has its origin not in
some sudden new idea or impulse on God's part but in His
eternal purpose of grace.

It will be convenient to leave discussion of ἱλαστήριον till after
the remaining elements of vv. 25 and 26 have been considered,
since they contribute to its clarification.

The first of these remaining elements is διὰ πίστεως which
has both a positive and a negative significance. Positively,
it indicates that a response of faith on men's part is definitely required: the benefit resulting from the fulfilment
of God's purpose that Jesus Christ should be ἱλαστήριον is to
be accepted, appropriated, by faith. But it also implies,
negatively, that no other way of appropriating this benefit
but faith alone is open to men: every thought of their earning
it by their works is excluded. [Nestle²⁶ adds τῆς before πίστεως.]

ἐν τῷ αὐτοῦ αἵματι is the second element. It is not to be
connected with πίστεως (Paul is not indicating by it that
the faith in question is faith in Christ's blood), but with
ἱλαστήριον:[1] it was by means of the shedding of His blood that,
according to the divine purpose, Christ was to be ἱλαστήριον.
With this reference to the blood of Christ we may compare
5.9; Acts 20.28; Eph 1.7; 2.13; Col 1.20; Heb 9.11ff; 10.19, 29;
13.12, 20; 1 Pet 1.2, 19; 1 Jn 1.7; 5.6; Rev 1.5; 5.9; 7.14; 12.11;
and also, of course, Mt 26.28 = Mk 14.24 = Lk 22.20; 1 Cor 11.25
and 10.16. In 5.9 ἐν τῷ αἵματι αὐτοῦ corresponds to διὰ τοῦ
θανάτου τοῦ υἱοῦ αὐτοῦ in the following verse, and in the
Ephesians and Colossians passages cited above the use of αἷμα
could perhaps be explained as simply a way of expressing the
idea of death; but in 1 Cor 11.25, the three Synoptic verses, and
the Hebrews, 1 Peter and 1 John passages, a sacrificial significance is clearly present, and it seems probable that in the
other passages cited above also a sacrificial significance
attaches to the use of the word αἷμα, whether felt more or less

---

[1] On the assumption that προέθετο is to be understood as meaning
'proposed', this is the only possibility. On the less likely assumption
that προέθετο means here 'set forth publicly', it would perhaps be just
possible to connect ἐν τῷ αὐτοῦ αἵματι with the verb ('set forth publicly
in His blood', i.e. in His violent death).

strongly. There is little doubt that this is so in the verse under consideration. Compare Lev 17.11, in the LXX version of which the verb ἐξιλάσκεσθαι which is cognate with ἱλαστήριον is twice used (ἡ γὰρ ψυχὴ πάσης σαρκὸς αἷμα αὐτοῦ ἐστιν, καὶ ἐγὼ δέδωκα αὐτὸ ὑμῖν ἐπὶ τοῦ θυσιαστηρίου ἐξιλάσκεσθαι περὶ τῶν ψυχῶν ὑμῶν· τὸ γὰρ αἷμα αὐτοῦ ἀντὶ τῆς ψυχῆς ἐξιλάσεται), and also 4 Macc 6.29; 17.22.

The third element is εἰς ἔνδειξιν τῆς δικαιοσύνης αὐτοῦ διὰ τὴν πάρεσιν τῶν προγεγονότων ἁμαρτημάτων ἐν τῇ ἀνοχῇ τοῦ θεοῦ. According to Nygren,[1] δικαιοσύνη both here and in its occurrence in v. 26 has the same sense as it had in 3.21 and 22 (and also in 1.17) and denotes the righteous status which God gives, and ἔνδειξις means 'showing' not in the sense of proving but in the sense of offering, making available, in both its occurrences in these two verses. But, while there is an obvious neatness about ascribing to δικαιοσύνη in vv. 25 and 26 the same meaning as it had in vv. 21 and 22, the reference to God's being righteous in the last part of v. 26 would seem to tell strongly in favour of understanding δικαιοσύνη in these two verses as referring to God's own righteousness, and ἔνδειξις as meaning 'proving'. The significance of the word πάρεσις[2] as used here is also debated.[3] In spite of opinions to the contrary, there seems to be little doubt that it is not just used as a synonym of ἄφεσις (cf. the Vulgate 'remissionem'), διά having the sense 'with a view to', but is intended to express the idea of passing over, leaving unpunished,[4] διά being used in its more usual sense of 'on account of'. The reference to God's ἀνοχή (cf. 2.4; Acts 17.30: see also the note on 2.4) affords support for this view. The idea of God's patiently holding back His wrath is familiar in Judaism. But for God simply to pass over sins would be altogether

[1] p. 160.
[2] The noun, found in Phalaris, Xenophon, Hippocrates, Philo, Josephus, Plutarch, Dionysius of Halicarnassus, Dio Chrysostomus, and in some other places, occurs in the Greek Bible only here; but the cognate verb παριέναι, which is quite a common word in secular Greek, occurs in Lk 11.42 and Heb 12.12, and nearly a score of times in the LXX (see especially Ecclus 23.2).
[3] See Sanday and Headlam, p. 90; Lietzmann, p. 51; A. Deissmann, *Paulus: eine Kultur- und religionsgeschichtliche Skizze*, Tübingen, ²1925, p. 134; R. Bultmann, in *TWNT* I, pp. 506–9; J. M. Creed, 'Πάρεσις in Dionysius of Halicarnassus and St Paul', in *JTS* 41 (1940), pp. 28–30; W. G. Kümmel, 'Πάρεσις und ἔνδειξις', in *ZTK* 49 (1952), pp. 154–67; Michel, p. 109f.
[4] Cf. Xenophon, *Eq. Mag.* 7.10: τὰ οὖν τοιαῦτα ἁμαρτήματα οὐ χρὴ παριέναι ἀκόλαστα. The meaning νέκρωσις which Chrysostom (col. 445) saw in πάρεσις (cf. LSJ, s.v. πάρεσις II; s.v. παρίημι III.1; Bauer, s.v. παρίημι 2.a) is not at all likely here.

incompatible with His righteousness. He would not be the good and merciful God, had He been content to pass over sins indefinitely; for this would have been to condone evil—a denial of His own nature and a cruel betrayal of sinners. God has in fact been able to hold His hand and pass over sins, without compromising His goodness and mercy, because His intention has all along been to deal with them once and for all, decisively and finally, through the Cross. Paul is saying in these two verses that God purposed (from eternity) that Christ should be ἱλαστήριον, in order that the reality of God's righteousness, that is, of His goodness and mercy, which would be called in question by His passing over sins committed up to the time of that decisive act,[1] might be established.

The fourth element is πρὸς τὴν ἔνδειξιν τῆς δικαιοσύνης αὐτοῦ ἐν τῷ νῦν καιρῷ. It repeats the main idea of the preceding element with the addition of ἐν τῷ νῦν καιρῷ. The time indicated by ὁ νῦν καιρός must be the period which embraces both the time of the gospel events and also the time of their proclamation in the on-going preaching of the gospel.[2]

[1] προγεγονότων must be intended to characterize the sins referred to as committed before the time of Christ's becoming ἱλαστήριον. Up to that time sins were neither punished as they deserved nor atoned for as they were going to be.

[2] ὁ νῦν καιρός is used again in 8.18 and 11.5 (also in 2 Cor 8.14). Whereas in using the phrase in 8.18 Paul would seem (whether he thought of the period as beginning with Christ's earthly life or with His ascension) to have specially in mind the end of the period (he is contrasting the time before the Parousia with the glory which the Parousia will inaugurate), he is here thinking particularly of the beginning of the period (the contrast in mind is between the time of God's passing over sins and the time of His decisive action in relation to them which may be said to have begun with the coming of Christ). In 11.5 ὁ νῦν καιρός is the time during which only a remnant of Israel believes: it began with the gospel events and was apparently expected by Paul (see on 11.15) to last till the Parousia. That in each of these three passages of Romans the time denoted by ὁ νῦν καιρός is thought of by Paul as specially significant and critical is certain; but the special significance attaching to the expression derives from the context rather than from any special associations of the word καιρός; for, while it is true that in classical Greek καιρός means characteristically the right time, the exact or critical time, opportunity, season, and in the Bible it can denote especially the critical time determined by God, the time which God's decision has filled with special significance (as, for example, in Mk 1.15; 13.33), it can also be used quite generally either of a point, or of a period, of time. On the word καιρός (which occurs also in 5.6; 9.9; 13.11—in addition to the Romans passages cited above) reference may be made to O. Cullmann, *Christ and Time*, Eng. tr., London, 1951, especially pp. 39–44; J. Marsh, *The Fulness of Time*, London, 1952, and also in *TWB*, pp. 258–67; G. Delling, in *TWNT* 3, pp. 456–65; J. Barr, *The Semantics of Biblical Language*, Oxford, 1961, especially p. 225f, and *Biblical Words for Time*, London, 1962 (while Barr is sometimes less than fair to those

The fifth and last element is εἰς τὸ εἶναι αὐτὸν δίκαιον καὶ δικαιοῦντα τὸν ἐκ πίστεως Ἰησοῦ. The sense will be substantially the same, whether we explain this grammatically as dependent on πρὸς τὴν ἔνδειξιν, κ.τ.λ. or as parallel with εἰς τὴν ἔνδειξιν, κ.τ.λ. and πρὸς τὴν ἔνδειξιν, κ.τ.λ. In either case, these words indicate the ultimate object of God's purposing Christ as ἱλαστήριον. Barrett's explanation of v. 26b as meaning that 'the demonstration of God's righteousness . . . was intended to show that God (a) was righteous in himself, and (b) justified the man who relied on faith'[1] is to be rejected, because it reads the thought of showing from εἰς τὴν ἔνδειξιν, κ.τ.λ. and πρὸς τὴν ἔνδειξιν, κ.τ.λ. into εἰς τὸ εἶναι αὐτόν, κ.τ.λ., to which it is quite foreign. The words εἰς τὸ εἶναι αὐτὸν δίκαιον mean not 'in order that He might show that He is righteous', but 'in order that He might be righteous'. Paul is not saying that God purposed Christ as ἱλαστήριον, in order to show His righteousness . . . (v. 26a), in order to *show* both that He is righteous in Himself and also that He justifies . . . (v. 26b); but that God purposed Christ as ἱλαστήριον, in order to show His righteousness . . . (v. 26a), in order that He might *be* righteous . . . (v. 26b). Paul recognizes that what was at stake was not just God's being seen to be righteous, but God's *being* righteous. God would not *be* righteous, if He neglected to show Himself to be righteous: it is essential to His being the righteous, the loving and merciful God, that He should show that He is righteous.

The further point must also be made that the variant reading (G *pc* Ambst) which omits καί, though it should not be accepted, is probably a pointer to the correct understanding of καί; for it is surely more natural to take καί adverbially here (as meaning 'even') than as the copulative 'and'. The Greek is very awkward, if it is meant to express the double purpose that God might be righteous and that He might justify (or that He might be righteous and the justifier); but is a quite natural way of expressing the meaning 'that God might be righteous even in justifying', i.e. that He might justify righteously, without compromising His own righteousness. So understood, the words afford an insight into the innermost meaning of the Cross as Paul understands it and into his use of ἱλαστήριον in v. 25. For God to have forgiven men's sins lightly—a cheap forgiveness which would have implied that moral evil does not

whom he criticizes, these two books of his are a salutary warning against the temptation to build too much on an author's vocabulary as opposed to his actual statements).

[1] p. 80.

matter very much—would have been altogether unrighteous, a violation of His truth and profoundly unmerciful and unloving toward men, since it would have annihilated their dignity as persons morally accountable. The purpose of Christ's being ἱλαστήριον was to achieve a divine forgiveness, which is worthy of God, consonant with His righteousness, in that it does not insult God's creature man by any suggestion that that is after all of but small consequence, which he himself at his most human knows full well (witness, for example, the Greek tragedians) is desperately serious, but, so far from condoning man's evil, is, since it involves nothing less than God's bearing the intolerable burden of that evil Himself in the person of His own dear Son, the disclosure of the fullness of God's hatred of man's evil at the same time as it is its real and complete forgiveness.

The words τὸν ἐκ πίστεως Ἰησοῦ specify as the object of God's justifying the man who believes in Jesus: compare παντὶ τῷ πιστεύοντι in 1.16 and δικαιοσύνη δὲ θεοῦ διὰ πίστεως [Ἰησοῦ] Χριστοῦ, εἰς πάντας τοὺς πιστεύοντας in v. 22 of the present chapter. For the expression compare οἱ ἐκ πίστεως in Gal 3.7 and 9; οἱ ἐκ νόμου in 4.14; οἱ ἐκ περιτομῆς in 4.12; Acts 11.2; Gal 2.12; and also τῷ σπέρματι, οὐ τῷ ἐκ τοῦ νόμου μόνον ἀλλὰ καὶ τῷ ἐκ πίστεως Ἀβραάμ in 4.16.[1] For the genitive Ἰησοῦ see on v. 22.

We must now return to ἱλαστήριον. Since this word is used of the kappōreṯ or mercy-seat in twenty-one out of its twenty-seven occurrences in the LXX and in its only other occurrence in the NT (Heb 9.5), the possibility that Paul is using it in that sense here and thinking of Christ as the anti-type of the OT mercy-seat must clearly be taken seriously. From early times Paul has often been so understood,[2] and this view of ἱλαστήριον is upheld by many recent writers.[3] But the arguments which have been urged in support of it have been shown by L. Morris to be not really very strong.[4] Thus the strongest of them (that from the LXX usage) is seriously diminished by the recognition that, wherever in the LXX ἱλαστήριον means 'mercy-seat', it is used with the definite article (cf. Heb 9.5), except in Exod 25.17, where the addition

[1] See Bauer, s.v. ἐκ 3.d.

[2] e.g. by Origen (Scherer, pp. 156ff).

[3] e.g. Nygren, pp. 156–8; T. W. Manson, 'ΙΛΑΣΤΗΡΙΟΝ', in *JTS* 46 (1945), pp. 1–10; S. Lyonnet, 'De notione expiationis', in *VD* 37 (1959), pp. 336–52; Bruce, p. 106f.

[4] 'The Meaning of ἱλαστήριον in Romans 3.25', in *NTS* 2 (1955–6), pp. 33–43. Cf. Hill, *GWHM*, p. 40f.

of ἐπίθεμα has the similar effect of removing ἱλαστήριον from the realm of the general, and there is always something in the context to make clear which of the things which could be denoted by ἱλαστήριον is intended. Here in Romans 3 ἱλαστήριον is anarthrous, and there is nothing in the context which can be said to indicate unambiguously that the mercy-seat is referred to. Morris further shows the weakness of Manson's contention that in its occurrences in Ezekiel and in early Christian literature outside the NT ἱλαστήριον denotes a place (it is the propitiatory character and purpose of the object, not its being a place, which is indicated by the use of ἱλαστήριον), and of the various arguments put forward to prove that Paul was thinking of the Day of Atonement ceremonies. There are, on the other side, considerations which weigh heavily against this interpretation of ἱλαστήριον. While it is an understandable paradox to refer to Christ as being at the same time both priest and victim, to represent Him as being the place of sprinkling as well as the victim is surely excessively harsh and confusing. Moreover, there seems to be something essentially improbable in the thought of Paul's likening Christ, for whom, personally, man's redemption was so infinitely costly, and to whom he felt so tremendous a personal indebtedness (cf., e.g., Gal 2.20), to something which was only an inanimate piece of temple furniture. The mercy-seat would surely be more appropriately regarded as a type of the Cross.

Before considering the other suggested meanings of ἱλαστήριον, it is necessary to refer to the question whether ἱλάσκεσθαι and its cognates, when used in the Bible, carry the idea of propitiation or appeasement which it is generally agreed that they express in pagan usage. C. H. Dodd argued in a well-known article[1] that practically no trace of this meaning attaches to these words as used in the LXX, the thought expressed being rather, where the subject of the action is human, that of the expiation of sin, or, where the subject is God, that of God's being gracious, having mercy, forgiving. But, while it is certainly true that the idea of a wrath of God which is capricious and vindictive and requires to be placated by bribery on men's part is alien to the OT, it is by no means true that all ideas of divine wrath are alien. Morris has shown that in many, if not all, of the passages in which ἱλάσκεσθαι or related words occur in the LXX the idea of God's wrath is

---

[1] 'Ἱλάσκεσθαι, its cognates, derivatives and synonyms in the Septuagint', in *JTS* 32 (1931), pp. 352–60 (reprinted in his *Bible and the Greeks*).

present.[1] (Dodd failed to pay adequate attention to the contexts of these words' occurrences.) In view of this fact, we cannot allow that the thought of propitiation is altogether foreign to the ἱλάσκεσθαι word-group in the LXX. Indeed, the evidence suggests that the idea of the averting of wrath is basic to this word-group in the OT no less than in extra-biblical Greek, the distinctiveness of the OT usage being its recognition first that God's wrath, unlike all human wrath, is perfectly righteous, and therefore free from every trace of irrationality, caprice and vindictiveness,[2] and secondly that in the process of averting this righteous wrath from man it is God Himself who takes the initiative.

The other meanings which have been suggested for ἱλαστήριον (that is, other than the meaning 'mercy-seat) must now be considered. We may set aside as unlikely to be correct, in view of what we have seen in the last paragraph and also of the fact that the wrath of God is prominent in the preceding section of Romans (see, especially, 1.18; 2.5, 8; 3.5), the various suggestions (whether taking ἱλαστήριον as a masculine adjective or as a masculine noun or as a neuter noun), which are expressly intended to exclude the idea of propitiation. The remaining possibilities are: (i) 'propitiatory' or 'propitiating' (a masculine adjective agreeing with ὅν); (ii) 'a propitiator'; (iii) 'a propitiation' or 'a means of propitiation'; (iv) 'a propitiatory sacrifice'. Of these (ii) should probably be rejected, in spite of the considerable support it has had (e.g. the rendering 'propitiatorem' in some Vulgate MSS and in Ambrose, Ambrosiaster, Jerome, Pelagius; also modern exegetes such as J. Haussleiter, G. Kittel, R. Seeberg), on the ground that there does not seem to be any independent attestation of such a use of ἱλαστήριος in ancient times (had this been Paul's meaning, he would probably have used the word ἱλαστής). Between the other three possibilities there would seem to be little substantial difference, since, even if the word is explained as having one of the more general senses (i) and (iii), the presence of ἐν τῷ αὐτοῦ αἵματι would still indicate that a propitiatory sacrifice is in mind. On the whole, it seems best to

---

[1] L. Morris, 'The Use of ἱλάσκεσθαι etc. in Biblical Greek', in *ET* 62 (1950–51), pp. 227–33; and *The Apostolic Preaching of the Cross*, London, 1955. Cf. Hill, *GWHM*, pp. 23ff. Sometimes, as in Exod 32.12–14 (παῦσαι τῆς ὀργῆς τοῦ θυμοῦ σου καὶ ἵλεως γενοῦ ... καὶ ἱλάσθη κύριος περὶ τῆς κακίας ἧς εἶπεν ποιῆσαι τὸν λαὸν αὐτοῦ) and Dan 9.16–19 (... ἀποστραφήτω ὁ θυμός σου καὶ ἡ ὀργή σου ἀπὸ τῆς πόλεώς σου ... κύριε, σὺ ἱλάτευσον) a prayer for God to turn away His wrath is actually expressed in the context.

[2] See on ὀργὴ θεοῦ in 1.18.

accept (iv).[1] We may compare the words σωτήριον, χαριστήριον, καθάρσιον, τελεστήριον. We take it that what Paul's statement that God purposed Christ as a propitiatory victim means is that God, because in His mercy He willed to forgive sinful men and, being truly merciful, willed to forgive them righteously, that is, without in any way condoning their sin, purposed to direct against His own very Self in the person of His Son the full weight of that righteous wrath which they deserved.

That Paul's thought of Christ as ἱλαστήριον has something in common with the speech of the youngest of the seven martyr brothers in 2 Macc 7.30–38,[2] the prayer of Eleazar in 4 Macc 6.27–29,[3] the statement about the seven in 4 Macc 17.20–22,[4] and also with the Jewish theology of the 'Binding of Isaac',[5] is clear. It is probable that the idea that the death of a martyr could be an atonement for the sins of Israel was well known to Paul. It is probable too that he was familiar with the belief in the redemptive efficacy of the binding of Isaac. The possibility that his thinking about the death of Christ was influ-

---

[1] That this is the way in which Chrysostom (col. 444) understood ἱλαστήριον would seem to be implied by his comment, Καὶ ἱλαστήριον δι' αὐτὸ τοῦτο καλεῖ, δεικνὺς ὅτι, εἰ ὁ τύπος τοσαύτην εἶχεν ἰσχύν, πολλῷ μᾶλλον ἡ ἀλήθεια τὸ αὐτὸ ἐπιδείξεται, in view of the preceding Τρίτον ἀπὸ τῶν θυσιῶν τῶν ἐν τῇ Παλαιᾷ· διὰ γὰρ τοῦτο εἶπεν, Ἐν τῷ αὐτοῦ αἵματι, ἀναμιμνήσκων αὐτοὺς τῶν προβάτων ἐκείνων καὶ τῶν μόσχων. Εἰ γὰρ ἀλόγων σφαγαί, φησίν, ἁμαρτίας ἔλυον, πολλῷ μᾶλλον τὸ αἷμα τοῦτο.

[2] Note especially the references in v. 33 to God's wrath and to His being reconciled again (ἐπώργισται and πάλιν καταλλαγήσεται), in v. 37 to His becoming gracious to the nation of Israel (the word ἵλεως which is related to ἱλαστήριον is used), and in v. 38 to the staying of God's wrath which had been justly brought upon the whole Jewish race.

[3] Specially v. 28f (ἵλεως γενοῦ τῷ ἔθνει σου ἀρκεσθεὶς τῇ ἡμετέρᾳ ὑπὲρ αὐτῶν δίκῃ. καθάρσιον αὐτῶν ποίησον τὸ ἐμὸν αἷμα καὶ ἀντίψυχον αὐτῶν λαβὲ τὴν ἐμὴν ψυχήν).

[4] The Greek is: καὶ οὗτοι οὖν ἁγιασθέντες διὰ θεὸν τετίμηνται, οὐ μόνον ταύτῃ τῇ τιμῇ, ἀλλὰ καὶ τῷ δι' αὐτοὺς τὸ ἔθνος ἡμῶν τοὺς πολεμίους μὴ ἐπικρατῆσαι καὶ τὸν τύραννον τιμωρηθῆναι καὶ τὴν πατρίδα καθαρισθῆναι, ὥσπερ ἀντίψυχον γεγονότας τῆς τοῦ ἔθνους ἁμαρτίας. καὶ διὰ τοῦ αἵματος τῶν εὐσεβῶν ἐκείνων καὶ τοῦ ἱλαστηρίου τοῦ θανάτου αὐτῶν ἡ θεία πρόνοια τὸν Ἰσραηλ προκακωθέντα διέσωσεν. In v. 22 ἱλαστηρίου is the genitive of the noun ἱλαστήριον, if τοῦ is read before θανάτου: if the τοῦ is not read, ἱλαστηρίου must be an adjective agreeing with θανάτου.

[5] On the 'Binding of Isaac' ('ᵃḳēḏaṭ Yiṣḥāḳ) see Schoeps, Paul. pp. 141–49; S. Spiegel, The Last Trial, Eng. tr. by J. Goldin, New York, 1967; G. Vermes, Scripture and Tradition in Judaism, Leiden, 1961, pp. 193–227; R. Le Déaut, La Nuit Pascale (Analecta Biblica 22), Rome, 1963, pp. 133–208, and also 'La présentation targumique du sacrifice d'Isaac et la sotériologie paulinienne', in Studiorum Paulinorum Congressus Internationalis Catholicus 2, Rome, 1963, pp. 563–74. In Jewish tradition the unconsummated sacrifice of Isaac atoned for Israel's sins. See also on 8.32.

enced by these ideas cannot be ruled out. But the fact that for
Paul Jesus was decisively distinguished alike from the Mac-
cabean martyrs and from the patriarch Isaac as being both
God's 'own Son' (8.32) and sinless (cf. 2 Cor 5.21) should not be
forgotten. The possibility that Isa 53.10 (*'im tāśîm 'āšām
napšô*) may have contributed to Paul's thought of Christ as
ἱλαστήριον also deserves to be seriously considered.[1]

IV. 3. ALL GLORYING IS EXCLUDED (3.27–31)

This short section is specially difficult. While its general sense
and its function in the over-all structure of the main division
(its contribution to the clarification of the 'from faith to faith'
and the 'by faith' of 1.17) are clear enough, it is extraordinarily
difficult to define the internal articulation of its argument
precisely. It affirms that all glorying, that is, all thinking to
establish a claim on God on the ground of one's works, has been
ruled out. So much is beyond question. For the rest, we may
indicate our understanding of the section as follows: It is
implied that the statement that glorying has been excluded is
a conclusion which must be drawn from what precedes (whether
vv. 21–26 or the whole of 1.18–3.26). At the same time it is
indicated that the exclusion has been brought about through
the law—not the law understood legalistically, but the law
recognized as the law of faith which it is. In support of the
statements that glorying has been excluded and that this has
been accomplished through the law Paul appeals to the fact
that believers know that men are justified by faith, apart from
works of the law. To deny that they are so justified would be
to imply that God is God of the Jews only, and that would be
a denial of the fundamental truth that God is one. Since He
is the one and only God, who is God of all men, He will
assuredly justify Jews and Gentiles alike by faith and only by
faith. The conclusion is that what has been said about faith,
so far from contradicting the law, is thoroughly consonant with
it, and is therefore confirmed.

[27]Where then is glorying? It has been excluded. By what kind of
law? By a law of works? No, but by the law of faith! [28]For we

[1] On ἱλαστήριον, in addition to the works already mentioned in this
connexion, reference may be made to: Lietzmann, p. 49f; SB 3, pp.
165–85; J. Herrmann and F. Büchsel, in *TWNT* 3, pp. 300–24; V. Taylor,
'Great Texts Reconsidered' [on Rom 3.25], in *ET* 50 (1938–39), pp.
295–300; Davies, *PRJ*, pp. 230ff; Bauer, s.v.; L. Morris, *The Cross in
The NT*, London, 1965; Cambier, *L'Évangile de Dieu* 1, pp. 92–94.

reckon that it is by faith that a man is justified apart from works of the law. ²⁹Or is God *the God* of Jews only? Is he not *the God* of the Gentiles also? Most certainly of the Gentiles also! ³⁰seeing that God is one, and he will justify the circumcision on the ground of faith and the uncircumcision through faith. ³¹Do we then invalidate the law through *our teaching about* faith? God forbid! Rather we uphold the law.

27. Ποῦ οὖν ἡ καύχησις;¹ ἐξεκλείσθη. It follows inevitably from what has been said (whether we think specially of vv. 21–26 or of 1.18–3.26 as a whole) that there can be no question of any man's putting God in his debt. This conclusion is stated by means of the rhetorical question 'Where then [i.e. Where, if what has been said is true] is glorying?' followed by the declaration 'It has been excluded'. On καυχᾶσθαι and its cognates and on Paul's use of them see on 2.17. Here the abstract noun καύχησις denotes the assertion of a claim upon God on the ground of one's works. The tense of ἐξεκλείσθη² indicates that the exclusion referred to has been accomplished once for all. In view of what follows it would seem that the reference is not simply to the fact that what has been said has demonstrated the absurdity of all such glorying, but to the exclusion effected by God Himself (the passive concealing a reference to a divine action), whether in the sense that God has rendered all such glorying futile and absurd by what He has done in Christ³ or—perhaps more probably, in view of the next few words—in the sense that He has shown it to be futile and absurd through the OT scriptures.

διὰ ποίου νόμου; τῶν ἔργων; οὐχί, ἀλλὰ διὰ νόμου πίστεως is difficult, and has been variously interpreted. Some explain νόμου πίστεως as a rhetorically-motivated formulation due simply to the desire to match [τοῦ νόμου] τῶν ἔργων.⁴ Others take it to refer to a special law under which Christians stand and compare ὁ . . . νόμος τοῦ πνεύματος τῆς ζωῆς in 8.2 and τὸν νόμον τοῦ Χριστοῦ in Gal 6.2 and the expression ἔννομος Χριστοῦ in 1 Cor 9.21.⁵ Others understand νόμος in

---

¹ *Pace* Zahn, p. 200, it is not very likely that the σου after καύχησις (attested by G lat) is original. A copyist might well have felt that it was required in view of the use of the second person singular in 2.17–27 (especially 2.17 in which the verb καυχᾶσθαι occurs); but intrinsic probability is against σου, for an apostrophizing of a representative of the unbelieving Jews does not fit the present context at all naturally.

² The only other occurrence of ἐκκλείειν in the NT is in Gal 4.17.

³ So Michel, p. 111 ('durch das Kreuz').

⁴ So, e.g., Lietzmann, p. 52; M. Dibelius, 'Synthetische Methoden in der Paulus-Forschung', in *TB* 3 (1924), col. 62. According to this view νόμου πίστεως means no more than πίστεως by itself would have meant.

⁵ Cf., e.g., E. Sommerlath, *Der Ursprung des neuen Lebens nach Paulus*, Leipzig, ²1927, pp. 37ff; Zahn, in loc.

this verse to have some sense other than 'law'. Thus it has been taken to mean 'principle', 'ethical norm', 'divine institution', 'system', and 'way of salvation'. But Friedrich's contention that by the νόμος πίστεως the OT law is intended¹ should probably be accepted; for this interpretation seems to fit the context best. We may then understand Paul's meaning to be that the correct answer to the question 'By what kind of law² (has such glorying been excluded)?' is 'By God's law (i.e. the law of the OT)—that is, by God's law, not misunderstood as a law which directs men to seek justification as a reward for their works,³ but properly understood as summoning men to faith'. There is confirmation of the rightness of this interpretation in 9.31f, where the complaint is made against Israel that it has pursued the νόμος of righteousness ἐξ ἔργων instead of ἐκ πίστεως, and in 10.6ff, where ἡ . . . ἐκ πίστεως δικαιοσύνη is pictured as speaking in Deuteronomy, as well as close at hand in v. 21f (δικαιοσύνη θεοῦ . . . μαρτυρουμένη ὑπὸ τοῦ νόμου . . ., δικαιοσύνη δὲ θεοῦ διὰ πίστεως . . .) and in v. 31.

28. λογιζόμεθα γὰρ⁴ δικαιοῦσθαι πίστει ἄνθρωπον χωρὶς ἔργων νόμου is best understood as intended to support v. 27 as a whole (that is, both in its basic statement that glorying has been excluded and also in its further statement that it is διὰ νόμου πίστεως that it has been excluded).⁵ λογίζεσθαι is here used to indicate a faith-judgment, a conviction reached in the light of the gospel (see also on 6.11; 8.18; 14.14).⁶ The use of the plural might be explained simply as an author's plural, but is perhaps better explained as indicating that this

¹ 'Das Gesetz des Glaubens Röm. 3,27', in *TZ* 10 (1954), pp. 401–17.

² On ποῖος see BDF, § 298 (2). But Friedrich (p. 415) may well be right in claiming that, as in 1 Cor 15.35 (its only other occurrence in Paul's letters), ποῖος has its proper sense here. He continues: 'Demnach fragt Paulus nicht, welches von verschiedenen Gesetzen das Rühmen ausschliesst, sondern nach der Beschaffenheit des Gesetzes. Wie muss der νόμος aussehen, der das Rühmen ausschliesst?'

³ It seems that to take the νόμος which is here described as τῶν ἔργων to be the law understood as a law which directs men to seek justification by works (i.e. as something which it is not at all) fits the context better than to take it to be the law understood merely as requiring works of obedience (i.e. as being what is only a part of what the OT law really is).

⁴ The attestation of γάρ (ℵ A D* G *al* lat) is stronger than that of οὖν (B C 𝔎 *pm*), and intrinsic probability seems also to be on the side of γάρ. The reading οὖν is perhaps to be explained (as Bengel suggested (p. 509)) as an accidental repetition of the οὖν of the previous verse.

⁵ This seems to be much more satisfactory than either connecting it with Ποῦ οὖν ἡ καύχησις; ἐξεκλείσθη only (and regarding the latter part of v. 27 as parenthetic) or connecting it only with the latter part of v. 27.

⁶ Cf. H. W. Heidland, in *TWNT* 4, pp. 287ff.

conviction is common to all believers (cf. καταργοῦμεν and ἱστάνομεν in v. 31). The words δικαιοῦσθαι πίστει ἄνθρωπον χωρὶς ἔργων νόμου sum up the substance of vv. 20a, 21–22,24,[1] the emphasis here—in connexion with v. 27—being on the fact that it is not on the ground of works[2] but only by faith[3] that men[4] are justified rather than on the fact that such justification has actually been made available.

29f is better understood as connecting with v. 28 than as connecting with v. 27 as a whole or with the first five words of it (v. 28 or vv. 27b–28 being explained as parenthetic). The question ἢ Ἰουδαίων ὁ θεὸς μόνον;[5] indicates what would necessarily follow, if what is stated in v. 28 were not true. If that were not true, then God would not be the God of all men in the sense that He desires and seeks the salvation of all with equal seriousness. No Jew of Paul's day would ever have thought of questioning that God is the God of all men in the sense of being their Creator and Ruler and Judge; but Paul clearly takes it for granted that God is not the God of any man

---

[1] With δικαιοῦσθαι cf., especially, δικαιούμενοι in v. 24, with πίστει cf. διὰ πίστεως [Ἰησοῦ] Χριστοῦ and εἰς πάντας τοὺς πιστεύοντας in v. 22, and with χωρὶς ἔργων νόμου the negative statement in v. 20a and the χωρὶς νόμου of v. 21.

[2] On the expression ἔργα νόμου see on v. 20. It is clear that it must have the same sense here as it has there.

[3] The reading πίστει ἄνθρωπον is no doubt to be preferred to the variant ἄνθρωπον διὰ πίστεως, since it is not only better attested but is also the *lectio difficilior*. This is the only occurrence of πίστει δικαιοῦσθαι in the NT. Elsewhere we have ἐκ πίστεως, διὰ τῆς πίστεως and ἐξ ἔργων used with δικαιοῦν or δικαιοῦσθαι, and also ἐν τούτῳ, ἐν Χριστῷ, ἐν τῷ ὀνόματι τοῦ κυρίου ἡμῶν, ἐν τῷ αἵματι αὐτοῦ, and ἐν νόμῳ: the only cases of the simple dative used with this verb, besides the present one, are τῇ αὐτοῦ χάριτι in v. 24 and τῇ ἐκείνου χάριτι in Tit 3.7. The fact that Luther translated πίστει here by 'allein durch den Glauben' is well known; but the expression *sola fide* is already found in Rufinus's translation of Origen's comment on vv. 27–28 (col. 952f), which contains the words '. . . ut requiramus quis sine operibus sola fide justificatus sit', and then, after a reference to the penitent thief on the cross, 'Nec aliud quidquam describitur boni operis ejus in Evangeliis, sed pro hac sola fide ait ei Jesus: "Amen dico tibi: Hodie mecum eris in paradiso"' and also in Ambrosiaster's comments on 3.24 (col. 79: 'Justificati sunt gratis, quia nihil operantes, neque vicem reddentes, sola fide justificati sunt dono Dei') and on 4.5 (col. 82f: 'Quomodo ergo Judaei per opera legis justificari se putant . . .; cum videant Abraham non per opera legis, sed sola fide justificatum?') and in Aquinas's comment (p. 59 (330)) on 4.5 ('. . . *reputabitur fides eius*, scilicet sola sine operibus exterioribus, *ad iustitiam* . . .').

[4] For the use of the singular ἄνθρωπος without the article in an indefinite and universal sense cf. 1 Cor 4.1; 7.1, 26; 11.28; Gal 2.16; 6.7; Jas 2.24.

[5] The reading μόνος found in D is clearly not original, and the μόνων attested by B *al* Cl is probably also a corruption.

without being his gracious and merciful God.[1] So he follows up his question with the further question, οὐχὶ καὶ ἐθνῶν; which is answered positively by ναὶ καὶ ἐθνῶν. Compare 3.22; 10.12: without in any way calling in question the reality of Israel's special place in God's purpose, which is attested by the Ἰουδαίῳ ... πρῶτον of 1.16 (cf. 2.9 and 10) and by such passages as 3.2; 9.4f; 11.1, 17ff, Paul insists on the fact that the divine purpose is equally for all men gracious and merciful.

εἴπερ εἷς ὁ θεός. In support of the affirmation ναὶ καὶ ἐθνῶν, Paul appeals to the fundamental fact of the oneness of God confessed in the Shema (šᵉma'), the creed of Israel, which begins with Deut 6.4. As in its two other occurrences in Romans (8.9 and 17), εἴπερ has here the sense 'if, as is indeed true', 'seeing that'.[2]

ὃς δικαιώσει περιτομὴν ἐκ πίστεως καὶ ἀκροβυστίαν διὰ τῆς πίστεως. The relative clause states what is for Paul the corollary to be drawn from the confession that God is one—namely, that He will justify Jew and Gentile alike by faith alone. The future indicative δικαιώσει is probably to be understood as simply logical. περιτομή and ἀκροβυστία here denote the communities of the circumcised and uncircumcised respectively (for the various meanings of these two words see on 2.25 and 26). Attempts to make out a substantial distinction between ἐκ πίστεως and διὰ τῆς πίστεως (e.g. by Origen[3] and Theodore of Mopsuestia,[4] and, in modern times, Zahn[5] and Schlatter[6]) are unconvincing. There is little doubt that Augustine[7] was right in explaining the variation as purely rhetorical (cf. ἐν τῇ ἀκροβυστίᾳ and δι' ἀκροβυστίας in 4.11; διὰ τοῦ θανάτου τοῦ υἱοῦ αὐτοῦ and ἐν τῇ ζωῇ αὐτοῦ in 5.10; διὰ δόξης and ἐν δόξῃ in 2 Cor 3.11).[8]

[1] It is instructive to set beside Paul's argumentation here the comment of Rabbi Simeon ben Jochai on 'I am the LORD thy God' in Exod 20.2 (quoted in SB 3, p. 185): 'God spake to the Israelites: "I am God over all who enter the world, but my name have I associated only with you; I have not called myself the God of the nations of the world, but the God of Israel " '.

[2] On εἴπερ see BDF, § 454 (2) and LSJ, s.v. II. The variant ἐπείπερ is an easier reading, since it expresses rather more obviously the sense 'seeing that', which the context requires.

[3] Scherer, pp. 170–73.

[4] col. 796: Ἐπὶ τῶν Ἰουδαίων τὸ "ἐκ πίστεως" τέθεικεν, ὡς ἂν ἐχόντων μὲν καὶ ἑτέρας ἀφορμὰς πρὸς δικαίωσιν, οὐ δυναμένων δὲ αὐτῆς μετέχειν πλὴν ἐκ τῆς πίστεως · ἐπὶ δὲ τῶν Ἑλλήνων "διὰ τῆς πίστεως".

[5] p. 205f.   [6] p. 155f.

[7] De Spir. et litt. 29.50: 'non ad aliquam differentiam ... sed ad varietatem locutionis'.

[8] Cf. Ambrosiaster, col. 81: 'Tam enim gentiles, quam Judaeos non aliter quam credentes justificavit; quia enim omnium unus est Deus, una ratione omnes justificavit'.

31. νόμον οὖν καταργοῦμεν διὰ τῆς πίστεως; μὴ γένοιτο, ἀλλὰ νόμον ἱστάνομεν. Here two related questions have to be answered: (i) Is this verse to be understood as the conclusion of the preceding section or as the opening of the following section? and (ii) How is the pair of opposites, *καταργεῖν/ἱστάνειν*, to be understood? With regard to (i), a good many interpreters[1] have favoured the view that this verse is to be connected with chapter 4. In support of it, it has been urged that it is unlikely that Paul would dismiss an extremely important objection by a mere opposite assertion, passing immediately to a new subject, which—on the contrary view—he would be doing; and, positively, that chapter 4 constitutes an appropriate scriptural proof of the statement made in this verse. But these arguments can be countered. The dismissal of an objection in 3.8 is no less abrupt than that which—if this verse is the end of the section—we have here; and chapter 4 may equally well be interpreted as a demonstration of the truth of the statement that glorying has been excluded. And there is something which weighs heavily against the view that chapter 4 was intended as the proof of 3.31—the use of the conjunction *οὖν* at the beginning of 4.1. It was surely not the natural conjunction to use, to introduce the proof of the immediately preceding statement; but it was entirely appropriate, if the purpose of 4.1 was to introduce a reference to the case of Abraham as the most obvious possible objection to another statement of the last section, namely, the statement that glorying has been excluded, in order that that statement (so vital to Paul's whole argument) might be powerfully confirmed by the demonstration that he who of all men might most plausibly be claimed as an exception to it was in fact no exception at all. We conclude that 3.31 is rightly taken, not as the beginning of the new section, but as the conclusion of 3.27ff.[2]

With regard to (ii), it seems natural to understand Paul to be using *καταργεῖν* and *ἱστάνειν* as equivalent to the Hebrew *biṭṭēl* (Aramaic: *baṭṭēl*) and *ḳiyyêm* (Aramaic: *ḳayyēm*),[3] and to mean that what he has been saying about faith is not in any way inconsistent with the law[4] but upholds it in the sense that

[1] e.g. Cornely, pp. 203ff; Meyer 1, p. 185f; Lagrange, p. 80; Huby, pp. 161, 163f.
[2] Cf., e.g., Calvin, p. 80f; Sanday and Headlam, p. 96f; Barrett, p. 84; Kuss, p. 178; Murray 1, pp. 124–26.
[3] Cf. Michel, p. 112; Daube, *NTRJ*, p. 60f; Gerhardsson, *Memory and Manuscript*, p. 287. This view is disputed by Cambier, *L'Évangile de Dieu* 1, p. 160.
[4] We take it that by *νόμος* here is meant the OT law in its full extent, i.e., the Torah or Pentateuch, as in v. 21, or—possibly—the whole OT, as in v. 19.

it is thoroughly consonant with it. According to this under-standing of καταργοῦμεν and ἱστάνομεν, Paul is declaring that his teaching about faith is confirmed by the law. It is, we believe, true that he thought that the law was also being established in another sense—in the sense of being rendered fully and decisively effective (cf. 8.1–16); but the establishing of the law in this sense of the verb 'establish' is something which he ascribes to God, not to men (not even apostles). It is accomplished by God through the gift of His Spirit consequent upon the work of Christ. To translate νόμον ἱστάνομεν 'we are placing law itself on a firmer footing', as the NEB does, is surely to put into Paul's mouth a self-important utterance which is quite out of character.

The question introduced by οὖν indicates a false conclusion which Paul recognizes could be drawn from what he has been saying. It could be thought that what has been said of faith is inconsistent with the law and calls it in question. Such a reading of the situation Paul emphatically rejects. The truth is rather that, rightly understood, the law supports and confirms the doctrine of faith.

IV. 4. THE CASE OF ABRAHAM AS CONFIRMATION OF THE STATEMENT THAT GLORYING HAS BEEN EXCLUDED (4.1–25)

The function of this section is to confirm the truth of what was said in the first part of 3.27. (At the same time it also adds an independent contribution of its own, particularly in vv. 17b–22, to the exposition of 'by faith'.) If anyone has a right to glory, Abraham must have—according to Jewish assumptions. So, if it can be shown that, according to Scripture, Abraham himself has no right to glory, it will have been proved that no one has such a right—that glorying has in fact been excluded.

The first verse introduces the subject of Abraham. The rest of the chapter falls into five parts. In the first (vv. 2–8) Paul, after admitting that, if Abraham was justified on the ground of his works, he certainly would have a right to glory, goes on to argue that, rightly understood, the basic biblical text for the righteousness of Abraham (Gen 15.6) itself implies that he was justified apart from works. In the second (vv. 9–12) he makes the point that, when his faith was reckoned to him for righteousness, Abraham was not yet circumcised, and draws out its significance. In the third (vv. 13–17a) Paul argues that it was not on the condition of its being merited through fulfilment of the law that the promise that he should be heir of the world was given to Abraham and his seed, but simply on the basis of the righteousness of faith. The fourth (vv. 17b–22) —though v. 17b is grammatically part of the sentence which began with v. 16, it belongs by reason of its content to what follows—is an expanded paraphrase of Gen 15.6. Apart from v. 22, it is a drawing out of the meaning of the words 'And Abraham believed God'. It is thus a positive statement concerning the essential character of Abraham's faith. The fifth and last part (vv. 23–25) underlines the relevance to all Christians of Abraham's faith as the paradigm of their own, and at the same time makes an appropriate conclusion to the whole main division which began with 1.18.[1]

¹What then are we to say that Abraham, our forefather according to the flesh, has found?

²For if Abraham was justified on the ground of works, then he does indeed have a right to glory. But this is not how God sees him; ³for what does the scripture say? 'And Abraham believed God, and it was reckoned to him for righteousness.' ⁴Now if a man does have works to his credit, his wages are not reckoned as a matter of grace but as a debt; ⁵but to the man who has no work to his credit but believes in him who justifies the ungodly his faith is reckoned for righteousness, ⁶even as David also pronounces the blessing of the man to whom God reckons righteousness apart from works: ⁷'Blessed are those whose iniquities have been forgiven and whose sins have been covered; ⁸blessed is the man whose sin the Lord will in no wise reckon.'

⁹Does this blessing then apply to the circumcision *only* or also to the uncircumcision? For we say: 'To Abraham his faith was reckoned for righteousness.' ¹⁰In what circumstances then was it reckoned? When he was circumcised or when he was still uncircumcised? It was not when he was circumcised, but when he was still uncircumcised. ¹¹And he received the sign of circumcision as a seal of the righteousness by faith which he had while still uncircumcised, so that he might be the father of all those who, in a state of uncircumcision, believe, so that righteousness is reckoned to them, ¹²and also the father of the circumcision for those who not only belong to the circumcision but also* walk in the steps of the faith of our father Abraham which he had while he was still uncircumcised.

¹³For it was not on the basis of *fulfilment of* the law that the promise was made to Abraham or to his seed that he should be heir of the world, but on the basis of the righteousness of faith. ¹⁴For if

---

* Not translating the τοῖς before στοιχοῦσιν: see note on the verse.

¹ In connexion with this section reference may be made to Käsemann, *Perspektiven*, pp. 140–77; G. Klein, 'Röm 4 und die Idee der Heilsgeschichte', in *EvTh* 23 (1963), pp. 424–47, and 'Heil und Geschichte nach Röm 4', in *NTS* 13 (1966–67), pp. 43–47; L. Goppelt, 'Paulus und die Heilsgeschichte: Schlussfolgerungen aus Röm 4 und 1 Kor 10.1–13', in *NTS* 13, pp. 31–42; U. Wilckens, 'Die Rechtfertigung Abrahams nach Röm 4', in R. Rendtorff and K. Koch (ed.), *Studien zur Theologie der alttestamentlichen Überlieferungen*, Neukirchen, 1961, pp. 111–27; O. Cullmann, *Salvation in History*, Eng. tr., London, 1967, pp. 261–64; Barrett, *From First Adam to Last*, pp. 22–45.

it is those *who have a claim* on the basis of *their fulfilment of* the law who are heirs, then faith has been rendered vain and the promise annulled; ¹⁵for the law works wrath, but where there is no law, there there is also no transgression. ¹⁶For this reason it is on the basis of faith, namely, in order that it may be according to grace, so that the promise may be certain of fulfilment for all the seed, not only for that which is of the law, but also for that which is of Abraham's faith, who is the father of us all, ¹⁷ᵃeven as scripture says, 'Father of many nations have I made thee'—

—¹⁷ᵇbefore God, in whom he believed, *the God* who quickens the dead and calls things which are not into being. ¹⁸He in hope against *all* hope believed, so that he became the father of many nations according to the word spoken to him, 'So shall thy seed be.' ¹⁹And without weakening in faith he considered his own body, which was *as good as* dead (for he was about a hundred years old), and the deadness of Sarah's womb, ²⁰and yet did not waver in unbelief with regard to God's promise, but was strengthened in faith, giving glory to God ²¹and being fully persuaded that he had the power to do what he had promised. ²²That is why 'it was reckoned to him for righteousness'.

²³But this statement of scripture that 'it was reckoned to him' was not written just for his sake, ²⁴but for our sakes also, to whom *our faith* is to be reckoned, who believe on him who raised Jesus our Lord from the dead, ²⁵who was delivered up for our trespasses and was raised for our justification.

1. Τί οὖν ἐροῦμεν εὑρηκέναι ᾿Αβραὰμ τὸν προπάτορα ἡμῶν κατὰ σάρκα; It has already been suggested above (in the discussion of 3.31) that the purpose of this verse is to raise the question of Abraham as the most obvious possible objection to the statement that glorying has been excluded (3.27), in order that the truth of that statement might be decisively confirmed by the subsequent demonstration that even he has no ground for glorying, since he too was justified ἐκ πίστεως.

The witnesses to the text vary (i) as between προπάτορα and πατέρα, and (ii) as to whether εὑρηκέναι should be (a) placed after ἐροῦμεν or (b) placed after ἡμῶν or (c) omitted. The reading προπάτορα should no doubt be preferred. It is the more difficult reading (προπάτωρ occurs nowhere else in the NT and in the LXX only in 3 Macc 2.21), and is anyway strongly attested. With regard to (ii), it is probable that (a), which is attested by ℵ D G *pm*, should be read. Readings (b) and (c) can be variously explained. Thus both could be independent attempts at improvement provoked by the strangeness of the way εὑρίσκειν is used according to (a); or (b) could have originated in an accidental transposition and then, because its natural meaning seemed nonsensical, been corrected to (c); or (c) could have been due to accidental omission and (b) could, conceivably, be an attempted improvement of (c), which is certainly very odd Greek; or, of course, one of them could be a deliberate attempt to correct (a) and the other an accidental alteration of it.

It seems likely that the use of εὑρίσκειν here was suggested by the common LXX expressions εὑρίσκειν χάριν (or ἔλεος) ἐναντίον τινός (or ἐνώπιόν τινος or ἐν ὀφθαλμοῖς τινος).[1]

κατὰ σάρκα is to be connected not with προπάτορα[2] but with ἡμῶν. The implicit thought is that, while we (i.e. the Jews) are Abraham's children κατὰ σάρκα, Abraham has other children who are his in a different way (cf. vv. 11, 16ff); not that we have another forefather who is our forefather otherwise than κατὰ σάρκα.[3]

2. εἰ γὰρ Ἀβραὰμ ἐξ ἔργων ἐδικαιώθη, ἔχει καύχημα. The point of γάρ here is that this sentence explains the relevance of the question about Abraham in v. 1 to Paul's purpose in this section which is, as will become clear from the course of the argument, to confirm the truth of the statement (in 3.27) that καύχησις has been excluded. (There is no need to think of any imaginary Jewish objector either here or in v. 1, as do some commentators.) That Abraham was justified on the ground of his works was indeed what Paul's Jewish contemporaries were accustomed to assume. According to Jub. 23.10, 'Abraham was perfect in all his deeds with the Lord, and well-pleasing in righteousness all the days of his life'; and in *Kidd.* 4.14 it is stated that 'we find that Abraham our father had performed the whole Law before it was given, for it is written, Because that Abraham obeyed my voice and kept my charge, my commandments, my statutes, and my laws [Gen 26.5]'. He was one of the righteous ones not needing repentance—'Thou therefore, O Lord, that art the God of the just, hast not appointed repentance to the just, to Abraham, and Isaac, and Jacob, which have not sinned against thee; but thou hast appointed repentance unto me that am a sinner' (Prayer of Manasses (8)).[4] On such a view Abraham clearly has ground for glorying.

[1] e.g. Gen 6.8; 18.3; 19.19; 30.27; 32.5 [LXX: 6]; 33.8, 10; 34.11.

[2] Some commentators (e.g. Meyer 1, p. 195f; Godet, *in loc.*) insist on taking κατὰ σάρκα with εὑρηκέναι (this is indeed the most natural interpretation, if the reading which has the infinitive after ἡμῶν is accepted); but the sense yielded (κατὰ σάρκα would presumably have to mean something like 'by his own natural powers') does not suit the sequel at all well.

[3] For κατὰ σάρκα see on 1.3. Here the sense is 'according to natural physical generation'. Cf. 9.3.

[4] On Abraham in Jewish thought see SB 3, pp. 186ff; O. Schmitz, 'Abraham im Spätjudentum und im Urchristentum', in *Aus Schrift und Geschichte: theologische Abhandlungen A. Schlatter dargebracht*, 1922, pp. 99–123; J. Jeremias, in *TWNT* 1, pp. 7–9; Barrett, *From First Adam to Last*, pp. 22–45.

ἀλλ' οὐ πρὸς θεόν has sometimes been understood as intended merely to limit the scope of the statement ἔχει καύχημα by indicating that Abraham's right to glory does not extend to his relation to God (the thought that he does have the right to glory in relation to men being implied). But there are two objections to this interpretation: (i) the idea that Abraham, while not having any right to glory in relation to God, does have such a right in relation to men is scarcely relevant here; and (ii) the fact that the preceding ἔχει καύχημα is the apodosis of a protasis (εἰ . . . Ἀβραὰμ ἐξ ἔργων ἐδικαιώθη) which it is quite clear Paul regards as totally untrue, makes it exceedingly unlikely that he had in mind here the positive thought that Abraham does as a matter of fact possess a ground of glorying in relation to men. It would seem most agreeable to the context either to understand ἀλλ' οὐ πρὸς θεόν to be rejecting the supposition of the protasis εἰ . . . Ἀβραὰμ ἐξ ἔργων ἐδικαιώθη (and according to Paul's argument at the end of chapter 3 this would carry with it the rejection of the conclusion ἔχει καύχημα), or else to understand it to be rejecting the conclusion ἔχει καύχημα (the rejection of which would necessarily carry with it the denial that Abraham ἐξ ἔργων ἐδικαιώθη). Of these two alternative interpretations, the latter may perhaps have the advantage, so long as we confine our attention to the present verse, but the references to justification, faith, and working and not working, in vv. 3–6 would seem to favour the former, since they suggest that in the verses which are introduced as support (note the γάρ in v. 3) for ἀλλ' οὐ πρὸς θεόν Paul is concerned to disprove the supposition that Abraham ἐξ ἔργων ἐδικαιώθη rather than the conclusion that Abraham ἔχει καύχημα. But the connexion in Paul's mind between being justified on the ground of works and having a right to glory is so very close that there is no really substantial difference between these two interpretations. In either case πρός should probably be understood as equivalent to the Hebrew *lipnê* (cf. ἐνώπιον in 3.20). We take it that, in so far as a contrast with πρὸς ἀνθρώπους is implicit, the point is that, whatever men's view of the matter may be, God's view (which is attested in Scripture —cf. v. 3) is not that Abraham was justified ἐξ ἔργων (or possesses καύχημα).

3. τί γὰρ ἡ γραφὴ λέγει; introduces an OT quotation in support of ἀλλ' οὐ πρὸς θεόν. That in God's sight Abraham was not justified on the ground of works (and does not have ground for glorying) is clear from the following statement of Scripture.

ἐπίστευσεν δὲ Ἀβραὰμ τῷ θεῷ, καὶ ἐλογίσθη αὐτῷ εἰς δικαιοσύνην is an exact quotation of LXX Gen 15.6, except for the substitution of δέ for καί and of the form Ἀβραάμ for Ἀβράμ. The LXX itself differs from the MT in that it has replaced the active by the passive (ἐλογίσθη). This verse, which refers to Abraham's believing God's word to him, God's promise (Gen 15.1, 4, 5), figured prominently in Jewish thought and discussion. Already in 1 Macc 2.52 (Αβρααμ οὐχὶ ἐν πειρασμῷ εὑρέθη πιστός, καὶ ἐλογίσθη αὐτῷ εἰς δικαιοσύνην;) the faith it records is understood as a meritorious act on Abraham's part, as the use of ἔργα in the previous verse indicates. More explicit are the words attributed to Rabbi Shemaiah (about 50 B.C.) in *Mekilta* on Exod 14.15 (35[b]): 'The faith with which their father Abraham believed in Me [it is God who is represented as speaking] merits[1] that I should divide the sea for them, as it is written: "And he believed in the LORD, and he counted it to him for righteousness"'. Subsequently this understanding of the verse was generally accepted in Rabbinic Judaism. Typical is the statement in *Mekilta* 40[b] (Exod 14.31): 'So you find that our father Abraham became the heir of this and of the coming world simply by the merit of[2] the faith with which he believed in the LORD, as it is written: "He believed in the LORD, and he counted it to him for righteousness"'. That to Rabbinic Judaism Gen 15.6 was no proof at all that Abraham was not justified on the ground of works is absolutely clear. And this is also true with regard to the Judaism represented in the Pseudepigrapha and to Philo, though the conception of faith to be found in them is rather less stridently legalistic (in these non-Rabbinic Jewish writings faith is not just one particular meritorious act alongside others, but rather something basic and inclusive, the motivation and power behind particular works, embracing both the fundamental belief in the one only true God, the Creator, Ruler and Judge of the world, and also the way of life which corresponds to this belief[3]). Thus it is apparent that, in appealing to Gen 15.6 in support of his contention that Abraham was not justified on the ground of works and has no right to glory before God, Paul was deliberately appealing to a verse of Scripture which his fellow Jews generally assumed to be clear support for the diametrically opposite view. That he did so is highly significant, but in no way surprising. It was clearly essential to the

[1] Hebrew: k⁽e⁾dāy.
[2] Hebrew: biz⁽e⁾kût. So the H. S. Horovitz ed. (Jerusalem, ²1960). The J. Z. Lauterbach ed. (Philadelphia, 1933) reads biś⁽e⁾kar ('as a reward for'). Whichever of these readings is correct, and even if whichever it is is used prepositionally (= 'for the sake of'), the sentence implies the meritoriousness of the faith. Further illustrative material in SB 3, pp. 199–201.
[3] See, e.g., Philo. *De Abr.* 262–74; *Quis rer. div. her.* 90–95: *De mig. Abr.* 43–44: *Leg. Alleg.* 3.228.

credibility of his argument that he should not by-pass a text
which would seem to many of his fellow Jews the conclusive
disproof of the point he was trying to establish and which was
on any showing a text of cardinal importance in the biblical
account of Abraham, but should show that, rightly interpreted,
it confirmed his contention. This he proceeds to do in vv. 4–8
by drawing out the significance of the statements contained
in it.

4f. τῷ δὲ ἐργαζομένῳ ὁ μισθὸς οὐ λογίζεται κατὰ χάριν ἀλλὰ κατὰ
ὀφείλημα· τῷ δὲ μὴ ἐργαζομένῳ, πιστεύοντι δὲ ἐπὶ τὸν δικαιοῦντα τὸν
ἀσεβῆ, λογίζεται ἡ πίστις αὐτοῦ εἰς δικαιοσύνην has been variously
explained. According to Barrett, Paul's interpretation of Gen
15.6 hinges on the use of the verb λογίζεσθαι. So he puts
'counted' in inverted commas in his translation of v. 4,[1] and in
his comment states that Paul's first step 'is to fasten upon the
verb "to count" '.[2] He understands Paul's argument to turn
on the assumption that λογίζεσθαι is appropriately joined with
πιστεύειν and χάρις, but not with ἐργάζεσθαι and ὀφείλημα, so
that 'since Abraham had righteousness *counted* to him, he
cannot have done works, but must have been the recipient of
grace'.[3] But this explanation runs foul of the fact that Paul
himself uses λογίζεσθαι in v. 4 with κατὰ ὀφείλημα as well as
with κατὰ χάριν.[4]

The explanation of H. W. Heidland,[5] which also assumes the
pivotal importance of λογίζεσθαι, is more subtle. According to
it, Paul is playing off the Hebrew meaning of λογίζεσθαι
(Hebrew ḥāšaḇ) in λογίζεται κατὰ χάριν against the Greek
meaning of the word in [λογίζεται] κατὰ ὀφείλημα.[6] But, while

---

[1] p. 85.
[2] p. 88.
[3] ibid. The same understanding of Paul's argument is implied by the
NEB translation, which also puts 'counted' in v. 4 in inverted commas,
and, further, introduces a different verb as a supplement in rendering
ἀλλὰ κατὰ ὀφείλημα—'they are paid as debt' (cf. Barrett's addition of
'is paid' to his lemma on p. 88).
[4] The NEB conceals this fact by inserting the supplement 'are paid'.
[5] *TWNT* 4, pp. 293–95. Cf. Michel, p. 116.
[6] In secular Greek λογίζεσθαι is characteristically used (i) of numerical
calculation (its primary sense), and so as a technical term in accounting
(with a personal dative it means to put something down to someone's
account, whether credit or debit), and (ii) of strictly rational thought
which is free from the influence of emotion, so with such meanings as
'consider', 'conclude'. But in the LXX it comes to have further con-
notations as a result of the fact that it is used (in all but five of its
occurrences) to represent the Hebrew ḥāšaḇ, which only rarely denotes
a counting or reckoning in the commercial sense, but is frequently used
in such senses as 'devise', 'plan', 'invent' (meanings which are not
proper to the Greek word) to denote a thinking in which feeling and will

this certainly has considerable theological attractiveness (for by it Paul is very neatly shown to be breaking free from the idea of Abraham's faith as a meritorious work), and while the distinction between the ordinary Greek connotation of λογίζεσθαι and its special 'Hebrew' connotation is indeed relevant to the interpretation of Gen 15.6 and of Rom 4.4f, it is by no means clear that Paul's explanation of Gen 15.6 really hinges on the meaning of λογίζεσθαι. It is very significant that in the other Pauline passage in which Gen 15.6 is appealed to, namely, Gal 3, it is to the word ἐπίστευσεν that Paul draws attention (Gal 3.6f). And in the present passage the emphatic contrast between τῷ . . . ἐργαζομένῳ and τῷ . . . μὴ ἐργαζομένῳ, πιστεύοντι δέ surely indicates that it is upon ἐπίστευσεν, not upon ἐλογίσθη, that Paul is fastening. This conclusion is confirmed by the fact that the meaning of ἐπίστευσεν is further drawn out by the addition of ἐπὶ τὸν δικαιοῦντα τὸν ἀσεβῆ after πιστεύοντι.

The best explanation of Paul's exposition of Gen 15.6 in these two verses would seem to be that which understands it to turn upon the fact that the Genesis verse makes no mention of any work of Abraham but simply refers to his faith. Had a work been referred to, then the counting of it to Abraham as righteousness would have been a matter of ὀφείλημα and μισθός; but that his faith was counted to him for righteousness can only be a matter of χάρις—that is, if his faith is understood (in accordance with the context of this verse in Genesis) as his reliance upon God's promise (cf. Gen 15.1, 4f), his response of trust to God's prior initiative of grace, and still more of course if it is understood in the light of the definition of faith which has been emerging in the course of the epistle up to this point (cf. 1.5, 17; 3.22–24, 27f, 30). But, when once the significance of ἐπίστευσεν in Gen 15.6 is brought out, it immediately becomes clear that the verb λογίζεσθαι (as used in that verse) must signify a counting which is not a rewarding of merit but a free and unmerited decision of divine grace. Thus, on this interpretation, while Paul does not start by assuming

are involved (e.g. Ps 140 [LXX: 139].2 [MT and LXX: 3]; Mic 2.1; Zech 8.17), or, again, in such senses as 'count (as)', 'count (something to someone as)', denoting a personal—often purely subjective—judgment (e.g. Gen 31.15; 1 Sam 1.13; Job 41.27, 29 [MT: 21, 24]; Isa 5.28; 29.17; 40.15, 17; 53.4). The use of ḥāšab/λογίζεσθαι in Ps 106 [LXX: 105].31 is interesting for its formal similarity to that in Gen 15.6; but, whereas Gen 15.6 speaks of Abraham's faith as being reckoned to him for righteousness, what the psalm-verse refers to as reckoned to Phinehas for righteousness is his zealous deed (cf. Num 25.7–13). See further H. W. Heidland, in *TWNT* 4, pp. 287–95.

a special 'Hebrew' sense of λογίζεσθαι, he does, by starting from
ἐπίστευσεν, bring out the fact that in Gen 15.6 λογίζεσθαι must
be understood in its 'Hebrew' rather than its ordinary Greek
sense.

Paul's completion of πιστεύοντι by ἐπὶ τὸν δικαιοῦντα τὸν
ἀσεβῆ[1] is highly significant. To say that Abraham was one who
had no claim on God on the ground of works (τῷ . . . μὴ
ἐργαζομένῳ)[2] is tantamount to saying that he was ungodly
(for the word ἀσεβής, which occurs again in 5.6, see on ἀσέβεια
in 1.18), a sinner: we may compare the equation of justification
χωρὶς ἔργων with the forgiveness of sins in vv. 6–8. So the
faith which he had in God was necessarily faith in the God
who justifies the ungodly. That God does do just this is the
meaning of His grace (cf. κατὰ χάριν). The words ἐπὶ τὸν
δικαιοῦντα τὸν ἀσεβῆ may be said to point both backward and
forward—backward to 1.18–3.20 and 3.21–26 and forward to
vv. 6–8 and 25 and also to 5.6. It is noticeable that Paul here
substitutes πιστεύειν ἐπί for the πιστεύειν with the simple
dative of the Genesis quotation (see on 1.16 (παντὶ τῷ
πιστεύοντι) particularly, p. 90, n. 2).

6–8. That we have here a conscious application of the

---

[1] We may recognize in these words an echo of the language of Exod
23.7; Prov 17.15; 24.24; Isa 5.23; but it is a misleading over-simplification
to say, as Barrett does (p. 88), that they 'describe God as doing what
the Old Testament forbids'. According to the LXX all these passages
refer to human judges: they are forbidden to acquit the guilty—
particularly for the sake of bribes. In the MT the last part of Exod 23.7
(which in the LXX is καὶ οὐ δικαιώσεις τὸν ἀσεβῆ ἕνεκεν δώρων) is a divine
declaration, 'for I will not justify the wicked'. That the justification
of the ungodly to which Paul's words refer differs *toto caelo* from the
sort of thing against which the OT warns human judges is obvious
enough. And, as regards the Hebrew form of Exod 23.7, Paul's language
must be seen in the light of what he has said in 3.24–26, which makes it
clear that God's forgiveness is no cheap forgiveness that condones
wickedness, but the costly, just and truly merciful forgiveness διὰ τῆς
ἀπολυτρώσεως τῆς ἐν Χριστῷ Ἰησοῦ, which does not violate the truth which
the Exodus verse attests.

[2] The sense intended by τῷ . . . μὴ ἐργαζομένῳ here would seem to be
'to him who does no works which establish a claim on God' or 'to him
who has no claim on God on the ground of works', and, by contrast,
τῷ . . . ἐργαζομένῳ in the previous verse would seem to mean 'to him
who does works which establish a claim on God' (there being no such
man, according to Paul, Jesus Christ alone excepted). To take these
expressions to mean 'to him who does not seek to establish a claim on
God' and 'to him who seeks . . .', respectively, does not fit the context
(*pace* Michel, p. 117). Calvin was of course right to observe that Paul
has no intention of discouraging the doing of good works (p. 84).
τῷ . . . μὴ ἐργαζομένῳ does not imply that Abraham did no good works,
but only that he did none which constituted a claim on God.

Rabbinic exegetical principle of *gᵉzērāh šāwāh*[1] is very probable; but it is certainly important to recognize that Paul's argument is not merely verbal but substantial. The validity of his appeal to Ps 32.1f as helping to interpret Gen 15.6 is not just a matter of the presence of a common term (λογίζεσθαι/*ḥāšāḇ*) in both places: his appeal to the psalm-passage has an inward and substantial validity, for God's reckoning righteousness to a man χωρὶς ἔργων is, in fact, equivalent to His forgiving of sins.

καθάπερ. See on 3.4.

Δαυὶδ λέγει. As in 11.9, Paul names David in introducing a quotation from a psalm. In both cases the psalm quoted is one specifically ascribed to David in its title. Compare Mk 12.36–37 and parallels; also Acts 2.25. In Acts 4.25 and Heb 4.7 passages from psalms which in the MT have no title are ascribed to David. By this time the Psalter as a whole was known by his name. The psalm-passage to which Paul is appealing (Ps 32.1f) is one that is often cited in Rabbinic literature.[2]

μακαρισμόν: 'blessing' (not 'blessedness' which would be *μακαριότητα*). Reference may be made to the article by G. Bertram and F. Hauck in *TWNT* 4, pp. 365–73.

ᾧ ὁ θεὸς λογίζεται[3] δικαιοσύνην χωρὶς ἔργων. By means of this relative clause, which gathers up the thought of vv. 4 and 5, Paul makes the connexion between the passage he is about to quote and Gen 15.6, identifying the forgiving of sins with the reckoning of righteousness χωρὶς ἔργων.

μακάριοι ὧν ἀφέθησαν αἱ ἀνομίαι καὶ ὧν ἐπεκαλύφθησαν αἱ ἁμαρτίαι· μακάριος ἀνὴρ οὗ οὐ μὴ λογίσηται κύριος ἁμαρτίαν. The quotation agrees exactly with the LXX. It is interesting to note that the verb ἀφιέναι is nowhere else used in the Pauline epistles in the sense 'forgive', though ἄφεσις in the sense 'forgiveness' occurs in Eph 1.7 and Col 1.14. ἀνομίαι here represents *pešaʿ*. Of the Hebrew roots denoting 'sin' *pšʿ* is the most active and positive, signifying, as it does, rebellion against the divine authority, the deliberate and open violation of God's commandment, transgression; and it is this positive

---

[1] Cf. J. Jeremias, 'Zur Gedankenführung in den paulinischen Briefen', in *Studia Paulina*, pp. 149–51; Barrett, p. 89f; Gerhardsson, *Memory and Manuscript*, p. 287f. On *gᵉzērāh šāwāh*, which is the second of Hillel's *middôṯ* and refers to the association of two passages of Scripture having a term in common and the interpretation of each in the light of the other, see Strack, *Introduction*, p. 94; Jastrow, *Dictionary* s.v. גְּזֵרָה 4.

[2] Examples are given in SB 3, p. 202f. It was particularly quoted in connexion with the Day of Atonement.

[3] λογίζεται, which in vv. 4 and 5 was passive, is here middle.

sense of open rebellion against God which ἀνομία expresses in its other Pauline occurrences (6.19 (twice); 2 Cor 6.14; 2 Th 2.3, 7; Tit 2.14). ἐπικαλύπτειν occurs only here in the NT (the noun ἐπικάλυμμα occurs in 1 Pet 2.16). The Hebrew behind ὧν ἐπεκαλύφθησαν αἱ ἁμαρτίαι means literally 'he who is covered in respect of sin' ('he who is covered' being the Qal passive participle of kāsāh). The Hebrew kāsāh, used of 'covering' sin in a bad sense (opposed to confessing it) in Job 31.33 and Prov 28.13, and in a good sense (with reference to a human action) in Prov 10.12 and 17.9, is used here and in Ps 85.2 of God's forgiving sin.[1] In v. 8 the reading οὗ should no doubt be preferred to the variant ᾧ; for not only is it the more strongly attested reading, but it is also much more likely that an original οὗ would have been assimilated to the construction which is to be found with λογίζεσθαι in vv. 3, 4, 5, 6, 9, 11, 22, 23, and 24, than that an original ᾧ would have been assimilated to the οὗ of the LXX[2] or to the genitives in v. 7. οὐ μὴ λογίσηται is emphatic: 'will in no wise reckon'.

9. ὁ μακαρισμὸς οὖν οὗτος ἐπὶ τὴν περιτομὴν[3] ἢ καὶ ἐπὶ τὴν ἀκροβυστίαν; We may assume that it would be generally taken for granted by the Rabbis of Paul's day that the blessing pronounced in Ps 32.1f applied exclusively to the Jews.[4] (For

---

[1] The suggestion is sometimes made (e.g. Barrett, p. 89) that ἐπεκαλύφθησαν might be thought of as recalling the description of Christ crucified as God's ἱλαστήριον in 3.25. But, while it is no doubt true that Paul understood Ps 32.1f generally in the light of the Cross, the connexion between ἐπεκαλύφθησαν in particular and ἱλαστήριον is scarcely clear (unless one should regard it as established by the fact that the Rabbis often cite Ps 32.1f with reference to the Day of Atonement), since the Hebrew root which ἱλαστήριον, and its cognates ἱλάσκεσθαι, ἱλασμός, ἐξιλάσκειν, ἐξιλασμός, and ἐξίλασμα, most commonly represent in the LXX, and which, according to one view, has 'cover' as its basic connotation, is not ksh, the root used in Ps 32.1, which is never represented in the LXX by ἱλαστήριον or any of its cognates, but kpr, which in turn is never represented in the LXX by ἐπικαλύπτειν or καλύπτειν.

[2] In the textual tradition of the LXX too there is a variant reading ᾧ here (ℵ^c), which is, of course, closer to the Hebrew original. Heidland (TWNT 4, p. 295) has suggested that in the LXX the choice of οὗ rather than ᾧ (in spite of the fact that the Hebrew had lô) may have been due to the desire to avoid the suggestion of a business relationship attaching to λογίζεσθαί τινι, the verb being used here rather in the sense 'regard'; but this does not seem very convincing. The content of the sentence anyway makes it clear that the 'not-reckoning' is a matter of grace rather than desert.

[3] The μόνον read by D (cf. vg^cl) after περιτομήν is doubtless a secondary clarification.

[4] Cf., e.g. (the of course later): Pesikta R. 45 (185b): 'On the Day of Atonement God cleanses Israel and atones for its guilt, as it is written, "For on this day shall atonement be made for you, to cleanse you",

περιτομή and ἀκροβυστία used concretely to denote the Jews and the Gentiles respectively see on 2.25 and 26.)

λέγομεν γάρ¹ ἐλογίσθη τῷ Ἀβραὰμ ἡ πίστις εἰς δικαιοσύνην. Paul rejects the Rabbis' assumption, appealing back to Gen 15.6 in support of his contention. The γάρ may be explained as implying an unexpressed answer καὶ ἐπὶ τὴν ἀκροβυστίαν to the foregoing question. Paul now appeals back to Gen 15.6 as serving to interpret Ps 32.1f.

10. πῶς οὖν ἐλογίσθη; ἐν περιτομῇ ὄντι ἢ ἐν ἀκροβυστίᾳ; οὐκ ἐν περιτομῇ ἀλλ' ἐν ἀκροβυστίᾳ. Abraham's state, at the time that his faith was reckoned to him for righteousness, was that of uncircumcision; for his circumcision is not related until two chapters later (in Gen 17.1ff, where he is said to be ninety-nine years old—in 16.16 he is said to be eighty-six at the time of Ishmael's birth, which is some time after what is recorded in 15.1ff: according to the chronology of the Jews Abraham's circumcision was twenty-nine years after the promise of Gen 15.6²). If then it is right to interpret Ps 32.1f by Gen 15.6, it follows that the blessing pronounced by the psalm cannot be limited to those who are circumcised.

11a. καὶ σημεῖον ἔλαβεν περιτομῆς σφραγῖδα τῆς δικαιοσύνης τῆς πίστεως τῆς ἐν τῇ ἀκροβυστίᾳ is taken by Barrett to be a parenthesis, vv. 11b–12 being understood as following on v. 10.³ But v. 10, while it could be said to be an adequate basis for v. 11b, can hardly be regarded as a natural basis for v. 12. It would perhaps be possible to take vv. 10 and 11a together as the basis on which vv. 11b and 12 are dependent; but it is more natural to understand vv. 11b and 12 to depend on v. 11a alone. Since the statement made in v. 11a affirms both that Abraham did receive circumcision and also that righteousness had already been reckoned to him while he was still uncircumcised, it provides an adequate basis both for v. 12 and for v. 11b.

σημεῖον, περιτομή and ἡ ἀκροβυστία all occur in LXX Gen 17.11–13, σημεῖον in v. 11 (your circumcision ἔσται ἐν σημείῳ

Lev 16.30. And, if thou wouldst say, "Another nation too [he cleanses]", know that] it is not so, but it is only Israel; for so spake the prophet Micah (7.18): "Who is a God like unto thee, that pardoneth iniquity, and passeth by the transgression of the remnant of his heritage?" It is only Israel that he forgives. When David saw how God forgives the sins of the Israelites and has mercy upon them, he began to pronounce them blessed and to glorify them: "Blessed is he whose transgression is forgiven, etc.", Ps 32.1.'

¹ ὅτι is inserted after γάρ by A C 𝔎 G *pl* vg.
² Cf. *Seder Olam R.* 1 (quoted in SB 3, p. 203).
³ p. 90.

διαθήκης¹ ἀνὰ μέσον ἐμοῦ καὶ ὑμῶν), περιτομή in v. 13 (περιτομῇ περιτμηθήσεται) and ἡ ἀκροβυστία in v. 11 (καὶ περιτμηθήσεσθε τὴν σάρκα τῆς ἀκροβυστίας ὑμῶν). περιτομῆς² is a genitive of apposition or identity: the sign consists in circumcision. Circumcision is an outward sign, a pointer to the reality of that which it signifies, namely (according to Gen 17.11) the covenant made by God with Abraham and his seed. By σφραγῖδα τῆς δικαιοσύνης τῆς πίστεως τῆς ἐν τῇ ἀκροβυστίᾳ Abraham's circumcision is characterized as the seal, that is, the outward and visible authentication, ratification and guarantee, of the righteousness by faith which³ was already his while he was still uncircumcised. It seems quite probable, though it is not certain, that the custom of referring to circumcision as a seal⁴ was already well established in Judaism by Paul's time.⁵ The words imply that Abraham's circumcision, while it did not confer a status of righteousness on him, was nevertheless valuable as the outward and visible attestation of the status of righteousness which he already possessed.

11b–12 is made up of two clauses composed of εἰς with the articular infinitive, the main one being εἰς τὸ εἶναι αὐτὸν πατέρα πάντων τῶν πιστευόντων δι' ἀκροβυστίας ... καὶ πατέρα περιτομῆς τοῖς οὐκ ἐκ περιτομῆς μόνον ἀλλὰ καὶ τοῖς στοιχοῦσιν τοῖς ἴχνεσιν τῆς ἐν ἀκροβυστίᾳ πίστεως τοῦ πατρὸς ἡμῶν Ἀβραάμ and εἰς τὸ λογισθῆναι αὐτοῖς [τὴν] δικαιοσύνην being dependent on the first part of it. The former clause is naturally understood as expressing a divine purpose⁶— it was God's intention in causing Abraham to be cir-

¹ MT: lᵉʾôṯ bᵉrîṯ.
² The variant περιτομήν is no doubt secondary, an attempt at clarification.
³ τῆς ἐν τῇ ἀκροβυστίᾳ is better understood as dependent on δικαιοσύνης than on πίστεως, since it is Abraham's righteousness, not his faith, which is directly at issue throughout this passage.
⁴ Cf. e.g., *Shab.* 137ᵇ ('He who pronounces the blessing [over the cup of wine] says: Blessed be He who hath sanctified the Beloved from the womb and set the statute in his flesh and sealed his offspring with the sign of the holy covenant': the words are still in use—cf. *ADPB*, p. 305); *Exod R.* 19 (81ᶜ) ('Unless the seal [ḥôṯām] of Abraham is in your flesh, you may not eat'); Targ. Ct 3.8 ('. . . and each one of them had the seal of circumcision [hᵃṯîmaṯ mîlāh] in his flesh, as it was imprinted in the flesh of Abraham . . .'); cf. also Barn. 9.6 (ἀλλ' ἐρεῖς· Καὶ μὴν περιτέτμηται ὁ λαὸς εἰς σφραγῖδα). The early Christian use of σφραγίς to denote baptism (see Bauer, s.v. 2.b.), perhaps anticipated by the use of σφραγίζεσθαι in 2 Cor 1.22; Eph 1.13; 4.30, is very probably to be connected with this Jewish use of the image of sealing.
⁵ Cf. Lietzmann, p. 53f; Michel, p. 119, n. 4: *contra*, e.g. Fitzer, in *TWNT* 7, p. 949, n. 85.
⁶ So, e.g., Michel, p. 120. Lagrange, p. 90, argues that a final clause, while it suits what is said in v. 12 very well, is inconsonant with v. 11b ('on ne peut pas dire: il reçut la circoncision afin d'être le père des

cumcised that he should be the point of union between all who
believe, whether circumcised or uncircumcised, being, on the
one hand, by virtue of his having been justified while still
uncircumcised, the father of all those who as uncircumcised[1]
believe, and, on the other hand, by virtue of the fact that he
subsequently received circumcision, the father of all those who,
being circumcised, are not only circumcised but are also
believers. The latter εἰς with the articular infinitive clause
would seem to be rather better explained as consecutive than
as final.[2] It depends on πιστευόντων.[3] In v. 12 the first περιτομῆς
is a case of the abstract used for the concrete. For περιτομή
used in this sense without the article compare 3.30; 15.8
(contrast v. 9; Gal 2.7, 8, 9). The omission of the article is in
no way surprising, especially as περιτομῆς is connected with the
anarthrous πατέρα. A puzzling feature of the verse is the
presence of the article before στοιχοῦσιν. It implies that a
different group of people altogether from that just referred to
is intended. But this is not only contrary to what seems to be
the clear sense of the sentence; it is also ruled out grammatically—this point is often not mentioned—by the position of
the earlier τοῖς in relation to οὐκ . . . μόνον. Since the objection
to the presence of the τοῖς before στοιχοῦσιν on the ground of the
sense of the passage is thus confirmed by the thoroughly
objective fact of its inconsistency with the grammar of the
sentence, it would seem that we are justified[4] in regarding it as
a simple mistake, whether of Paul himself or of Tertius or of a
very early copyist,[5] and ignoring it in interpretation.

incirconcis'); but this is to treat vv. 11b and 12 as though they expressed
two quite separate purposes, whereas in reality they express a single purpose, namely, that Abraham might be the one who is both this and that.

[1] διά with the genitive here expresses attendant circumstances.

[2] *Pace* Michel, p. 120; Barrett, p. 86, *et al.*

[3] There is textual variation at two points in this clause. C ℵ D G *pm*
have καί after λογισθῆναι. It is a moot question whether it is more likely
that this was omitted by accident or added in order to bring out the
point that having righteousness reckoned is something common to them
and to Abraham. It is also very difficult to decide whether to read or
to omit τήν (attested by B C* ℵ G *pm*) before δικαιοσύνην. [N²⁶ adds the
καί in square brackets.]

[4] *Pace* Cambier 1, p. 171, n. 1.

[5] Since it has the unanimous support of the extant textual witnesses,
it must—if it is to be attributed to a copyist—be attributed to one so
early as to have been in a position to corrupt the whole textual tradition.
The suggestion has naturally been made that an original καὶ αὐτοῖς could
easily (especially if the καί had been abbreviated to its initial letter)
have been misread as καὶ τοῖς. In the sixteenth century Beza proposed
the omission of τοῖς. The difficulty of managing 'not only . . . but also . . .'
(not only in Greek!) is notorious, and a simple mistake by Tertius or
by Paul himself can scarcely be ruled out.

Both the placing of πατέρα πάντων τῶν πιστευόντων δι᾽ ἀκροβυστίας[1] before πατέρα περιτομῆς and also the qualification of the latter by τοῖς οὐκ ἐκ περιτομῆς μόνον,[2] κ.τ.λ. have the effect of emphasizing the fact that it is faith, not circumcision, which is decisive. But, while recognizing that Paul is here concerned with a kinship with Abraham which depends on the sharing of his faith, we must be careful to avoid the mistake of concluding from what is said here that Paul intended to deny the reality of the kinship κατὰ σάρκα (cf. v. 1) with Abraham of those Jews who did not share his faith or that he believed that such Jews were altogether excluded from the promises (cf. what was said of 2.28f).

13. Οὐ γὰρ διὰ νόμου ἡ ἐπαγγελία τῷ Ἀβραὰμ ἢ τῷ σπέρματι αὐτοῦ, τὸ κληρονόμον αὐτὸν εἶναι κόσμου, ἀλλὰ διὰ δικαιοσύνης πίστεως. This verse has been variously interpreted, matters particularly at issue being the reference of the anarthrous νόμου, the meaning of the repeated διά, and the thought behind the insertion of ἢ τῷ σπέρματι αὐτοῦ. Some[3] maintain that the reference of νόμου is quite general, to any system of law requiring obedience, while others[4] insist that it is specific, the Mosaic law being intended. The latter view is surely to be preferred in the context (cf. the occurrences of νόμος in vv. 14, 15 and 16). With regard to διά, the question is whether it is to be explained as signifying instrumentality or attendant circumstances. On the assumption that it signifies attendant circumstances, it is possible to understand Paul's meaning to be either that the promise does not fall within the scope of the law but within that of the righteousness of faith,[5] or—a simple matter of chronology— that it was at a time when the law had not yet been given but Abraham had already been justified through faith (Gen 15.6), that the promise was given to him (Gen 18.18; 22.17f).[6] But it

---

[1] What Paul means by these words clearly differs radically from what was meant by the Rabbis when they referred to Abraham as the first proselyte (e.g. *Mekilta* Exod 22.20 (101a)) or as the first of those who believe (cf. material quoted by Delitzsch, p. 80).

[2] τοῖς οὐκ ἐκ περιτομῆς μόνον must clearly mean 'for those who not only belong to the circumcision' (cf. Michel, p. 119; Kuss, p. 184), and not 'of those . . . who do not rely on circumcision only' (Barrett, p. 86: cf. NEB; and also the paraphrase in Sanday and Headlam, p. 106). That Paul would imply that a Jewish Christian must necessarily *rely on* circumcision is most unlikely.

[3] e.g., Kühl, p. 143; Sanday and Headlam, p. 110; Zahn, p. 230; Murray 1, p. 141.

[4] e.g., Calvin, p. 91; Lagrange, p. 91f; Barth, *Shorter*, p. 51; Michel, p. 121; Kuss, p. 187.

[5] Cf. Barrett, p. 94

[6] Cf. Gal 3.17.

is probably preferable to take διά as instrumental. Paul's meaning may then be understood to be, not that it was not through the instrumentality of the law but through that of the righteousness of faith that the promise was given, but that it was not through the instrumentality of the law but through that of the righteousness of faith that the promise was to be appropriated, or—to put it differently—that the promise was not given on the condition of its being merited by fulfilment of the law but simply on the basis of the righteousness of faith. Paul's statement stands in striking contrast to the Rabbis' assumption that all the promises were made to Abraham on the basis of his fulfilment of the law (which, according to them, was already known by him and performed in its completeness, although it had not yet been promulgated) and to their understanding of his faith as itself a meritorious work.[1] With regard to the words ἤ[2] τῷ σπέρματι αὐτοῦ, it has been suggested that Paul may perhaps be thinking of Christ as the true seed of Abraham (cf. Gal 3.16); but in view of vv. 16 and 17 this is not likely.[3] His thought, as he uses the expression 'thy seed' which recurs again and again in the record of God's promises to Abraham (Gen 12.7; 13.15f; 15.5, 18; 17.8; 22.17f), is rather of all those of whom Abraham is said in vv. 11 and 12 to be the father (cf. v. 16f). Nowhere in the OT is the promise to Abraham couched in terms at all close to τὸ κληρονόμον αὐτὸν εἶναι κόσμου. What is promised in the various Genesis passages is a numberless progeny,[4] possession of the land of Canaan,[5] and that all the nations of the earth shall be blessed (or shall bless themselves) in Abraham[6] or in his seed.[7] But Judaism came to interpret the promise to Abraham as a much more comprehensive promise. Thus Ecclus 44.21 contains the words: 'Therefore he assured him by an oath, . . . That he would . . . exalt his seed as the stars, And cause them to inherit from sea to sea, And from the River unto the utmost part of the earth'. Compare *Mekilta* Exod 14.31 (40ᵇ), already quoted in the note on v. 3, and the further material in SB 3, p. 209. Perhaps the best comment on the meaning of the promise as understood by

---

[1] Cf. the passages already quoted in the notes on vv. 2 and 3, and the further material in SB 3, pp. 186ff and 204ff.

[2] For the copulative sense which ἤ can have, especially in a negative clause, see BDF, § 446.

[3] And in the case of Christ διὰ δικαιοσύνης πίστεως would hardly be appropriate.

[4] Gen 12.2; 13.16; 15.5; 18.18.

[5] Gen 12.7; 13.14f, 17; 15.7, 18–21; 17.8.

[6] Gen 12.3; 18.18.

[7] Gen 22.18.

Paul is provided by 1 Cor 3.21b–23 (πάντα γὰρ ὑμῶν ἐστιν, εἴτε Παῦλος εἴτε Ἀπολλῶς εἴτε Κηφᾶς, εἴτε κόσμος εἴτε ζωὴ εἴτε θάνατος, εἴτε ἐνεστῶτα εἴτε μέλλοντα, πάντα ὑμῶν, ὑμεῖς δὲ Χριστοῦ, Χριστὸς δὲ θεοῦ). It is the promise of the ultimate restoration to Abraham and his spiritual seed of man's inheritance (cf. Gen 1.27f) which was lost through sin.[1] We may now look back to the γάρ at the beginning of the verse. It may now be explained as marking the introduction of a further consideration in support of what has already been said by way of proof that Abraham is no exception to the statement in 3.27 that boasting has been ruled out.

14. εἰ γὰρ οἱ ἐκ νόμου κληρονόμοι, κεκένωται ἡ πίστις καὶ κατήργηται ἡ ἐπαγγελία. This verse too has been understood in a number of different ways. The simplest and most natural interpretation, especially in view of v. 15, is surely that which takes Paul's point (made in support of what he has just said in v. 13) to be that, if it were true[2] that it is those who have a claim to the inheritance on the basis of their fulfilment of the law[3] who are the heirs, faith would be vain[4] and the promise a mere dead letter (since, on this condition, there could be no heirs at all, except for Christ Himself, there being none, Christ alone excepted, who actually have—as opposed to imagining that they have—a claim on God on the basis of their obedience).[5]

[1] Calvin's comment on these words (p. 91f) includes the following suggestive sentences: 'The godly have a taste of this in the present life, for however often they may be oppressed by difficulty and want, yet because they partake with a peaceable conscience of those things which God created for their use, and enjoy earthly blessings from a favourable and willing Father as pledges and foretastes of eternal life, their poverty does not prevent them from acknowledging earth, sea, and heaven as their right. Although the ungodly devour the riches of the world, they can call nothing their own, but rather snatch what they have by stealth, for they usurp it under the curse of God.'

[2] The condition is unfulfilled according to the author's thought, though not according to the grammatical form in which it is expressed. Cf. 4.2, and see Burton, *MT*, § 245. The 'real case' form is used for the sake of greater vividness.

[3] That this is what is meant by οἱ ἐκ νόμου here is confirmed by the parallel protasis in Gal 3.18 (εἰ . . . ἐκ νόμου ἡ κληρονομία). Other views are: that the reference is to those who rely on the law (so, e.g., Barrett, p. 92); that the reference is simply to the Jews as such as being the people of the law (so, e.g., Kuss, p. 188). Some (e.g. Sanday and Headlam, p. 111; Murray 1, p. 142) insist on understanding νόμου in a general sense.

[4] For the meaning of κεκένωται ἡ πίστις cf. 1 Cor 15.14 (εἰ δὲ Χριστὸς οὐκ ἐγήγερται, κενὸν ἄρα τὸ κήρυγμα ἡμῶν, κενὴ καὶ ἡ πίστις ὑμῶν).

[5] Cf., e.g., Calvin, p. 92f. Others (e.g. Barrett, p. 94f) explain that Paul is here justifying what he has said in the previous verse by an appeal to the proper meanings of the words πίστις and ἐπαγγελία (if the promise which, according to Genesis, is related to Abraham's faith, is

15. If the interpretation of v. 14 given above is accepted, then the connexion between the first half of v. 15 and v. 14 is perfectly clear. ὁ γὰρ νόμος ὀργὴν κατεργάζεται confirms v. 14 by drawing attention to the fact that, so far from the law's being something which a man might hope so adequately to fulfil as thereby to establish a claim on God, its actual effect, men being what they are, is to bring God's wrath upon them by turning their sin into conscious transgression and so rendering it more exceeding sinful. We may compare 3.20b; 5.20a; 7.7–13; Gal 3.19a.

οὗ δὲ οὐκ ἔστιν νόμος, οὐδὲ παράβασις is added in clarification[1] of the first half of the verse. It highlights the essential character-istic of the situation obtaining in the absence of the law, in order to suggest the process (the conversion of sin into conscious transgression)[2] by which the law's advent works wrath.

16. Διὰ τοῦτο ἐκ πίστεως, ἵνα κατὰ χάριν, εἰς τὸ εἶναι βεβαίαν τὴν ἐπαγγελίαν παντὶ τῷ σπέρματι, οὐ τῷ ἐκ τοῦ νόμου μόνον ἀλλὰ καὶ τῷ ἐκ πίστεως Ἀβραάμ. It is widely assumed that Διὰ τοῦτο is to be understood as referring backward, whether to v. 15, or to v. 14 (if v. 15 is taken to be a parenthesis), or to vv. 14 and 15 as a whole, and so meaning 'wherefore'. This is certainly possible; but, in view of the ἵνα which follows almost immediately, it is surely preferable to understand it as referring forward (cf. 2 Cor 13.10; Philem 15; 1 Tim 1.16), and so to take Διὰ τοῦτο ... ἵνα to mean 'For this reason . . ., namely, in order that'.[3] The

really conditional upon the fulfilment of the law, then 'the terms "faith" and "promise" have lost their meaning'). But, while it is of course true that from Paul's point of view there is an essential incongruity in using the words πίστις and ἐπαγγελία in connexion with a blessing which is understood to be conditional on fulfilment of the law (cf., e.g., 3.28; Gal 3.18a), this explanation of v. 14 is surely less likely than the one given above, since it involves a rather strained interpretation of κεκένωται, κ.τ.λ. and the treatment of v. 15 as parenthetic. The natural connexion between vv. 14 and 15 is also destroyed by the explanation (found already in Pelagius, p. 38: 'Si [illi] soli . . . circumcisi heredes sunt, non impleuit deus promissum Abrahae, ut "pater esset multarum gentium", et, si ita est, iam uidebitur deo sine causa cre[di]disse'), according to which Paul's meaning is that, if it is only the Jews who are heirs, then God's promise to Abraham which is quoted in v. 18 has been dishonoured and Abraham's faith proved vain.

[1] The variant γάρ (א D G pl lat syp) is easily explicable as due to a desire to make the connexion of thought clearer. Some, however (e.g. von Soden; Lagrange, p. 93f) prefer to read γάρ.

[2] On παράβασις see on 2.23.

[3] The expression διὰ τοῦτο occurs more than sixty times in the NT. It can have either a backward or a forward reference. Paul uses it in both ways, though in his epistles, as in the NT as a whole, the backward reference is more common. The proportion is about the same in the

first part of the verse is strikingly elliptic. It is possible to supplement ἐκ πίστεως by ἡ ἐπαγγελία (ἐστίν) from v. 13 or by ἡ κληρονομία from v. 14, or—and this is probably best—one can follow Sanday and Headlam,[1] Lagrange,[2] Barrett,[3] and others, in understanding Paul to have in mind something more comprehensive—the divine plan of salvation. With ἵνα κατὰ χάριν it is natural to supply γένηται. God has made His plan of salvation to depend, on man's side, not on fulfilment of the law but solely on faith, in order that, on His side, it might be a matter of grace.[4]

With regard to the second purpose clause it is necessary to decide whether the main emphasis falls on βεβαίαν or on παντὶ . . ., οὐ τῷ ἐκ τοῦ νόμου μόνον ἀλλὰ καὶ τῷ ἐκ πίστεως 'Αβραάμ. If it is on the former, Paul's point is that God's plan is ἐκ πίστεως in order that it may be κατὰ χάριν in order that the promise may be sure of fulfilment, instead of being an empty promise (as it would have been, had God's plan been dependent on men's performance of the law), for all the seed. If, however, it is on the latter, then Paul's point is that God's plan is ἐκ πίστεως in order that it may be κατὰ χάριν in order that the promise may be sure of fulfilment for all the seed, instead of being so merely for that which is ἐκ τοῦ νόμου (as it would have been, had God's plan been dependent on men's performance of the law). Of these alternatives the former fits the context better; for the implication of v. 15 is not that only some of Abraham's seed would inherit but that no one at all would inherit, if inheriting were really to be limited to οἱ ἐκ νόμου. The fact that παντί does indeed get considerable emphasis, being expanded in the words which follow, need not mean that it is the main thought which Paul wishes to express here: rather is it a subsidiary thought, but, once mentioned, it is expanded and developed, as being important in itself.

Sometimes τῷ ἐκ τοῦ νόμου is taken to refer to the Jews: more probably Paul means by it the Jewish Christians, who possess the law as well as sharing Abraham's faith, and by τῷ ἐκ πίστεως 'Αβραάμ the Gentile Christians, who share Abraham's faith without possessing the law. Compare vv. 11b and 12. If this interpretation is correct, τῷ ἐκ τοῦ νόμου is used

Pauline corpus as in the rest of the NT—roughly two backward references to every one forward reference. Where the reference is forward, διὰ τοῦτο is naturally followed by a clause indicating purpose or cause.
[1] p. 112.
[2] p. 94.
[3] p. 95f.
[4] Cf. Barrett, p. 95.

here in a different sense from that in which ἐκ νόμου is used in
v. 14. (The possibility of taking ἐκ τοῦ νόμου in the same sense as
ἐκ νόμου in v. 14, explaining τῷ ἐκ τοῦ νόμου as meaning that
part of Abraham's seed which really has a claim on the
ground of its fulfilment of the law—that is, according to Paul's
understanding, only Jesus Christ—and then taking τῷ ἐκ
πίστεως 'Αβραάμ to denote all those who, like Abraham, are
righteous by faith, whether Jews or Gentiles, may at least be
mentioned; but it is less probable than the interpretation just
given.)

ὅς ἐστιν πατὴρ πάντων ἡμῶν repeats with a certain solemnity[1]
the thought of vv. 11b–12, presupposed by the words παντὶ
τῷ σπέρματι, κ.τ.λ. Abraham is not only the father according to
the flesh of all Jews (cf. v. 1); he is also the father in a different,
but no less real, sense of all believers without exception.

17a. καθὼς γέγραπται ὅτι πατέρα πολλῶν ἐθνῶν τέθεικά σε provides
scriptural confirmation of what has just been said. The words
are quoted exactly from LXX Gen 17.5, where they are an
explanation of the significance of the name 'Abraham'. In
Genesis the thought may be simply of the Ishmaelites and
Edomites and the descendants of Abraham and Keturah,
though it is not impossible that a more far-reaching thought is
already present. Among the Rabbis there were some who
claimed on the basis of this Genesis verse that Abraham can be
said to be the father of proselytes and even the father of all men.[2]

17b. κατέναντι οὗ ἐπίστευσεν θεοῦ is equivalent to κατέναντι τοῦ
θεοῦ ᾧ ἐπίστευσεν (on the attraction of the relative see BDF,
§ 294). The words are naturally connected with ὅς ἐστιν πατὴρ
πάντων ἡμῶν, v. 17a being a parenthesis. (This is better than
taking them with εἰς τὸ εἶναι βεβαίαν τὴν ἐπαγγελίαν παντὶ τῷ
σπέρματι, οὐ τῷ ἐκ τοῦ νόμου μόνον ἀλλὰ καὶ τῷ ἐκ πίστεως 'Αβραάμ
and treating the whole of ὅς ἐστιν, κ.τ.λ. right down to the end of
the OT quotation as the parenthesis.) Abraham is father of us
all in God's sight. This is how God sees him, whatever some
Jews may think, and it is God's view which matters. For
κατέναντι see BDF, § 214, especially (4), and Bauer, s.v. It can
mean either 'opposite' or 'in the sight of'. It is used here in the
latter sense.[3] Compare the only other occurrences of the word
in Paul—2 Cor 2.17; 12.19; and also the use of *lipnê* in such

---

[1] On ὅς ἐστιν introducing a solemn statement reference may be made
to E. Norden, *Agnostos Theos*, Leipzig and Berlin, 1913, pp. 168ff.
[2] Cf. SB 3, p. 211.
[3] *Pace* Sanday and Headlam, who claim (p. 113) that it describes
'the posture in which Abraham is represented as holding colloquy with
God' in Gen 17.1ff. SB 3, p. 212, compares *Mekilta* Exod 15.1 (41ᵃ):
'Great is faith before [*lipnê*] God'.

places as Ps 19.14 [MT: 15]; 143.2. While these words properly belong to the relative clause ὅς ἐστιν πατὴρ πάντων ἡμῶν, they serve to lead into the positive statement about the nature of Abraham's faith which follows.

The remainder of the verse characterizes the God in whom Abraham believed by reference to two attributes of the divine sovereignty exhibited in the story of Abraham and acknowledged in Judaism. Abraham's faith was faith in *this* God.

τοῦ ζῳοποιοῦντος τοὺς νεκρούς. Compare the second benediction of the Shemoneh Ezreh (the Eighteen Benedictions): 'Blessed art Thou, O LORD, who quickenest the dead' (*Bārûḵ 'attāh YHWH mᵉḥayyēh hammēṯîm*)[1]; also Wisd 16.13; Tob 13.2 (cf. also Deut 32.39; 1 Sam 2.6; 2 Kgs 5.7). Paul has in mind the quickening of the body of Abraham and the womb of Sarah, which from the point of view of raising a family were as good as dead (cf. νενεκρωμένον and νέκρωσιν in v. 19), conceivably also the sparing of Isaac's life related in Gen 22 (cf. Heb 11.19), and certainly in the background the raising of Jesus (cf. vv. 24 and 25).

καὶ καλοῦντος τὰ μὴ ὄντα ὡς ὄντα. There is little doubt that the reference is to God's *creatio ex nihilo*. Sanday and Headlam[2] list four suggested interpretations, which may be summarized as follows: (i) 'who names things non-existent as if they existed'; (ii) 'who calls into being things which do not exist';[3] (iii) 'who issues His summons to things not yet existing as if they existed'; (iv) 'who calls (to life and salvation) things not yet existing as if they existed'. Sanday and Headlam rightly dismiss the last as remote from the context; but neither (i) nor (iii), between which they think the choice is to be made (they prefer (iii) and in their paraphrase represent the words by 'who issues His summons (as He issued it then) to generations yet unborn'), is at all convincing. The difficulty in the way of accepting (ii) is ὡς ὄντα; but this is probably not insuperable. The ὡς may perhaps be explained as expressing consequence (see LSJ, s.v., B.III.1), a participle being used instead of the infinitive or indicative in order to express vividly the immediacy of the result.[4] For the thought and also the language

[1] Käsemann, *Perspektiven*, p. 159, suggests that it is because Paul has in mind this benediction that he uses ζῳοποιεῖν (which occurs in the Pauline corpus otherwise only in 8.11) instead of ἐγείρειν.

[2] p. 113.

[3] For God's creating call cf. Isa 48.13.

[4] Otherwise it might be explained as comparative as in (i), (iii) and (iv), καλοῦντος still being understood to denote God's creative call. The idea would then be that God, in calling into being what does not exist, addresses His creating word to it, thus in a sense treating it as though it already existed.

compare Philo *Spec. Leg.* 4.187 (τὰ γὰρ μὴ ὄντα ἐκάλεσεν εἰς τὸ εἶναι);[1] also 2 Macc 7.28 (ἀξιῶ σε, τέκνον, ἀναβλέψαντα εἰς τὸν οὐρανὸν καὶ τὴν γῆν καὶ τὰ ἐν αὐτοῖς πάντα ἰδόντα γνῶναι ὅτι οὐκ ἐξ ὄντων ἐποίησεν αὐτὰ ὁ θεός, . . .); 2 Bar. 21.4; 48.8; and in Rabbinic Judaism the description of God as 'He who spoke and the world came into being' (mî šeʼāmar wᵉhāyāh hāʻôlām) found on the lips of various teachers (e.g. *Mekilta* Exod 18.3 (65ᵇ); 21.37 (95ᵃ); 22.22 (101ᵇ)). God's promise that Abraham shall be the father of many nations exemplifies His creating power.

18. ὃς παρ' ἐλπίδα ἐπ' ἐλπίδι ἐπίστευσεν. Chrysostom no doubt gives the general sense of these words correctly, when to his own question, Πῶς παρ' ἐλπίδα ἐπ' ἐλπίδι ἐπίστευσε; he replies suggestively, Παρ' ἐλπίδα τὴν ἀνθρωπίνην, ἐπ' ἐλπίδι τῇ τοῦ Θεοῦ.[2] But the words require further clarification. The expression παρ' ἐλπίδα[3] can mean either 'beyond hope' (cf. Latin *praeter spem*) or 'against hope' (cf. the Latin *contra spem*).[4] If it is used in the former sense here, Paul's point will be that Abraham believed God at a time when it was no longer a human possibility for him to go on hoping—human hope's utmost limit had already been reached and passed, and, so far as hope as a human possibility was concerned, he had given up hoping. And, since the promise of offspring recorded in Gen 15.5 (the verse before the one which Paul is expounding and will quote again in v. 22) is not substantially something quite new but substantially a repetition of the promise recorded in Gen 12.2f, which (according to Genesis) was made something like a quarter of a century earlier (cf. Gen 12.4 and 17.1), a reference to the limit's having been passed as far as Abraham's hope was concerned could hardly be said to be inappropriate. But perhaps it is rather more likely that Paul is thinking simply of the sheer impossibility (according to human calculations) of the promise recorded in Gen 15.5, without any reference to the fact that Abraham had already been hoping for a very long time without receiving the object of his hope, and that we should therefore understand παρά to mean 'against' (as does the Vulgate with its 'contra spem') rather than 'beyond'. The point will then be that Abraham's believing ἐπ' ἐλπίδι is a defiance of

[1] See also, e.g., Philo, *Op. Mund.* 81; *Vit. Mos.* 2.100: the conception of God's *creatio ex nihilo* is particularly characteristic of Hellenistic Judaism.

[2] col. 461.

[3] It occurs in extra-biblical Greek in, e.g., Aeschylus, *Ag.* 899 (καὶ γῆν φανεῖσαν ναυτίλοις παρ' ἐλπίδα); Sophocles, *Ph.* 882; Dionysius of Halicarnassus, 6.25; Philo, *Vit. Mos.* 1.250; Josephus, *B. J.* 3.183.

[4] For Paul's use of παρά in the sense 'beyond' cf. 12.3; 2 Cor 8.3; for his use of it in the sense 'against', 'contrary to', cf. 11.24.

all human calculations: his hope (signified by ἐλπίδι) is contrary to all human expectation (signified by ἐλπίδα). A good comment on παρ' ἐλπίδα is then supplied by Charles Wesley's lines:

> 'In hope, against all human hope,
> Self-desperate, I believe; . . .
>
> Faith, mighty faith, the promise sees,
> And looks to that alone;
> Laughs at impossibilities,
> And cries: It shall be done!'[1]

The next phrase, ἐπ' ἐλπίδι, is understood by Bauer[2] as meaning 'on the basis of hope' (on this view we may take Paul's thought to be that Abraham's faith was based on his God-given hope—in other words, the basis of his faith was simply the divine promise); but other occurrences of ἐπ' ἐλπίδι might encourage us rather to understand it here as describing Abraham's condition, his state of mind, at the time of his faith.[3] In either case, the hope must be understood as God-given, as a hope which was altogether independent of human possibilities and human calculations.

εἰς τὸ γενέσθαι αὐτὸν πατέρα πολλῶν ἐθνῶν. Some prefer to place no mark of punctuation after ἐπίστευσεν and to understand these words as expressing the content of Abraham's faith, i.e. the content of the divine promise which he believed; but πιστεύειν εἰς followed by the articular infinitive would be a very surprising construction. It is much better (pace, among the most recent commentators, Michel, p. 125, and Kuss, p. 192) to put a comma after ἐπίστευσεν and take these words as a consecutive clause ('so that he became the father of many nations')—or, less probably, a final clause. The result of his hopeful faith is that he is the father of us all (cf. v. 16f, where the statement that Abraham is father of us all is confirmed by quotation of five words from LXX Gen 17.5, three of which are again quoted here in v. 18, namely, πατέρα πολλῶν ἐθνῶν).

The effect of the addition of κατὰ τὸ εἰρημένον· οὕτως ἔσται τὸ σπέρμα σου is to connect the preceding seven words (which include the phrase from Gen 17.5) with Gen 15.5, and so with the actual promise to which Gen 15.6, the verse which is basic

---

[1] Hymn 561 in *The Methodist Hymn-Book*, London, 1933.
[2] s.v. ἐλπίς 1; ἐπί II.1.b.γ. His expression is: 'Auf Grund von Hoffnung'.
[3] Cf. Jülicher's rendering (quoted by Michel, p. 125): 'Er hat, wo nichts zu hoffen war, hoffnungsvoll zu glauben gewagt'. For ἐπ' ἐλπίδι cf. 5.2; 8.20; also Acts 2.26; 26.6; 1 Cor 9.10; Tit 1.2; in the LXX, Judg 18.7, 10 and 27 in the B text; Ps 4.8 [LXX: 9]; Ps 16 [LXX: 15].9; Hos 2.18 [LXX: 20]; Zeph 2.15.

to this whole chapter of Romans, refers. The additional words read by G after τὸ σπέρμα σου (cf. Gen 15.5; 22.17; 32.12; and also Heb 11.12) are no doubt secondary, a clarification of οὕτως.

19. καὶ μὴ ἀσθενήσας τῇ πίστει. The simple dative is better attested than the ἐν τῇ πίστει of D* G Or, and may be explained as a dative of respect (see BDF, § 197). To have taken God's promise less seriously than the circumstances contradicting it would have been ἀσθενεῖν τῇ πίστει. Compare the positive statement ἐνεδυναμώθη τῇ πίστει in the following verse.

κατενόησεν. There is an interesting variation here in the textual tradition between κατενόησεν and οὐ κατενόησεν (ℵ D G *pm* it vgᶜˡ). Both readings are patient of interpretations which suit the context thoroughly well. If the negative is read, Paul's meaning may be understood to be that, because of his un-weakened faith, Abraham did not concentrate all his attention on his own unpromising circumstances: if the positive reading is accepted, Paul's meaning may be taken to be that, because of his unweakened faith, Abraham considered steadily, with-out attempting to deceive himself, his unpromising circum-stances, but, as v. 20 goes on to indicate, did not allow what he saw to make him doubt God's promise. The reading κατενόησεν (without the negative particle) has strong textual support and is also to be preferred on the ground that it is the less obvious reading. There is little doubt that it should be accepted. We may see in κατενόησεν, κ.τ.λ. Paul's attempt to do justice to Gen 17.17—he apparently understood what is there recorded of Abraham as the expression not of unbelief but of an honest and clear-sighted recognition of the facts of the situation.[1]

τὸ ἑαυτοῦ σῶμα νενεκρωμένον, ἑκατονταέτης που ὑπάρχων, καὶ τὴν νέκρωσιν τῆς μήτρας Σάρρας. For the emphasis on deadness com-pare the reference in v. 17 to God's quickening the dead. For the age attributed to Abraham compare Gen 17.17 (in 17.1 he is said to be ninety-nine). The difficulty of Abraham's sub-sequent marriage to Keturah and begetting of six sons by her (Gen 25.1f) need not worry us unduly. The difficulty concerns Gen 17.17 as much as Paul. Augustine, who drew attention to it,[2] argued that it was only Sarah who was incapable of becoming a parent, while Calvin concluded that 'When Abraham, who before had been like a dry, withered tree, was revived by the heavenly blessing, he not only had the power to beget Isaac, but having been restored to the age of virility,

[1] Cf. Lagrange, p. 96.
[2] *De Civ. Dei* 16.28.

was afterward able to produce other offspring'.[1] The ἤδη which many authorities read after σῶμα is probably a secondary clarification. [Nestle[26] adds it but in square brackets.]

20. εἰς δὲ τὴν ἐπαγγελίαν τοῦ θεοῦ οὐ διεκρίθη τῇ ἀπιστίᾳ, ἀλλὰ ἐνεδυναμώθη τῇ πίστει. The preposition εἰς here means 'with reference to', 'with regard to':[2] the RV and Barrett[3] by introducing the idea of looking which is not present in the Greek (the RV has 'yea, looking unto the promise of God, he wavered not . . .') destroy the grammatical connexion which exists in the original between εἰς . . . τὴν ἐπαγγελίαν τοῦ θεοῦ and οὐ διεκρίθη (and probably also ἐνεδυναμώθη τῇ πίστει). The reference to the divine promise at this point is vitally important. It makes it clear that the faith with which Paul is concerned is not belief in the impossible simply because it is impossible (as though faith and paradox were interchangeable concepts), nor any other anthropocentric mental stance of man, but is wholly based on, and controlled by, the divine promise. It is the promise on which it rests which is its power. It exists because a man has been overpowered, held and sustained by God's promise. For the use of διακρίνεσθαι in the sense 'be divided within oneself', 'waver,' 'doubt' (the NT provides the earliest known examples of it) compare 14.23; also Mt 21.21; Mk 11.23; Acts 10.20; Jas 1.6; 2.4; Jude 22. Michel rightly makes the point that ἀπιστία denotes more than just the absence of faith: it denotes the active rejection of faith, the positive refusal to give credence to God's offered promise.[4] τῇ πίστει is sometimes taken as instrumental or causal (so, e.g., Euthymius, Godet, Sanday and Headlam), and Paul's thought taken to be that Abraham's faith gave him new strength for the begetting of Isaac;[5] but, in view of the immediate context (the contrast between διεκρίθη τῇ ἀπιστίᾳ and ἐνεδυναμώθη τῇ πίστει and the sequel in the last four words of the verse and in v. 21) in which attention seems to be concentrated on the nature of faith itself, it is much more probable that τῇ πίστει should be understood as a dative of respect: 'in faith'.[6] ἐνεδυναμώθη will then refer not to Abraham's bodily strength but to the confirmation of his faith. ἐνεδυναμώθη could mean 'became strong', and is often so understood; but it seems rather more likely that it is intended to have its proper passive force—

[1] p. 97f.
[2] See LSJ, s.v. IV; Bauer, s.v. 5.
[3] p. 97.
[4] p. 126.
[5] Cf. Heb 11.11f.
[6] So Chrysostom, col. 461, and many others.

'was strengthened', that is, by God. The juxtaposition of the negative statement οὐ διεκρίθη τῇ ἀπιστίᾳ and the positive ἐνεδυναμώθη τῇ πίστει serves to bring out more clearly the true nature of faith by showing it in its opposition to, and its victory over, unbelief. In a situation in which everything seems to be ranged against the promise, faith is a being enabled to rest on the promise alone, refusing to demand visible or tangible signs and proofs. Chrysostom's comment is to the point: Οὐδὲ γὰρ ἀπόδειξιν ἔδωκεν, οὔτε σημεῖον ἐποίησεν ὁ Θεός, ἀλλὰ ῥήματα ἦν ψιλὰ μόνον, ἐπαγγελλόμενα ἅπερ οὐχ ὑπισχνεῖτο ἡ φύσις.[1]

δοὺς δόξαν τῷ θεῷ. For the expression διδόναι δόξαν τῷ θεῷ compare, e.g., Josh 7.19; 1 Sam 6.5; 1 Chr 16.28, 29; Isa 42.12; Jer 13.16; Jn 9.24; Acts 12.23; Rev 11.13; 16.9; 19.7. A man gives glory to God when he acknowledges God's truthfulness and goodness and submits to His authority. '. . . no greater honour can be given to God than by sealing His truth by our faith' is Calvin's comment.[2] By embracing His promise and believing it faith does that which the men, of whom 1.21–23 speaks, failed to do.[3]

21. καὶ πληροφορηθεὶς ὅτι ὃ ἐπήγγελται δυνατός ἐστιν καὶ ποιῆσαι completes this description of Abraham's faith. It underlines the fact that Abraham's faith was faith in the God who had promised, not merely in what had been promised.[4] It was a humble acknowledgement of the faithfulness and omnipotence which guaranteed the promise. He believed the promise because God had spoken it, and was delivered from 'the supposition that God promises more in His Word than He can perform'.[5] We may render πληροφορηθείς by some such expression as 'being fully persuaded'. On πληροφορεῖν (used in the same sense also in 14.5, and in different senses in Lk 1.1; Col 4.12; 2 Tim 4.5, 17: compare also the occurrences of

---

[1] col. 461. It is worth recalling also Calvin's eloquent words (p. 99): 'Let us also remember that we are all in the same condition as Abraham. Our circumstances are all in opposition to the promises of God. He promises us immortality: yet we are surrounded by mortality and corruption. He declares that He accounts us just: yet we are covered with sins. He testifies that He is propitious and benevolent towards us: yet outward signs threaten His wrath. What then are we to do? We must close our eyes, disregard ourselves and all things connected with us [Calvin read οὐ κατενόησεν in v. 19], so that nothing may hinder or prevent us from believing that God is true.'

[2] ibid.

[3] Cf. Nygren, p. 182.

[4] Cf. Leenhardt, p. 126.

[5] Calvin, p. 99. The whole of his comment on this verse is interesting and valuable.

πληροφορία in Col 2.2; I Th 1.5; Heb 6.11; 10.22) see Bauer, s.v. πληροφορέω. ἐπήγγελται is here middle, not passive. For δυνατός used of God compare 9.22; 11.23; Mk 10.27=Mt 19.26=Lk 18.27; Mk 14.36; Lk 1.49; 2 Tim 1.12; Heb 11.19: compare also the passages where δύναμις, δύνασθαι, and δυνατεῖν are used with reference to God (e.g. 1.16, 20; 9.17; Mt 3.9; 10.28; 22.29; 26.64; 2 Cor 9.8).

22. διὸ [καὶ]¹ ἐλογίσθη αὐτῷ εἰς δικαιοσύνην concludes the subsection. The preceding verses have drawn out the meaning of the first five words of LXX Gen 15.6, and now the διό, with which Paul introduces his quotation of the last part of that verse, makes the point that it was because Abraham's faith in God referred to in the first part of the verse was the sort of thing that Paul has just shown it to have been that God counted it to him εἰς δικαιοσύνην.

23-25. Οὐκ ἐγράφη δὲ δι' αὐτὸν μόνον ὅτι ἐλογίσθη αὐτῷ, ἀλλὰ καὶ δι' ἡμᾶς makes the point that what Scripture says about Abraham (ἐλογίσθη αὐτῷ is probably intended to call to mind the whole of Gen 15.6) was not recorded just for his sake—that is, as a memorial of him, that he might live on in men's remembrance² —but for our sakes too, because his faith in God and its being reckoned εἰς δικαιοσύνην have a direct relevance to us.

οἷς μέλλει λογίζεσθαι explains the relevance of Abraham's story to Paul and those to whom he is writing: to them too faith—their faith—is to be reckoned for righteousness. Some commentators³ insist that μέλλει λογίζεσθαι must refer to the final judgment. That this interpretation is possible should not be denied—the future tense (δικαιώσει) in 3.30 may perhaps afford some support for it. But, in view of the general tendency of Paul's language with regard to justification and especially of 5.1 and 9, and also in view of the past tense (ἐλογίσθη) in the Genesis verse which Paul has been expounding, it is surely more probable that the reference is to justification not as the eschatological hope of Christians but as the fact which they are confidently to assume as the basis of their present life. The use of the present tense of μέλλειν with the infinitive may be explained as signifying something which has to happen in accordance with a divine decision (cf. Bauer, s.v. μέλλω, I.c. δ).

τοῖς πιστεύουσιν: not 'if we believe', but 'to us who believe'.

ἐπί. For πιστεύειν ἐπί followed by the accusative compare

---

¹ καί, though attested by ℵ K pl, is omitted by B D* G syᴾ, and is perhaps secondary (assimilation to the LXX—cf. v. 3, where Gen 15.6 is quoted as a whole).
² Cf. Ecclus 44.8, 10, 14f.
³ e.g. Schlatter, p. 172; Michel, p. 127, n. 2; Barrett, p. 99.

v. 5; also Mt 27.42; Acts 9.42; 11.17; 16.31; 22.19 (followed by the dative, it occurs in 9.33; 10.11; 1 Tim 1.16; 1 Pet 2.6).

τὸν ἐγείραντα Ἰησοῦν τὸν κύριον ἡμῶν ἐκ νεκρῶν may be compared with θεοῦ τοῦ ζωοποιοῦντος τοὺς νεκροὺς καὶ καλοῦντος τὰ μὴ ὄντα ὡς ὄντα in v. 17, understood in relation to the reference to Abraham's σῶμα νενεκρωμένον and the νέκρωσις of Sarah's womb in v. 19. Between the quickening of Abraham's and Sarah's deadness for the purpose of procreation and the raising of Jesus Christ from the dead there is an inward connexion which is much more than the similarity between two events both of which may be spoken of in terms of ζωοποίησις; for what gave unique and absolute significance to Abraham's begetting, and Sarah's bearing, of Isaac was the fact that it was of this child that Christ Himself was eventually to be a descendant κατὰ σάρκα. In connexion with Paul's description of God as ὁ ἐγείρας Ἰησοῦν, it should be noted that the NT characteristically refers to the resurrection of Jesus as God's act (cf., e.g., 8.11; 10.9; also Acts 3.15; 4.10; 1 Cor 6.14; 15.15; 2 Cor 4.14; 1 Pet 1.21).[1] On the designation of Jesus as ὁ κύριος ἡμῶν see on 1.4 (and also on 10.9). With the close juxtaposition here of the reference to the Resurrection and of the use of the κύριος title compare 10.9. There is a noticeable solemnity about the latter part of v.24, which prepares the way for what is the solemn conclusion (v. 25) both of the whole section (4.1ff) and of the whole main division (1.18–4.25).

ὃς παρεδόθη διὰ τὰ παραπτώματα ἡμῶν καὶ ἠγέρθη διὰ τὴν δικαίωσιν ἡμῶν looks like a quotation of a traditional formula. That it was formulated under the influence of Isa 52.13–53.12 is hardly to be doubted. παραδιδόναι is too obvious a verb to use in this connexion (it is used in the NT with reference to Jesus' being delivered up by Judas to the representatives of the chief priests, by the Sanhedrin to Pilate, by Pilate to the soldiers, and in Rom 8.32 it is used of God's delivering up Jesus to the power of men and to death—the reference it probably has here) for its occurrence here to prove by itself reminiscence of the Isaiah passage, in which it occurs three times (in 53.6 and twice in 53.12). But the conjunction of παραδιδόναι with διὰ τὰ παραπτώματα ἡμῶν is significant: compare καὶ κύριος παρέδωκεν αὐτὸν ταῖς ἁμαρτίαις ἡμῶν in Isa 53.6 and καὶ διὰ τὰς ἁμαρτίας αὐτῶν παρεδόθη in Isa 53.12. We may compare also v. 5: αὐτὸς δὲ ἐτραυματίσθη διὰ τὰς ἀνομίας ἡμῶν καὶ μεμαλάκισται διὰ τὰς ἁμαρτίας ἡμῶν. In addition, there is a striking parallel (though it is not generally noticed) between

[1] Only in Jn 2.19, 21; 10.17, 18 is it referred to as accomplished by Jesus Himself.

the association of justification with Christ's resurrection in the latter half of v. 25 and the reference in the Hebrew text of Isa 53.11 to the Servant's justifying many (the LXX has the word δικαιῶσαι, but differs widely from the MT here) in the course of the song's final strophe which seems to speak of the Servant's resurrection, though it does not use the term.

It is to be noted that διά is used in this verse in two different senses, first in a causal, and then in a final, sense.[1]

The two clauses are, of course, not to be understood 'woodenly' (as Bruce puts it),[2] as though a rigid separation between the function of Christ's death and the function of His resurrection were intended (5.9 makes it clear that there is a connexion between Christ's death and our justification). At the same time, it would be a mistake to conclude that the formation of the two clauses has been controlled solely by rhetorical considerations. For what was necessitated by our sins was, in the first place, Christ's atoning death, and yet, had His death not been followed by His resurrection, it would not have been God's mighty deed for our justification.

V

THE LIFE PROMISED FOR THOSE WHO ARE RIGHTEOUS BY FAITH—'SHALL LIVE' EXPOUNDED (5.1–8.39)

The point at which the new main division begins is disputed. Some see the first eleven verses,[3] others the whole,[4] of chapter

---

[1] The suggestion that the first διά should be understood as final ('in order to deal with') is not very probable. Still less probable is the suggestion that the second διά should be taken as causal (the meaning being that Jesus was raised up because we had been justified through His death). In view of the fact that τὰ παραπτώματα ἡμῶν and τὴν δικαίωσιν ἡμῶν, though grammatically parallel, are by no means parallel as far as their significance is concerned (the one denoting something profoundly regrettable, the other something altogether desirable), it is hardly surprising that διά should be used with them in different senses.

[2] p. 119.

[3] e.g., Leenhardt, p. 131 (Fr., 77).

[4] e.g., Sanday and Headlam, p. xlviii; Lagrange, p. 99f; Gaugler 1, p. viif; Bruce, p. 67f.

5 as belonging to what precedes, while others see the significant break as occurring between chapters 4 and 5.[1] In support of taking some or all of chapter 5 with what precedes, it is noted that the vocabulary of chapter 5 (this applies mainly but not exclusively to vv. 1–11) shows significant connexions with chapters 1 to 4.[2] These may be set out as follows:

δίκαιος occurs four times in chapters 1 to 4 (1.17; 2.13; 3.10, 26), twice in chapter 5 (vv. 7 and 19), and elsewhere in Romans only in 7.12;

δικαιοῦν occurs, respectively, nine times (2.13; 3.4, 20, 24, 26, 28, 30; 4.2, 5), twice (5.1, 9), and in 6.7; 8.30 (twice), 33;

δικαιοσύνη fourteen times (1.17; 3.5, 21, 22, 25, 26; 4.3, 5, 6, 9, 11 (twice), 13, 22), twice (5.17, 21), and eighteen other times (five or six times denoting moral righteousness);

δικαίωμα twice (1.32; 2.26), twice (5.16, 18), and in 8.4;

δικαίωσις once (4.25), once (5.18), and nowhere else;

καυχᾶσθαι twice (2.17, 23), three times (5.2, 3, 11), and nowhere else;

καύχημα occurs in Romans only in 4.2;

καύχησις in 3.27 and 15.17;

ὀργή six times in chapters 1 to 4 (1.18; 2.5, 8; 3.5; 4.15), once in chapter 5 (v. 9), and five other times;

ἐν τῷ αὐτοῦ αἵματι occurs in 3.25, ἐν τῷ αἵματι αὐτοῦ in 5.9, and there is no other reference to the blood of Christ in Romans. It has also been suggested that τὴν χάριν ταύτην and ἐπ' ἐλπίδι τῆς δόξης τοῦ θεοῦ in 5.2 should be seen as recalling 3.24 and 3.23, respectively, and συνίστησιν . . . τὴν ἑαυτοῦ ἀγάπην in 5.8 as corresponding to θεοῦ δικαιοσύνην συνίστησιν in 3.5; but, as far as these last three expressions are concerned, the connexions with later chapters would seem to be at least as significant as the ones with chapter 3.

That there is a significant linguistic affinity between chapter 5 and chapters 1 to 4 is not to be denied. But this is no proof that the whole, or part, of chapter 5 must be included in the same main division with what precedes it. It is just as easily explicable on the assumption that the new main division consists of 5.1–8.39, these four chapters being intended to describe the life which those who are righteous by faith are to live, or, put in a different way, to draw out what having been

[1] e.g., Bengel, p. 494; Cornely, p. 251; Nygren, p. 188; Barth, *Shorter*, p. 55; Michel, p. 129.
[2] Cf. Lagrange, p. 100; A. Feuillet, 'Le Plan salvifique de Dieu d'après l'épître aux Romains', in *RB* 57 (1950), p. 356, n. 1; Leenhardt, p. 131.

justified by faith means. That much of the language of the previous division should reappear in 5.1–8.39 is only to be expected in view of the fact that 5.1–8.39 is actually drawing out the meaning of the justification with which 1.18–4.25 is concerned.[1] And it is not surprising that chapter 5 should be specially closely linked with the preceding division, since, while the whole of 5.1–8.39 is drawing out the meaning of justification, Paul's method in chapters 5 to 8 is not in each successive section of this division to go back and derive his argument directly from the preceding main division, but rather to lead on from chapter 5 to chapter 6, from chapter 6 to chapter 7, and from chapter 7 to chapter 8.

The chief reason for associating chapter 5 with the following, rather than with the preceding, chapters is the nature of its contents. In our view, it is parallel by virtue of its substance with the three following chapters, the chapters in this stretch of Romans coinciding exactly with the logical sections. In each of the four chapters the first sub-section is a basic statement concerning the life promised for the man who is righteous by faith or concerning the meaning of justification. The four initial sub-sections affirm that being justified means being reconciled to God, being sanctified, being free from the law's condemnation, and being indwelt by God's Spirit; and in each case what follows the initial sub-section is a necessary clarification of what has been said in it.

But, in addition to the argument from the contents, two formal points may be mentioned. The first is that the occurrence of one or other of the formulae 'through our Lord Jesus Christ', 'through Jesus Christ our Lord' and 'in Christ Jesus our Lord' at the beginning, in the middle and at the end, of chapter 5, and at the end of each of the three succeeding chapters has the effect of binding the four chapters together. The second is that the solemn formula which concludes chapter 4 strongly suggests that 4.25 marks the end of a major division of the epistle.[2]

---

[1] It is to be noted that, as far as the occurrences of ζωή are concerned, chapter 5 stands with chapters 6 to 8 rather than with chapters 1 to 4 (it occurs once in chapters 1 to 4, four times in chapter 5, and eight times in chapters 6 to 8). See also p. 102.

[2] Cf. Michel, p. 129.

V. 1. A LIFE CHARACTERIZED BY PEACE WITH GOD (5.1–21)

A truly remarkable variety of suggested titles for this section and its component sub-sections is to be seen in the commentaries. Thus, for example, Lagrange heads the section 'La grâce de la justification dans l'âme et dans l'humanité', and the sub-sections 'La justification gage du salut' and 'Le péché et la justification dans l'histoire, et l'épisode de la Loi'; Nygren heads the section 'Free from wrath', and the sub-sections 'Redeemed from God's wrath by God's love' and 'The two aeons: Adam and Christ'; Gaugler heads them 'Die aus der Rechtfertigung erfliessende Heilsgewissheit', 'Die durchgreifende Hoffnung', and 'Der in Christus überwundene Tod'; Michel, who does not suggest a title for chapter 5 as a whole, calls vv. 1–11 'Die Gaben der Gnade', and vv. 12–21 'Der neue Mensch und die neue Menschheit'; Barrett calls them 'Justification and salvation' and 'Adam and Christ'; and Bruce 'The blessings which accompany justification: peace, joy, hope' and 'The old and the new solidarity'. That there is nothing like a consensus with regard either to the exact function of this section within the structure of the epistle or to the exact functions within this section of its component sub-sections, is obvious. But the contents of vv. 1, 10 and 11 are surely sufficient warrant for claiming that Paul himself has given a fairly clear indication that his main concern in the first sub-section is with the fact that those who are justified are at peace with God. And a comparison of the structures of chapters 5, 6, 7 and 8 strongly suggests the likelihood that the rest of this chapter will be in some way a clarification of the first sub-section or a drawing out of what is implicit in it or to be inferred from it. That it is, in fact, at any rate formally, a conclusion from it is indicated by the $\Delta\iota\grave{a}$ $\tauο\hat{υ}\tauο$ with which v. 12 begins—if we allow that expression its natural meaning. It would seem then that the indications Paul himself has provided concerning the movement of his thought point to the conclusion that the fact of our peace with God should be regarded as the subject which gives the section as a whole its unity.[1] In our view, a detailed examination of the text bears out this conclusion.

---

[1] Cf. the title which Barth, *Shorter*, gives to chapter 5: 'The Gospel as Man's Reconciliation with God'.

(i) *Peace with God*
(5.1–11)

¹Having been justified then on the basis of faith, we have peace with God through our Lord Jesus Christ, ²through whom also we have obtained access [by faith] to this grace in which we stand, and we exult* in hope of the glory of God. ³And not only so, but we even exult in afflictions, knowing that affliction works endurance, ⁴and endurance provedness, and provedness hope. ⁵And this hope does not put us to shame, for God's love has been poured out in our hearts through the Holy Spirit who has been given to us. ⁶For,** when we were still powerless, Christ died at the appointed time for ungodly men. ⁷For someone will scarcely die for a righteous man; for a benefactor perhaps someone might bring himself to die. ⁸But God proves his own love for us by the fact that Christ died for us when we were still sinners.⁹Since, then, we have now been justified by his blood, we shall much more be saved through him from the wrath. ¹⁰For if when we were enemies we were reconciled to God through the death of his Son, much more, having been reconciled, shall we be saved by his life. ¹¹And not only this; we also exult in God through our Lord Jesus [Christ], through whom we have now already received reconciliation.

These verses make the point that the life promised for the man who is righteous by faith is a life characterized by peace with God ('we have peace with God' in v. 1; 'we were reconciled to God' and 'having been reconciled' in v. 10; 'we have . . . received reconciliation' in v. 11). They affirm the amazing truth that God's undeserved love has through Christ transformed people from being God's enemies into being at peace with Him, being His friends. The reconciliation Paul is speaking of is not to be understood as simply identical with justification (the two terms being understood as different metaphors denoting the same thing), nor yet as a consequence of justification, a result following afterwards. The thought is rather that—in the case of the divine justification of sinners—justification necessarily involves reconciliation. Whereas between a human judge and an accused person there may be no really deep personal relationship at all, the relation between God and the sinner is altogether personal, both because God is the God He is and also because it is against God Himself that the sinner has sinned. So God's justification of sinners of necessity involves also their reconciliation, the removal of

---

* In our translation we have normally used the verb 'glory' to represent καυχᾶσθαι; but here, in view of the presence of δόξα, for which we wanted the noun 'glory', we preferred to use 'exult', and it then seemed desirable to use 'exult' also in vv. 3 and 11.

** Reading ἔτι γάρ rather than εἴ γε. The double ἔτι can hardly be reproduced in an English translation—in Greek it is a little easier.

enmity, the establishment of peace. This sub-section, then, is drawing out something already implicit in 3.21–26. The fact that men have been justified means that they must also have been reconciled. The fact that they are righteous by faith means that they now live as God's friends.

Verses 2b–5 are descriptive of this life at peace with God, emphasizing particularly the hope which is a characteristic feature of it. Verses 6–8 take up the reference to God's love in the latter part of v. 5 and draw out the nature of God's love for us as altogether undeserved and spontaneous. Verses 9 and 10 take up again the theme of hope, and confidently affirm in two parallel statements the certainty of our hope's fulfilment, of our final salvation, while v. 11 refers to our present jubilant exultation in God through Christ, through whom we have received reconciliation with God.

It is noteworthy that this whole sub-section is in the first person plural.

1. Δικαιωθέντες οὖν ἐκ πίστεως gathers up the thought of 1.18–4.25, and so connects what follows with the preceding main division of the epistle. The result of the argument of the main division IV, thus summed up in a participial clause, is the basis of all that is said in the present main division. For the inclusion at the beginning of a new section of a summary of the substance of the previous section we may compare 3.23 (summing up 1.18–3.20) and 8.1 (summing up 7.1–6).

εἰρήνην ἔχομεν[1] πρὸς τὸν θεόν states the theme of the section —that those who have been justified by God have peace with

---

[1] Though the indicative ἔχομεν is a good deal less strongly attested than the subjunctive ἔχωμεν, it is almost certainly to be preferred on the ground of intrinsic probability. It is clear from v. 10f that Paul regards the believers' peace with God as a fact. It would therefore be inconsistent for him to say here 'let us have peace', meaning thereby 'let us obtain peace' (Paul would anyway hardly think of peace with God as something to be obtained by human endeavour). If the subjunctive is read, we must understand it in some such sense as 'let us enjoy the peace we have' or 'let us guard the peace we have' (cf., e.g., Origen, Chrysostom). But this is not free from objection; for it would surely be strange for Paul, in such a carefully argued writing as this, to exhort his readers to enjoy or to guard a peace which he has not yet explicitly shown to be possessed by them. While it is of course true that considerations such as have just been mentioned could easily have led to the substitution of the indicative for the subjunctive, a deliberate alteration in the opposite direction would also be understandable, since a copyist might well have felt that, after so much doctrinal statement, an element of exhortation was called for. But, since the difference in pronunciation between o and ω was slight, a change in either direction could easily occur, whenever in the transmission of the text dictation was employed (cf. the textual variations in, e.g., 6.2; 14.19; 1 Cor 15.49).

God. That εἰρήνη here denotes, not subjective feelings of peace (though these may indeed result), but the objective state of being at peace instead of being enemies, is made clear by the parallel statements of v. 10f (. . . ἐχθροὶ ὄντες κατηλλάγημεν τῷ θεῷ . . . καταλλαγέντες . . . τὴν καταλλαγὴν ἐλάβομεν). The question arises: What is the significance of the combination of Δικαιωθέντες and εἰρήνην ἔχομεν? or, to put it otherwise, What did Paul understand to be the relation between reconciliation and justification? The correct answer would seem to be neither that reconciliation is a consequence of justification,[1] nor that 'Justification and reconciliation are different metaphors describing the same fact',[2] but that *God's* justification involves reconciliation because God is what He is. Where it is God's justification that is concerned, justification and reconciliation, though distinguishable, are inseparable. Whereas between a human judge and the person who appears before him there may be no really personal meeting at all, no personal hostility if the accused be found guilty, no establishment of friendship if the accused is acquitted, between God and the sinner there is a personal relationship, and God's justification involves a real self-engagement to the sinner on His part.[3] He does not confer the status of righteousness upon us without at the same time giving Himself to us in friendship and establishing peace between Himself and us—a work which, on account of the awful reality both of His wrath against sin and of the fierce hostility of our egotism against the God who claims our allegiance, is only accomplished at unspeakable cost to Him. Thus Δικαιωθέντες . . . εἰρήνην ἔχομεν . . . is not a mere collocation of two metaphors describing the same fact, nor does it mean that, having been justified, we were subsequently reconciled and now have peace with God; but its force is that the fact that we have been justified means that we have also been reconciled and have peace with God.

διὰ τοῦ κυρίου ἡμῶν Ἰησοῦ Χριστοῦ. As it is through Christ that we are justified (cf. 3.24), so it is also through Him that we are reconciled to God (cf. v. 10; 2 Cor 5.18f). It is to be noted that this formula is repeated in v. 11 (possibly without Χριστοῦ), and (with a slightly different word-order) in v. 21 and in 7.25, and that ἐν Χριστῷ Ἰησοῦ τῷ κυρίῳ ἡμῶν occurs in 6.23 and 8.39. This placing of the same or similar formulae at the beginning, in the middle (i.e., at the end of the first sub-section)

---

[1] So Barrett, p. 101.
[2] Barrett, p. 108.
[3] It is not surprising that this sub-section contains a statement about God's ἀγάπη (vv. 6–8).

and at the end, of chapter 5, and at the ends of chapters 6, 7 and 8 in turn, is scarcely accidental. It has the double effect of marking off these four sections of the epistle and at the same time underlining the fact of their belonging together as a single main division.[1]

2. δι' οὗ καὶ τὴν προσαγωγὴν ἐσχήκαμεν [τῇ πίστει] εἰς τὴν χάριν ταύτην ἐν ᾗ ἑστήκαμεν. It seems better to take τὴν χάριν ταύτην (i.e. this state of being the objects of favour) to refer to our justification (Δικαιωθέντες) than to our peace with God, since in the latter case the whole relative clause δι' οὗ, κ.τ.λ. would be tautologous after εἰρήνην ἔχομεν . . . διὰ τοῦ κυρίου ἡμῶν Ἰησοῦ Χριστοῦ. The use of προσαγωγή was quite probably intended to evoke the thought of 'the privilege of . . . being introduced into the presence of someone in high station',[2] though the word is, of course, a common one which occurs in a wide variety of connexions. ἐσχήκαμεν is perhaps to be explained as a perfect used for the aorist, but can be taken as a pure perfect (see BDF, § 343 (2)). The question whether τῇ πίστει (which has both Alexandrian and Byzantine attestation and also the support of the Vulgate and the Syriac versions, but is omitted by B D G it Or^lat) should be read is not very important, since, in any case, there is no doubt that Paul thought that this προσαγωγή had been obtained by faith. It is possible that ἑστήκαμεν simply denotes situation and is thus little more than a synonym of ἐσμέν (cf. Bauer, s.v. ἵστημι II.2.c.β); but, in view of Pauline usage, it is more probable that it carries something of the sense 'stand firm' or 'abide'.[3]

καὶ καυχώμεθα ἐπ' ἐλπίδι τῆς δόξης[4] τοῦ θεοῦ is better taken as co-ordinate with εἰρήνην ἔχομεν . . . Χριστοῦ than with τὴν προσαγωγὴν ἐσχήκαμεν, κ.τ.λ.[5] The question whether καυχώμεθα (both here and in v. 3) is to be understood as indicative or subjunctive depends on whether ἔχομεν or ἔχωμεν is read in v. 1 (it would of course have to be indicative, if this clause were taken as co-ordinate with τὴν προσαγωγήν, κ.τ.λ.). On καυχᾶσθαι see on 2.17. Here it is used in a good sense, and denotes exultant rejoicing, jubilation. We may compare the use of ἀγαλλιᾶν in Lk 1.47; 10.21, and of ἀγαλλίασις in Acts 2.46

[1] Cf. Nygren, pp. 194, 206.
[2] Bruce, p. 123. Cf. Eph 2.18; 3.12; 1 Pet 3.18; Xenophon, Cyr. 1.3.8; 7.5.45.
[3] Cf. 11.20; 1 Cor 7.37; 15.1; 2 Cor 1.24; Eph 6.11, 13, 14; Col 4.12; 2 Tim 2.19; 1 Pet 5.12. In 14.4 and 1 Cor 10.12 the sense is rather of standing as opposed to falling.
[4] The 'filiorum' of Vg Ambst Aug is no doubt due to assimilation to 8.21.
[5] Pace Lagrange, p. 101; Barrett, p. 100; Moffatt, RSV, etc.

as well as a good many of the NT occurrences of χαίρειν and χαρά (e.g. 12.12 and 15.13, in both of which joy is mentioned in connexion with hope). Michel has rightly drawn attention to the exalted style and overflowing joy which characterize this section;[1] but his assertion that Paul, in mentioning καύχησις here and in vv. 3 and 11, undoubtedly had in mind the church's prayer of thanksgiving and Spirit-inspired shouts of joy[2] is perhaps an undue limitation of Paul's meaning. This exulting is an exulting in the confident expectation of the glory of God. The noun ἐλπίς (used three times in vv. 2–5 and occurring also in 4.18 (twice); 8.20, 24 (three times); 12.12; 15.4, 13 (twice)) denotes the confident anticipation of that which we do not yet see. Calvin's comment on this verse includes the sentence: 'Paul's meaning is that, although believers are now pilgrims on earth, yet by their confidence (fiducia ... sua) they surmount the heavens, so that they cherish their future inheritance in their bosoms with tranquillity'.[3] By the δόξα τοῦ θεοῦ is meant here (cf. 3.23; 8.17, 18, 21, 30; 9.23) that illumination of man's whole being by the radiance of the divine glory which is man's true destiny but which was lost through sin, as it will be restored (not just as it was, but immeasurably enriched through God's own personal participation in man's humanity in Jesus Christ—cf. 8.17), when man's redemption is finally consummated at the parousia of Jesus Christ.[4]

3. οὐ μόνον δέ, ἀλλὰ καὶ καυχώμεθα ἐν ταῖς θλίψεσιν. Not only do we exult in hope of the glory of God, but we also actually exult in tribulations. For οὐ μόνον δέ, ἀλλὰ καί (cf. v. 11; 8.23; 9.10; 2 Cor 8.19) see Bauer, s.v. μόνος, 2.c.; BDF, § 479 (1). The expression is elliptical: with οὐ μόνον has to be understood that which immediately precedes—here καυχώμεθα ἐπ᾽ ἐλπίδι τῆς δόξης τοῦ θεοῦ. The ἐν ταῖς θλίψεσιν could mean 'in afflictions' in the sense of 'in the midst of afflictions' (i.e. indicating the situation in which the exultation takes place), but it is much more probable that it indicates the basis of the exultation (cf. ἐπ᾽ ἐλπίδι in v. 2, and the occurrences of ἐν with καυχᾶσθαι in v. 11; 1 Cor 1.31; 3.21; 2 Cor 10.17; 12.9 (in the light of the following verse); Gal 6.13; Phil 3.3; Jas 1.9; 4.16). With καυχώμεθα ἐν ταῖς θλίψεσιν compare the reference to exulting ἐν ταῖς ἀσθενείαις in 2 Cor 12.9 (cf. 2 Cor 11.30).[5] For θλῖψις see on 2.9.

[1] p. 130 and n. 1.
[2] p. 131.
[3] p. 105.
[4] Reference should be made to the valuable discussion of the glory of God in Barth, CD II/1, pp. 640–77 (= KD II/1, pp. 722–64).
[5] Cf. Prov 3.11; Ps. Sol. 3.4; 10.1; 1QH 9.10, 23–25.

εἰδότες (cf. 6.9; 13.11; 1 Cor 15.58; 2 Cor 4.14; 5.6, 11; Gal
2.16; Eph 6.8, 9; Col 3.24; 4.1; 1 Pet 1.18: the reference is to a
knowledge given to faith and for which an absolute validity is
claimed)[1] ὅτι ἡ θλῖψις ὑπομονὴν κατεργάζεται shows that the
exulting in tribulations to which this verse refers is not an
exulting in them as in something meritorious on our part—this
would of course be closely akin to the καυχᾶσθαι rejected in
3.27f—but an exulting in them as in that to which God
subjects us as part of the discipline by which He teaches us to
wait patiently for His deliverance. As a general statement
ἡ θλῖψις ὑπομονὴν κατεργάζεται would lack validity; for, as
Calvin points out, tribulation 'provokes a great part of mankind to murmur against God, and even to curse Him'.[2] But
Paul is here thinking of what it achieves, when it is met by
faith in God which receives it as God's fatherly discipline.
Where God sustains faith, tribulation produces ὑπομονή. For
ὑπομονή (also in 8.25; 15.4, 5) see on 2.7. For κατεργάζεσθαι see
on 1.27: with its use here compare 4.15; also 2 Cor 4.17; 7.10;
Jas 1.3. ἡ θλῖψις ὑπομονὴν κατεργάζεται is the first member of a
climax[3] which extends through the next verse.

4. **ἡ δὲ ὑπομονὴ δοκιμήν.** Such patient endurance as faith
exhibits under the discipline of tribulation is in its turn the
source of δοκιμή, that is, the quality of provedness which is
possessed by faith when it has stood up to testing, like the
precious metal which is left when the base metals have been
refined away. The word δοκιμή occurs a number of times in
Paul's letters (2 Cor 2.9; 8.2; 9.13; 13.3; Phil 2.22), but there is
no known occurrence of it earlier than Paul.[4] Compare the use
of δοκίμιον in Jas 1.3; 1 Peter 1.7.[5]

ἡ δὲ δοκιμὴ ἐλπίδα. To have one's faith proved by God in the
fires of tribulation and sustained by Him so as to stand the
test is to have one's hope in Him and in the fulfilment of His
promises, one's hope of His glory (v. 2), strengthened and
confirmed.

5. **ἡ δὲ ἐλπὶς οὐ καταισχύνει**[6] completes the climax. The hope
which is thus strengthened and confirmed does not put those

---

[1] Cf. Michel, p. 131, n. 3.
[2] p. 106.
[3] cf. 8.30; 10.14f, 17; and see BDF, § 493 (3).
[4] See further W. Grundmann, in *TWNT* 2, pp. 258–64.
[5] A comparison of this and the preceding verse with Jas 1.2f and 1 Pet
1.6f suggests the possibility that a common parenetic tradition lay
behind these passages.
[6] The verb could of course be accentuated καταισχυνεῖ; but it is
probably better to read it as present, the present being in the context
rather more forceful than the future would be.

who cherish it to shame by proving illusory.[1] The language is reminiscent of the OT. Compare Ps 22.5 [LXX: 21.6] (πρὸς σὲ ἐκέκραξαν καὶ ἐσώθησαν, ἐπὶ σοὶ ἤλπισαν καὶ οὐ κατῃσχύνθησαν); 25 [LXX: 24].3, 20; 119 [LXX: 118].116 (... μὴ καταισχύνῃς με ἀπὸ τῆς προσδοκίας μου); and also Isa 28.16 (LXX: ... καὶ ὁ πιστεύων ἐπ᾽ αὐτῷ οὐ μὴ καταισχυνθῇ).

It is possible to connect the statement introduced by ὅτι with v 3a, placing a comma at the end of v. 4 so as to make vv. 3b–5a a single participial clause: in this case it gives the reason why καυχώμεθα ἐν ταῖς θλίψεσιν. But it is much more probable that v. 5b is intended as a proof of v. 5a.

ἡ ἀγάπη τοῦ θεοῦ. This is the first occurrence of ἀγάπη in Romans (the verb ἀγαπᾶν does not occur till 8.28, but ἀγαπητός was used in 1.7). The phrase has sometimes been understood to mean 'love to God' (τοῦ θεοῦ objective genitive), as by Augustine and Pelagius for example, and it is true that on this view it is rather easier to explain the use of ἐκκέχυται; but a reference to God's love to us fits the context much better,[2] and τοῦ θεοῦ is therefore no doubt to be understood as a subjective genitive (so Origen, Ambrosiaster, Chrysostom, Calvin, and most modern exegetes).

ἐκκέχυται ἐν ταῖς καρδίαις ἡμῶν διὰ πνεύματος ἁγίου τοῦ δοθέντος ἡμῖν. The fact that ἐκχεῖν (ἐκχύννειν) is used in Acts 2.17f (LXX Joel 3.1f), 33; 10.45; Tit 3.6 of God's giving the Holy Spirit to men, together with the presence here in association with ἐκκέχυται of ἐν ταῖς καρδίαις ἡμῶν (cf. Gal 4.6) and of διὰ πνεύματος ἁγίου, has led some exegetes to suggest that Paul was actually thinking of the Spirit's being poured out.[3] But

---

[1] That v. 5a is not intended as a general statement (in spite of the sapiential style), but refers only to the hope which is grounded in faith in Christ, ought to be clear. Michel, p. 133, n. 2, rightly dismisses the explanation given by Zahn, p. 247, which applies Paul's statement to human hopes generally, as mistaken.

[2] A statement of the fact of God's love for us is a more cogent proof of the security of our hope than a statement of the fact of our love for Him would be (it would also be more suitable as an explanation why we exult in our tribulations, if this clause were connected with v. 3a instead of with v. 5a); and it is God's love for us which vv. 6–8 go on to describe.

[3] So, e.g., M. Dibelius, 'Vier Worte des Römerbriefes', in *SBU* 3, 1944, p. 6 (quoted by Michel, p. 133, n. 4): 'ἐκκέχυται ist gesagt von der Liebe, gedacht vom heiligen Geist. Die Liebe ist nach Paulus gar nicht dadurch bestimmt, dass sie "ausgegossen" wird, sondern indem der heilige Geist den Gläubigen geschenkt, d.h. ausgegossen wurde, tat ihnen Gott seine Liebe kund'; Barrett, p. 105: 'Paul's meaning would perhaps have been somewhat clearer if he had said that the Spirit had been poured out in our hearts, and that by this means God's love for us had there become fully operative, both in making us aware of its presence, and in transforming us'.

ἐκχεῖν is used much more often in the LXX (and also as a
matter of fact in the NT—nine occurrences in Rev 16) of the
pouring out of God's wrath, and—what is more particularly
relevant—it is used in Ecclus 18.11 of the pouring out of God's
mercy (ἔλεος) and in Mal 3.10 of the pouring out of His blessing
(εὐλογία). There is therefore nothing very strange in Paul's
speaking of God's love as having been poured out. The metaphor may well have been chosen in order to express the idea
of unstinting lavishness.[1] The words ἐν ταῖς καρδίαις ἡμῶν and
διὰ πνεύματος ἁγίου τοῦ δοθέντος ἡμῖν, which on this view
present a difficulty, are best explained by assuming that we
have here a pregnant construction, and that the meaning is
that God's love has been lavished upon us (as will be spelled out
in vv. 6–8), and actually brought home to our hearts (so that
we have recognized it and rejoice in it) by the Holy Spirit who
has been given to us.[2] (For Paul's assumption that the Holy
Spirit has certainly been given to him and the Roman
Christians, cf. 8.9 and see notes there.) The proof that our hope
will not disappoint us in the end is the fact of the amazing
generosity of God's love for us—a fact which we have been
enabled to know and understand by the gift of His Spirit to us.[3]

The next three verses describe the nature of the divine love
to which v. 5 referred.

6. εἴ γε ('if so be that', 'if indeed', so 'seeing that') is read by
Nestle, but the reading ἔτι γάρ seems more likely to be original.[4]
It looks as if ἔτι was placed at the beginning of the sentence in
order to give it special emphasis, and then repeated after the
genitive absolute to which it belongs for the sake of clarity.[5]

ὄντων ἡμῶν ἀσθενῶν ἔτι. Christ's work was not according to
the 'God helps them that helps themselves' of *Poor Richard's*

---

[1] Cf. Chrysostom, col. 470: Καὶ οὐκ εἶπε, Δέδοται, ἀλλ' Ἐκκέχυται . . ., τὸ
δαψιλὲς ἐμφαίνων, and Bengel, p. 514: 'abundantissime'.

[2] I.e. by the Holy Spirit, in the sense that the Holy Spirit has worked
in our hearts the knowledge of God's love for us, rather than in the
sense (as has sometimes been suggested) that the fact of the Spirit's
presence is a proof that God loves us (or that the Spirit's presence is
the gift given by God's love or an earnest of the fulfilment of our hope).

[3] About the gift of the Spirit Paul will have more to say in chapter 8
(see also on 1.4; 2.29; 7.6, 14).

[4] εἴ γε is attested by B sa; ἔτι γάρ has Alexandrian, Western and
Byzantine support. Other variants are: εἰς τί γάρ (G lat Ir^lat); εἰ γάρ
(201 vg^codd); εἰ δέ (sy^p); and εἴπερ has been conjectured. On the assumption
that ἔτι γάρ is original, the other readings can be explained as various
attempts to improve the sentence by getting rid of a redundant ἔτι.
[N^26 reads ἔτι γάρ.]

[5] Unless—just conceivably?—the first ἔτι was intended to carry some
such sense as 'actually' (see LSJ, s.v. II), and only the second the sense
'still'.

Almanac. He did not wait for us to start helping ourselves, but died for us when we were altogether helpless.

κατὰ καιρόν. Compare Mk 1.15; Gal 4.4. It was at the time appointed by God in His sovereign freedom that Christ accomplished His work. For the word καιρός see on 3.26.

ὑπὲρ ἀσεβῶν ἀπέθανεν. For Christ's death on behalf of sinners compare, in this epistle, 3.25; 4.25; 6.10; 7.4; 8.32; 14.15 (in the last two of these passages ὑπέρ is used, as it is here and also in a good many other NT passages dealing with the same subject). The ἀσεβεῖς (see on 1.18) referred to here are not to be distinguished from the 'we' who have just been described as ἀσθενεῖς and will be described as ἁμαρτωλοί (v. 8) and ἐχθροί (v. 10). Paul's meaning is that, in dying for us, Christ died for those who were helpless, ungodly, sinners, enemies. What Paul is here concerned to bring out is the fact that the divine love is love for the undeserving, love that is not the result of any worth in its objects but is self-caused and in its freedom itself confers worth upon them.

7. μόλις γὰρ ὑπὲρ δικαίου τις ἀποθανεῖται· ὑπὲρ γὰρ τοῦ ἀγαθοῦ τάχα τις καὶ τολμᾷ ἀποθανεῖν. That the purpose of this verse is to set off the ὑπὲρ ἀσεβῶν of v. 6 and so emphasize the extraordinariness of Christ's self-sacrifice is clear, but its exact interpretation is disputed. Of those who take δικαίου and τοῦ ἀγαθοῦ as more or less synonymous, some regard the second sentence as a clarification of the first intended to exclude a possible misunderstanding of it (as a denial that any man at all would give his life on behalf of a righteous man),[1] while others suggest that Paul may have meant v. 7b not as a complement to v. 7a but as a replacement of it, and that Tertius may have left v. 7a standing by mistake.[2] Of those who see a distinction in meaning between δικαίου and τοῦ ἀγαθοῦ, some take both as neuter ('a just cause' and 'the public good'), others take δικαίου as masculine and τοῦ ἀγαθοῦ as neuter (claiming that the presence of the article indicates the difference); but, if τοῦ ἀγαθοῦ meant 'the public good', then τάχα would be a serious understatement, since many have voluntarily died for their countries.[3] Yet others have understood τοῦ ἀγαθοῦ to mean 'his benefactor',[4]

---

[1] Cf., e.g., Estius, who paraphrases thus: 'Dico vix reperiri qui pro justo moriatur; non simpliciter nego reperiri quia forsitan reperiatur aliquis qui id faciat' (quoted with approval by Huby, p. 185).

[2] So, e.g., Lietzmann, p. 59; Barrett, p. 105.

[3] Cf. Lagrange, p. 103.

[4] For the use of ἀγαθός in this sense cf., e.g., Ps 73 [LXX: 72].1 ('Ὡς ἀγαθὸς τῷ Ἰσραηλ ὁ θεός, τοῖς εὐθέσι τῇ καρδίᾳ); 118 [LXX: 117].1 ('Ἐξομολογεῖσθε τῷ κυρίῳ, ὅτι ἀγαθός, ὅτι εἰς τὸν αἰῶνα τὸ ἔλεος αὐτοῦ), 2, etc.: that this is the force of ἀγαθός is manifest in the light of the content of

and this seems to give the best sense. We understand Paul's meaning then to be that, whereas it is a rare thing for a man deliberately and in cold blood to lay down his life for the sake of an individual just man, and not very much less rare for a man to do so for the sake of an individual who is actually his benefactor, Christ died for the sake of the ungodly.[1]

8. συνίστησιν δὲ τὴν ἑαυτοῦ ἀγάπην εἰς ἡμᾶς ὁ θεὸς[2] ὅτι ἔτι ἁμαρτωλῶν ὄντων ἡμῶν Χριστὸς ὑπὲρ ἡμῶν ἀπέθανεν. For συνιστάναι meaning 'prove', 'demonstrate', compare 3.5. The use of the present tense is noteworthy: the event of the Cross is a past event (ἀπέθανεν), but the fact that it occurred remains as a present proof. ἑαυτοῦ is emphatic, God's love being contrasted with that shown by men (v. 7). *Pace* Sanday and Headlam, p. 128, εἰς ἡμᾶς is probably to be connected with ἀγάπην rather than with the verb (compare Eph 1.15; Col 1.4; 1 Th 3.12; 2 Th 1.3, in which εἰς is used in specifying the objects of ἀγάπη: it is also significant that in Rom 16.1; 2 Cor 4.2; 5.12 the indirect objects of συνιστάναι/συνιστάνειν are indicated by a dative or by πρός with the accusative, not by εἰς). ὅτι here means 'in that', 'by the fact that' (see BDF, § 394). For Paul the death of Christ is the proof of the fact, and the revelation of the nature, of *God's* love.

9. πολλῷ οὖν μᾶλλον δικαιωθέντες νῦν ἐν τῷ αἵματι αὐτοῦ σωθησόμεθα δι' αὐτοῦ ἀπὸ τῆς ὀργῆς. Having described in vv. 6–8 the nature of God's love for us, to the reality of which (brought home to our hearts by the Holy Spirit) he had appealed in v. 5 as proof that our hope will not disappoint us, he now returns to the subject of our hope's not disappointing and affirms the certainty of our hope's fulfilment, of our final salvation, in two parallel statements (vv. 9 and 10), both in the form of the *argumentum a minori ad maius* (called by the Rabbis *ḳal wāḥômer*, i.e. 'light and heavy'—see SB 3, pp. 223–6). The

these two Psalms. Cf. also LSJ, svv. ἀγαθόω, ἀγαθύνω, III, IV, ἀγαθωσύνη; and Irenaeus, *Haer.* 1.27.1, for the Gnostics' characterization of the God of the OT and the God of the NT as δίκαιος and ἀγαθός, respectively.

[1] Evidence of the recognition among pagans of an obligation to defend one's friends and relatives at the cost of one's own life is to be seen in, e.g., Arrian, *Epict.* 2.7.3; Philostratus, *V.A.* 7.12. The Herculaneum papyrus 1044 (Deissmann, *Light*, p. 118) cited by Michel, p. 134, n. 1, is specially interesting as a parallel: 'For the best-loved of his friends or relatives he would indeed be ready to risk his life'.

[2] The variant ὁ θεὸς εἰς ἡμᾶς instead of εἰς ἡμᾶς ὁ θεός (D G L *pc* lat sy^h Mcion Ir^lat) is probably due to a natural feeling that the reference of ἑαυτοῦ should not be left in doubt any longer than necessary. The omission of ὁ θεός (B Ephr) is understandable in view of the naturalness (after v. 6) of the assumption that the subject of συνίστησιν must be Χριστός.

first of these is couched in a somewhat abbreviated form, the protasis having been compressed into a participial clause (δικαιωθέντες νῦν ἐν τῷ αἵματι αὐτοῦ) and explicit reference to the state in which we were when we were justified omitted (what it was has of course been indicated in vv. 6 and 8). The point made is that, since God has already done the really difficult thing, that is, justified impious sinners, we may be absolutely confident that He will do what is by comparison very easy, namely, save from His wrath at the last those who are already righteous in His sight. It was put succinctly by Pelagius: 'Si peccatores tantum dilexit, quanto magis iam custodiet iustos!'[1] For πολλῷ μᾶλλον compare vv. 10, 15, 17; also Mt 6.30; 1 Cor 12.22; 2 Cor 3.11; Phil 2.12: compare also πολὺ μᾶλλον in Heb 12.9, 25, and πόσῳ μᾶλλον (e.g. Mt 7.11; 10.25; Rom 11.12, 24). The participle δικαιωθέντες picks up again the first words of v. 1, in which the argument of 1.18–4.25 was gathered up. νῦν here denotes the present time in contrast both with the time before the δικαιοσύνη θεοῦ was manifested and also with the future to which σωθησόμεθα refers (cf. v. 11; also, e.g., 3.26; 8.1, 18). For ἐν τῷ αἵματι αὐτοῦ in connexion with δικαιωθέντες compare 3.24–26 (δικαιούμενοι . . . διὰ τῆς ἀπολυτρώσεως τῆς ἐν Χριστῷ Ἰησοῦ · ὃν προέθετο ὁ θεὸς ἱλαστήριον . . . ἐν τῷ αὐτοῦ αἵματι, εἰς ἔνδειξιν τῆς δικαιοσύνης αὐτοῦ . . ., εἰς τὸ εἶναι αὐτὸν δίκαιον καὶ δικαιοῦντα . . .). The preposition ἐν is here used in the sense 'by means of' or 'by virtue of' (cf. the parallel phrase διὰ τοῦ θανάτου τοῦ υἱοῦ αὐτοῦ in v. 10). For σωθησόμεθα see on 1.16 (εἰς σωτηρίαν). The verb is here used in its narrower sense, of deliverance in the final judgment (cf., e.g., 1 Cor 3.15; 5.5), and that from which we are to be saved is specified as the divine wrath, as in 1 Th 5.9 (cf. 1 Th 1.10).[2] For ὀργή see on 1.18. δι' αὐτοῦ stands in parallel to ἐν τῇ ζωῇ αὐτοῦ in v. 10; but it would be wrong to infer from these verses that Paul intended any rigid distinction between what Christ's death, and what His resurrection and exaltation, accomplished (it is to be noted that in 4.25 it was with His resurrection that our justification was connected, and Christ's death would indeed have accomplished but little to our benefit, had it not been followed by His resurrection).

10. εἰ γὰρ ἐχθροὶ ὄντες κατηλλάγημεν τῷ θεῷ. A new term—reconciliation—is introduced here, though the thought was present already in v. 1 (εἰρήνην ἔχομεν πρὸς τὸν θεόν). It is

[1] p. 44.
[2] Mt 1.21 should perhaps also be compared—if ἀπὸ τῶν ἁμαρτιῶν αὐτῶν there means 'from the consequences of their sins'.

hardly surprising that καταλλάσσειν and its cognates play no significant part in the language of Greek or Hellenistic religion even in connexion with rites of propitiation,[1] since the relation between deity and man was not conceived of in ancient paganism as the deeply personal thing that it is in the Bible. In the NT they are used with reference to the relation of God and men only in the Pauline epistles (cf. 11.15; 2 Cor 5.18–20), and there they express the quality of personal relationship which is integral to *God's* justification of men but which the word 'justification' does not as such necessarily suggest.[2] The enmity which is removed in the act of reconciliation is both sinful man's hostility to God (cf. 8.7; probably also 1.30— θεοστυγεῖς) and also God's hostility to sinful man (this aspect of it is particularly clear in 11.28), though the removal of God's hostility is not to be thought of as involving a change of purpose in God (God's purpose with regard to man is constant, and it is an altogether merciful purpose, but the accomplishment of His merciful purpose involves both unrelenting opposition to man's sin and also His self-giving to man). The initiative in reconciliation is God's, and His too is the determinative action: Paul in fact uses the active voice of the verb only of God, the passive only of men. Yet the fact that he can in 2 Cor 5.20 represent God as calling upon men to be reconciled is a clear indication that he does not think of men's part as merely passive: indeed to have done so would have been inconsistent with that very recognition that God in redeeming man deals with him as a person which led to the use of the language of reconciliation. The close connexion that there is between reconciliation and justification—and indeed their inseparability—is shown by the parallelism between vv. 9 and 10, but to conclude that the two terms are merely synonymous would be a false inference, as we have already seen (cf. the note on v. 1).[3]

It was διὰ τοῦ θανάτου τοῦ υἱοῦ αὐτοῦ that we were reconciled to God, because, on the one hand, Christ's death was the means by which God pardoned us without in any way condoning our sin and so laid aside His hostility towards us in a way that was worthy of His goodness and love and consistent with His constant purpose of mercy for us, and, on the other

---

[1] The verb καταλλάσσειν is used in Sophocles, *Ajax* 744, with a religious reference.

[2] It is significant that in this section which is concerned with reconciliation the idea of God's love is prominent.

[3] On καταλλάσσειν and its cognates see further F. Büchsel, in *TWNT* I, pp. 254–9.

hand, it was the means by which He demonstrated His love for us and so broke our hostility toward Himself.

πολλῷ μᾶλλον καταλλαγέντες σωθησόμεθα ἐν τῇ ζωῇ αὐτοῦ. As in v. 9, the point made is that, since God has already done the much more difficult thing (in this case, reconciled us, when enemies, to Himself),[1] we can with absolute confidence expect that He will do what by comparison is but a little thing, namely, at the last save us who are now His friends.[2]

11. οὐ μόνον δέ,[3] ἀλλὰ καί. Compare v. 3. It is surely more natural to supply σωθησόμεθα, the main verb of the previous sentence, with οὐ μόνον than to supply καταλλαγέντες, as do many commentators.[4] We take it that the tense of the following participle is intended to be stressed (not only shall we be saved hereafter, but we already exult now).

καυχώμενοι[5] ἐν τῷ θεῷ. For the use of καυχᾶσθαι here see on v. 2. That this jubilant exultation was expressed in early Christian worship is not to be doubted; but there is no good reason for limiting the reference of καυχώμενοι to something occurring in a context of worship. We should rather understand Paul as thinking of it as characteristic of the Christian life as a whole (combined—paradoxically—with that στενάζειν to which 8.23 refers). We may compare, but must also contrast, Paul's use of καυχᾶσαι ἐν θεῷ in 2.17, where there is a suggestion of complacency and self-righteousness, which is certainly not intended here.

διὰ τοῦ κυρίου ἡμῶν Ἰησοῦ [Χριστοῦ],[6] δι' οὗ νῦν τὴν καταλλαγὴν ἐλάβομεν. It is through Christ (for the formula see on v. 1), through whom we have already received the gift of reconcilia-

---

[1] The inclusion of 'our peace, our reconciliation' in 'The smaller thing' in Barth, *Shorter*, p. 60 (so too in the German p. 72) was no doubt a slip.

[2] Chrysostom, col. 543, put it neatly: Ὁ γὰρ τὸ μεῖζον τοῖς ἐχθροῖς δεδωκὼς πῶς τὰ ἐλάττονα οὐ δώσει τοῖς φίλοις;

[3] As in v. 3, D* (here also G it) adds τοῦτο. It is not likely to be original, and anyway makes no difference to the sense.

[4] e.g. Lagrange, p. 104; Huby, p. 187.

[5] The reading καυχώμεθα (L 69 *al* lat sy^p) is an obvious attempted improvement and almost certainly secondary. On the assumption that the participle is to be read, we have here an example of the use of a participle where a finite verb would be normal which occurs quite often in Paul's letters (cf., e.g., 2 Cor 5.12; 7.5; 8.4; Phil 3.4) possibly under the influence of Semitic usage (see Moule, *Idiom-Book*, p. 179f; BDF, §468 (1)). To join vv. 10 and 11 together as a single sentence, treating καυχώμενοι as parallel to καταλλαγέντες, is unsatisfactory, the result being intolerably awkward.

[6] Χριστοῦ is omitted by B 1739 *pc*; but the fact that the name Χριστός is present in the formulae found in 5.1, 21; 6.23; 7.25, and 8.39 might be taken to suggest the likelihood that its absence from B etc. is due to accidental omission. [N²⁶ rightly discarded the square brackets here.]

tion with God, that we exult; for this gift which we have received through Him is ground enough for ceaseless exultation.[1]

(ii) *Christ and Adam*
(5.12–21)

[12]Wherefore, as through one man sin entered the world, and through sin death, and so death came to all men in turn, because all have sinned—[13]for sin was already in the world before the law was given, but, in the absence of the law, sin is not registered *with full clarity*. [14]But death reigned from Adam to Moses even over those who had not sinned in the same way as Adam, by transgression *of a definite commandment*. Now Adam is the type of him who was to come. [15]But it is not a matter of 'As is the misdeed, so [also] is the gracious gift'. For if by the misdeed of the one the many died, much more have the grace of God and the gift *which has come* by the grace of the one man Jesus Christ abounded unto the many. [16]And it is not a matter of 'As is the result of one man's sinning, so is the gift'; for the judgment followed one misdeed and issued in condemnation, but the gracious gift followed many misdeeds and issued in justification. [17]For if death reigned through the one man by the misdeed of the one, much more shall those who receive the abundance of grace and of the gift of righteousness reign in life through the one man, Jesus Christ. [18]So then as the result of one man's misdeed has been for all men condemnation, so also the result of one man's righteous conduct is for all men justification issuing in life. [19]For as through the disobedience of the one man the many were made sinners, so also through the obedience of the one will the many be made righteous. [20]But the law came in as a new feature of the situation in order that the misdeed might increase; but where sin increased, grace superabounded, [21]in order that, as sin reigned in death, so also grace might reign through righteousness unto eternal life through Jesus Christ our Lord.

Verses 12–21 indicate the conclusion to be drawn from the previous sub-section. The fact that there are those who, being justified by faith, are also now God's friends means that something has been accomplished by Christ which does not just concern believers but is as universal in its effects as was the sin of Adam. The existence of Jesus Christ does not only determine the existence of believers: it is also the innermost secret of the life of every man. Significantly the first person plural, used throughout vv. 1–11, gives place to the third person plural.

Paul begins to draw his parallel between Christ and Adam in v. 12, but breaks off at the end of the verse without having stated the apodosis of his sentence, because, realizing the danger of his comparison's being very seriously misunderstood,

---

[1] Cf. Chrysostom, col. 471: Οὐδὲν γὰρ ἴσον εἰς δόξης λόγον καὶ παρρησίας τοῦ φιλεῖσθαι παρὰ τοῦ Θεοῦ καὶ τοῦ φιλεῖν αὐτὸν τὸν ἀγαπῶντα.

he prefers to indicate as emphatically as possible the vast dissimilarity between Christ and Adam before formally completing it. Verses 13 and 14 are a necessary explanation of the use of the verb 'sin' at the end of v. 12; and vv. 15–17 drive home the dissimilarity between Christ and Adam. Then in v. 18 Paul repeats in a briefer form the substance of v. 12, and now completes it with the long-delayed apodosis. Verse 19 is explanatory of v. 18, bringing out as it does the connecting links between Adam's misdeed and the condemnation of all men, and between Christ's righteous conduct and men's final justification unto life. Verses 20 and 21 refer to the part played by the law in God's purpose. The effect of the gift of the law to Israel was to make sin abound—to turn men's wrong-doing into conscious and wilful rebellion by confronting them with the clear manifestation of God's will; but at the very place where sin most fully and most outrageously abounded (in Israel's rejection of Jesus Christ), there grace abounded more exceedingly and triumphed gloriously. The relevance of the reference to the law at this point lies in the fact that it is the law which makes manifest the full magnitude of sin and so also at the same time the full magnitude of the triumph of grace.[1]

---

[1] From the great mass of modern literature relevant to the discussion of vv. 12–21 the following may be mentioned: A. Kirchgässner, *Erlösung und Sünde im Neuen Testament*, Freiburg i.B., 1950; G. Friedrich, ''Ἁμαρτία οὐκ ἐλλογεῖται, Röm 5.13', in *TLZ* 77 (1952), cols. 523–28; K. Barth, *Christ and Adam: Man and Humanity in Romans 5*, Edinburgh, 1956 (original German 1952); M. Black, 'The Pauline Doctrine of the Second Adam', in *SJT* 7 (1954), pp. 170–79; Davies, *PRJ*, pp. 31–57; S. Lyonnet, 'Le sens de ἐφ' ᾧ en Rom 5.12', in *Biblica* 36 (1955), pp. 436–56; A. M. Dubarle, 'Le péché originel dans S. Paul', in *RechSR* 44 (1956), pp. 64–84; G. Lafont, 'Sur l'interprétation de Rom 5.15–21', in *RechSR* 45 (1957), pp. 481–513; S. Lyonnet, 'Le péché originel et l'exégèse de Rom 5.12–14', in Huby, pp. 521–57; Kuss, pp. 241–75; Cullmann, *Christology*, pp. 170–74; R. Bultmann, 'Adam and Christ according to Rom 5' (original German 1959), in W. Klassen and G. F. Snyder (ed.), *Current Issues in New Testament Interpretation*, New York, 1962, pp. 143–65; J. Jervell, *Imago Dei: Gen 1.26f im Spätjudentum, in der Gnosis und in den paulinischen Briefen*, Göttingen, 1960; L. Ligier, *Péché d'Adam et péché du monde*, Paris, 1960; Barrett, *From First Adam to Last*; E. Brandenburger, *Adam und Christus: exegetisch-religionsgeschichtliche Untersuchung zu Röm 5.12–21*, Neukirchen, 1962; E. Jüngel, 'Das Gesetz zwischen Adam und Christus', in *ZTK* 60 (1963), pp. 42–74; J. Cambier, 'Péchés des Hommes et Péché d'Adam en Rom 5.12', in *NTS* 11 (1964–65), pp. 217–55; P. Lengsfeld, *Adam und Christus: die Adam-Christus-Typologie im Neuen Testament und ihre dogmatische Verwendung bei M. J. Scheeben und K. Barth*, Essen, 1965; R. Scroggs, *The Last Adam: a study in Pauline anthropology*, Oxford, 1966; Cambier, *L'Évangile de Dieu* I, pp. 195–338; H. Müller, 'Der rabbinische Qal-Wachomer-Schluss in paulinischer Typologie (Zur Adam-Christus-Typologie in Röm 5)', in *ZNW* 58 (1967), pp. 73–92;

12. Διὰ τοῦτο (see on 4.16) must here refer backward, since
there is no following clause capable of picking it up.[1] It has
been suggested that it indicates only a loose relation between
what follows and what precedes;[2] that it looks back to 5.11; to
5.9–11; to 5.1–11; to 1.17–5.11.[3] Of these suggestions, the
best is surely that which takes the connexion to be with
5.1–11 as a whole. Verses 1–11 have affirmed that those who
are righteous by faith are people whom God's undeserved love
has transformed from the condition of being God's enemies into
that of being reconciled to Him, at peace with Him. The point
of Διὰ τοῦτο is that Paul is now going on to indicate in vv. 12–21
the conclusion to be drawn from what has been said in vv.
1–11.[4] The fact that this reconciliation is a reality in the case of
believers does not stand by itself: it means that something has
been accomplished by Christ which is as universal in its
effectiveness as was the sin of the first man.[5] Paul is no longer
speaking just about the Church: his vision now includes the
whole of humanity. Significantly, the first person plural of
vv. 1–11 has given place to the third person plural.[6] The
existence of Jesus Christ not only determines the existence of
believers: it is also the innermost secret of the life of every man.
Διὰ τοῦτο indicates that Paul is inferring Christ's significance
for all men from the reality of what He now means for

F. W. Danker, 'Rom 5.12: Sin under Law', in *NTS* 14 (1967–68),
pp. 424–39; C. E. B. Cranfield, 'On Some of the Problems in the
Interpretation of Rom 5.12', in *SJT* 22 (1969), pp. 324–41; A. J. M.
Wedderburn (to whom I am indebted for drawing my attention to
several references in connexion with 5.12ff), 'The Body of Christ and
Related Concepts in 1 Corinthians', in *SJT* 24 (1971), pp. 74–96, and
'The Theological Structure of Romans 5.12', in *NTS* 19 (1972–73),
pp. 339–54.
[1] The sense which Barrett, p. 110, says the sentence would bear ('For
this reason, namely, that sin and death entered the world through
Adam, . . .') if Διὰ τοῦτο were taken as anticipatory (though he himself
rejects this way of taking it as straining Paul's language) could not be
justified as an even remotely possible meaning of the Greek.
[2] Cf., e.g., Barrett, p. 110; Bultmann, 'Adam and Christ', p. 153;
Scroggs, op. cit., p. 77.
[3] Sanday and Headlam, p. 131, list supporters of these various
suggestions.
[4] Cf. Michel, p. 138, n. 1.
[5] Nygren, p. 209, rejects the translation 'therefore' on the ground
that Paul gives no intimation that he regarded Adam's position so
highly that he would be likely to want to prove that Christ may be
compared to him. But the point is Adam's significance for *all* men, and
it is surely understandable that Paul should wish to prove that Christ
is significant not just for believers but, like Adam, for *all* men—only for
blessing instead of for ruin.
[6] Cf. Barth, *Christ and Adam*, p. 42.

believers. The connexion, then, between vv. 12–21 and vv.
1–11 is definite and close.

That ὥσπερ introduces a protasis which has no apodosis,
the sentence having been broken off, has been generally
agreed from ancient times down to the present,[1] and this
view, though it has recently been challenged by Cerfaux,[2]
Barrett[3] and Scroggs,[4] must be upheld as the only feasible
explanation of the structure of the verse.[5] The latter half of

---

[1] Cf., e.g., Origen, col. 1005f; Augustine, col. 2068; the Vulgate ('et
ita': contrast 'ita et' in vv. 15, 16, 19, 21, and 'sic et' in v. 18); Calvin,
p. 111; AV; RV; RSV.

[2] Le Christ, p. 178.

[3] p. 109f. His translation ('Therefore as through one man sin entered
the world (and through sin came that man's death), so also death came
to all men, because they all sinned') shows that he understands the part
of the verse beginning with καὶ οὕτως as the apodosis of the ὥσπερ clause;
but he does not discuss the matter.

[4] op. cit., p. 79, n. 13 (continued on p. 80).

[5] In support of this judgment the following points may be made:
(i) In Greek a definite distinction is observed between καὶ οὕτως and
οὕτως καί (as far as I have been able to check the matter, it is consistently
observed). To introduce the apodosis answering to a protasis beginning
with ὥσπερ or another word of similar meaning, the simple οὕτω(ς) or
the stronger οὕτω(ς) καί (in this order) is used. By contrast, καὶ οὕτω(ς)
is equivalent to our 'and so', 'and thus', meaning 'and so (as a result)'
or 'and so (in this way)'. (For καὶ οὕτως cf. 11.26; 1 Cor 7.36; 11.28;
Gal 6.2. For οὕτως καί introducing an apodosis answering to a protasis
introduced by ὡς, ὥσπερ or similar word, see in this chapter vv. 15
(though here καί is omitted by B), 18, 19, 21; also 6.4; 11.31; 1 Cor 12.12;
15.22; Eph 5.24; Col 3.13; 2 Tim 3.8. On the καί after οὕτως reference
may be made to Kühner-Gerth II/2, p. 256). (ii) The comparison which
results from taking v.12b as the apodosis of v.12a (a comparison
between the entry of sin and death into the world through one man
and the coming of death to all men severally because [if that is the
correct translation of ἐφ' ᾧ] all men have sinned) is intrinsically unsatisfactory. (Even Barrett's supplement 'came that man's' before the first
'death' does not turn it into a satisfactory comparison in this context,
and this supplement is anyway unjustifiable—what must be understood
is rather 'entered the world'.) (iii) The emphatic position of δι' ἑνὸς
ἀνθρώπου in v. 12a suggests that in the corresponding apodosis the
emphasis would be on something answering to it. (iv) The argument of
the section as a whole suggests that the comparison between Christ and
Adam was already in Paul's mind from the beginning, and that the
intended analogue of the 'one man' (Adam) of v. 12a is not the 'all' of
the last clause of the verse but the one man (Christ) who will be
mentioned later. (v) The fact that, while, on the assumption that v. 12
is a complete sentence, there is nothing in it which could be said to
follow from what has been said in vv. 1–11, it is possible, on the
assumption that the construction is broken off, to see a connexion
between vv. 1–11 and the thought of the unexpressed—or rather post-
poned—apodosis which fully justifies the use of διὰ τοῦτο, is—though
not by itself a conclusive argument—an additional support for the view
we have upheld.

the verse is a continuation of the protasis. Paul then breaks off his construction, in order to give a necessary explanation (v. 13f) of what he has said in that continuation of his protasis and to drive home with much emphasis (vv. 15–17) the vast dissimilarity between Adam and Christ. Finally, instead of just expressing at last the apodosis which he has all along intended, he now, as his parenthesis has become so excessively long (it is five whole verses), repeats the substance of his original protasis in v. 18a, and then immediately completes it with its proper apodosis in v. 18b.[1] The anacoluthon reflects a real theological difficulty, and is a valuable clue to the right understanding of vv. 12–21 as a whole. Paul wants to draw the comparison between Christ and Adam—and indeed must draw it—in order to bring out clearly the universal significance of Christ's work, but is vividly conscious of the danger of its being misunderstood. He is therefore reluctant to complete his statement of the comparison (though in the course of his long parenthesis he certainly does give a hint—at the end of v. 14—of the comparison he has in mind), before he has hedged it about with qualifications emphasizing that this is no comparison of like with like but a comparison of two persons who are utterly dissimilar except in respect of the actual point of comparison. Even such a term as 'antithetical typology' (Michel[2]) is liable to be misleading in this connexion, since, while it indicates that Paul is contrasting Christ and Adam, it is liable to suggest that he sees a close correspondence between them and is balancing the one against the other. The truth is that he desires, while drawing the analogy, at the same time to deny emphatically that there is even the remotest semblance of an equilibrium between them; for, as Chrysostom observes,[3] 'Sin and grace are not equivalents, nor yet death and life, nor yet the devil and God; but the difference between them is infinite'.

A preliminary discussion of the rest of the verse except for

[1] The explanation of Sanday and Headlam (p. 132), according to which Paul, having brought up by the words διὰ τῆς ἁμαρτίας ὁ θάνατος in v. 12a the subject he was intending to raise, namely, the connexion of sin and death with the fall of Adam, 'goes off upon this, and when he has discussed it sufficiently for his purpose, . . . does not return to the form of sentence which he had originally planned, but . . . attaches the clause comparing Christ to Adam by a relative (ὅς ἐστιν τύπος τοῦ μέλλοντος) to the end of his digression: and so what should have been the main apodosis of the whole paragraph becomes merely subordinate', is surely a much less natural analysis of the situation.

[2] p. 137.

[3] col. 475 (οὐκ ἴσον ἁμαρτία καὶ χάρις, οὐκ ἴσον θάνατος καὶ ζωή, οὐκ ἴσον διάβολος καὶ Θεός, ἀλλ' ἄπειρον τὸ μέσον).

the last clause is possible now: a more general discussion of the contents of the verse will follow consideration of the specially difficult last clause. δι' ἑνὸς ἀνθρώπου ἡ ἁμαρτία εἰς τὸν κόσμον εἰσῆλθεν states that one man's (Adam's) transgression gave sin entrance into the world—that is, most probably, the world in the sense of 'mankind', so 'human life'.[1] A tendency to personify sin is perhaps to be discerned here, as in 6.12ff and 7.8ff; but here (as v. 13b shows) it is not sustained. The further words καὶ διὰ τῆς ἁμαρτίας ὁ θάνατος indicate that sin's entry meant also the entry of death, which followed sin like a shadow. For the language used here compare Wisd 2.24 (φθόνῳ δὲ διαβόλου θάνατος εἰσῆλθεν εἰς τὸν κόσμον . . .); Apoc. Mos. 32 (in which Eve declares: '. . . all sin is come into the creation through me'); Deut R. 9 (206a) ('. . . for he [namely, Adam] brought death into the world'). Verse 12b then goes on to state explicitly what is already implicit in v. 12a—that the entry of sin and death into the world of men was in due course followed by its natural consequence (καὶ οὕτως), death's taking hold of each individual man in turn, as the generations succeeded one another.[2] Here, instead of speaking first of sin and then of death (as in the first half of the verse), Paul mentions first death's taking hold of each individual man, and then adds the reference to each individual's sinning in the last clause of the verse. The result is a chiasmus—sin, death, death, sin.

ἐφ' ᾧ πάντες ἥμαρτον has given rise to an enormous volume of discussion. At any rate four basic grammatical explanations have to be considered;[3] but, since it is possible to base three quite distinct interpretations of Paul's meaning on one of them, it will be best to set out the alternatives as six main lines of interpretation. They are as follows:

(i) to take ᾧ as masculine with ὁ θάνατος as its antecedent.

(ii) to take ᾧ as masculine with ἑνὸς ἀνθρώπου as its antecedent, and ἐπί as equivalent to ἐν.

(iii) as (ii), but taking ἐπί in the sense 'because of'.

(iv) to take ἐφ' ᾧ as a conjunction meaning 'because',

---

[1] That κόσμος here means 'mankind' or 'human life' is often treated as self-evident by commentators. For an interesting statement of argument in support of this interpretation see Luther, p. 165f.

[2] Pace Cambier, 'Péchés des Hommes et Péchés d'Adam', p. 238f, it is natural to give to the δια- of διῆλθεν here this distributive force. See LSJ, s.v. διά, D.II; and cf. Lk 9.6 (also 5.15); Acts 8.4.

[3] The statement of Scroggs, op. cit., p. 79, n. 12, that 'It is the clear consensus of modern scholars that ἐφ' ᾧ is to be understood as "because" ' is quite misleading.

understanding ἥμαρτον to refer not to men's sinning in their own persons but to their participation in Adam's transgression (thus combining the essential theological idea of (ii) with the grammatical explanation of ἐφ' ᾧ as a conjunction).

(v) as (iv), but understanding ἥμαρτον to refer to men's sinning in their own persons quite independently of Adam, though after his example.

(vi) as (iv), but understanding ἥμαρτον to refer to men's sinning in their own persons but as a result of the corrupt nature inherited from Adam.[1]

Interpretation (i) is mentioned as a third alternative by Augustine in his *Contra duas epistolas Pelagianorum*[2] but immediately set aside as improbable. It is also mentioned by the ninth-century Patriarch Photius as maintained by some.[3] In modern times it has been supported by Héring[4] and Stauffer, the latter explaining ἐπί as meaning 'in Richtung auf' (he compares Phil 4.10; 2 Tim 2.14; Wisd 2.23) and paraphrasing thus: 'der Tod, dem sie Mann für Mann durch ihr Sündigen verfielen'.[5] Though it is true that ὁ θάνατος is near at hand, that ἐπί can bear this meaning, that ἐπ' ἀφθαρσίᾳ in Wisd 2.23 (a verse which together with its sequel Paul seems to have had in mind in writing this verse) may be adduced as support, and that a sense is yielded which is not inconsistent with Paul's argument, this interpretation should, we think, be rejected on the ground that it is difficult and forced (the very fact that Stauffer in paraphrasing to bring out the sense has to alter the grammatical structure radically is itself a pointer to its forcedness). The way in which πάντες picks up εἰς πάντας ἀνθρώπους in the previous clause strongly suggests that the last clause of the verse was intended to explain why death came to all men. It seems perverse, in view of this, to explain it as a relative clause adjectival to ὁ θάνατος, when other explanations, according to which the grammatical structure would

[1] Other suggestions have of course been made, but many of them may be regarded as variations on one or other of the alternatives we have listed (so, for example, the interpretation put forward by Lyonnet in Huby, pp. 521ff, in which 'étant remplie la condition que' is preferred to 'parce que' as a translation of ἐφ' ᾧ, is a variation on (vi)). The suggestion of Danker (*NTS* 14, pp. 424–39) that the clause means 'on the legal basis in terms of which all (including the Gentiles) sinned' (p. 431) seems very unlikely: his attempt to wrest support for it from the other Pauline occurrences of ἐφ' ᾧ (and ἐφ' οἷς) is unconvincing. See now also J. A. Fitzmyer, in *NTS* 39 (1993), pp. 321–39.

[2] 4.4.7.

[3] PG 101, col. 553.

[4] *Le Royaume de Dieu et sa venue* (Neuchâtel, 1937), p. 157.

[5] *Theologie*, p. 248f.

agree more closely with the structure of the thought, are possible.

(ii) is specially associated with Augustine, though it did not originate with him.[1] In the *De peccatorum meritis et remissione*[2] he put forward two alternative explanations of 'in quo': either 'in peccato' or 'in Adam' (since the sin referred to is of course Adam's, there is no substantial difference of meaning between these two). Some of the later Latin interpreters were content to let these two alternatives stand side by side, but Augustine himself later came down decisively on the side of 'in Adam'. Thus in the *Contra duas epistolas Pelagianorum* passage, to which reference was made earlier,[3] he first set out three alternatives, and then dismissed 'in morte' (as we have seen) as improbable, and 'in peccato' on the ground that the Greek word ἁμαρτία is feminine and so cannot be the antecedent of ᾧ, and concluded that 'in quo' can only refer to Adam, appealing to Ambrosiaster (whom he believed to be Hilary) as supporting this interpretation.[4] The implications of the clause for Augustine are made clear by such passages as: 'Omnes enim fuimus in illo uno, quando omnes fuimus ille unus'[5] and 'Per unius illius voluntatem malam omnes in eo peccaverunt, quando omnes ille unus fuerunt, de quo propterea singuli peccatum originale traxerunt'.[6] We must of course distinguish between acceptance of Augustine's general understanding of the thought of the clause and acceptance of his grammatical explanation of 'in quo'. The former (see on (iv) below) is much more widespread than the latter. But the latter has been widespread in the west, and still has its supporters. It is defended by, for example, W. Manson[7] and N. Turner.[8] But it should surely be rejected; for ἑνὸς ἀνθρώπου is too far away to be a natural antecedent, ἐν rather than ἐπί would be appropriate if this were the meaning, and—an argument which tells equally against (i), (ii) and (iii)—it is much more natural

---

[1] On Augustine's interpretation reference should be made to G. I. Bonner, 'Augustine on Romans 5,12', in F. L. Cross (ed.), *Studia Evangelica* 5, Berlin, 1968, pp. 242–7.

[2] 1.10.11 (*PL* 44, col. 115).

[3] 4.4.7 (*PL* 44, col. 614).

[4] The relevant passage in Ambrosiaster is col. 92. It includes the words, 'Manifestum itaque est in Adam omnes peccasse quasi in massa'.

[5] *De civitate Dei* 13.14.

[6] *De nupt. et concup.* 2.15.

[7] 'Notes', p. 159.

[8] *Insights*, pp. 116–18. However, his intention is not quite clear, since, while he claims that his interpretation of ἐφ' ᾧ is that of Augustine, he also offers the suggestion that ἐπί here means 'under the power of' or 'within the jurisdiction of'.

to understand ἐφ' ᾧ here as a conjunctional expression, as did a number of Greek interpreters.[1]

Interpretation (iii) is interesting, as having, apparently, the support of John Damascene[2] and Theophylact,[3] and perhaps of their master, Chrysostom.[4] In recent times it has been favoured by Cerfaux[5] and Cambier.[6] It has an advantage over (ii), in that it takes account of the difference between ἐπί and ἐν; but it is open to the other objections which lie against (ii) which were noted above, and is hardly to be accepted.

Of the remaining three lines of interpretation, (v), that of Pelagius, though we may recognize in it the intention of doing justice to a vital element of the truth which certainly ought not to be obscured, namely, that we all are ourselves responsible for our own re-enactment of Adam's sin, must surely be rejected on the grounds that it reduces the scope of the analogy between Christ and Adam to such an extent as virtually to empty it of real significance, and fails to do justice to the thought of vv. 18 and 19 and to that solidarity of men with Adam which is clearly expressed in 1 Cor 15.22.

Interpretation (iv) has been, and still is, very widely supported. It is possible that Chrysostom should be counted among its supporters (cf. on (iii) above). It is the view of, among others, Bengel,[7] Lagrange,[8] Prat,[9] Huby,[10] Bruce.[11] According to this interpretation, the reference of ἥμαρτον is to a collective sin: death has come to all men in their turn because they all sinned collectively in the primal transgression of Adam. Thus the theological substance of Augustine's interpretation is combined with the grammatical explanation

[1] The discussion of the clause by Photius (*PG* 101, cols. 553 and 556) is particularly interesting. He explains ἐφ' ᾧ without any apparent hesitation as equivalent to διότι.

[2] col. 477.

[3] col. 404.

[4] col. 474. Unfortunately, his words do not make clear exactly how he understood the grammar of the clause. It has sometimes been suggested that Chrysostom understood ἐφ' ᾧ in the sense 'in whom', but there seems to be no justification for this contention (cf. Lyonnet, in Huby, p. 535, n. 2.).

[5] *Le Christ*, p. 178: he takes ἐφ' ᾧ to mean 'à cause de celui par qui'.

[6] 'Péchés des Hommes et Péché d'Adam', p. 253: he concludes that ἐφ' ᾧ means 'à cause du seul homme à cause de qui'.

[7] p. 516.

[8] p. 106f.

[9] *Theology*, 1, pp. 214–17, though he stresses that the original sin is not to be isolated from its whole stream of consequences which include actual sins.

[10] p. 190f.

[11] p. 129f: cf. p. 126.

of ἐφ' ᾧ as meaning 'because'. Before considering the claims of this interpretation, we must set beside it the remaining alternative.

According to (vi), ἥμαρτον refers to men's actual sinning (death has come to all men in their turn because all men have sinned in their own persons voluntarily), but—contrast the Pelagian view (i.e. (v) above)—their sinning is related to Adam's transgression not merely externally, as being an imitation of it, but also internally, as being its natural consequence, the fruit of the desperate moral debility and corruption which resulted from man's primal transgression and which all succeeding generations of mankind have inherited. According to this interpretation, while men did not sin in Adam in Augustine's sense, they certainly do sin in Adam in the sense that they sin in a real solidarity with him, as a result of the entail of his transgression. Cyril of Alexandria seems to have understood the clause in this way.[1]

The main argument which can be adduced as an objection to (vi) and as favouring (iv) is that the parallel which Paul is drawing between Adam and Christ requires that, as Christ is alone responsible for our salvation, so too Adam must alone be responsible for our ruin.[2] But in answer to this it may be pointed out that Paul in this passage insists on the dissimilarity as well as on the similarity between Christ and Adam, and that therefore we have no right to insist that, because he saw the righteousness which we have through Christ to be quite independent of our works, Paul must necessarily have held that the guilt which is ours through Adam must also be quite independent of our actual sinning. It is surely enough for the justification of the analogy that in both cases the act of one man has far-reaching consequences for all other men: it is not necessary that the ways in which the consequences follow from the acts should also be exactly parallel. It is also argued by the adherents of interpretation (iv) that vv. 13 and 14 support it. Paul has shown, it is said, that the cause of death is sin; but the universality of death cannot be explained on the basis of actual sins, since there was a period between Adam's transgression and the giving of the law when there was no law which forbade sin under pain of death, and sins committed during that period were therefore not punishable by death. The fact that nevertheless the men of that time died shows therefore, it is argued, that the cause of death cannot be men's

[1] col. 784: cf. col. 789 (on v. 18).
[2] Cf., e.g., Calvin, p. 112; W. Manson, 'Notes', p. 159; Bruce, pp. 125–30.

actual sins but their participation in the primal sin of Adam.[1]
But against this it may be said that, according to 1.32, even
those who do not know the law have enough moral perception
to know τὸ δικαίωμα τοῦ θεοῦ . . ., ὅτι οἱ τὰ τοιαῦτα πράσσοντες
ἄξιοι θανάτου εἰσίν, and 2.12a seems to connect the death of
those who sinned 'without the law' with the fact of their
sinning, i.e. of their actual sins. A more probable interpretation
of vv. 13–14 is given below. A further argument in favour of
(iv) is furnished by v. 19; but it is not necessary to assume that
the manner in which the many were made sinners must be
closely parallel to the manner in which the many were made
righteous (cf. what was said with reference to the first argument). We may understand that the many were made sinners
through the disobedience of the one man, in that his transgression gave sin entrance into mankind and meant that the
nature passed on by him to his descendants was a nature
weakened and corrupted. It has also sometimes been argued
that πάντες must include those who have died in infancy, and
that the contention that infants participate by seminal
identity in the primal sin of Adam is more intelligible than the
contention that they commit actual sins. But those who die in
infancy are a special and exceptional case, and Paul must
surely be assumed to be thinking in terms of adults. While the
arguments in favour of (iv) and against (vi) are thus by no
means compelling, there is on the other side the important
consideration that there is nothing in the context or in this
verse to suggest that ἥμαρτον is being used in an unusual
sense and that in every other occurrence of this verb in the
Pauline epistles the reference is quite clearly to actual sin. We
conclude that πάντες ἥμαρτον has the same meaning here as it
has in 3.23, and that interpretation (vi) is to be accepted as
most probable.

We must now look at v. 12 as a whole. Its first two clauses
state only that through Adam sin gained entrance to mankind
and that as a result death also gained entrance. So far it has
not been said that death actually reached all men either as the
direct result of Adam's sin or as the result of their own sinning.
Thus these two clauses do not go beyond what is explicit in
Gen 2.17b and 3.3, 19. The third and fourth clauses of the
verse, however, say something which is not explicit in the
Genesis narrative or anywhere else in the OT,[2] though it is the

[1] Cf., e.g., Lagrange, p. 107f; Huby, pp. 191ff: cf. also Chrysostom,
col. 475.
[2] Apart from Gen 2–5 the only certain reference to Adam by name
in the OT seems to be in 1 Chr 1.1. There are several passages where

natural inference to be drawn from the Genesis narrative and
is surely its intention, namely, that, as a result of the entrance
of sin followed by death, death in time reached all men because
they all sinned.[1] What is implicit in the OT account was, of
course, made fully explicit in later Jewish writings (Ecclus
25.24 is the earliest passage to assert that physical death is
due to the Fall and to connect all men's sinfulness with the
sin of Adam and Eve), and it is significant that in these
writings both the ideas expressed (if our interpretation is
correct) in the third and fourth clauses of this verse, namely,
that Adam's sin was the cause of the death of all men and
that men did not die simply because of Adam's sin without
their contributing their own sinning by their own fault, are
frequently expressed.[2] But other ideas are also present: so,
for example, the blame is sometimes put on Eve rather than
on Adam, or else on Satan or on the angels of Genesis 6; or
the origin of sin is traced back to creation itself, as in 2 Esdr
4.30 and 7.[92] (cf. 1QS 3.17f). Particularly important is the
tendency to exalt Adam as the first patriarch, the father of
Israel, and to allow the imagination to run riot in extravagant
descriptions of his superlative size, beauty and wisdom before

it is not clear whether '$\bar{a}\underline{d}\bar{a}m$ is a proper name or generic (see Deut 32.8;
Job 31.33; Hos 6.7). There are other passages where Adam is not referred
to by name but where the Genesis narrative about Adam seems to have
been in the author's mind (see Ps 8 and Ezek 28). One may wonder
whether in Isa 43.27 the reference is to Adam.

[1] That the Genesis narrative is intended as an account of the origin
of human sinfulness and death can hardly be denied. Note the way in
which Gen 4 follows Gen 3, the explicit involvement of Eve's seed in
3.15 and the implicit involvement of future generations in what is said
in 3.17–19.

[2] Thus 2 Bar. 54.15 contains both ideas ('For though Adam first
sinned and brought untimely death upon all, yet of those who were
born from him each one of them has prepared for his own soul torment
to come, . . .'), while v. 19 declares: 'Adam is therefore not the cause,
save only of his own soul, but each of us has been the Adam of his own
soul'; and 17.3; 19.8; 23.4 speak of Adam's bringing death to men (cf.
48.42ff), while 48.46 refers to the sins of individual men. Cf. 2 Esdr
7.48 [118] ('O thou Adam, what hast thou done? for though it was
thou that sinned, the evil is not fallen on thee alone, but upon all of
us that come of thee') and 49 [119] ('For what profit is it unto us, if
there be promised us an immortal time, whereas we have done the
works that bring death?'); also 3.7 and 8; 3.21 and 7.[72]. The same
ambivalence is to be seen in Rabbinic literature (see, e.g., on the one
side, *Siphre Deut* 323 (138b), where Rabbi Judah's interpretation of Deut
32.32 as meaning 'You are sons of Adam who brought death upon you
and upon all his descendants coming after him until the end of all
generations' is given, and, on the other side, such passages as *Num R.*
19.18, where it is affirmed that all men die because all men sin). See
further material collected in SB 3, pp. 227–29.

his fall.[1] That Paul was familiar with many of the ideas concerning Adam to be found in the Apocrypha and Pseudepigrapha and in Rabbinic literature is probable; but the restraint and sobriety of his own references to Adam are noticeable. Here in Rom 5.12ff his attention is firmly centred on Christ, and Adam is only mentioned in order to bring out more clearly the nature of the work of Christ. The purpose of the comparison is to make clear the universal range of what Christ has done. Though Paul does elsewhere refer by implication to the glory which was Adam's before the fall (3.23), he is here concerned with Adam only as the man who has affected all other men disastrously but whose effectiveness for ill has been far surpassed by Christ's effectiveness for good.[2]

According to this verse, human death is the consequence of human sin. This is stated first in the words καὶ διὰ τῆς ἁμαρτίας ὁ θάνατος with reference to Adam's primal sin, and then again in the second half of the verse with reference to the subsequent sinning of all individual men (if our understanding of the last clause is correct). That it is difficult for those who are in the habit of thinking of death as natural to come to terms with this doctrine of death is obvious—and it is not only in modern times that the difficulty of this doctrine has been felt.[3] But it will be convenient to reserve discussion of the problems raised for the concluding essay in volume 2.

13f may be understood differently according as the first or the second sentence of v. 13 is stressed. If the latter is stressed and the former regarded as virtually equivalent to a concessive

---

[1] Cf., e.g., Ecclus 49.16; *Pesikta R.* 23 (115a) (SB 3, p. 325); *Gen R.* 8.1; b. *Baba Bathra* 58a; Philo, *Op. Mund.* 135–52; also passages cited in SB 3, p. 681.

[2] Bultmann (in the essay cited on p. 270) has argued that the Christology of vv. 12–21 'is actually Gnostic' (p. 150). Paul, he maintains, is not content with having in vv. 1–11 described life as anticipated in hope but wants to depict it as already present with Christ, and to this end 'reaches for the gnostic myth of the original man' (p. 154), though correcting it in certain respects by the introduction of salvation-historical motifs. Brandenburger also (in the work referred to on p. 270) assumes a gnostic influence (a Corinthian *Urmensch*-Saviour Christology). But, while in the present inadequate state of our knowledge of pre-Christian 'gnosis' we cannot say categorically that Paul cannot have been in any way influenced by it in any form, we certainly have no justification for assuming a gnostic background whether as something polemized against or as something influencing him positively, when the evidence can be equally well explained without any such assumption. In this connexion reference may be made to the judicious discussion in R. McL. Wilson, *Gnosis and the New Testament*, Oxford, 1968, and, with regard to these verses in particular, to R. Scroggs, op. cit.

[3] See, e.g., Aquinas, p. 75f (§ 416).

clause, then v. 13f as a whole may be understood in a way favourable to interpretation (iv), as against interpretation (vi), of ἐφ' ᾧ πάντες ἥμαρτον (see on v. 12). But, if the first sentence of v. 13 is stressed and the second treated as virtually equivalent to a concessive clause, it is then the fact that sin was already present and active in mankind before the law was given that is introduced as explanation of something in v. 12. This second alternative, which seems to be a perfectly natural way of taking v. 13, has the advantage of suiting what on other grounds is the most probable interpretation of the last clause of v. 12. ἄχρι γὰρ νόμου ἁμαρτία ἦν ἐν κόσμῳ may then be understood as intended to explain how it is true that 'all sinned' in spite of the fact that for a time there was no law: even during that time sin was present in mankind and men actually sinned. The sentence ἁμαρτία δὲ οὐκ ἐλλογεῖται μὴ ὄντος νόμου is added in acknowledgment of the fact that in the absence of the law sin is not the clearly defined thing, starkly shown up in its true character, that it becomes when the law is present (cf. 3.20b; 4.15). By οὐκ ἐλλογεῖται Paul does not mean that it is not registered in the sense of being charged to men's account, reckoned against them, imputed; for the fact that men died during this period of the law's absence (v. 14) shows clearly enough that in this sense their sin was indeed registered. οὐκ ἐλλογεῖται must be understood in a relative sense: only in comparison with what takes place when the law is present can it be said that, in the law's absence, sin οὐκ ἐλλογεῖται. Those who lived without the law were certainly not 'innocent sinners'[1]—they were to blame for what they were and what they did. But, in comparison with the state of affairs which has obtained since the advent of the law, sin may be said to have been, in the law's absence, 'not registered', since it was not the fully apparent, sharply defined thing, which it became in its presence. It is only in the presence of the law, only in Israel and in the Church, that the full seriousness of sin is visible and the responsibility of the sinner stripped of every extenuating circumstance.

The ἀλλά at the beginning of v. 14 (at first sight rather surprising on the assumption that the verse states the conse-quence of the presence of sin affirmed in v. 13a) is to be explained as due to the fact that v. 13b, instead of being subordinated to v. 13a in the form of a concessive clause, has been made co-ordinate with it: instead of being connected with v. 13a (which would have agreed better with the thought),

---

[1] *Pace* Leenhardt, p. 187, n. *.

v. 14 has been connected by an adversative conjunction with v. 13b (a connexion for which there is, of course, some justification). The words ἐβασίλευσεν ὁ θάνατος ἀπὸ 'Αδὰμ μέχρι Μωϋσέως express the truth that as a result of sin's presence death reigned (cf. vv. 17a, 21a, and contrast vv. 17b, 21b) over mankind throughout the period from Adam to the giving of the law, and the following καὶ ἐπὶ τοὺς μὴ¹ ἁμαρτήσαντας ἐπὶ τῷ ὁμοιώματι τῆς παραβάσεως 'Αδάμ is added in order to bring out the fact that those over whom sin reigned throughout this period were actually men who, while they had indeed sinned and were punished for their sin, had not sinned after the likeness of Adam's transgression, that is, by disobeying a clear and definite divine commandment such as Adam had (Gen 2.17) and Israel was subsequently to have in the law. The relative clause ὅς ἐστιν τύπος τοῦ μέλλοντος is a very clear hint of the comparison, for the completion of the formal statement of which we have still to wait until v. 18f. The word τύπος denotes a mark made by striking (it is cognate with τύπτειν), an impression made by something, such an impression used in its turn as a mould to shape something else (e.g. in 6.17), hence a form, figure, pattern, example, and— a specialized use in biblical interpretation—a type in the sense of a person or thing prefiguring (according to God's design) a person or thing pertaining to the time of eschatological fulfilment.² It is in this sense that it is used here and also in 1 Cor 10.6 (cf. τυπικῶς in v. 11). Adam in his universal effectiveness for ruin is the type which—in God's design— prefigures Christ in His universal effectiveness for salvation. It is to be noted that it is precisely his παράβασις (which has just been mentioned) and its results which constitute him the τύπος τοῦ μέλλοντος. The expression τοῦ μέλλοντος ('of him who was to come', not 'of him who is to come') may remind us of ὁ ἐρχόμενος in Mt 11.3 = Lk 7.20; but its use here is explicable simply on the basis of the contents of this paragraph by itself.³ (On Adam as the type of Christ see further on vv. 18, 19 and 21.)

---

¹ The omission of μή (385 424² d* Or Ambst codd. latini apud Aug) is a very understandable 'improvement' originating in a failure to see the point intended and a not unnatural assumption that it must have been a reference to the likeness of men's sins to that of Adam.

² See further L. Goppelt, in TWNT 8, pp. 246ff (bibliography on p. 246).

³ The fact that Paul elsewhere speaks of Christ as ὁ ἔσχατος 'Αδάμ (1 Cor 15.45) is scarcely justification enough for assuming that here 'Αδάμ is to be supplied with τοῦ μέλλοντος (as is done by, e.g., Bauer, s.v. τύπος, 6). Even more unlikely, in view of the argument of this sub-

The purpose of **15–17** is to drive home the vast dissimilarity between Christ and Adam, before the formal comparison between them is made in v. 18f, and so to preclude possible misunderstanding of that comparison. Ἀλλ' οὐχ ὡς τὸ παράπτωμα, οὕτως [καὶ]¹ τὸ χάρισμα is the first of two statements of this dissimilarity (the second being v. 16a), each of which is followed by supporting argument. The Ἀλλ' is due to the presence of the last clause of v. 14, which gave such a strong hint of the comparison about to be made. With each part of the sentence ἐστίν is to be understood. The sense might be brought out by some such rendering as 'But it is not a matter of "As is the misdeed, so [also] is the gracious gift"'. παράπτωμα is wrongly taken by Michel to be synonymous with παράβασις.² It is actually more closely equivalent to ἁμάρτημα; for it does not focus attention on the fact that Adam's sin was a transgression of a definite commandment, but rather characterizes it simply as a false step, a going astray (it is cognate with παραπίπτειν), and so a misdeed which violated his relationship with God.³ By τὸ χάρισμα Paul possibly meant the undeserved gift of God, which is Jesus Christ and His work for men, as a whole; but, in view of the presence of τῆς δωρεᾶς τῆς δικαιοσύνης in v. 17 and of εἰς δικαίωσιν ζωῆς, δίκαιοι κατασταθήσονται and διὰ δικαιοσύνης in vv. 18, 19 and 21, respectively, it seems more probable that he had specially in mind the gracious gift of a status of righteousness before God.

εἰ γὰρ τῷ τοῦ ἑνὸς παραπτώματι οἱ πολλοὶ ἀπέθανον, πολλῷ μᾶλλον ἡ χάρις τοῦ θεοῦ καὶ ἡ δωρεὰ ἐν χάριτι τῇ τοῦ ἑνὸς ἀνθρώπου Ἰησοῦ Χριστοῦ εἰς τοὺς πολλοὺς ἐπερίσσευσεν. The statement of the dissimilarity between Adam's sin and God's gracious gift (v. 15a) is now supported (γάρ) by an appeal to the infinitely superior effectiveness of the latter. For the structure of the sentence (εἰ . . ., πολλῷ μᾶλλον . . .) compare vv. 10 and 17, and for πολλῷ μᾶλλον see on v. 9. The articles before ἑνός, πολλοί, ἑνὸς ἀνθρώπου and πολλούς are not otiose, and should be retained in translation: the AV's omission of them is seriously misleading. The contrast is not just between one man and many, but between Adam and Christ, respectively, and 'the many',

section as a whole, is the suggestion of J. A. T. Robinson (*The Body*, London, 1952, p. 35, n. 1), which Scroggs (op. cit., p. 80f) is inclined to accept, that τοῦ μέλλοντος refers to Moses or, possibly, to 'man under the law'.

¹ καί should perhaps be omitted with B syᵖ [though N²⁶ omits the square brackets].
² p. 140. His words are: 'Der Begriff der Übertretung (παράπτωμα) hebt die Besonderheit der Schuld Adams hervor: er übertritt ein bestimmtes Gebot Gottes'.
³ On παράπτωμα see W. Michaelis, in *TWNT* 6, pp. 170–73.

that is, the rest of mankind. οἱ πολλοί and τοὺς πολλούς are
practically equivalent to πάντας ἀνθρώπους in vv. 12 and 18.[1]
Such an inclusive use of 'many' (as opposed not to 'all', but to
'one' or 'some') is of course to be found in the OT.[2] For the
substance of the protasis compare v. 12. The πολλῷ μᾶλλον here
rests on the fact that what stands over against the sin of Adam
is nothing less than the grace of God.[3] How could God not be
infinitely stronger than man, and His grace infinitely more
effective than man's sin? At first sight it is tempting to try to
make ἐν χάριτι τῇ τοῦ ἑνὸς ἀνθρώπου Ἰησοῦ Χριστοῦ parallel to
τῷ τοῦ ἑνὸς παραπτώματι and so to connect it with the verb
ἐπερίσσευσεν, and some explain the sentence in this way. But a
closer consideration of the sentence reveals the fact that the
structures of the protasis and the apodosis are not alike. The
subject of the apodosis is not the οἱ πολλοί which we might have
expected (answering to the οἱ πολλοί of the protasis): instead we
have ἡ χάρις, κ.τ.λ., and 'the many' mentioned in a different
place in the clause (εἰς τοὺς πολλούς). Thus it is the subject of
the apodosis which logically corresponds to the τῷ τοῦ ἑνὸς
παραπτώματι of the protasis, and the real parallelism of
thought between the apodosis and the protasis is actually a
very strong reason for connecting ἐν χάριτι, κ.τ.λ. not with the
verb but with ἡ δωρεά. Having accepted this connexion, we
prefer, in view of Paul's τῇ after χάριτι, not to follow Bauer,
s.v. ἐν IV.4.b and Michel, p. 141, n. 2, in explaining ἡ δωρεὰ ἐν
χάριτι as equivalent to ἡ δωρεὰ τῆς χάριτος (had Paul meant by
ἡ δωρεά, κ.τ.λ. 'das Gnadengeschenk des einen Menschen Jesus
Christus', as Michel translates it on p. 136f, would he not have
written ἡ rather than τῇ after χάριτι?), but to understand
ἡ δωρεά, κ.τ.λ. as meaning 'the gift (which has come) by the
grace of the one Man Jesus Christ'.[4] After ἡ χάρις τοῦ θεοῦ καί

[1] Cf. Calvin, A Harmony of the Gospels of Matthew, Mark and Luke 2,
Eng. tr. by T. H. L. Parker, Edinburgh, 1972, p. 277 (on Mt 20.28):
' "Many" is put, not for a definite number, but for a large number, in
that He sets Himself over against all others. And this is its meaning
also in Rom v. 15, where Paul is not talking of a part of mankind but
of the whole human race.'
[2] The suggestion that Paul's τοὺς πολλούς in this verse is a deliberate
echo of Isa 53.11 (cf. Bruce, p. 132) is possible, but more can hardly
be claimed for it.
[3] Cf. the first part of Chrysostom's comment on v. 15b (col. 475):
Ὁ γὰρ λέγει, τοιοῦτόν ἐστιν· Εἰ ἡ ἁμαρτία τοσοῦτον ἴσχυσε, καὶ ἀνθρώπου
ἁμαρτία ἑνός, χάρις, καὶ Θεοῦ χάρις, καὶ οὐ Πατρὸς μόνου, ἀλλὰ καὶ Υἱοῦ, πῶς
οὐ περιέσται μειζόνως; (The rest of his comment strikes us as decidedly
weak.)
[4] While Paul mentions the grace of Christ specially frequently in
the conclusions of his letters (e.g. 16.20; 1 Cor 16.23; 2 Cor 13.13), he
also refers to it in other contexts (e.g. 2 Cor 8.9; Gal 1.6).

it is natural to understand the gift to be the gift of God rather than of Christ, and, in view of v. 17, we should probably identify it with δικαιοσύνη. For the use of περισσεύειν compare 3.7; 15.13; and also v. 17 (περισσεία).[1] The teaching of Rabbi Jose (about A.D. 150) quoted in *Siphra* Lev 5.17 (120a),[2] which argues on the basis of the principle that the measure of God's kindness exceeds the measure of punishments that the greatness of the evil effects of Adam's disobedience for himself and his descendants proves the even greater ('how much more') good effects which a just man's acts of obedience must have, may be regarded as to a very limited extent a parallel to the thought of this sentence. But it is to be noted that, whereas Rabbi Jose's confidence in the superiority of God's kindness serves to support a thoroughly legalistic trust in the efficacy of human merit, Paul's sentence expresses a confidence that is confidence in nothing but the triumph of divine grace.

καὶ οὐχ ὡς δι' ἑνὸς ἁμαρτήσαντος[3] τὸ δώρημα: 'And it is not a matter of "As is the result of [more literally: As is (that which came about) through] one man's sinning, so is the gift" '. This is the second of the two statements of the dissimilarity between Christ and Adam. The gift of God given through Jesus Christ is no mere equivalent of the result of Adam's sin.

τὸ μὲν γὰρ κρίμα ἐξ ἑνὸς εἰς κατάκριμα, τὸ δὲ χάρισμα ἐκ πολλῶν παραπτωμάτων εἰς δικαίωμα[4] is added in support of v. 16a. It draws attention to two decisive differences between the judgment[5] which followed Adam's misdeed and the gracious gift of God by Christ. The first concerns their external circumstances or contexts: the judgment was the consequence of but one misdeed,[6] but the gift was God's answer to a numberless multitude of misdeeds, to all the accumulated sins of the centuries. (That one single misdeed should be answered by judgment, this is perfectly understandable: that the accumulated sins and guilt of all the ages should be answered by God's free gift, this is the miracle of miracles, utterly beyond human comprehension.) The second concerns the ends to which they

---

[1] Words of this group occur frequently in the NT: it is instructive to consult MG, p. 798f.

[2] Quoted in SB 3, p. 230.

[3] The reading ἁμαρτήσαντος is to be preferred to the reading ἁμαρτήματος (D G *pc* it vg^d syp) as being the more difficult.

[4] The addition of ζωῆς (D*) is doubtless assimilation to v. 18 (εἰς δικαίωσιν ζωῆς).

[5] By κρίμα is meant the actual sentence pronounced on Adam.

[6] Some understand ἑνός as masculine, but the fact that it is parallel to πολλῶν παραπτωμάτων suggests that παραπτώματος should be supplied. Cf. Augustine, col. 2068: '*Ex uno* ergo quod dictum est, subauditur, delicto . . .'

lead: the judgment pronounced on Adam issues in condemnation[1] for all men, but the gift of God issues in justification.[2]

Verse 17 is better understood as further support for v. 16a than as supporting v. 16b. It is reminiscent of v. 15b both in structure (εἰ . . ., πολλῷ μᾶλλον . . .) and substance. τῷ τοῦ ἑνὸς[3] παραπτώματι repeats v. 15b, but for οἱ πολλοὶ ἀπέθανον is substituted the more vivid and forceful ὁ θάνατος ἐβασίλευσεν (cf. v. 14),[4] and διὰ τοῦ ἑνός together with the corresponding διὰ τοῦ ἑνὸς Ἰησοῦ Χριστοῦ[5] in the apodosis are added in order to give extra emphasis to what is for Paul the one real point of likeness between Christ and Adam, namely, the fact of one man's action's being determinative of the existence of the many. The way in which the substance of the apodosis of v. 15b is re-expressed in the latter half of v. 17 is particularly interesting and suggestive. The structure of the apodosis of v. 15b was itself an inversion of the structure of the protasis: instead of making οἱ πολλοί the subject of it (as of the protasis), Paul made ἡ χάρις, κ.τ.λ. the subject—probably because he wanted at this point to emphasize the initiative of the divine grace. In v.17 there is once again an inversion of structure between protasis and apodosis; for now, instead of saying

[1] While κρίμα tended to encroach on the domain of κατάκριμα (for, though it properly denotes simply a judgment pronounced, it was used specially often with reference to a negative judgment, condemnation), κατάκριμα is nevertheless to be distinguished from it as being the stronger term, meaning specifically 'condemnation'. Where the condemnation referred to is condemnation by God, κατάκριμα often signifies not only the pronouncement of the sentence but also its execution. So here the reference is probably not just to the sentence of condemnation pronounced on all men by God but also to the far-reaching consequences issuing from it. See further F. Büchsel, in *TWNT* 3, pp. 943f, 953f; Bauer, s.vv. κρίμα and κατάκριμα. (Bauer in the latter place goes so far as to suggest that κατάκριμα does not denote the actual pronouncement of the sentence of condemnation but simply the consequent punishment.)

[2] δικαίωμα is apparently used in preference to δικαιοσύνη or δικαίωσις (used in v. 18) because a counterpart to κατάκριμα is desired (see Bauer, s.v. δικαίωμα, 3). It is used here (as is also δικαίωσις in v. 18) to denote justification in the sense not of the action of justifying but of the result of the action, i.e. the condition of having been justified, of possessing a righteous status before God.

[3] The readings ἐν ἑνός (1739 vg^codd), ἐν ἑνί (A G) and ἐν τῷ ἑνί (D) are probably to be explained as different attempts to make the phrase τῷ τοῦ ἑνὸς παραπτώματι correspond more obviously with ἐν ζωῇ by introducing an ἐν.

[4] The aorist ἐβασίλευσεν is perhaps better explained, in view of the natural sense of the parallel future βασιλεύσουσιν, as complexive (the action being thought of as a whole irrespective of its duration: cf. vv. 14 and 21) than (with Michel, p. 142) as ingressive ('zur Herrschaft kam').

[5] B has Χριστοῦ Ἰησοῦ.

ἡ ζωὴ βασιλεύσει in correspondence to the ὁ θάνατος ἐβασίλευσεν of the protasis, he says οἱ τὴν περισσείαν τῆς χάριτος καὶ τῆς δωρεᾶς τῆς δικαιοσύνης λαμβάνοντες ἐν ζωῇ βασιλεύσουσιν, which is much more.[1] The effectiveness and the unspeakable generosity of the divine grace are such that it will not merely bring about the replacement of the reign of death by the reign of life, but it will actually make those who receive its riches to become kings themselves, that is, to live 'the true kingly life'[2] purposed by God for man. It is no doubt correct to say with Michel[3] that Paul has taken up 'an old apocalyptic tradition' (the idea of the reign of the saints); but he has not done so for the sake of a literary allusion, but because he wanted at this point to bring out as vividly as possible the measureless generosity of God's grace and the inexpressible glory of God's purpose for man. The expression ἡ δωρεὰ[4] τῆς δικαιοσύνης[5] is strong support for the interpretation which we gave of δικαιοσύνη θεοῦ in 1.17. The tense of βασιλεύσουσιν is to be noted: the reference is to the eschatological fulfilment. Not yet do the recipients of God's grace reign: to suppose that they do is the illusion of a false piety (cf. 1 Cor 4.8). But to recognize this is not to belittle the splendour and the wonder of what they receive even now.[6]

In vv. 15–17 Paul has made clear the essential dissimilarity between Christ and Adam which has to be firmly grasped if the comparison between them is not to be altogether misunderstood. He has shown that, apart from the one point of the formal similarity between the relation of Christ to all men and the relation of Adam to all men, they stand over against each other in utter dissimilarity. This having been made clear, Paul can now go on to make his comparison.

18f. Ἄρα[7] οὖν is used to introduce the formal statement of the comparison. This is understandable, since the preceding verses have been preparing the way for it, and it may be thought of as

---

[1] Cf. Gaugler i, p. 134.

[2] Barth, *Christ and Adam*, p. 14.

[3] p. 142. Cf., e.g., Ps. Sol. 3. 12b [Rahlfs. Charles: 16]; 1 Cor 6.2; Rev 20.4.

[4] τῆς δωρεᾶς could have been omitted (B Ir^lat Or^pt Aug) by accident or perhaps because it seemed redundant.

[5] The omission of τῆς δικαιοσύνης by C is perhaps to be explained as assimilation to v. 15.

[6] The present participle λαμβάνοντες could, of course, refer to the future, the time of their reigning, but is probably better taken as referring to the present.

[7] ἄρα, which in classical Greek is never the first word of a sentence, occurs eleven times in Romans (this being its first occurrence), on eight occasions in combination with οὖν.

drawing them together. Like vv. 15a and 16a, v. 18 is characterized by a highly condensed style, a kind of note-form, and has no verbs expressed.

ὡς δι' ἑνὸς παραπτώματος εἰς πάντας ἀνθρώπους εἰς κατάκριμα repeats the substance of the original protasis (v. 12). Since ἑνός is masculine in its three occurrences in v. 17 and also in its two occurrences in v. 19, and since the whole subsection is concerned with the relation of the one man Adam and one Man Christ to the many, while, apart from v. 16b, the fact that just one misdeed was decisive for ill is not stressed unless it is in the present verse, it is surely better to take ἑνός here as masculine than as agreeing with παραπτώματος.[1]

οὕτως καί (contrast the καὶ οὕτως of v. 12) introduces the apodosis.

ἑνός is again better taken as masculine.

δικαιώματος is variously understood as meaning 'act of justifying' or 'condition of possessing a status of righteousness' or 'righteous act'—so 'righteous conduct'. Of these suggested meanings the last is surely to be accepted, as giving a natural contrast with παραπτώματος and also agreeing with the parallel τῆς ὑπακοῆς in v. 19. The doubt expressed by Sanday and Headlam, p. 142, as to 'whether δικαίωμα can quite = "a righteous act"' may be set aside; for we may compare Aristotle, *Rh.* 1359ᵃ25,[2] where it is contrasted with ἀδίκημα; Bar 2.19; Rev 19.8; and perhaps 2 Sam 19.29. We take it that by Christ's δικαίωμα Paul means not just His atoning death but the obedience of His life as a whole, His loving God with all His heart and soul and mind and strength, and His neighbour with complete sincerity, which is the righteous conduct which God's law requires.

εἰς πάντας ἀνθρώπους εἰς δικαίωσιν ζωῆς. The noun δικαίωσις (its only other occurrence in the NT is in 4.25) probably denotes here not just the act of justification but also the condition resulting from it of possessing a status of righteousness before God (cf. what was said above on κατάκριμα and δικαίωμα in v. 16). ζωῆς is to be explained as a genitive of result (see BDF, § 166): this righteous status has life, eternal life, for its result (cf. v. 17: οἱ τὴν περισσείαν . . . τῆς δωρεᾶς τῆς δικαιοσύνης λαμβάνοντες ἐν ζωῇ βασιλεύσουσιν, and v. 21: διὰ

---

[1] *Pace* Sanday and Headlam, p. 141 (cf. p. 142 on ἑνὸς δικαιώματος). Some witnesses (א* *pc*) actually insert ἀνθρώπου here after ἑνός, while others (D G 69 syp) read τὸ παράπτωμα instead of παραπτώματος and also τὸ δικαίωμα later in the verse instead of δικαιώματος.

[2] In *E.N.* 1135a12–13, however, he distinguishes between δικαίωμα as applied to the correction of an injustice and δικαιοπράγημα as the general term for a just action.

δικαιοσύνης εἰς ζωὴν αἰώνιον). The repetition of εἰς πάντας ἀνθρώπους gives rise to such questions as 'How can Paul speak of both κατάκριμα and δικαίωσις as resulting for *all* men?' and 'Does he really mean "all"?' The important thing here is to remember that vv. 15–17 have specially stressed the vast superiority of Christ to Adam, and made it abundantly clear that Adam's sin and Christ's obedience are not on an equal footing and that there is no equilibrium between their respective consequences. κατάκριμα does indeed result for all men from Adam's sin, but this κατάκριμα is no absolutely irreversible, eternal fact: on the contrary, Christ has in fact already begun the process of its reversal, and therefore the πάντας of the protasis, while it really does mean 'all', is no eternally unalterable quantity. What then of the πάντας of the apodosis? It will be wise to take it thoroughly seriously as really meaning 'all', to understand the implication to be that what Christ has done He has really done for all men, that δικαίωσις ζωῆς is truly offered to all, and all are to be summoned urgently to accept the proffered gift, but at the same time to allow that this clause does not foreclose the question whether in the end all will actually come to share it.

ὥσπερ γὰρ διὰ τῆς παρακοῆς τοῦ ἑνὸς ἀνθρώπου ἁμαρτωλοὶ κατεστάθησαν οἱ πολλοί, οὕτως καὶ διὰ τῆς ὑπακοῆς τοῦ ἑνὸς δίκαιοι κατασταθήσονται οἱ πολλοί. The γάρ should be carefully noted; for v. 19 is not a mere repetition in other words of v. 18, but 'a necessary explanation' of it, as Calvin pointed out.[1] For it indicates the connecting links between Adam's misdeed and the condemnation of the many, and between Christ's perfect fulfilment of God's righteous requirements and the possession by the many of that righteous status which means eternal life. The many have not been condemned for someone else's transgression, for Adam's sin, but because, as a result of Adam's transgression, they have themselves been sinners; and they will not finally inherit that righteous status which carries with it eternal life on account of something which remains altogether apart from themselves, but because, as a result of Christ's obedience, they have actually themselves been made to be men who in God's sight are righteous. At this point the question of course arises: What exactly is meant by ἁμαρτωλοὶ κατεστάθησαν and δίκαιοι κατασταθήσονται, respectively? If what was said about the last clause of v. 12 was right, we may assume that by the former statement Paul means that all other men (Jesus alone excepted) were constituted sinners through

[1] p. 118.

Adam's misdeed in the sense that, sin having once obtained
entry into human life through it, they all in their turns lived
sinful lives. There seems to be no justification whatever for the
assumption of many that Paul's ὥσπερ . . ., οὕτως καί . . . implies that he thought that the ways in which Adam's sin and
Christ's obedience were effective for other men must correspond
exactly. All that is implied surely is that in both cases what
one man does affects all other men and is determinative of their
existence. Michel's 'Ganz entsprechend' (p. 143) is not warranted by the text.[1] With regard to the other statement
(δίκαιοι κατασταθήσονται), we assume that what is meant is
that the many will be constituted righteous through Christ's
obedience in the sense that, since God has in Christ identified
Himself with sinners and taken upon Himself the burden of
their sin, they will receive as a free gift from Him that status
of righteousness which Christ's perfect obedience alone has
deserved. The use of παρακοή and ὑπακοή in this verse makes
explicit the fact that Adam's παράπτωμα and Christ's δικαίωμα
are both to be understood in relation to the revealed will of
God, the one as disobedience to it, the other as obedience.
For Christ's ὑπακοή compare Phil 2.8.[2] The term covers His
whole life, not just His passion and death. As to the future
(δίκαιοι κατασταθήσονται), while it could refer to the final
judgment, it is probably better understood, in agreement with
5.1 and 9, as referring to the present life of believers.

20. νόμος[3] δὲ παρεισῆλθεν. It has been very widely assumed
that παρεισῆλθεν must here have a more or less disparaging
sense. Thus Sanday and Headlam paraphrase: 'Then Law came
in, as a sort of "afterthought", a secondary and subordinate
stage, in the Divine plan';[4] and Barrett translates: 'The law

---

[1] Michel refers to the fact that καθιστάναι can have 'geradezu recht-
lichen Sinn', and cites LXX Deut 25.6; Plato, *Phlb.* 16b; Euripides,
Andr. 635; 3 Macc 1.7; 3.5, and J. de Zwaan (on this verse) in *TS* 31
(1913), pp. 85ff. But a consideration of LSJ, s.v. καθίστημι, might suggest
that Paul may have chosen to use this word here as being equally
appropriate in both clauses precisely by reason of its generalness. The
passive of this verb could serve simply as a true passive equivalent of
γίνεσθαι.

[2] Where (*pace* F. W. Beare, *The Epistle to the Philippians*, London,
1959, p. 84) ὑπήκοος is to be understood of Christ's obedience to God
(cf. J. B. Lightfoot, *Saint Paul's Epistle to the Philippians*, London,
reprinted 1908, p. 113).

[3] That the OT law is meant may be regarded as certain. To infer
from the absence of the article that the meaning is more general is
quite unjustified.

[4] p. 139.

took its subordinate place'.[1] But παρεισέρχεσθαι, while it probably does mean something like 'insinuate oneself in' or 'intrude' in Gal 2.4 (its only other occurrence in the NT), need not have a depreciatory sense. It is used, for example, in Galen of fingers or instruments being inserted,[2] in Vettius Valens of an idea occurring to someone.[3] One of the meanings which παρά can have in composition is 'alongside of', 'beside',[4] and the most natural way of understanding παρεισῆλθεν[5] here is surely to take it as a simple reference to the undisputed fact that the law was given at a later date than that of Adam's fall, namely, in the time of Moses. To refer to this fact is not, in itself, to say anything about the worth of the law depreciatory or otherwise.[6]

ἵνα πλεονάσῃ τὸ παράπτωμα. This ἵνα is not to be explained as merely ecbatic.[7] The clause it introduces states not, of course, the whole purpose of God in giving the law but an important part of it—an intermediate object, not the ultimate goal of the divine action. If sin, which was already present and disastrously active in mankind, though as yet nowhere clearly visible and defined, were ever to be decisively defeated and sinners forgiven in a way worthy of the goodness and mercy

---

[1] p. 110. Cf. also, for example, Leenhardt, p. 149, n. †: 'Παρεισῆλθεν is somewhat pejorative: the law was not foreseen in the original plan of God; it was the disobedience of Adam which rendered its promulgation necessary'; Gaugler 1, p. 136: 'Das ist eine deutliche Herabsetzung. . . . Es ist ganz allgemein an die untergeordnete Bedeutung des Gesetzes beim Heilsvorgang zu denken'; Michel, p. 143: 'Das Gesetz ist "daneben hineingekommen", ist also keine legitime Antwort auf die Frage nach dem "Leben"' (contrast Jesus' replies to the rich man's question in Mk 10.17ff and to the lawyer's question in Lk 10.25ff); NEB: 'Law intruded into this process'. But the assumption that παρεισῆλθεν was intended to be disparaging is not limited to modern times. It is to be seen, for instance, in Chrysostom, col. 478: Διὰ τί δὲ οὐκ εἶπε, Νόμος ἐδόθη, ἀλλά, Νόμος δὲ παρεισῆλθε; Πρόσκαιρον αὐτοῦ δεικνὺς τὴν χρείαν οὖσαν, καὶ οὐ κυρίαν οὐδὲ προηγουμένην.
[2] 18 (1). 323, 332.   [3] 357.9.
[4] Cf., e.g., παρεισφέρειν in 2 Pet 1.5; παρεισδέχεσθαι in Sophocles, Tr. 537, and Aristotle, P.A., 662ᵃ9 (LSJ gives more than twenty words compounded with παρεισ- under παρεισβαίνω); παρατρέφειν meaning 'to feed beside one', 'to maintain in addition'.
[5] Cf. Cyril, col. 789: τὸ δὲ Παρεισῆλθεν ἀντὶ τοῦ Παρεισβέβληκε μεταξὺ τῆς τε ἐν Ἀδάμ κατακρίσεως καὶ τῆς ἐν Χριστῷ δικαιοσύνης.
[6] To say, as Barrett does (p. 117) that Paul meant 'to indicate that it [i.e. the law] came in beside what was already in position, and consequently enjoyed an inferior status' is bad logic. Is the Queen of England inferior in status to the peers and commons assembled for the opening of Parliament because they are already in position before she arrives and takes her place?
[7] Pace Chrysostom, col. 478 (τὸ δὲ Ἵνα ἐνταῦθα οὐκ αἰτιολογίας πάλιν, ἀλλ' ἐκβάσεώς ἐστιν).

of God and recreated in newness of life, it was first of all necessary that sin should increase somewhere among men in the sense of becoming clearly manifest. So the law was given in order that πλεονάσῃ[1] τὸ παράπτωμα, in order that in one people (for their own sake and also for the sake of all others) sin might be known as sin. But πλεονάσῃ covers more than this; for, when the advent of the law makes sin increase in the sense of becoming manifest as sin, it also makes it increase in the sense of being made more sinful, since the law by showing men that what they are doing is contrary to God's will gives to their continuing to do it the character of conscious and wilful disobedience.[2] It is possible that Paul also had in mind here (see on 7.5) a third sense in which sin would increase as a result of the coming of the law, namely, that it would actually increase in quantity, since the response of man's egotism to the law's attack upon it would be to seek to defend itself by all sorts of feverish activity including even (indeed, above all!) the attempt to exploit in its own interest the very law of God itself. But the purpose ἵνα πλεονάσῃ τὸ παράπτωμα is only rightly understood, when it is recognized as a purpose of God, an intermediate purpose within (and not outside or contrary to) His merciful purpose for the salvation of men, an intermediate object which has to be fulfilled, if the ultimate goal expressed in v. 21 is to be achieved. When this is realized, it is possible to see that the law, even in its apparently negative and disastrous effects, is for Paul, the instrument of the mercy of God; and the theological justification for insisting on a depreciatory interpretation of παρεισῆλθεν disappears.

οὗ δὲ ἐπλεόνασεν ἡ ἁμαρτία: that is, in Israel to which God's gracious will has been clearly revealed in His law and to which His generosity and forbearance have been most signally shown. Nowhere else does the sin of man increase to such fearful proportions, nowhere else is it so exceedingly sinful, as in Israel (and, since the days of the apostles, in the Christian Church). Oppression and torture, for example, are monstrous evils when practised by pagans and atheists, but when practised by Jews or Christians they are infinitely more evil. But Paul no doubt had in mind the climax of sin's πλεονάζειν, when the people of Israel, because of their stubborn refusal to submit to their law and their insistence on trying instead

---

[1] πλεονάσῃ could here be transitive with τὸ παράπτωμα as its object; but, in view of the fact that it must be intransitive in the next clause, it is more probably intransitive.

[2] Cf. Pelagius, p. 48: '. . . dum scienter peccatur, coepit abundare delictum; . . .'

to exploit it for the satisfaction of their own egotism, rejected God's Messiah and handed Him over to the pagans to be crucified, and when the Gentile world in the person of Pilate responded to Israel's challenge by the deliberate prostitution of justice to expediency. It was then and there, above all, that ὑπερεπερίσσευσεν ἡ χάρις in mercy for Israel and also for all other peoples. ὑπερεπερίσσευσεν forms a climax to the series of terms expressive of abundance and superabundance which have been a prominent feature of this section (πολλῷ μᾶλλον and ἐπερίσσευσεν in v. 15, πολλῷ μᾶλλον and περισσείαν in v. 17, πλεονάσῃ and ἐπλεόνασεν in this verse).

21. ἵνα ὥσπερ ἐβασίλευσεν ἡ ἁμαρτία ἐν τῷ θανάτῳ, οὕτως καὶ ἡ χάρις βασιλεύσῃ διὰ δικαιοσύνης εἰς ζωὴν αἰώνιον διὰ Ἰησοῦ Χριστοῦ τοῦ κυρίου ἡμῶν. The triumph of grace described in v. 20b was not itself the end of the matter. Its goal was the dispossession of the usurper sin and the replacement of its reign by the reign of grace. In expressing the divine purpose in the triumphant overflowing of grace, Paul has for the last time in this section made use of a comparison—this time comparing the never-ending reign of the divine grace with the passing reign of sin. Once again it is a comparison of things which in almost every respect are utterly dissimilar. By ἐν τῷ θανάτῳ is probably meant 'with death as its result and accompaniment'. For Paul, with Gen 2.17 not far from his mind, death is the result of sin, willed not by sin but by God. So it is hardly likely that the ἐν is instrumental. *Pace* Chrysostom,[1] death is not sin's soldier or servant or instrument: death is the sign of God's authority, appointed by God as the inseparable, inescapable accompaniment of sin. In v. 14 it was death, not sin, that was said to have reigned. Corresponding to the single phrase ἐν τῷ θανάτῳ in the protasis are three distinct phrases in the apodosis. διὰ δικαιοσύνης indicates that it is through the gift to men of righteousness (i.e. of a status of righteousness before God)[2] that grace reigns; εἰς ζωὴν αἰώνιον indicates the result of its reign; and διὰ Ἰησοῦ Χριστοῦ τοῦ κυρίου ἡμῶν indicates that it is through Christ that the reign of grace is both established and sustained. On the use of this last phrase see further on v. 1. On v. 20f see my *On Romans*, 1998, pp. 15–22.

It remains to draw attention to a highly significant implication of Paul's argument in vv. 12–21.[3] The fact, which these

[1] col. 479.
[2] That this is the sense of δικαιοσύνη here is clear in view of vv. 16, 17, 18 and 19. The subject of the sanctification of believers is introduced as a fresh subject in the following chapter.
[3] Cf. Barth, *Christ and Adam*, to which this paragraph is much indebted.

verses clearly attest, that, in spite of the vast and altogether decisive dissimilarity between Christ and Adam, there is nevertheless a real likeness between them consisting in the correspondence of structure between the Christ-and-all-men relationship and the Adam-and-all-men relationship, a likeness which makes it possible and appropriate to compare them, to refer to Adam as the τύπος of Christ (v. 14) and to argue from the one relational structure to the other with a πολλῷ μᾶλλον (vv. 15 and 17)—this fact must surely mean that human existence as such cannot avoid bearing witness to the truth of Christ and of His saving work. Because the structure of the Adam-and-all-men relationship, that is, of mankind's solidarity in sin, corresponds to the structure of that other relationship, the concrete reality of human existence cannot help being a constant pointer to that other relationship of all men with Christ; and, since not even the deepest degradation can remove a human being from the solidarity of mankind, no man whatsoever can help being, simply by virtue of his being human, a τύπος of Christ, in the sense that—however far this may be from his intention or consciousness—his life must needs be, in spite of its sin and wretchedness, an authentic witness to the truth and grace of Jesus Christ.

V. 2. A LIFE CHARACTERIZED BY SANCTIFICATION (6.1–23)

On the main burden of this section there is widespread agreement, though there is plenty of controversy about some of the details. Paul is here concerned to insist that justification has inescapable moral implications, that our righteous status before God involves an absolute obligation to seek righteousness of life, that to imagine that we can 'receive righteousness in Christ without at the same time laying hold on sanctification'[1] is a profane absurdity. The word ἁγιασμός may be taken as the key-word of the section, though it does not occur till v. 19 (cf. v. 22).

The importance of this section for the understanding of the theological basis of the Christian's moral obligation is apparent. But it must not be forgotten that as a general account of that basis it is incomplete, since, containing no explicit reference to the work of the Spirit (Paul's plan being to treat of the gift

---

[1] Calvin, p. 8. Cf. p. 121 ('Throughout this chapter the apostle maintains that those who imagine that Christ bestows free justification upon us without imparting newness of life shamefully rend Christ asunder').

of the Spirit in a later section), it lacks an essential element of such an account. While Romans 6 makes the point that the life promised for the man who is righteous by faith is a life characterized by sanctification, it is not in this chapter by itself but in the whole of 6.1–8.39 that the meaning of the believer's sanctification is set forth.

(i) Dead to sin, alive to God
(6.1–14)

[1]What then are we to say? Are we to continue in sin, in order that grace may increase? [2]God forbid! Seeing that we have died to sin, how shall we still live in it? [3]Or are you ignorant of the fact that all of us who have been baptized into Christ Jesus have been baptized into his death? [4]So then we have been buried together with him through baptism into *his* death, in order that, as Christ was raised from the dead through the glory of the Father, so we also might walk in newness of life. [5]For if we have been conformed to his death, we are certainly also to be to his resurrection. [6]And we know that our old self was crucified with *him*, that the body of sin might be destroyed, so that we might cease to be slaves of sin. [7]For the man who has died has been justified from sin. [8]But if we have died with Christ, we believe we are also to live with him: [9]and we know that Christ, now that he has been raised from the dead, dies no more, *and* death exercises lordship over him no more. [10]For the death which he died he died to sin once and for all; but the life which he lives he lives to God. [11]So then recognize *the truth* that you yourselves are dead to sin but alive to God in Christ Jesus. [12]Stop, then, allowing sin to reign *unopposed* in your mortal selves in such a way that you obey the self's desires, [13]and stop placing your members at the disposal of sin as tools of unrighteousness; instead, place yourselves at the disposal of God as being alive from the dead and your members at God's disposal as tools of righteousness. [14]For sin shall no longer be lord over you; for you are not under the law, but under grace.

In v. 1 Paul refers to a false inference which he knows some people will be inclined to draw from what he has said in 5.20b, namely, that we should go on sinning so that grace may be multiplied all the more, and rejects it emphatically. Verses 2–11, the purpose of which is to justify his repudiation of this false inference, are all concerned with the Christian's death and resurrection with Christ; and the key to their right understanding is the recognition that there are different senses in which our death and resurrection with Christ may properly be spoken of, and that these require to be carefully distinguished. In more than one sense the Christian has already died and been raised with Christ; but in another sense his dying and being raised with Christ is a matter of present obligation, something which ought now to be in process of being fulfilled, and in yet another sense it lies ahead of him as eschatological promise.

Paul's thought in these verses moves between these different senses of death and resurrection with Christ. Verses 12–13 indicate that the conclusion which the Roman Christians are to draw from the preceding argument and, in particular, from that fact which they have been bidden in v. 11 to recognize and take seriously, is that they are under obligation to stop allowing sin to reign unopposed over their lives and to revolt in the name of their rightful ruler, God, against sin's usurping rule. The first part of v. 14 supports the imperatives of the two preceding verses by promising that sin will no longer have absolute lordship over the Roman Christians so as to have them helpless in its power; and the latter part of the verse adds in support of the promise an assurance that they are not under the law, that is (as we understand it), not under God's condemnation pronounced by the law, but under God's gracious favour. On this section see my *On Romans*, 1998, pp. 23–31.

1. For **Tί ... ἐροῦμεν**; see on 3.5. Here (as in 3.5; 7.7; 9.14) it introduces an indication of a false inference which Paul recognizes could be drawn from what he has said and which he desires to repudiate before stating his own understanding of the matter.[1]

ἐπιμένωμεν[2] **τῇ ἁμαρτίᾳ, ἵνα ἡ χάρις πλεονάσῃ**; looks back to 5.20b (*οὗ δὲ ἐπλεόνασεν ἡ ἁμαρτία, ὑπερεπερίσσευσεν ἡ χάρις*), which the bogus logic of the man who has not yet submitted to the discipline of the gospel could very easily twist into an invitation to continue in sin.[3] Compare 3.7–8. (Unlike the questions introduced by *τί ... ἐροῦμεν*; in 3.5 and 9.14, which are stamped from the start as expressing false inferences by their *μή* form, the actual form of the question here, as in 7.7, is neutral, though an emphatic repudiation follows immediately.) Gaugler rightly warns against regarding this question with complacent detachment.[4] For of how much

---

[1] That Paul's concern here is to counter the danger of antinomianism in the church, to bring home to any of its members who might be unaware of it, or inclined to forget it, the inseparability of justification and sanctification, rather than to rebut an objection to his teaching from the side of Christian or Jewish legalists (to the effect that it was likely to encourage licence), is surely clear (*pace*, e.g., Sanday and Headlam, pp. 153, 155; Michel, p. 152f) from the contents of the rest of this chapter.

[2] For the use of *ἐπιμένειν* cf. 11.22, 23; Phil 1.24; Col 1.23; 1 Tim 4.16. Neither of the variant readings *ἐπιμενοῦμεν* (181 *al* lat sy) and *ἐπιμένομεν* (ℵ and Byzantine text) seems likely to be original.

[3] Cf. Chrysostom, col. 479: . . . *ἐδόκει παρὰ τοῖς ἀνοήτοις προτροπὴ τὸ λεγόμενον εἰς ἁμαρτίαν εἶναι*.

[4] 1, p. 147f.

ostensibly Christian living is the thought behind this question the real if unacknowledged presupposition!

2. μὴ γένοιτο. See on 3.4.

οἵτινες ἀπεθάνομεν τῇ ἁμαρτίᾳ, πῶς ἔτι ζήσομεν[1] ἐν αὐτῇ; The relative clause is placed at the beginning of the sentence in order to give the more emphasis to 'the consideration which contains within itself the answer to the false inference'.[2] Though usually in the NT no distinction seems to be made between ὅστις and the simple relative pronoun, it is possible that here and in a few other places a distinction was intended since it would be particularly appropriate:[3] if so, the shade of meaning intended here would be brought out by using 'seeing that' (cf. the Latin 'quippe qui') to translate it. That the statement ἀπεθάνομεν τῇ ἁμαρτίᾳ is of fundamental importance in this section is abundantly clear and generally agreed; but there is far from being agreement about what exactly Paul meant by it. A striking testimony to its difficulty is to be seen in the introductory summary of this sub-section in the commentary of Sanday and Headlam, in which they say: 'The baptized Christian cannot sin. Sin is a direct contradiction of the state of things which baptism assumes. . . . As Christ by His death on the Cross ceased from all contact with sin, so the Christian, united with Christ in his baptism, has done once for all with sin, and lives henceforth a reformed life dedicated to God. [This at least is the ideal, whatever may be the reality.]'[4] The curious sentence enclosed in square brackets betrays their sense of embarrassment and seems to imply that they cannot see in the statement any meaning which really requires to be taken at all seriously. It is hard to understand how they can go on three pages later to speak of Paul's 'profound and original argument' in vv. 4ff.[5] But simply to omit the contents of the square brackets of the above quotation while sticking to a dogged reiteration of its categorical assertions—as some other interpreters seem inclined to do—is scarcely to do more justice to Paul's thought; for the issue of such a procedure is likely to be either the conclusion that, according to Paul, there are no real Christians at all, or else a quite arbitrary and illegitimate restriction of the meaning of 'sin'. Such an

---

[1] The variant ζήσωμεν (𝔓⁴⁶ C G L *pm*) is clearly inferior (due perhaps to an unthinking assimilation to ἐπιμένωμεν). ζήσομεν not only has stronger attestation but is also intrinsically more probable.

[2] Murray I, p. 213.

[3] Cf. Moule, *Idiom-Book*, pp. 123–25; see also Bauer, s.v. ὅστις and BDF, § 293.

[4] p. 153.

[5] p. 156.

interpretation falls foul of the sober recognition of the continuing sinfulness of Christians to be found (according to what we are convinced is the more probable exegesis) in chapter 7. While it is reasonable to infer from πῶς ἔτι ζήσομεν ἐν αὐτῇ; that the death to sin which Christians are here said to have died is, according to Paul, an event which has rendered their continuing in sin something essentially absurd, both 7.14–25 and also the imperatives in this present chapter alike forbid us to conclude that he thought that it had actually made it impossible for genuine believers to continue to sin seriously. We shall not do justice to Paul's meaning here or to his thought in this chapter as a whole, unless we recognize that in his understanding of the situation there are four quite different senses in which Christians die to sin and, corresponding to them, four different senses in which they are raised up, and that these different senses need to be carefully distinguished but at the same time understood in the closest relation to one another. They may be listed as follows:

(i) They died to sin *in God's sight*, when Christ died on the cross for them. This is a matter of God's decision. His decision to take their sins upon Himself in the person of His dear Son may be said to be tantamount to a decision to see them as having died in Christ's death. (Cf. perhaps 2 Cor 5.14: . . . κρίναντας τοῦτο, ὅτι εἷς ὑπὲρ πάντων ἀπέθανεν· ἄρα οἱ πάντες ἀπέθανον). Similarly they may be said to have been raised up in His resurrection on the third day, since His resurrection was, according to God's merciful will, for them. Compare Col 3.1ff, where Christians are exhorted to seek the things above where Christ is living His exalted life, because they have died and their life, that is, their real life, the life which God mercifully regards as their life, is hidden with Christ in God, is in fact the sinless life which Christ (who according to Col 3.4 is their life) lives for them. We may call this first sense the *juridical sense*.

(ii) They died to sin, and were raised up, in their baptism, which was at the same time both their ratification of their own acceptance of God's decision on their behalf (to regard Christ's death for their sins as their death and His risen life as their life) and also God's bestowal of His seal and pledge of the fact that His decision really concerned them individually, personally. We may call this the *baptismal sense*.[1]

---

[1] Looking at an ecclesiastical situation in which the administration of baptism is commonly quite separated from the believer's own ratification of his decision of faith, we may well be inclined to break the unity of sense (ii) into two distinct senses, one sacramental and the other relative to conversion; but, as far as the exegesis of Romans is concerned, this inclination must surely be resisted.

(iii) They are called, and have been given the freedom, to die daily and hourly to sin by the mortification of their sinful natures, and to rise daily and hourly to newness of life in obedience to God. This we may call the *moral sense*. And in this connexion we may borrow the words of Pindar, *Pyth.* 2.72, γένοι' οἷος ἐσσὶ μαθών, though using them with a different sense from the anthropocentric sense in which Pindar himself wrote them. The man who has learned through the gospel message the truth of God's gracious decision on his behalf is now to strive with all his heart to approximate more and more in his actual concrete daily living to that which in God's decision of justification he already is.

(iv) They will die to sin finally and irreversibly when they actually die, and will—equally finally and irreversibly—at Christ's coming be raised up to the resurrection life. This is the *eschatological sense*.

In the course of the following verses Paul moves freely from one to another of these different senses, these different dyings and risings with Christ, implying all the time both their distinctness and their real and essential relatedness. The question whether ἀπεθάνομεν in this verse was intended in sense (i) or sense (ii) is not of vital importance. That Paul was already thinking particularly of baptism is possible, and some have argued that his use of the aorist points to this reference; but an aorist would be equally appropriate, if the reference were to the divine decision, and, on the whole, it seems rather more probable that the sense intended was sense (i).

3. ἢ ἀγνοεῖτε (compare 7.1; also 6.16; 11.2; 1 Cor 3.16; 5.6; 6.2, 3, 9, 15, 16, 19; 9.13, 24; Jas 4.4; also Jn 19.10) implies that the author thinks that the Christians in Rome are likely to know at least the truth stated in the rest of this verse— perhaps also some of the doctrine which he sets out in the following verses as following from it. The use of this formula here has special significance, since the Roman church was not founded by Paul and has not as yet even been visited by him. The inference that the belief that baptism into Christ involved baptism into His death must therefore have belonged to the common primitive Christian teaching (as opposed to being a Pauline contribution), while not absolutely certain, is highly probable.[1]

---

[1] If the belief that 'Christ died for our sins according to the scriptures' was as central to the faith of the primitive Church as 1 Cor 15.3 implies that it was, then it certainly is not at all surprising that a connexion should have been made at a very early date between the believer's baptism and Christ's death.

ὅσοι ἐβαπτίσθημεν εἰς Χριστὸν Ἰησοῦν.[1] It is unlikely that the choice of εἰς Χριστὸν (Ἰησοῦν) rather than εἰς τὸ ὄνομα Χριστοῦ Ἰησοῦ (cf. Mt 28.19; Acts 8.16; 19.5) or ἐν τῷ ὀνόματι Χριστοῦ Ἰησοῦ (cf. Acts 10.48) or ἐπὶ τῷ ὀνόματι Χριστοῦ Ἰησοῦ (cf. Acts 2.38, though there is a variant ἐν) is particularly significant either here or in Gal 3.27; for in both places the context requires a purely factual statement and this is immediately followed by a further statement which goes beyond it and offers an interpretation of the objective fact. We take it then that βαπτί-ζεσθαι εἰς Χριστὸν Ἰησοῦν here is synonymous with βαπτίζεσθαι εἰς τὸ ὄνομα Χριστοῦ Ἰησοῦ (Paul's familiarity with this formula is indicated by 1 Cor 1.13, 15) and also βαπτίζεσθαι ἐν (or ἐπὶ) τῷ ὀνόματι Χριστοῦ Ἰησοῦ,[2] and that all that Paul wishes to convey in this clause is the simple fact that the persons concerned have received Christian baptism.[3] But at the same time the expression which he uses implies (as do also the expressions involving the use of the word ὄνομα)[4]—what was no doubt generally acknowledged throughout the primitive Church—that baptism has to do with a decisive personal relationship between the individual believer and Christ.

εἰς τὸν θάνατον αὐτοῦ ἐβαπτίσθημεν makes the point—which Paul apparently expects the Christians in Rome to accept without demur as a truth already well known to them—that the relationship to Christ with which baptism has to do includes, in particular, a relationship to His death.

At this point the question arises: How did Paul understand the relation between baptism and this relationship of the Christian to Christ and, in particular, to His death? The suggestion has been made—and it has been fairly widely accepted—that Paul was deeply influenced in his understanding of baptism (and indeed of the Christian's relationship to Christ as a whole) by the pagan mystery cults.[5] It was characteristic of these cults that of central importance was a god who died and rose again, and that the initiation rites were supposed to accomplish the union of the postulant with

---

[1] Ἰησοῦν is omitted by B al Marcion.

[2] On these formulae see A. Oepke, in *TWNT* 1, p. 537; H. Bietenhard, in *TWNT* 5, p. 274f.

[3] To claim, as Gaugler does (1, p. 156), that the sense of the first of the two clauses is to be inferred from the content of the second, is surely not justified.

[4] It need hardly be said that the use of 'in (or 'into') the name of Christ Jesus' was not intended merely to draw attention to the formal use of the name in the rite.

[5] Cf., e.g., Bousset, *Kyrios Christos*; Reitzenstein, *Mysterienreligionen*; G. Bornkamm, 'Baptism and New Life in Paul: Romans 6', in *Early Christian Experience*, p. 85, n. 5.

the god. But, in spite of certain obvious resemblances, there are such significant differences between baptism as understood by Paul and the essential characteristics of these cults, as to make it extremely unlikely that Paul ever conceived baptism as a mystery of this sort. While the mysteries were concerned with the union of the participant with a nature-deity, baptism had to do with the relationship of the believer to the historical event of God's saving deed in Christ; while the dying and rising of a nature-deity were conceived as something recurring again and again, the historical event to which baptism pointed was a once for all, unique event; while the mysteries were inclusive (one could be initiated into several without offence, since they were recognized as varying forms of the same fundamental, age-old religion), baptism was altogether exclusive; while the mystery rites were magical, setting forth symbolically the god's experiences and being thought of as effecting the union with the god which they depicted, in the case of baptism the symbolism, if it was conscious at all (and as far as Paul is concerned it is far from certain that it was), was clearly not of decisive importance, since, while Rom 6.4 and Col 2.12 might suggest the thought that the Christian's immersion in the water of baptism portrays his burial with Christ (and his emergence from it his resurrection with Christ), Paul could also write 1 Cor 12.13 (. . . πάντες ἐν πνεῦμα ἐποτίσθημεν) and Gal 3.27 (. . . Χριστὸν ἐνεδύσασθε) with reference to baptism, and an *ex opere operato* view of baptism is ruled out by such a passage as 1 Cor 10.1–12; while the mysteries reflected Hellenistic dualism (the initiate being thought of as transported out of the temporal and material world into an eternal and spiritual), baptism had to do with eschatology, with the relation of the believer to the events of the salvation-history and his membership of the Church of God; and, while in the mystery cults the initiate could be regarded as having become divine (in some of them after initiation he was actually worshipped), any idea of a divinization of the believer is completely alien to Paul's thought.[1] Another view

---

[1] Cf., e.g., Gaugler I, pp. 156–61; Davies, *PRJ*, pp. 88–93; also H. A. A. Kennedy, *St Paul and the Mystery Religions*, London, 1913; W. F. Flemington, *The New Testament Doctrine of Baptism*, London, 1948, pp. 76–81. The suggestion of E. R. Goodenough, *By Light, Light: the Mystic Gospel of Hellenistic Judaism*, Newhaven, 1935, that the mysteries had already gained a firm foothold in Judaism, so that Paul could have been indebted to the pagan mysteries not directly but at second hand through the mediation of Hellenistic Judaism, is hardly more convincing (cf. the criticism of it in Davies, *PRJ*, pp. 93–98).

is that of A. Schweitzer.[1] In most respects altogether different
from the suggestion we have just been considering, it nevertheless agrees with it in attributing to Paul a magical understanding of baptism as effecting *ex opere operato* what it
signifies (in Paul's view, according to Schweitzer, 'in the
moment when' a man 'receives baptism, the dying and rising
again of Christ takes place in him without any co-operation, or
exercise of will or thought, on his part'[2]), which we have
seen to be incompatible with such a passage as 1 Cor 10.1–12.

What then did Paul mean by his claim that Christian
baptism is essentially baptism into Christ's death? Not that it
actually relates the person concerned to Christ's death, since
this relationship is already an objective reality before baptism
takes place, having been brought into being by God's gracious
decision, which is implied by the ὑπὲρ ἡμῶν in 5.8;[3] but that it
points to, and is a pledge of, that death which the person
concerned has already died—in God's sight. On God's side, it
is the sign and pledge that the benefits of Christ's death for all
men really do apply to this individual in particular, while, on
man's side, it is the outward ratification (we are thinking of
course of adult baptism here) of the human decision of faith, of
the response already begun to what God has done in Christ.
That Paul thought of it (in its aspect of divine pledge) as an
automatic, mechanical, magical guarantee is impossible in view
of 1 Cor 10. But it does not therefore follow that he thought of
it as a 'mere sign', a *signum nudum*. It seems likely that he
thought of Christ Himself as present and active personally in
freedom and in power in the visible word of baptism as well as
in the spoken word of the preached message (cf., e.g., 10.14:
πῶς δὲ πιστεύσωσιν οὗ οὐκ ἤκουσαν; πῶς δὲ ἀκούσωσιν χωρὶς
κηρύσσοντος;).[4]

---

[1] *Paul and his Interpreters*, London, 1912; *The Mysticism of Paul the
Apostle*, London, 1931.

[2] *Paul and his Interpreters*, p. 225f.

[3] The theory that Paul's understanding of baptism derives from the pagan
mysteries fails altogether to do justice to the implication of the Χριστὸς ὑπὲρ
ἡμῶν ἀπέθανεν that at the level of the divine decision our death with Christ
was contemporaneous with Christ's death (cf. 2 Cor 5.14: . . . ὅτι εἷς ὑπὲρ
πάντων ἀπέθανεν · ἄρα οἱ πάντες ἀπέθανον).

[4] The following works, which ought to be mentioned in addition to
those already cited in the commentary on this and the previous verse,
may conveniently be listed here: G. R. Beasley-Murray, *Baptism in the
New Testament*, London, 1962; G. Wagner, *Das religionsgeschichtliche
Problem von Römer 6.1–11*, Zurich, 1962 (Eng. tr. under the title,
Pauline Baptism and the Pagan Mysteries, Edinburgh, 1967); R. C.
Tannehill, *Dying and Rising with Christ: a study in Pauline Theology*,
Berlin, 1967; Barth, *CD* IV/4; E. Schweizer, 'Dying and Rising with

4. By συνετάφημεν οὖν αὐτῷ διὰ τοῦ βαπτίσματος εἰς τὸν θάνατον Paul draws out and clarifies the meaning of the last clause of v. 3. Through the baptism into Christ's death to which it referred (εἰς τὸν θάνατον is better taken with βαπτίσματος than with συνετάφημεν,[1] since τοῦ βαπτίσματος εἰς τὸν θάνατον corresponds closely to εἰς τὸν θάνατον αὐτοῦ ἐβαπτίσθημεν in v. 3, and to speak of burial into death would be strange) we have been buried with Christ. By stating that we have been buried with Christ (cf. Col 2.12) Paul expresses in the most decisive and emphatic way the truth of our having died with Christ; for burial is the seal set to the fact of death—it is when a man's relatives and friends leave his body in a grave and return home without him that the fact that he no longer shares their life is exposed with inescapable conclusiveness.[2] So the death which we died in baptism was a death ratified and sealed by burial, an altogether unambiguous death. Baptism, according to Paul, while (as we have seen) it is no magical rite effecting *ex opere operato* that which it signifies, is no empty sign but a decisive event by which a man's life is powerfully and unequivocally claimed by God.

ἵνα introduces a statement of the purpose (the reference being of course to God's purpose) of our burial with Christ in baptism.

ὥσπερ ἠγέρθη Χριστὸς ἐκ νεκρῶν διὰ τῆς δόξης τοῦ πατρός serves to characterize the action denoted by the last five words of the verse (which indicate the substance of the purpose) as in some way analogous to Christ's being raised from the dead. By δόξα[3] here is meant no doubt the power of God gloriously exercised. God's use of His power is always glorious, and His use of it to raise the dead is a specially clear manifestation of His glory. Commentators appropriately compare Jn 11.40 (in the light of v. 23). But glory and power are very often closely associated in the Bible (e.g. Exod 15.6; 1 Chr 16.28; Ps 145.11; Mt 6.13 (TR); Col 1.11; 1 Pet 4.11; Rev 1.6; 4.11; 5.12f; 7.12; 19.1), and the thought of power is often present in the word 'glory' (so much was this felt to be so, that in the LXX δόξα was sometimes

---

Christ', in *NTS* 14 (1967–68), pp. 1–14; J. D. G. Dunn, *Baptism in the Holy Spirit*, London, 1970. Special mention should also be made of Kuss, pp. 307–81, and of A. J. M. Wedderburn, *Baptism and Resurrection*, Tübingen, 1987.

[1] So numerous commentators, among them Sanday and Headlam, p. 157 (though with considerable hesitation): the opposite view is maintained by, e.g., Lagrange, p. 145; Gaugler 1, p. 161f. On the non-repetition of the article after βαπτίσματος see BDF, § 272.

[2] Cf. K. Barth, *Dogmatics in Outline*, London, 1949, p. 117f.

[3] See on 1.23; 3.23; 5.2. The whole phrase διὰ τῆς δόξης τοῦ πατρός sounds like an echo of a solemn confessional or doxological formula.

used to represent Hebrew words denoting power specifically).[1]

ἡμεῖς ἐν καινότητι ζωῆς περιπατήσωμεν. The reference is to the moral life. The use of περιπατεῖν to denote a man's conduct occurs frequently in the Pauline epistles (e.g. 8.4; 13.13; 14.15; 1 Cor 3.3) but also elsewhere in the NT (e.g. Mk 7.5): it reflects a common use of hālak in the OT (e.g. Exod 16.4; Deut 8.6; Ps 101.6; Prov 6.12; Dan 9.10) and in Judaism. The use of the aorist περιπατήσωμεν perhaps indicates that the thought is of the beginning of the new way of life which contrasts with the old (cf. παραστήσατε in v. 13 and περιπατήσωμεν in 13.13).[2] The quality of this way of life is indicated by the phrase ἐν καινότητι ζωῆς. Though the distinction between καινός and νέος[3] was not by any means always maintained,[4] there is no doubt that the proper significance of καινός attaches to καινότης here, and that the thought of the transcendent worth of the new way of life, as compared with the old, is present. This newness of life is the moral aspect of that life which is really life which is promised in the scriptural quotation in 1.17 (cf. 6.11, 13; 12.1). In the NT the word καινός is particularly associated with the eschatological hope (cf., e.g., Mk 14.25; 2 Pet 3.13; Rev 2.17; 3.12; 5.9; 21.1, 5), and καινότητι ζωῆς here and τῇ ἀνακαινώσει τοῦ νοός in 12.2, as also καινὴ κτίσις in 2 Cor 5.17 and Gal 6.15, and the statement τὰ ἀρχαῖα παρῆλθεν, ἰδοὺ γέγονεν καινά in 2 Cor 5.17, have to be understood in the light of NT eschatology. The newness of life, of which Paul speaks here, is a foretaste of the final renewal.

In this verse there is a movement from (death and) burial in baptism (i.e. in sense (ii) as listed above—see on v. 2) to resurrection in the moral sense (i.e. sense (iii) in our list), the former being said to have taken place in order that the latter may take place. It is to be noted that Paul does not speak here

---

[1] Cf. G. Kittel, in *TWNT* 2, p. 247.

[2] See further BDF, § 337 (1), but see also the rest of § 337.

[3] It is brought out with admirable clarity by J. Behm, in *TWNT* 3, p. 450, lines 7–14 (Eng. tr.: p. 447: 'Of the two most common words for "new" since the classical period, namely, νέος and καινός, the former signifies "what was not there before," "what has only just arisen or appeared," the latter "what is new and distinctive" as compared with other things. νέος is new in time or origin, i.e., young, with a suggestion of immaturity or of lack of respect for the old. καινός is what is new in nature, different from the usual, impressive, better than the old, superior in value or attraction . . .').

[4] For example, compare Eph 4.23 with Rom 12.2. In the case of Col 3.10 a distinction between νέος and ἀνακαινούμενος could conceivably be maintained—νέος used of the new man thought of as one who was not there a short time before, ἀνακαινούμενος of the continual renewal by the Spirit.

of both death and resurrection in baptism and of both death and resurrection in the moral sense, but of death (burial) alone in the former case and of resurrection alone in the latter. Paul here (and also in v. 5) sets forth the twofold fact of our dying and being raised in baptism by means of the single term death (burial) and the twofold fact of our ethical dying to sin and being raised to newness of life by means of the single term resurrection, because—we suggest—at this point he particularly wants to bring out the positive content of the new obedience.[1]

5. εἰ γὰρ σύμφυτοι γεγόναμεν τῷ ὁμοιώματι τοῦ θανάτου αὐτοῦ, ἀλλὰ καὶ τῆς ἀναστάσεως ἐσόμεθα. The γάρ indicates that the sentence is intended as a confirmation of the preceding one. As far as its structure is concerned, it is clear that σύμφυτοι τῷ ὁμοιώματι and αὐτοῦ have to be supplied in the apodosis from the protasis. The ἀλλά in the apodosis has the force of 'certainly' (see BDF, § 488(5)). But the exegesis of the verse turns on several questions which have been variously, and perhaps cannot now be definitively, answered. They are:

(i) In what sense is σύμφυτος used here?

(ii) Is the dative τῷ ὁμοιώματι directly dependent on σύμφυτοι, or is αὐτῷ to be supplied and τῷ ὁμοιώματι taken as either instrumental or a dative of respect?

(iii) What is meant by τὸ ὁμοίωμα τοῦ θανάτου αὐτοῦ?

(iv) How is the future indicative ἐσόμεθα to be understood?

With regard to (i), σύμφυτος (not from συμφυτεύω, 'plant along with', 'plant together', but from συμφύω, 'make to grow

---

[1] We might apply to what Paul does here the term 'appropriation' which was used in the older dogmatics with reference to the Persons of the Trinity (see Barth, *CD* I/1, p. 428f (= *KD* I/1, p. 393f)); for he is appropriating to baptism the language of death/burial which belongs just as much to the description of the Christian's obedience, and to the Christian's obedience the language of resurrection which belongs equally to the interpretation of baptism, much as he himself in 2 Cor 13.13 appropriates χάρις to Christ, ἀγάπη to God, and κοινωνία to the Holy Spirit, though each of these terms could quite properly be connected with any of the three Persons. The fact that Paul does elsewhere use a past tense with reference to the resurrection of Christians (Col 2.12; 3.1: cf. Eph 2.5f) and also speaks of their dying as something still to be accomplished (so 8.13; Phil 3.10; Col 3.5), while it supports our explanation, according to which Paul thought of Christians as both dying and being raised in each of the senses which we listed in the notes on v. 2, but tended to appropriate the language of dying to senses (i) and (ii) and that of resurrection to senses (iii) and (iv), tells strongly against the commonly given explanation of the use of future tenses in this chapter in respect of the resurrection of Christians, that Paul, while he can say that they have already died, cannot affirm that they have already been raised up (see, for example, Leenhardt, p. 156f: cf. Schweizer, in *NTS* 14, pp. 6–8).

together', 'unite', and, in the passive, 'grow together', 'unite', 'become assimilated', 'become natural') is attested as early as Pindar (*Isthm.* 3.14) and Aeschylus (*Ag.* 107 and 152). It bears such meanings as 'born with one', 'congenital', 'innate', 'natural', 'cognate', 'grown together', 'united'.[1] If it is understood here in the sense 'grown together' and the thought of growth is pressed, and if αὐτῷ (see under (ii)) is supplied, the support of this verse may then be claimed for the idea of an organic union with Christ. Thus it has often been assumed (e.g. by Calvin, p. 123f, and Sanday and Headlam, especially p. 154, but also p. 157) that Paul had in mind the imagery of grafting. But, while σύμφυτος would of course be an appropriate word to describe a graft in relation to the tree into which it is grafted, the quite numerous occurrences of the word do not provide the evidence of its having had special associations with grafting which would justify this assumption. It seems appropriate to ask whether there has not been a tendency among exegetes and theologians generally to read more into this verse than the language used in it really warrants. It seems quite likely that some such translation as 'united' or 'assimilated' would better represent Paul's meaning than 'grown together'.

With regard to (ii), the presence of συνετάφημεν . . . αὐτῷ in v. 4, of ἀπεθάνομεν σὺν Χριστῷ and συζήσομεν αὐτῷ in v. 8, and of συνεσταυρώθη (with which Χριστῷ must be supplied) in v. 6 provide considerable support for the view that αὐτῷ is to be supplied here, and τῷ ὁμοιώματι understood as instrumental or as a dative of respect. But the presence of τῷ ὁμοιώματι in close proximity to the συν-compound weighs heavily on the other side, and should probably be regarded as decisive.

With regard to (iii), some maintain that by τὸ ὁμοίωμα τοῦ θανάτου αὐτοῦ Paul simply means baptism, others[2] that he means the death of Christ as sacramentally present in baptism (distinguished by the use of ὁμοίωμα from the death as actually taking place on Golgotha). But both these interpretations are beset with serious difficulty when the second clause comes into consideration; for the context seems to require in the main sentence a movement away from the subject of baptism rather than another statement about it. The meaning, 'For if we have become united to Christ's death as sacramentally present in baptism, it follows that we must also be (taking the future ἐσόμεθα as logical—see (iv) below) united to His resurrection as

[1] Cf. LSJ, s.v.; and also W. Grundmann in *TWNT* 7, pp. 786, 790f.

[2] Cf. J. Schneider, in *TWNT* 5, p. 194f.

sacramentally present in baptism' (i.e. one cannot be joined by baptism to Christ's death without also being joined to His resurrection), is perhaps just conceivable; but it is extremely clumsy, and not really apposite to the context. The explanation which Denney gives ('if we have become vitally one with the likeness of his death; i.e., if the baptism, which is a similitude of Christ's death, has had a reality answering to its obvious import, so that we have really died in it as Christ died, then we shall have a corresponding experience of resurrection')[1] surely puts too much weight on σύμφυτοι. It seems preferable to take ὁμοίωμα to mean here 'form' cf. Rev 9.7; LXX Deut 4.12 and Josh 22.28[2]) or—though this is less satisfactory—'likeness' in the sense of the quality of being like (cf. 5.14).

With regard to (iv), the choice is between three possibilities: taking ἐσόμεθα as a purely logical future or understanding it as referring to the moral life or taking it to refer to the eschatological fulfilment. In view of v. 4 (ἐν καινότητι ζωῆς περιπατήσωμεν) and v. 6 (τοῦ μηκέτι δουλεύειν ἡμᾶς τῇ ἁμαρτίᾳ), we must surely, choose the second of these.

We conclude that the key to the understanding of this verse is the recognition that, as Paul uses it here, the expression σύμφυτος γίνεσθαι τῷ ὁμοιώματι followed by a genitive means simply 'to be assimilated to the form of', 'to be conformed to', and is thus equivalent to συμμορφίζεσθαι as used in Phil 3.10[3] (cf. the use of σύμμορφος in Rom 8.29 and Phil 3.21). The verse as a whole may then be given an interpretation which perfectly suits the context (see on vv. 4 and 6): 'For if (in baptism) we have become conformed to His death, we are certainly also to be conformed (in our moral life) to His resurrection'. On ἐσόμεθα see my *On Romans*, 1998, p. 28, n. 7.

6. τοῦτο[4] γινώσκοντες, ὅτι. More probable than the view that Paul is appealing to the experimental knowledge of believers as confirmation of what he has just said is the suggestion that this is Paul's way of introducing another fact relevant to his argument (cf. εἰδότες ὅτι in v. 9).[5]

ὁ παλαιὸς ἡμῶν ἄνθρωπος denotes the whole of our fallen

---

[1] p. 633.

[2] In Josh 22.28 the RV renders the Hebrew *tabnît* by 'pattern'.

[3] I assume that συμμορφιζόμενος in Phil 3.10 is passive, and not middle. Paul is there using συμμορφίζεσθαι τῷ θανάτῳ αὐτοῦ with reference not to baptism but to the present life of the Christian.

[4] The insertion of καί before τοῦτο in B may perhaps be due to a mistaken assumption that Paul must have intended to use the καὶ τοῦτο idiom (see on 13.11, where we have καὶ τοῦτο followed by a participle of similar meaning to γινώσκοντες here).

[5] Cf. Murray 1, p. 219.

human nature, the whole self in its fallenness.[1] It is the whole man, not merely a part of him, that comes under God's condemnation, and that died in God's sight in Christ's death. For the expression compare Eph 4.22–24; Col 3.9–11, and see the note on 7.22 (κατὰ τὸν ἔσω ἄνθρωπον).

συνεσταυρώθη: sc. Χριστῷ (cf. Gal 2.19 [RV: 20]). The reference to crucifixion is a stark reminder—the harsh word 'cross' had not yet been rendered mellow by centuries of Christian piety! —of the vast distance separating what Paul is saying about dying and being raised with Christ from the mysticism of the contemporary mystery-cults.

Our fallen human nature was crucified with Christ in our baptism in the sense that in baptism we received the divinely-appointed sign and seal of the fact that by God's gracious decision it was, in His sight, crucified with Christ on Golgotha.[2] It is not implied that the old man no longer exists. *Pace* Murray I, p. 219f, the old fallen nature lingers on in the believer. That is why in Col 3.9 *believers* have to be exhorted to put off the old man.[3] The Christian has still to fulfil on the moral level, by daily dying to sin, the death which in God's merciful decision and in the sacrament of baptism he has already died.

ἵνα καταργηθῇ τὸ σῶμα τῆς ἁμαρτίας. Two interrelated questions need to be answered. The more easily dealt with is that of the meaning of τὸ σῶμα τῆς ἁμαρτίας. The word σῶμα here has often been understood figuratively, the phrase being taken to mean either the totality of sin viewed as a body having many members, an organism, or else simply the mass of sin. But this line of interpretation is surely to be rejected as over-subtle. Others have taken the phrase to mean the body, i.e., the material, physical body, as controlled by sin. But this is too narrow an interpretation in view of other passages where σῶμα is used and of Paul's understanding of man generally. The phrase denotes rather the whole man as controlled by sin (cf. the notes on, e.g., τοῦ σώματος τοῦ θανάτου τούτου in 7.24; also on 8.10). τὸ σῶμα τῆς ἁμαρτίας and ὁ παλαιὸς ἡμῶν ἄνθρωπος are thus identical, the only difference being that the use of σῶμα places more stress on the aspect of the sinful man as an individual, the self as an organized whole.

---

[1] As Calvin rightly emphasizes (p. 125). Such a paraphrase as Theodoret's ἡ προτέρα πολιτεία (*PG* 82, col. 617 (on Col 3.9)) misrepresents Paul's meaning.

[2] The use of the word 'ideal' in this connexion ('the one decisive ideal act which he [i.e. Paul] regards as taking place in baptism') in Sanday and Headlam, p. 158, introduces confusion.

[3] So Barrett, p. 125, rightly (*contra* RV 'seeing that ye have . . . ').

The other question concerns the clause as a whole. Does this first of the two final clauses which follow συνεσταυρώθη refer to what happened in baptism or (as the second final clause clearly does) to the moral life of Christians? At first sight it is tempting to take it in the latter way—and so as parallel to ἵνα . . . ἡμεῖς ἐν καινότητι ζωῆς περιπατήσωμεν in v. 4 and ἀλλὰ καὶ τῆς ἀναστάσεως ἐσόμεθα (according to our interpretation) in v. 5. But the fact that the old man, the self as controlled by sin, is still very much alive in the Christian is a difficulty in the way of this interpretation. And, even if this could be got over either by taking καταργεῖν in the weaker sense of 'put out of action', 'disable' (with Augustine and Tertullian before him) or by explaining the aorist tense along the lines of the περιπατήσωμεν of v. 4 (in the case of καταργηθῇ this is less satisfactory), there still is the further difficulty that the double statement of the purpose on the ethical level seems tautological. It is much better to take the reference of the ἵνα clause (as well as of the previous clause) to be to what takes place in baptism. It may be suggested that, following the statement ὁ παλαιὸς ἡμῶν ἄνθρωπος συνεσταυρώθη, this purpose clause is by no means redundant, since crucifixion and the resulting death are not really just one event; for a man was not immediately killed by being crucified, but was indeed crucified, in order that he might die—hours, even days, later. So there is real point in saying, whether with reference to our baptism or with reference to that which lies behind it, of which it is the sign and seal, that our sinful self was hanged on the cross with Christ, in order that it might die.

With **τοῦ μηκέτι δουλεύειν ἡμᾶς τῇ ἁμαρτίᾳ** we are definitely on the level of the moral life. In baptism our sinful selves were crucified and died (in the sense we have indicated) in order that we might in our practical living cease to be the slaves of sin.[1]

7. ὁ γὰρ ἀποθανὼν δεδικαίωται ἀπὸ τῆς ἁμαρτίας. It is quite likely that these words are consciously reminiscent of a well-known Rabbinic legal principle (cf. the material assembled in SB 3, p. 232), but (*pace* a number of commentators) it is not at all clear that Paul is really clinching his argument by appealing to a general principle of the Rabbis. In the sense that 'death pays all debts' this principle is valid only in relation to a human court: it is certain that Paul did not think that a man's death atoned for his sins in relation to God, or that a dead

---

[1] Chrysostom expressed the moral challenge presented by baptism in the memorable sentence (col. 485): Εἰ τοίνυν ἀπέθανες ἐν τῷ βαπτίσματι, μένε νεκρός.

man was no longer accountable to God for his sins. The Rabbinic principle is, in fact, singularly inappropriate as a confirmation of what has just been said. It is therefore much more likely that Paul, though quite probably aware of the use of similar language by the Rabbis, was using the words in his own sense, and that he meant them not as a general statement about dead men, but as a specific theological statement that the man, who has died with Christ in God's gracious decision with regard to him, that is, who has died that death in God's sight to which his baptism points back and of which it is the sign and seal, has been justified from his sin.[1] To state this fact is indeed to confirm v. 6; for it is the fact that God has justified us that is the firm basis of that new freedom to resist the bondage of sin in our practical living, to which the last six words of v. 6 refer.[2]

8. εἰ δέ:[3] 'But if (it is really true that)'. On the use of εἰ with the indicative of reality in logical reasoning see BDF, § 372 (2b).

ἀπεθάνομεν: sc. that death in God's sight which is attested by baptism. (Or it may be that Paul has primarily the sacramental death in mind, though thinking also of that other death to which baptism bears witness. But our impression is that with v. 7 he has moved from sense (ii) to sense (i) in our list in the notes on v. 2.)

The actual phrase σὺν Χριστῷ occurs in Romans only here; but this formula is virtually present in certain occurrences of συν-compounds (vv. 4 and 6, the latter part of the present verse, and 8.17). σὺν αὐτῷ occurs in 8.32, but this is a quite

[1] If our understanding of v. 7 as a theological, and not a general, statement is right, then δεδικαίωται ἀπὸ τῆς ἁμαρτίας must clearly mean 'has been justified from sin' rather than 'has been freed from sin' (the meaning proposed for it by some commentators: cf. Bauer, s.v.), since, while (as the last clause of v. 6 indicates) the Christian is no longer the completely helpless and unresisting slave of sin, he is not in this life, according to Paul (cf. especially 7.14ff), actually free from sin. It would be perverse indeed to give any weight to 1 Pet 4.1 (the interpretation of which is notoriously problematic) as an argument in favour of understanding here so characteristic a Pauline word as δικαιοῦν in an un-Pauline sense (Barrett, *A Commentary on the First Epistle to the Corinthians*, London, 1968, p. 142, rightly decides in favour of taking ἐδικαιώθητε in 1 Cor 6.11 in its ordinary Pauline sense). For δικαιοῦσθαι ἀπό cf. Acts 13.38, where the verb is best taken in its Pauline sense (*pace* Bauer, ibid.).
[2] For other views of this verse see, e.g. G. Schrenk, in *TWNT* 2, p. 222f; Michel, p. 155; Huby, p. 210f and pp. 591–94 (Lyonnet).
[3] There is a variant reading γάρ instead of δέ, in 𝔭⁴⁶ and G, which is intrinsically unsuitable and is perhaps due to the γάρ at the beginning of v. 7, an instance of parablepsis.

distinct use. (Outside Romans compare 2 Cor 4.14; 13.4; Gal 2.19; Eph 2.5; Col 2.13, 20; 3.3, 4; 1 Th 4.14, 17; 5.10; 2 Tim 2.11f.) The formula, which as such seems to have originated with Paul,[1] is used by him most often with reference to fellowship with Christ in the eschatological glory, but it is also used with past tenses with reference to baptism and to that to which baptism is the witness (i.e. senses (ii) and (i) in our note on v. 2), and in a few passages refers to the Christian's fellowship with Christ in this present life (see below on the latter part of this verse and also on 8.17).[2] The antecedents of the Pauline formula probably include the thought of such OT passages as Ps 21.6; 73.23ff; 139.18b; 140.13b, especially as they are interpreted in the LXX, and perhaps also the thought underlying, for example, the 'with thy God' of Mic 6.8.[3]

πιστεύομεν ὅτι is inserted at the cost of disturbing the balance of the sentence, not in order to weaken in any way the following statement (by suggesting that it is made with something less than certainty), but rather to emphasize it by indicating the personal and inward commitment of the members of the Church to its truth. In 10.9 πιστεύειν ὅτι is associated intimately with ὁμολογεῖν, Paul linking together the public confession by the mouth and the inward belief of the heart of which it is the expression. πιστεύειν ὅτι occurs in Paul's letters only here, in 10.9 and in 1 Th 4.14. But, while various other usages feature more prominently, πιστεύειν ὅτι has a secure place; for belief in God necessarily involves belief that certain things are true about Him, and it is in fact upon the 'belief that' that the 'belief in' is based. *Fides qua* cannot exist in the complete absence of *fides quae*. (See on 1.5.)

That καὶ συζήσομεν αὐτῷ refers to the present life is clear from the whole structure of the argument in this paragraph and especially from the content of v. 11, which is closely related to this verse (λογίζεσθε ἑαυτοὺς εἶναι . . . ζῶντας . . . τῷ θεῷ ἐν Χριστῷ Ἰησοῦ corresponding to καὶ συζήσομεν αὐτῷ).[4] The

---

[1] Cf. W. Grundmann, in *TWNT* 7, p. 781, lines 49 and 50, and n. 79.
[2] To claim that the formula is used only with a sacramental or an eschatological reference is arbitrary and doctrinaire.
[3] On σὺν Χριστῷ see further: W. Grundmann, in *TWNT* 7, pp. 780–95; also A. R. George, *Communion with God in the New Testament*, London, 1953, pp. 150–55. See also on ἐν Χριστῷ in v. 11.
[4] So, e.g., Lagrange, p. 147f; Gaugler 1, p. 170f: the contrary view (that the primary reference at any rate is to the eschatological future) is maintained by, e.g., Huby, p. 211, n. 4; Barrett, p. 126; C. F. Evans, *Resurrection and the New Testament*, London, 1970, p. 163, but without (as far as we can see) any convincing argument in support.

Christian's present life is to be a life with Christ (cf. the 'with thy God' of Mic 6.8) in the power of His resurrection, a walking ἐν καινότητι ζωῆς (v. 4).[1] For the future tense compare ἐσόμεθα in v. 5. But, while the reference to the present is clearly primary, it is quite possible, since the present life of Christians is a foretaste of the life with Christ in glory, that the thought of the eschatological fulfilment of the life already begun is also present.

9. εἰδότες ὅτι. It would seem better to punctuate with a colon at the end of v. 8 (as at the end of v. 5) than with a comma, and to understand εἰδότες as meaning 'and we know' (i.e., as introducing another consideration relevant to what has just been said)[2] than to understand it as meaning 'since we know' (i.e., as stating the ground of the belief just mentioned in v. 8).[3] This further consideration (stated in the rest of the verse and in v. 10 which is closely connected with it), being concerned with the true nature of Christ's resurrection, has light to throw upon the meaning of συζήσομεν αὐτῷ.

Χριστὸς ἐγερθεὶς ἐκ νεκρῶν οὐκέτι ἀποθνῄσκει. Christ was not raised, like Lazarus, to a mere extension of natural life, only to succumb once more to death; for His resurrection was the final, eschatological resurrection uniquely anticipated. Nor was His resurrection like that of a nature-god, part of an endlessly recurring cycle of death and renewal.

θάνατος αὐτοῦ οὐκέτι κυριεύει reinforces the preceding statement. For a brief period death really did exercise lordship over Him (this is implied by οὐκέτι), but now it has no power over Him, no hold on Him any more. The use of κυριεύειν is possibly a reflection of the Jewish use of šālaṭ in connexion with the angel of death.[4]

10. ὃ γὰρ ἀπέθανεν, τῇ ἁμαρτίᾳ ἀπέθανεν ἐφάπαξ· ὃ δὲ ζῇ, ζῇ τῷ θεῷ. For the construction—ὃ γάρ stands for τὸν γὰρ θάνατον, ὃν and ὃ δέ for τὴν δὲ ζωήν, ἥν—compare Gal 2.20b (ὃ δὲ νῦν ζῶ ἐν σαρκί, ἐν πίστει ζῶ τῇ τοῦ υἱοῦ τοῦ θεοῦ . . .), and see BDF, § 154 (also 153). The verse explains (γάρ) v. 9. Death has no more any hold on Christ, because the death He died was death to

---

[1] It should be noted that συζήσομεν αὐτῷ, while as a statement in the first person plural it is of course a statement about us, is in a sense even more a statement about God, since our living with Christ will not be our own achievement but God's doing (it is significantly preceded by πιστεύομεν ὅτι). It is God who will establish and maintain our life as life with Christ. How He does this will become clearer in chapter 8.

[2] Cf. Michel's translation: 'und wir wissen' (p. 148); and see on v. 6 (τοῦτο γινώσκοντες).

[3] As do, e.g., Barrett, p. 120; Murray I, p. 223.

[4] See SB 3, p. 232f, for examples.

sin¹ ἐφάπαξ (i.e., once for all, an altogether decisive and unrepeatable event), while the life He now lives is life τῷ θεῷ (and therefore eternal). The expression τῇ ἁμαρτίᾳ ἀποθνήσκειν was used in v. 2, but it is now used in a quite different sense (though in both places τῇ ἁμαρτίᾳ is a dative of the person affected,² and may be translated 'to sin', i.e. in relation to sin). What is actually meant here by 'dying to sin' has to be understood from what Paul says elsewhere about the relation of Christ's death to sin (e.g. 3.24–26; 4.25; 5.6–8; 8.3; 1 Cor 15.3; 2 Cor 5.21; Gal 3.13). He died to sin, that is, He affected sin by His dying, in that, as the altogether sinless One who identified Himself with sinful men, He bore for them the full penalty of their sins and so—in the pregnant sense in which the words are used in 8.3—'condemned sin in the flesh'. But at this point Paul is not concerned to draw out the meaning of Christ's death as death to sin, but simply to stress its once for all character as an event which was so utterly decisive and final that there can be no question of its being repeated. For ἐφάπαξ compare Heb 7.27; 9.12, 26, 28; 10.10; 1 Pet 3.18 (also the use of εἷς in Heb 10.12 and 14). To this once for all quality of Christ's death to sin corresponds the fact that His risen life is lived τῷ θεῷ. Once more we have a dative of the person affected. His risen life belongs pre-eminently to God, and is therefore everlasting.³

Verses 9 and 10, then, together do not just state the reason for our belief that we are to live with Christ: they also throw a flood of light on the character of this new life which is to be ours; for they reveal the transcendent security of its basis in the absolute finality of His death to sin and in His risen life which He lives to God, which is for ever beyond the reach of death.⁴

11. οὕτως καὶ ὑμεῖς may be understood as meaning either (i) 'Even so (or 'So also' or 'Likewise also') (do) you . . .' (οὕτως bringing out the correspondence between the death and risen life of Christians and Christ's death and risen life)⁵ or (ii) 'So

---

¹ In the Clementine Vulgate the punctuation is different, τῇ ἁμαρτίᾳ being taken with the first ἀπέθανεν instead of with the second—'Quod enim mortuus est peccato, mortuus est semel'; but the superiority of the punctuation of the Greek is generally recognized.

² Cf. BDF, § 188 (2).

³ Cf. Chrysostom, col. 486: Ὁ δὲ ζῇ, τῷ θεῷ ζῇ, φησί · τουτέστιν ἀκαταλύτως, ὡς μηκέτι κρατεῖσθαι ὑπὸ τοῦ θανάτου.

⁴ Chrysostom, col. 485, has the memorable epigram: θανάτου γὰρ θάνατος ὁ θάνατος αὐτοῦ γέγονε.

⁵ Cf., e.g., Mt 17.12. Cf. also the use in the apodosis of a comparison (e.g. 5.18).

then (or 'Wherefore') (do) you also . . .' (οὕτως indicating that what is about to be said follows from what has just been said).[1] In either case the thought of the correspondence is present (if (ii) is accepted, the καί is a pointer to it), but only according to (i) is it formally emphasized. As at this point there is a transition to exhortation, to the drawing of practical conclusions, it is perhaps better to accept (ii).

λογίζεσθε (pace Bengel and some others) is surely an imperative (so most commentators). The verb λογίζεσθαι, as used here, denotes not a pretending ('as if'),[2] nor a mere ideal, but a deliberate and sober judgment on the basis of the gospel, a reasoning which is subject to the discipline of the gospel in that it accepts as its norm what God has done in Christ, the gospel-events which are only recognizable as such by faith. Compare 3.28; 8.18; 14.14.[3] So here the imperative followed by ἑαυτοὺς εἶναι[4] means something like 'Recognize that the truth of the gospel means that you are . . .' This seeing oneself as one is revealed to oneself by the gospel and understanding and taking seriously what one sees is a first step—and a decisively important one—on the way of obedience.

νεκροὺς μὲν τῇ ἁμαρτίᾳ ζῶντας δὲ τῷ θεῷ ἐν Χριστῷ Ἰησοῦ:[5] that is, dead to sin and alive to God (the actual formulation is influenced by v. 10) in sense (i) of the notes on v. 2. The Pauline formula 'in Christ' has given rise to a great deal of discussion,[6] and has been variously explained. The fact that the present context is, as Gaugler has rightly noted,[7] so very heilsgeschichtlich should discourage us from accepting local,[8]

[1] Cf. 1.15; and see Bauer, s.v. οὕτως 1.b (with reference to these two passages of Romans).

[2] Contra Bruce, p. 139 ('live as though you had already entered the resurrection life').

[3] Cf. H.-W. Heidland, in TWNT 4, pp. 287ff; Michel, p. 156.

[4] εἶναι is omitted by a number of textual witnesses.

[5] א C K, vgᶜˡ syᵖʰ add τῷ κυρίῳ ἡμῶν.

[6] Bibliographies in TWNT 2, p. 534, and Bauer, s.v. ἐν I.5.d. In addition to the literature listed in them, the following may be mentioned: A. R. George, Communion with God in the New Testament, London, 1953, pp. 147–64; F. Neugebauer, 'Das paulinische "in Christo"', in NTS 4 (1957–58), pp. 124–38, and In Christus/EN ΧΡΙΣΤΩΙ: Eine Untersuchung zum paulinischen Glaubensverständnis, Göttingen, 1961; M. Bouttier, En Christ: étude d'exégèse et de théologie paulinienne, Paris, 1962; A. J. M. Wedderburn, article cited in bibliography on 5.12ff, especially pp. 86–90. Valuable also for their suggestiveness in relation to this subject are the works of T. Preiss: La Vie en Christ, Neuchâtel, 1951, part of which is available in English (Life in Christ, London, 1954), and Le Fils de l'Homme 1 and 2, Montpellier, 1951–53.

[7] I, p. 174f.

[8] The local explanation, according to which Christians are thought of as being in the spiritual, glorified Christ rather in the way that men

mystical or sacramental-realistic explanations. A clue to what is surely the most probable explanation of Paul's ἐν Χριστῷ has, in fact, already been given in the note on v. 2 (in what was said about sense (i)). We said there that God's decision to take our sins upon Himself in the person of His dear Son was tantamount to a decision to see us as having died in Christ's death. It was also a decision to see Christ's risen life as our true life—in other words to see us as living in Him. Paul's ἐν Χριστῷ has to do with God's decision as our gracious Judge to see us, not as we are in ourselves, but 'in Him'. The reality of our being in Christ is a matter not of locality nor of mysticism (unless we use the word in the sense of Théo Preiss's highly paradoxical expression, 'juridical mysticism'[1]) nor of sacramental realism (though the sacraments are pledges of that reality), but of a divine decision. We are in Christ, inasmuch as God accepts Christ's death as having been died for us and His risen life as being lived for us; for this means that in God's sight we died in His death, that is, we died in Him, and were raised up in His resurrection, that is, in Him, and now live in Him. Paul himself gives us a clue to the meaning of his ἐν Χριστῷ in 2 Cor 5.14, when he says: . . . . . . κρίναντας τοῦτο, ὅτι εἷς ὑπὲρ πάντων ἀπέθανεν · ἄρα οἱ πάντες ἀπέθανον. The nos in Christo is all the time implicit in the Christus pro nobis, and the basis of the nos in Christo and the Christus pro nobis alike is God's gracious decision. So here Paul's exhortation to the Roman Christians is to reckon seriously with the fact (disclosed by the gospel) that by virtue of God's gracious decision Christ's death and risen life are counted as theirs, so that, in God's sight, they are 'in Christ' dead to sin but alive to God.

12. μὴ οὖν βασιλευέτω ἡ ἁμαρτία ἐν τῷ θνητῷ ὑμῶν σώματι. The conclusion to be drawn (οὖν) from the fact which they have just been bidden to recognize and take seriously (ἑαυτοὺς εἶναι νεκροὺς μὲν τῇ ἁμαρτίᾳ ζῶντας δὲ τῷ θεῷ ἐν Χριστῷ Ἰησοῦ) is not that, secure in God's gracious decision for them, they may go on contentedly living just as they have always lived, but rather that now they must fight—they must not let sin go on reigning unopposed over their daily life,[2] but must revolt in the name

live in the atmosphere, goes back to G. A. Deissmann, *Die neutestament-liche Formel in Christo Jesu*, Marburg, 1892, and has enjoyed consider-able popularity. It is accepted, e.g., by Sanday and Headlam, p. 160f.

[1] *Life in Christ*, London, 1954, pp. 52ff.

[2] On the significance of the present imperative see BDF, §§ 336 and 337 (1) n. Murray's objection ('It is not to be supposed that sin is conceived of as reigning in the believer and that now he is exhorted to terminate that reign of sin. This would run counter to all that has been

of their rightful ruler, God, against sin's usurping rule. Some would limit the reference of ἐν τῷ θνητῷ ὑμῶν σώματι to the physical body,[1] but it is better to understand Paul to mean by σῶμα the whole man in his fallenness (see on v. 6). It is not only the physical body that is mortal: the whole man, as the fallen human being that he is, is subject to death. And it is over the whole of our fallen nature, not just over our bodies, that sin has established its rule. So it is in the whole field of our life as the fallen human beings we are that we are called to resist sin's dominion.

εἰς τὸ ὑπακούειν ταῖς ἐπιθυμίαις αὐτοῦ[2] is added as a reminder of the consequences which would result from allowing sin to go on reigning unchallenged ἐν τῷ θνητῷ . . . σώματι. If they do not obey the command Paul has just given, then they will be driven hither and thither in obedience to the lusts of their fallen nature. On the view taken above concerning the meaning of σῶμα in this verse, these lusts will include not just what we would call 'bodily lusts', but also such things as the will to dominate other people—in fact, all the desires of the ego in its state of rebellion against God.

13. μηδὲ παριστάνετε: 'And stop (or 'do not go on') placing . . . at the disposal of . . .'

τὰ μέλη ὑμῶν. The primary meaning of μέλος is 'limb', but the word came to be used in a wider sense covering organs as well as limbs (so, for example, in 1 Cor 12.14ff the ear and the eye are included among the μέλη), so that often it requires to be translated 'member' rather than 'limb'. But here it is perhaps used in an even wider sense to include any natural capacity. In 7.23 ἐν τοῖς μέλεσίν μου seems to be more or less equivalent to ἐν ἐμοί in 7.17 and 20 (see the relevant notes); and in the

set forth in the preceding verses regarding the status of the believer as dead to sin and alive to God'—1, p. 226) seems to stem mainly from failure to reckon with the several different senses in which Paul speaks of the Christian's death to sin and of his new life. We have introduced the word 'unopposed' because it seems to us very clear that Paul did not think of the Christian's positive response to his μὴ . . . βασιλευέτω as actually bringing to an end sin's reign over his fallen nature (see especially 7.14, where we take πεπραμένος ὑπὸ τὴν ἁμαρτίαν to refer to the Christian). What it does bring to an end is sin's unchallenged, unresisted reign.

[1] e.g., Murray 1, p. 227: 'The mortal body is without question the physical organism as subject to dissolution'.

[2] The textual witnesses vary here, 𝔓⁴⁶ D G it Ir Tert attesting αὐτῇ (referring to ἁμαρτία), the Byzantine text attesting αὐτῇ ἐν ταῖς ἐπιθυμίαις αὐτοῦ, while the text as printed above is supported by the Hesychian text-form and by vg syᵖ. Of these, the first appears to be an attempt to improve the sense, and the second an attempt to conflate the other two readings.

present verse there is probably not much substantial difference between τὰ μέλη ὑμῶν and ἑαυτούς. We might perhaps say that in 7.23 and here τὰ μέλη denotes the self under the aspect of its capacities.[1] We might translate here: 'your natural capacities'.

It is a moot question whether ὅπλα has here its general sense of 'instruments', 'tools', or its particular sense of 'weapons'. Pauline usage is in favour of the latter, and the thought of fighting may plausibly be said to be implicit in μὴ βασιλευέτω. But perhaps (*pace* Chrysostom, Calvin, Sanday and Headlam, Lagrange, Michel and many others) the general sense is rather more appropriate here in view of the references to the service of slaves in this chapter (vv. 6, 16, 17, 18, 19, 20, 22). The thought of the slave's members and capacities as being his master's tools is a natural one (compare Aristotle's famous definition of a slave as ἔμψυχον ὄργανον in E.N. 1161b).

ἀδικίας is not possessive (the possessor is indicated by τῇ ἁμαρτίᾳ), but a genitive of purpose (see BDF, § 166)—'for the doing of unrighteousness'.[2] The word is used in its most general sense, to contrast with δικαιοσύνης later in the verse.

παραστήσατε. For the significance of the aorist see on v. 4 (περιπατήσωμεν).

ἑαυτοὺς τῷ θεῷ ὡσεὶ ἐκ νεκρῶν ζῶντας καὶ τὰ μέλη ὑμῶν ὅπλα δικαιοσύνης τῷ θεῷ. The formulation of the positive command varies from that of the negative, in that before τὰ μέλη ὑμῶν, κ.τ.λ., which answers to the formulation of the preceding sentence, there is inserted ἑαυτοὺς τῷ θεῷ ὡσεὶ ἐκ νεκρῶν ζῶντας καί. The most likely reason for this double formulation is that Paul wanted at this point to refer to the fact of their new life already mentioned in v. 11. To have attached this reference to τὰ μέλη ὑμῶν, κ.τ.λ. would have been rather clumsy and would anyway have destroyed the parallelism: it was therefore preferable to introduce ἑαυτούς in co-ordination with τὰ μέλη ὑμῶν. The sense of ὡσεί is not 'as if you were', but 'being, as you are'.[3]

14. ἁμαρτία γὰρ ὑμῶν οὐ κυριεύσει is difficult, and has—not surprisingly—been variously interpreted.[4] The view that it is

---

[1] See also Bauer, s.v. μέλος 2, with reference to Col 3.5.

[2] This is surely preferable to Michel's explanation of it as a genitive of quality (p. 157, n. 2).

[3] Cf. Lagrange, p. 154; Michel, p. 157.

[4] We proceed here as elsewhere on the principle that, while the possibility of Paul's having been illogical or inconsistent should not be ruled out dogmatically, we ought, in expounding Paul as in expounding any other writer whose intelligence and competence we have good reason to respect, where a sentence taken by itself is patient of various interpretations, to accept as most probable that which both suits its immediate context best and also agrees best with what the same author has said in other places.

a promise that those whom Paul is addressing will never again yield to sin may be set aside as altogether improbable, since Paul has elsewhere made it abundantly clear that he was under no such illusion about himself or his fellow Christians. The suggestion that κυριεύσει was intended in an imperatival sense ('is not to . . .'), though attractive at first sight, should be rejected on the grounds that the sentence would then be a lame repetition of the substance of v. 12, which would be quite out of place at this point, and that the conjunction γάρ would be inappropriate. Unsatisfactory too is the suggestion that ἁμαρτία refers only to that fundamental sin which consists in the attempt to use the law to establish one's own righteousness, and not material sin, that is, sinful acts,[1] for there is no support in the context for limiting the meaning of ἁμαρτία in this way. But we are on the way to a satisfactory explanation, when we recognize, on the one hand, that here (as often in this chapter) Paul is thinking of sin as a power, that is, personifying it, and, on the other hand, that κυριεύειν is to be understood in its primary sense, 'be lord of'. The sentence may then be interpreted as a promise that sin will no more be their lord, because another lord has taken possession of them, namely, Christ (it is instructive to compare the use of κυριεύειν in 14.9). That does not mean that sin will have no power at all over them (Paul can state the fact of sin's continuing hold on Christians with relentless frankness, if our understanding of 7.14 is correct); but it does mean that they will never again be left helpless in sin's power—unless, of course, they wantonly turn their backs on the Lord who has redeemed them (an unconditional promise is hardly in question). Though sin will still have a hold upon them until they die (in the natural sense), they will henceforth, as subjects of Christ over whom He has decisively reasserted His authority, be free to fight against sin's usurped power, and to demonstrate their true allegiance.[2] So understood the sentence makes good sense as support (γάρ) for the imperatives of vv. 12 and 13.

οὐ γάρ ἐστε ὑπὸ νόμον ἀλλὰ ὑπὸ χάριν is widely taken to mean that the authority of the law has been abolished for believers and superseded by a different authority.[3] And this, it must be

---

[1] So Leenhardt, pp. 166–68 (= Fr.: p. 96f).
[2] Cf. 8.2, and the notes on it.
[3] Some remarkably rash statements have been made in connexion with this half-verse. Barrett, for example, writes (p. 129): 'Law means the upward striving of human religion and morality, and therefore colours all human activity with sin, for it represents man's attempt to scale God's throne'; but it is legalism, man's abuse of God's law, not the law itself, which represents man's upward striving. And Michel,

admitted, would be a plausible interpretation, if this sentence stood by itself. But, since it stands in a document which contains such things as 3.31; 7.12, 14a; 8.4; 13.8–10, and in which the law is referred to more than once as God's law (7.22, 25; 8.7) and is appealed to again and again as authoritative, such a reading of it is extremely unlikely. The fact that ὑπὸ νόμον is contrasted with ὑπὸ χάριν suggests the likelihood that Paul is here thinking not of the law generally but of the law as condemning sinners; for, since χάρις denotes God's undeserved favour, the natural opposite to ὑπὸ χάριν is 'under God's disfavour or condemnation'. And the suggestion that the meaning of this sentence is that believers are not under God's condemnation pronounced by the law but under His undeserved favour receives strong confirmation from 8.1 (οὐδὲν ἄρα νῦν κατάκριμα τοῖς ἐν Χριστῷ Ἰησοῦ), which, in Paul's argument, is closely related (through 7.1–6) to this half-verse. Moreover, this interpretation suits the context well; for an assurance that we have been set free from God's condemnation and are now the objects of His gracious favour is indeed confirmation (γάρ) of the promise that henceforth sin shall no more be lord over us, for those who know themselves freed from condemnation are free to resist sin's usurped power with new strength and boldness. It is perhaps possible that in Paul's ὑπὸ νόμον here there was also another thought present, namely, the thought of labouring (as so many of his Jewish contemporaries were doing) under the illusion with regard to the law that a man has to earn a status of righteousness before God by his obedience. Since χάρις denotes God's *free, undeserved* favour, the contrast with ὑπὸ χάριν might perhaps be not unreasonably claimed as support for this suggestion.

(ii) *A choice between masters*
(6.15–23)

[15]What then? Are we to sin, because we are not under the law but under grace? God forbid! [16]Do you not know that, whoever it is at whose disposal you place yourselves as slaves to obey him, you are the slaves of the one whom you obey, whether it be of sin with death as the consequence or of obedience with righteousness as the consequence? [17]But thanks be to God that you, who once were slaves of sin, have from the heart become obedient to the pattern of teaching to which you were delivered, [18]and having been set free from sin you have been made slaves to righteousness. [19](I have to put this in a

---

p. 157, has the statement: 'Die Herrschaft der Gnade bricht sowohl die Macht der Sünde als auch des Gesetzes'. Even Sanday and Headlam could speak of 'Law, Sin's ally' (p. 153).

very human way because of the weakness of your flesh.*) For just as you once placed your members as slaves at the disposal of uncleanness and lawlessness for *a life of* lawlessness, so now place your members as slaves at the disposal of righteousness for sanctification. ²⁰For when you were slaves of sin, you were free in relation to righteousness. ²¹What fruit did you then obtain? Things of which you now are ashamed! For their end is death. ²²But now, having been set free from sin and made slaves to God, you obtain your fruit unto sanctification, and as the end eternal life. ²³For the wage which sin pays is death, but the free gift which God gives is eternal life in Christ Jesus our Lord.

This sub-section underlines the fact that the question of a man's being free in the sense of having no master, of not being a slave at all, simply does not arise. Only two alternatives present themselves, to have sin for one's master or to have God (this second alternative is variously expressed in these verses); there is no third possibility. The Roman Christians have been freed from the slavery of sin and made slaves of God; and they must act accordingly and not try to combine incompatibles. Paul is aware that the figure of slavery is unworthy, inadequate and apt to be grievously misleading, as a way of indicating the believer's relation to God. Hence his apology in v. 19a. But, in spite of the fact that in so many respects it is altogether inappropriate, he cannot dispense with it, because it does express the total belongingness, total obligation and total accountability which characterize the life under grace, with a vigour and vividness which no other image seems able to equal.

15. Τί οὖν; ἁμαρτήσωμεν,¹ ὅτι οὐκ ἐσμὲν ὑπὸ νόμον ἀλλὰ ὑπὸ χάριν; μὴ γένοιτο recalls v. 1. But the false conclusions dealt with in the two verses are not the same. Whereas in v. 1 the false inference from the truth stated in 5.20 was that one should continue in sin so as to make grace abound still more, here the false inference from the truth stated in v. 14b is that sinful acts do not matter any more as far as we are concerned. The pains Paul is at in the following verses to drive his point home indicate that the danger of such misunderstanding was not merely hypothetical.

16. οὐκ² οἴδατε ὅτι. Compare 1 Cor 3.16; 5.6; 6.2, 3, 9, 15, 16,

* Or 'your weakness of the flesh' (see p. 326, n. 1).
¹ For the tense-form compare 5.14, 16, and see BDF, § 75. The variant ἁμαρτήσομεν is parallel to the variant ἐπιμενοῦμεν in v. 1. The nonsensical variant ἡμαρτήσαμεν is no doubt due to Latin influence, a Latin reading 'peccavimus' being a mistake (due to similarity of pronunciation) for 'peccabimus' (cf. Lagrange, p. 155).
² The ἤ (before οὐκ) attested by D* G it may be explained as assimilation to those Pauline passages in which ἢ οὐκ οἴδατε or ἢ ἀγνοεῖτε occurs (1 Cor 6.2, 9, 16, 19; Rom 6.3; 7.1).

19; 9.13, 24; Jas 4.4; also οὐκ οἴδατε . . . τί in Rom 11.2, and ἢ ἀγνοεῖτε ὅτι in Rom 6.3; 7.1; and see on v. 3.

ᾧ παριστάνετε ἑαυτοὺς δούλους εἰς ὑπακοήν, δοῦλοί ἐστε ᾧ ὑπακούετε, ἤτοι ἁμαρτίας εἰς θάνατον[1] ἢ ὑπακοῆς εἰς δικαιοσύνην; Here two distinct points are being made: (i) that whatever is the power to which you yield yourselves as slaves to obey it, you are the slaves of that power which you obey;[2] and (ii) that you have only two alternatives from which to choose, being the slaves of sin (with death as the result) or being the slaves of obedience (with righteousness as the result). The expression of (i) seems rather clumsy. If the point is simply—as it appears to be—that you are the slaves of whatever power you obey, then there is some unnecessary repetition and δούλους in the relative clause would seem to be a premature indication of the point to be made in the main clause. The cardinal term 'obedience' (εἰς ὑπακοήν and ᾧ ὑπακούετε) probably denotes here a willing obedience (for example, what is contemplated in the deliberative question ἁμαρτήσωμεν, κ.τ.λ. in v. 15) and is not meant to include the unwilling yielding to sin of those who are resisting it such as is depicted in chapter seven. This first point is the answer to the question in v. 15: for those who are 'under grace' committing sinful acts does indeed matter, for to commit such acts willingly is to be the slave of sin. With regard to (ii), several things should be noticed. The phrases εἰς θάνατον and εἰς δικαιοσύνην amount to two subsidiary statements indicating that these slaveries lead in the end, the one to death (cf. v. 23),[3] the other to final justification.[4] The use of ὑπακοῆς as opposite to ἁμαρτίας is unexpected, and specially interesting. In vv. 18 and 20 (cf. 19) the opposition is between ἁμαρτία and δικαιοσύνη; and it is easy to see that in v. 16 δικαιοσύνης was virtually ruled out, if εἰς δικαιοσύνην was to be used (instead of the more obvious εἰς ζωήν) as opposite to εἰς θάνατον. However, in vv. 13, 22 and 23 the opposition is between sin and God Himself. Why then did not Paul put τοῦ θεοῦ here? To this the correct answer would seem to be that, while the fundamental decision for Paul was indeed between being slaves to sin and

---

[1] εἰς θάνατον is omitted by D 1739 it vg^codd syp sa.

[2] Neither the suggestion that the second ᾧ stands for καὶ ἐκείνῳ, nor the suggestion that it stands for διὰ τούτου ὅτι, commends itself as at all likely.

[3] 'Death' here denotes not the death which all men have to die as the result of sin (cf. 5.12ff) but death as God's final eschatological judgment of condemnation, which even for the baptized remains a possibility. Cf. Michel's valuable note (p. 159, n. 3).

[4] That δικαιοσύνη has here its forensic, rather than its moral, sense is clear from the contrast with θάνατος.

being slaves to God, he wanted at this point specially to emphasize the thought of obedience (to God), because he wanted to make his readers see that to be under God's grace is to be under obligation to obey Him.

The burden of the verse as a whole may be expressed in some such way as this: The question of a man's being free in the sense of having no master at all simply does not arise. The only alternatives open to him are to have sin, or to have God, as his master (the man who imagines he is free, because he acknowledges no god but his own ego, is deluded; for the service of one's own ego is the very essence of the slavery of sin). The one alternative has as its end death, but the other life with God.

17. χάρις δὲ τῷ θεῷ ὅτι. This verse and—if a comma is read after διδαχῆς—v. 18 have the form of a prayer of thanksgiving to God. Compare 7.25a; 1 Cor 15.57; 2 Cor 2.14; 8.16; 9.15. Nygren notes that, instead of praising the Roman Christians, Paul thanks God.

ἦτε δοῦλοι τῆς ἁμαρτίας is logically equivalent to a concessive clause subordinate to the clause which follows (Paul does not mean to thank God that they were slaves of sin—what he thanks God for is that, in spite of their having been slaves of sin, they now have obeyed . . .), but is grammatically co-ordinate with it (an example of parataxis).

ὑπηκούσατε δὲ ἐκ[1] καρδίας εἰς ὃν παρεδόθητε τύπον διδαχῆς has given rise to a great deal of discussion. According to Bultmann,[2] it is a very early gloss, a 'stupid insertion' which destroys the clear antithesis presented by v. 17a+v. 18, and which is, in addition, suspect on the grounds that it contains two un-Pauline expressions ἐκ καρδίας and τύπος διδαχῆς, and that the thought which it expresses is trivial in comparison with that of the context; and some commentators have indicated their inclination to agree with him.[3] It must be freely admitted that v. 17a+v. 18 would make a neat antithesis, that the text as it stands does give a certain impression of overcrowding, and that the δέ at the beginning of v. 18 comes a little un-expectedly after v. 17b. But, if v. 17b proves to be patient of a sense which can plausibly be regarded as Pauline, we may be reasonably confident that what we have here is not a gloss, but an example of that overburdening of literary structure into which Paul is sometimes betrayed by the richness and

---

[1] A *pc* add καθαρᾶς. Cf. 1 Tim 1.5; 2 Tim 2.22; 1 Pet 1.22 (variant reading). It is clearly not original here.

[2] 'Glossen', col. 202.

[3] e.g. Leenhardt, p. 172, n. * (Fr.: p. 99, n. 1); Michel, p. 160.

vivacity of his thought. If we can also discern a good reason for Paul's insertion of v. 17b, this will be an important confirmation of our confidence.

The fact that ἐκ καρδίας does not occur elsewhere in Paul's epistles (ἐκ καθαρᾶς καρδίας is a different expression, and occurs only in the Pastorals) should not worry us unduly: it is found in I Pet 1.22, and is a perfectly good Greek expression exactly suited to the purpose for which it is here used (ἐκ τῆς καρδίας occurs in Aristophanes, Nu. 86, with the same sense as is required here). τύπος διδαχῆς would indeed be incredible in a Pauline epistle, if it meant, as Bultmann and others have supposed, 'type of teaching' in the sense of one type of Christian teaching over against other types; but a much more natural meaning is 'pattern of teaching', that is, the pattern consisting of teaching (appositive genitive), which is to mould the lives of those who have received it.[1] We may compare the reference to the teaching (τὴν διδαχὴν ἣν ὑμεῖς ἐμάθετε) in 16.17. The words εἰς ὃν παρεδόθητε τύπον διδαχῆς, which are to be explained as an abbreviation of τῷ τύπῳ τῆς διδαχῆς εἰς ὃν παρεδόθητε,[2] become intelligible as soon as one ceases to be mesmerized by the association of παραδιδόναι and διδαχή, and realizes that here 'the verb παραδίδωμι is to be interpreted wholly in relation to the figure of the transfer of the slave from one master to another, without any thought, without even an overtone, of the transmitting of tradition'.[3] What is being said in v. 17b is that the persons addressed have obeyed from the heart (not merely formally but with inward commitment) that teaching (concerning the way of life demanded by the gospel—that teaching which is the mould by which their lives are to be shaped), to which they were delivered up (in their baptism?) as slaves to a new master. There does not seem to be anything in this which is difficult to imagine Paul saying to the Christians in Rome. And, thus understood, v. 17b seems to fit into the thought of the context perfectly well, though admittedly having a disturbing effect on the grammatical structure of vv. 17 and 18.

It remains to ask whether any motive can be suggested which is likely to have led Paul to interpolate these words between v. 17a and what seems to be its appropriate sequel in

---

[1] On τύπος see on 5.14; on its use in the present passage see especially F. W. Beare, 'On the interpretation of Rom 6.17', in NTS 5 (1958–59), pp. 206–10.

[2] Zahn's suggestion (p. 322) that they are equivalent to εἰς τὸν τύπον τῆς διδαχῆς ὃν παρεδόθητε and that ὃν παρεδόθητε is to be explained on the analogy of πιστεύομαί τι and ἐπιτρέπομαί τι is ingenious, but surely unlikely.

[3] Beare, op. cit., p. 207.

v. 18. We think such a motive can indeed be suggested, and that it is the same motive as led Paul to put the unexpected ὑπακοῆς in v. 16, namely, Paul's special concern at this point to stress the place of obedience in the Christian life—the fact that to be under God's grace involves the obligation to obey Him (cf. what was said above on v. 16).[1]

18-19a. It is probably better to punctuate with a comma at the end of v. 17 than by putting a full stop there to make v. 18 a quite independent sentence. In either case, δέ is a little surprising. It is better explained as marking the connexion between v. 18 and v. 17a (compare, for example, 1 Cor 6.11, where ἀλλά is used three times to introduce parallel statements, the adversative connexion in each case being with what preceded the first ἀλλά) than as connecting v. 18 with v. 17b.[2] The variant οὖν is an understandable attempt to improve the structure (it implies a full stop at the end of v. 17, and makes the connexion with v. 17b).

ἐλευθερωθέντες . . . ἀπὸ τῆς ἁμαρτίας. They have already been set free from sin in the sense that they have been transferred from the possession of sin to the possession of a new master and so are now in a position to resist sin's continuing hold upon them. See on v. 14 and on 8.2.

ἐδουλώθητε τῇ δικαιοσύνῃ. ἀνθρώπινον λέγω διὰ τὴν ἀσθένειαν τῆς σαρκὸς ὑμῶν. Paul is clearly aware of the fact that the figure of slavery is inadequate, unworthy and misleading as a way of speaking about the believer's relation to δικαιοσύνη (here used, of course, in its moral sense)—that is why he apologizes for the all too human nature of his language, as soon as he has made the statement that they have been enslaved to righteousness. (There are similar apologies in 3.5; 1 Cor 9.8; Gal 3.15, and in each case the apology is introduced, as here, asyndetically.) In almost every respect the image is inappropriate for Paul's purpose. Of course, the Christian's relation to righteousness, to obedience (v. 16), to God (v. 22), is not at all the unjust, humiliating, degrading, grievous thing that slavery has always been. On the contrary, it is 'perfect freedom',[3] or, as Chrysostom put it, 'better than any freedom'.[4] But because of their human

---

[1] Among the literature on the subject of v. 17b may be mentioned, in addition to the article by Beare, Bultmann, 'Glossen', col. 202; A. Fridrichsen, 'Exegetisches zum Neuen Testament', in *Coniectanea Neotestamentica* 7, 1942, pp. 6–8; J. Kürzinger, 'τύπος διδαχῆς und der Sinn von Röm 6.17f', in *Biblica* 39, 1958, pp. 156–76.

[2] A possible alternative is to explain δέ along the lines of Bauer, s.v. δέ 2.

[3] The Second Collect, for Peace, in 'The Order of Morning Prayer', in *The Book of Common Prayer*.

[4] col. 489 (Δύο ἐνταῦθα δείκνυσι τοῦ Θεοῦ δωρεάς, τό τε ἁμαρτίας ἐλευθερῶσαι, καὶ τὸ δουλῶσαι τῇ δικαιοσύνῃ, ὅπερ ἐλευθερίας ἁπάσης ἄμεινόν ἐστι).

weakness[1] Paul cannot dispense with the figure of slavery, harsh and unworthy though it is. They are prone—the whole passage reflects his consciousness of the fact—to forget the obligations involved in being under grace. But in this they are only like all other believers, so that Paul's figure seems no less necessary today; for it is doubtful whether there is any other which can so clearly express the total belongingness, the total obligation, the total commitment and the total account-ability, which characterize the life under grace. We shall be wise to accept it and at the same time heed Paul's warning of its unworthiness.[2]

19b largely repeats the thought of v. 13, but with significant nuances.

ὥσπερ ... οὕτως ... underlines the parallel between their old self-dedication to uncleanness and lawlessness and the new self-dedication to which they are being summoned.

The tense of παρεστήσατε is perhaps to be explained as a complexive aorist indicating a linear action which, having been completed, is regarded as a whole.[3] If so, it is consonant with a desire to emphasize the fact that this phase of their lives is a thing of the past.

τὰ μέλη ὑμῶν. See on v. 13.

δοῦλα. The adjective δοῦλος is used in the NT only in this verse, but is found in Sophocles, Euripides, Plato, and in the LXX.

τῇ ἀκαθαρσίᾳ. See on 1.24.

τῇ ἀνομίᾳ. See on 4.7.

---

[1] Michel, p. 161, n. 2, is quite possibly right in thinking that ὑμῶν depends not just on σαρκός but on the expression τὴν ἀσθένειαν τῆς σαρκός as a whole. For the language cf. Mk 14.38=Mt 26.41; Gal 4.13; but the meaning here is different. What is meant is the incomprehension, insensitiveness, insincerity and proneness to self-deception, which characterize the fallen human nature even of Christians, the marks of a mind which is as yet only just beginning to be renewed (cf. 12.2)—surely, not just, as Barrett (p. 132) states, that 'frailty of human nature, which cannot grasp profound truth unless it is presented in human analogies'.

[2] Beare, op. cit., p. 207f, seems to blame Paul for using this figure at all. But it seems to us that Paul was right to use the image which expresses most clearly a vital point, even though that image is unworthy, and at the same time to indicate (as he has done here) its inadequacy, and also provide in other passages the necessary correctives (as he has done in, for example, the passages Beare mentions, 8.15 and 29, and Gal 4.7). The question may well be asked whether the expurgation of our exposition of the Christian life by the removal of the slavery figure is not more likely to prove a serious impoverishment and distortion than a genuine purification.

[3] See BDF, § 332 (1).

The omission of εἰς τὴν ἀνομίαν (B 1912 syᵖ Tert) was probably due to a mistaken impression that it merely repeated τῇ ἀνομίᾳ. The phrase indicates what was the end in view of their action; it was for the doing of lawlessness and would have as its consequence more and more lawlessness.[1]

νῦν is emphatic. Compare 3.26; 5. 9, 11; 6.21,22 (νυνί); 8.1, etc. The present time in its eschatological context is the time of opportunity and of decision.

παραστήσατε. For the tense see on v. 4 (περιπατήσωμεν). The use of the imperative following the passive indicatives of v. 18 is interesting: it points to the human response demanded by the divine action, while the aorist passive indicatives point to the basis on which alone the imperative is really meaningful.

εἰς ἁγιασμόν is parallel to εἰς τὴν ἀνομίαν, and indicates the end in view of the action commanded. The noun ἁγιασμός occurs in the NT nine other times (v. 22; 1 Cor 1.30; 1 Th 4.3, 4, 7; 2 Th 2.13; 1 Tim 2.15; Heb 12.14; 1 Pet 1.2). It denotes God's work in the believer, his ethical renewal. In spite of some opinions to the contrary,[2] the word, as used by Paul, indicates a process rather than a state, and is better represented by 'sanctification' than by 'holiness' or 'consecration'. See on 1.7 (ἁγίοις).[3]

20. ὅτε γὰρ δοῦλοι ἦτε τῆς ἁμαρτίας, ἐλεύθεροι ἦτε τῇ δικαιοσύνῃ. The γάρ is probably best understood as indicating the connexion not of v. 20 by itself, but of vv. 20 and 21 together, with v. 19b.[4] Together they serve to support the command just given, reinforcing its urgency. τῇ δικαιοσύνῃ is a dative of respect—'in respect of (or 'in relation to') righteousness'. See BDF, § 197. The general sense of the verse would seem to be that one cannot be the slave of sin and the slave of righteousness at the same time. Compare Mt 6.24.

21. τίνα οὖν καρπὸν εἴχετε τότε; ἐφ'οἷς νῦν ἐπαισχύνεσθε. τὸ⁵ γὰρ

---

[1] The RSV rendering of τῇ ἀνομίᾳ εἰς τὴν ἀνομίαν by 'to greater and greater iniquity' is unlikely to be correct; for—not to mention other considerations—the parallelism between εἰς τὴν ἀνομίαν and εἰς ἁγιασμόν is surely too pronounced to be ignored.

[2] e.g. Murray I, p. 234, n. 21.

[3] See further O. Procksch, in *TWNT* I, p. 114f; Bauer, s.v. (includes some bibliographical information); K. Stalder, *Das Werk des Geistes in der Heiligung bei Paulus*, Zurich, 1962; W. Pfister, *Das Leben im Geist nach Paulus*, Fribourg, 1963.

[4] Cf. Murray I, p. 235. This is surely preferable to the suggestion (Barrett, p. 133) that some such supplement as 'These are mutually exclusive attitudes' is to be supplied between vv. 19 and 20.

[5] The μέν read by B D* G 33 *pc* after τό is not likely to be original: it is inappropriate here, and was probably introduced by mistake as correlative to the first δέ of v. 22.

τέλος ἐκείνων θάνατος. There is not much doubt (*pace* Sanday and Headlam,[1] Murray,[2] *et al.*) that this punctuation, which is explicitly supported by Theodore of Mopsuestia,[3] is to be preferred to the alternative which places no stop or just a comma after τότε, and a question mark after ἐπαισχύνεσθε.[4] According to the punctuation printed above, (ἐκεῖνα) ἐφ᾿ οἷς νῦν ἐπαισχύνεσθε is the answer to the initial question, and τὸ γὰρ τέλος, κ.τ.λ. contributes an explanation of their sense of shame. The fruit which they used to have from their slavery to sin consisted of things (Paul doubtless has in mind evil deeds, evil habits, evil characters), of which they now are ashamed, since the end to which such things lead is death. The mention of their being ashamed is by no means otiose; for to be ashamed of one's past evil ways is a vital element in sanctification, as Calvin emphasized in his comment on this verse ('Only those . . . who have learned well to be earnestly dissatisfied with themselves, and to be confounded with shame at their wretchedness, are imbued with the principles of Christian philosophy').[5] For the last sentence of the verse compare v. 16 (εἰς θάνατον).

22. νυνὶ δέ. It is more natural to take νυνί as part of the main clause than to connect it with the participles. It is therefore appropriate to place a comma after δέ (with WH). νυνί probably has its proper temporal force.

ἐλευθερωθέντες ἀπὸ τῆς ἁμαρτίας δουλωθέντες δὲ τῷ θεῷ. Compare v. 18. It is to be noted that here Paul speaks quite directly of slavery to God (τῷ θεῷ), and not indirectly as when he referred to slavery to righteousness (ἐδουλώθητε τῇ δικαιοσύνῃ) in v. 18 or to slavery to obedience (δοῦλοι . . . ὑπακοῆς) in v. 16.

ἔχετε τὸν καρπὸν ὑμῶν εἰς ἁγιασμόν. The RSV rendering ('the return you get is sanctification') and Barrett's 'your fruit proves to be sanctification'[6] telescope Paul's meaning, destroy-

[1] p. 169f.
[2] p. 235f.
[3] col. 804: Κατ᾿ ἐρώτησιν ἀναγνωστέον τὸ Τίνα οὖν καρπὸν εἴχετε τότε; εἶτα κατὰ ἀπόκρισιν ᾿Εφ᾿ οἷς νῦν ἐπαισχύνεσθε.
[4] The alternative punctuation involves supplying ἐκείνων as antecedent of οἷς. The arguments in favour of it, most of which are mentioned either by Sanday and Headlam or by Murray, seem to have little substance in comparison with those in favour of the punctuation printed above, viz., that it yields a smoother and clearer sequence of thought, and that it produces a distinction between the immediate and the ultimate results of slavery to sin ((ἐκεῖνα) ἐφ᾿ οἷς νῦν ἐπαισχύνεσθε and θάνατος) corresponding to that in v. 22 between ἁγιασμός and ζωὴ αἰώνιος as the immediate and ultimate results of slavery to God (cf. Barrett, p. 133).
[5] p. 135.
[6] p. 131.

ing the distinction between τὸν καρπὸν ὑμῶν and ἁγιασμόν. But εἰς surely implies a distinction between them, and is not here to be explained on the analogy of γίνεσθαι εἰς in, for example, 11.9 or 1 Cor 15.45. What Paul is saying is that they are now obtaining fruit (of their slavery to God) which is a contribution to—indeed, a beginning of—the process of their sanctification: but this is not to imply that their sanctification may simply be equated with the fruit which they are obtaining at the present time (νυνὶ . . . ἔχετε).

τὸ δὲ τέλος ζωὴν αἰώνιον: 'and as the end (of your slavery to God)[1] (you have—i.e. you will have) eternal life'. There is a contrast (indicated by δέ) between τὸ . . . τέλος and νυνί. But ζωὴ αἰώνιος is, of course, to be distinguished not only from the fruit which they receive now, but also from the sanctification to which that fruit contributes.

23 provides both clarification of vv. 21-22 and also a solemn conclusion to the section as a whole.

τὰ . . . ὀψώνια τῆς ἁμαρτίας: 'the wages which sin pays' (not 'the wages paid for sin'). Sin is still personified, and is here represented either as a general who pays wages to his soldiers (some who understand ὅπλα in v. 13 in the sense of 'weapons' see here the recalling of military imagery already present there) or—and this suits the prominence of δοῦλος in the preceding verses—as a slave-owner who pays his slaves an allowance.[2] The word ὀψώνιον (from ὄψον meaning 'cooked (or otherwise prepared) food' and ὠνεῖσθαι meaning 'to buy'—so wages with which to buy food) denotes a wage paid in money,[3] and is most frequently used of soldiers' pay, but was also used in connexion with slaves.[4]

[1] The fact that τὸ . . . τέλος in v. 21 is associated with ἐκείνων makes it unlikely, in view of the parallelism, that τὸ . . . τέλος here is to be understood as adverbial. It also raises the question whether the reference here is to the end of the fruit rather than to the end of the slavery. While this is possible, it seems rather more natural here to think of the end, the goal, of their slavery to God.

[2] Among the Romans it was normal for a slave to receive a *peculium* or pocket-money, and, according to Cicero, *Phil.* 8.32, a good slave could save enough in seven years to buy his freedom. See also Varro, *R.R.* 1.2.17; Seneca, *Ep. mor.* 80.7; T. Frank (ed.), *An Economic Survey of Ancient Rome* 1, Baltimore, 1933, pp. 383–86; 5, 1940, p. 182; and S. H. Travis, *Divine Retribution in the thought of Paul*, Cambridge Ph.D. thesis, 1970, p. 100, n. 7, to which I am indebted for reminding me of information I had forgotten.

[3] This, as the form of the word suggests, is the word's basic meaning: the justification for 'eigtl. die Ration, die der Soldat erhält' in Bauer, s.v., is surely questionable. ὀψώνιον occurs in the NT also in Lk 3.14; 1 Cor 9.7; and 2 Cor 11.8.

[4] See MM, s.v.; also LSJ, s.v. 3 *fin.*

θάνατος. The wage which sin pays is death.[1]

τὸ ... χάρισμα τοῦ θεοῦ. God does not pay wages, since no man can put Him in his debt; but the free gift which He gives is nothing less than eternal life. The idea that Paul, in using χάρισμα here in contrast with ὀψώνια, was thinking of the *donativum* or largess given to each soldier by the emperor or by an imperial heir on his accession, introduction to public life or other extraordinary occasion, goes back to Tertullian, *De res. carn.* 47 ('Stipendia enim delinquentiae mors, donativum autem Dei vita aeterna').[2] It is perhaps possible that he was; but, picturesque though the suggestion may be, it is by no means as well-founded as some commentators seem to assume. It is not as though χάρισμα could be shown to be a well-established first century equivalent of *donativum*. And if Paul really did have the imperial *donativum* in mind, it can only have been as a passing allusion; for it was not a particularly illuminating or edifying comparison. His own use of the word elsewhere (e.g. in 5.15, 16) is surely a much more probable clue to his meaning here.

ἐν Χριστῷ Ἰησοῦ τῷ κυρίῳ ἡμῶν. See on 5.1.

V. 3. A LIFE CHARACTERIZED BY FREEDOM FROM THE LAW'S CONDEMNATION (7.1–25)

The life promised for the man who is righteous by faith is, in the third place, described as a life characterized by freedom from the law, that is, from the law in the limited sense of the-law-as-condemning or the law's condemnation (cf. 8.1). The point is made in the first sub-section (7.1–6), which takes up and elucidates the statement 'you are not under the law, but under grace' made in 6.14. The second sub-section (7.7–25) is a necessary clarification of 7.1–6, intended to elucidate

---

[1] The suggestions in *TWNT* 5, p. 592 (H. W. Heidland), that there is a consciously intended contrast between 'death' and the idea of a wage meant to provide the means of life, and that, since ὀψώνια properly denotes not a once for all, but a recurring, payment, θάνατος cannot here mean just death as the end of life or as eschatological penalty but must also include the baleful effects which death produces before its time, the deadly shadow which it casts before itself over life, are both of them over-subtle.

[2] See Sanday and Headlam, p. 170; Zahn, p. 328; Michel, p. 163. For references to the *donativum* see, e.g., Tacitus, *Ann.* 12.41; 14.11; *Hist.* 1.5; Suetonius, *Aug.* 10; *Claud.* 10; *Nero* 7; Dio Cassius 56.32.2; 59.2.1ff; Josephus, *Ant.* 19.247.

certain matters relating to the law and to guard against possible misunderstanding.[1]

(i) *Freedom from the law's condemnation*
(7.1-6)

[1]Or are you ignorant, brethren, of the fact—it is to men who know the law that I am speaking—that the law has authority over a man so long as he lives? [2]For a married woman is bound by the law to her husband as long as he is living; but, if her husband dies, she is released from the law in so far as it binds her to her husband. [3]So then, while her husband is living, she will be accounted an adulteress, if she becomes another man's; but, if her husband dies, she is free from the law so that she is not an adulteress, if she becomes another man's. [4]Therefore, my brethren, you too were made dead to the law through the body of Christ, so that you might belong to another, even to him who has been raised from the dead, in order that we might bear fruit unto God. [5]For, when we were in the flesh, the sinful passions stimulated by the law were active in our members so that we bore fruit to death; [6]but now we have been released from the law, having died to that by which we were held, so that we serve in newness of the Spirit, not in oldness of the letter.

Paul has told the Roman Christians in 6.14 that they are 'not under the law, but under grace', in order to encourage them to obey the imperatives of 6.12-13. Now in 7.1-6 he elucidates that statement, showing how it is true, how it has come about that they are free from the law's condemnation. They have been freed from it by their death, that is, by the death which in God's sight and by God's gracious decision they themselves have died ('you . . . were made dead' in v. 4: cf. 'having died' in v. 6) in Christ's death on their behalf ('through the body of Christ' in v. 4). In this explanation what has been said in 6.2-11 and, behind that, in 3.21-26 and also in chapter 5 is of course presupposed.

Paul begins (v. 1) by appealing to the legal principle that the law's authority over a man lasts so long, but only so long, as he lives. Then in vv. 2 and 3 he gives an example which serves to clarify this principle by illustrating its corollary, namely, that the occurrence of a death effects a decisive change in respect of relationship to the law. Verse 4 is Paul's conclusion from v. 1 as clarified by vv. 2 and 3. In view of what has been said in vv. 1-3, the death which the Roman Christians have died must be understood to mean that they have been freed from the law's condemnation, so that they might henceforth belong to Christ, and, along with all other believers, render service to God. Verses 5 and 6, in which the

[1] In connexion with the whole of chapter 7 reference may be made to W. G. Kümmel, *Römer 7 und die Bekehrung des Paulus*, Leipzig, 1929.

use of the first person plural, introduced abruptly in v. 4, is
continued, are added in elucidation of v. 4. While v. 5 looks
back at the past from which we have been delivered, v. 6,
anticipating what is to be said in chapter 8, focuses attention
on the fact that, in consequence of their liberation from the
law's condemnation, believers serve God not in that oldness
which is the perverse way of legalism, of misunderstanding and
misuse of God's law, but in the God-given newness which is
the power of God's indwelling Spirit.

1. Ἢ ἀγνοεῖτε, ἀδελφοί, γινώσκουσιν γὰρ νόμον λαλῶ, ὅτι ὁ νόμος
κυριεύει τοῦ ἀνθρώπου ἐφ'ὅσον χρόνον ζῇ; The implication of the
formula ἢ ἀγνοεῖτε or ἢ οὐκ οἴδατε as used by Paul (6.3; 1 Cor
6.2, 9, 16, 19) seems always to be that, if the people addressed
really know—the assumption is that they surely must—the
truth which is about to be stated (in every case a ὅτι-clause
follows), then they ought to recognize the truth, or agree with
the sentiment, expressed or implicit in something that has
been said already (usually immediately before the formula is
introduced). It is generally agreed that here Paul looks back
as far as 6.14b, and this is surely right. We take it then that
the thought behind the use of the ἢ ἀγνοεῖτε formula here is
that, if those who are being addressed accept the conclusion
which is drawn in vv. 4–6 from the principle stated in the
ὅτι-clause of v. 1 and illustrated in vv. 2–3,[1] then they must
surely be able to understand and accept what was said in
6.14b together with—that this should be added, and that the
backward reference includes not only 6.14b but also the intermediate verses, seems probable—what has been said in
clarification of it in 6.15–23. Such would seem to be the
connexion of thought between this verse and its context.
But, while 7.1–6 is thus introduced as support for what has
already been said in the previous chapter, it is also, as a
statement in some detail of the Christian's freedom from the
law as condemning, a new paragraph of the exposition of the
life which the man who is righteous by faith is to live.

For ἀδελφοί see on 1.13. It is noteworthy that this address,
which has not been used since 1.13, occurs twice in this short
paragraph, here and in v. 4 (ἀδελφοί μου).

The parenthesis γινώσκουσιν γὰρ νόμον λαλῶ has been
variously interpreted, some taking the reference to be to
their knowledge of law in general (e.g. Sanday and Headlam,
p. 172), others taking it to be to their knowledge of Roman

---

[1] That the appeal is not just to the principle stated in v. 1, but to
the conclusion drawn from it, is clear, since the principle in itself
certainly does not prove the point.

law (e.g. B. Weiss), and others taking it to be to the OT law.
Of these interpretations the last is by far the most probable.[1]
Gentile Christians as well as Jewish could no doubt be assumed
to have some knowledge of the OT law. By γινώσκειν something more than mere acquaintance is probably meant—
some measure of understanding.

The ὅτι-clause sounds like a legal maxim (see on 6.7). The
meaning is that the law's authority over a man lasts so long,
but only so long, as he lives.

2-3. Paul goes on to give an illustration of the principle to
which he has just referred. The law binds a married[2] woman
to her husband; but the husband's death releases[3] her from
the law in so far as it binds her to her husband (see below).
While she would be accounted[4] an adulteress, were she to
marry another man[5] during her husband's life, if her husband
dies, she is free from the law (in so far as it binds her to her
husband),[6] and so is not an adulteress, if she marries another.

The phrase τοῦ νόμου τοῦ ἀνδρός has been understood in
different ways. Thus it has been understood as 'the law of the
husband' in the sense of that part of the law which deals with
the rights and duties of husbands (on the analogy of 'the law
of the leper' in Lev 14.2 and 'the law of the Nazirite' in
Num 6.13);[7] or as 'the law of her husband' in the sense of the
law which (or, in so far as it) binds her to her husband;[8] while
Barrett has suggested that τοῦ ἀνδρός should 'be taken in
apposition with' τοῦ νόμου (he explains: 'in the analogy as a
whole the husband represents the law').[9] Of these interpretations the last is surely extremely unlikely; for, had Paul really
wanted to insert such an interpretative hint at this point

[1] Cf. Aquinas, p. 95 (520): 'Sed hoc [that *lex naturalis* is meant] non
videtur esse secundum intentionem Apostoli qui, absolute et indeterminate de lege loquens, semper loquitur de lege Moysi'.
[2] For ὕπανδρος (in the NT only here) cf. LXX Prov 6.24,29; Ecclus 9.9;
Polybius 10.26.3; Plutarch, *Pel.* 9.2; Aelian, *N.A.* 3.42, etc. The similar
ὑπ' ἀνδρὸς οὖσα occurs in LXX Num 5.20,29.
[3] καταργεῖν (see on 3.3) is here, as also in v. 6, used in the passive with
ἀπό in the sense 'be released from' ('be taken out of the sphere of activity
of').
[4] For this sense of χρηματίζειν cf. Acts 11.26; Josephus, *Ant.* 8.157;
13.318; *B.J.* 2.488. For the word's interesting range of meanings see
LSJ, s.v. On the gnomic future see BDF, § 349 (1).
[5] For the expression γίνεσθαι ἀνδρί cf., e.g., LXX Num 36.11; Deut
24.2; Hos 3.3. It is the Hebrew idiom hāyetāh le (see BDB, s.v. היה II.2.h).
[6] The variant reading which adds τοῦ ἀνδρός here, though clearly to
be rejected, gives the correct meaning.
[7] Cf., e.g., Sanday and Headlam, p. 173; Gaugler 1, p. 189.
[8] Cf., e.g., Lagrange, p. 161; Michel, p. 165.
[9] p. 136.

and really been content to do so by simply placing one term in apposition to the other, he would surely at least have put the two terms in what (on this explanation) would be the natural order, i.e. τοῦ ἀνδρὸς τοῦ νόμου. Of the others the second seems rather more simple and straightforward than the first, and should probably be accepted.

It remains to ask what was Paul's intention in these two verses. From early times it has usually been assumed to be allegorical. On this assumption, the natural interpretation would seem to be to take the husband to represent the law and the woman the Christian or the company of believers as a whole[1] set free by the removal of the law to form a new union with Christ. But this interpretation comes up against a serious difficulty in the fact that in v. 4 Paul goes on to speak not of the death of the law (as on this interpretation one would expect) but of Christians' having died to the law. Its exponents have sought to meet the difficulty by suggesting that Paul refrained from speaking of the death of the law, as the logic of his allegory demanded, and spoke instead of Christians' having died to the law, in order to avoid offending Jewish sentiment.[2] In modern times another form of the allegorical interpretation has been proposed, according to which the husband stands not for the law but for the Christian's old self (ὁ παλαιὸς ἡμῶν ἄνθρωπος of 6.6), while the wife stands for the continuing self of the Christian which through the death of the old self is translated into a new condition of life.[3] But this seems extremely complicated and forced. It is not surprising that Dodd grew impatient at this point in his commentary; but it would have been wiser to lose patience with an unpromising line of interpretation than, becoming impatient with Paul, to decide that 'The illustration . . . has gone hopelessly astray. . . . We shall do best to ignore the illustration as far as may be, and ask what it is that Paul is really talking about in the realm of fact and experience'.[4] A less unpromising line is taken when vv. 2–3 are understood

---

[1] Cf., e.g., Chrysostom, col. 497 (. . . ἐν τάξει δὲ τῆς γυναικὸς τοὺς πιστεύοντας ἅπαντας). It is more difficult to take the reference to be to the individual Christian; for, as Kümmel has pointed out (op cit., p. 41), Paul nowhere else has the idea of the individual Christian as being married to Christ—in fact this is an idea which occurs nowhere else in the Bible (cf. H. S. Pretorius, *Bijdrage tot de exegese en de geschiedenis der exegese van Romeinen 7*, Amsterdam, 1915, p. 85).

[2] e.g., Chrysostom, col. 497f; Augustine, cols. 2069–70; Pelagius, p. 55 ('Noluit iuxta comparationem legem illis dicere mortuam, sed quod inter Iudaeos dicere non audebat, intellectui dereliquit'); Calvin, p. 138.

[3] e.g., Gifford; Sanday and Headlam, p. 172; Barth, *Shorter*, pp. 77ff.

[4] p. 120.

as a parable rather than as an allegory. But the decisive clue
to the right interpretation of these verses is the recognition
that they were not intended to be connected directly with
v. 4 but with v. 1.[1] They are not an allegory (nor yet a parable),
the interpretation of which is to be found in v. 4, but an
illustration designed to elucidate v. 1. Verse 4 is the conclusion
drawn from vv. 1–3 as a whole, that is, from v. 1 as clarified
by vv. 2–3: it is not an interpretation or application of vv. 2–3.
The rightness of this view of the matter is confirmed by the
fact that v. 4 is introduced by ὥστε, and not by οὕτως; for,
had Paul thought of v. 4 as interpreting vv. 2–3, it would
have been much more natural to introduce it by a word
expressive of similarity or correspondence,[2] than by a word
which (as used here) can only mark a conclusion drawn from
what has been said.[3] We take it then that these two verses
are simply intended as an illustration of the principle stated
in the ὅτι-clause of v. 1 or—rather more accurately—of its
corollary, namely, that the occurrence of a death effects a
decisive change in respect of relationship to the law.

4. ὥστε: 'Therefore', 'So' (inferential, not the 'so' which is
correlative to 'as', which in Greek would be οὕτως). Paul is
drawing his conclusion from the principle stated in v. 1 as
clarified by vv. 2 and 3; he is not treating his illustration as
an allegory to be interpreted.

ἀδελφοί μου. See on v. 1.

καὶ ὑμεῖς ἐθανατώθητε. In the case of Christians and their
relation to the law's condemnation also a death has occurred,
not, as one might in view of the foregoing illustration be
inclined to expect, the death of the law or of the law's condemnation, but the death of the Christians themselves which
is to be understood in the light of 6.2ff (see notes *in loc.*). Paul
uses here not ἀπεθάνετε (cf. 6.2) but ἐθανατώθητε, possibly
because the thought of Christ's being put to death on the
cross is in his mind,[4] more probably because he has in mind,
and wants to suggest to his readers, the fact that this blessed

---

[1] Cf. Kümmel, op. cit., p. 41.
[2] Cf. the use of οὕτως in, e.g., Mt 13.40, 49; 24.27; Mk 4.26.
[3] Gaugler's reference (1, p. 190) to ὥστε . . . καὶ ὑμεῖς as a 'comparison-
formula' (*Vergleichsformel*) is surely a mistake. See LSJ and Bauer, s.v.
ὥστε. German and English interpreters need to be on their guard against
the danger of being unconsciously misled by the fact that 'so,' which in
both languages is (in its sense of 'therefore') a correct translation of
ὥστε here, can also in both languages be used as correlative to the word
which introduces a comparison (in English 'as'), whereas ὥστε is not
so used.
[4] So Huby, p. 228.

death in the Christians' past is God's doing (cf. the similar passive, κατηργήθημεν, in v. 6).

τῷ νόμῳ: a dative of advantage or disadvantage (cf. BDF, §188 (2)). The death to sin (6.2ff) is necessarily also a death to the law's condemnation.[1]

διὰ τοῦ σώματος τοῦ Χριστοῦ: 'through the body of Christ', through His person put to death on the cross. The assumption that the idea of the Church as the body of Christ is also present here is unwarranted.[2] Their being made dead to the law's condemnation through the body of Christ is a matter of God's merciful decision: they died in His death in that the death which He died was died for them. Paul is not saying that they have a share in Christ's death because they now are united to Him (in His body), but that Christ died for them (and this means that they also died in God's sight) in order that they might be united to Him (cf. the following clause).

εἰς τὸ γενέσθαι ὑμᾶς ἑτέρῳ indicates the purpose for which they were put to death. They were thus set free from the condemnation pronounced by the law, in order that they might belong to Christ. The expression is less naturally explained as reflecting the preceding illustration, the union with Christ being presented in terms of marriage to a second husband, than (with Thomas Aquinas, Lipsius, Cornely et al.) as simply signifying the transference to another master.[3]

τῷ ἐκ νεκρῶν ἐγερθέντι stands in apposition to ἑτέρῳ, being added to clarify the reference to the risen Christ.

ἵνα καρποφορήσωμεν τῷ θεῷ is best taken as dependent on ἐθανατώθητε, in spite of the fact that this involves a harsh combination in the same sentence of the second and first persons plural. To take it as dependent on ἐγερθέντι (cf. the alternative punctuation given in the Nestle apparatus) would certainly make the transition to the first person easy, but the sense yielded would be less satisfactory. To make the ἵνα-clause dependent on γενέσθαι would also give a less satisfactory sense. A transition in successive sentences from the second person plural to the first or vice versa would, of course, present no difficulty (cf., for example, 6.14–16; 8.11–13, 15–16; 13.11, 13–14). Some (e.g. Sanday and Headlam,[4] Barrett[5]) maintain

---

[1] Cf. Augustine, De diversis quaestionibus ad Simplicianum 1, quaest, 1.17 (PL 40, col. 110): 'Sic ergo dictum est, Mortui estis legi, ac si diceretur, Mortui estis supplicio legis. . .' .

[2] Pace J. A. T. Robinson, The Body, London, 1952, p. 47. See also on 12.5.

[3] In this sentence the view expressed in the first two impressions is reversed.

[4] p. 174.

[5] p. 137.

that in using καρποφορεῖν here Paul had in mind the image of
bearing children; but, whether or not the illustration of v. 2f is
taken to be reflected in the clause εἰς τὸ γενέσθαι ὑμᾶς ἑτέρῳ,
we judge that this explanation of καρποφορήσωμεν is surely
to be rejected; for (i) the image of our bearing offspring to
God is altogether grotesque; (ii) had Paul had this image in
mind here, he would have written (τῷ) Χριστῷ and not
τῷ θεῷ, in view of the preceding clause; (iii) the same verb
is used in the next verse with τῷ θανάτῳ, and the idea of a
marriage to death would be quite foreign to the context. We
may compare the use of καρπός in 6.21f. The general sense
of καρποφορεῖν in the present verse is probably much the same
as is expressed by δουλεύειν in v. 6.

5f. ὅτε γὰρ ἦμεν ἐν τῇ σαρκί. The γάρ indicates the relation of
v. 5f as a whole to v. 4: the function of vv. 5 and 6 together is
to elucidate v. 4. In 2 Cor 10.3; Gal 2.20; Phil 1.22 (cf. 24:
ἐπιμένειν[1] τῇ σαρκί) ἐν σαρκί is used of the life which Christians
as well as other men must live in this world; but here Paul uses
ἐν τῇ σαρκί, as he uses ἐν σαρκί in 8.8, 9, to denote the condition
which for Christians belongs to the past. They are no longer in
the flesh in the sense of having the basic direction of their lives
determined and controlled by their fallen nature (cf. Paul's use
of κατὰ σάρκα περιπατεῖν in 8.4, of κατὰ σάρκα εἶναι in 8.5, and
of κατὰ σάρκα ζῆν in 8.12, 13), although the σάρξ in the sense of
fallen human nature is still an element—and a far from powerless element—in their lives (cf., e.g., 7.14, 18, 25). But, when
we were altogether under the domination of the flesh, then that
condition prevailed in our lives which the rest of v. 5 describes.

τὰ παθήματα τῶν ἁμαρτιῶν. The noun πάθημα, when it is used
of an emotion or affection, is in itself neutral. In the two places
in the NT where it occurs in this sense it is clear that the
reference is to bad affections or passions, in Gal 5.24 from the
fact that the παθήματα referred to are those which belong to
the σάρξ which has just been mentioned, and here from the
following τῶν ἁμαρτιῶν. The genitive could be either a genitive
of quality or an objective genitive ('which lead to sins'). In
either case, the significance of the plural is that it is concrete
acts of sin rather than sin as a condition or principle which are
intended.

τὰ διὰ τοῦ νόμου. The παθήματα τῶν ἁμαρτιῶν were stimulated
and intensified by the law. Calvin says in his comment on this
verse: 'The work of the law, in the absence of the Spirit, . . . is
to inflame our hearts still more, so that they burst forth into

---

[1] ἐν is read before τῇ σαρκί by 𝔭⁴⁶ B 𝕶 D G *al.*

such lustful desires', and adds that the 'perversity and lust' of man's corrupt nature 'break forth with greater fury, the more they are held back by the restraints of righteousness'.[1] Challenged by the law which claims man for God and for his neighbour, man's self-centredness—the sinful ego—recognizes that it is being called in question and attacked, and so seeks all the more furiously to defend itself.

ἐνηργεῖτο: 'worked', 'were active'. For the use of the middle compare 2 Cor 1.6; 4.12; Gal 5.6; Eph 3.20; Col 1.29; 1 Th 2.13; 2 Th 2.7.

ἐν τοῖς μέλεσιν ἡμῶν indicates the sphere of this activity. For the meaning of μέλη here see on 6.13.

εἰς τὸ καρποφορῆσαι τῷ θανάτῳ is better taken as consecutive than as final. The subject of καρποφορῆσαι which has to be understood is no doubt ἡμᾶς.[2] For the general idea compare 6.21c.

νυνί here does not mean merely 'as it is',[3] but has its temporal force. Used with the aorist, it can denote the beginning of a present, contrasted with a previous, state of affairs or action (cf. 5.11; 11.30, 31; Eph 3.5).[4] So here the reference is to the time when we came to believe in Christ as the beginning of our present state as believers.

κατηργήθημεν. The verb has here a similar sense to that which it had in v. 2.

ἀπὸ τοῦ νόμου. ὁ νόμος is here used in a limited sense—'the law (as condemning us)', 'the law('s condemnation)'. That this is what is mainly intended is suggested by the way in which Paul continues his argument in 8.1 with οὐδὲν ἄρα νῦν κατάκριμα τοῖς ἐν Χριστῷ Ἰησοῦ (7.7–25 is to be understood as a necessary clarification of 7.1–6). But perhaps there is the further thought of the law, in so far as, by men's misuse of it, it has become a bondage. That—pace many commentators—the meaning is not that we have been discharged from the law simpliciter is clear enough from v. 25b (cf. vv. 12 and 14a; also 3.31; 8.4; 13.8–10).

ἀποθανόντες[5] ἐν ᾧ κατειχόμεθα. It is natural to understand ἀποθανόντες by reference to ἐθανατώθητε in v. 4, and the fact that ἐθανατώθητε was followed by τῷ νόμῳ suggests that the

---

[1] p. 141.
[2] Though the Vulgate has the third person plural 'fructificarent'.
[3] So, e.g., Sanday and Headlam, p. 175.
[4] Cf. Bauer, s.v. νῦν 1.a.γ.
[5] The Western variant τοῦ θανάτου reflects the influence of 8.2. The reading ἀποθανόντος in Beza's edition of 1565, which is presupposed by the AV translation 'that being dead wherein we were held', has no manuscript authority apart from that of the minuscule 242.

τούτῳ or ἐκείνῳ to be supplied as antecedent to ᾧ must refer to the law, and this is in fact the view taken by most commentators, and it should probably be accepted. The other possibility is to take the neuter τούτῳ or ἐκείνῳ to be supplied as antecedent to ᾧ to refer to the flesh or the 'old man' (so Lipsius, Sanday and Headlam, Jülicher, Lagrange).[1] If the reference is to the law, it will be to the law in a limited sense, as in the main clause. The image suggested by κατειχόμεθα is that of captivity.

ὥστε δουλεύειν [ἡμᾶς]. Whether ἡμᾶς should be read or omitted is disputable; but, in either case, the sense must be the same. It is difficult to decide whether ὥστε δουλεύειν expresses (i) an actual result, or (ii) a potential result, or (iii) a purpose. The confidence of Sanday and Headlam that only (ii) is possible[2] is unjustified; for it is clear that ὥστε with the infinitive quite often indicates an actual consequence (e.g. Mt 13.2, 54; 15.31; Acts 1.19; Rom 15.19; Phil 1.13). On the whole it seems best to choose (i), as agreeing best with the course of the argument; for, while Paul is fully aware of the Christian's need of exhortation to live according to his faith (12.1–15.13) and of the painful fact of his continuing sinfulness (7.7–25), he nevertheless maintains that, if one is a Christian at all, one has the Spirit of Christ (8.9) and walks according to the Spirit (8.4). With δουλεύειν here τῷ θεῷ is, of course, to be understood. In accordance with the insight of 6.15–23, the new life is spoken of in terms of δουλεία.

ἐν καινότητι πνεύματος καὶ οὐ παλαιότητι γράμματος contains a double contrast, καινότης being opposed to παλαιότης (cf. 6.4 and 6; 2 Cor 3.6 and 14; Eph 4.22–24; Col 3.9f) and πνεῦμα to γράμμα (cf. 2.29; 2 Cor 3.6), while at the same time καινότης and πνεῦμα are linked together, and παλαιότης and γράμμα. The genitives πνεύματος and γράμματος are probably to be explained as genitives of apposition (so Sanday and Headlam[3]): in newness, that is, in the Spirit (cf. ἐν πνεύματι in 8.9 and κατὰ πνεῦμα in 8.4) and not in oldness, that is, according to the letter. Another possibility would be to understand the genitives as expressing origin: Paul would then be characterizing the newness as the gift of the Spirit and the oldness as the result of dependence on the mere letter. That Paul is not opposing the law as such and in itself to the Spirit is clear, since only a few verses later he affirms that the law is 'spiritual' (v. 14). He does not use 'letter' as a simple equivalent of 'the law'. 'Letter'

---

[1] Or to sin (so, e.g., Chrysostom, col. 498).
[2] p 175f.
[3] p. 176.

is rather what the legalist is left with as a result of his misunderstanding and misuse of the law. It is the letter of the law
in separation from the Spirit. But, since 'the law is spiritual'
(v. 14), the letter of the law in isolation from the Spirit is not
the law in its true character, but the law as it were denatured.
It is this which is opposed to the Spirit whose presence is the
true establishment of the law (cf. notes on 8.1ff). Life in the
Spirit is the newness of life which belongs to the new age: life
according to 'the letter' (in the sense which we have indicated)
belongs, by contrast, to this age which is passing away.

(ii) *A necessary clarification of what has been said*
concerning the law
(7.7–25)

⁷What then shall we say? Is the law sin? God forbid! but I should
not have come to know sin had it not been for the law; for indeed
I should not know coveting, had not the law said, 'Thou shalt not
covet'; ⁸but sin having obtained a base for its operations worked in
me through the commandment all manner of covetousness; for in
the absence of the law sin is dead. ⁹But I was alive once in the absence
of the law; but when the commandment came sin sprang to life, ¹⁰and
I died, and the commandment which was unto life proved to be, as
far as I was concerned, unto death. ¹¹For sin having obtained a base
of operations deceived me through the commandment and through
it killed me. ¹²So then in itself the law is holy, and the commandment
holy and righteous and good.
¹³Did then that which is good become death to me? God forbid!
but sin, in order that it might be manifest as sin, *was* working death
for me through that which is good, in order that sin might through
the commandment become sinful beyond measure. ¹⁴For we know
that the law is spiritual; but I am carnal, a slave under sin's power.
¹⁵For that which I work I do not acknowledge; for I do not practise
what I will, but I do what I hate. ¹⁶But if I do that which I do not
will, I am agreeing with the law that it is good. ¹⁷But, this being so,
it is then not I who work that which I do, but sin which dwells in
me. ¹⁸For I know that good does not dwell in me, that is, in my flesh;
for, while I can will to do that which is good, to work what is good
is beyond my reach. ¹⁹For I do not do the good which I will, but the
evil which I do not will, this I practise. ²⁰But, if I do what I do not
will, then in these circumstances it is not I who work it but sin
which dwells in me. ²¹So then I prove by experience the law that,
though I will to do what is good, it is that which is evil which is
within my reach. ²²For I, in so far as the inner man is concerned,
delight in God's law, ²³but I see in my members a different law,
which is waging war against the law of my mind and making me a
prisoner of the law of sin which is in my members.
²⁴Wretched man that I am! Who will deliver me from this body of
death? ²⁵Thanks be to God through Jesus Christ our Lord! So then
I myself serve with my mind the law of God, but with my flesh the
law of sin.

Several things which Paul has said in the course of his argument (5.20; 6.14 and 7.1–6, in particular, come to mind) could give the impression that the law is actually an evil, in some way to be identified with sin. So in the first of the three paragraphs of which this sub-section is made up (vv. 7–12) Paul seeks to deal with this possible misunderstanding. In v. 7 he repudiates the suggestion that the law is sin and asserts that, far from being sin, it is that which makes him recognize his sin for what it is. (Throughout this sub-section the first person singular is used. In the present summary we assume that Paul is not just speaking about his own experience, but is taking himself as representative, first (in vv. 7–13) of mankind generally, and then (in vv. 14–25) of Christians. We shall discuss the matter fully below.) In vv. 8–11 Paul goes on to explain that, while the law certainly is not sin, it is true that sin has been able to exploit it for its own evil purpose to deadly effect. Paul seems to have in mind here the narrative of Genesis 3, in which the divine commandment which is God's good and gracious gift for man's preservation is seen to be also an opportunity which the serpent can exploit in order to ruin man. Sin has wrought man's death through the commandment. So a true understanding of the situation with regard to the law must include the recognition of the fact that it has been effectively exploited by sin for sin's purpose, but must never lose sight of the fundamental truth, which is affirmed with emphasis in v. 12, that in itself the law is God's law, holy, righteous and good.

In the second paragraph (vv. 13–23) Paul deals with the false inference which can be drawn from what has been said in vv. 9–12, namely, that the law, which is truly good, is to blame for man's death. The truth is rather that sin has made use of the good thing in order to accomplish man's death. This is stated in v. 13, which also indicates that sin's exploitation of the law actually fulfils two elements of the divine purpose in giving the law, namely, that sin might be shown to be sin and that by means of the commandment its sinfulness might be enhanced. With v. 14, which introduces evidence in confirmation of what was said in v. 13, the past tenses give way to present, and, as the sequel makes clear, Paul is thinking specifically of Christians. The verses which follow depict vividly the inner conflict characteristic of the true Christian, a conflict such as is possible only in the man, in whom the Holy Spirit is active and whose mind is being renewed under the discipline of the gospel. In the man who understands the law not legalistically but in the light of Christ and so recognizes the real seriousness of its requirement, and who truly and sincerely wills to obey it, to do what is good and to avoid the evil, the man in whom the power of sin is really being seriously and resolutely challenged, in him the power of sin is clearly seen. The more he is renewed by God's Spirit, the more sensitive he becomes to the continuing power of sin over his life and the fact that even his very best activities are marred by the egotism still entrenched within him.

The third and final paragraph of the sub-section (vv. 24–25), in which the real anguish of severe and relentless warfare (not despair!), the earnest longing for final deliverance, thankful confidence in God, sincere commitment to God's law, and an honest recognition of the fact of continuing sinfulness, all come to expression and are held together, forms a conclusion to the verses (14–23) describing the conflict of the Christian life; and the fact that Paul sums them up in this way is an indication that he sees them not just as being support for what he has said in v. 13 but also as contributing an indispensable element of the description of the life promised for the man who is righteous by faith. In fact, the latter part of the sub-section has a dual role: on the one hand, it is an integral part of the necessary clarification of 7.1–6; on the other hand, it is to be related to chapter eight, as supplying an important insight without which what is said there would be very seriously misleading. 7.14–25 and chapter eight are necessary to each other. Neither, if read in isolation from the other, gives a true picture of the Christian life.

Paul's Use of the First Person Singular in 7.7–25. In view of the fact that there is a significant difference between vv. 7–13 and vv. 14–25 in that past tenses are characteristic of vv. 7–13, whereas in vv. 14–25 the present tense is used, we must consider these two passages separately.

As far as vv. 7–13 are concerned, the main suggestions which have to be considered are:

(i) that the passage is strictly autobiographical;

(ii) that Paul is using the first person singular to depict the experience of the typical Jewish individual;

(iii) that he is speaking in the name of Adam;

(iv) that he is presenting the experience of the Jewish people as a whole;

(v) that he speaks in the name of mankind as a whole;

(vi) that Paul is using the first person singular in a generalizing way without intending a specific reference to any particular individual or clearly defined group, in order to depict vividly the situation of man in the absence of the law and in its presence.

Of these, both (i) and (ii) should surely be rejected in spite of the support they have commanded in ancient and especially in modern times. The objections which lie against them, even when what is said in these verses is clearly recognized as being said from the point of view of Christian faith and not from that of the youthful Paul or of the typical young Jew, are, in our judgment, insuperable. The most obvious is the difficulty (pointed out by Origen)[1] of seeing how Paul could conceivably say either of himself or of any other Jew who had been circumcised on the eighth day ἐγὼ δὲ ἔζων χωρὶς νόμου ποτέ. The explanation, which is often given, that Paul is referring to the period before he became a bar-miṣwāh is unconvincing; for though it is true that the Jewish boy who had not yet become a bar-miṣwāh was not under obligation to keep the whole law, it would not be at all accurate to describe him as χωρὶς νόμου.[2]

While both (iv) and (v) may be said to contain elements of truth (for on the one hand Paul is certainly concerned with the OT law, and on the other hand what he is saying has a universal relevance), it seems probable that the choice should be between (iii) and (vi), or perhaps a modification of the latter. The view that Paul is specifically speaking in the name of Adam, maintained by Methodius,[3] Theodore of Mopsuestia,[4] and Theodoret[5] in the ancient Church, by Cajetan in the sixteenth century, and by Feine, Holtzmann, Dibelius, et al. in modern times, seems to us forced; but (unlike Kümmel)[6] we think there is little doubt that, when Paul was writing these verses, the narrative of Genesis 3 was present to his mind. That he should draw on the drama of Genesis 2 and 3 in depicting man's situation in relation to the Mosaic law is in no way surprising; for he has already indicated in 5.14 his awareness of the correspondence of the commandment of Gen 2.17 to the Mosaic law. The most probable explanation of Paul's use of the first person in vv. 7-13 would seem to be a modified form of (vi). We may recognize Paul's use of the first person singular here as an example of the general use of the first person

---

[1] col. 1082.
[2] Kümmel, op. cit., p. 81, cites Philo, Leg. ad Gaium 210, which refers to Jews as being taught the law ἐκ πρώτης ἡλικίας, and 115 (ἐξ αὐτῶν τρόπον τινὰ σπαργάνων); Josephus, Contra Ap. 2.178 (ἀπὸ τῆς πρώτης αἰσθήσεως).
[3] PG 18, cols. 296ff.
[4] cols. 809ff.
[5] col. 117.
[6] op. cit., p. 86f. For an important answer to Kümmel's objection that Paul's citation of the tenth commandment shows that he does not have Genesis 2 and 3 in mind, see S. Lyonnet, ' "Tu ne convoiteras pas" (Rom 7.7)', in Neotestamentica et Patristica, pp. 157-65.

singular;[1] but at the same time we shall probably be right to assume that his choice of this form of speech is, in the present case, due not merely to a desire for rhetorical vividness but also to his deep sense of personal involvement,[2] his consciousness that in drawing out the general truth he is disclosing the truth about himself. We may also accept that in his description he draws upon the fundamental narrative of Genesis 2 and 3.

We turn now to vv. 14–25. With regard to the first person singular in these verses we may distinguish at least seven possibilities:

(i) that it is autobiographical, the reference being to Paul's present experience as a Christian;

(ii) that it is autobiographical, the reference being to his past experience (before his conversion) as seen by him at the time referred to;

(iii) that it is autobiographical, the reference being to his pre-conversion past but as seen by him now in the light of his Christian faith;

(iv) that it presents the experience of the non-Christian Jew, as seen by himself;

(v) that it presents the experience of the non-Christian Jew, as seen through Christian eyes;

(vi) that it presents the experience of the Christian who is living at a level of the Christian life which can be left behind, who is still trying to fight the battle in his own strength;

(vii) that it presents the experience of Christians generally, including the very best and most mature.

We may set (ii) aside at once on the ground that what is said in these verses is altogether contrary to the verdict which, according to Phil 3.6b (cf. Gal 1.14), Paul before his conversion passed upon his own life.[3] And (iv) may also be set aside, as inconsistent with the picture of Jewish self-complacency which Paul gives in chapter 2.[4] Against (iii), and also against (ii), the use of present tenses throughout vv. 14–25 weighs heavily; for the use of the present is here sustained too consistently and for too long and contrasts too strongly with the

---

[1] Cf. Ambrosiaster, col. 109: 'Sub sua persona quasi generalem agit causam'.

[2] Cf. Michel, p. 170: '. . . von einer an seine Person gebundene Erfahrung'.

[3] It is clear that Phil 3.6b cannot be Paul's Christian view of his former life: it must reflect his pre-conversion view of himself.

[4] For Jewish complacency cf. Mk 10.20; and see SB 1, p. 814. It is true that a more pessimistic view is to be found in 2 Esdras; but this does not seem to have been the characteristic view of Paul's contemporaries.

past tenses characteristic of vv. 7–13 to be at all plausibly explained as an example of the present used for the sake of vividness in describing past events which are vividly remembered. Moreover v. 24 would be highly melodramatic, if it were not a cry for deliverance from present distress. A further objection to (iii), which also lies against (ii) and (iv) and (v) and also against (vi), is the order of the sentences in vv. 24–25. Verse 25b is an embarrassment to those who see in v. 24 the cry of an unconverted man or of a Christian living on a low level of Christian life and in v. 25a an indication that the desired deliverance has actually arrived, since, coming after the thanksgiving, it appears to imply that the condition of the speaker after deliverance is just the same as it was before it. All the attempts so far made to get over this difficulty have about them an air of desperation.

The difficulty in the way of accepting (i) or (vii), which has been felt by very many from early days on, is of course that the acceptance of either of them has seemed to involve altogether too dark a view of the Christian life and, in particular, to be incompatible with what is said of the believer's liberation from sin in 6.6, 14, 17f, 22 and 8.2. And this objection to both (i) and (vii) has seemed to a great many interpreters completely conclusive. But there have also been those who have accepted one or other of these two explanations. They include, among the Greeks, Methodius,[1] the Latins, Ambrose,[2] Ambrosiaster,[3] and Augustine,[4] in the Middle Ages, Aquinas,[5]

---

[1] *Ex libro de resurrectione*, in *PG* 18, cols. 299ff.

[2] *De Abraham* 2.6.27, in *PL* 14, col. 467: 'Cum caro repugnat adversus spiritum, et spiritus adversus carnem, non mediocris pugna est, quando ipse Apostolus vas electionis dominicae dicit: Video legem carnis meae repugnantem legi mentis meae, et captivantem me in lege peccati, quod est in membris meis. Sedare hanc pugnam ipse nequiverat, et ideo ad Christum confugit dicens: Infelix ego homo: quis me liberabit de corpore mortis hujus?'

[3] cols. 111–16.

[4] Augustine at one time understood Paul to be speaking in the name of the unregenerate man (e.g. *PL* 35, col. 2071: 'homo . . . sub lege positus ante gratiam'), but later he retracted his earlier view (see especially *Retract.* 1.23.1 and 2.1.1 (*PL* 32, cols. 620f and 629f)) and maintained that Paul was speaking in his own name as a Christian.

[5] So, in commenting on v. 14, he mentions Augustine's two different explanations, but states his preference for the later one (p. 101 (558): 'Et potest hoc verbum dupliciter exponi. Uno quidem modo, ut Apostolus loquatur in persona hominis in peccato existentis. Et ita hoc Augustinus exponit in libro *LXXXIII quaestionum*. Postea vero in libro *Contra Iulianum*, exponit hoc ut Apostolus intelligatur loqui in persona sua, id est, hominis sub gratia constituti. Prosequamur ergo declarando qualiter haec verba et sequentia diversimode possunt utroque modo exponi, quamvis secunda expositio melior sit').

the sixteenth century Reformers,[1] and, among recent commentators, Barth,[2] Nygren,[3] Barrett,[4] Murray.[5] That it is these latter interpreters rather than the others who have rightly understood Paul's mind, we do not doubt; for it is only along the lines of either (i) or (vii) that we can really do justice to the text. The man who speaks here is one who wills the good and hates the evil (vv. 15, 16, 19, 20), who as far as his inner man is concerned delights in God's law (v. 22), who serves it with his mind (v. 25b). Not so does Paul describe the unregenerate man. It is particularly instructive to set the statement in v. 25b ('So then I myself with my mind serve (δουλεύω) the law of God') alongside 6.17, 18, 20, according to which the Roman Christians were δοῦλοι of sin before their conversion, but have now become the slaves (ἐδουλώθητε) of righteousness, and also 8.7 which states that the φρόνημα of the flesh is not subject to God's law and indeed cannot be. In the ego which wills the good and hates the evil, in the νοῦς of vv. 23 and 25b, in the 'inner man' of v. 22, we must surely recognize the human self which is being renewed by God's Spirit, not the self, or any part of the self, of the still unconverted man. In fact, a struggle as serious as that which is here described can only take place where the Spirit of God is present and active (cf. Gal 5.17).

With regard to the objection that it is incredible that Paul should speak of a Christian as πεπραμένος ὑπὸ τὴν ἁμαρτίαν, we ought to ask ourselves whether our inability to accept this expression as descriptive of a Christian is not perhaps the result of failure on our part to realize the full seriousness of the ethical demands of God's law (or of the gospel).[6] Are we not all of us all too prone still to understand them legalistically, as did the young man who could say: 'Master, all these things have I observed from my youth' (Mk 10.20)? And is it not

---

[1] e.g. Luther, pp. 200ff; Calvin, pp. 146ff.
[2] 1933, pp. 257ff; *Shorter*, pp. 84–87.
[3] pp. 284ff.
[4] pp. 146ff.
[5] I, pp. 256ff.
[6] The way in which Kümmel dismisses Romans 12–16 as irrelevant to the interpretation of chapter 7 on the ground that in these chapters 'von ethischen und praktischen Fragen die Rede ist, die zum mindesten äusserlich mit dem ersten Teil nur lose zusammenhängen' and states: 'Wollen wir also die Stellung des 7. Kapitels im Ganzen des Römerbriefs erörtern, so brauchen wir nur Kap. 1–11 zu betrachten' (op. cit., p. 5) is surely most revealing. It would seem to indicate the presence of a blind-spot in the author's theological thinking serious enough to have bedevilled a good deal of the discussion in what is in many respects a valuable and informative book.

true that the more the Christian is set free from legalistic ways of thinking about God's law and so sees more and more clearly the full splendour of the perfection towards which he is being summoned, the more conscious he becomes of his own continuing sinfulness, his stubborn all-pervasive egotism, and also of the fact that there is none among his Christian acquaintance—even among those whose real sincerity shines most brightly—of whom it would be untrue to say:

> 'but I can see his pride
> Peep through each part of him'?[1]

On the question of the compatibility of interpretations (i) and (vii) with various statements in other parts of Romans the reader must be referred to the detailed commentary on this passage and on the other passages concerned (e.g. on 8.2).

As to the relatively unimportant question whether (i) or (vii) is to be preferred, it seems, in view of the fact that in vv. 7–13 it is hardly possible to understand the first person singular as strictly autobiographical, rather more natural to accept the latter than the former. But again, as with regard to vv. 7–13, we may assume that Paul's use of the first person singular throughout vv. 14–25 reflects not only his desire to state in a forceful and vivid manner what is generally true—in this case, of Christians—but also his sense of his own deep personal involvement in what he is saying.

7. Τί οὖν ἐροῦμεν; As in 6.1 and 9.14, this formula introduces, as a preliminary to the statement of Paul's own understanding of the matter in hand, an indication of a false inference which could be drawn from what has just been said. See further on 3.5.

ὁ νόμος ἁμαρτία; A number of things Paul has said in the course of the epistle could indeed suggest that the law is actually an evil, in some way to be identified with sin. The last six verses and 5.20 and 6.14, in particular, come to mind. It is time for Paul to deal with this possible false conclusion. That the danger of misunderstanding here was not merely theoretical, subsequent Church history was to prove again and again.

If ἀλλά indicates the relation of what follows to μὴ γένοιτο, the thought will be that what follows limits its force: while the conclusion ὁ νόμος ἁμαρτία must be rejected, it is nevertheless true that . . . (cf. Kümmel[2]). But it is probably better

---

[1] Shakespeare, *King Henry the Eighth* 1.1.68f.
[2] p. 47: so too Michel, p. 172.

to understand ἀλλά as indicating the relation of what follows to ὁ νόμος ἁμαρτία (compare the ἀλλά after μὴ γένοιτο in 3.31), the thought being of the opposition between what is about to be said and the false inference that the law is sin.

τὴν ἁμαρτίαν οὐκ ἔγνων εἰ μὴ διὰ νόμου· τήν τε γὰρ ἐπιθυμίαν οὐκ ᾔδειν εἰ μὴ ὁ νόμος ἔλεγεν· οὐκ ἐπιθυμήσεις. It is possible to take οὐκ ἔγνων as a statement of fact ('it was only through the law that I came to know . . .'), but more natural to take it, as well as οὐκ ᾔδειν,[1] as hypothetical. It is doubtful whether any distinction of meaning between γινώσκειν and εἰδέναι was intended here; but the difference of tense should not be ignored ('I should not have come to know', 'I should not know'). The use of the pluperfect of οἶδα, which is equivalent to an imperfect, implies that the action of the verb is still continuing: so this sentence may be compared with the statements in the present tense in vv. 14ff. Both ἔγνων and ᾔδειν are often taken to refer to practical knowledge, experience (compare the use of γινώσκειν in 2 Cor 5.21).[2] If this is correct, the thought expressed here may be compared with that expressed in 5.20; 7.5 (τὰ παθήματα τῶν ἁμαρτιῶν τὰ διὰ τοῦ νόμου), and of course vv. 8 and 9b. But, since Paul elsewhere recognizes that even in the absence of the law men do actually sin (cf., e.g., 2.12; 5.12–14), he can hardly have meant to imply by τὴν ἁμαρτίαν οὐκ ἔγνων εἰ μὴ διὰ νόμου here that there is no experience of sin at all except through the law, or by τήν τε γὰρ ἐπιθυμίαν οὐκ ᾔδειν εἰ μὴ ὁ νόμος ἔλεγεν· οὐκ ἐπιθυμήσεις that in the absence of the tenth commandment men do not have experience of coveting. Rather, we should have to understand him to mean that, in comparison with experience of sin in the presence of the law, the experience of it where the law is not present would scarcely count as experience of sin, so much more serious is the experience where the law is given. But this is rather forced. It is more straightforward to understand Paul's meaning to be that, while men do actually sin in the absence of the law, they do not fully recognize sin for what it is, apart from the law (cf. 3.20),[3] and that, while they do indeed experience covetousness even though they do not know the tenth commandment, it is only in the light of that commandment that they recognize their

---

[1] οὐκ ᾔδειν has also sometimes been explained as factual, but in view of the form of what follows it this is hardly possible.

[2] e.g., by Lagrange, p. 168; Michel, p. 172; Gaugler 1, p. 199; Barrett, p. 141.

[3] The point made by v. 7a is then well expressed in Ambrosiaster's words (col. 108): 'Non ergo peccatum est Lex, sed index peccati'.

coveting for what it is—that coveting which God forbids, a deliberate disobeying of God's revealed will. On this interpretation v. 8 does not repeat more explicitly something which has already been said in v. 7, but makes a different point (though one that has been hinted at in v. 5).

Paul introduces the tenth commandment as an example, and it is a particularly instructive example in that it directs attention to the inward root of man's outward wrong-doing. The formulation of the commandment in Exod 20.17 and Deut 5.21 only refers explicitly to covetousness in the modern English sense of the word, that is, the culpable desire of anything which belongs to another man. Paul's omission to specify any object of οὐκ ἐπιθυμήσεις both here and in 13.9 could be explained as a simple abbreviation (the rest of the commandment being intended to be understood); but more probably it reflects the consciousness, which is evidenced in the OT and in Judaism as well as elsewhere in the NT,[1] of the sinfulness of all inordinate desires as the expression of man's self-centredness and self-assertion over against God. We may compare 4 Macc 2.6, where . . . μὴ ἐπιθυμεῖν εἴρηκεν ἡμᾶς ὁ νόμος . . . could, since the commandment has been given in the previous verse in a fuller form, be taken to be a simple abbreviation, but in view of the general context is more probably a generalizing of the commandment like that to be found in Philo, *Decal.* 142ff.[2]

8. ἀφορμὴν δὲ λαβοῦσα ἡ ἁμαρτία διὰ τῆς ἐντολῆς κατειργάσατο ἐν ἐμοὶ πᾶσαν ἐπιθυμίαν. ἀφορμή means 'starting-point', and hence comes to have such meanings as 'origin', 'occasion', 'pretext', 'base of operations' or 'bridgehead'. In the NT, besides its two occurrences in this chapter, it is found in 2 Cor 5.12; 11.12; Gal 5.13; 1 Tim 5.14, and in a variant at Lk 11.54. The expression ἀφορμὴν λαμβάνειν is found as early as Isocrates,

[1] In the NT ἐπιθυμία and ἐπιθυμεῖν are sometimes used of a good desire (e.g. Matt 13.17; Phil 1.23; 1 Tim 3.1) or a desire that is natural and legitimate (e.g. Lk 15.16; 16.21), but more often of desires which are bad.

[2] On the subject of ἐπιθυμία, ἐπιθυμεῖν, see further F. Büchsel, in *TWNT* 3, pp. 168–72; also S. Lyonnet, ' "Tu ne convoiteras pas" (Rom 7.7)', in *Neotestamentica et Patristica*, pp. 157–65. The radicalization and generalization of the tenth commandment was taken just about as far as possible by question 113 of the Heidelberg Catechism: '*What is required in the tenth commandment?* That even the least inclination or thought against any of God's commandments should never enter into our heart; but that with our whole heart we are continually to hate all sin, and to take pleasure in all righteousness' (as translated in T. F. Torrance, *The School of Faith: the catechisms of the Reformed Church*, London, 1959, p. 92).

and is common in Hellenistic Greek (cf. ἀφορμὴν εὑρίσκειν). *Pace* Lagrange, Huby, Gaugler, Michel, Barrett, Kümmel (op. cit., p. 44), AV, Ostervald, RSV, NEB, *inter al.*, it is preferable to connect διὰ τῆς ἐντολῆς with κατειργάσατο (so Vulgate, Bengel, Sanday and Headlam, RV, Weymouth, Segond *et al.*). For (i) the order of the words favours it (cf. the order of the words in v. 13b); (ii) the use of the preposition διά also favours it (διά is natural with κατειργάσατο (cf. v. 13b), but not with ἀφορμὴν λαβοῦσα, for Paul surely intends to suggest not that the commandment is the means by which sin obtained an ἀφορμή but that the commandment actually is that ἀφορμή); (iii) in v. 11 (which is substantially similar to v. 8a), where διά occurs twice, the fact that δι' αὐτῆς must be taken with ἀπέκτεινεν makes it natural to connect διὰ τῆς ἐντολῆς with ἐξηπάτησεν rather than with λαβοῦσα; and (iv) the description of sin in v. 13b as διὰ τοῦ ἀγαθοῦ μοι κατεργαζομένη θάνατον (it is to be noted that v. 13b is explicatory of what has been said in vv. 7–12) is further support.

In the divine commandment οὐκ ἐπιθυμήσεις sin received its chance, its foothold in man's life, its bridgehead, which it was able to take advantage of, to make use of, in order to produce in man all sorts of inordinate desires. How was this so? Why was the divine commandment an opportunity for sin? We shall not do justice to Paul's thought here, if we settle for a merely psychological explanation along the lines of Ovid's 'Nitimur in vetitum semper cupimusque negata',[1] the proverbial wisdom that speaks of forbidden fruits as sweetest. It is rather that the merciful limitation imposed on man by the commandment and intended to preserve his true freedom and dignity can be misinterpreted and misrepresented as a taking away of his freedom and an attack on his dignity, and so can be made an occasion of resentment and rebellion against the divine Creator, man's true Lord. In this way sin can make use of the commandment not to covet as a means of arousing all manner of covetousness. It is to be noted that in this verse and in the following verses sin is personified,[2] being spoken of as an active power with a malicious purpose: Paul no doubt has the narrative of Genesis 3 in mind. In fact, these verses are best understood as exposition of the Genesis narrative. It was perhaps with that narrative in mind that Paul chose the tenth commandment as his example; for there is a specially close relationship between the tenth commandment, understood in the generalized way we have noted (which brings it into close

[1] *Am.* 3.4.17.
[2] See on 5.12; 6.12ff.

contact with the first commandment), and the prohibition of Gen 2.17, and between the ἐπιθυμία which the commandment forbids and what is described in Gen 3.6 (with 'ye shall be as God'—Gen 3.5—in the background).

χωρὶς γὰρ νόμου ἁμαρτία νεκρά. Even without the law sin is indeed present, but it is inactive—or at least relatively so.[1] For this use of νεκρός in the sense of 'inactive' compare Jas 2.17, 26.[2] In the absence of the law sin is relatively powerless (compare 1 Cor 15.56: ἡ δὲ δύναμις τῆς ἁμαρτίας ὁ νόμος). In the Genesis narrative the serpent was only able to attack man because the commandment of Gen 2.17 had been given. The contrast between νεκρά here and ἀνέζησεν in the next verse well suits the serpent lying motionless and hidden, and then stirring itself to take advantage of its opportunity. 'Nothing', Leenhardt has observed,[3] 'resembles a dead serpent more than a living serpent so long as it does not move!'

9f. ἐγὼ δὲ ἔζων χωρὶς νόμου ποτέ. Calvin gave a strikingly daring interpretation of this sentence, referring it to the time before Paul's conversion, when, though the law was indeed very much before his eyes, he did not properly understand it but imagined that he was fulfilling all its requirements (cf. Phil 3.6b). According to Calvin, Paul refers to himself as having been 'without the law' during the time in which he did not understand it aright.[4] Others have thought of Paul's boyhood before he became a 'son of the commandment'. But much more likely than either of these explanations is the view that Paul is using the first person in a general sense, and refers to man's situation before the giving of the law, along with which Paul probably has in mind the state of man pictured in Gen 1.28ff. In view of the contrast with ἀπέθανον in v. 10, it is probable that ζῆν is used, not in the weak sense of 'pass one's life', but in the strong sense of 'be alive'. In the primal state described in Genesis 1 man 'was alive', and in the time before the law was given through Moses, while man certainly could not be said to be alive in the full sense which ζῆν has for example in 1.17 or 8.13, he may be said to have been alive in the sense that his condition then was life, in comparison with his condition after the law had been received[5] (this seems a

---

[1] Cf. Augustine (PL 35, col. 2070): 'Quod autem dicit, Sine Lege enim peccatum mortuum est, non quia non est, dixit mortuum est, sed quia latet: . . .'
[2] Gaugler, 1, p. 201, compares also the use in Rom 6.11; but that is rather different.
[3] p. 186.   [4] p. 144.
[5] It was so, as far as the period between Adam and Moses was concerned, only in this relative sense; for, according to 5.13–14, during

more natural interpretation than to take the point to be that, not yet knowing himself to be a sinner, he seemed to himself to be possessed of life).[1]

In ἐλθούσης δὲ τῆς ἐντολῆς we may see a double reference—both to the giving of the law represented by the tenth commandment (hence the use of ἐντολή rather than νόμος) and also to the commandment of Gen 2.16f.

ἡ ἁμαρτία ἀνέζησεν: 'sin sprang to life'. The verb does not here have its proper meaning ('return to life', 'be alive again', as, e.g. in Lk 15.24), but means simply 'come to life'.

ἐγὼ δὲ ἀπέθανον. Compare 5.12, 14; 6.23; Gen 2.17b. Though he continues to live, he is dead—being under God's sentence of death (cf. v. 24b). Physical death, when it comes, is but the fulfilment of the sentence already passed. It need scarcely be said that the death referred to here is, of course, something entirely different from the good death of 6.2, 7, 8; 7.4.

καὶ εὑρέθη μοι ἡ ἐντολὴ ἡ εἰς ζωήν, αὕτη εἰς θάνατον. The true and proper purpose alike of the commandment of Gen 2.16f and of the tenth commandment (representing the whole law) was that man might have life.[2] But the actual effect of the commandment has been death.[3]

11. As in v. 8, it is better to connect διὰ τῆς ἐντολῆς with the following indicative than with the participle λαβοῦσα.

ἐξηπάτησεν. In LXX Gen 3.13 the woman says: Ὁ ὄφις ἠπάτησέν με, . . ., but the compound verb ἐξαπατᾶν, which is used here, is also used by Paul in 2 Cor 11.3 (cf. 1 Tim 2.14), where he is quite definitely echoing Gen 3.13. In Genesis 3 the serpent is represented as deceiving the woman in at least three respects: first, by distorting and misrepresenting the divine commandment by drawing attention only to the negative part of the commandment and ignoring the positive (Gen 3.1b: contrast 2.16f, in which 'Of every tree of the garden thou mayest freely eat' is included in what 'the LORD God commanded the man')[4]; secondly, by making her believe that God

that time death already reigned. What Paul is here concerned to bring out is the fact that fallen man is much more 'morti obligatus'—to use Aquinas's phrase (p. 100 (548))—in the presence of the law than in its absence.

[1] Cf. Augustine's 'vivere mihi videbar' contrasted with 'mortuum me esse cognovi' (PL 35, col. 2070).

[2] See, e.g., Gen 2.17b; Lev 18.5; Deut 30.15ff; and for Paul's expression cf. Ps. Sol. 14.2 (. . . ἐν νόμῳ, ᾧ ἐνετείλατο ἡμῖν εἰς ζωὴν ἡμῶν).

[3] For this use of the passive of εὑρίσκειν in the sense 'prove to be' cf. 1 Cor 4.2; 15.15; 2 Cor 5.3; Gal 2.17. See further Bauer, s.v. εὑρίσκειν, 2; BDB, s.v. מָצָא, Niph. 2.f. The participle οὖσα is to be supplied with εἰς θάνατον.

[4] Cf. Leenhardt, p. 188f, n. ‡ (Fr.: p. 108f, n. 3).

would not punish disobedience by death (v. 4); and thirdly, by using the very commandment itself (actually deceiving and seducing her by means of God's commandment—διὰ τῆς ἐντολῆς ἐξηπάτησεν), in order to insinuate doubts about God's good will and to suggest the possibility of man's asserting himself in opposition to God (v. 5). The case with the law of Israel is similar. Sin deceives man concerning the law, distorting it and imposing a false image of it on his understanding, and also deceives him by means of the law, in particular by making use of it in order to suggest that man is in a position so to fulfil it as to put God under an obligation to himself. Thus sin by deception succeeds in accomplishing man's death by means of that which God gave 'unto life'—δι' αὐτῆς ἀπέκτεινεν.

12. ὥστε introduces the conclusion to be drawn from the argument of the preceding verses—'So then'. This verse is Paul's final and definitive reply to the question raised in v. 7a.

ὁ μὲν νόμος: 'the law itself' or 'the law for its part'. The μέν is not followed by a δέ; but there is an implicit contrast between the law and sin. The presence of the law has actually resulted in death for man, but for this result the law is not at all to blame. (It is no more to blame for this result than is the gospel for the fact that those who reject it or try to make use of it for their own evil purposes come under a severer condemnation than would have been theirs, had they never heard the gospel.)[1] The blame is to be laid at sin's door.

ἅγιος. The law is holy. For Paul, as for Jesus, it is God's law (cf. 7.22, 25; 8.7; 1 Cor 7.19; Mt 15.3, 6; Mk 7.8f, etc.),[2] deriving from Him and bearing the unmistakable marks of its origin and authority.

ἡ ἐντολή would, of course, be appropriate, if the commandment of Gen 2.16f were intended; but here in Paul's definitive answer to the question ὁ νόμος ἁμαρτία; the reference is no doubt to the individual commandments contained in the law. Paul virtually repeats his statement that ὁ . . . νόμος ἅγιος, and then piles up the adjectives, because he wants to make his denial of the false inference that the law is sin as strong and emphatic as possible. Not only the law as a whole, but also each individual commandment it contains, is holy.

δικαία. God's commandments are just,[3] both in that they require just conduct among men and also in that, being

---

[1] Cf. the interesting discussion in Chrysostom, col. 500f, in the course of which he appeals to Jn 15.22.

[2] On the Rabbinic understanding of the holiness of the law reference may be made to *TWNT* 1, p. 100.

[3] Cf. especially Deut 4.8.

merciful and not burdensome, they bear witness to God's own justice.

ἀγαθή. They are good, in that they are intended for men's benefit (cf. εἰς ζωήν in v.10).

It is difficult to understand how, in the face of this verse, so many interpreters of Paul can persist in treating as axiomatic the assumption that he regarded the law as an enemy in the same class with sin and death (cf., e.g., the heading of Rom 5.12–7.25 in JB—'Deliverance from sin and death and law').

13. Τὸ οὖν ἀγαθὸν ἐμοὶ ἐγένετο θάνατος; The new paragraph begins with a question parallel to that raised in v. 7. For the Rabbinic treatment of 'the good' as a designation of the law (e.g. *Aboth* 6.3) reference may be made to SB 1, p. 809; but here the use of τὸ ἀγαθόν picks up the ἀγαθή of v. 12, as the use of θάνατος picks up the ἀπέθανον and εἰς θάνατον of v. 10 and the ἀπέκτεινεν of v. 11. If the law is good and yet death has resulted from its presence, does this mean that that which is good has become death to me—that it is to blame for my death? To this question as to that in v. 7, the answer is the emphatic denial **μὴ γένοιτο.** The good thing is certainly not to blame for my death.

ἀλλὰ ἡ ἁμαρτία, ἵνα φανῇ ἁμαρτία, διὰ τοῦ ἀγαθοῦ μοι κατεργαζομένη θάνατον, ἵνα γένηται καθ' ὑπερβολὴν ἁμαρτωλὸς ἡ ἁμαρτία διὰ τῆς ἐντολῆς. The sentence is incomplete, and ἐμοὶ ἐγένετο θάνατος has to be supplied from the earlier part of the verse, or else ἐγένετο understood with κατεργαζομένη. On the whole, the latter alternative seems simpler (cf. the Vulgate: 'operatum est').[1] The true conclusion to be drawn is not that the good thing is responsible for my death but that sin made use of the good thing in order to accomplish my death. The sentence further contains two final clauses, ἵνα φανῇ ἁμαρτία and ἵνα γένηται, κ.τ.λ., the former of them expressing the purpose that sin might be shown to be sin (by the fact of its misusing God's good gift to men), the latter expressing the further purpose that by means of the commandment sin's sinfulness might actually be enhanced.[2] These purposes are God's, though they are neither the whole, nor yet the ultimate element, of God's intention in

---

[1] If, however, the former alternative is preferred, the question arises whether διὰ τοῦ ἀγαθοῦ μοι κατεργαζομένη θάνατον is to be connected with what precedes ('But sin (became death to me), in order that it might be shown to be sin, by working death to me by means of that which is good' . . .'—cf. RV) or with what follows ('But sin (became death to me), in order that it might be shown to be sin, working death to me by means of that which is good, in order that sin might become . . .'). Of these the former should probably be preferred.

[2] καθ' ὑπερβολήν (cf. 1 Cor 12.31; 2 Cor 1.8; 4.17; Gal 1.13) is adverbial and qualifies ἁμαρτωλός, here used as an adjective.

giving the law.[1] But the fact that they are embraced within God's intention does not mean that God and His law are to blame for man's death, any more than the fact that it was part of His purpose in sending His Son into the world that men's sin should be revealed in its true colours as enmity to God by the reaction which Christ's ministry of love would provoke means that God is to blame for the rejection and crucifixion of Christ. The two final clauses are an indication that the dire results of men's encounter with the law, so far from being a proof of the triumph of sin or of the imperfection of the law, are a sign that God's purpose finally and completely to overthrow sin is being advanced.

14. οἴδαμεν γάρ. The reading of οἴδαμεν as οἶδα μέν, adopted in Jerome, *Contra Jovin.* 1.37, has been accepted by some modern commentators; but it is surely to be rejected. The argument supporting it on the ground of the prominence of the first person singular in vv. 7–25, which at first sight seems very impressive, is seen on closer consideration to be far from cogent; for what is required at this point in Paul's argument as support (γάρ) for the contention of v. 13 is not the confession of the ἐγώ of this passage, but a statement which it can be assumed will command the general assent of Paul's readers— in fact, the sort of statement which Paul is in the habit of introducing by οἴδαμεν.[2] For οἴδαμεν γάρ compare 8.22; 2 Cor 5.1; also οἴδαμεν δέ in 2.2; 3.19; 8.28; 1 Tim 1.8. See note on 2.2. It may also be asked whether Paul is really likely to have written οἶδα μέν . . . ἐγὼ δὲ . . .[3] The reason for γάρ here is that the statement it introduces is intended as support for the contention of the previous verse as a whole.

ὁ νόμος πνευματικός ἐστιν is basically an affirmation of the divine origin of the law, the meaning of which may be illustrated by comparison with such passages as Mt 22.43; Mk 12.36; Acts 1.16; 4.25; 28.25; 2 Pet 1.21, which refer to the work of the Holy Spirit in connexion with the Scriptures. That this was a fundamental dogma of Judaism is of course clear (cf., e.g., *Sanh.* 10.1: 'And these are they that have no share in the world to come: . . ., and [he that says] that the Law is not from Heaven, . . .'). But an affirmation of the divine origin of the law is also by implication an affirmation of its divine authority,

---

[1] To explain the purposes as being sin's is perverse, and attempts to weaken the final sense of ἵνα here are misguided, in view of the evidence of chapters 9–11 (e.g. 11.32).

[2] Cf. Chrysostom's Ὡσανεὶ ἔλεγεν · Ὡμολογημένον τοῦτο καὶ δῆλόν ἐστιν, ὅτι . . . (col. 507).

[3] That a contrast between οἶδα and εἰμί was intended is clearly impossible.

of the majesty with which it confronts men, and of the correspondence to its source of its character, mode of operation and effectiveness. We should probably see here a further implication, namely, that, being spiritual, it cannot be properly understood except by the help of the same Spirit by whom it was given (cf. 1 Cor 2.10–16). It is only those who have the Spirit who can truly acknowledge the law and consent to it with their minds (cf. vv. 16, 22, 23, 25b) and also in their lives make a beginning of real obedience to it (cf. 8.1ff). Those who do not have the Spirit grasp only the letter (cf. v. 6), and the letter bereft of the Spirit kills (cf. 2. Cor 3.6). We may also note the associations of πνεῦμα with life (e.g. 8.1f, 6, 10f, 13; 2 Cor 3.6b) and compare v. 10 (ἡ ἐντολὴ ἡ εἰς ζωήν).[1]

ἐγὼ δὲ σάρκινός εἰμι, πεπραμένος ὑπὸ τὴν ἁμαρτίαν. The first person singular is again used, but now for the first time in this chapter with a present tense.[2] The only natural way to understand this ἐγὼ . . . εἰμι is surely the way indicated by Calvin's comment on the following verse: 'Paul . . . is depicting in his own person the character and extent of the weakness of believers'.[3] The faithful often refuse this natural interpretation on the ground that it involves—so they argue—a gross belittling of the victory vouchsafed to the believer, and hanker after an interpretation which regards 7.14–25 and chapter 8 as describing two successive stages, before and after conversion. Even those who see that what is depicted in 7.14–24 does not fit the pre-conversion life are liable to argue that it belongs to a stage of the Christian life which can be left behind, a stage in which the Christian is still trying to fight the battle in his own strength, and to see 8.1ff as describing a subsequent deliverance.[4] But we are convinced that it is possible to do justice to the text of Paul—and also to the facts of Christian living wherever they are to be observed—only if we resolutely hold chapters 7 and 8 together, in spite of the obvious tension between them, and see in them not two successive stages but two different aspects, two contemporaneous realities, of the Christian life, both of which continue so long as the Christian is in the flesh.

The adjective σάρκινος (σάρκινος as the more difficult

---

[1] Cf. Gaugler I, p. 214.   [2] Though note ᾔδειν in v. 7.

[3] p. 149. Calvin himself, however, seems to want to distinguish between v. 14b and vv. 15ff, and to understand Paul in v. 14b as simply setting forth the nature of man generally in contrast with the law of God, and then in v. 15 going on to set before his readers the example of a regenerate man.

[4] So, for example, Bruce, pp. 150–53, 155f; and C. L. Mitton, 'Romans vii Reconsidered', in ET 65 (1953–54), pp. 78ff, 99ff and 132ff.

reading is to be preferred to the σαρκικός of 𝕶 al), meaning 'composed of flesh', is a quite common word, but occurs in the NT only three times in Paul and once in Hebrews, whereas σαρκικός (the pre-Pauline attestation of which is uncertain)[1] is commoner in Paul and means 'determined by the flesh', 'carnal'. In 2 Cor 3.3 (in an OT quotation) σάρκινος clearly has its ordinary sense, being contrasted with λίθινος. It is argued by some[2] that here in Rom 7.14 also it should be interpreted in accordance with the ordinary usage as meaning simply ἐν σαρκί in the sense that phrase has in Gal 2.20: Paul, it is argued, does not describe Christians as 'carnal' (in the sense of carnal-minded). But against this it must be said (i) that the last four words of the verse appear to interpret σάρκινος in the sense of 'carnal', and (ii) that in 1 Cor 3.1, where σάρκινος stands in contrast to πνευματικός, it is natural to understand it as equivalent to σαρκικός in v. 3. We take it then that Paul is here describing the Christian as carnal and implying that even in him there remains, so long as he continues to live this mortal life, that which is radically opposed to God (cf. 8.7), though chapter 8 will make it abundantly clear that he does not regard the Christian as being carnal in the same unqualified way that the natural man is carnal.[3]

With πεπραμένος ὑπὸ τὴν ἁμαρτίαν we may compare v. 23 which speaks of the other law as ἀντιστρατευόμενον τῷ νόμῳ τοῦ νοός μου καὶ αἰχμαλωτίζοντά με ἐν τῷ νόμῳ τῆς ἁμαρτίας . . .[4] The sense of ὑπό here is 'under the power (or authority) of' (cf., e.g., ἔχων ὑπ' ἐμαυτὸν στρατιώτας in Mt 8.9 and Lk 7.8). Understood in isolation from the teaching of chapters 6 and 8 and 12ff, these words would certainly give a thoroughly wrong impression of the Christian life; but, taken closely together with it, they bring out forcefully an aspect of the Christian life

[1] Cf. E. Schweizer, in *TWNT* 7, p. 101, n. 25.
[2] e.g. by Nygren, p. 299.
[3] See further *TWNT* 7, pp. 101f, 144f; Bauer, s.vv. σαρκικός and σάρκινος ; BDF, § 113 (2); Kümmel, op. cit., p. 58f.
[4] The verb πέρνημι (πιπράσκω is a late form of the present active) was most frequently used in Epic of exporting captives to foreign parts for sale as slaves: later it was used of selling quite generally. πιπράσκειν is used in Mt 18.25 of selling someone into slavery (for its use in this sense in the LXX see, e.g., Exod 22.3 [MT and LXX: 2]). But the passive is used in the LXX version of 1 Kgs 21.20, 25 [3 Regn. 20.20, 25]; 2 Kgs 17.17; and in 1 Macc 1.15 of selling oneself to doing evil, i.e. giving oneself with abandon to it. The passive is also used in Polybius 3.4.12 in the sense 'fall under the control of' (εἰς τὴν τῶν Ῥωμαίων ἐξουσίαν). It would seem probable, though in view of the above evidence not absolutely certain, that the thought of slavery is present here. In any case, the intention is to describe the person referred to as being under the power of sin and not in a position to free himself.

which we gloss over to our undoing. When Christians fail to take account of the fact that they (and all their fellow Christians also) are still πεπραμένοι ὑπὸ τὴν ἁμαρτίαν, they are specially dangerous both to others and to themselves because they are self-deceived. The more seriously a Christian strives to live from grace and to submit to the discipline of the gospel, the more sensitive he becomes to the fact of his continuing sinfulness, the fact that even his very best acts and activities are disfigured by the egotism which is still powerful within him—and no less evil because it is often more subtly disguised than formerly. At the same time it must be said with emphasis that the realistic recognition that we are still indeed πεπραμένοι ὑπὸ τὴν ἁμαρτίαν should be no encouragement to us to wallow complacently in our sins.

15. ὃ γὰρ κατεργάζομαι οὐ γινώσκω· οὐ γὰρ ὃ θέλω τοῦτο[1] πράσσω, ἀλλ' ὃ μισῶ τοῦτο ποιῶ. While the second γάρ simply indicates the relation of v. 15b to v. 15a, the first γάρ indicates the relation of vv. 15–23 as a whole to v. 14—they explain what it means to be πεπραμένος ὑπὸ τὴν ἁμαρτίαν. It is possible that κατεργάζομαι (used also in vv. 17, 18, 20), πράσσω (used also in v. 19) and ποιῶ (used also in vv. 16, 19, 20, and 21) are in this passage simply used as synonyms; but perhaps rather more likely that a distinction is intended between κατεργάζομαι and ποιῶ on the one hand and πράσσω on the other. The verb πράσσειν is less definite than κατεργάζεσθαι and ποιεῖν, and so more appropriate for denoting an inconclusive activity. In the NT, unlike κατεργάζεσθαι and ποιεῖν, it is never used with reference to an action of God or Christ, and it is used predominantly of an activity which is disapproved of. In this verse πράσσω is negatived, while in v. 19 it is used of practising the evil I do not will. On the other hand, where κατεργάζομαι or ποιῶ is used in this passage, we are probably right to assume that the thought of the effectiveness of the action, the completion of what is undertaken, is in mind.[2] By οὐ γινώσκω Paul can hardly mean 'I do not know'; for the subject of the verb knows only too well what he does. It is not much more likely that the meaning is 'I do not understand';[3] for the subject of the verb is depicted in vv. 15–24 as having a very clear comprehension of his position. The best explanation is along the lines of the sense 'acknowledge' (cf. the use of γινώσκειν of a father's acknowledging a child as his

[1] The omission of the first τοῦτο in D G it was probably intended as a stylistic improvement, giving the sentence more variety.

[2] See further TWNT 6, pp. 632ff (esp. 635 and 637).

[3] Pace Lagrange, p. 175; Kümmel, op. cit., p. 59; et al.

own)[1]—so 'I do not acknowledge', that is, 'I do not approve', 'I do not condone'.[2] This interpretation finds confirmation in v. 15b. What is depicted already in v. 15a is an inner conflict within—according to our understanding of the chapter—the Christian man.

As illustrations of vv. 15b, 18b and 19 such passages from ancient pagan literature as the words of Medea in Ovid's *Metamorphoses* 7. 19ff ('. . . aliudque cupido,

mens aliud suadet: video meliora proboque,

deteriora sequor') have only a limited relevance;[3] for, while they are a moving testimony to the phenomenon of inward conflict in human life, the sort of inner struggle which they describe is not really commensurate with what is depicted by Paul. For in the conflict which Paul is describing two factors of decisive importance are present which are absent from that depicted by Ovid: first, the knowledge of the revelation of God's will for man in the divine law, and, secondly, the activity of the Holy Spirit, who, on the one hand, clarifies, interprets and applies the law, and, on the other hand, creates and sustains man's will to obey it. It is where these two are present, that is, in the Christian believer, that the corruption of fallen human nature appears conspicuously. Here battle is joined in earnest in a way that is not possible before a man is sanctified by the Holy Spirit. For in the Christian there is a continual growth in understanding of the will of God and therefore also an ever-deepening perception of the extent to which he falls short of it; and this growing knowledge and the deepening hatred of sin which accompanies it are not merely phenomena of the Christian's human psychology but the work of the Spirit of God. The Holy Spirit Himself is active in him in opposition to the continuing power of his egotism. While the subject of κατεργάζομαι, οὐ πράσσω and ποιῶ in v. 15 is also the subject of οὐ γινώσκω, θέλω and μισῶ, in the actions denoted by οὐ γινώσκω (the negative expression here implies a positive refusal to 'know'), θέλω and μισῶ there is also another subject involved—a divine

---

[1] e.g. Plutarch, *Ages.* 3.1 (597a).

[2] Cf. Augustine, col. 2071: '*ignoro*, sic dictum est hoc loco, ut intelligatur, non approbo'; Pareus, *in loc.*: 'Pii quod perpetrant, non agnoscunt, non approbant, non excusant, non palliant'.

[3] The sentences about the thief in Arrian's *Discourses of Epictetus* 2. 26. 1, 2 and 4 (. . . δῆλον ὅτι ὃ μὲν θέλει οὐ ποιεῖ. . . . Οὐκ οὖν . . . ὃ μὲν θέλει ποιεῖ. . . . πῶς ὃ θέλει οὐ ποιεῖ καὶ ὃ μὴ θέλει ποιεῖ), while verbally closer to Rom 7, are, understood in the light of their context, much less relevant. Plautus, *Trin.* 657 ('Scibam ut esse me deceret; facere non quibam miser') is more relevant. Other references in Wettstein. p. 57.

Subject whose action is, so to speak, behind, under, and within, these human actions.

16. εἰ δὲ ὃ οὐ θέλω τοῦτο ποιῶ, σύμφημι τῷ νόμῳ ὅτι καλός. The fact that there is such a conflict in the Christian proves that there is within him that which acknowledges the goodness and rightness of the law. And this something within the Christian, this centre of commitment to God's law, is the work of the Holy Spirit, who, coming from without, yet works within the human personality not as an alien force but in such a way that what He does may truly be spoken of as the action of the man (hence the first person singular οὐ θέλω and σύμφημι).[1]

17. νυνὶ δὲ οὐκέτι ἐγὼ κατεργάζομαι αὐτὸ ἀλλὰ ἡ ἐνοικοῦσα ἐν ἐμοὶ ἁμαρτία. Both νυνί[2] and οὐκέτι[3] are here used in a logical, rather than a temporal, sense, the meaning of the first four words of the verse being 'But, this being so (that is, in the circumstances indicated by v. 16), it is then not I who'. This verse is not intended as an excuse, but is rather an acknowledgment of the extent to which sin, dwelling[4] in the Christian, usurps control over his life. But, while neither what is stated in this verse nor the οὐ θέλω and the σύμφημι τῷ νόμῳ ὅτι καλός of v. 16 is any excuse (the latter is no excuse, since God requires not ineffectual sentiments but obedient deeds), the fact that there is real conflict and tension is a sign of hope.

18 confirms the view that v. 17 was not intended as excuse of the self; for it is a confession of the self's powerlessness for good, but the γάρ with which it is introduced shows that it is thought of as supporting v. 17.[5]

τοῦτ' ἔστιν ἐν τῇ σαρκί μου is a necessary qualification of

---

[1] Calvin rightly emphasizes (p. 150) that what is denoted by σύμφημι here is something very different from that approval of the better course to which Ovid refers ('video meliora proboque')—a thoroughly serious consent 'with most eager desire of his heart', that is, a real inward engagement to God's law.

[2] Cf. 1 Cor 13.13. See Bauer, s.v. 2.a.

[3] Cf. v. 20; 11.6a; 14.15; Gal 3.18. See Bauer, s.v. 2. It is scarcely possible to take οὐκέτι as temporal and to understand the implication to be that, whereas once (i.e., before the person spoken of became a Christian) it was he who did what now he does not will, now that he is a Christian it is no longer he that does it.

[4] Whether we read ἐνοικοῦσα or the strongly supported variant οἰκοῦσα makes no substantial difference to the sense; but the variant is probably to be explained as assimilation to v. 20 [though it is read by Nestle[26]].

[5] To supply 'The fault must lie with sin' before v. 18, as Barrett (p. 148) does, obscures the movement of the thought; for it is the implication of v. 17 that the self is powerless for good, not the idea that it is sin rather than the self that is to blame, which is supported by v. 18.

ἐν ἐμοί, since in the Christian the Holy Spirit dwells, who it is
that works that willing what is good and acknowledging the
rightness of the law to which reference has been made.[1] By
σάρξ here Paul means not the 'lower self' as a 'part of the
man' contrasted with another part of his own nature,[2] but
the whole fallen human nature as such—in Calvin's words,
'all the endowments of human nature, and everything that is
in man, except the sanctification of the Spirit'.[3] (See also on
vv. 22, 23 and 25b.)

τὸ γὰρ θέλειν παράκειταί μοι, τὸ δὲ κατεργάζεσθαι τὸ καλὸν οὔ.[4]
Basic to the knowledge referred to in the first part of the verse
is the fact that the Christian, while he can will to do good, is
unable to carry out the good he wills. There is little doubt
that we should, with Calvin,[5] understand Paul to mean by
these words not that the Christian has absolutely nothing
beyond an ineffectual desire, but that what he actually does
never fully corresponds to his will. Sometimes he may fail to
carry it out at all, sometimes he may even do the very opposite
of what he wills; but even his best actions, in which he comes
nearest to accomplishing the good he wills, are always stained
and spoiled by his egotism.

19 repeats the substance of v. 15b.

20 is a repetition of the substance of vv. 16a and 17.

21. εὑρίσκω ἄρα τὸν νόμον τῷ θέλοντι ἐμοὶ ποιεῖν τὸ καλόν, ὅτι ἐμοὶ
τὸ κακὸν παράκειται. One of the features which make the last
five verses of chapter 7 specially difficult is the repeated use
of the word νόμος (in vv. 21–23 and 25b), and it is τὸν νόμον
which is the main problem of this verse. Many interpreters,
both ancient and modern, have insisted that the reference
must be to the OT law, but the various explanations of the
verse which have been offered on this assumption are so

---

[1] The presence of this qualification, implying as it does that there is
more to be said about the man who is being spoken of than that he is
flesh, is an indication that Paul is here speaking of the Christian (cf.
Aquinas, p. 104 (576): 'Si vero hoc referatur ad hominem sub peccato
existentem, superflue additur quod dicit *hoc est in carne mea*'). The
statements of some commentators (e.g. Michel, p. 178; Leenhardt, p. 191,
n. *) to the effect that it is not restrictive but only explanatory are true,
if what is meant is that it does not imply that the σάρξ is only a part of
the man's human self, but not, if what is meant is that it is not inserted
in order to exclude the work of the Spirit in the Christian.
[2] As Sanday and Headlam, p. 182, seem to suggest.
[3] p. 151.
[4] There is little doubt that the variants οὐχ εὑρίσκω and οὐ γινώσκω
instead of the simple οὐ are secondary.
[5] p. 151f.

forced as to be incredible.[1] Moreover, since in v. 23 a law different from the law of God is explicitly spoken of, the possibility of explaining τὸν νόμον in v. 21 otherwise than as referring to the OT law is clearly open to us. And the presence of τοῦ θεοῦ after τῷ νόμῳ in v. 22 suggests the probability that νόμος has just been used with a different reference. Some have understood νόμος here in v. 21 in the sense 'norm' or 'principle'. Thus NEB has 'this principle', and JB 'the rule' (which is explained in a note saying, 'Lit. "law", in the sense of regular experience'). But more probable is the view that by τὸν νόμον is meant that law which will be referred to more clearly in v. 23—the ἕτερος νόμος.[2]

Other matters relating to this verse are less difficult. The sense of ἄρα may be expressed by 'so then'; εὑρίσκω is best understood as meaning something like 'I prove for myself by experience' (cf. the use of the passive in v. 10); τῷ θέλοντι ἐμοὶ ποιεῖν τὸ καλόν could be taken as a dative of disadvantage with εὑρίσκω, but is probably better explained as belonging to the ὅτι clause but placed before the conjunction for the sake of emphasis;[3] and the ὅτι clause states the substance of the law under discussion.

22. συνήδομαι γὰρ τῷ νόμῳ τοῦ θεοῦ. The γάρ indicates that the sentence contained in vv. 22 and 23 is an explanation of the situation described in v. 21. The meaning of συνήδεσθαι with the dative here is probably not 'rejoice with'[4] but 'rejoice in' (see LSJ, s.v. I. 2; and compare the use of συγχαίρειν in I Cor 13.6[5]). The Christian delights in God's law, embraces it with gladness, loves it as the revelation of God's good and merciful will. Compare Ps 19.8; 119.14, 16a, 24a, 35b, 47, 70b,

---

[1] The following examples may be mentioned: (i) 'I find then with regard to the Law, that to me who would fain do that which is good, to me (I say) that which is evil is present' (so Vaughan p. 143); (ii) the explanation that Paul starts to speak about the law of God, and then breaks off under the stress of emotion to say τῷ θέλοντι, κ.τ.λ., returning to the subject of the divine law in v. 22 (so Moule, p. 200); (iii) 'This is what I find the law—or life under the law—to come to in experience: when I wish to do good, evil is present with me' (so Denney, p. 642; (iv) 'I find then that to me who would fain do the law, that is, the good thing, to me evil is present'; (v) 'I find then by the law (i.e. by its instruction) that to me who would fain do that which is good, evil is present' (so, e.g., Erasmus, p. 353). But many other interpretations taking τὸν νόμον to mean the OT law have been suggested.

[2] So Cornely (p. 383f), Lagrange (p. 177f), et al.

[3] Cf., e.g., the word-order of 11.2 (ἐν Ἠλίᾳ before τί) and see on 11.31 and examples given there.

[4] Pace, e.g., Michel, p. 169 ('ich stimme dem Gesetz . . . mit Freuden zu'); Barrett, pp. 139, 150 (his 'I agree with' is anyway too weak); Bauer, s.v.   [5] See Bauer, s.v. συγχαίρω, I (fin.).

77b, 92a, etc. The τοῦ θεοῦ is required for clarity after the use of νόμος in v. 21 with reference to another law.[1]

κατὰ τὸν ἔσω ἄνθρωπον qualifies the first person singular of the verb. The subject is 'I in so far as the inner man is concerned', 'I in so far as I am that inner man'. For ὁ ἔσω ἄνθρωπος compare 2 Cor 4.16; Eph 3.16; and also Rom 6.6 (the reference to the new man implied by what is said about the old); Col 3.10 (τὸν νέον [sc. ἄνθρωπον], τὸν ἀνακαινούμενον . . .); Eph 4.24 (τὸν καινὸν ἄνθρωπον τὸν κατὰ θεὸν κτισθέντα . . .). The meaning of ὁ ἔσω ἄνθρωπος here must be much the same as that of ὁ νοῦς μου in v. 23 and ὁ νοῦς in v. 25, which must be understood in the light of the reference to the ἀνακαίνωσις τοῦ νοός in 12.2. The mind which recognizes, and is bound to, God's law is the mind which is being renewed by God's Spirit; and the inner man of which Paul speaks is the working of God's Spirit within the Christian.[2] (Compare what was said above

[1] The variant νοός (B) for θεοῦ is no doubt to be explained as assimilation to the following verse.

[2] This interpretation of κατὰ τὸν ἔσω ἄνθρωπον is naturally rejected by those who deny that Paul in 7.14ff refers to the Christian. So, according to Leenhardt, p. 193f, for example, while in 2 Cor 4.16 ὁ ἔσω [ἄνθρωπος] denotes the man as renewed by the Holy Spirit, the human personality in so far as it has been regenerated and transformed by the divine action, and so so is equivalent to 'the new man', the same expression must here in Rom 7 be understood in a psychological and secular sense as referring merely to the higher part of man, since (according to him) 'the action of the Holy Spirit is absent from the drama of the man who speaks in Rom 7'. The conception of an inner man is to be found in classical Greek philosophy, in Hellenistic Judaism, and in Hellenistic mysticism. Thus, for example, Plato (R. 589a) refers to ὁ ἐντὸς ἄνθρωπος (Plotinus at a much later date actually attributes to him Paul's very phrase: οἷον λέγει Πλάτων τὸν εἴσω ἄνθρωπον (Enn. 5.1.10)); Philo (Congr. 97) refers to the mind (νοῦς) as ἄνθρωπος ἐν ἀνθρώπῳ, while in Plant. 42 he calls it ὁ ἐν ἡμῖν πρὸς ἀλήθειαν ἄνθρωπος, and in Det. Pot. ins. 22f he refers to the λογικὴ διάνοια as ὁ πρὸς ἀλήθειαν ἄνθρωπος and as ὁ ἄνθρωπος ἐν ἑκάστου τῇ ψυχῇ κατοικῶν; and in the Hermetic literature the ἔξω ἄνθρωπος of Adam is distinguished from ὁ ἔσω αὐτοῦ ἄνθρωπος ὁ πνευματικός (Zosimus, in Reitzenstein, Poimandres, p. 104f). For further references see J. Jeremias, in TWNT i, p. 366. But the likelihood is that Paul, though he may well have been aware that others used this language differently (the suggestion of Fuchs, p. 61f, that he was actually adapting a Gnostic lament does not seem likely), was using it in his own sense. It is, in fact, a weakness in Leenhardt's position that he is compelled to argue that Paul uses ὁ ἔσω ἄνθρωπος here in a quite different sense from that in which he uses it in 2 Cor 4.16. The view of Kümmel (op. cit., p. 136), according to which the ἔσω ἄνθρωπος or νοῦς and the σάρξ are the same man seen from different viewpoints (as the willing subject and the acting subject respectively), though it is opposed to the interpretation of νοῦς and σάρξ as two parts of man that together add up to the whole, is to be rejected because it too understands the inner man or νοῦς of this passage in purely psychological terms.

with regard to the subject of οὐ γινώσκω, θέλω and μισῶ in v. 15.)

23. βλέπω δὲ ἕτερον νόμον ἐν τοῖς μέλεσίν μου ἀντιστρατευόμενον τῷ νόμῳ τοῦ νοός μου καὶ αἰχμαλωτίζοντά με ἐν τῷ νόμῳ τῆς ἁμαρτίας τῷ ὄντι ἐν τοῖς μέλεσίν μου. That by ἕτερος νόμος a law different from, and contrasted with, the law of God mentioned in v. 22 is meant, is clear enough. Since ἕτερον νόμον is followed by ἐν τοῖς μέλεσίν μου, and τῷ νόμῳ τῆς ἁμαρτίας later in the verse is qualified by τῷ ὄντι ἐν τοῖς μέλεσίν μου, it seems natural to identify the ἕτερος νόμος with the νόμος τῆς ἁμαρτίας (explaining τῷ νόμῳ τῆς ἁμαρτίας, κ.τ.λ. as substituted for the ἑαυτῷ one might have expected, in order to clarify the indefinite ἕτερον νόμον). Moreover, it is quite natural to understand τοῦ νοός μου to mean 'which my mind acknowledges'[1] and to identify the νόμος τοῦ νοός μου with the νόμος τοῦ θεοῦ of v. 22. Understood in this way, vv. 22 and 23 depict two laws in opposition to each other.[2] The identity of one of them, 'the law of God', is not in doubt; but the identity of the other, 'the law of sin', requires some clarification. It would seem that Paul is here using the word 'law' metaphorically, to denote exercised power, authority, control, and that he means by 'the law of sin', the power, the authority, the control exercised over us by sin.[3] It is a forceful way of making the point that the power which sin has over us is a terrible travesty, a grotesque parody, of that authority over us which belongs by right to God's holy law. Sin's exercising such authority over us is a hideous usurpation of the prerogative of God's law.

[1] This interpretation (as against, e.g., JB: 'which my reason dictates') is supported by the first half of v. 25b and also by v. 22.

[2] To distinguish here four laws ((i) the law of God; (ii) the law of the mind, i.e. 'the readiness of the faithful mind to obey the divine law'; (iii) the law of unrighteousness, i.e. 'the power which iniquity exercises not only in a man who is not yet regenerate, but also in the flesh of the man who is'; (iv) the law in the members, i.e. 'the concupiscence which resides in his members'), as Calvin, for example, does, p. 152, is surely to introduce a complication not required by Paul's language.

[3] Chrysostom's interesting comment (col. 511) is worth recalling: Νόμον ἐνταῦθα πάλιν ἀντιστρατευόμενον τὴν ἁμαρτίαν ἐκάλεσεν, οὐ διὰ τὴν ἀξίαν, ἀλλὰ διὰ τὴν σφοδρὰν ὑπακοὴν τῶν πειθομένων αὐτῇ. Ὥσπερ οὖν κύριον τὸν μαμμωνᾶν καλεῖ, καὶ θεὸν τὴν κοιλίαν, οὐ διὰ τὴν οἰκείαν ἀξίαν, ἀλλὰ διὰ τὴν πολλὴν τῶν ὑποτεταγμένων δουλείαν· οὕτω καὶ ἐνταῦθα νόμον ἐκάλεσεν ἁμαρτίαν, διὰ τοὺς οὕτως αὐτῇ δουλεύοντας καὶ φοβουμένους ἀφεῖναι αὐτήν, ὥσπερ δεδοίκασιν οἱ νόμον λαβόντες ἀφεῖναι τὸν νόμον. Chrysostom rightly saw whyPaul used νόμος in this connexion; but his identification of 'the law of sin' with sin itself (making τῆς ἁμαρτίας a genitive of apposition) seems on the whole a less satisfactory way of explaining Paul's language than that which we have adopted above. But in any case, the relation between the exercised authority of sin and sin as exercising authority is extremely close. (See also on 8.2.)

Understood thus, Paul's use of νόμος here, so far from obscuring Paul's meaning, is surely—for any one who is attending at all closely to what he is saying—an extremely apposite and forceful way of representing sin as the hateful usurper that it is.[1] That νόμος should be consistently translated by 'law' throughout this passage should go without saying; for, while it is true that, when Paul uses νόμος with reference to sin, he is specially referring to the authority or constraint which it exercises over us, the power of his language would be greatly impaired if νόμος were in some cases rendered by a different word.

For the use of military metaphors in this connexion (ἀντιστρατευόμενον and αἰχμαλωτίζοντα) compare the use of ἀφορμή in vv. 8 and 11, and of στρατεύεσθαι in 1 Pet 2.11 (cf. also Gal 5.17—ἀντίκειται). For the ἐν after αἰχμαλωτίζοντά με compare the use of εἰς with the same verb in 2 Cor 10.5: in these two verses there seems to be no difference in meaning between αἰχμαλωτίζειν ἐν and αἰχμαλωτίζειν εἰς.[2] The variant reading of A C L etc. (without ἐν) is probably to be explained as an attempt at improvement (αἰχμαλωτίζειν is used with a simple dative in Ignatius, *Phld.* 2.2: compare also the use of the simple dative with δουλοῦν). With the thought expressed by αἰχμαλωτίζοντα, κ.τ.λ. we may compare the phrase πεπραμένος ὑπὸ τὴν ἁμαρτίαν in v. 14.

24. Ταλαίπωρος ἐγὼ ἄνθρωπος· τίς με ῥύσεται ἐκ τοῦ σώματος τοῦ θανάτου τούτου; So Paul begins the third and final paragraph of the sub-section. Many commentators,[3] including— surprisingly —not a few in the Reformed tradition, have stated quite dogmatically that it cannot be a Christian who speaks here. But the truth is, surely, that inability to recognize the distress

---

[1] Barrett (pp. 149–53) seems to assume the following equations: 'the law of sin' = the law of God as taken possession of and perverted by sin = religion as it exists. But this is surely to interpret 'the law of sin' too narrowly. While it is true that religion, in so far as it is a human activity, is always permeated by sin, and to the extent that it is a human attempt to put God under an obligation to man it is peculiarly sinful, and that Christians—and especially those among them who like to be called 'Church leaders'—ought always to remember the warning words of Lucretius, 'Tantum religio potuit suadere malorum', it is surely quite untrue that religion, even in all the multiplicity of its different forms, is the whole of what Paul means by 'the law of sin'.

[2] The alternative rendering in the NEB margin ('by means of the law') is hardly feasible, if both ἕτερον νόμον and τῷ νόμῳ τῆς ἁμαρτίας refer to the same law (as we have argued above).

[3] e.g. Denney, p. 643 ('The words are not those of the Apostle's heart as he writes; . . . not the cry of the Christian Paul, but of the man whom sin and law have brought to despair'); Kümmel, op. cit., p. 98; Gaugler I, p. 230; Leenhardt, p. 195.

reflected in this cry as characteristic of Christian existence argues a failure to grasp the full seriousness of the Christian's obligation to express his gratitude to God by obedience of life. The farther men advance in the Christian life, and the more mature their discipleship, the clearer becomes their perception of the heights to which God calls them, and the more painfully sharp their consciousness of the distance between what they ought, and want, to be, and what they are. The assertion that this cry could only come from an unconverted heart, and that the apostle must be expressing not what he feels as he writes but the vividly remembered experience of the unconverted man, is, we believe, totally untrue. To make it is to indicate— with all respect be it said—that one has not yet considered how absolute are the claims of the grace of God in Jesus Christ. The man, whose cry this is, is one who, knowing himself to be righteous by faith, desires from the depths of his being to respond to the claims which the gospel makes upon him (cf. v. 22). It is the very clarity of his understanding of the gospel and the very sincerity of his love to God, which make his pain at this continuing sinfulness so sharp. But, be it noted, v. 24, while it is a cry of real and deep anguish, is not at all a cry of despair. To interpret it as the cry of the 'religious' man 'who longs for a help from outside himself, but knows no helper', as Kümmel has done,[1] is unjustified; for ταλαίπωρος can indicate distress, affliction, suffering, without in any way implying hopelessness,[2] and the question τίς με ῥύσεται, κ.τ.λ. may be understood as expressing the speaker's earnest longing for something which he knows is surely coming (cf. 8.23).[3]

The expression, τὸ σῶμα τοῦ θανάτου τούτου, has still to be discussed. It is best understood as signifying, like τὰ μέλη μου in the previous verse, the speaker's human nature in its condition of occupation by that 'other law' which is the usurping authority of sin.[4] We may compare τῇ σαρκί in v. 25b and τὸ σῶμα τῆς ἁμαρτίας in 6.6 (see also 6.12; 8.10, 11, 13, 23). It is possible, grammatically, to take τούτου either

---

[1] op. cit., p. 98.

[2] cf. LSJ, s.v., and also under ταλαιπωρέω, and HR, under ταλαιπωρεῖν, ταλαιπωρία and ταλαίπωρος.

[3] cf: Ps 14.7 [LXX: 13.7] and 53.6 [LXX: 52.7], in which the wish, expressed in both the Hebrew and the Greek as a question, is followed by the confident statement that, when God brings back the captivity of His people, then Jacob shall rejoice and Israel shall be glad. Here in Romans it is natural to assume that the speaker of v. 24 speaks in the confidence expressed in v. 25a.

[4] The suggestion that the reference is to 'the mass of unredeemed mankind' (Manson, p. 946) is surely improbable.

with σώματος ('this body of death') or with θανάτου ('the body of this death'). The demonstrative adjective serves to define, in the former case, the body referred to, in the latter case, the death, as the one which has already been mentioned. The fact that there have been references to a death in vv. 10, 11, and 13, and the possibility of regarding vv. 14–23 as explanatory of that death, have inclined some commentators to prefer the latter alternative. But, since an equivalent of σῶμα has twice been used in v. 23 (the repeated ἐν τοῖς μέλεσίν μου) and since vv. 14–23 may perhaps rather more naturally be considered a drawing out of the meaning of bodily life (note the prominence of σάρκινος in v. 14), we judge it better to take τούτου with σώματος. That from which the speaker longs to be delivered is the condition of life in the body as we know it under the occupation of sin which has just been described, a life which, because of sin, must succumb to death.

25a. The exclamation **χάρις τῷ θεῷ**[1] **διὰ Ἰησοῦ Χριστοῦ τοῦ κυρίου ἡμῶν** is an indirect answer to the question in v. 24. It apparently implies that the speaker knows either that God has already fulfilled for him the wish expressed by the question or that God will surely fulfil it for him in the future. Those commentators who are quite convinced that, while it is a Christian who speaks in v. 25a, v. 24 is the cry of an unconverted man, not unnaturally tend to assume that the man who thanks God in v. 25a must be conscious of having already been delivered from the body of death.[2] But this assumption is responsible for a great deal of confusion in the exegesis of this passage and has bedevilled in particular the interpretation of v. 25b. Moreover, it is inconsistent with Paul's thought as expressed elsewhere. We may for example refer to 8.10, according to which even for the man in whom Christ dwells, while it is indeed true that τὸ ... πνεῦμα ζωὴ διὰ δικαιοσύνην, it is still also true that τὸ ... σῶμα νεκρὸν διὰ ἁμαρτίαν. The implication of v. 25a then is not that the speaker has already been delivered ἐκ τοῦ σώματος τοῦ θανάτου τούτου, but that he

---

[1] There is little doubt that the reading of B, χάρις τῷ θεῷ, is original. The two Western readings, ἡ χάρις τοῦ θεοῦ and ἡ χάρις κυρίου which replace the exclamation by a direct reply to the question in v. 24. and the reading of Ψ and 33 (the addition of δέ after χάρις), which gives a less abrupt text, are all explicable as attempted improvements of χάρις τῷ θεῷ. The εὐχαριστῶ τῷ θεῷ of the TR is also less abrupt than the reading of B, but may perhaps have originated in an accidental duplication of τω, the mistake being later corrected by the addition of εὐ before χαριστω instead of by the deletion of the extra τω. [N²⁶ has δέ.]

[2] So, e.g., Denney, p. 643: 'The exclamation of thanksgiving shows that the longed-for deliverance has actually been achieved'.

knows that God will surely deliver him from it in the future. Deliverance in the limited sense of separation from the body could come with death, deliverance in all its positive fullness would come with the eschatological redemption of the body of death, the ἀπολύτρωσις τοῦ σώματος (8.23).

The key to the right understanding of v. 25a is the recognition that the man who speaks in v. 24 is already a Christian; for that saves us from the necessity of imagining a drastic change between vv. 24 and 25a.

25b. Ἄρα¹ οὖν αὐτὸς ἐγὼ τῷ μὲν νοῒ δουλεύω νόμῳ θεοῦ, τῇ δὲ σαρκὶ νόμῳ ἁμαρτίας. It is hardly surprising that many of those who have seen in v. 24 the cry of an unconverted man (or of a Christian on a low level of Christian life) and in v. 25a an indication that the longed for deliverance has actually been accomplished, have felt this sentence to be an embarrassment, since, coming after the thanksgiving, it appears (on this understanding of vv. 24–25a) to imply that the condition of the speaker after his deliverance is exactly the same as it was before it. A favourite way of dealing with the difficulty has been to posit a disarrangement of the sentences at a very early stage and to re-arrange the verses in the order 23, 25b, 24, 25a.² Another suggestion which has been made is that v. 25b is a secondary gloss (intended as a summary of vv. 15–23), which should therefore be omitted.³ But, while the possibility of a primitive corruption which has affected all the surviving witnesses to the text cannot of course be ruled out absolutely, an exegesis which rests on a re-arrangement of sentences or on the exclusion of an alleged gloss, when there is not the slightest suggestion of support in the textual tradition for either procedure, is exceedingly hazardous, and, when sense can be made of the text as it stands, has little claim to be regarded as responsible. A good many, of course, even of those who do take

¹ The capital letter in the Nestle text reflects a particular understanding of the movement of the argument at the end of chapter 7 and the beginning of chapter 8. In our view the lower case would be preferable, since we consider v. 25b to be more closely related to v. 25a than to 8.1.

² So, for example, the eighteenth century Dutch scholar, Herman Venema; Moffatt; Dodd, p. 132f; F. Müller, 'Zwei Marginalien im Brief des Paulus an die Römer, in ZNW 40 (1941), pp. 249–54; Michel, pp. 144, 154f (though Dodd and Michel also take seriously the suggestion that v. 25b is a gloss). Müller's view is that the order intended by Paul was 7.22, 23, 25b, 24, 25a; 8.2, 1, 3; but that 7.24–25a and 8.2 were originally written in the margin, being an addition by Paul himself in order to make a satisfactory connexion between 7.25b and 8.1, and were then misplaced when the original was copied.

³ So, for example, Michelsen; Jülicher; Bultmann, 'Glossen', cols. 197–99.

v. 24 to express the situation of the unconverted have managed to explain v. 25b without having resort to such dubious methods. Some,[1] for example, have explained v. 25a as anticipatory, a momentary glance forward to what is to be made clear in chapter 8: in that case v. 25a would not imply that the speaker of v. 24 has already been delivered, and v. 25b would be quite natural as a summing up of the situation described in vv. 15–24. Others,[2] who have taken v. 25a to imply that deliverance has already been accomplished, have taken the αὐτὸς ἐγώ in v. 25b to mean 'I myself apart from Jesus Christ', and so have understood Paul to mean that, left to himself, he would still be in the position already described: according to this view, v. 25b does not describe the actual condition of the man who has been delivered (for he is not left to himself), but what would be his condition still, had it not been for God's intervention. But, when once it is recognized that the one who speaks in v. 24 is a Christian (and a mature Christian—not merely one who is still on some specially low level of Christian existence), and also that v. 25a expresses not consciousness of having already been delivered ἐκ τοῦ σώματος τοῦ θανάτου τούτου but certainty that God will in the future deliver him from it, a straightforward and satisfying interpretation of v. 25b becomes possible. Far from being an anticlimax or an incongruous intrusion at this point, it is an altogether appropriate conclusion[3] to the preceding verses (including vv. 24–25a). For it sums up with clear-sighted honesty—an honesty which is thoroughly consonant both with the urgency of the longing for final deliverance expressed in v. 24 and also with the confidence that God will surely accomplish that deliverance in His good time reflected in v. 25a— the tension, with all its real anguish and also all its real hopefulness, in which the Christian[4] never ceases to be involved so long as he is living this present life. To read into this sentence any suggestion of a complacent acceptance on the part of the

[1] e.g., Gaugler I, p. 232, who thinks of vv. 24 and 25a as an interjection by which Paul interrupts his argument in Jewish fashion.

[2] e.g. Sanday and Headlam, p. 178; Denney, p. 643.

[3] For ἄρα οὖν cf. 5.18; 7.3; 8.12; 9.16, 18; 14.12, 19; Gal 6.10; Eph 2.19; 1 Th 5.6; 2 Th 2.15. Zahn's accentuation of ἄρα as ἆρα (p. 370f) was surely a counsel of despair.

[4] The words αὐτὸς ἐγώ would seem to be best explained neither as emphasizing that Paul is speaking of himself nor as indicating that the sentence is stating what is true apart from Christ's intervention, but rather as underlining the full personal involvement of the Christian as the subject of both statements, both τῷ . . . νοΐ δουλεύω νόμῳ θεοῦ and τῇ . . . σαρκὶ (δουλεύω) νόμῳ ἁμαρτίας.

Christian of his continued sinfulness[1] would be quite unfair.
For—not to mention the evidence of moral earnestness contained in v. 24—the words τῷ μὲν νοΐ δουλεύω νόμῳ θεοῦ
express clearly enough the Christian's engagement, in the very
depths of his personality as one who is being renewed by God's
Spirit,[2] to God's holy law, his sense of being altogether bound
to it.[3] And it is fully congruous with this deep sense of commitment to God's will that this conclusion does not cloak the
painful fact of continuing sinfulness, but goes on to acknowledge frankly that the Christian, so long as he remains in this
present life, remains in a real sense a slave of sin (δουλεύω—
compare v. 14b), since he still has a fallen nature (τῇ . . . σαρκί).

V. 4. A LIFE CHARACTERIZED BY THE INDWELLING OF GOD'S SPIRIT (8.1–39)

The life promised for the man who is righteous by faith is, in
the fourth place, described as a life characterized by the

---

[1] Such as is sometimes in evidence where Luther's *simul peccator
et justus* is repeated without Luther's deep understanding of the gospel.
[2] The NEB translation of τῷ . . . νοΐ by 'as a rational being' is misleading. It is not his rationality as such but its renewal by the Holy
Spirit which binds the Christian to God's law. For τῷ . . . νοΐ here
compare what was said on v. 22 under κατὰ τὸν ἔσω ἄνθρωπον. By νοῦς
Paul means the mind in so far as it is renewed by the Spirit of God.
[3] For the use of δουλεύειν in connexion with God's law cf. 6.16, 18, 19,
22; 7.6. The associations of humiliation, compulsion and human injustice, which necessarily adhere to words indicative of slavery, clearly
make them unsatisfactory for use in this connexion, and Paul himself
apologizes in 6.19 for making use of them. But they have the great
advantage of suggesting an absolute obligation and the fact that the
Christian is not his own but God's. Bultmann, 'Glossen', col. 198f,
claims that the statement τῷ . . . νοΐ δουλεύω νόμῳ θεοῦ is inconsistent
with the position described in vv. 15–23 and is, therefore, a proof that
v. 25b is a secondary gloss. But his argument that, whereas τῷ . . . νοΐ
δουλεύω νόμῳ θεοῦ means: 'ich habe die Absicht, die Forderung des νόμος
zu erfüllen', the statements σύμφημι τῷ νόμῳ, ὅτι καλός in v. 16 and
συνήδομαι . . . τῷ νόμῳ τοῦ θεοῦ κατὰ τὸν ἔσω ἄνθρωπον in v. 22 mean no more
than 'ich bejahe die Intention, den Zweck, des Gesetzes (nämlich, dass
es εἰς ζωήν ist, V. 10), einerlei ob ich es erfülle oder nicht', is scarcely
cogent; for it is quite arbitrary—in the face of the repeated use of θέλειν
in vv. 15, 16, 18, 19, 20, 21, even perverse—to suppose that vv. 15–23
imply that the man who acknowledges the goodness of the law and
delights in it κατὰ τὸν ἔσω ἄνθρωπον does not also have the 'Absicht' to
fulfil its requirement. It seems to us that τῷ . . . νοΐ δουλεύω νόμῳ θεοῦ
and συνήδομαι . . . τῷ νόμῳ τοῦ θεοῦ κατὰ τὸν ἔσω ἄνθρωπον are saying
substantially the same thing, the former stressing the element of
absolute obligation, and the latter the element of real freedom, in the
Christian's commitment to God's law.

indwelling of the Spirit of God. The key-word of this section is πνεῦμα, which, while it is used only five times in chapters 1 to 7 and eight times in chapters 9 to 16, occurs twenty-one times in chapter 8, that is, much more often than in any other single chapter in the whole NT. In the majority of its occurrences in Romans 8 it quite certainly denotes the Holy Spirit, and in two of them it clearly does not. In the remaining instances it is a matter of some controversy whether the reference is, or is not, to the Holy Spirit:[1] in all of them, in our judgment, it is.

Being characterized by the indwelling of God's Spirit, this life which is promised for the man who is righteous by faith is necessarily also a life in which God's law is being established and fulfilled (vv. 4, 12–16), a life which here and now bears the promise of resurrection and eternal life (vv. 6, 10f), a life in hope (vv. 17–30). The last sub-section (vv. 31–39) is at the same time both the conclusion to this section, underlining the certainty of the believer's hope, and also the conclusion to the whole argument of the epistle up to this point.[2]

(i) *The indwelling of the Spirit* (8.1–11)

[1]So then there is now no condemnation for those who are in Christ Jesus. [2]For the law of the Spirit of life has in Christ Jesus set thee free from the law of sin and of death. [3]For God, having sent his own Son in the likeness of sinful flesh and to deal with sin, condemned sin in the flesh (the thing which the law was unable to do, because it was weak through the flesh), [4]so that the righteous requirement of the law might be fulfilled in us who do not walk according to the flesh but according to the Spirit. [5]For those whose lives are determined

---

[1] The English translator has to decide in which of the twenty-one occurrences of πνεῦμα in this chapter he is to represent it by 'Spirit' and in which by 'spirit', and a similar problem faces the editor of the Greek text who is in the habit of using a capital π when he understands πνεῦμα to refer to the Holy Spirit (cf. BFBS): those editions of the Greek (like Nestle) which always use a lower case π for πνεῦμα (just as they regularly print θεός with a lower case θ) avoid the difficulty.

[2] Among the discussions of this section of Romans that by Barth in his shorter commentary stands out for its theological perceptiveness in spite of its brevity. Reference may also be made here (in connexion with the subject of the Spirit) to: E. Schweizer, *et al.*, in *TWNT* 6, pp. 330–453 (including a bibliography of earlier work on pp. 330–33); N. Q. Hamilton, *The Holy Spirit and Eschatology in Paul*, Edinburgh, 1957; I. Hermann, *Kyrios und Pneuma: Studien zur Christologie der paulinischen Hauptbriefe*, Munich, 1961; K. Stalder, *Das Werk des Geistes in der Heiligung bei Paulus*, Zurich, 1962; W. Pfister, *Das Leben im Geist nach Paulus: der Geist als Anfang und Vollendung des christlichen Lebens*, Fribourg, 1963; Hill, *GWHM*, pp. 202–93; and (on this chapter generally) M. Loane, *The Hope of Glory: an exposition of the eighth chapter in the Epistle to the Romans*, London, 1968. Also my *On Romans*, 1998, pp. 33–49.

by the flesh are on the flesh's side, but those whose lives are determined by the Spirit are on the Spirit's side. ⁶For the flesh's mind is
death, but the Spirit's mind is life and peace. ⁷For the mind of the
flesh is enmity toward God; for it is not subject to God's law—indeed,
it cannot be; ⁸and those who are in the flesh cannot please God. ⁹But
you are not in the flesh but in the Spirit, seeing that God's Spirit
dwells in you. (If someone does not possess Christ's Spirit, then he
does not belong to Christ.) ¹⁰But, if Christ is in you, though your body
is indeed mortal because of *your* sin, the Spirit is life because of *your*
justification. ¹¹But, if the Spirit of him who raised Jesus from the
dead dwells in you, he who raised from the dead Christ Jesus shall
quicken your mortal bodies also through his Spirit who dwells in you.

The first sub-section of V. 4 consists of 8.1–11. It connects not
with 7.25a or 7.25b but with 7.6 (7.7–25 being, as we have seen,
a necessary clarification of 7.1–6). Verse 1 draws out the
significance of 7.1–6: those who are in Christ Jesus are freed
from the divine condemnation pronounced by God's law.
Verse 2, which takes up a point already hinted at in 7.6b,
confirms the truth of v. 1 by appealing to the fact that the
further liberation which deliverance from God's condemnation
makes possible, namely, the liberation of the believer by the
power of God's Spirit from the power of sin and of its inevitable
concomitant, death, has actually taken place as a result of the
work of Christ. Verse 3 takes up and elucidates the ἐν Χριστῷ
Ἰησοῦ of v. 2, clarifying the basis of the freedom referred to in
v. 1 and also of the resulting freedom described in v. 2. Verse 4
indicates what was God's purpose in sending His Son—a
purpose which, according to v. 2, is actually being fulfilled.
What God's gift of His Spirit has brought about (v. 2) is
nothing less than a beginning of the fulfilment of the divine
purpose of Christ's work, namely, the establishment of God's
law in the life of believers (what this means will be elucidated
in the next sub-section). Verses 5–8 bring out forcefully the
absolute opposition existing between the Spirit of God and all
that belongs to Him, on the one hand, and, on the other hand,
the flesh, that is, our fallen, ego-centric human nature and all
that belongs to it. Verse 9 underlines the decisive fact that
God has given His Spirit to indwell believers. And, finally,
vv. 10 and 11, taking up the καὶ τοῦ θανάτου of v. 2, bring out
the truth that the life which is characterized by the indwelling
of the Spirit of God is necessarily a life which breathes the
promise of resurrection and of eternal life.

The closely-knit character of the argument of this sub-
section, which at first sight is not at all obvious but becomes
apparent when the verses are carefully analysed, should be
noted.

8.1–11   373

1. οὐδὲν ἄρα νῦν κατάκριμα τοῖς ἐν Χριστῷ Ἰησοῦ. Some of those
who have removed 7.25b from between 7.25a and 8.1 (whether
by transposition or by excision) have understandably felt that,
while 8.1 does not seem a very natural sequel to 7.25a, 8.2 is
just the sort of sequel which seems to be required, since it can
be taken as a statement of the ground for the thanksgiving,
and so have proceeded either to transpose 8.1 and 8.2[1] or to
excise 8.1 as a gloss.[2] But 8.1 makes excellent sense where it
stands, provided we recognize that it connects neither with
7.25a nor with 7.25b but with 7.6.[3] It draws out the significance
(ἄρα) of the paragraph 7.1–6 in which Paul took up and elucidated the statement he had made in 6.14, οὐ γάρ ἐστε ὑπὸ νόμον.
We saw that that statement was to be understood in a strictly
limited sense—'for you are not under the law *as condemning
you*'—and that interpretation of 6.14b is now confirmed by the
content of 8.1. For those who are in Christ Jesus (cf. 6.2–11;
7.4) there is no divine condemnation, since the condemnation
which they deserve has already been fully borne for them by
Him. The reference of the νῦν[4] is not to some moment of
conversion thought of as having occurred between v. 24 and
v. 25a but to the gospel events themselves: 'now'—that is,
since Christ has died and been raised from the dead.[5]

2. ὁ γὰρ νόμος τοῦ πνεύματος τῆς ζωῆς ἐν Χριστῷ Ἰησοῦ ἠλευθέρωσέν σε ἀπὸ τοῦ νόμου τῆς ἁμαρτίας καὶ τοῦ θανάτου. Since v. 1 is
the conclusion drawn from 7.1–6 and v. 2 is connected with it

[1] So F. Müller in the article cited with reference to 7.25b, followed,
for example, by Michel, p. 187.
[2] So Bultmann, 'Glossen', col. 199.
[3] Cf., e.g., Bengel, p. 527: 'Nunc etiam plane ex diverticulo eximio in
viam redit, quae habetur c.7,6' (though it is of the greatest importance
to recognize that 7.7–25 is an excursus only in the sense that it interrupts
the flow of the argument at this point, and not at all in the sense of
being a mere appendage which is not an integral part of the argument
as a whole: it is a necessary interruption, a clarification, without which
the argument would be unsatisfactorily stated and chapter 8 open to
grievous misunderstanding); Gaugler 1, p. 249f; Barrett, p. 154. For
this connexion of 8.1ff with 7.1–6 rather than with 7.7–25 compare the
way in which 7.1–6 in its turn connects not so much with 6.1–14 as
with 6.15–23. It is a characteristic of the sections comprising chapters
5, 6, 7 and 8, that the opening paragraph is the basic statement of the
main point which is to be made and what follows is added by way of
further elucidation or to guard against possible misunderstanding.
[4] The originality of νῦν is not seriously called in question by its
omission by D* 1908mg syp. It is surely to be understood in its temporal,
and not merely in its logical, sense. Cf. the νυνί in 7.6.
[5] The words μὴ κατὰ σάρκα περιπατοῦσιν which follow Ἰησοῦ in A, etc.
(as also the still longer addition in the TR) are clearly not original here,
but have been interpolated under the influence of v. 4, where they are
in place.

by γάρ, it would not be surprising if v. 2 picked up or repeated or was in some way parallel to something in 7.1–6. In fact it states the truth which was hinted at in the last part of the concluding sentence of 7.1–6. The last clause of 7.6 spoke of a δουλεύειν . . . ἐν καινότητι πνεύματος[1] as the result of liberation from the law as condemning us: the present verse expresses this result in a different way, describing it as a further liberation. To say that we have been set free from the law of sin and of death by the νόμος τοῦ πνεύματος τῆς ζωῆς is another way of saying that we now serve ἐν καινότητι πνεύματος. The implication of the γάρ is that the fact that this further liberation has taken place is confirmation of the reality of the fundamental liberation described in v. 1.

But with regard to the first few words of this verse three basic questions have to be answered (in addition to the question—just considered—of the relation of the verse as a whole to what has preceded it):

(i) What is signified here by ὁ νόμος?

(ii) Is τῆς ζωῆς dependent on τοῦ πνεύματος, or is it, as well as τοῦ πνεύματος, dependent on ὁ νόμος?

(iii) Is ἐν Χριστῷ Ἰησοῦ to be taken (a) with τῆς ζωῆς, or (b) with ἠλευθέρωσεν, or—perhaps just conceivably—either (c) with τοῦ πνεύματος τῆς ζωῆς, or (d) with ὁ νόμος?

We shall not attempt to indicate all the conceivable combinations of answers or the various interpretations of which each combination might be patient, but shall simply consider the three questions in turn.

It will be convenient to take (iii) first. Of the four alternatives mentioned, (c), which might perhaps give some such sense as 'the νόμος which in Christ Jesus is τοῦ πνεύματος τῆς ζωῆς', and (d), which might perhaps give some such sense as 'the νόμος in Christ Jesus which is also a νόμος τοῦ πνεύματος τῆς ζωῆς',[2] should probably be rejected as being unnatural. A good many interpreters have favoured (a),[3] and 6.23 has been claimed as

---

[1] In view of 7.6 it is hardly permissible to say of 8.2 with Bruce (p. 160) that 'Apart from the anticipatory mention of the Spirit in Romans v. 5, where His coming is said to flood the hearts of believers with the love of God (and the brief reference in i.4 to the "spirit of holiness" in connexion with Christ's being raised from the dead), this is the first place in the Epistle where the Spirit of God enters the argument'.

[2] Barrett's translation (p. 153), 'the religion which is made possible in Christ Jesus, namely that of the life-giving Spirit', would seem to be based on acceptance of this last alternative.

[3] e.g. Denney, p. 644; Lagrange, p. 191; Moffatt (followed without questioning by Dodd, p. 135); Michel, p. 189. (On the question whether τῆς would have had to be repeated, were this the meaning, reference may be made to BDF, § 269.)

support for it; but (b) seems a more natural way of understanding the Greek,[1] and the fact that in the following sentence (joined as it is with this verse by γάρ) the sending of the Son is the method by which God accomplishes the action described argues strongly in its favour. We conclude that it is most likely that ἐν Χριστῷ Ἰησοῦ should be connected with ἠλευθέρωσεν, and understood to indicate the basis of the operation which the verse describes.

With regard to (i), ὁ νόμος here has been variously explained as signifying the Holy Spirit Himself[2] or faith[3] or the gospel[4] or the authority exercised by the Holy Spirit[5] or—more vaguely—the spiritual life resulting from union with Christ[6] or the religion which is possible in Christ.[7] But in view of the fact that the νόμος τῆς ἁμαρτίας καὶ τοῦ θανάτου mentioned later in this verse is most naturally understood to be identical with the νόμος τῆς ἁμαρτίας referred to in 7.23 and 25 (νόμῳ ἁμαρτίας) and the ἕτερος νόμος mentioned at the beginning of 7.23, it seems natural to ask whether we should not also identify the νόμος τοῦ πνεύματος τῆς ζωῆς with the νόμος τοῦ θεοῦ mentioned in 7.22 (compare νόμῳ θεοῦ in 7.25 and also τῷ νόμῳ τοῦ νοός μου in 7.23) to which the law of sin is opposed. This explanation has the advantage of economy, since by accepting it we should avoid having to attribute to Paul a reference to yet another different law. It may also be said in its support that the association of God's law with πνεῦμα and ζωή looks as if it

---

[1] It seems to be presupposed by Ambrosiaster's comment (col. 116): 'Haec itaque Lex in Christo Jesu, hoc est, per fidem Christi, liberat credentem a lege peccati et mortis', and also by Chrysostom's explanation, in the course of which, after saying that in reply to 7.24b Paul shows (in 7.25a) the Father acting through the Son, he goes on to say with regard to 8.2: εἶτα πάλιν τὸ Πνεῦμα τὸ ἅγιον μετὰ τοῦ Υἱοῦ [sc. τοῦτο ποιοῦντα] (col. 513).

[2] So Chrysostom, for example, comments: νόμον Πνεύματος ἐνταῦθα τὸ Πνεῦμα καλῶν. Ὥσπερ γὰρ νόμον ἁμαρτίας τὴν ἁμαρτίαν, οὕτω νόμον Πνεύματος τὸ Πνεῦμά φησι (col. 513). Cf. Aquinas, p. 110 (602) ('Quae quidem lex potest dici, uno modo, Spiritus Sanctus, ut sit sensus: Lex spiritus, id est lex quae est spiritus'); Calvin, p. 156.

[3] Cf. Aquinas, p. 110 (603): 'Alio modo lex spiritus potest dici proprius effectus Spiritus Sancti, scilicet fides per dilectionem operans. Quae quidem et docet interius de agendis, . . .'.

[4] So Bengel, p. 528, explains νόμος τοῦ πνεύματος as 'evangelium cordi inscriptum'.

[5] Cf., e.g., Sanday and Headlam, p. 190.

[6] Cf., e.g., Lagrange, p. 192 ('la loi ou le régime de l'esprit, la vie spirituelle'); Huby, p. 277. They do not take πνεῦμα here to refer to the Holy Spirit (Lagrange, ibid., states: 'l'esprit de la vie dans le Christ n'est pas l'Esprit-Saint, mais l'esprit que nous tenons de notre union au Christ').

[7] So Barrett, p. 153.

might have been intended to recall 7.14a (οἴδαμεν γὰρ ὅτι ὁ νόμος πνευματικός ἐστιν) and 7.10 (ἡ ἐντολὴ ἡ εἰς ζωήν).[1] But this explanation is not free from objection. A statement to the effect that God's law ἠλευθέρωσέν σε ἀπὸ τοῦ νόμου τῆς ἁμαρτίας καὶ τοῦ θανάτου seems hardly to accord with the thought of this section, the theme of which is God's establishment of His law by His gift of His Spirit to men (see on vv. 4 and 15), and which speaks (v. 3) of τὸ . . . ἀδύνατον τοῦ νόμου, ἐν ᾧ ἠσθένει διὰ τῆς σαρκός. The subject which, in the light of the context, seems appropriate to this predicate is not God's law but the new factor in the human situation, namely, the Holy Spirit's presence and exercised authority and constraint.[2] We conclude that the most probable interpretation of ὁ νόμος here is that which understands it to refer to the authority and constraint exercised upon believers by the Holy Spirit.

Question (ii) may be dealt with more briefly. While it is possible that τῆς ζωῆς, as well as τοῦ πνεύματος, should be understood as dependent on ὁ νόμος ('the Spirit's life-giving law', the law which is of the Spirit and which is also of life),[3] it is perhaps on the whole rather more likely that τῆς ζωῆς was meant to depend on τοῦ πνεύματος ('the law of the life-giving Spirit').[4]

For τοῦ νόμου τῆς ἁμαρτίας see on 7.23. The addition of καὶ τοῦ θανάτου is to be understood in the light of 7.10f, 13. The ultimate end of sin's lordship over us is death.

The tense of ἠλευθέρωσεν is surely to be explained not as 'a kind of gnomic aorist' to be translated 'by an English present'[5] but as indicating that the reference is to the gift of the Spirit to the Christian as an event in the past. This liberation has actually been accomplished.

At this point the ancient witnesses to the text present an interesting variety of readings: με, ἡμᾶς, σε, and, finally, no expressed object at all. The first and second of these readings should be set aside on the ground that they are easily explicable

---

[1] One might indeed be tempted, in spite of what was said on (iii) above, to take ἐν Χριστῷ Ἰησοῦ with τοῦ πνεύματος τῆς ζωῆς, and understand Paul to mean that it is God's law, now established by Christ's work in its true and original character and office as 'spiritual' and 'unto life' (taking both τοῦ πνεύματος and τῆς ζωῆς as dependent on ὁ νόμος), which has effected the believer's liberation.

[2] Even if we think of the law as qualified in the way indicated in the previous foot-note, it still seems a less natural subject of ἠλευθέρωσεν, κ.τ.λ. than the exercised authority of the Spirit.

[3] So, e.g., Bruce, p. 160. Cf. Lk 1.78; 2 Cor 5.1; possibly 1 Tim 1.11.

[4] See BDF, § 168.

[5] As Barrett, p. 153, n. 1, thinks it should be, on the assumption that the reading which omits the object is to be accepted.

as assimilations to the first person singular used in 7.7–25 and to the first person plural used in 8.4, respectively.[1] The possibility that originally the object was unexpressed (the reader being left to supply it from v. 1) cannot be ruled out altogether: there is some slight textual evidence to support it, and the σε could be explained as being the result of an accidental repetition of the final syllable of the verb. But, as far as the possibility of accidental error is concerned, σε could just as easily have been omitted by haplography as added by dittography; and it is so unexpected here that it can hardly be a deliberate attempt at improvement by a copyist. In these circumstances the reading σε, which is the best-attested reading (BℵG 1739 it sy^p), must surely be accepted.[2] Instances of the singling out of the individual as representative of the group for the sake of greater vividness are not uncommon in Romans (cf. 2.1, 3–5, 17–27; 9.19f; 10.9; 11.17–24; 13.3f; 14.4, 10, 15, 20–22); but the present example of the use of the second person singular is specially interesting, because it is so unexpected and is confined to the one word. It would seem that Paul, being aware of the momentousness and amazingness of the truth he was stating (with its significant past tense), wanted to make sure that each individual in the church in Rome realized that what was being said in this sentence was something which really applied to him personally and particularly.[3]

Verse 2 then, as we understand it, states that God's gift of His Spirit to believers, by which His (i.e. the Spirit's) authority and constraint have been brought to bear on their lives, has freed them from the authority and control of sin. But how is this confident affirmation to be understood alongside 7.14b, 23, 25b (τῇ δὲ σαρκὶ νόμῳ ἁμαρτίας)? We have excluded the solution according to which 7.14ff refers to the pre-conversion state. How then can the same man be at the same time both a prisoner of 'the law of sin', and also one who has been freed from 'the law of sin and of death'? In this connexion there are several things which must be said:

(i) Both 7.14b, etc., and 8.2 are indeed true of the Christian life, and neither is to be watered down or explained away.

(ii) While the Christian never in this life escapes entirely

---

[1] The decision of the editors of UBS (1967) to read με is very surprising.
[2] As it is by Nestle, Merk, and BFBS.
[3] It is to be noted that such recent English translations as NEB and JB, having jettisoned the second person singular in favour of 'the plural of politeness' (the latter altogether and the former except in prayer) are unable here to bring out the full significance of the original.

from the hold of egotism, that is, of sin, so that even the best things he does are always marred by its corruption, and any impression of having attained a perfect freedom is but an illusion, itself the expression of that same egotism, there is a vast difference between the ways in which the believer and the unbeliever are prisoners of the law of sin—a difference which fully warrants, we believe, the ἠλευθέρωσεν of 8.2. The believer is no longer an unresisting, or only ineffectually resisting, slave, nor is he one who fondly imagines that his bondage is emancipation. In him a constraint even stronger than that of sin is already at work, which both gives him an inner freedom (cf. 7.22, 25b (τῷ μὲν νοΐ δουλεύω νόμῳ θεοῦ)) and also enables him to revolt against the usurper sin with a real measure of effectiveness. He has received the gift of the freedom to fight back manfully.

(iii) The present effectiveness of the authority of the Spirit in those who are in Christ is the pledge of their future complete freedom from the authority of sin. Between the pressure still exerted on their lives by sin, to which 7.14b, etc., bear witness, and the pressure exerted already by the Holy Spirit, to which 8.1ff testifies, there is no equilibrium: the former is destined to pass away, the latter to be fully realized hereafter.[1]

3–4. The γάρ indicates the connexion between vv. 3–4 and v. 2: the presupposition and basis of the liberating bestowal of the Spirit (and of the absence of condemnation for those who are in Christ) are God's decisive deed in Christ.

τὸ ... ἀδύνατον τοῦ νόμου is to be explained, together with the following clause which is dependent on it, as an accusative in apposition to κατέκρινεν τὴν ἁμαρτίαν ἐν τῇ σαρκί or—less probably—to this together with the whole of v. 4.[2] What the sentence goes on to affirm that God has done is characterized by anticipation as 'what was impossible for the law'.[3]

---

[1] In connexion with this verse I may refer to my contribution, 'The Freedom of the Christian according to Rom 8.2', in M. E. Glasswell and E. W. Fasholé-Luke (ed.), *New Testament Christianity for Africa and the World* (a volume in honour of Professor Harry Sawyerr), London, 1974. See now my *On Romans*, 1998, pp. 33–49.

[2] Cf. τὴν λογικὴν λατρείαν ὑμῶν (in apposition to παραστῆσαι τὰ σώματα ὑμῶν θυσίαν ζῶσαν ἁγίαν τῷ θεῷ εὐάρεστον) in 12.1. See BDF, § 480 (6), and also the earlier discussion in Sanday and Headlam, p. 191f. There seems to be no justification here for pronouncing Paul's sentence incomplete and suggesting supplements, as do, e.g., Michel (p. 189) and Barrett (p. 155).

[3] There has been much discussion as to whether ἀδύνατον is active ('unable') or passive ('impossible'). In spite of the considerable patristic support (e.g. Tertullian, *De res. carn.* 46; Origen (*JTS* 14), p. 17; Cyril of Alexandria, col. 817)—and patristic opinion on a matter of this sort

ἐν ᾧ ἠσθένει διὰ τῆς σαρκός depends on ἀδύνατον, and was added in order to make clear that the fault was not in the law but in men's fallen nature. Compare the comment of Pelagius: 'In quo infirmabatur per carnem. In illis [i.e. in men] infirmabatur, non in se'.[1] ἐν ᾧ more probably (pace Sanday and Headlam[2]) means 'because'[3] than 'in which', 'wherein'.

ὁ θεὸς τὸν ἑαυτοῦ υἱὸν πέμψας. ἑαυτοῦ is emphatic: compare τοῦ ἰδίου υἱοῦ in v. 32. For the use of the terminology of sending in this connexion compare Gal 4.4 (ἐξαποστέλλειν); and, outside the Pauline corpus, Lk 20.13; Jn 4.34; 5.23, 24, 30, 37; 6.38, 39, 44; 7.16, 18, 28, 33; 8.16, 18, 26, 29; 9.4; 12.44, 45, 49; 13.20b; 14.24; 15.21; 16.5, in all of which πέμπειν is used; and (with ἀποστέλλειν) Mt 10.40; 15.24; 21.37; Mk 9.37; 12.6; Lk 4.18, 43; 9.48; Jn 3.17, 34; 5.36, 38; 6.29, 57; 7.29; 8.42; 10.36; 11.42; 17.3, 8, 18, 21, 23, 25; 20.21; 1 Jn 4.9, 10, 14.[4] For υἱόν see on 1.3.

ἐν ὁμοιώματι σαρκὸς ἁμαρτίας. By σάρξ ἁμαρτίας Paul clearly meant 'sinful flesh', i.e., fallen human nature. But why did he say ἐν ὁμοιώματι σαρκὸς ἁμαρτίας rather than just ἐν σαρκὶ ἁμαρτίας? At any rate five alternative solutions to this problem have to be considered:

(i) that he introduced ὁμοίωμα in order to avoid saying ἐν σαρκί, because he did not wish to imply the reality of Christ's human nature. But this solution which attributes a docetic sense to the phrase must of course be rejected, as inconsistent with Paul's thought—it is in fact contradicted in this very verse by ἐν τῇ σαρκί (according to the most likely interpretation of that phrase).

is certainly not to be set aside lightly—for taking it as active, we should almost certainly understand it as passive, since (i) this affords a better sense and a much easier construction (if ἀδύνατον is taken as active, the phrase cannot be in apposition to κατέκρινεν, κ.τ.λ., but has to be explained as a sort of nominative absolute ('the impotence of the law being this that it was weak through the flesh') or perhaps as an accusative of respect ('as to the impotence of the law . . .'); (ii) it agrees with the usage of the Greek Bible, in which this adjective is regularly active in the masculine or feminine, but passive in the neuter (cf. Greek usage generally as illustrated by LSJ, s.v.); (iii) what influenced the Fathers was probably the use of the genitive τοῦ νόμου rather than the dative, but Paul's choice of the genitive here is probably to be explained as due to his partiality for the use of the neuter singular of an adjective with a dependent genitive (see BDF, § 263 (2)).

[1] p. 61.
[2] p. 192.
[3] So BDF, § 219 (2): cf., e.g., Lagrange, p. 193.
[4] On πέμπειν, ἀποστέλλειν and ἐξαποστέλλειν, see K. H. Rengstorf, in TWNT 1, pp. 397ff; also E. Schweizer, 'Zum religionsgeschichtlichen Hintergrund der "Sendungsformel" Gal 4.4f, Röm 8.3f, Joh 3.16f, 1 Joh 4.9', in ZNW 57 (1966), pp. 199–210.

(ii) that he introduced ὁμοίωμα in order to avoid implying that the Son of God assumed *fallen* human nature, the sense being: like our fallen flesh, because really flesh, but only like, and not identical with, it, because unfallen. This, though it is the traditional solution,[1] is open to the general theological objection that it was not unfallen, but fallen, human nature which needed redeeming.[2]

(iii) that he introduced ὁμοίωμα in order to avoid implying that Christ actually sinned, the sense being: like our fallen human nature, because really fallen human nature, and yet only like ours, because not guilty of actual sin by which everywhere else our fallen nature is characterized.[3]

[1] Cf., e.g., Ambrosiaster, col. 117f ('Haec est similitudo carnis: quia quamvis eadem caro sit, quae et nostra; non tamen ita facta in utero est et nata, sicut et caro nostra. Est enim sanctificata in utero, et nata sine peccato, et neque ipse in illa peccavit. Ideo enim virginalis uterus electus est ad partum Dominicum, ut in sanctitate differret caro Domini a carne nostra; in causa enim similis est, non in qualitate peccati substantiae. Propterea ergo similem dixit, quia de eadem substantia carnis, non eamdem habuit nativitatem; quia peccato subjectum non fuit corpus Domini'); Chrysostom, col. 514f (Εἰ δὲ ἐν ὁμοιώματι σαρκός φησι πέμψαι τὸν Υἱόν, μὴ διὰ τοῦτο ἄλλην ἐκείνην σάρκα εἶναι νόμιζε· ἐπειδὴ γὰρ εἶπεν ἁμαρτίας, διὰ τοῦτο καὶ τὸ ὁμοίωμα τέθεικεν. Οὐδὲ γὰρ ἁμαρτωλὸν σάρκα εἶχεν ὁ Χριστός, ἀλλ' ὁμοίαν μὲν τῇ ἡμετέρᾳ τῇ ἁμαρτωλῷ, ἀναμάρτητον δέ, καὶ τῇ φύσει τὴν αὐτὴν ἡμῖν. Ὥστε καὶ ἐντεῦθεν δῆλον ὅτι οὐκ ἦν πονηρὰ τῆς σαρκὸς ἡ φύσις. Οὔτε γὰρ ἑτέραν ἀντὶ τῆς προτέρας λαβὼν ὁ Χριστός, οὔτε αὐτὴν ταύτην μεταβαλὼν κατ' οὐσίαν, οὕτως αὐτὴν ἀναμαχήσασθαι παρεσκεύασεν· ἀλλ' ἀφεὶς μένειν ἐπὶ τῆς αὐτῆς φύσεως, τὸν στέφανον ἀναδήσασθαι ἐποίησε κατὰ τῆς ἁμαρτίας...); Cyril of Alexandria, cols. 817 and 820; Aquinas, p. 111 ('... non est sic intelligendum, quasi veram carnem non habuerit, ... Unde non subdit solum, *in similitudinem carnis*, sed *in similitudinem carnis peccati*. Non enim habuit carnem peccati, id est, cum peccato conceptam, ... Sed habuit similitudinem carnis peccati, id est, similem carni peccatrici in hoc quod erat passibilis. Nam caro hominis, ante peccatum, passioni subiecta non erat'); Calvin, p. 159 ('Christ, he says, came *in the likeness of sinful flesh*. Although the flesh of Christ was unpolluted by any stain, it had the appearance of being sinful, since it sustained the punishment due to our sins, and certainly death exerted every part of its power on the flesh of Christ as though it were subject to it. Because our High Priest had to learn by His own experience what it means to assist the weak, Christ was willing to undergo our infirmities, in order that He might be more inclined to sympathy. In this respect too there appeared in Him a certain resemblance to our sinful nature'); Bengel, p. 528 ('Nos cum carne nostra peccato penitus infecta debueramus morti dedi: sed *Deus in similitudine carnis* illius (nam similitudinem requirebat justitia) i.e. in carne Filii sui vera eademque sancta, *et* (quidem) *pro peccato, condemnavit peccatum* illud, (quod erat) in *carne* (nostra,) ut nos liberaremur'); Sanday and Headlam, p. 193; Dodd, p. 136f.

[2] Cf. the discussion of the question whether the Son of God assumed unfallen or fallen human nature, in Barth, *CD* I/2, pp. 151–59 (= *KD* I/2, pp. 165–73).

[3] Cf., e.g., Gaugler 1, p. 260f.

(iv) that ὁμοίωμα is here to be understood as meaning 'form' rather than 'likeness'—that is, as without any suggestion of mere resemblance.[1]

(v) that the intention behind the use of ὁμοίωμα here (cf. its use in Phil 2.7, where there is no specific mention of sin) was to take account of the fact that the Son of God was not, in being sent by His Father, changed into a man, but rather assumed human nature while still remaining Himself. On this view, the word ὁμοίωμα does have its sense of 'likeness'; but the intention is not in any way to call in question or to water down the reality of Christ's σὰρξ ἁμαρτίας, but to draw attention to the fact that, while the Son of God truly assumed σὰρξ ἁμαρτίας, He never became σὰρξ ἁμαρτίας and nothing more, nor even σὰρξ ἁμαρτίας indwelt by the Holy Spirit and nothing more (as a Christian might be described as being), but always remained Himself.[2]

We have already ruled out (i), and have indicated the serious theological objection which lies against (ii). Against (iv) it must be said that, on this view, it is difficult to understand why Paul was not content simply to say ἐν σαρκὶ ἁμαρτίας. With regard to (iii), it may be suggested that the use of the expression ἐν ὁμοιώματι σαρκὸς ἁμαρτίας was not a satisfactory way of indicating that, though sharing our fallen human nature, Christ never actually sinned; for the effect of the use of ὁμοίωμα is to indicate a difference between Christ's human nature and ours (that His human nature was like, but only like, ours), but the difference between Christ's freedom from actual sin and our sinfulness is not a matter of the character of His human nature (of its being not quite the same as ours), but of what He did with His human nature. And, if this suggestion is right, it may be further suggested that the natural place for Paul to refer to Christ's sinlessness was not in the participial clause which is concerned with God's sending of His Son, but in the main sentence (ὁ θεὸς . . . κατέκρινεν τὴν ἁμαρτίαν ἐν τῇ σαρκί), and that, rightly interpreted, κατέκρινεν, κ.τ.λ. does indeed include the affirmation of Christ's sinlessness. We conclude that (v) is to be accepted as the most probable explanation of Paul's use of ὁμοίωμα here, and understand

[1] So Barrett, p. 156, who understands Paul as thinking that 'Christ took precisely the same fallen nature that we ourselves have' and yet 'remained sinless because he constantly overcame a proclivity to sin'.
[2] Reference may be made here to J. Schneider, in TWNT 5, pp. 195-97; R. P. Martin, Carmen Christi: Philippians ii.5-11 in recent interpretation and in the setting of early Christian worship (Cambridge, 1967), pp. 197ff, 227; Barth, CD I/2, pp. 132-71 (=KD I/2, pp. 145-187).

Paul's thought to be that the Son of God assumed the selfsame fallen human nature that is ours, but that in His case that fallen human nature was never the whole of Him—He never ceased to be the eternal Son of God.

καὶ περὶ ἁμαρτίας¹ belongs to the participial clause: to connect it with κατέκρινεν (taking καί in the sense 'even'), as has sometimes been done,² is forced. Since the expression περὶ ἁμαρτίας is frequently used in the LXX to denote a sin offering (e.g. Lev 14.31—ḥaṭṭā't; Ps 40.6 [LXX: 39.7]—ḥᵃṭā'āh; Isa 53.10—'āšām) or with the meaning 'for a sin offering' (e.g. Lev 9.2—lᵉḥaṭṭā't), it has quite often been understood here to mean 'as an offering for sin'.³ But the context does not seem to support this sacrificial interpretation. So it is better to take it in a general sense as indicating that with which the mission of the Son had to do.⁴

κατέκρινεν τὴν ἁμαρτίαν ἐν τῇ σαρκί. There are two main questions which need to be answered here: (i) How is ἐν τῇ σαρκί to be construed? and (ii) What is meant by κατέκρινεν?

Of these the former is quite easily answered. ἐν τῇ σαρκί is to be connected not with τὴν ἁμαρτίαν (Paul surely did not mean to suggest that only sin dwelling in man's flesh was affected, and that in so far as sin is a power external to man it was unscathed), but with κατέκρινεν. It tells us where God's 'condemnation' of sin took place. It took place in the flesh, i.e., in Christ's flesh, Christ's human nature.

The latter is more difficult. In view of τὸ ἀδύνατον τοῦ νόμου, the verb κατακρίνειν must here denote something more than the pronouncing of sentence of condemnation, for this the law was certainly able to do. As F. Büchsel has pointed out,⁵ where God's κατακρίνειν is concerned, the distinction between the pronouncement of sentence and its execution may lose its importance, and the verb may denote both of these together as one single act. We may therefore understand it here as meaning such a combination of sentence and execution as constitutes a final and altogether decisive dealing with its object—so God's

---

¹ The omission of these words (110 pc) is no doubt accidental (after ἁμαρτίας). To regard them as a gloss as did Jülicher is quite unjustified.

² e.g. by Calvin, who translated: 'etiam de peccato damnavit peccatum in carne'.

³ e.g. Origen, col. 1095; Aquinas, p. 111 (609); Bruce, p. 161; RV, NEB.

⁴ Cf., e.g., Lagrange, p. 193; Gaugler 1, p. 262f; Michel, p. 190; Barrett, p. 156.

⁵ In TWNT 3, p. 953. His treatment of κατακρίνειν includes a suggestive discussion of this clause.

effective breaking of sin's power.[1] That Paul had in mind Christ's death as the event in which the full weight of God's wrath against sin (see on 1.18) was, in the flesh of Christ, that is, in His human nature, so effectively brought to bear upon all the sin of all mankind, as to rule out its ever having to be brought to bear upon it in any other flesh—this is scarcely to be doubted. But, if we recognize that Paul believed it was fallen human nature which the Son of God assumed, we shall probably be inclined to see here also a reference to the unintermittent warfare of His whole earthly life by which He forced our rebellious nature to render a perfect obedience to God.[2]

ἵνα τὸ δικαίωμα τοῦ νόμου πληρωθῇ ἐν ἡμῖν τοῖς μὴ κατὰ σάρκα περιπατοῦσιν ἀλλὰ κατὰ πνεῦμα expresses the purpose of God's 'condemnation' of sin. And, since final clauses which express God's purposes carry also a consecutive sense (for all God's purposes come in the end to fulfilment), we may say that it has this as its result—it leads to this. This ἵνα-clause at the same time clarifies the significance of the liberation spoken of in v. 2. This is the meaning of the believer's liberation. This is what we have been set free for.

By δικαίωμα is meant here not 'righteousness', 'act of

[1] To explain that the ἵνα- clause (v. 4) is to be connected specially closely with κατέκρινεν, κ.τ.λ. so that it becomes simply a clarification of the meaning of κατέκρινεν (this condemnation being defined as such a condemnation as has this for its effect), and that τὸ ἀδύνατον . . . διὰ τῆς σαρκός stands in apposition not just to κατέκρινεν τὴν ἁμαρτίαν ἐν τῇ σαρκί but to that together with the following ἵνα-clause (the sense being that what the law could not do was so to condemn sin as to produce this effect), though it seems at first sight rather attractive, is surely much less natural.

[2] In this connexion it is interesting to refer to *Credo*, p. 73, where Barth draws attention to the striking contrast between Calvin's Geneva Catechism of 1545, in which in reply to the question why the Creed passes straight from Christ's birth to His death the scholar has to say: 'Here there is mentioned only what belongs to the real substance of our Redemption', and the Heidelberg Catechism which understands the word 'suffered' to cover the whole of Christ's earthly life (though, in fairness to Calvin, it should be said that in the first few sentences of *Institutes* 2.16.5 he does himself show awareness of the redemptive significance of the 'whole course' of Christ's obedience). Those who believe that it was fallen human nature which was assumed have even more cause than had the authors of the Heidelberg Catechism to see the whole of Christ's life on earth as having redemptive significance; for, on this view, Christ's life before His actual ministry and death was not just a standing where unfallen Adam had stood without yielding to the temptation to which Adam succumbed, but a matter of starting from where we start, subjected to all the evil pressures which we inherit, and using the altogether unpromising and unsuitable material of our corrupt nature to work out a perfect, sinless obedience.

righteousness' as in 5.18, nor 'justification'[1] as in 5.16 (this word is only chosen there because Paul has just used other words ending in -μα), but 'requirement', 'righteous requirement', as in 2.26. The use of the singular is significant. It brings out the fact that the law's requirements are essentially a unity, the plurality of commandments being not a confused and confusing conglomeration but a recognizable and intelligible whole, the fatherly will of God for His children.[2] God's purpose in 'condemning' sin was that His law's requirement might be fulfilled in us, that is, that His law might be established in the sense of at last being truly and sincerely obeyed—the fulfilment of the promises of Jer 31.33[3] and Ezek 36.26f. But πληρωθῇ is not to be taken to imply that the faithful fulfil the law's requirement perfectly. Chapter 7 must not be forgotten. They fulfil it in the sense that they do have a real faith in God (which is the law's basic demand), in the sense that their lives are definitely turned in the direction of obedience, that they do sincerely desire to obey and are earnestly striving to advance ever nearer to perfection. But, so long as they remain in this present life, their faith is always in some measure mixed with unbelief, their obedience is always imperfect and incomplete. And this means of course that there can never be any question of their being able to make their new obedience a claim on God. Grace was indeed given, in order that the law might be fulfilled, as Augustine says,[4] but not in order that by their fulfilment of the law the faithful might justify themselves. The gospel was certainly not given in order that a new legalism might be established more securely than the old. It has been suggested[5] that ἐν ἡμῖν should be translated 'among us'; but, while ἐν can of course mean 'among' as well as 'in', this sense does not seem appro-

---

[1] *Pace*, e.g., Calvin, p. 160 (and see his translation). Calvin rightly saw that Paul was not likely to have meant that those who are renewed by the Spirit fulfil the law's requirement perfectly, but this insight should have led him, not to give δικαίωμα a meaning which in this clause is thoroughly forced, but to give πληρωθῇ a limited sense.

[2] Cf. such OT passages as Lev 19.18b; Deut 6.4f; Mic 6.8: also Mk 12.28–34; Rom 13.9, etc.

[3] Jer 31.31–34 is often understood as a promise of a new law to take the place of the old (cf. Michel, p. 189: 'Gemeint ist, . . . dass das mosaische Gesetz durch den Christus in ein Gesetz ganz anderer und neuer Art verwandelt wird (Jer 31,31–34)') or else as a promise of a religion without law at all. But the new thing promised in v. 33 is, in fact, neither a new law nor freedom from law, but a sincere inward desire and determination on the part of God's people to obey the law already given to them ('my law').

[4] 'Gratia data est, ut lex impleretur' (*De Spir. et litt.* 19.34).

[5] e.g., by Gaugler 1, p. 265f.

priate here, since there can hardly be a corporate fulfilment of the law's requirement independently of its fulfilment in the obedience of the several members of the believing community.

The words τοῖς μὴ κατὰ σάρκα περιπατοῦσιν ἀλλὰ κατὰ πνεῦμα are not to be understood as expressing a condition of the law's requirement's being fulfilled in us (as though the meaning were 'in order that the righteous requirement of the law might be fulfilled in us, provided we walk . . .'), nor yet as describing us as we are independently of the fulfilment of the law's requirement and independently also of the divine action described in v. 3 (as though our so walking were our own doing, our independent and meritorious work), but rather as indicating the manner of the fulfilment of the law's require-ment (God's purpose in sending His Son and condemning sin was that the requirement of the law might be fulfilled by our walking not according to the flesh but according to the Spirit).[1] Thus these words serve to clarify the meaning of πληρωθῇ. The law's requirement will be fulfilled by the determination of the direction, the set, of our lives by the Spirit, by our being enabled again and again to decide for the Spirit and against the flesh, to turn our backs more and more upon our own insatiable egotism and to turn our faces more and more toward the freedom which the Spirit of God has given us.

5. οἱ γὰρ κατὰ σάρκα ὄντες τὰ τῆς σαρκὸς φρονοῦσιν, οἱ δὲ κατὰ πνεῦμα τὰ τοῦ πνεύματος. The γάρ may be said to indicate the relation to v. 4 not just of v. 5 but of vv. 5–11 as a whole. They provide an explanation of the reference in v. 4 to walking not κατὰ σάρκα but κατὰ πνεῦμα.

Though it might seem rather tempting to press the use of the verb εἶναι in this verse as referring to being rather than conduct, on the ground that this would afford a somewhat bigger difference of meaning between οἱ κατὰ σάρκα ὄντες and τὰ τῆς σαρκὸς φρονοῦσιν, it is more probable that Paul simply used οἱ κατὰ σάρκα ὄντες as synonymous with οἱ κατὰ σάρκα περιπατοῦντες (that he has not developed a carefully fixed technical terminology is clear from, for example, his use of ἐν σαρκί in v. 8—contrast Gal 2.20).

In view of the widespread attestation of τά τινος φρονεῖν meaning 'to be of someone's mind', 'to be on someone's side',

---

[1] For the metaphorical use of περιπατεῖν with reference to someone's way of life, moral conduct, see on 6.4. For its use with κατά cf. Mk 7.5 (κατὰ τὴν παράδοσιν τῶν πρεσβυτέρων); Rom 14.15 (κατὰ ἀγάπην); Eph 2.2 (κατὰ τὸν αἰῶνα τοῦ κόσμου τούτου, κατὰ τὸν ἄρχοντα τῆς ἐξουσίας τοῦ ἀέρος, κ.τ.λ.); 2 Jn 6 (κατὰ τὰς ἐντολὰς αὐτοῦ).

'to be of someone's party',¹ and the appropriateness of such a meaning here, it is natural to understand τὰ τῆς σαρκὸς φρονοῦσιν and τὰ τοῦ πνεύματος (φρονοῦσιν) in this sense. We take Paul's meaning in this verse then to be that those who allow the direction of their lives to be determined by the flesh are actually taking the flesh's side in the conflict between the Spirit of God and the flesh, while those who allow the Spirit to determine the direction of their lives are taking the Spirit's side.

6 is linked to v. 5 by γάρ, because it is intended as explanation of the opposition between the Spirit and the flesh presupposed in v. 5. *Pace* the AV,² Barrett,³ *et al.*, the expressions τὸ φρόνημα τῆς σαρκός and τὸ φρόνημα τοῦ πνεύματος are not equivalents of τὸ τὰ τῆς σαρκὸς φρονεῖν and τὸ τὰ τοῦ πνεύματος φρονεῖν, but denote, respectively, the flesh's (i.e., fallen human nature's) mind, that is, its outlook, assumptions, values, desires and purposes, which those who take the side of the flesh share, and the Spirit's mind, which those who take the side of the Spirit share.⁴ We may compare the use of φρόνημα in v. 27, though there its meaning is more specific. The genitives τῆς σαρκός and τοῦ πνεύματος are subjective. The predicates θάνατος and ζωὴ καὶ εἰρήνη characterize the mind of the flesh and the mind of the Spirit in terms of their respective fruits. For θάνατος compare especially 7.10, 11, 13, 24; 8.2; for ζωή compare especially 7.10; 8.2, 10, 11; and for εἰρήνη compare 1.7; 2.10; 5.1; 14.17; 15.13, 33 (see notes on 1.7).

7. διότι τὸ φρόνημα τῆς σαρκὸς ἔχθρα εἰς θεόν explains why the mind of the flesh has death for its fruit: it is because (διότι) it is essentially enmity toward God.

τῷ γὰρ νόμῳ τοῦ θεοῦ οὐχ ὑποτάσσεται, οὐδὲ γὰρ δύναται⁵ is, in its turn, explanatory (γάρ) of the statement that the mind of the flesh is enmity toward God. Fallen man's fierce hostility to God is the response of his egotism (which is the essence of his

---

¹ e.g. Herodotus 2.162.6; 7.102.2; Sophocles, *Aj.* 491; Aristophanes, *Pax* 640; Xenophon, *Hell.* 6.3.4; 7.4.40; Demosthenes 18.161; *In Phil.* 3.56; Diodorus Siculus 20.35.2; Add. Esth 16.1 [LXX: 8.12b]; 1 Macc 10.20; Josephus, *Ant.* 14.450; Polyaenus (2nd cent. A.D.) 8.14.3; Herodian (3rd cent. A.D.) 8.6.6. See also Cranfield, *The Gospel according to Saint Mark*, Cambridge, ⁴1972, p. 28of, on Mk 8.33.

² 'to be carnally minded', 'to be spiritually minded', and, in the margin, 'the minding of the flesh', 'the minding of the Spirit'.

³ 'to have one's mind set on the flesh', 'to have one's mind set on the Spirit'.

⁴ The Vulgate renderings of φρόνημα, *prudentia* in v. 6 and *sapientia* in v. 7, are not far from the mark, if the words *prudentia* and *sapientia* are understood in the same sort of sense as σοφία has in Jas 3.15 and 17.

⁵ The infinitive ὑποτάσσεσθαι is, of course, to be supplied.

fallenness) to God's claim to his allegiance. Determined to assert himself, to assert his independence, to be the centre of his own life, to be his own god, he cannot help but hate the real God whose very existence gives the lie to all his self-assertion. His hatred of God and his rebellion against God's claim upon him expressed in God's law are inseparable from each other. As a rebel against God he hates God, and as one who hates God he rebels against Him. That mind of our fallen nature (its assumptions, desires, outlook, etc.) which is enmity toward God is also unsubmissive to His law, and indeed by its very nature is incapable of submitting to it. Even in the Christian this is still true, as 7.14–25 has made clear: but in the Christian fallen human nature is not left to itself.

8. The δέ is correctly rendered by 'and' (not 'so then', as in the AV, nor 'It follows that', as Barrett, p. 158, translates). The verse simply repeats the substance of v. 7 in a personal form, which prepares the way for the direct address to the readers in v. 9.

Here and in v. 9 ἐν σαρκί is used (as was ἐν τῇ σαρκί in 7.5) in the sense which was expressed by κατὰ σάρκα in vv. 4 and 5, and not, as, for example, in Gal 2.20, to denote the condition in which even those who are walking κατὰ πνεῦμα have still to live in this present life.[1] Those who allow the direction of their lives to be determined by their fallen nature are, so long as they do so, unable to please God, because they are fundamentally hostile to Him and opposed to His will. For θεῷ ἀρέσαι compare 12.1, 2; 14.18; 1 Cor 7.32; 2 Cor 5.9; Eph 5.10; Phil 4.18; Col 3.20; 1 Th 4.1; also Jn 8.29; Heb 13.21; 1 Jn 3.22.

9. ὑμεῖς δὲ οὐκ ἐστὲ ἐν σαρκὶ ἀλλὰ ἐν πνεύματι. Paul now addresses the Roman Christians directly. They are not ἐν σαρκί (in the sense in which the expression was used in v. 8) and consequently unable to please God: on the contrary, they are ἐν πνεύματι. The direction of their life is determined not by the flesh but by the Spirit of God.[2] The double statement is made as a statement of fact, of their actual situation which has been brought about by God.[3] The very fact of their

---

[1] In 2 Cor 10.3 ἐν σαρκί and κατὰ σάρκα are actually opposed to each other.

[2] ἐν πνεύματι has often been understood to refer to the human spirit or to the spiritual enrichment of the human spirit effected by the presence of the Holy Spirit (e.g., among modern commentators, Sanday and Headlam, p. 196; Cornely, p. 407; Zahn, p. 390f); but it is much more satisfactory to take πνεῦμα throughout vv. 1–11 to refer to the Holy Spirit (cf., e.g., Michel, p. 192f).

[3] Cf. Gaugler 1, p. 272 ('Es handelt sich . . . um eine wirkliche Situation, die von Gott geschaffen wurde . . .').

faith in Christ, their justification, their baptism, involves also their being not 'in the flesh' but 'in the Spirit'. This is not called in question by the following clause; for εἴπερ πνεῦμα θεοῦ οἰκεῖ ἐν ὑμῖν is not to be understood as making the assertion of the main clause conditional, as a discreet warning of the possibility that some of them may not be indwelt by the Spirit after all, but as an appeal to a fact acknowledged by them[1] in confirmation of that assertion. It indicates a *fulfilled* condition.[2] For the use of οἰκεῖν ἐν[3] to denote 'a settled permanent penetrative influence' (Sanday and Headlam, p. 196), possession by a power superior to the self, compare 7.18, 20; 8.11; 1 Cor 3.16; also (ἐνοικεῖν) 7.17; 8.11; Col 3.16; 2 Tim 1.5, 14.[4] Used of the Holy Spirit, it denotes the mystery of His presence.

εἰ δέ τις πνεῦμα Χριστοῦ οὐκ ἔχει, οὗτος οὐκ ἔστιν αὐτοῦ is paren-thetic. Whether or not Michel is right in thinking of it as a formula of exclusion (cf. 1 Cor 16.22a) already in use in the Church which Paul cites as a witness to the truth that belong-ing to Christ carries with it the possession of the Spirit,[5] it is clear that its purpose here is the positive one of asserting that every Christian is indwelt by the Spirit. The sentence has also, of course, a negative significance, namely, that the man who does not have the Spirit (whose life bears no evidences of the Spirit's sanctifying work) is no Christian, however much he may claim to be one (compare what was said above on chapter 6)—though this is not the point which Paul wishes to stress here. That the same Spirit is meant by both πνεῦμα θεοῦ and πνεῦμα Χριστοῦ is evident. The ease with which Paul can pass from the one expression to the other is one more indica-tion of his recognition of the divine dignity of Christ. (See the essay in volume 2 on the theology of Romans.) Paul's choice

---

[1] Cf. 1 Cor 3.16 and 6.19, where the οὐκ οἴδατε form suggests that Paul regards the doctrine of the Spirit's indwelling of believers as a fundamental Christian truth.

[2] So Chrysostom, col. 518, and many others. Cf. the Old Latin rendering of εἴπερ here by 'si quidem' (contrast Vulgate 'si tamen'). For this use of εἴπερ cf. 3.30; 8.17; 2 Th 1.6. Εἰ is used with the same sense in vv. 10 and 11 (cf., e.g., 6.8; 8.31; Mt 6.30). We may translate by 'seeing that' or 'since' or 'if, as is the fact'. See LSJ, s.v. εἴπερ II, and εἰ B.VI; Bauer, s.v. εἰ III and VI.11.

[3] On the ἐν Bengel, p. 529, observes well: '*In*, particula valde observanda hoc capite, v. 1-4. 8-11. 15. de statu carnali et spirituali'. That the sense conveyed by it varies in the course of these verses is of course clear: it is particularly clear in this verse.

[4] For illustrations of the Jewish use of šārāh (Aramaic: šĕrā') meaning 'rest', 'dwell' see SB 3, p. 241; also Jastrow, *Dictionary*, p. 1629f.

[5] p. 192f.

here in particular of πνεῦμα Χριστοῦ—if the sentence is his own construction and not a pre-Pauline formula—may perhaps have been decided by consideration of what he intended to say in the apodosis.[1]

10. εἰ δὲ Χριστὸς ἐν ὑμῖν. On the significance of εἰ here see on v. 9 (εἴπερ). The fact that Paul, after referring to the Spirit's dwelling in Christians in v. 9, now goes on to speak of Christ's being in them, has led some to conclude that he was unable to distinguish between the exalted Christ and the Spirit. But neither this passage nor 2 Cor 3.17f demands such an interpretation, and both passages contain phrases which are inconsistent with the identification of the Spirit and the exalted Christ (πνεῦμα Χριστοῦ in v. 9 and πνεῦμα κυρίου in 2 Cor 3.17). Paul's thought is rather that through the indwelling of the Spirit Christ Himself is present to us, the indwelling of the Spirit being 'the manner of Christ's dwelling in us'.[2]

τὸ μὲν σῶμα νεκρὸν διὰ ἁμαρτίαν, τὸ δὲ πνεῦμα ζωὴ διὰ δικαιοσύνην. If νεκρόν is taken to refer to the death to sin in God's sight of which baptism is the seal or to baptism itself or to the moral death to sin to which baptism engages the Christian, it is natural to understand both parts of this carefully balanced formulation as stating consequences of Christ's indwelling.[3] But an explanation along these lines is unlikely, since these deaths are (according to chapter 6) 'to sin' rather than 'because of sin'.[4] We take the reference to be then to the fact that the Christian must still submit to death as the wages of sin, because he is a sinner. The word νεκρός is used instead of θνητός for the sake of vividness and emphasis.[5] This interpretation is confirmed by v. 11 (τὰ θνητὰ σώματα ὑμῶν). But, if this is right, the first of the two parallel clauses is not properly consequential on εἰ . . . Χριστὸς ἐν ὑμῖν—those in whom Christ does not dwell are equally mortal—and we must recognize an example of parataxis where, according to the thought, one clause is subordinate. We may translate the μέν clause as concessive.[6]

---

[1] Cf. Gaugler 1, p. 275.
[2] Calvin, p. 165. On the question of Paul's understanding of the relation of the exalted Christ to the Holy Spirit reference may be made to Taylor, *Person of Christ*, pp. 53–55; N. Q. Hamilton, *The Holy Spirit and Eschatology in Paul*, Edinburgh, 1957, pp. 3–16; E. Schweizer, in *TWNT* 6, pp. 413ff.
[3] So, e.g., Barrett, p. 159.
[4] Cf. Zahn, p. 389; Michel, p. 193, n. 1.
[5] Cf. Augustine, col. 2073: '*Corpus mortuum* dicitur, mortale'.
[6] Cf., e.g., Lagrange, p. 198; Bruce, p. 164; RSV; NEB.

The term πνεῦμα is here often understood anthropologically as denoting the Christian's inner life as opposed to his body,[1] but Barrett rightly objects that, had Paul meant by πνεῦμα the human spirit, he would have said that it was alive, not that it was life (he aptly compares 1 Cor 15.45).[2] Both the use of ζωή and the rest of the occurrences of πνεῦμα in vv. 1–11 favour the view that πνεῦμα here signifies the Holy Spirit. Paul's meaning is that, since Christ is in them through the indwelling of the Spirit, they, though they[3] still have to die because they are sinners, have the presence of the Spirit (who is essentially life-giving) as the assurance that they will finally be raised up from death. The significance of διὰ δικαιοσύνην is that, just as their having to die is due to the fact of their sin, so their being indwelt by the life-giving Spirit as the pledge of their future resurrection (that is, the Spirit's being ζωή *for them*, not, of course, His being ζωή *in itself*) is due to the fact of their justification.[4]

11 spells out more precisely the affirmation already made in v. 10.

εἰ δὲ τὸ πνεῦμα τοῦ ἐγείραντος τὸν[5] Ἰησοῦν ἐκ νεκρῶν οἰκεῖ ἐν ὑμῖν. After his reference to Christ as indwelling (v. 10), Paul once again refers to the Spirit's indwelling. But, instead of using πνεῦμα θεοῦ or πνεῦμα Χριστοῦ (as in v. 9), he now calls the Spirit τὸ πνεῦμα τοῦ ἐγείραντος τὸν Ἰησοῦν ἐκ νεκρῶν (for the title of God compare 4.24), because he wants to bring out the close connexion between the resurrection of Christ and the resurrection of Christians (compare 1 Cor 6.14; 15.20, 23; 2 Cor 4.14; Phil 3.21; 1 Th 4.14). The name Ἰησοῦς is here preferred, since it is the historical event of the Resurrection as such on which attention is being focused.

ὁ ἐγείρας ἐκ νεκρῶν Χριστὸν Ἰησοῦν.[6] The solemn repetition

[1] So, e.g., Sanday and Headlam, p. 198; Zahn, p. 391; Gaugler 1, p. 276; RSV; NEB; JB.

[2] p. 159.

[3] When it is recognized that πνεῦμα is not to be taken anthropologically, it becomes clear that σῶμα does not mean a mere part of the man but the man himself as a whole.

[4] This interpretation (cf. Vulgate 'propter justificationem') is surely more natural, in view of the parallelism with διὰ ἁμαρτίαν and also in view of what seems to be the course of the argument (it is not till v. 12 that Paul explicitly returns to the subject of the Christian's ethical obligation), than that which understands δικαιοσύνην as referring to moral righteousness and this second διά as expressing purpose (so, e.g., Lietzmann, p. 80; Lagrange, p. 199).

[5] τόν is omitted by C Ӿ D G *pl* Cl.

[6] The words ἐκ νεκρῶν Χριστὸν Ἰησοῦν appear in four different orders in the textual tradition, and, in addition, sometimes the word Χριστόν, and sometimes the word Ἰησοῦν, is omitted, and sometimes the definite

and the use of titles describing God by reference to His mighty works or His attributes are both characteristics of Jewish and early Christian prayer and hymnody. There is a certain appropriateness in the use of the title Χριστός here (contrast the simple proper name earlier in this verse), since it is in this part of the sentence that the close connexion between the resurrection of Christ and the resurrection of those who belong to Him comes more clearly into view, and so the fact that He was raised as the head of a people,[1] whether or not Paul was actually influenced by this consideration in varying his language.

ζωοποιήσει was understood by Calvin to refer to 'the continual operation of the Spirit, by which He gradually mortifies the remains of the flesh and renews in us the heavenly life';[2] but, in view of the probable meaning of v. 10, the use of θνητά here, the way in which the thought of dying and living is picked up in v. 13 (μέλλετε ἀποθνήσκειν and ζήσεσθε), and also the fact that the subject of ethics seems to be introduced in v. 12 as something which has not been referred to for some verses, it is better to understand it as referring to the final resurrection, as did, for example, Chrysostom[3] and Augustine.[4]

καὶ τὰ θνητὰ σώματα ὑμῶν. The point which καί[5] is intended to emphasize is, of course, not that their bodies will be quickened in addition to their spirits, but that they will be quickened in addition to Christ. For the meaning of τὰ . . . σώματα ὑμῶν see on σῶμα in v. 10.

διὰ τοῦ ἐνοικοῦντος αὐτοῦ πνεύματος ἐν ὑμῖν. The textual authorities are divided between this reading and διὰ τὸ ἐνοικοῦν αὐτοῦ πνεῦμα ἐν ὑμῖν. In view of the facts that both readings have strong and early attestation and that other considerations here cannot be said to be conclusive, there is a considerable element of doubt as to which should be adopted. But, although the opposite view is taken by some (e.g. E. Schweizer, in *TWNT* 6, p. 419, n. 591), we are fairly confident that the genitive reading is what Paul dictated, for the following reasons: (i) While the

article is inserted before Χριστόν. The UBS editors have accepted the reading [τὸν] Χριστὸν ἐκ νεκρῶν; but, against their decision (and in favour of the Nestle text), it may be said that the placing of ἐκ νεκρῶν after the name is plausibly explicable as assimilation to the τὸν Ἰησοῦν ἐκ νεκρῶν earlier in the verse. Concerning this textual question there remains (as the UBS editors indicate) a very high degree of doubt, but no substantial difference of meaning is involved. [Nestle[26] reads Χριστὸν ἐκ νεκρῶν.]

[1] Cf. Loane, p. 43.
[2] p. 166.
[3] col. 519.
[4] col. 2073.
[5] καί is omitted by ℵ A *pc*.

support for the accusative is undoubtedly impressive, the attestation of the genitive has perhaps, all things considered, rather more weight; (ii) The alteration of the genitive to the accusative is explicable as assimilation to διὰ ἁμαρτίαν and διὰ δικαιοσύνην in the previous verse; (iii) It is not easy to think of a really plausible explanation of either the accidental or the deliberate alteration of the accusative to the genitive (the Macedonian controversy is of course too late to be adduced); (iv) The genitive ('by the agency of') seems to fit the statement of v. 10 that the Spirit is life rather better than the accusative ('on account of', 'for the sake of'), while this advantage is not obvious enough to have been a likely motive for changing an original accusative into a genitive.

Whereas, if the accusative reading were accepted, the meaning would be that the Spirit indwelling Christians now will be a reason for God's raising them up hereafter,[1] if the genitive is adopted, the meaning is that the Spirit who now dwells in them will hereafter be the agent of God in raising them up.[2]

(ii) *The indwelling of the Spirit—the establishment of God's law* (8.12–16)

[12]So then, brothers, we are debtors, not to the flesh to live according to the flesh. [13]For if you live according to the flesh, you will certainly die; but if by the Spirit you put to death the activities of the body, you shall live. [14]For as many as are led by the Spirit of God, these are sons of God. [15]For you have not received a spirit of slavery to lead you back into fear, but you have received the Spirit of adoption, by whose enabling we cry, 'Abba, Father'. [16]The Spirit himself assures our spirit that we are children of God.

[1] Cf. the use (in connexion with the Spirit) of ἀπαρχή (8.23), and ἀρραβών (2 Cor 1.22; 5.5; Eph 1.14).

[2] The fact that no other Pauline passage explicitly ascribing to the Spirit a role in the resurrection of the dead can be adduced in support of this is not (*pace* E. Schweizer, in *TWNT* 6, p. 419, n. 591) an adequate ground for rejecting the genitive. We may compare, in addition to v. 10 (τὸ δὲ πνεῦμα ζωή), 1.4 and 1 Tim 3.16, which appear to make *some* connexion between the Spirit and Christ's resurrection; 2 Cor 3.6, where ζωοποιεῖν is used of the Spirit; 1 Cor 6.14, where possibly διὰ τῆς δυνάμεως αὐτοῦ should be understood as parallel to διὰ τοῦ . . . αὐτοῦ πνεύματος here; and 1 Cor 15.45, which is perhaps indirect evidence of the association of the Spirit with resurrection. In the OT Ezek 37.14 is of course relevant, and relevant also is the Rabbinic teaching derived from it, e.g. *Exod R.* 48 (102d): 'In this world my Spirit has given wisdom within you, but in the future my Spirit will make you alive again'. That the Spirit had an important role in creation was of course well established doctrine (e.g. Gen 1.2; Job 33.4; Ps 104.30); and the analogy between creation and resurrection is an obvious one.

The sub-section begins by referring to the obligation which rests on Paul and the recipients of the letter (the first person plural is used here), making the negative point that this obligation is not to the flesh to live according to it. After breaking off to warn the recipients (second person plural) of the consequence which will follow, if they do yield allegiance to the flesh, Paul then, instead of going on to speak positively of the believers' obligation to the Spirit, promises life to the Roman Christians if they mortify the flesh. Verse 14 clarifies v. 13b, repeating its substance in different terms and as a general third person plural statement: the life promised for believers is no mere not-dying, but life as sons of God. Verse 15 with its positive assertion, 'you have received the Spirit of adoption', harks back to the basic indicatives of vv. 1–11 which are the presupposition of what is said in vv. 12–16, and gives to the obligation to the Spirit to live according to the Spirit, which was implied in v. 12 but never expressed, definitive expression in the relative clause, 'by whose enabling we cry, "Abba, Father" '. The implication of this verse understood in its context is that it is in the believers' calling God 'Father' that God's holy law is established and its 'righteous requirement' (v. 4) fulfilled, and that the whole of Christian obedience is included in this calling God 'Father'. The verse, in fact, states in principle everything that there is to say in the way of Christian ethics; for there is nothing more required of us than that we should do just this—with full understanding of what it means, with full seriousness and with full sincerity. For to address the true God by the name of Father with full sincerity and seriousness will involve seeking wholeheartedly to be and think and say and do that which is pleasing to Him and to avoid everything which displeases Him. (But Paul knows, of course, that Christians continue to be sinners so long as they live this present life (cf. 7.14ff), and so he knows how necessary it is also to spell out in concrete and particular exhortation what is involved in calling God 'Father' truly—a task he will attempt to fulfil for the Roman church in 12.1–15.13.) Paul speaks of this calling God 'Father' as something which is actually happening ('we cry'). Believers do this, and their doing it is God's gift given in His gift of His Spirit. The indicative, of course, contains an implicit imperative—that they must continue to do it, and do it ever more and more sincerely, consistently and resolutely. But Paul sees the imperative as being essentially God's gift, the freedom which He has given us in His gift of His Spirit on the basis of Christ's completed work, the freedom which we are permitted to enjoy.

Finally, v. 16 points to our warrant for daring to call God 'Father'—the fact that He, whose testimony is in this matter the only testimony which carries weight, Himself assures us that we are God's children.[1]

12. Ἄρα οὖν (see on 7.25b) here introduces a new paragraph setting forth the practical conclusion to be drawn from vv. 1–11.

ἀδελφοί. See on 1.13.

ὀφειλέται ἐσμέν, οὐ τῇ σαρκὶ τοῦ κατὰ σάρκα ζῆν. The position of the negative strongly suggests that Paul intended to continue with something like ἀλλὰ τῷ πνεύματι τοῦ κατὰ πνεῦμα ζῆν, but broke off in order to insert the warning of v. 13a, and then, after adding a natural complement to v. 13a, failed to complete the sentence begun in v. 12. For ὀφειλέται see on 1.14. It follows from what has been said in vv. 1–11 that we have no duty to the flesh to allow our lives to be determined by it. For κατὰ σάρκα see on vv. 4 and 5. The genitive of the articular infinitive here may be explained as approximating to the consecutive sense (cf. BDF, § 400 (2)) or simply as epexegetic.

13. The two contrasted conditional clauses indicate the two possibilities of human existence. Compare Deut 11.26ff; 30.15ff: in the latter passage, as here, life and death are presented as the consequences of the alternative ways.

μέλλετε ἀποθνήσκειν. The periphrastic future is used to emphasize that the consequence is necessary and certain, since it is God's judgment. ἀποθνήσκειν is pregnant: the meaning is not merely that they will die (those who live according to the Spirit have also to die—compare v. 10), but that they will die without hope of life with God.

πνεύματι is an instrumental dative. The Spirit of God—and only the Spirit of God—is to be the means of the destruction of the flesh and its activities.[2] But the dative is not to be taken to imply that the Holy Spirit is to be a tool in the hands of Christians, wielded and managed by them. A safeguard against such a misunderstanding is afforded by πνεύματι θεοῦ ἄγονται in the next verse.

πράξεις is used quite often by Polybius to denote political intrigues and treacheries (cf. Lagrange, p. 200; LSJ, s.v. V. 2), and it is possible that something of this pejorative significance adheres to it here. (See also on πράσσω in 7.15.)

[1] On the history of exegesis of this sub-section reference may be made to C. M. Kempton Hewitt, *Life in the Spirit: a study in the history of interpretation of Romans 8.12–17*, Durham University Ph.D. thesis, 1969.

[2] Cf. Barth, 1933, p. 295.

τοῦ σώματος. The word σῶμα here is best understood as used in the sense of σάρξ, by which it is actually replaced in some authorities (D G latt, etc.). It is not the body's activities (which include such things as sleeping and walking) which are intended, but the activities or schemings of the sinful flesh, of human self-centredness and self-assertion. See on 6.6.

θανατοῦτε. Compare Col 3.5; also 3.9. In SB 3, p. 241f, the Rabbinic use of *kābaš* of the subduing of the evil impulse is compared; but the Pauline language is stronger, and reflects the thought of 6.1ff. What is envisaged is an action which is continuous or again and again repeated, not an action which can be done once for all.

ζήσεσθε: i.e. eternally. See on 1.17.

14. ὅσοι γὰρ πνεύματι θεοῦ ἄγονται, οὗτοι υἱοί εἰσιν θεοῦ. The γάρ is best taken as indicating that this verse is explanatory of v. 13b, which it may be said to repeat in different terms. ὅσοι has sometimes been understood in an exclusive sense ('only those who'), and sometimes as carrying both an inclusive and an exclusive sense ('all those who . . . but only those who . . .'). Had Paul continued differently after v. 14, the latter view might, in view of the presence of two alternatives in v. 13, have been plausible. But the fact that vv. 15–17 carry forward only the positive side makes it likely that v. 14 is to be connected only with v. 13b and not with v. 13a as well, and that ὅσοι must therefore be understood in the inclusive sense.[1] This is confirmed by the emphatic position of υἱοί in the reading accepted by Nestle;[2] for it strongly suggests that the point of the sentence is the positive one, that those referred to are actually sons of God. The words ὅσοι . . . πνεύματι θεοῦ ἄγονται interpret εἰ . . . πνεύματι τὰς πράξεις τοῦ σώματος θανατοῦτε. The daily, hourly putting to death of the schemings and enterprises of the sinful flesh by means of the Spirit is a matter of being led, directed, impelled, controlled by the Spirit. Though the active participation of the Christian is indeed involved (θανατοῦτε), it is fundamentally the work of the Spirit (hence the passive ἄγονται). For the use of ἄγειν compare Lk 4.1 (cf. Mt 4.1—ἀνάγειν); Gal 5.18: also Rom 2.4; 1 Cor 12.2; 2 Tim 3.6. It is used by classical authors of being led, controlled, by reason, anger, desire, pleasure, etc. The words υἱοί εἰσιν θεοῦ interpret the ζήσεσθε of the

---

[1] *Pace* Lagrange (p. 201), Michel (p. 196f), *et al.*
[2] This is the reading of B and G. The Egyptian text form and also D have υἱοὶ θεοῦ εἰσιν, while the TR has εἰσιν υἱοὶ θεοῦ: neither of these puts as much emphasis on υἱοί as does the reading accepted by Nestle. [Nestle[26] has υἱοὶ θεοῦ εἰσιν.]

previous verse. The life which God promises is not a mere not-dying: it is to be a son of God, to live as a son of God, both now and hereafter.[1]

15. οὐ γὰρ ἐλάβετε πνεῦμα δουλείας πάλιν εἰς φόβον, ἀλλὰ ἐλάβετε πνεῦμα υἱοθεσίας. The γάρ is perhaps best understood as indicating that vv. 15 and 16 are intended as a confirmation and clarification of the statement just made in v. 14. The contrast between πνεῦμα δουλείας and πνεῦμα υἱοθεσίας has been variously explained. Some have argued that πνεῦμα δουλείας is most naturally understood as denoting a human disposition, and that πνεῦμα υἱοθεσίας, since it is contrasted with it (the same verb, ἐλάβετε, being used in both cases), can scarcely be the Holy Spirit but must also be here a human disposition (albeit one inspired by the Holy Spirit), a filial sentiment; others, assuming that πνεῦμα υἱοθεσίας must refer to the Holy Spirit, have felt obliged to understand πνεῦμα δουλείας also of the Holy Spirit (seeing a reference to life under the Old Dispensation). In either case the tendency has been to see a connexion between πνεῦμα δουλείας and the law. Another way has been to disallow the argument that πνεῦμα must have the same sort of meaning in both parts of the sentence and to understand the first πνεῦμα to denote a disposition and the second the Holy Spirit. Yet another explanation which has been given—and this seems the most probable—is that the sentence does not imply the actual existence of a πνεῦμα δουλείας but means only that the Holy Spirit whom they have received is not a spirit of bondage but the Spirit of adoption. We may compare 1 Cor 2.12 and 2 Tim 1.7 for the form of sentence. The reference of the aorist ἐλάβετε is no doubt to the beginning of their Christian life— in particular, probably, to their baptism. πάλιν is to be taken not with ἐλάβετε (a previous receiving is not implied) but closely with εἰς φόβον: the Spirit whom they have received has not led them back into bondage, and so into that anxiety which is its inseparable characteristic (φόβος here means anxiety, not of course the proper fear which is a mark of the true Christian); He has not betrayed their hopes by subjecting them to the same sort of anxious fear as they had experienced

---

[1] *Pace* Sanday and Headlam, p. 202, who maintain (following Westcott) that 'whereas τέκνον denotes the natural relationship of child to parent, υἱός implies, in addition to this, the recognized *status* and legal privileges reserved for sons', it seems doubtful whether Paul had any such distinction in mind. In this passage he seems to use them without distinction (υἱός in vv. 14 and 19, υἱοθεσία in vv. 15 and 23, τέκνον in vv. 16, 17 and 21). Cf. Michel, p. 199.

before (whether in paganism or in Judaism).[1] Instead, He
has proved Himself to be the Spirit of adoption, that is, the
Spirit who brings about adoption, uniting men with Christ
and so making them sharers in His sonship.[2] Barrett's translation of πνεῦμα υἱοθεσίας by 'the Spirit which anticipates our
adoption as sons' on the ground that v. 23 'makes quite clear
that our adoption . . . lies in the future' (p. 163) must be
firmly rejected. It makes nonsense of the present tenses in
vv. 14 (εἰσιν) and 16 (ἐσμέν), and implies that in crying 'Abba'
we use this form of address only by anticipation. (See further
on vv. 19 and 23.)

The word υἱοθεσία occurs in the NT only here and in v. 23
and in 9.4; Gal 4.5; Eph 1.5. It is not found in the LXX.
The earliest known occurrences of it are in inscriptions of
the second century B.C., its first known literary appearances
in Diodorus Siculus and Nicolaus Damascenus (both of the
first century B.C.). The expression υἱὸς θετός, however, is
found as early as Pindar (Ol. 9.62), θετὸν παῖδα ποιεῖσθαι is used
by Herodotus (6.57), and υἱὸν θέσθαι τινά by Plato (Lg. 929c),
while παῖδα ποιεῖσθαί τινα is used in Homer, Il. 9.494f. On the
institution of adoption (as distinct from the use of the word
υἱοθεσία) information is available in Isaeus 7 (and also 2) from
the fourth century B.C. and in Menander, Dysc. (see LSJ Suppl.,
p. viii). Adoption was also common among the Romans (see
Lewis and Short, s.vv. adoptio, adoptivus, adopto). On Greek
and Roman adoption see further TWNT 8, p. 400f; OCD, s.vv.
'Adoptio' and 'Adoption, Greek', with further bibliography
under 'Law and procedure, Roman. I'; also A. N. Sherwin-
White, Roman Society and Roman Law in the New Testament
(Oxford, 1963). Since adoption as a legal act was not a Jewish
institution, Paul may reasonably be assumed to have had
Greek or Roman adoption in mind. At the same time, in view
of Gen 15.2-4; Exod 2.10; Esth 2.7; and also Exod 4.22f;
2 Sam 7.14; 1 Chr 28.6; Ps 2.7; 89.26f; Jer 3.19; Hos 11.1, it is
unwise to claim that the background of the metaphor is exclusively Graeco-Roman. When Paul used the word υἱοθεσία in
9.4, he must surely have had OT material very much in mind.
Moreover, while it is true that the Jews did nct practise

[1] It should not, of course, be inferred from Paul's recognition that
Judaism was characterized by such an anxious fear that he was of the
opinion that such a fear belonged properly to the law: passages like
10.6ff make it clear that he saw it rather as the fruit of a radical
misunderstanding and misuse of the law.

[2] In Gal 4.6, however, it seems to be implied that adoption precedes
the gift of the Spirit, and the gift of the Spirit is a kind of seal confirming
the adoption. (Cf. Gaugler 1, p. 287.)

adoption in the legal form familiar in the Gentile world, it should not be forgotten that the phenomenon of a man's bringing up someone else's child and treating him as his son was by no means unknown among the Jews (cf. SB 3, p. 340). And, in view of the last words of this verse, we must not forget that Paul was aware of the fact that Jesus had taught His disciples to address God as 'Father'. While the term Paul used came undoubtedly from the Hellenistic world, and he was certainly familiar with the Gentile institution denoted by it, we should allow for the probability that in his mind it also had other associations.[1]

ἐν ᾧ κράζομεν· ἀββὰ ὁ πατήρ. Moffatt and the RSV (following WHmg) connect these words with v. 16. But against this punctuation (i.e. a full stop after υἱοθεσίας and a comma after πατήρ), and in favour of the usual punctuation with a comma after υἱοθεσίας and a full stop after πατήρ, the following points may be made: (i) If a full stop is placed after υἱοθεσίας, the sentence οὐ γὰρ ἐλάβετε, κ.τ.λ. seems incomplete both stylistically, since there is nothing to balance πάλιν εἰς φόβον, and also as far as the meaning is concerned, since πνεῦμα υἱοθεσίας is a new, and not an easy, expression, which seems to require some measure of explanation within the same sentence. (ii) If the last words of the verse are connected with οὐ γὰρ ἐλάβετε, κ.τ.λ., they not only serve to balance πάλιν εἰς φόβον and to clarify the meaning of πνεῦμα υἱοθεσίας, but they also (construed in this way) state what may be regarded as a theological truth of the greatest importance, namely, that the Spirit enables us to call God 'Father'. (iii) If these words are taken with v. 16, and ἐν ᾧ is understood in the sense of 'when' (as in the RSV), the resulting sentence, consisting of these words together with v. 16, seems to imply that the Spirit's testimony is dependent on our initiative—or, at least, that the only testimony of the Spirit mentioned is so dependent. (The sense obtained by adopting the punctuation presupposed by the RSV but understanding ἐν ᾧ as having a causal significance seems to us quite unsatisfactory.) If, however, the other punctuation is adopted, the sentence about the Spirit's witness is not limited, and our crying 'Abba' is represented as a result of the gift of the Spirit. That this is more

[1] That in υἱοθεσίας here the thought of the status of sonship resulting from the act of adoption is present may be taken as certain. (Reference may be made to E. Schweizer's discussion in *TWNT* 8, p. 402.) But to translate it 'of sonship', as the RSV does, is to blur Paul's meaning rather than to clarify it; for it is not likely that the thought of the divine act of grace from which the believer's status of sonship derives was absent from his mind. Cf. the formulation in Jn 1.12f.

consonant with Paul's thought as expressed elsewhere can
scarcely be doubted.[1]

We assume then that these words are to be taken with the
rest of v. 15. The relative clause serves to clarify the use of
πνεῦμα υἱοθεσίας as a description of the Spirit of God. He is
the One in whom, i.e. enabled by whom, Christians cry
'Abba'.

The use of κράζειν here has given rise to various suggestions.
It has been suggested that Paul had in mind 'the cry *Abba!*
uttered by Christians under obvious spiritual stress. . . . The
conditions which Paul has in view are those associated with
what is called "religious revival", when many of the customary
restraints and inhibitions are broken up, and the inner life is
much nearer to the surface than at ordinary times',[2] and 'the
use of the violent word, "cry out" ' is said to be support for
the view that Paul's reference is 'to Spirit-inspired prayers
(cf. I Cor. xiv. 15)'.[3] Others, noting that κράζειν was sometimes used to denote a loud, public proclamation, have
suggested that the reference may be to the invocation with
which Christian prayer begins as a kind of liturgical proclamation.[4] Yet another suggestion is that it indicates a praying
aloud, expressive of confidence and joy, contrasted with the
whispered prayer prescribed by Jewish custom.[5] But the true
explanation is surely rather the simple one that κράζειν is
used again and again in the LXX of urgent prayer, being so
used in Psalms alone more than forty times (e.g. 3.4 [LXX:5];
4.3 [LXX: 4]; 18.6 [LXX: 17.7]; 22.2, 5 [LXX: 21.3, 6]; 34.6
[LXX: 33.7]). It is used to represent several different Hebrew
words. So here it is best taken to denote an urgent and sincere
crying to God irrespective of whether it is loud or soft (or
even unspoken), formal or informal, public or private.

For the use of ἀββά compare Mk 14.36; Gal 4.6. The Aramaic
word '*abbā*', used by Jesus, continued for a while to be used

[1] Jeremias's argument for the other punctuation that 'To begin the
sentence at v. 16 would produce a very harsh asyndeton' (*The Prayers
of Jesus*, London, 1967, p. 65, n. 75, seems hardly cogent. Is this
asyndeton any harsher than the one produced by putting a full stop
after υἱοθεσίας?

[2] Dodd, p. 145.

[3] Barrett, p. 164. He mentions the possibility that the reference is
to such prayers as an alternative to the possibility that it is to the use
of the Lord's Prayer in Christian worship, but goes on to suggest that
'the contrast between a liturgical prayer and a free prayer spontaneously
inspired by the Spirit may well have been less marked in the first- than
in the twentieth-century mind'.

[4] e.g. Leenhardt, p. 214.

[5] Schlatter, p. 265.

in the Greek-speaking Church. In origin an exclamatory form used by small children, it had by the time of Jesus come to be used more extensively, being no longer confined to the speech of children. It had replaced the form *'ăḇî* ('my father') both in its vocative and in its non-vocative use, and had also replaced the emphatic *'āḇā'*. But its homely and affectionate origin was not forgotten, and it was not used as a form of address to God in ancient Judaism (its non-vocative use with reference to God is found only extremely rarely). Its use by Jesus expressed His consciousness of a unique relationship to God, and His authorizing His disciples to address God in this way is to be understood as His giving them a share in His relationship to God.[1]

It is perhaps rather more likely that ὁ πατήρ was added for the sake of emphasis than that it was added as an explanation which might be necessary for some in the Roman church. On the use of the nominative with the definite article instead of the vocative see BDF, § 147, especially (3).

That the thought of the recital of the Lord's Prayer was present to Paul's mind, when he used the words ἐν ᾧ κράζομεν· ἀββά ὁ πατήρ, is of course highly likely,[2] but there seems to be no good reason for thinking that he had this in mind exclusively.

Now that we are in a better position to see v. 15 as a whole, we must try to understand its function in the structure of this sub-section. According to Dodd, there is a break in the thought between vv. 13 and 14: in vv. 12–13 'We are already thoroughly on the plane of moral practice, and we seem to be well launched on a course of direct ethical teaching. But Paul remembers that there is much more that should be said of life in the Spirit, on the purely religious plane. In particular, he has said nothing of the fact that the man who has the Spirit is a son . . . of God . . . Accordingly, the true sequel to 12–13 is held up for a time.'[3] Dodd sees that 'true sequel' in chapters 12 and following. We believe that there is here a serious misunderstanding of Paul's thought. It is, of course, true that chapters 12 and following are, in view of the facts of the human situation, a necessary explication of what is said in the present sub-section. But we are convinced that—so far from it's being true that v. 15 is a statement 'on the purely religious

---

[1] See further Jeremias, *The Prayers of Jesus*, London, 1967, *passim*, but especially pp. 57–65. But see also Davies and Allison, ICC *Matthew* 1, pp. 600–02; 3, p. 497.

[2] The observations of Jeremias, op. cit., pp. 82–85, on 'The Lord's Prayer in the Ancient Church' are illuminating in this connexion.

[3] p. 143.

plane'—Barth is justified in understanding it as stating *in principle* all that has to be said about ethics—and so as the altogether appropriate sequel to vv. 12–13.[1]

In v. 12 Paul stated the negative obligation which follows from what was said in vv. 1–11. He omitted to express the complementary positive obligation, though he expressed the negative obligation in such a way as to suggest that the positive was also in his mind. In v. 13a he gave a warning of the consequences of ignoring the negative obligation; and then in v. 13b, instead of going on to state the positive obligation directly, he put it into the form of a conditional clause (here the positive obligation which was implied in v. 12 is expressed by πνεύματι τὰς πράξεις τοῦ σώματος θανατοῦν), with an apodosis stating the promise contingent on its fulfilment. Verse 14 takes up the conditional clause of v. 13b (πνεύματι θεοῦ ἄγεσθαι is synonymous with πνεύματι τὰς πράξεις τοῦ σώματος θανατοῦν), though by its use of the passive instead of the active bringing out the point that what is meant is in the last resort the work of God's Spirit, and asserts that those who fulfil it—or, rather, in whom it is fulfilled—are God's sons. Verse 15 (which in its turn will be confirmed by v. 16) harks back with its confident positive assertion, ἐλάβετε πνεῦμα υἱοθεσίας, to the fundamental indicatives of vv. 1–11 which are the context and presupposition of vv. 12ff, and gives to the obligation τῷ πνεύματι τοῦ κατὰ πνεῦμα ζῆν, which was implied but never expressed in v. 12, its final and definitive expression in the relative clause ἐν ᾧ κράζομεν· ἀββὰ ὁ πατήρ. This then is what it means to live after the Spirit, to mortify by the Spirit the deeds of the body, and to be led by the Spirit of God—simply to be enabled by that same Spirit to cry, 'Abba, Father'. And it is here expressed not as an imperative but as an indicative: Christians do as a matter of fact do this. The implicit imperative is that they should continue to do just this, and do it more and more consistently, more and more sincerely, soberly and responsibly. This is all that is required of them. It is what the whole law of God is aimed at achieving. All that must be said about the Christian's obedience has been already said in principle when this has been said. Nothing more is required of us than that we should cry to the one true God 'Abba, Father' with full sincerity and with full seriousness. That this necessarily includes seeking with all our heart to be and think and say and do what is well-pleasing to Him and to avoid all that displeases Him, should go without saying. In the accomplishment of this work

---

[1] *Shorter*, p. 95f.

of obedience the δικαίωμα τοῦ νόμου is fulfilled (cf. v. 4) and God's holy law established.

16. αὐτὸ τὸ πνεῦμα συμμαρτυρεῖ τῷ πνεύματι ἡμῶν ὅτι ἐσμὲν τέκνα θεοῦ. The asyndeton has the effect of giving this sentence extra weight and solemnity.

Two interrelated questions have here to be asked: (i) What is the relation of this verse to v. 15? and (ii) Does συμμαρτυρεῖν with the dative here mean 'witness together with' or 'witness to', 'assure'? With regard to (i), the mistake has often been made (and it has by no means been confined to those who punctuate with a full stop after υἱοθεσίας) of turning things upside down by looking to ἐν ᾧ κράζομεν· ἀββὰ ὁ πατήρ to explain v. 16, instead of seeing that v. 16 explains the υἱοθεσίας and ἐν ᾧ of v. 15. So, for example, Barrett inserts the words 'in this way' in his translation ('The Spirit himself in this way bears witness . . .'),[1] and apparently identifies the Spirit's witness with the Church's prayer.[2] But this we regard as an unjustifiable strait-jacketing of Paul's meaning. The truth is surely rather that v. 16 is intended to confirm and clarify the υἱοθεσίας and the ἐν ᾧ of v. 15 by indicating that our crying 'Abba, Father' rests upon something prior to it[3] and independent of it, namely the fact that no less an authority than God Himself in His Spirit has assured us—and continues to assure us—that we are His children. The knowledge that we are God's children (not to be confused with any merely natural desire of weak human beings to feel that there is someone greater and stronger than themselves who is kindly disposed to them) is something which we cannot impart to ourselves: it has to be given to us from outside and beyond ourselves—from God. Verse 16 is Paul's solemn and emphatic statement that this knowledge has been given to us. This knowledge is not to be identified with our calling God 'Father': it is rather the warrant for it.[4] And the Spirit's imparting of it is not to be identified simply with His immediate inspiration of the prayer 'Abba, Father' (not even when that is understood, as we have suggested it should be, in the widest sense, as em-

[1] p. 160.
[2] On p. 164 he comments: 'The prayers of the Church (cf. v. 26) confirm the personal conviction of the Christian'.
[3] We take it that the use of the present tense (συμμαρτυρεῖ) does *not* imply that the action it describes is to be thought of as only taking place at the same time as our crying.
[4] Chrysostom (col. 527) rightly speaks of the Spirit's witness as the αἰτία of our crying 'Abba'; but he then goes on to interpret αἰτία in what seems to us too narrow a sense by the sentence: τοῦ γὰρ Πνεύματος ὑπαγορεύοντος, ταῦτα λέγομεν.

bracing all the obedience of Christians), but rather with His whole work of enabling us to believe in Jesus Christ, through whom alone we may rightly call God 'Father'.

With regard to (ii), it may be said that, if συμμαρτυρεῖν is taken to mean 'witness together with' (as it is by many commentators both ancient and modern, and by NEB and JB) and if, at the same time, τὸ πνεῦμα ἡμῶν is given its natural meaning of 'our (own human) spirit', then the sense of the verse is that the Holy Spirit and our own human spirit are linked together as two witnesses to the fact that we are children of God. But what standing has our spirit in *this* matter? Of itself it surely has no right at all to testify to our being sons of God. To get over this very serious objection, recourse has often (from early times) been had to such suggestions as that by τὸ πνεῦμα ἡμῶν is meant the χάρισμα that has been given to us (e.g. Chrysostom, col. 527) or our new nature, the self regenerated by Christ (e.g. Schlatter, p. 266; Lagrange, p. 202); but explanations of this sort seem over-subtle. Even when full allowance has been made for the influence exercised by Deut 19.15 in primitive Christian thought, it seems better here to follow the example of the Vulgate and take συμμαρτυρεῖν with the dative in its other (well established) sense of 'testify to', 'assure'.[1] We may then give to τῷ πνεύματι ἡμῶν its natural meaning. (It may be noted as an interesting feature of the middle part of this chapter that nine different συν-compounds occur within fourteen verses, namely, vv. 16–29.)

(iii) *The indwelling of the Spirit—the gift of hope* (8.17–30)

[17]And if children, then also heirs: heirs of God and fellow-heirs of Christ, seeing that we are *now* suffering with him, in order that we may *hereafter* be glorified with him. [18]For I reckon that the sufferings of the present time are not worthy to be compared with the glory which is to be revealed in us. [19]For the eager expectation of the creation is waiting for the revelation of the sons of God. [20]For the creation was subjected to vanity, not of its own will but because of him who subjected it, in hope, [21]because the creation itself too shall be set free from the bondage of decay into the liberty of the glory of the children of God. [22]For we know that the whole creation groans and travails with one accord even until now. [23]And not only this,

---

[1] Cf., e.g., Lietzmann, p. 84; Althaus, p. 76; Leenhardt, p. 215; Strathmann, in *TWNT* 4, p. 515f. Whether or not Paul actually had in mind the fact that a Roman adoption ceremony was carried out in the presence of witnesses who could afterwards vouch for the truth of the adoption (see, e.g., Barclay, p. 111) seems scarcely important. In any case, it is clear that the Spirit's testimony referred to here is thought of as addressed to the adopted son himself and not to any other party.

but we also ourselves who have the firstfruits of the Spirit, even ourselves, groan within ourselves, waiting for our adoption, that is, the redemption of our bodies. ²⁴For it was in hope that we were saved; but when once something hoped for is seen it ceases to be the object of hope; for why indeed should a man hope for something which he actually sees?* ²⁵But since we hope for what we do not see, we wait for it with steadfast patience. ²⁶And in like manner the Spirit also helps our weakness; for we do not know what it is right for us to pray for, but the Spirit himself intercedes for us with unspoken groanings, ²⁷and he who searches the hearts knows what is the intention of the Spirit, that he is interceding for the saints according to God's will. ²⁸And we know that all things prove advantageous for *their true* good to those who love God, that is, to those who are called according to his purpose. ²⁹For whom he foreknew, he also foreordained to be conformed to the image of his Son, so that he might be the firstborn among many brothers; ³⁰and whom he foreordained, these he also called; and whom he called, these he also justified; and whom he justified, these he also glorified.

Verse 17 by its movement of thought from sonship to heirship makes the transition to the subject of Christian hope, with which this sub-section is concerned. The life which is characterized by the indwelling of the Spirit of God, which is a life in which God's law is established, is a life characterized by hope. Verses 18, 19, 21 and the latter part of v. 23 give some indication of the content of this hope, of the transcendent worth of the glory to be hoped for, and of the fact that it touches not only believers, not even only mankind as a whole, but God's whole creation. An indication of the painfulness of the present context of this hope, of the circumstances in which it must be exercised, is given by v. 20; and this painfulness of hope's present context is emphasized by the reference to the groaning of creation (v. 22) and to the groaning of believers (vv. 23–25). In vv. 26–27, while their formal function seems to be to set alongside the groanings just mentioned a third groaning, namely, that of the Spirit (so v. 26 begins with 'And in like manner . . . also'), the thought of the Spirit's groaning ('with unspoken groanings') is mastered by the positive thought of what the Spirit's groaning accomplishes for believers. Verses 28–30 express the certainty of Christian hope.

This sub-section will hardly be properly understood, unless the poetic quality displayed in it, particularly in vv. 19–22, is duly recognized. What is involved in these verses is not what belongs to the outward form of poetry, such things as artistic arrangement and rhythm, but rather those things which belong to its inner essence, imaginative power (to be seen, for instance, in the use of images), feeling for the richly evocative

* So the Nestle text: what seems to us the most probable reading may be rendered: 'for who hopes for what he actually sees?' [N²⁶ reads it.]

word, a deep sensitivity, catholicity of sympathy, and a true generosity of vision and conception. That the passage owes something to the Jewish apocalyptic tradition is not to be denied (various parallels to Paul's language may be adduced in apocalyptic and elsewhere); but, when such debts have been fully allowed for, the whole has certainly not been told. What is to be seen in these verses is an attempt by a poetic imagination, which is at the same time both altogether obedient to, and splendidly liberated by, the gospel, to suggest something of the glory of that future, worthy of Himself, which God has in store for His creation.

17 by its movement of thought from sonship to heirship effects the transition to the subject of Christian hope (already hinted at in vv. 10–11, 13b and, of course, earlier in the epistle), with which the rest of the chapter is concerned. Its abrupt style (omission of the copula) is noteworthy.[1]

εἰ δὲ τέκνα, καὶ κληρονόμοι· κληρονόμοι μὲν θεοῦ, συγκληρονόμοι δὲ Χριστοῦ. In the Pauline Epistles there are three main passages in which the language of inheriting is used: Gal 3–4; Rom 4, and this passage.[2] There are interesting parallels between these passages (e.g. between this verse and Gal 4.7); but there are also quite definite differences, and it is important to distinguish carefully the various uses of the language of inheriting in Paul, and not to scramble them.[3] In Rom 4 the language of inheriting is used twice—v. 13 states that it was not διὰ νόμου but διὰ δικαιοσύνης πίστεως that the promise was made to Abraham τὸ κληρονόμον αὐτὸν εἶναι κόσμου (the reference is to the repeated promise of Gen 12.2f; 17.4–8; 18.18; 22.16–18), and v. 14 that, if οἱ ἐκ νόμου κληρονόμοι, then faith is made void and the promise of no effect. There are also references to Abraham's seed not only in v. 13 but also in vv. 16 and 18, and it is clearly implied that inheriting is connected with being Abraham's seed. So heirship is here connected with sonship, but the sonship referred to is sonship *of Abraham*: nothing is here said of being sons or heirs *of God*.

---

[1] Michel, p. 199, compares the style of the exposition of law in the Mishnah.

[2] Outside these passages, κληρονόμος occurs only once in the Corpus Paulinum (in Tit 3.7); κληρονομία three times in Ephesians and once in Colossians; κληρονομεῖν four times in 1 Corinthians and once in Galatians (all five times of inheriting the kingdom of God or ἀφθαρσία which is used in parallelism with 'the kingdom of God'); and συγκληρονόμος occurs once in Ephesians.

[3] As, e.g., Dodd, p. 147; Barrett, p. 164, are inclined to do. The effect of scrambling (by explaining the use in Rom 8 on the basis of Rom 4 and/or Gal 3–4) is seriously to obscure the transcendent significance of what is being said in Rom 8.

In Gal 3–4 the situation is more complicated. In 3.7 it is stated that it is οἱ ἐκ πίστεως who are Abraham's sons, in vv. 13 and 14 that Christ has redeemed us from the curse of the law, so that the Gentiles also may share Abraham's blessing in Christ. Verse 16 makes the point that in Genesis the word 'seed' is used in the singular ('and to thy seed', Gen 13.15: cf. 12.7, etc.), and that it is to be understood to refer to Christ— He is the seed to whom the promise is made (cf. v. 19). According to v. 18, the inheritance was granted to Abraham by God δι' ἐπαγγελίας; it cannot be ἐκ νόμου. In v. 26 Paul affirms that all whom he is addressing are 'sons of God, through faith, in Christ Jesus'. Then in v. 29 he returns to the theme of Abraham's seed as inheritor of God's promise, but the singular 'seed' now includes all who belong to Christ ('And if ye are Christ's, then are ye Abraham's seed, heirs according to promise'). Chapter 4 begins by asserting the likeness of an heir's circumstances while he is not yet of age to those of a slave, and then proceeds (vv. 4–6) to contrast with such a restricted lot the situation of the Christian who has been redeemed in order that he may receive τὴν υἱοθεσίαν, and into whose heart God has sent His Spirit crying, 'Abba, Father'. Verse 7 concludes: 'So thou art no longer a bondservant but a son; and if a son, then an heir through God'. It is to be noted that, while the thought of the Christian's being a son of God by adoption is clearly present here, he is not said to be an heir of God, but an heir *through* God (κληρονόμος διὰ θεοῦ)[1]—i.e. presumably an heir of the promise made to Abraham (cf. 3.29 together with 3.26). The remaining reference to inheriting is in v. 30, but it adds nothing of substance so far as our present purpose is concerned. The position may then be summed up thus: Rom 4 speaks of sons of Abraham and heirs of Abraham, but says nothing about sons of God or heirs of God; Gal 3–4 speaks of sons of Abraham and heirs of Abraham, of sons of God and of heirs through God, but not of heirs of God; and Rom 8 does not mention Abraham at all, but speaks of Christians' being sons (or children) of God and also of their being heirs of God and joint-heirs with Christ. There are the further contacts between Rom 8 and Gal 3–4 that both passages make use of the term υἱοθεσία, both mention the 'Abba, Father' invocation and the Holy Spirit's work in connexion with it, and both indicate a connexion between the heirship of Christians and Christ's heirship. But the differences between

---

[1] There are several variant readings here, including one which is clearly an assimilation to Rom 8.17. The reading διὰ θεοῦ is surely to be preferred.

these three passages are such that it is better not to assume
that Rom 8.17 is to be explained simply on the basis of one or
other or of both the other two passages, but to explain it
independently of them. We shall then not be inhibited from
recognizing the full import of what is being said. The term
'heirs of God' is not to be explained as meaning simply 'heirs
of Abraham, who are to receive in due course the blessings
which God promised to him and to his seed', nor is the paradox
involved in referring to 'heirs of [the eternal] God' to be
removed by appealing to the fact that the Hebrew verbs
yāraš and *nāḥal*, which were used when hereditary succession
was referred to, mean primarily and most often not 'obtain by
hereditary succession' but, respectively, 'possess' and 'have
divided out to one as one's share'; for here in Rom 8.17 there
is the closest possible relationship between heirship and sonship, and the sonship in question is quite clearly (cf. v. 16) that
of God's children. The imagery, of course, breaks down; for,
since the eternal God does not die (the thought which is
present in Heb 9.15–17 is not present here), there is no question
of God's heirs' succeeding Him. But it points extraordinarily
effectively to the facts that Christians are men who have great
expectations, that their expectations are based upon their
being sons of God, that these expectations are of sharing not
just in various blessings God is able to bestow but in that which
is peculiarly His own, the perfect and imperishable glory of
His own life, and that the determination of the time when their
expectations will be realized is outside their control (the
appointment of the time by God's free personal decision
answering to the determination of the time of succession by the
death of the testator in the case of an ordinary inheritance).
The addition of συγκληρονόμοι δὲ Χριστοῦ expresses the
certainty of our hope. Our sonship and our heirship rest on our
relation to Him, on His having claimed us for His own. But He
has already entered upon the inheritance for which we have
still to wait, and this fact is the guarantee that we too, who are
His joint-heirs, will enjoy the fulfilment of our expectations.[1]

εἴπερ συμπάσχομεν ἵνα καὶ συνδοξασθῶμεν is not to be understood
as introducing a condition, but rather as stating a fact which
confirms what has just been said. As in v. 9, εἴπερ means here
'seeing that' (cf. Old Latin 'si quidem'), and is roughly
equivalent to γάρ. We may bring out the sense by some such
paraphrase as the following: 'for the fact that we are now
suffering with Him, so far from calling the reality of our

[1] On the use of κληρονόμος, συγκληρονόμος, see further W. Foerster and
J. Herrmann, in *TWNT* 3, pp. 757–86.

heirship in question, is a pledge of our being glorified with Him hereafter'. The reference of συμπάσχομεν is not to our suffering with Christ in the sense of our having died with Him in God's sight, nor to our having suffered (sacramentally) in baptism. Had either of these 'sufferings' been in mind, a past tense would have been natural. The reference is rather to that element of suffering which is inseparable from faithfulness to Christ in a world which does not yet know Him as Lord (cf. v. 35f, and see on 1.16: cf. also, e.g., Mt 5.11f; Mk 8.34f, 38; Jn 15.18–20; 16.33; Acts 14.22). It would be prosaic to try to define precisely what is meant by the συν- of συμπάσχομεν: but we may understand it to include the thoughts, 'for His sake', 'in conformity with the pattern of His earthly life' (though not implying that our sufferings are redemptive in the sense in which His are), and 'in union with Him' (i.e., being bound to Him by God's merciful decision so that we share His destiny)—perhaps also the thought that the exalted Christ participates in His brethren's sufferings (cf. Acts 9.5b?). On the formula σύν Χριστῷ see on 6.8. The conjunction ἵνα indicates not the subjective motive of the sufferers (so, e.g. Cornely, p. 420: 'eo fine ut (ἵνα) conglorificemur'), but the objective connexion according to God's will between suffering now with Christ and being glorified with Him hereafter (so, e.g., Lagrange, p. 203; Huby, p. 293, n. 4). Gaugler has rightly pointed out that συνδοξασθῶμεν refers not to life after death merely, but to something far more wonderful—the glory of the final consummation.[1] On the meaning of the 'glory', which is the content of the hope with which vv. 17–30 are concerned, see especially on 3.23; 5.2; 8.18. With εἴπερ . . . συνδοξασθῶμεν as a whole it is natural to compare 2 Tim 2.11–12a—as far as content is concerned, more particularly v. 12a.

18. Λογίζομαι. On this verb see on 3.28. It denotes here, as in 3.28 and 6.11, a firm conviction reached by rational thought on the basis of the gospel.

The γάρ is accounted for by the fact that v. 18 explains how the sufferings and the glory referred to in v. 17 (συμπάσχομεν, συνδοξασθῶμεν) stand in relation to each other.

ὅτι οὐκ ἄξια τὰ παθήματα τοῦ νῦν καιροῦ πρὸς τὴν μέλλουσαν δόξαν ἀποκαλυφθῆναι εἰς ἡμᾶς. From his understanding of the gospel Paul is convinced that the sufferings of the present time are only a very slight thing in comparison with the glory which is to be revealed. We might translate οὐκ ἄξια . . . πρός by 'bear no comparison with'. The basic meaning of ἄξιος is 'weighing as much', 'of like value', 'of equal worth'. The use of πρός ('in

[1] I, p. 292.

comparison with'—cf. LSJ, s.v. C. III. 4) with the accusative after ἄξια instead of the usual simple genitive may perhaps be explained as due to a desire to avoid another genitive immediately after καιροῦ. For the thought compare 2 Cor 4.17. The παθήματα which Paul has in mind here are no doubt, in view of συμπάσχομεν in v. 17, those of Christians, though in vv. 19–22 the range of interest is much wider. They are τοῦ νῦν καιροῦ, that is, they are characteristic of the period of time which began with the gospel events and will be terminated by the Parousia.[1] From the fact that Paul had said τὴν μέλλουσαν[2] δόξαν ἀποκαλυφθῆναι (and not τὴν μέλλουσαν δόξαν ἔσεσθαι) John Chrysostom concluded that he thought of the glory as already existing, though as yet concealed,[3] and this contention seems to have some substance. In addition to Col 3.3, which Chrysostom himself quoted in support, we may refer to vv. 16 and 19 of this present chapter according to which, while the revelation of our sonship is still in the the future, we are already sons of God, and to v. 17 according to which, though we have not yet inherited, we are already heirs. The fact that in 5.2 our share in God's glory is spoken of as the object of hope need not imply that that glory is not yet ours in any sense at all, but (in the light of 8.25) may indicate only that we do not yet see it, do not yet possess it palpably. The being glorified to which v. 17 refers may be understood as signifying not the reception of a glory not possessed before, but the manifestation of a glory previously concealed. In 8.30 Paul even uses the aorist indicative of δοξάζειν. That Paul thought of the glory which is to be revealed εἰς ἡμᾶς as being in some senses already ours is not

[1] If we are right in thinking that the sufferings referred to are specifically those of Christians who may be said to suffer with Christ (συμπάσχομεν in v. 17), it is better to understand ὁ νῦν καιρός in this way than to take it in the wider sense of ὁ αἰὼν οὗτος. See also on 3.26 and 13.11. Whereas in 3.26 the interest is in the fact that the period indicated has begun, the interest here is more in the certainty that it will one day be terminated (the sufferings will occur until that point).

[2] It would scarcely be justifiable to maintain that the use of μέλλουσαν here specially conveys the idea of certainty, since the tendency to use a periphrasis with μέλλειν as a substitute for the disappearing future infinitive and future participle was strong in Paul's time (see BDF, § 356); but it is possibly fair to see the position of μέλλουσαν in this group of words as giving special emphasis to the futurity of the revelation (for the order of words cf. Gal 3.23).

[3] Col. 529: Εἶτα, ἐπειδὴ μέλλουσαν αὐτὴν εἶπε, δείκνυσιν αὐτὴν ἤδη οὖσαν. Οὐ γὰρ εἶπε, " Πρὸς τὴν μέλλουσαν ἔσεσθαι " ἀλλὰ " Πρὸς τὴν μέλλουσαν ἀποκαλυφθῆναι ", ὡς καὶ νῦν οὖσαν μὲν κρυπτομένην δέ· ὅπερ καὶ ἀλλαχοῦ σαφέστερον ἔλεγεν, ὅτι "Ἡ ζωὴ ἡμῶν κέκρυπται σὺν τῷ Χριστῷ ἐν τῷ Θεῷ". Θάρρει τοίνυν ὑπὲρ αὐτῆς· παρεσκεύασται γὰρ ἤδη τοὺς σοὺς ἀναμένουσα πόνους.

to be denied. But it is important not to stress this in such a way as to obscure the vastness of the difference between our present condition and that which is to be ours. The words εἰς ἡμᾶς are hardly to be understood as equivalent to the simple dative whether in the sense 'for us' (cf. I Pet 1.4) or in the sense 'to us'. They are naturally understood as indicating where the revelation of the glory is to occur, the persons whose condition will be transformed by it. Perhaps εἰς ἡμᾶς was used in preference to ἐν ἡμῖν because it seemed more apt to suggest the truth that the revelation of the glory will be, not something merely internal to us nor something brought about by our own activity, but something outwardly manifest as well as affecting our inward life, done to us by the decisive action of God. But, while the RV 'to us-ward' (cf. Michel, p. 201: 'in Richtung auf uns') represents an attempt to do justice to the use of εἰς ἡμᾶς, it is doubtful whether it expresses Paul's meaning as accurately as the 'in us' of the AV (cf. Vulgate 'in nobis').

19. ἡ γὰρ ἀποκαραδοκία τῆς κτίσεως[1] τὴν ἀποκάλυψιν τῶν υἱῶν τοῦ θεοῦ ἀπεκδέχεται. This sentence is introduced as support for the statement made in v. 18, but, once introduced, it itself requires expansion and elucidation. In fact, the whole of vv. 19–30 may be said to be in one way or another support for, and elucidation of, v. 18. In the course of these verses Paul indicates more fully the content of the Christian hope (vv. 19 and 21), its present painful context (vv. 20, 22–27), and its certainty (vv. 28–30). But v. 19 and vv. 20–22 which follow it are certainly not to be understood as merely an inference from the observable and generally recognized fact of the prevalence of fear and suffering in nature. What these verses affirm is something which can only be known by faith.

The noun ἀποκαραδοκία occurs elsewhere in the NT only in Phil 1.20, where it is associated with ἐλπίς and signifies confident expectation. The words ἀποκαραδοκεῖν (Polybius, Josephus, Aquila), καραδοκεῖν (quite common in classical Greek) and καραδοκία (Aquila) do not occur in the NT. The basic idea in all these words is that of stretching the neck, craning forward (κάρα is a poetical synonym for κεφαλή). The ἀπο- is intensive, as it is also in ἀπεκδέχεσθαι later in the verse and in v. 23.[2]

[1] The variant πίστεως (69 pc) is no doubt simply an accidental mistake.

[2] Cf. Chrysostom, col. 529: ἀποκαραδοκία γὰρ ἡ σφοδρὰ προσδοκία ἐστίν (cf. col. 604, where he comments on ἀποστυγοῦντες in 12.9: Σφόδρα μισοῦντες. Τὸ γὰρ " ἀπὸ " τοῦτο πολλαχοῦ ἐπιτάσεώς ἐστι παρ' αὐτῷ· ὡς ὅταν λέγῃ " ἀποκαραδοκίαν ", καὶ " ἀπεκδεχόμενοι ", καὶ " ἀπολύτρωσιν ").

ἡ κτίσις in this and the following verses has been variously interpreted in the course of the centuries as signifying the whole creation, including mankind both believing and unbelieving and also the angels;[1] all mankind;[2] unbelieving mankind only;[3] believers only;[4] the angels only;[5] sub-human nature together with the angels;[6] sub-human nature together with mankind in general;[7] sub-human nature only.[8] But believers must almost certainly be excluded, since in v. 23 they are contrasted with the creation. Moreover, οὐχ ἑκοῦσα in v. 20, if it is given the sense which seems natural in the context, namely, 'not by its own choice',[9] seems to rule out mankind generally; for, if Paul meant to include mankind when he used κτίσις here, he can hardly have intended to exclude Adam, the created man *par excellence* (had he intended to make so strange an exception, he must surely have indicated it), and Adam at any rate clearly cannot be said to have been subjected οὐχ ἑκών to ματαιότης. Against the suggestion that only unbelieving mankind is referred to, it may be urged that this would involve an extremely unnatural distinction; for, while it is understandable that κόσμος should sometimes be used to denote unbelievers in contrast with believers, it is very hard to imagine a NT writer using κτίσις in this way, a term specifically indicating a relation to God, which is not only one in which Christians stand no whit less than non-Christians but is also one which they above all men must acknowledge and delight in. A reference to angels seems not very likely. The use of κτίσις to denote the angels alone and the use of it to denote the angels in addition to sub-human nature with mankind excluded would seem about equally unlikely. Moreover, it is hardly possible to give any really convincing interpretation of τῇ . . . ματαιότητι . . . ὑπετάγη, οὐχ ἑκοῦσα in respect of the angels. The only interpretation of κτίσις in these verses which is really probable seems to be that which understands the reference to be to the sum-total of sub-

[1] e.g., Origen, cols. 1109ff.
[2] e.g., Augustine, col. 2074f.
[3] e.g., Schlatter, pp. 269–75.
[4] This view was held by some eighteenth- and nineteenth-century interpreters.
[5] Given as one possibility by Pelagius, p. 65f, it has been taken up recently by Fuchs, p. 109.
[6] e.g., Theodore, cols. 824ff.
[7] e.g., W. Foerster, in *TWNT* 3, p. 1030; Barth, *Shorter*, p. 99f.
[8] e.g., Ambrosiaster, col. 124f; Cyril, col. 821; Chrysostom, cols. 529–31; Euthymius, pp. 91–93; Calvin, pp. 172–74; Sanday and Headlam, p. 207; Lietzmann, p. 84; Lagrange, p. 207; Gaugler 1, p. 299.
[9] See below on v. 20.

human nature both animate and inanimate.[1] The objection that Paul's use here of personal language (ἀποκαραδοκία, ἀπεκδέχεται, οὐχ ἑκοῦσα, ἐφ᾽ ἐλπίδι, συστενάζει) is inconsistent with his intending a reference to irrational nature is not to be sustained; for, as Chrysostom for example noted,[2] there is here a personification such as is often found in the OT.[3] With poetic boldness and with a penetrating prophetic insight Paul sees the whole splendid theatre of the universe together with all sub-human life within it as eagerly awaiting the time when the sons of God will be made manifest in their true glory. The further objection that, if ἡ κτίσις refers only to the sub-human creation, there is then no reference in this passage to unbelieving mankind, is not as weighty as it seems at first sight. It may be suggested that Paul may have omitted to mention unbelievers here as a separate class contrasted with believers, because he did not accept that human unbelief presents God with an eternal fact but saw believers as the first fruits of mankind.

For τὴν ἀποκάλυψιν τῶν υἱῶν τοῦ θεοῦ compare the comments on v. 15 (πνεῦμα υἱοθεσίας), particularly p. 397, on v. 16, and also on v. 23 (υἱοθεσίαν ἀπεκδεχόμενοι). Believers are already sons of God in this life, but their sonship is veiled and their

---

[1] On the history of exegesis reference may be made to H. Gieraths, *Knechtschaft und Freiheit der Schöpfung: eine historisch-exegetische Untersuchung zu Röm 8, 19–22* (a doctoral dissertation at the Faculty of Catholic Theology of the University of Bonn, dated 1950). In connexion with vv. 19–22 see also M. Goguel, 'Le caractère et le rôle de l'élément cosmologique dans la sotériologie paulinienne', in *RHPR* 15 (1935), pp. 335–59; W. Foerster, in *TWNT* 3, pp. 999–1034; H. Biedermann, *Die Erlösung der Schöpfung beim Apostel Paulus*, Würzburg, 1940; R. Guardini, *Das Harren der Schöpfung: eine Auslegung von Röm 8,12–39*, Würzburg, 1940; A. Viard, 'Exspectatio creaturae', in *RB* 69 (1952), pp. 337–54; A.-M. Dubarle, 'Le gémissement des créatures dans l'ordre divin du Cosmos (Rom viii, 19–22)', in *RSPT* 38 (1954), pp. 445–65; N. A. Dahl, 'Christ, Creation and the Church', in W. D. Davies and D. Daube, *The Background of the NT and its Eschatology*, Cambridge, 1956, pp. 422–43; Barth, *CD* IV/2, p. 329; IV/3, p. 532 (= *KD* IV/2, p. 367f; IV/3, p. 611f); R. Prenter, *Schöpfung und Erlösung*, 2 volumes, Göttingen, 1958–60; W. Schrage, 'Die Stellung zur Welt bei Paulus, Epiktet und in der Apokalyptik', in *ZTK* 61 (1964), pp. 125ff; U. Gerber, 'Röm. viii.18ff. als exegetisches Problem der Dogmatik', in *NT* 8 (1966), pp. 58–81; S. Lyonnet, 'Redemptio "cosmica" secundum Rom 8.19–23', in *VD* 44 (1966), pp. 225–42; J. G. Gibbs, *Creation and Redemption: a study in Pauline theology*, Leiden, 1971; H. R. Balz, *Heilsvertrauen und Welterfahrung: Strukturen der paulinischen Eschatologie nach Römer 8.18–39*, Munich, 1971; Cranfield, 'Some Observations on Romans 8.19–21', in R. Banks (ed.), *Reconciliation and Hope* (Leon Morris *Festschrift*), Exeter, 1974.

[2] col. 529.

[3] e.g. Ps 65.12f; Isa 24.4, 7; Jer 4.28; 12.4.

incognito is impenetrable except to faith. Even they themselves have to believe in their sonship against the clamorous evidence of much in their circumstances and condition which seems to be altogether inconsistent with the reality of it.

20-21. τῇ γὰρ ματαιότητι ἡ κτίσις ὑπετάγη. The γάρ indicates the relation of these two verses to v. 19: they explain why the creation waits so eagerly for the revealing of the sons of God. The aorist ὑπετάγη refers to a particular event. The use of the passive veils a reference to God. There is little doubt that Paul had in mind the judgment related in Gen 3.17–19, which includes (v. 17) the words 'cursed is the ground for thy sake'. Special emphasis is given to τῇ ματαιότητι by its position in the sentence. The parallelism between τῇ . . . ματαιότητι . . . ὑπετάγη and τῆς δουλείας τῆς φθορᾶς has led some to assume that ματαιότης must here be used as a simple synonym of φθορά[1] and encouraged others to understand ματαιότης and φθορά to mean respectively the mutability and mortality which characterize creaturely existence as we know it. Some have taken τῇ ματαιότητι as an example of the use of the abstract for the concrete and understood Paul to mean that the creation was subjected to οἱ μάταιοι, i.e. vain men. Others have thought to see the clue to the meaning of ματαιότης here in the use of the cognate verb in 1.21, and so have suggested that the thought is of subjection to man's idolatry which exploits the sub-human creation for its own purposes (cf. 1.23, 25): they have then gone on to explain φθορά as signifying the moral corruption resulting from idolatry (cf. 1.24, 26ff) and the δουλεία τῆς φθορᾶς as the creation's bondage to man's corrupt abuse of it. Others, noting that ματαιότης could be used actually to denote a god of the heathen, have suggested that by subjection to ματαιότης Paul meant subjection to various celestial powers: in support of this view Gal 4.9, which refers to bondage to τὰ ἀσθενῆ καὶ πτωχὰ στοιχεῖα, has been adduced. Yet others have interpreted ματαιότης here along the lines of its use in Ecclesiastes, which contains the majority of its occurrences in the LXX and where it denotes the futility, the disorder, the sheer absurdity, of things. But the simplest and most straightforward interpretation would seem to be to take ματαιότης here in the word's basic sense as denoting the ineffectiveness of that which does not attain its goal (cf. the adverb μάτην),[2] and to understand Paul's meaning to be that the sub-human creation has been subjected to the frustration of not being able properly to fulfil the purpose of its existence,

[1] e.g. Euthymius, p. 92.
[2] Cf. Sanday and Headlam, p. 208.

God having appointed that without man it should not be made perfect. We may think of the whole magnificent theatre of the universe together with all its splendid properties and all the chorus of sub-human life, created to glorify God but unable to do so fully, so long as man the chief actor in the drama of God's praise fails to contribute his rational part.

On the assumption that ἡ κτίσις signifies the sub-human creation, οὐχ ἑκοῦσα is naturally understood as meaning 'not through its own fault'. (If ἡ κτίσις is taken to mean mankind or to include mankind, it would seem to be necessary to explain οὐχ ἑκοῦσα along the lines of Augustine's interpretation as referring to the involuntariness of the creation's submission to the penalty imposed on it.)[1]

ἀλλὰ διὰ τὸν ὑποτάξαντα. ὁ ὑποτάξας can only be God, not Adam, nor man in general, nor Satan; for (i) it would be intolerably harsh to take the participle to refer to any one other than the agent implied by the passive ὑπετάγη earlier in the verse, and this must surely be God, since no one else could naturally be said to have subjected the creation ἐφ' ἐλπίδι, and (ii) ὑποτάσσειν here clearly denotes an authoritative action, which could not be effected by Adam or man in general or Satan, but only by God.[2] The διά with the accusative indicates the cause or occasion. The sense is well expressed by Gaugler's paraphrase: 'because of the judicial decision pronounced by God on account of Adam's sin'.[3]

ἐφ' ἐλπίδι[4] is no doubt better connected with ὑπετάγη than with ὑποτάξαντα. The creation was not subjected to frustration without any hope: the divine judgment included the promise of a better future, when at last the judgment would be lifted. Paul possibly had in mind the promise in Gen 3.15 that the woman's seed would bruise the serpent's head (cf. Rom 16.20). Hope for the creation was included within the hope for man.

διότι. As far as transcriptional probability is concerned, there is not much to choose between διότι and the variant ὅτι (the

---

[1] col. 2075: 'Non sponte autem dicit esse subjectam vanitati creaturam, quoniam poenalis est ista subjectio. Non enim homo sicut sponte peccavit, sic etiam sponte damnatus est: . . .'

[2] Cf. Bengel, p. 531: 'Adamus eam obnoxiam vanitati fecit, non subjecit'. Barth's suggestion (Shorter, p. 99f) that Paul was thinking of Jesus Christ as having subjected 'man, and with him the whole creation, to vanity' by the judgment pronounced and executed on Golgotha seems forced—though it is true that the Cross was the final revelation of the ματαιότης to which the creation was subjected on account of man's sin, just as it was the final revelation of the ὀργὴ θεοῦ (cf. on 1.18).

[3] I, p. 303.

[4] The MSS vary between ἐφ' ἐλπίδι and ἐπ' ἐλπίδι. See BDF, § 14. For the expression cf. 1 Cor 9.10.

former could be explained as due to dittography after the final δι of ἐλπίδι, the latter as due to haplography). But ὅτι is the easier reading since it would be the obvious word to use to introduce a statement of the content of the hope. The more difficult διότι should probably be read.*.It is conceivable that it is used in the sense 'that', since the use of διότι in this sense is attested in Hellenistic Greek;[1] but, as it is not used elsewhere in Paul (or indeed in the rest of the NT) in this sense, it seems preferable to understand it here to mean 'because' or 'for'— that is, as introducing a statement explaining why the creation is said to have been subjected ἐφ' ἐλπίδι (the subjection was ἐφ' ἐλπίδι, because the creation is going to be set free . . .).

καὶ αὐτὴ ἡ κτίσις: 'the creation itself also'. The implied contrast is with the children of God. That Paul's main interest in these verses is in the certainty of the coming glory of believers (cf. εἰς ἡμᾶς in v. 18) is no doubt true; but to state categorically that 'He [i.e. Paul] is not concerned with creation for its own sake', as Barrett does in his comment on v. 19,[2] is surely to go beyond what is warranted by the evidence—even when full weight is given to the existence of 1 Cor 9.9.

ἐλευθερωθήσεται: at the time of the revelation of the sons of God.

ἀπὸ τῆς δουλείας τῆς φθορᾶς: 'from the bondage of decay', i.e., from the condition of being the slaves of death and decay, of corruption and transitoriness, which is the very opposite of the condition of glory.[3] For the genitive compare τὴν τῶν κρεισσόνων δουλείαν in Thucydides, 1.8. The genitive with the abstract noun δουλεία here indicates the same relationship as would be indicated by the genitive with the cognate concrete noun δοῦλος.

εἰς τὴν ἐλευθερίαν signifies the condition which is to replace that of servitude: the creation will be freed from a state of slavery into a state of freedom.

τῆς δόξης τῶν τέκνων τοῦ θεοῦ. The first of these genitives has often been understood as adjectival (so the AV: 'the glorious liberty'); but to take it to have a sense roughly corresponding to that of τῆς φθορᾶς agrees better with the structure of the

---

*[though N²⁶ has adopted ὅτι.]   [1] Cf. Bauer, s.v. 4; MM, s.v.
[2] p. 165. Contrast with his statement Sanday and Headlam, p. 212; Huby, pp. 297–301; Gaugler I, p. 303f. For the expectation in Judaism of a renewal and transformation of nature cf., e.g., Isa 11.6–9; 65.17,25; 66.22; 2 Esdr 7.[75]; 2 Bar. 3.7–4.1; 31.5–32.6; 44.12; 51.3; 57.2; 73.6–74.4; Jub. 1.29; 4.26; 1 Enoch 45.4f; 72.1; 91.16f; 1QS 4.25; 1QH 11.13–14; 13.11–13; and SB 3, pp. 247ff, 840ff.
[3] For other interpretations of φθορά see above on τῇ ματαιότητι.

sentence and also with the thought of the passage. As the δουλεία τῆς φθορᾶς is a bondage to corruption, a bondage which corruption may be said to impose, so the ἐλευθερία τῆς δόξης, κ.τ.λ. is a liberty which results from, is the necessary accompaniment of, the (revelation of the) glory of the children of God.[1] Paul's meaning is hardly that the creation will share the same liberty-resulting-from-glory as the children of God will enjoy, but that it will have its own proper liberty as a result of the glorification of the children of God. We may, however, assume that the liberty proper to the creation is indeed the possession of its own proper glory—that is, of the freedom fully and perfectly to fulfil its Creator's purpose for it, that freedom which it does not have, so long as man, its lord (Gen 1.26, 28; Ps 8.6), is in disgrace.

22. οἴδαμεν γάρ. See on 7.14 and also on 2.2. (οἴδαμεν δέ).

πᾶσα ἡ κτίσις συστενάζει καὶ συνωδίνει ἄχρι τοῦ νῦν, introduced as something generally known among Christians, represents an OT insight (compare especially Gen 3.17), reflected in the apocalyptic tradition, and confirmed and sharpened by the gospel. It serves to sum up the contents of vv. 20 and 21, and so (with those verses) to support what was said in v. 19. Two thoughts, already implicit in v. 19, are here expressed more clearly, on the one hand, the thought of the creation's present painful condition, and on the other hand, the thought that that painful condition is not to no purpose but will have a worthwhile issue (expressed by the image of travail).[2] The sense of the συν- of the two compound verbs is not 'with us (believers)', for this would be inappropriate in view of v. 23; nor is it 'with Christ', for Christ has not been named since

---

[1] In grammatical terms, τῶν τέκνων τοῦ θεοῦ is dependent on τῆς δόξης, not directly on τὴν ἐλευθερίαν.

[2] For the personification involved in the use of συστενάζειν and συνωδίνειν see on v. 19. With the use of συστενάζειν compare the use of the simple verb in 2 Cor 5.2 and 4. A connexion between Paul's use of these words and Hermetic ideas (see Stobaeus 1.389f, 395.5ff) has sometimes been seen; but, if we were right in maintaining that the κτίσις in this passage means the sub-human creation, such OT passages as Isa 24.4, 7; Jer 4.28; 12.4 are closer parallels to this verse. The words στενάζειν and στεναγμός occur frequently in the LXX. The idea of the groaning of the whole sub-human creation is not a very big step from the basic statement of Gen 3.17 that the ground is cursed for man's sake. With Paul's use of συνωδίνειν compare the Rabbinic expression, 'the birth-pang of the Messiah' (see SB 1, p. 950), which refers not to the sufferings of the Messiah but to the sufferings preceding his coming. The origin of the expression is to be seen in such OT passages as Isa 26.17; 66.8; Jer 4.31; Hos 13.13; Mic 4.9f. Compare Mk 13.8; Jn 16.21; 1 Th 5.3. The metaphor is a very natural one to express the thought of severe distress from which a happy and worthwhile issue is to be looked for.

v. 17; nor is it 'with mankind (in general)' nor yet 'with unbelieving mankind', there being nothing in the context to support either of these meanings. Nor is it likely, in the case of these two verbs, that the συν- has simply an intensive force (though the Vulgate does have simply 'ingemiscit et parturit'). The sense must be 'together', 'with one accord'.[1] The words ἄχρι τοῦ νῦν serve to emphasize the long continuance (until now without having ceased) of this groaning and travailing (cf. Phil 1.5): Barrett's explanation of this νῦν as denoting 'the decisive moment, when God's purposes are fulfilled'[2] is unjustified.

23. οὐ μόνον δέ, ἀλλὰ καί. See on 5.3. Not only does the sub-human creation groan, but even Christians groan too.

αὐτοὶ τὴν ἀπαρχὴν τοῦ πνεύματος ἔχοντες [ἡμεῖς] καὶ αὐτοί.[3] The αὐ-τοὶ . . . καὶ αὐτοί is extremely emphatic. The first αὐτοί as well as the second is to be connected with the following indicative, not with the participle.[4] Christians already possess the ἀπαρχή of the Spirit.

The word ἀπαρχή[5] (in the NT also in 11.16; 16.5; 1 Cor 15.20, 23; 16.15; 2 Th 2.13; Jas 1.18; Rev. 14.4) is used in extra-biblical Greek of firstlings or first-fruits for sacrifice or offering, or, as in Herodotus, 1.92, of a part of the worshipper's property dedicated to a god, or of the first part of a sacrifice, the hairs cut from the victim's forelock (e.g. Euripides, *Or.* 96). It is also used rather more generally of various offerings to the gods and metaphorically (as of an inheritance-tax paid to the

---

[1] Cf. Theodore, col. 828: βούλεται δὲ εἰπεῖν ὅτι συμφώνως ἐπιδείκνυται τοῦτο πᾶσα ἡ κτίσις. . . . The fact that in vv. 16–29 there occur nine different συν-compounds has already been pointed out.

[2] p. 166. He compares the νῦν καιρός of v. 18, which he explains as meaning 'the unique moment of eschatological time anticipated in the present' (p. 165). But in both these places it is surely the 'not yet' aspect of the present rather than the fulfilment aspect (as in 3.21 and 26) which is in mind.

[3] There is a good deal of textual variation here. D G lat sy sa support the addition of ἡμεῖς before the first αὐτοί, 104 has it after it, while 𝔓⁴⁶ omits the first αὐτοί together with the καί which precedes it; and B *pc* vg omit the ἡμεῖς before the second καὶ αὐτοί, while 𝔓⁴⁶ and the representa-tives of the Egyptian text-form generally, place it before, and the Byzantine text places it after, καὶ αὐτοί. In view of the variety of position in which ἡμεῖς occurs and the fact that the addition of ἡμεῖς is so very much easier to understand than its omission, it is best to follow B and read αὐτοὶ τὴν ἀπαρχὴν τοῦ πνεύματος ἔχοντες καὶ αὐτοί.

[4] *Pace* Michel, p. 205 ('. . . so dass das erste καὶ αὐτοί zu ἔχοντες, das zweite zu στενάζομεν zu ziehen ist'): his own translation on p. 200, however, seems to presuppose the way of understanding the words supported above.

[5] See also on 11.16; and Delling, in *TWNT* I, p. 483f; Bauer, s.v.; LSJ, s.v.

state). In the LXX it is used mainly in connexion with the cultus (see, for example, Exod 22.29 [LXX: 28]; 23.19; Num 18.12; Deut 18.4; Neh 10.37 [Εσδρ Β′ 20.38]), but also occasionally in non-cultic connexions (e.g. Deut 33.21; Ps 78[LXX: 77].51; 105[LXX: 104].36; and the variant ἀπαρχήν in Ecclus 24.9). Here in Rom 8 it is used with reference not to something offered by man to God but to something given by God to man, and the idea conveyed is that of the gift of a part as a pledge of the fuller gift yet to come. What the believer has already received is a foretaste and a guarantee of what he has still to hope for. Compare the use of ἀρραβών in 2 Cor 5.5.[1]

The genitive τοῦ πνεύματος is puzzling. Different possible explanations of it have to be considered:

(i) That it is partitive. On this view, the word πνεῦμα must here mean not the Holy Spirit Himself as such, but the Holy Spirit as affecting us, so His work in relation to us. The fact that this verse goes on to mention the redemption of our body gives a certain plausibility to the explanation along these lines, according to which Paul's thought is that the present work of the Spirit in us is a first instalment of His total work in relation to us, the completion of which will be the raising up of our bodies as σώματα πνευματικά.

(ii) That it is appositive. On this view too, πνεῦμα will not mean the Holy Spirit Himself as such, but rather His present work in us. The thought will be that the Spirit's present work in us is the first-fruits, the foretaste and pledge of the full glory which God has in store for us.

(iii) That it is possessive. On this view, πνεῦμα will denote the Holy Spirit Himself, and the thought will be of the Spirit's present work in us as His first-fruits, that is, as the foretaste and pledge, belonging to Him and effected by Him, of the full glory which is still to come.

Of these, (i) seems the least likely: the fact that it implies that the totality looked forward to is exclusively the work of the Spirit tells against it. Explanation (ii) is probably to be preferred to explanation (iii); but in any case they both yield substantially the same sense.

ἐν ἑαυτοῖς στενάζομεν. Of the various proposed interpretations of ἐν ἑαυτοῖς, 'within ourselves' (in contrast to the creation's groaning outside us)[2] would seem to be the most natural, and

---

[1] There is an interesting use of ἀπαρχή in Barn. 1.7: . . . ὁ δεσπότης . . . τῶν μελλόντων δοὺς ἀπαρχὰς ἡμῖν γεύσεως. . . .

[2] The objection which has been urged against it, that it is not a necessary mark of the Christian's groaning that it should be exclusively internal, is not cogent; for the words, if given this interpretation, may

should therefore be preferred to 'among ourselves' (i.e. in the Christian community gathered for worship) and 'with regard to ourselves'. στενάζομεν picks up the συστενάζει of v. 22, and is in turn picked up by στεναγμοῖς in v 26: the bolder metaphor of travail (συνωδίνει) is not taken up again.

υἱοθεσίαν[1] ἀπεκδεχόμενοι. The key to the resolution of the apparent tension between these words and the present tenses, εἰσιν and ἐσμέν, in vv. 14 and 16 is provided by the phrase τὴν ἀποκάλυψιν τῶν υἱῶν τοῦ θεοῦ in v. 19. We are already sons of God, but our sonship is not yet manifest. We have been adopted, but our adoption has yet to be publicly proclaimed. υἱοθεσίαν here denotes the final manifestation of our adoption, our revelation as sons of God. The same forceful verb is used both in v. 19 of the creation's longing and in v. 23 of the believers' longing, and the objects of ἀπεκδέχεται and of ἀπεκδεχόμενοι are identical in meaning.

τὴν ἀπολύτρωσιν τοῦ σώματος ἡμῶν interprets υἱοθεσίαν. The full manifestation of our adoption is identical with the final resurrection of our bodies at the Parousia, our complete and final[2] liberation from the ματαιότης and φθορά to which we (like the sub-human creation) have been subjected. We may (with Chrysostom) compare 1 Cor 15.54; Phil 3.21.

24. τῇ ... ἐλπίδι is probably to be explained neither as equivalent to ἐφ' ἐλπίδι in v. 20,[3] nor as instrumental (whether ἐλπίς be understood as subjective, denoting our hoping, or as objective, denoting that for which we hope),[4] but as a modal dative serving to qualify ἐσώθημεν.[5] Paul's use of the aorist tense is justified, because the saving action of God has already taken place; but it would be misleading, were it not accompanied by some indication that the final effect of God's action,

be assumed to have the positive purpose of indicating our real inward involvement rather than the negative one of implying that the inward groaning must never be outwardly expressed.

[1] The omission of υἱοθεσίαν by 𝔓⁴⁶vid D G it probably (pace P. Benoit, '"Nous gémissons, attendant la délivrance de notre corps" (Rom 8.23)', in RechSR 39 (1951–52), pp. 267–80; also JB) reflects the presence of bewilderment in the face of the apparent inconsistency between the present tenses of vv. 14 and 16 and the future sense conveyed by ἀπεκδεχόμενοι. The omission of υἱοθεσίαν leaves τὴν ἀπολύτρωσιν τοῦ σώματος ἡμῶν as the quite straightforward object of ἀπεκδεχόμενοι.

[2] Chrysostom, col. 531, draws attention to the intensive ἀπο-: Τοῦτο γάρ ἐστιν ἀπολύτρωσις, οὐχ ἁπλῶς λύτρωσις, ἀλλ᾽ ὥστε μηκέτι πάλιν ὑποστρέψαι ἐπὶ τὴν προτέραν αἰχμαλωσίαν.

[3] So, e.g., Lietzmann, p. 85; Lagrange, p. 211.

[4] So, e.g., Zahn, p. 411.

[5] Cf. Bengel, p. 531: 'Dativus, non medii, sed modi'; and the translation of the Luther Bible, 'Denn wir sind wohl selig, doch in der Hoffnung'.

namely, our enjoying salvation, still lies in the future: τῇ . . . ἐλπίδι makes this necessary qualification. (See on σωτηρία in 1.16.) The γάρ indicates that this sentence is intended as explanation of v. 23: the fact that even we who have the first-fruits of the Spirit have to groan and wait now is understandable when it is remembered that we were saved τῇ . . . ἐλπίδι.

The second sentence of the verse, ἐλπὶς δὲ βλεπομένη οὐκ ἔστιν ἐλπίς, is complementary to the first, drawing out the implication of τῇ . . . ἐλπίδι. To use the word 'hope' (in the sense of what is hoped for) with reference to an object which is already seen involves, Paul argues, a contradiction in terms; and this is clearly true, provided that we take 'seen' in a slightly pregnant sense.

The third sentence of the verse, printed in Nestle in the form ὃ γὰρ βλέπει τις, τί καὶ ἐλπίζει; supports the second. It appears in varying forms in the textual tradition. That attested by 𝔭⁴⁶ B* (and, apart from the last word, also by 1908ᵐᵍ Or)—ο γαρ βλεπει τις ελπιζει—seems to have the strongest claim to be regarded as original. This itself is patient of two different punctuations: either a comma after βλέπει, so that τις is read as τίς (i.e. 'who'), or a comma after τις which must then be read as τις (i.e. 'someone'). Of these, the former seems more probable. The textual variations may in fact be explained as having originated in a mistaken acceptance of the latter way of reading the words, followed by different attempts to make the resulting question smoother. The variant ὑπομένει for ἐλπίζει looks like a slip due to the presence of ὑπομονῆς in the next verse: the form of the next sentence seems to require ἐλπίζει here. [N²⁶ has what is argued for above.]

25. εἰ δὲ ὃ οὐ βλέπομεν ἐλπίζομεν, δι᾽ ὑπομονῆς ἀπεκδεχόμεθα: 'But since we hope for what we do not see we wait for it with steadfast patience'. Thus Paul comes back to the affirmation which was made in v. 23 and which v. 24 was intended to support; but, whereas in v. 23 the accent fell rather on the negative aspect (στενάζομεν) than on the positive, in this verse it is the positive aspect which stands out, the fact that the Christian life is characterized by steadfast hope for that glory which has not yet been openly revealed. To see here, as Michel does,[1] the influence of the Hellenistic-philosophical contrast between the seen and the unseen is uncalled for. On ὑπομονή see on 2.7 and 5.3.[2]

26. ὡσαύτως δὲ καὶ τὸ πνεῦμα. The intended comparison

---

[1] p. 206.

[2] Chrysostom observes (col. 532) in connexion with its occurrence here: τὸ γὰρ τῆς ὑπομονῆς ὄνομα ἱδρώτων ἐστὶν ὄνομα καὶ καρτερίας πολλῆς.

(ὡσαύτως) can hardly be 'as we wait patiently, so the Spirit helps', nor yet 'as hope sustains us, so the Spirit also sustains us', but must surely be between the creation's and our groaning (vv. 22, 23) and the Spirit's groaning, in spite of the fact that the key-word στεναγμός is not introduced in the first part of the verse, but only at the very end.

συναντιλαμβάνεται: 'helps'. For the verb see Bauer, s.v. It occurs in the LXX in Exod 18.22; Num 11.17; Ps 89.21 [LXX: 88.22], and in the NT in Lk 10.40. The συν- does not here mean 'together with', but is simply intensive: the meaning is not that the Spirit joins our weakness in helping the creation by intercession for it or by adding further groanings (ours and His) to its groaning,[1] but simply that the Spirit helps our weakness. The question of the nature of His help will be discussed below.

τῇ ἀσθενείᾳ[2] ἡμῶν. Even in our praying (that this is what is in mind is clear from the next sentence) we are weak.

τὸ[3] γὰρ[4] τί προσευξώμεθα καθὸ δεῖ οὐκ οἴδαμεν. It is not easy to decide whether τί προσευξώμεθα means 'what to pray' or 'what to pray for' (i.e. whether the accusative denotes the content of the prayer (cf. Lk 18.11; also Mk 12.40; Lk 20.47) or the thing prayed for (cf. Mk 11.24; perhaps Phil 1.9)): the latter is perhaps rather more likely (cf. Bauer, s.v. προσεύχομαι). But, in any case, τί is not to be reduced to a virtual equivalent of πῶς, as it is by Sanday and Headlam,[5] Lagrange,[6] Huby,[7] RV, NEB. καθὸ δεῖ is to be taken with προσευξώμεθα (the suggestion that it should be taken with οὐκ οἴδαμεν must be rejected as forced); but the words τί προσευξώμεθα καθὸ δεῖ are not to be understood as indicating two distinct things as unknown, namely, what to pray for (or what to pray) and how to present our prayers to God,[8] but one thing, namely, what it is right, i.e. according to God's will (καθὸ δεῖ is parallel to κατὰ θεόν in v. 27), for us to pray for (or to pray). Käsemann has insisted with particular forcefulness on the singularity and

[1] See, e.g., Bengel, p. 531.
[2] The variants τῆς δεήσεως and τῇ ἀσθενείᾳ τῆς δεήσεως make explicit the implied reference to prayer. The variant ταῖς ἀσθενείαις looks like a slip (note the -ται which immediately precedes).
[3] For the use of the article before an indirect question see BDF, § 267.
[4] The γάρ is better understood as indicating that these words together with all that follows down to the end of v. 27 are explanation of v. 26a as a whole than as indicating that these words by themselves explain τῇ ἀσθενείᾳ ἡμῶν.
[5] p. 213.
[6] p. 211f.
[7] p. 303.
[8] Cf., e.g., Origen, De orat. 2 (PG 11, col. 417B).

strangeness (in view of the encouragement of confidence and joyfulness in prayer characteristic of the NT generally and the fact that Paul himself shows no sign of being inhibited with regard to prayer) of this statement,[1] and has concluded that Paul's making such a statement is explicable only on the assumption that he had in mind a particular concrete phenomenon, namely the phenomenon of glossolaly in the church. As a conclusion drawn by Paul from the occurrence of glossolaly in Christian worship it is, he thinks, understandable. What many Christians were admiring as a glorious heavenly manifestation, as angelic tongues, Paul saw—paradoxically— as evidence of the Church's deep weakness and ignorance.[2] But Käsemann's basic assumption that Paul could not possibly have had in mind in this statement Christian prayer quite generally must be firmly rejected. To assert, as he does,[3] that to predicate this not-knowing of Christian prayer in general is simply absurd and contradicts everything which the NT says elsewhere on this subject, and that it would rob prayer of its meaning and assurance, is to fail to take properly into account that element of paradox which is characteristic of the Christian's life in this world (see especially 2 Cor 6.8–10). Käsemann has in fact failed to reckon with Paul's being as radical here as he actually is. We take Paul's meaning to be that all praying of Christian men, in so far as it is *their* praying, remains under the sign of this not-knowing, of real ignorance, weakness and poverty, and that even in their prayers they live only by God's justification of sinners.[4] It would indeed be strange if the continuing sinfulness of Christians (cf. 7.14–25) were altogether without effect in the matter of their knowledge of what to pray. Pelagius's 'frequenter obsunt quae prodesse arbitramur' (p. 67) shows greater perceptiveness.

ἀλλὰ αὐτὸ τὸ πνεῦμα ὑπερεντυγχάνει[5] στεναγμοῖς ἀλαλήτοις

---

[1] *Perspektiven*, pp. 219–21. The need to reconcile this statement with the fact that Christians have been taught how to pray by Christ Himself (Mt 6.9ff) was felt by Cyril of Alexandria (cols. 824f and 828). The explanation he offers is that, while Christ has taught us how to pray (καθ' ὃν ἂν πρέποι τρόπον ποιεῖσθαι τὰς ἱκετείας), the good things which God has in store for us and for which we ought to pray are, according to 1 Cor 2.9, 'Things which eye saw not, and ear heard not, And which entered not into the heart of man', and therefore beyond our understanding.

[2] Cf. pp. 221ff (especially 222, 226, 228, 231, 233f).

[3] p. 226.

[4] Gaugler's discussion of this verse (1, pp. 312–24) is particularly penetrating and perceptive.

[5] There is little doubt that the words ὑπὲρ ἡμῶν after ὑπερεντυγχάνει (attested by C K *pm* lat sy) are a secondary improvement.

explains the positive content of the first sentence of the verse (just as the preceding words explained the reference to our weakness). The Spirit Himself helps our weakness by interceding for us.[1] (The explanation of πνεῦμα here as meaning our human spirit, supported in ancient (e.g. by Cyril, col. 824) and in modern times (e.g. by Oltramare, 2, p. 170 (cf. pp. 136 and 139)) must be rejected as inconsistent with the natural sense of ὑπερεντυγχάνει and also of ὑπὲρ ἁγίων in v. 27 and with the confidence expressed in κατὰ θεόν in v. 27.) Käsemann is quite sure that στεναγμοῖς ἀλαλήτοις must refer to the ecstatic utterances of glossolaly[2]—an interpretation with a long history going back to Origen[3] and Chrysostom.[4] But, while he has succeeded in showing weaknesses in some of the arguments urged against this interpretation, he has offered little in the way of positive argument in support of it, apart from his argument (already referred to) from the words τὸ γὰρ τί προσευξώμεθα καθὸ δεῖ οὐκ οἴδαμεν. On the other side there seems to be force in the contention that the στεναγμοί mentioned here are not likely to be the utterances of glossolaly, since they clearly have to do with bringing the needs and longings of Christians before God, whereas glossolaly was pre-eminently praise.[5] But more decisive is the argument that, coming after the words αὐτὸ τὸ πνεῦμα ὑπερεντυγχάνει (cf. ἐντυγχάνει ὑπὲρ ἁγίων in v. 27), στεναγμοῖς ἀλαλήτοις must refer to the Spirit's own στεναγμοί, and it is highly unlikely that Paul would think of the ecstatic utterances of certain Christians, inspired by the Spirit though these utterances might be, as being the Spirit's own στεναγμοί. It is surely much more probable that the reference is to groanings imperceptible to the Christians themselves.[6] Whether by ἀλαλήτοις Paul meant 'ineffable', 'that cannot be expressed in ordinary human speech', intending to indicate the transcendence of these groanings, or whether he meant 'unspoken', is a further question. Verse 27 suggests that the latter possibility is more likely. The Spirit's groanings are not spoken, because they do

[1] The double compound verb ὑπερεντυγχάνειν occurs nowhere else in the Greek Bible, and is not known to occur in any Greek writer before the Christian era. The single compound ἐντυγχάνειν, however, is quite common from the 5th century B.C. onwards (in the NT: Acts 25.24; Rom 8.27, 34; 11.2; Heb 7.25): it means 'fall in with', 'chance upon', 'obtain an audience with', 'converse with', and so 'petition', 'appeal to', 'entreat'.

[2] p. 224.
[3] col. 1120.
[4] col. 533.
[5] Cf. Gaugler 1, p. 323.
[6] Cf. Gaugler 1, p. 323.

not need to be, since God knows the Spirit's intention without its being expressed.[1]

27. ὁ δὲ ἐρευνῶν τὰς καρδίας οἶδεν τί τὸ φρόνημα τοῦ πνεύματος. For this description of God compare, for example, 1 Sam 16.7; 1 Kgs 8.39; Ps 7.9; 17.3; 26.2; 44.21; 139.1, 2, 23; Prov 15.11; Jer 17.10; Acts 1.24; 15.8. Implicit in its use here is the thought that, since God searches the secrets of men's hearts, He must *a fortiori* be supposed to know the unspoken desires of His own Spirit (cf. 1 Cor 2.10f, where it is the Spirit's knowledge of God's secrets that is referred to). The sense of τὸ φρόνημα τοῦ πνεύματος is well expressed by the Vulgate rendering, 'quid desideret Spiritus'. See on v. 6.

ὅτι is better taken to mean 'that' than 'because' or 'for', since the clause it introduces explains not *why* God knows the Spirit's intention but *what* He knows in knowing it.

κατὰ θεόν: 'according to God's will'.

ἁγίων. See on 1.7.

28.[2] Paul's use of οἴδαμεν δέ (see on 2.2) suggests that he is stating in this sentence something which he knows to be generally recognized as true. The language used and the fact that Jewish parallels can be adduced make it likely that he is deliberately incorporating a piece of traditional teaching.

τοῖς ἀγαπῶσιν[3] τὸν θεόν. By being placed at the beginning of the clause these words have been given special emphasis. They have a rich OT and Jewish background.[4] The love to God, which is commanded in Scripture, is nothing less than

---

[1] Cf. Barrett, p. 168. On this and the next verse reference may be made to W. Bieder, 'Gebetswirklichkeit und Gebetsmöglichkeit bei Paulus: das Beten des Geistes und das Beten im Geist', in *TZ* 4 (1948), pp. 22–40; J. Schniewind, 'Das Seufzen des Geistes, Röm 8.26, 27', in *Nachgelassene Reden und Aufsätze*, Berlin, 1952, pp. 81–103; E. Gaugler, 'Der Geist und das Gebet der schwachen Gemeinde', in *IKZ* 51 (1961), pp. 67–94; K. Niederwimmer, 'Das Gebet des Geistes', in *TZ* 20 (1964), pp. 252–65.

[2] For a fuller discussion of this verse see Cranfield, 'Romans 8.28', in *SJT* 19 (1966), pp. 204–15.

[3] The verb ἀγαπᾶν occurs here for the first time in Romans: it occurs also in v. 37; 9.13, 25; 13.8, 9. The noun ἀγάπη has already occurred twice (5.5, 8).

[4] Cf. in the OT Exod 20.6; Deut 5.10; 6.5; 7.9; 10.12; 11.1, 13, 22; 13.3; 19.9; 30.6, 16, 20; Josh 22.5; 1 Kgs 3.3; Neh 1.5; Ps 31.23 [LXX: 30.24]; 97 [LXX: 96].10; 116 [LXX: 114].1; 145 [LXX: 144].20; Dan 9.4 (also Ps 5.11 [LXX: 12]; 69.36 [LXX: 68.37]; 119 [LXX: 118]. 132; Isa 56.6); in the Apocrypha Ecclus 1.10; 2.15f; 7.30; 34 [LXX: 31].16; 47.8, 22; 1 Macc 4.33; in the Pseudepigrapha Ps. Sol. 4.25; 6.6; 10.3; 14.1; Test. Benj. 4.5; Test. Iss. 5.2; and in the Qumran texts C.D. 3.2f; 1QH 15.9. In the NT cf. Mt 22.37 = Mk 12.30; Mk 12.33; Lk 10.27; 11.42; Jn 5.42; 1 Cor 2.9; 8.3; Jas 1.12; 2.5; 1 Jn 4.10, 20f; 5.1f.

the response of a man in the totality of his being to the prior love of God. It thus includes the whole of true religion.[1]

The question how πάντα συνεργεῖ should be construed is complicated by a variation in the textual tradition. While the majority of witnesses attest the shorter reading, 𝔓⁴⁶ B A sa syᵖᵃˡ arm attest the addition of ὁ θεός after συνεργεῖ. Some support for the longer reading is also to be found in Origen, though not in his commentary on Romans as translated by Rufinus, in which the shorter reading is followed without question.[2] At least eight possibilities have to be considered:

(i) to accept the longer reading and explain πάντα as an accusative of respect ('in all things', 'in all respects');

(ii) to accept the longer reading and explain συνεργεῖ as transitive and πάντα as its object (so, for example, Sanday and Headlam translate: 'causes all things to work',[3] while the RV margin gives 'worketh all things with them');

(iii) to accept the shorter reading and supply ὁ θεός, explaining πάντα as in (i);

(iv) to accept the shorter reading and supply ὁ θεός, explaining συνεργεῖ and πάντα as in (ii);

(v) to accept the shorter reading and take πάντα as the subject of συνεργεῖ;

(vi) to accept the shorter reading and understand the subject of συνεργεῖ to be the same as the subject of the last verb of v. 27, namely, τὸ πνεῦμα, explaining πάντα as in (i);

(vii) as in (vi), but explaining συνεργεῖ and πάντα as in (ii);

(viii) to accept the shorter reading with the emendation of πάντα to πνεῦμα or τὸ πνεῦμα.[4]

J. P. Wilson argued for (vi) or (viii) in 1949,[5] the NEB adopted (vi), and M. Black has taken up the case for (vi) or (viii).[6] Both Wilson and Black seem rather inclined to prefer (viii) to (vi). It must at once be admitted, in favour of (vi) and (vii), that τὸ πνεῦμα, as the subject of the verbs συναντιλαμβάνεται, ὑπερεντυγχάνει, and ἐντυγχάνει, in vv. 26–27, is near to hand to be supplied. But a serious objection, which applies

---

[1] Cf. Calvin, p. 179.
[2] col. 1121f. The Greek fragments do not include his comments on this verse.
[3] p. 215.
[4] W. L. Knox, St. Paul and the Church of the Gentiles, Cambridge, 2nd ed. 1961, p. 105, n. 2, has suggested a further possibility—that the 𝔓⁴⁶ variant παν for πάντα might point to an original τὸ πᾶν συνεργεῖ = 'the Universe co-operates'; but it seems more likely that this variant is simply a slip.
[5] In ET 60, p. 110f.
[6] In Neotestamentica et Patristica, pp. 169ff.

to all these last three proposals alike, is that they involve a change of subject (without any indication given in the text) between v. 28 and vv. 29–30. No subject is expressed in vv. 29–30; but it is clear that all the finite verbs in those two verses must have the same subject and that it must be God, not the Spirit, in view of the reference to 'his Son' in v. 29. If the subject of συνεργεῖ is the Spirit, a much harsher unannounced change of subject is involved than, for example, that involved between vv. 27 and 28, if one were to accept either proposal (iii) or proposal (iv); for, whereas the proximity of τὸν θεόν makes it easy to supply ὁ θεός in v. 28, the presence of a verb with another personal subject between τὸν θεόν in v. 28 and the beginning of v. 29 makes the supplying of ὁ θεός as the subject of the verbs of vv. 29–30 difficult.[1] (It might perhaps be argued that, since τοῖς κατὰ πρόθεσιν κλητοῖς picks up τοῖς ἀγαπῶσιν τὸν θεόν, there is an implicit τοῦ θεοῦ with πρόθεσιν, and that this makes the supplying of ὁ θεός in v. 29 easier. But in reply to this it must be pointed out that, if the subject of συνεργεῖ be τὸ πνεῦμα understood (or, according to (viii), expressed), then it is by no means clear that the 'purpose' is God's and not the Spirit's.)

Against (viii) there is the strong objection that, as far as the NT is concerned (for which there is such a wealth of textual evidence), conjectural emendation is a drastic expedient always requiring very special justification. Here it is quite unnecessary.

Against both (i) and (ii) it may be said that ὁ θεός looks very much like an insertion by a scribe, who understood the subject of συνεργεῖ to be God and felt it desirable to make the matter unambiguous, or else a marginal gloss which has come to be incorporated in the text. Stylistically τοῖς ἀγαπῶσιν τὸν θεὸν πάντα συνεργεῖ ὁ θεὸς εἰς ἀγαθόν is extremely clumsy; and Black's opinion that Paul 'was not so poor a stylist as to write' it is probably correct.[2]

A serious objection to (ii), (iv) and (vii) is the difficulty of adducing examples of συνεργεῖν used transitively in a sense

[1] It is interesting that the NEB, after preparing the way for the change of subject in v. 29 by placing 'with those who love God' after, instead of before, 'in everything . . . he co-operates for good' (thus producing an order of words which makes the supplying of 'God' in v. 29 very much easier) as well as supplying 'his' before 'purpose' (as do the other English versions), still feels it necessary actually to insert the word 'God' at the beginning of v. 29. This supplement is surely itself an indication of the harshness of the unannounced change of subject at this point, which the NEB translation involves.

[2] op. cit., p. 168. J. M. Ross has recently argued for (i) in TZ 33 (1977), pp. 82–85. [N[26] has rightly omitted ὁ θεός, which was printed in square brackets in N[25].]

which would be appropriate here. We have not found anything to support either the RV margin or the translation suggested by Sanday and Headlam.[1]

Of the eight explanations listed above, the two most likely would seem to be (iii) and (v). Against (iii) there are two objections, which apply also to (i) and (vi): first, that πάντα here in the sense 'in all things' is difficult (one would have expected ἐν πᾶσιν);[2] and, secondly, a sentence like this introduced by οἴδαμεν and making a statement expected to command general agreement is the sort of sentence which one expects to be rather carefully formulated and therefore not the sort in which the subject could at all naturally be left unexpressed.[3] It would be a point in favour of it, if J. P. Wilson's statement that it is 'the interpretation generally accepted by the old Greek commentators of the Eastern Church' could be sustained; but it must rather be called in question.[4]

The support of the Latin tradition for interpretation (v) is unambiguous, since in Latin a neuter plural subject requires a plural verb. There is no doubt at all that the subject of the Vulgate 'cooperantur' must be 'omnia'. C. H. Dodd has objected to this interpretation on the ground that it expresses an 'evolutionary optimism' altogether foreign to Paul's ways of thinking;[5] but it seems doubtful whether 'evolutionary optimism' can at all credibly be attributed to either Jerome or the English translators of 1611. That 'evolutionary optimism' is foreign to Paul is of course true, but there is no need to understand the statement according to interpretation (v) in any such sense. What is expressed is a truly biblical confidence in the sovereignty of God. Dodd's objection seems to have no cogency, and we can see no other objection. This being so, and since it can hardly be doubted that the sentence as a Greek sentence is most naturally understood in this way, we conclude that interpretation (v), which is the interpretation

[1] Perhaps a more likely meaning of πάντα συνεργεῖ, on the assumption that πάντα is the object of συνεργεῖ, would be 'affords every assistance' (cf. Xenophon, *Mem.* 3.5.16; Polybius, 11.9.1; Plutarch, *Moralia* 769D; Heliodorus 9.11).

[2] Though Bauer does quote a close parallel from the 2nd/3rd century writer Alexander Aphrodisiensis (*De fato* 31) for πάντα (understood as accusative of respect) συνεργεῖ εἰς ἀγαθόν.

[3] There would be no parallel among the other examples of this use of οἴδαμεν in Paul's epistles (in 3.19 the subject is placed in the relative clause, in 2 Cor 5.1 it is indicated by the inflexion of the verb: in every other case the subject is expressed).

[4] See the fuller discussion in *SJT* 19 (1966), p. 209f.

[5] p. 152f.

of the Latin Vulgate and of the AV and RV, is to be accepted as almost certainly right.

The primary reference of πάντα is, no doubt, to 'the sufferings of the present time' (v. 18), to what Calvin in his comment calls 'adversities' or 'the cross'. That this is so is confirmed by vv. 35–39. Sins committed against believers by other people are clearly included (compare 'persecution' and 'sword' in v. 35). Paul might perhaps, if pressed, have said that even believers' own sins were included in this πάντα (the question whether they are included, or not, has been discussed from patristic times). It is certainly true that the believer will often be made 'cautior et humilior', as Aquinas puts it, by his falls.[1] But it is, at any rate, to be noted that the words τοῖς ἀγαπῶσιν τὸν θεόν do set an effective limit to the scope of πάντα in this direction.

To insist on translating the verb συνεργεῖν here by 'work together with' is to give undue weight to the separate meanings of the components of a compound word. It should rather be translated by some such expression as 'assist', 'help on', 'profit'.[2] Paul's meaning is that all things, even those which seem most adverse and hurtful, such as persecution or death itself, are profitable to those who truly love God.

But not every sort of profit is meant. So συνεργεῖ has to be made more precise. Hence the addition of εἰς ἀγαθόν, with which we should compare εἰς τὸ ἀγαθόν in 13.4. Paul does not mean that all things serve the comfort or convenience or worldly interests of believers: it is obvious that they do not. What he means is that they 'assist our salvation'.[3]

We understand the first part of the verse, then, to mean that nothing can really harm—that is, harm in the deepest sense of the word—those who really love God, but that all things which may happen to them, including such grievous things as are mentioned in v. 35, must serve to help them on their way to salvation, confirming their faith and drawing them closer to their Master, Jesus Christ. But the reason why all things thus assist believers is, of course, that God is in control of all things. The faith expressed here is faith not in things but in God. Why then, it may be asked, does Paul make 'all things', and not 'God', the subject of his sentence? It is, we suggest, because he wants to draw attention to the transcendent power of Him who helps us. His power, His authority, is such that all things,

---

[1] p. 126 (698).
[2] Cf. LSJ and Bauer, s.v.; and also Chrysostom's use of ὠφελεῖ as a synonym (col. 541).
[3] Calvin, p. 179.

even the actions of those who are disobedient and set themselves against Him, must subserve His will. To say that all things assist believers is thus—in a *biblical* context—a heightening of the statement that God assists them; for it is to assert not only that He assists them, but also that His help is triumphantly and utterly effective.

This conviction that no evil which happens to the God-fearing or the good man can really harm him, but that all things, even those which seem most adverse and are most painful, must somehow result in good for him, was very widespread indeed.[1] But it is necessary to add that this traditional teaching is radically transformed, as it is taken over by Paul and other Christian writers, because it is now grounded in God's revelation of Himself in Jesus Christ.

τοῖς κατὰ πρόθεσιν κλητοῖς οὖσιν. With regard to these words three questions arise: (i) Why did Paul further define 'those who love God'? (ii) Why did he qualify κλητοῖς by κατὰ πρόθεσιν? and (iii) To what does πρόθεσιν refer?

It will be convenient to take (iii) first. The 'his' before 'purpose' in the RV has no equivalent in the original. Origen (according to Rufinus's translation), while he is aware of the possibility of taking the πρόθεσις to be God's, and actually thinks it worth while pointing out that, even if this alternative be accepted, his general interpretation of the words need not be invalidated, clearly prefers to refer πρόθεσις to men. He says: 'For these who are called according to a good choice and a good will which they have with regard to the service of God, these are they who are said to be called "according to choice".'[2] And this interpretation, which refers κατὰ πρόθεσιν to the free act of choice by which the called respond to God's call, is to be found in Chrysostom,[3] Theodoret,[4] Oecumenius,[5] and other Greek commentators. The opposite view, that the purpose

---

[1] Cf., e.g., Gen 50.20; Eccles 8.12; Ecclus 39.24–27 (especially 27); Test. Benj. 4.5; the saying attributed to Rabbi Akiba: 'Let a man accustom himself to say: "All the Almighty does, He does for good" ' (*Ber.* 60b); 'This too is for good' (attributed to Rabbi Nahum in *Taan.* 21a); *Hermetica* 9.4: 'For such a man [i.e. a godly man] all things, even though for others they are evils, are beneficial'; Plato, *Apol.* 41c–d: 'But you too, gentlemen of the jury, must cherish a good hope with regard to death, and be convinced of this one truth, that no evil befalls a good man either in life or after death, nor are his affairs neglected by the gods'; also 30c–d (cf. Epictetus, *Ench.* 53 *fin.*).

[2] col. 1126.

[3] col. 541.

[4] col. 141.

[5] col. 489.

referred to is God's, was taken by Augustine.[1] There can scarcely be any doubt that Augustine was right. Not only does 9.11 (the only other verse in Romans in which πρόθεσις occurs) support him; vv. 29 and 30 of the present chapter are also strong support. For the qualification of κλητοῖς by κατὰ πρόθεσιν in v. 28 is closely paralleled by the way in which v. 29 indicates what lies behind the τούτους . . . ἐκάλεσεν of v. 30. To put it otherwise, the meaning of πρόθεσις in v. 28 is defined by the verbs προέγνω and προώρισεν in v. 29. The purpose referred to is God's eternal purpose of mercy.[2]

Question (ii) may be put in another way. Did Paul qualify κλητοῖς by κατὰ πρόθεσιν simply in order to bring out the meaning of κλητοῖς, or did he want to distinguish one sort of calling from another, a calling κατὰ πρόθεσιν from a calling which is not κατὰ πρόθεσιν? With Mt 22.14 ('For many are called, but few chosen') in mind, patristic commentators tended to accept the latter alternative, those who took κατὰ πρόθεσιν to refer to human choice understanding Paul's intention to be to indicate not all the called but a smaller number who meet the divine call with obedience, and those who took it to refer to God's purpose seeing a distinction between those who are not only called but also foreknown and foreordained, and those who are merely called. But the position of ἐκάλεσεν (which is cognate to κλητός) in the fivefold chain of vv. 29 and 30 tells decisively against this; for it clearly denotes an effectual calling (compare for example, 9.24 and 1 Cor 7.17ff; and κλητός in 1.6, 7; 1 Cor 1.2, 24). We take it, then, that κατὰ πρόθεσιν is added simply in order to bring out the meaning of κλητοῖς.

[1] col. 2076. He says: 'Propositum autem Dei accipiendum est, non ipsorum'; but, unfortunately, after having recognized that the purpose must be God's and connected it with His foreknowing and foreordaining, goes on to speak of His foreknowledge as a foreknowledge of what particular men will do ('. . . nec praedestinavit aliquem, nisi quem praescivit crediturum et secuturum vocationem suam . . .'), just as Pelagius (p. 68) does.

[2] The word πρόθεσις (other occurrences in the NT: Mt 12.4 = Mk 2.26 = Lk 6.4; Acts 11.23; 27.13; Rom 9.11; Eph 1.11; 3.11; 2 Tim 1.9; 3.10; Heb 9.2) denotes in extra-biblical Greek a 'placing in public', the 'statement' of a case, a 'statement', 'proposition', that which one sets before oneself, so 'purpose'. It is used in the LXX in connexion with the shew-bread laid before God, in 2 and 3 Maccabees of a man's purpose, but never to represent the Hebrew 'ēṣāh; but, as used by Paul, it denotes that which in the OT is quite frequently expressed by 'ēṣāh—the counsel or purpose of God (e.g. Ps 33.11; Prov 19.21; Isa 14.26; 19.17; 25.1; 46.10f; Jer 49.20; 50.45; Mic 4.12). The word 'ēṣāh occurs very frequently in the Qumran texts, sometimes of God's purpose (e.g. 1QS 1.13; 11.18; 1QH 4.13), but often apparently in the sense of 'council' (e.g. 1QS 1.8; 3.6). See also on 9.11; and on 3.25 (προέθετο).

So we come back to question (i), the question of the purpose of the addition of these last five words of the verse. There is little doubt about the correct answer. We saw above that the purpose of vv. 28–30 was to underline the certainty of that hope of which vv. 17–27 had spoken. This certainty is indicated by the first part of v. 28; but, had Paul said no more, its fullness would not have been expressed. This only begins to be seen, when it is realized that behind the love which those who are righteous by faith have for God—and far transcending it in significance—is God's prior choice of them (compare 1 Jn 4.19). So Paul in a way corrects himself (compare Gal 4.9): 'to those who love God'—that is, 'to those who are called according to his purpose'. Their love for Him is a sign and token of His prior love for them. The certainty of the hope, of which Paul has spoken, rests on nothing less than the eternal purpose of God.

29. ὅτι: 'For'. It seems better to understand vv. 29–30 as supporting v. 28 as a whole than as explaining just the last five words of it.

οὓς προέγνω. Compare 11.2; 1 Pet 1.2. The -εγνω is to be understood in the light of the use of *yāḍaʻ* in such passages as Gen 18.19; Jer 1.5; Amos 3.2, where it denotes that special taking knowledge of a person which is God's electing grace.[1] The thought expressed by the προ- is not just that God's gracious choice of those referred to preceded their knowledge of Him, but that it took place before the world was created (cf. Eph 1.4; 2 Tim 1.9).[2]

[1] The interpretation of προέγνω as denoting God's foreknowledge of men's future moral fitness, which is common in patristic writers (e.g. Theodoret, cols. 141, 144: he argues that God's foreknowledge of what men will be is not the cause of their being such, any more than the man who sees a ferocious horse with a rider who cannot control it approaching a precipice and guesses that horse and rider will fall over it is the cause of their fall) is clearly un-Pauline. Origen recognized clearly that Paul was here using 'foreknow' in a special biblical sense (col. 1125: 'secundum consuetudinem Scripturae sacrae'): he explains it as meaning 'in affectum recipere sibique sociare' (col. 1127; cf. 1125, where he says, with reference to 2 Tim 2.19, 'cognovisse suos dicitur, hoc est in dilectione habuisse, sibique sociasse'). But there is a weakness in his grasp of the nature of grace; for he sees this special divine knowledge as resting upon a divine knowledge according to the ordinary sense of the word 'know' ('istam communem scientiam'—col. 1125)— 'illos . . . praecognitos a Deo, in quibus, sciens quales essent, amorem suum Deus affectumque posuisset . . .' (col. 1125). Aquinas (p. 127 (703)) rightly recognized that to make God's foreknowledge of our good deeds the cause of His predestination 'nihil est aliud quam gratiam ponere dari ex meritis nostris'.

[2] We reserve fuller discussion of Paul's doctrine of election and of predestination for the notes on chapters 9–11.

καὶ προώρισεν συμμόρφους τῆς εἰκόνος τοῦ υἱοῦ αὐτοῦ is the second link of the fivefold chain. Whereas προέγνω denoted God's gracious election, προώρισεν denotes His gracious decision concerning the elect, the content of which is indicated by the words which follow. For προορίζειν compare Acts 4.28; 1 Cor 2.7; Eph 1.5, 11. This divine predestination or decision which appoints for the elect their goal is, like their election, to be thought of as taking place πρὸ καταβολῆς κόσμου. Behind the words συμμόρφους τῆς εἰκόνος τοῦ υἱοῦ αὐτοῦ there is probably the thought of man's creation κατ᾽ εἰκόνα θεοῦ (Gen 1.27) and also the thought (cf. 2 Cor 4.4; Col 1.15) of Christ's being eternally the very εἰκὼν τοῦ θεοῦ (not, be it noted, just κατ᾽ εἰκόνα θεοῦ). The believers' final glorification is their full conformity to the εἰκών of Christ glorified; but it is probable (*pace* Sanday and Headlam, Lagrange, *et al.*) that Paul is here thinking not only of their final glorification but also of their growing conformity to Christ here and now in suffering and in obedience —that is, that συμμόρφους, κ.τ.λ. is meant to embrace sanctification as well as final glory, the former being thought of as a progressive conformity to Christ, who is the εἰκών of God, and so as a progressive renewal of the believer into that likeness of God which is God's original purpose for man (cf. Col 3.9f).[1]

εἰς τὸ εἶναι αὐτὸν πρωτότοκον ἐν πολλοῖς ἀδελφοῖς indicates God's purpose in foreordaining His elect to be conformed to the likeness of His Son. It was in order that His only-begotten Son might not be alone in enjoying the privileges of sonship, but might be the Head of a multitude of brothers, of the company of those who in, and through, Him have been made sons of God. It is as their conformity to Christ is perfected in glory that believers finally enter into the full enjoyment of the privileges of their adoption in fellowship with Him (cf. v. 17). The word πρωτότοκος (cf. Col 1.15, 18; Heb 1.6; Rev 1.5) expresses here at the same time both the unique pre-eminence of Christ and also the fact that He shares His privileges with His brethren.

30. οὓς δὲ προώρισεν, τούτους καὶ ἐκάλεσεν. With this third link of the chain we are in the realm of historical time. By καλεῖν here is meant not just 'call' but 'call effectually' (see on v. 28— κλητοῖς). When God thus calls effectually, a man responds with the obedience of faith. Indeed, calling in this sense and conversion might be likened to the obverse and reverse of the

---

[1] See further on εἰκών *TWNT* 2, pp. 378–96 (especially 393–96); also on 1.23. On the whole phrase συμμόρφους, κ.τ.λ., reference may be made to J. Kürzinger, 'συμμόρφους τῆς εἰκόνος τοῦ υἱοῦ αὐτοῦ (Röm 8.29)', in *BZ* 2 (1958–59), pp. 294–99; A. R. C. Leaney, ' "Conformed to the Image of His Son" (Rom 8.29)', in *NTS* 10 (1963–64), pp. 470–79.

same coin: they are the same event seen from two different points of view (cf., e.g., 1 Cor 7.17ff).[1]

καὶ οὓς ἐκάλεσεν, τούτους καὶ ἐδικαίωσεν is the fourth link. It is that divine gift of a status of righteousness before God with which so much of the epistle has been concerned.

οὓς δὲ ἐδικαίωσεν, τούτους καὶ ἐδόξασεν. The fifth, and last, link is God's glorification of His elect. The use of the aorist here is significant and suggestive. In a real sense, of course, their glory is still in the future, still the object of hope (cf. 5.2), and this 'not yet' with regard to their glory is certainly not to be explained away or glossed over. But their glorification has already been foreordained by God (cf. v. 29); the divine decision has been taken, though its working out has not been consummated. Moreover, Christ, in whose destiny their destiny is included, has already been glorified, so that in Him their glorification has already been accomplished. So it can be spoken of as something concealed which has yet to be revealed (cf. v. 18—μέλλουσαν δόξαν ἀποκαλυφθῆναι). We may compare the use of the aorist ἐσώθημεν in v. 24.

The fact that sanctification is not mentioned as an intermediate link between justification and glorification certainly does not mean that it was not important to Paul: the earlier part of this chapter—not to mention chapter 6 and 12.1–15.13—is clear evidence to the contrary. It may be that he felt that sanctification had already been sufficiently emphasized in the course of the section for it to be unnecessary to refer to it again here explicitly—an implicit reference is of course present, since, according to what has already been said in the epistle, sanctification is both the natural sequel to justification and also the earthly road which leads to the heavenly glory. He may perhaps have felt that ἐδόξασεν covered sanctification as well as glorification, since there is a real sense in which it is a beginning of glorification[2] (cf. 2. Cor 3.18—μεταμορφούμεθα ἀπὸ δόξης εἰς δόξαν, and also the way in which—if our interpretation was right—the words συμμόρφους τῆς εἰκόνος τοῦ υἱοῦ αὐτοῦ in v. 29 referred not only to conformity to Christ's glory hereafter but also to being conformed to Him here and now in sufferings and obedience).

---

[1] Cf. Barrett, p. 170.
[2] Cf. Bruce, p. 178.

*(iv) Conclusion both to section V. 4 and also at the same
time to the whole of the foregoing argument of the epistle
(8.31–39)*

[31]What then shall we say in view of these things? Seeing that God
is for us, who is against us? [32]He who did not spare his own Son,
but gave him up for us all, how shall he not also with him give us
all things? [33]Who shall lay a charge against God's elect? It is God
who justifies: [34]who shall condemn? It is Christ Jesus who died, and,
more than that, who was also raised from the dead, who is at the
right hand of God, who also intercedes for us. [35]Who shall separate
us from the love of Christ? Affliction or anguish or persecution or
famine or nakedness or peril or sword?—[36]even as it is written in
Scripture: 'For thy sake we are being done to death all the day long,
we have been reckoned as sheep to be slaughtered'. [37]But in all these
things we are more than conquerors through him who loved us. [38]For
I am persuaded that neither death nor life nor angels nor principalities
nor things present nor things to come nor powers [39]nor height nor
depth nor any other created thing shall be able to separate us from
the love of God which is in Christ Jesus our Lord.

While the primary reference of 'these things' in v. 31a is, no
doubt, to what has just been said in vv. 29(or 28)–30, it is
clear from the contents of vv. 32–34 that it has also a wider
reference, and that this sub-section serves not only as the
conclusion of section V. 4 underlining the certainty of the
Christian hope (the occurrence of the formula 'in Christ Jesus
our Lord' in v. 39 is a pointer to its being an integral part of
V. 4—compare 5.1, 11, 21; 6.23; 7.25), but also as a conclusion
to the whole course of the theological exposition up to this
point. The words 'God is for us' in v. 31b are a concise summary
not only of vv. 28–30 but also of 1.16b–8.30 (or, at the least, of
3.21–8.30).

This sub-section is a first person plural passage, except for
vv. 38–39 which are a personal statement in the first person
singular. It is clear that the whole sub-section has been
carefully constructed with an eye to rhetorical considerations.
Verses 31b–39 fall naturally into four strophes consisting of
vv. 31b–32, 33–34, 35–37, 38–39.[1] The elevated eloquence of
the sub-section is outstanding.

Attention has been drawn to the similarity of thought and
style to be observed between this passage and a number of
passages in the writings of Greek and Latin moralists, especially
Stoics, which list obstacles besetting the way of virtue over

---

[1] Cf., e.g., J. Weiss, 'Beiträge zur paulinischen Rhetorik', in
*Theologische Studien Herrn Prof. D. Bernhard Weiss zu seinem 70.
Geburtstage dargebracht*, Göttingen, 1897, p. 33; Lagrange, p. 217f;
Michel, p. 213.

which the truly wise man triumphs.[1] What distinguishes this passage from the others is, as Lagrange has pointed out,[2] the fact that the confidence expressed in it is confidence not in the power of human virtue but in the grace of God in Christ.

31. Τί οὖν ἐροῦμεν. See on 3.5. Here, as in 9.30, it is used to introduce, not a false inference which is going to be rejected, but Paul's own conclusion from what he has been saying.[3]

πρός: 'about', 'in view of'. See Moule, *Idiom-Book*, p. 63.

ταῦτα may be understood as referring primarily to the content of vv. 29–30 (or 28–30); but, in view of the nature of vv. 32–34, the reference of ταῦτα should not be restricted to the immediately preceding verses. Verses 31–39 may justifiably be regarded as the conclusion not only to chapter 8 but also to the whole argument of the epistle so far.

εἰ ὁ θεὸς ὑπὲρ ἡμῶν, τίς καθ' ἡμῶν; Compare Ps 23.4 ('. . . I will fear no evil; for thou art with me: . . .'); 56.9 ('. . . This I know, that God is for me') and 11 ('In God I have put my trust, I will not be afraid; What can man do unto me?'); also 118.6 and 7. The εἰ here does not introduce a condition which may or may not be fulfilled, but states what Paul is altogether convinced is a fact as the ground of the confidence expressed in the following rhetorical question. The words ὁ θεὸς ὑπὲρ ἡμῶν are a concise summary of the gospel. For the use of ὑπέρ in the sense 'on the side of' compare Mk 9.40 = Lk 9.50. What is meant is, of course, that God is on our side in the way indicated by the gospel events, that is, as our Lord, and not as a subservient ally who can be mobilized by us for the accomplishment of our purposes.

The rhetorical question (τίς καθ' ἡμῶν;) is equivalent to an emphatic statement that there is no one whose hostility we need fear.[4] Enemies we certainly have, who are against us and seek our ruin; but with God on our side we need not fear them. Though they may indeed cause us to suffer grievously (as Paul

---

[1] Cf. Bultmann, *Stil*, p. 19.

[2] p. 218.

[3] Vv. 31–39 are indeed a declaration of defiance (Barth, *CD* II/2, p. 493, uses the phrase, 'truly reverent defiance', in connexion with v. 31), and presuppose the existence of hostile forces; but, *pace* Gaugler i, p. 342, and Michel, p. 213, it is not necessary to suppose (whether on this ground or because of the use of the τί . . . ἐροῦμεν formula) that Paul is here actually meaning to answer objections.

[4] Some interpreters (e.g., Michel, p. 214) insist that the thought of a trial is already in Paul's mind (since God has acquitted, who will dare to come forward to accuse us?); but it may be suggested that the thought here is quite general (ὑπέρ and κατά simply meaning 'on the side of' and 'against'), and that, as far as this paragraph is concerned, the forensic imagery is introduced in v. 33 as something fresh.

well knew, witness 2 Cor 11.23ff), they cannot snatch us from Him.

32. ὅς γε τοῦ ἰδίου υἱοῦ οὐκ¹ ἐφείσατο is quite probably an intentional echo of Gen 22.12, 16 (LXX: . . . καὶ οὐκ ἐφείσω τοῦ υἱοῦ σου τοῦ ἀγαπητοῦ . . .): like Abraham, God has not spared His own Son. (On the subject of Isaac-Christ typology and on the question of the possible influence of Jewish thought concerning the 'Binding of Isaac' see on 3.25.) The γε (it is the only time that it is used in the NT with the relative) has the effect of drawing special attention to the idea expressed in the clause. For ἰδίου compare v. 3—τὸν ἑαυτοῦ υἱόν. The thought of the contrast between the only-begotten Son and the adopted sons is perhaps present: in any case, the adjective serves to heighten the poignancy of the clause, emphasizing the cost to the Father of delivering up His dearest and most precious.

ἀλλὰ ὑπὲρ ἡμῶν πάντων παρέδωκεν αὐτόν. The same verb was used in the passive in this connexion in 4.25. Compare also Isa 53.12. The traditional language of the primitive Church is echoed here. It is noteworthy that παραδιδόναι was also used in 1.24, 26, 28 of God's delivering up idolatrous men to the consequences of their sin. Isaac was rescued by divine intervention (Gen 22.11–13), but for Jesus there was no such intervention, no other lamb could take the place of the Lamb of God; and the delivering up meant making to drink to the very dregs the cup of wrath (see on 1.18). And this was ὑπὲρ ἡμῶν, 'for us', 'for our benefit'. For the πάντων which strengthens ἡμῶν compare, for example, 10.11, 12, 13; 15.33; 1 Cor 1.2.

πῶς οὐχὶ καὶ σὺν αὐτῷ τὰ πάντα ἡμῖν χαρίσεται; The argument is similar both in form and content to that of 5.9–10: since God has done the unspeakably great and costly thing, we may be fully confident that He will do what is by comparison far less. It has been suggested that the verb χαρίζεσθαι here should be understood in the sense 'forgive' (cf., e.g., 2 Cor 2.7, 10; Eph 4.32).² But this sense does not really fit the thought of the sentence, and σὺν αὐτῷ, in particular, would become problematic.³ It is surely to be taken in the sense 'give' (cf.,

---

¹ The variant supported by D (G), οὐδὲ τοῦ ἰδίου υἱοῦ for γε τοῦ ἰδίου υἱοῦ οὐκ perhaps originated in an accidental omission of the οὐκ. The substitution of οὐδέ for γε would then be explicable as an attempt to restore the sense by introducing the necessary negative.

² D. M. Baillie, *God was in Christ: an essay on Incarnation and Atonement*, London, 1948, p. 178, n. 2, cited by Loane, p. 132.

³ The explanation of σὺν αὐτῷ as associating the exalted Christ with God in the act of χαρίζεσθαι must surely be rejected on the ground that

e.g., Phil 1.29; 2.9; Philem 22). God's delivering up His Son to death on our behalf may be thought of as a giving of His Son to us (cf. Jn 3.16): the fact that 'deliver up' is in Greek a compound of the verb 'to give' makes the movement of thought the easier. God has delivered up His dear Son for us: therefore we may be confident that, together with His supreme Gift of His Son, He will also give us τὰ πάντα. A comparison with 1 Cor 3.21–23 suggests the possibility that by giving 'all things' is meant giving a share in Christ's lordship over the universe, and the phrase συγκληρονόμοι . . . Χριστοῦ in v. 17 might perhaps be claimed as possible support for this view; but it seems more probable that 'all things' should be understood as denoting the fullness of salvation (cf. 5.10) or else 'all that is necessary for our salvation' (Sanday and Headlam, p. 219: cf. Bengel, p. 533: 'πάντα omnia) salutaria').

33f. There is disagreement about the punctuation of these verses. There is ancient support for the view that question marks should be placed, not only after ἐκλεκτῶν θεοῦ and κατακρινῶν, but also after δικαιῶν, ἀποθανών, ἐγερθείς, τοῦ θεοῦ and ὑπὲρ ἡμῶν. (A modification of this punctuation, omitting the question marks after ἀποθανών, ἐγερθείς and τοῦ θεοῦ, and so making one big question out of Χριστὸς Ἰησοῦς, κ.τ.λ., is given in the RV margin and is favoured by Barrett, p. 172.) The punctuation accepted by Nestle, which is also that presupposed by the RV text, has the support of Origen and Chrysostom. Another punctuation is similar to that of Nestle, except for having a full stop instead of a colon after δικαιῶν, thus making τίς ἐγκαλέσει κατὰ ἐκλεκτῶν θεοῦ; and τίς ὁ κατακρινῶν; into two parallel questions with two parallel answers.

Of these, the punctuation of Nestle (question marks after ἐκλεκτῶν θεοῦ and κατακρινῶν, colon after δικαιῶν, commas after ἀποθανών, ἐγερθείς, and τοῦ θεοῦ, and full stop at the end of v. 34) is to be preferred for the following reasons:

(i) θεὸς ὁ δικαιῶν· τίς ὁ κατακρινῶν; looks like an echo of the first part of Isa 50.8 (ὅτι ἐγγίζει ὁ δικαιώσας με· τίς ὁ κρινόμενός μοι;), and, if it is a conscious echo, it is unlikely that Paul intended to break it up, which would be the effect of putting a question mark or a full stop after δικαιῶν. (Even if it was not a conscious echo, it is still true that ὁ δικαιῶν and ὁ κατακρινῶν form a natural antithesis which it seems perverse to break up.)

---

it involves assuming a change of thought from the preceding clause in which Christ is the object of παρέδωκεν, which, in the absence of any indication to prepare the reader, is intolerably harsh.

(ii) The views of Greek-speaking Fathers on a matter of this sort deserve special respect.

(iii) This punctuation gives the simplest and most natural development of thought.[1]

The argument that because in vv. 31, 32 and 35 we have a series of rhetorical questions, it is likely that vv. 33 and 34 are also made up only of questions[2] seems to lack force. Paul is just as likely to have varied his form as to have maintained it for so many verses without change.

τίς ἐγκαλέσει κατὰ ἐκλεκτῶν θεοῦ; is probably better taken as a rhetorical question equivalent to an emphatic denial that any one will dare to do so, and so not requiring an answer, than as a genuine question answered by vv. 33b and 34. Compare v. 31b. The verb ἐγκαλεῖν occurs elsewhere in the NT only in Acts. A judgment scene is envisaged.[3] The term ἐκλεκτοὶ θεοῦ picks up the thought of κατὰ πρόθεσιν κλητοῖς in v. 28 and οὓς προέγνω in v. 29.

θεὸς ὁ δικαιῶν[4] and τίς ὁ κατακρινῶν; belong closely together. As we have seen, they are probably a conscious echo of Isa 50.8. For their substance compare v. 31b. Pace Sanday and Headlam, p. 221, it is better to accentuate κατακρινῶν than κατακρίνων: the combination of the future participle of κατακρίνειν with the present δικαιῶν is perfectly natural, and the future is required by the parallel ἐγκαλέσει.

Χριστὸς Ἰησοῦς. The sentence so beginning is best taken as a statement—'It is Christ Jesus . . . who . . .' The words ἅμα δέ placed before Χριστός by 𝔭[46] (supported by d* Ir) appear to be an explicatory, improving addition. It is possible that Ἰησοῦς should be omitted, in view of the strong combination of authorities which do not have it.

ὁ ἀποθανών, μᾶλλον δὲ ἐγερθείς,[5] ὅς[6] ἐστιν ἐν δεξιᾷ τοῦ θεοῦ forms an ascending series. It seems on the whole rather better to take all three terms as adjectival to Χριστὸς Ἰησοῦς than to

---

[1] It is surprising that Barrett, p. 172, does not even mention as a possibility the RV text interpretation of the Greek as punctuated in Nestle.

[2] Barrett, p. 172.

[3] The thought of Satan's role of accuser (cf. Job 1 and 2; Zech 3.1; Rev 12.10) was possibly in Paul's mind.

[4] Loane, p. 138, notes that this is the last occurrence in the epistle of δικαιοῦν, which has been one of the main key-words of the first eight chapters.

[5] It is possible that ἐκ νεκρῶν should be read after ἐγερθείς (with ℵ* A C Ψ 33, etc.—for fuller list see UBS apparatus).

[6] The καί after this ὅς, attested by 𝔭27.46 B ℵ D G pm it, etc., is certainly not required, and would hardly have been added deliberately: it is perhaps due to assimilation to the following clause. [N²⁶ includes it.]

connect the third with what follows as part of the main framework of the sentence, in spite of the fact that the use of the relative pronoun and indicative forms a link with the following clause and contrasts with the two participles. The third term reflects the influence of Ps 110.1, which seems to be the OT verse most frequently echoed in the NT.[1] That its language is picture-language should go without saying (cf. Calvin, *Institutes* 2.16.15: a 'comparison . . . drawn from kings who have assessors at their side to whom they delegate the tasks of ruling and governing' and 'a question, not of the disposition of his body, but of the majesty of his authority'). In a real sense the chronological order in which the three terms are arranged represents also, for Paul, an ascending order of theological significance (note the μᾶλλον δέ): for him, as for the primitive church generally, the focus-point of faith is the present glory of the One who once was crucified (cf. the credal statement, κύριος Ἰησοῦς). (For stimulating brief discussions of the *Sessio ad dexteram* reference may be made to Barth, *Credo*, pp. 105ff, and *Dogmatics in Outline*, pp. 124ff.)

ὅς καὶ ἐντυγχάνει ὑπὲρ ἡμῶν. On the verb ἐντυγχάνειν see on v. 26 (ὑπερεντυγχάνει). For the thought of Christ as our Intercessor at God's right hand compare the reference to Him as our Advocate with the Father in 1 Jn 2.1, and also the reference to His intercession as our High Priest in Heb 7.25.[2] Pelagius's comment on this clause contains a striking and suggestive reference to the fact that Christ's high priestly intercession is accomplished as He continually shows and offers to His Father as our pledge that human nature which he assumed.[3]

35. τίς ἡμᾶς χωρίσει ἀπὸ τῆς ἀγάπης τοῦ Χριστοῦ; is yet another rhetorical question. No one will ever separate us (the position of ἡμᾶς gives it a slight emphasis) from the love of Christ, that is, from Christ's love of us (cf. v. 37—τοῦ ἀγαπήσαντος ἡμᾶς). The variant θεοῦ for Χριστοῦ is probably assimilation to v. 39, as the longer variant θεοῦ τῆς ἐν Χριστῷ Ἰησοῦ quite clearly is. The fact that Paul can speak here of Christ's love (cf. 2 Cor 5.14; Eph 3.19), whereas in v. 39 and in 5.5 he speaks of God's

---

[1] Cf. O. Cullmann, *The Earliest Christian Confessions*, Eng. tr., London, 1949, p. 58.

[2] Bruce, p. 180, sees here an echo of Isa 53.12, where the MT, but not the LXX, has a reference to the Servant's making intercession for the transgressors. He notes that in the Targum of Jonathan this is mentioned in vv. 4 and 11 as well as in v. 12.

[3] p. 70: '. . . in hoc interpellare eum, dum semper pat[r]i hominem, quem suscepit, quasi nostrum pignus ostendit et offert, ut uerus pontifex et aeternus'.

440 COMMENTARY ON ROMANS

love (cf. 2 Cor 13.13) led Chrysostom to observe: οὕτως ἀδιάφορον αὐτῷ καὶ Χριστὸν καὶ Θεὸν ὀνομάζειν (col. 544). It is another pointer to the nature of Paul's Christology.

The latter part of the verse is not a fresh question, but a supplement to, or indeed a continuation of, the preceding. Paul had himself already experienced all the trials which he here enumerates as threatening the Christian, except the last. On θλῖψις and στενοχωρία see on 2.9. For διωγμός compare I Cor 4.12; 2 Cor 4.9; 12.10; Gal 5.11; for λιμός and γυμνότης I Cor 4.11; 2 Cor 11.27; for κίνδυνος I Cor 15.30; 2 Cor 11.26; for μάχαιρα Acts 12.2; Heb 11.34, 37.

36. The ὅτι is no doubt to be taken as ὅτι recitativum introducing the quotation (cf., e.g., 3.10; 4.17; 9.17), and not as part of the quotation, although there does happen to be a ὅτι at the beginning of this particular OT verse in the LXX.[1]

The main effect of the quotation of Ps 44.22 [LXX: 43.23] is to show that the tribulations which face Christians are nothing new or unexpected, but have all along been characteristic of the life of God's people. The Rabbis applied this verse of the psalm to the death of martyrs (e.g. to the martyrdom of the mother and her seven sons described in 2 Macc 7), but also quite generally to the life of the godly who give themselves wholeheartedly to God.[2] Paul probably thought of it as applicable not just to the last item (μάχαιρα) but to all the things listed in v. 35.[3] For ἕνεκεν σοῦ compare, for example, 2 Macc 7.9 ('for his [i.e. God's] laws'), 11 ('for his law's sake'); Mk 8.35 ('for my sake and the gospel's'); Rev 1.9 ('for the word of God and the testimony of Jesus'). For θανατούμεθα ὅλην τὴν ἡμέραν compare I Cor 15.30f; 2 Cor 4.11.

37. ἀλλ'. Paul's magnificent declaration begins with a triumphant 'But'. Its force may be brought out by the paraphrase, 'So far from its being possible for any of these things to separate us from Christ's love'.

ἐν τούτοις πᾶσιν: just possibly a Hebraism meaning 'in spite of all these things',[4] but more probably 'in all these things',

[1] *Pace* Sanday and Headlam, p. 221.
[2] Cf. SB 3, pp. 258–60.
[3] Barrett, p. 173, remarks that 'It is noteworthy that Paul makes no cross-reference to Isa.liii.7', presumably meaning to imply that the absence of a reference to it here is support for his view that Isa 52.13–53.12 was not nearly as important to Jesus and to the primitive Church as has often been thought (cf., his contribution in *NT Essays* (T. W. Manson memorial volume), pp. 1–18). But in reply it must be said that, if this Isaiah passage was already applied to Jesus Himself, that would be a strong reason for not applying it directly to Christians.
[4] Cf. Bruce, p. 181; and see BDB, s.v. בְּ, III.7.

that is, not evading them or being spared them, but meeting them steadfastly, in the very experiencing of them.

ὑπερνικῶμεν. The felicitous AV translation 'we are more than conquerors' derives from the Geneva Bible. The ὑπερ- has an intensive force (cf., e.g., ὑπερπερισσεύειν in 5.20).[1] The verb was used with a different nuance by Menander (fourth century B.C.) in a shrewd epigram (proved true again and again wherever there has been a 'total victory' of one human being, or of one group or nation, over another), καλὸν τὸ νικᾶν, ὑπερνικᾶν δὲ σφαλερόν.[2] It also occurs in the Hippocratic corpus.[3]

διὰ τοῦ ἀγαπήσαντος[4] ἡμᾶς indicates that it is not through any courage, endurance or determination of our own, but through Christ, and not even by our hold on Him but by His hold on us, that we are more than conquerors. The use of the aorist participle indicates that the reference is to a particular historic act, namely, that act by which He proved His love to us (cf. 5.6–8; also Gal 2.20).

38f. Paul now adds in the first person singular his own personal declaration in support of v. 37.

πέπεισμαι as used by Paul (cf. 14.14; 15.14; 2 Tim 1.5, 12) indicates a firm and settled conviction, a confident certainty. Compare Pelagius, p. 71: 'Pro certo confido'.[5]

The powers listed are mentioned in pairs, apart from δυνάμεις and τις κτίσις ἑτέρα. θάνατος is mentioned first, probably because of θανατούμεθα in the psalm-verse just quoted. Death, the dreaded separator of loved ones, had for most of the OT period been thought even by the people of God to separate men from God's fellowship (cf., e.g., Ps 6.5; 30.9; 88.5, 10–12; 115.17; Isa 38.18); but for Paul to die was to 'be with Christ', and therefore could even be spoken of as 'gain' and something 'very far better' than life in this present world (Phil 1.21–23; cf. 2 Cor 5.8). With θάνατος is coupled ζωή. If death, the

---

[1] See LSJ, s.v. ὑπέρ, F. in Compos., 3.

[2] *Mon.*299 (in A. Meineke, *Fragmenta Comicorum Graecorum* 4, Berlin, 1841, p. 348).

[3] *Hebd.*50.

[4] The reading τὸν ἀγαπήσαντα is weakly attested as far as the Greek text is concerned, and is perhaps to be explained as having originated in an incorrect translation into Latin.

[5] Incidentally, the whole of his interpretation of these two verses is interesting in its own way: 'Pro certo confido quia nec si mihi [quis] mortem minetur, nec si uitam promittat, nec si se angelum dicat a domino destinatum, nec si angelorum principem mentiatur, nec si in praesenti honorem conferat, neque si polliceatur gloria[m] futurorum, neque si uirtutes operetur, nec si caelum promittat et inferno deterreat, uel profunditate[m] scientiae suadere conetur, umquam nos poterit a Christi secernere caritate'.

'praecipuum inter terribilia', as Aquinas called it,[1] cannot separate us from God's love, neither can life, the 'praecipuum inter appetibilia',[2] in spite of the trials and distresses, enticements and distractions, it may bring, and the fact that in it the believer has to 'walk by faith, not by sight' (2 Cor 5.7), and is in a real sense 'absent from the Lord' (2 Cor 5.6). Whether dying or living, we are equally 'the Lord's' (14.8), since He is Lord of the living and dead alike (14.9). The second pair is οὔτε ἄγγελοι οὔτε ἀρχαί. ἀρχαί could of course (simply as a Greek word) denote 'civil authorities', 'magistrates'; but, coupled with ἄγγελοι, it clearly signifies a category of angelic beings. There are a number of lists of such beings in the NT epistles, and ἀρχή figures in all except one of them, being always, apart from this present passage, associated with ἐξουσία[3] (1 Cor 15.24; Eph 1.21; 3.10; 6.12; Col 1.16; 2.10, 15). Other nouns used in these lists are δύναμις (1 Cor 15.24; Eph 1.21; 1 Pet 3.22), κυριότης (Col 1.16; Eph 1.21) and θρόνος (Col 1.16). These names were current in Judaism (cf., e.g., 1 Enoch 61.10; 2 Enoch 20.1). In the NT epistles they seem to be applied both to angelic beings which are thought of as obediently fulfilling their divinely-appointed roles in the ordering of the universe and in the affairs of men and also to spiritual forces of evil which have to be resisted by Christians (cf., e.g., Eph 6.12). What Paul is here concerned to say is simply that there is no spiritual cosmic power, whether benevolent or malevolent, which will be able to separate us from God's love in Christ. And this he can say with confidence, because he knows that Christ has once and for all won the decisive battle against the rebellious powers (cf. Col 2.15: also Eph 1.21, 22a; 1 Pet 3.22), so that their effectiveness has been drastically curtailed and their final complete subjection assured.[4] The third pair consists of ἐνεστῶτα and μέλλοντα, which are most naturally understood as signifying present and future (including eschatological) events and circumstances. The same pair figures in the list in 1 Cor 3.22, where it is associated, as here, with ζωή and θάνατος, but also with Παῦλος, Ἀπολλῶς, Κηφᾶς and κόσμος.[5] δυνάμεις stands by

---

[1] p. 131 (727).   [2] Aquinas, ibid.

[3] The variants noted in Nestle show that there was a tendency to introduce ἐξουσία here.

[4] On the subject of the spiritual powers see further on 13.1; also *TWNT* I, pp. 72ff; 481f; *VB*, pp. 16–19, 26–31; and the discussion—which cannot be ignored in any serious study of the subject—in Barth, *CD* III/3, pp. 369–531 (= *KD* III/3, pp. 426–623).

[5] It seems plausible to see a correspondence between the mention of ἄγγελοι, ἀρχαί and δυνάμεις (as various categories of cosmic spiritual powers) here in Romans and the mention of the κόσμος in 1 Cor 3.22.

itself. It is not very likely that the reference is to miracles (Pelagius, p. 71, paraphrases: 'neque si uirtutes operetur'). It is probably here another angelic designation like ἄγγελοι and ἀρχαί (it appears in angelic lists in 1 Cor 15.24; Eph 1.21 and 1 Pet 3.22, and also outside the Bible). Its separation from them here is noteworthy—it seems to come rather as an afterthought; but the suggestion that originally it stood next to ἀρχαί, was accidentally omitted and then restored in the wrong position, though of course possible, is hardly necessary.[1] ὕψωμα and βάθος have been variously explained. In ancient times they were commonly taken to refer to things above the heavens and things beneath the earth respectively. Origen (both as quoted in Cramer, p. 292, and in Rufinus's translation, col. 1135f) explained ὕψωμα by reference to the πνευματικὰ τῆς πονηρίας ἐν τοῖς ἐπουρανίοις of Eph 6.12 and βάθος as indicating infernal spirits. In modern times the suggestion has been made, on the basis of the use of ὕψωμα and βάθος as technical terms in ancient astronomy and astrology,[2] that the reference is to sideral spirits ruling in the sky above the horizon and in that part of the sky that is below it.[3] But, while such an interpretation is not to be ruled out, it is surely more probable that the reference here is to places than that it is to spirit-powers associated with them, and that the meaning is simply that neither the highest height nor the deepest depth (or should we say 'neither heaven nor hell'?) will be able to separate us from God's love. We might perhaps compare Ps 139.8 (where the context is concerned with the impossibility of getting beyond the reach of God): 'If I ascend up into heaven, thou art there: If I make my bed in Sheol, behold thou art there'. (The assumption of many that all the items of this list must refer to spiritual powers of one sort or another must be challenged. In the case of θάνατος and ζωή and also of ἐνεστῶτα and μέλλοντα such an interpretation is far from being natural. Moreover, the fact that v. 38f is intended as confirmation (as is indicated by the γάρ) of the statement in v. 37 that we are more than conquerors in all these things, that is, in all the trials and tribulations referred to in v. 35f, makes it unlikely (in view of the things mentioned in v. 35f) that the list in v. 38f is intended to refer to nothing but spiritual powers. The movement of thought surely requires that the list in these two verses should

---

[1] οὔτε δυνάμεις is actually placed immediately after ἀρχαί in the Byzantine text; but this reading is no doubt to be explained as an attempted improvement.

[2] See, e.g., *TWNT* 8, p. 611f; Bauer, s.v. βάθος, 1, and ὕψωμα, 1.

[3] Cf., e.g., Lietzmann, p. 88f.

be *all*-embracing, and the presence of the next phrase shows
that it is intended to be so.) οὔτε τις κτίσις ἑτέρα stands, like
οὔτε δυνάμεις, by itself, and concludes the list. It is apparently
added in order to make the list completely comprehensive. For
this use of ἕτερος compare 13.9.

δυνήσεται ἡμᾶς χωρίσαι. In v. 35 we had χωρίσει: the effect of
the substitution of the future indicative of δύνασθαι and the
infinitive of χωρίζειν for the future indicative of χωρίζειν is to
bring out the fact that the things which have been mentioned
do indeed threaten to separate us from God's love.

τῆς ἀγάπης τοῦ θεοῦ τῆς ἐν Χριστῷ Ἰησοῦ τῷ κυρίῳ ἡμῶν. See on
v. 35. Neither the phrase used there nor that used in 5.5 is as
precise and definitive as the present phrase; for the love of
Christ is not truly known until it is recognized as being the
love of the eternal God Himself, and it is only in Jesus Christ
that the love of God is fully manifest as what it really is. This
main division of the epistle is thus concluded with the solemn
mention of the same name and title with which it began
(διὰ τοῦ κυρίου ἡμῶν Ἰησοῦ Χριστοῦ in 5.1), and which were
repeated at the end of its sections (διὰ Ἰησοῦ Χριστοῦ τοῦ κυρίου
ἡμῶν in 5.21; ἐν Χριστῷ Ἰησοῦ τῷ κυρίῳ ἡμῶν in 6.23; and διὰ
Ἰησοῦ Χριστοῦ τοῦ κυρίου ἡμῶν in 7.25).